COMMUNICATION
IN THE FAMILY

COMMUNICATION IN THE FAMILY

Seeking Satisfaction in Changing Times

SECOND EDITION

JUDY C. PEARSON
Ohio University

HarperCollins*CollegePublishers*

Acquisitions Editor: Daniel F. Pipp
Project Editor: Thomas R. Farrell
Design Supervisor: Heather A. Ziegler
Text Design: Heather A. Ziegler
Cover Design: Delgado Design Inc.
Cover Photo: Peter Correz/Tony Stone Worldwide
Photo Researcher: Mira Schachne
Production Manager: Valerie A. Sawyer
Compositor: Express 93
Printer and Binder: R. R. Donnelley & Sons Company
Cover Printer: The Lehigh Press, Inc.

For permission to use copyrighted material, grateful acknowledgment is made to the copyright holders on page 488, which is hereby made part of this copyright page.

Communication in the Family: Seeking Satisfaction in Changing Times, Second Edition

Library of Congress Cataloging-in-Publication Data

Pearson, Judy C.
   Communication in the family : seeking satisfaction in changing
times / Judy C. Pearson. — 2nd ed.
   p. cm.
   Includes bibliographical references and index.
   ISBN 0-06-500047-1
   1. Communication in the family—United States. 2. Family—United
States. 3. Social change. I. Title
HQ536.P38 1993   92-39940
306.87—dc20   CIP

93 94 95 96 9 8 7 6 5 4

CONTENTS IN BRIEF

CONTENTS IN DETAIL

PREFACE

Communication students, teachers, and reseachers have shown an increased interest in family communication in the past decade. This book is written for individuals interested in family communication within the communication, sociology, psychology, home economics, counseling, and health professions. The book is intended as a textbook, but lay readers may find it useful as well.

In the past, theorists and practitioners attended to dysfunctional families; today, people have turned their attention to the functional family. A wide variety of communicative behaviors occurs in the functional family, however. Some of these behaviors are more likely to result in satisfaction for family members, while others may lead to distress, dissatisfaction, or dissolution.

The central idea of this text is that families in our changing times can seek satisfaction through their communicative behavior. All families are involved in change. The individual family goes through developmental phases, each of which presents unique problems and stresses. In addition, the family unit may change from one form to another through predictable and unpredictable events. These changes call upon individuals to develop large communicative repertoires in order to gain satisfying relationships among family members.

This text is divided into three parts. Part One introduces us to communication in the family and includes Chapter 1, an introduction; Chapter 2, on the many types of contemporary American families; Chapter 3, on the changing roles in current families; Chapter 4, on verbal rules in the family; and Chapter 5, on nonverbal rules. Whereas other books have used a systems approach to understand family communication, this text presents an alternative perspective.

Part Two focuses on changing times. Chapter 6 begins our discussion of the development of the family and covers the stages from meeting to mating; Chapter 7 extends our discussion by considering families from the time they have added a child until the oldest child begins school; Chapter 8 deals with the important topic of adolescence within the family unit; and Chapter 9 considers the final stages of the family.

Part Three considers specific communicative behaviors that allow family members to seek satisfaction. Chapters 10 through 14 are concerned with achieving autonomy and intimacy, understanding and supporting others, managing conflict among family members, and managing power, stress, and decision making. Communication occurs in both functional and dysfunctional families; we may achieve more satisfying relationships to the extent that we can engage in specific communicative behaviors and develop increasingly large repertoires of behavior.

Communication in the Family: Seeking Satisfaction in Changing Times,

Second Edition, relies on two kinds of sources. As the reader will observe, one set of sources is the increasing literature of family communication. Journals as diverse as *Family Process, Communication Monographs,* and *Sex Roles,* popular books such as Bill Cosby's writings, and scholarly texts and treatises were consulted. The endnotes at the conclusion of this book demonstrate the number and variety of published materials in this area.

In the preparation of the two editions of this book, a number of people assisted me in finding sources, correcting errors in the endnotes, and typing the final bibliography. I wish to thank especially the following people for their assistance with the bibliographical work involved with the book: Lois Lukens, Roberta Davilla, Tracy Corrigan, Amy Haskins, Wanda Sheridan, Karen Merkel, Xin Xin Song, Sue Manderick, Rob Reindl, Cheryl Heflin, Jeff Ringer, Linda Davis, Jill Rhea, Cheryl Forbes, Kimberlee Duran, Anne Nicotera, Charles Korn, and Patricia Cambridge.

The sseond set of sources was my own past and present students, without whose insightful and provocative comments this text could not have been written. Throughout the book, these men and women add their voices to clarify concepts. The following pseudonyms are used throughout for individual students: Adams, 1985; Anderson, 1985; Bell, 1985; Berger, 1985; Cook, 1985; Dehn, 1985; Elias, 1985; Evans, 1985; Fix, 1985; George, 1985; Gerber, 1985; Hart, 1985; Hoey, 1985; Ice, 1985; Jones, 1985; Jurma, 1985; Kirk, 1985; Krause, 1985; Lang, 1985; Rainey, 1985; Schmidt, 1985; Ticer, 1985; Zecchino, 1985; Bruggemeyer, 1986; Forman, 1986; Petrucelli, 1986; Rush, 1986; Stoppelbein, 1986; Vecchio, 1986; Abbott, 1987; Alassaf, 1987; Clarke, 1987; Cox, 1987; Ford, 1987; Good, 1987; Hoffman, 1987; Jenson, 1987; Knop, 1987; Kretch, 1987; LeMieux, 1987; Lempka, 1987; Mead, 1987; O'Shea, 1987; Reed, 1987; Remy, 1987; Shaw, 1987; Smith, 1987; Sole, 1987; Stone, 1987; Stickmaker, 1987; Thesing, 1987; Thompsen, 1987; Tocci, 1987; Ventrelli, 1987; Wagner, 1987; Wentworth, 1987; Young, 1987; Barzicchini, 1991; Baumgard, 1991; Beaumont, 1991; Black, 1991; Block, 1991; Cain, 1991; Dennis, 1991; Edwards, 1991; Emde, 1991; Fraleey, 1991; Goldstein, 1991; Gregori, 1991; Hamm, 1991; Hensley, 1991; Kloos, 1991; Moore, 1991; Pittman, 1991; Polk, 1991; Robertson, 1991; Rogalsi, 1991; Rohrback, 1991; Simms, 1991; and Turks, 1991. The author has attempted to substitute names of similar ethnic origin in order that the reader may draw conclusions, from different ethnic perspectives, about the similarity or divergence of views of the families described.

The actual names of some of these contributors are offered here. The author warmly appreciates the words of Ginny Hackman, Sharon Bodenschatz, JoAnne Lipsey, Lorayne Wright, Elizabeth Ploeger, Jack Ortizano, Sharon Mullen, Kara Bauer, Matthew Uram, Cassandra Parker, Sharon Stotz, Denise Cugini, J. Corey Henderson, Terry L. Frazier, Patricia S. Slonaker, Al Garrison, Terry Hill, James A. Lanning, Veronica Provo, Geoff Petersen, Dan Cencula, Todd Nolette, Stephen J. Rucki, Adam Sams, Jennifer Threm, Jane A. Willman, Christina M. Wolfe, Alison Dick, Kim Kelley, Brenda J. Williams, Loay Abukamil, Melinda Howard, Richard Rader, William

Pohovey, John Bickham, Gayle Wissinger, Trevor Phillips, Janice Neal, Kimberlee Duran, Gerri Smith, Jill Rhea, Charles Korn, Kellye, Jones, Verna Chapman, Jen Cox, Julia Graham, Joline Pinto, Jennifer Felderbau, Jeff and Sonja Stafford, Brian Davis, S. Haning, J. Stebelton, D. and S. Shonks, the Stoppenhagens, Karen Mitchell, Troy Burns, Doug and Lori Dawe, Lacy and Mary Ellen Rice, Lois and Burt DeVeau, Robert and Jeanette Schroer, the Anestenis, the Hinshaws, the Johnsons, the Guinthers, the Shonborns, and the Bojanowskis. The author sincerely thanks them for their honesty and clarity.

Finally, I wish to thank the reviewers who spent long hours helping to improve this text. They include Arthur Buchner, University of South Florida; Edith LeFebvre, California State University, Sacramento; Don Morlan, University of Dayton; Larry Miller, Wayne State University; David Natharius, California State University, Fresno; Laura Stafford, Ohio State University; Lea Stewart, Rutgers University; Vincent Bloom, California State University, Fresno; Jean Brodey, Temple University; Marvin Cox, Boise State University; Patricia Downing, Valparaiso University; Robert Field, University of Texas at Arlington; Sharon Kirk, LaSalle University; Linda Rea, Hiram College; Teresa Sabourin, University of Cincinnati; and Anthony Schroeder, Eastern New Mexico University.

This book represents a distillation of considerable material. As much information was deleted as included. First, the reader should be warned that the text deals primarily with middle-class white families in the United States. Families of different social classes, of different ethnic origins, or of different countries may operate with markedly different communication patterns. Although an attempt at diversity was made and despite my appreciation of the wonderful heterogeneity of the world's and America's families, restrictions of length did not allow an analysis of all the multitude of existing family types in our current world.

Furthermore, a variety of topics that are highly interesting, such as the history of the family, or salient in our contemporary society, such as homosexual families, or of concern, such as spousal abuse, have been omitted because they are less pertinent to the subject than those topics selected for inclusion. Reviewers encouraged me to focus on communication in the family rather than on general information on families such as might be included in a sociology textbook.

The research and writing of the two editions of this text have spanned over ten years. During that time I sometimes became discouraged by the large quantity of research being done on family communication and by the seemingly contradictory findings of that research. My enthusiasm for helping people achieve more satisfying family lives was the primary factor that encouraged me not to abort the project. You, too, may feel my frustration as you examine an area that suggests as many questions as it provides answers. I sincerely hope that this book will help all of us to seek, and perhaps achieve, more satisfying family relationships.

JUDY C. PEARSON

PART ONE

COMMUNICATION IN THE FAMILY

CHAPTER 1

AN INTRODUCTION TO COMMUNICATION IN THE FAMILY

The most beautiful thing we can experience is the mysterious. It is the source of all true art and science.

ALBERT EINSTEIN

After you have read this chapter, you will be able to

1. Define and explain family satisfaction and family stability.

2. List and explain factors associated with family satisfaction—premarital factors, social and economic factors, and interpersonal and dyadic factors.

3. Summarize conclusions from research on what constitutes a successful and satisfying marital relationship.

4. Construct and explain definitions for communication, family, and family communication.

5. Identify predicted and unpredicted changes that today's American family experiences.

6. Describe the relationship between communication and family satisfaction.

7. Discuss how meaning arises out of social interaction.

Although Albert Einstein was not referring specifically to family satisfaction, his observation has important implications for our understanding of this

3

phenomenon. This text considers the role of communication in family satisfaction. You will discover information that may lead you to more satisfying family relationships, but you will also learn that a great deal of satisfaction lies within the realm of the mysterious. Some observers have suggested that family satisfaction may be no more than luck and one has stated that it is merely an "idiot lottery." We are far from having all the answers to the question of how to achieve family satisfaction, but communication appears to play an important role. In this book you will be provided with our current understanding of the relationship between family satisfaction and communication.

Most of us understand the importance of our families and we desire satisfying family lives. Family theorist Sven Wahlroos observes, "The greatest happiness and the deepest satisfaction in life, the most intense enthusiasm and the most profound inner peace, all come from being a member of a loving family."[1] Marital researcher Graham Spanier, on a PBS program entitled *Love and Marriage,* observed, "Because we live in such an impersonal society, we are trying to personalize our lives through families." Yet, families are coming apart at historically unprecedented rates. Further, their forms are changing dramatically. How can we have satisfying family relationships in these changing times? This question serves as the organizer for this text.

❖ SATISFACTION

Tolstoy wrote, "All happy families are alike; every unhappy family is unhappy in its own way." Nabokov responded, "All happy families are more or less dissimilar; all unhappy ones are more or less alike." Family satisfaction is difficult to achieve in theory or practice. As you read this text you will understand the complexity of family life, but you will also untangle some of the contradictions. You may share the author's conclusion that satisfying marriages and families are possible and that our communicative behavior can assist us to that end.

Family satisfaction is our positive or negative assessment of marriage and family life. Although family satisfaction may be defined in a number of ways,[2] in all cases the family member is asked to assess his or her satisfaction. Family satisfaction is therefore a perceptual variable; that is, our perceptions are typically used to measure family satisfaction. You may question the subjective nature of such measurement. However, countless studies have demonstrated that people's *perceptions* of their relationships are most useful in measuring satisfaction.[3]

In recent times, researchers have shown that we gain a great deal of information when we explore family members' perceptions of their own family life.[4] They have coined the term *relationship awareness* to refer to "a person's thinking about interaction patterns, comparisons, or contrasts between himself or herself and the other partner in the relationship."[5] People are surprisingly able to describe and discuss their personal and familial relationships. A side benefit of such research is that family members seem to appreciate opportunities to share their feelings and the effect of the sharing may be to enhance or improve the relationship.[6]

Since satisfaction is based on individual evaluations, we find that wide variations exist. One spouse needs a great deal of sexual activity in order to claim satisfaction while the partner prefers little or no sexual contact. An adolescent equates living like a hermit with satisfaction while the parent needs a great deal of interaction. People's backgrounds, their observations of others, their developmental period, and their own experiences alter their understanding of family satisfaction.

■ Factors Associated with Family Satisfaction

Even though people's perceptions vary, some factors seem to be generally related to family satisfaction. A classic study by Lewis and Spanier summarized the factors that predict marital satisfaction. The predictors were divided into three categories: premarital factors, social and economic factors, and interpersonal and dyadic factors.[7] Premarital factors included *homogamy,* or similarity between the two members of the couple on such features as religion, ethnic group, family background, attitudes, and values;[8] *resources* such as education, social class, and physical health; *parental models;* and *support from significant others.*

Social and economic factors included *socioeconomic issues, the wife's employment,* and such issues as whether the union of the couple was approved by friends and neighbors (*community embeddedness*), and whether members of the family other than the couple would occupy the family home (*household composition*). Interpersonal and dyadic factors were identified as the expression of *positive regard,* the *gratification of emotional needs,* the *effectiveness of communication, role fit,* and the *amount of interaction.*[9]

Lewis and Spanier's classic work has been supplemented with recent surveys. For example, the marital couple Lauer and Lauer, who are also marital researchers, asked 350 satisfied marital couples about their perceptions.[10] Table 1.1 includes the reasons for marital satisfaction offered by husbands and wives, listed in order of frequency. The reasons offered are intriguing in their high level of similarity (the first seven reasons for husbands and wives are identical). Men and women in successful relationships tend to agree with each other, or reach consensus, on a variety of issues. In addition, some differences emerge.

What conclusions can we draw about successful marriages beyond the levels of agreement and disagreement between husbands and wives? Clearly, both men and women have positive attitudes toward their spouses. The first two reasons cited by both—"My spouse is my best friend" and "I like my spouse as a person"—reinforce this notion. In addition, the statement "My spouse has grown more interesting" suggests that the partners truly appreciate their spouse's qualities. "Liking" one's spouse may be as important as "loving" him or her.

TABLE 1.1 MARITAL SUCCESS: REASONS PROVIDED BY HUSBANDS AND WIVES, LISTED IN ORDER OF FREQUENCY	
HUSBANDS	WIVES
My spouse is my best friend.	My spouse is my best friend.
I like my spouse as a person.	I like my spouse as a person.
Marriage is a long-term commitment.	Marriage is a long-term commitment.
Marriage is sacred.	Marriage is sacred.
We agree on aims and goals.	We agree on aims and goals.
My spouse has grown more interesting.	My spouse has grown more interesting.
I want the relationship to succeed.	I want the relationship to succeed.
An enduring marriage is important to social stability.	We laugh together.
We laugh together.	We agree on a philosophy of life.
I am proud of my spouse's achievements.	We agree on how and how often to show affection.
We agree on a philosophy of life.	An enduring marriage is important to social stability.
We agree about our sex life.	We have a stimulting exchange of ideas.
We agree on how and how often to show affection.	We discuss things calmly.
I confide in my spouse.	We agree about our sex life.
We share outside hobbies and interests.	I am proud of my spouse's achievements.

Source: Lauer & Lauer (1985). Reprinted with permission from *Psychology Today*.

Another important factor is the couple's commitment to marriage. Successful couples are committed to making their marriage work—"Marriage is a long-term commitment," "Marriage is sacred," "I want the relationship to succeed," and "An enduring marriage is important to social stability." Individuals who enter the marital relationship with the idea that it does not matter a great deal to them if it works out or not probably have less success than do those couples who are highly committed to their marital relationship. By contrast, people in long-term happy marriages are committed. One man whose children had already left home said about his marriage, "Whatever it takes is what you have to do."

A third factor worth noting is the kinds of agreement that the couple feels are important. They feel that agreement on a philosophy of life, on their sex life, and on how to, and how often to, show affection are important aspects in their success. In other words, both their general outlook on life as well as their personal demonstrations of love are determined to be important matters on which to reach consensus. In addition, as we noted above, the couples are clear in their agreement on the relative importance of all the factors that contribute to a successful marriage.

Most recently, *Lasting Love: What Keeps Couples Together,* a study of happily married couples who had been together between 40 and 70 years, identified eight factors that marked the happy couples: lowered expectations, unconditional acceptance, positive distortion, becoming one, remaining two, sexual satisfaction, coping with conflict, and persistence.[11] Lowered expectations means that the couple did not have unrealistic notions of what the other person or the relationship could do for them. Unconditional acceptance means that the two not only accepted, but learned to appreciate, the idiosyncrasies of their partner. Positive distortion suggests that the members of the couple do not view each other realistically or objectively, but rather they see each other through "rose-colored glasses."

The couples became one as they explained that they were essentially "a two-headed animal," who shared not only experiences but aches and pains. They remained two as they transcended their common identity with separate values, attitudes, and beliefs. Although sexual activity varies dramatically among couples, a sense that the amount of sexual activity is satisfying is important. Couples showed a variety of conflict resolution techniques, but they all learned to cope with the "slings and arrows" of their relationship. Finally, the couples were persistent in remaining married and in remaining happily married. These factors were illustrated in the interaction patterns of the couples as well as in their specific comments describing their highly satisfying marriages.

Studies on marital satisfaction are useful to family members who desire more positive relationships. However, two limitations should be noted. First, little research has been conducted that examines satisfaction among family members other than the marital couple. However, the research that has been done generally supports similar variables as important predictors.

Second, investigations have identified many factors other than communicative behaviors or perceptions of communicative behaviors as important to family satisfaction. For example, marriages are less satisfying and stable when people marry very young, have little education, and cohabit.[12] In addition, well-being is associated with satisfying family relationships.[13]

Gender also affects one's assessment of marital satisfaction. "Her" marriage is not viewed as positively as "his" marriage. When husbands and wives evaluate their marital happiness, the husbands are more likely to give it high marks than are the wives.[14] Women may have higher expectations of their marriage, or the married state may not be as advantageous for them as it is for men.

Marital satisfaction also changes over the life cycle. People are generally happier in their marriages in the early years and in the period following retirement. They are less happy during the middle stages of their marriage.[15]

Most studies suggest that satisfaction has a curvilinear relationship to the length of the marriage—higher at the beginning and end and lower in the middle.

The topic of this text is the role of communication in family satisfaction. Nonetheless, as communication researchers Fitzpatrick and Badzinski write, "Communication *alone* can not explain all of the variance in family outcomes."[16] While our interest is in the relationship between communication and satisfaction, we should keep in mind that other factors are important, too.

What communication behaviors, or perceptions of behaviors, are related to satisfaction? Later in this chapter, and in Chapters 10 through 14, we will identify the specific clusters of communicative behaviors that are related to family satisfaction. These behaviors allow us to demonstrate understanding and support; establish autonomy and intimacy; manage conflict, power, and stress; and make decisions.

■ Family Satisfaction as Distinguished from Family Stability

In the past, satisfaction was often equated with *family stability*—the endurance or likelihood of endurance of the family unit. However, we have determined that family satisfaction and family stability are not identical.[17] The authors of the well-known book *The Mirages of Marriage,* William Lederer and Don Jackson, clarified this difference when they categorized marriages along the two primary continua of satisfaction and stability.[18] This distinction is crucial to our understanding of satisfaction and is illustrated in Figure 1.1.

Figure 1.1

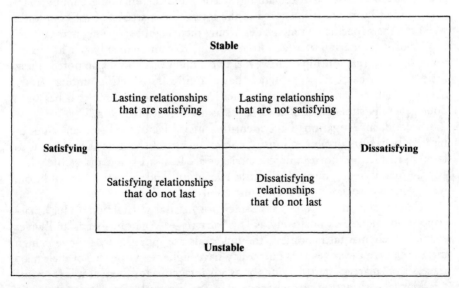

Relationships can be distinguished on a continuum from satisfying to dissatisfying and from stable to unstable.

Marriages can be stable (they endure the test of time), but are not necessarily satisfying to the couple. Similarly, they can be both stable and satisfying, which may be an ideal toward which individuals strive. Relationships can be neither stable nor satisfying: the bad relationship that ends. They may even be satisfying but not stable. Marital couples who are physically separated for their individual professions may terminate their relationships, even though they care deeply for each other and have had satisfying relational lives. The stability of a marriage and its satisfying nature have a moderate positive relationship,[19] but clearly these are different dimensions that can vary independently of each other.

One young woman clarified the difference between satisfaction and stability:

> I grew up in a middle class family in the suburbs of Columbus, Ohio. Our home was one in which stability reigned and satisfaction was secondary. My parents raised my sister, brother and I with the idea that commitment to hard work would create happiness and deep fulfillment. But upon reflection, I now see that often our satisfaction was sacrificed for the sake of stability. To us, stability sold itself as a success and an outward beauty of a harmonious family. But the picture we painted to the world was only a false replica of the true portrait that I could see in my mind's eye.[20]

Another woman described her aunt and uncle, who she felt were lacking in both satisfaction and stability:

> My Aunt and Uncle are the perfect example of a couple lacking in both marital satisfaction and marital stability. Over the years I have watched their marriage slowly deteriorate in many crucial areas. But I believe that this particular marriage was doomed at the very beginning. During their engagement, Tom would frequently call Louise from bars around the city. This was the beginning of his alcoholism. Once they were married, the alcohol problem escalated—even affecting Tom's ability to bear children—which he blamed on Louise. Although financially she was provided for, and although she had a fine home, she was totally unsatisfied with their marriage. Tom was always cold, angry, and drunk. Communication was distant and lovemaking had become a task for them. She decided to leave him.[21]

Marriages may be both stable and satisfying. A woman from New York City wrote:

> I have been very lucky to grow up with such good role models in my parents. I can best represent my parents' satisfactory marriage through an example:
>
> > My cousin Ross got married and my parents, Carole and Arnie, were at the wedding. My Mother wished Ross congratulations and commented on how happy he looked. Ross explained that he was very happy and that he now understood how Arnie felt every day.[22]

In this text we will be interested in relationships that are satisfying. Family satisfaction, rather than family stability, is our goal because many relationships have an enduring quality, but are hurtful to the participants. Marriages and families that are rated high in quality are superior to those that can boast several anniversaries. Television documentaries, newspaper headlines, and social service newsletters provide ample information of violence and abuse among family members in lasting relationships. Satisfying relationships are more likely to endure than are dissatisfying relationships, but the link between satisfaction and stability is sometimes broken.

❖ CHANGING TIMES

Twenty years ago Bob Dylan sang, "The times, they are a'changing." Futurists of our own era remark on the dramatic changes that are occurring all around us. John Naisbitt, author of *Megatrends,* labeled the 1980s a "decade of unprecedented diversity."[23] The alterations may be felt in no social group to the extent they are realized in the family. Families can no longer be categorized simply, and many family types replace the relatively fewer family types of the past. In Chapter 2 we will specifically consider the changes occurring in contemporary American families, and we will identify the major new family types. Corresponding changes in role behavior will be identified in Chapter 5.

Even if your family has not been affected by the revolutionary reconstitution of the family, you will still observe changes in your family. As you moved from childhood into adolescence and early adulthood, you may have recognized that your parents no longer interacted with you or with each other in the same way. Such developmental changes occur in all families and are part of the changing times to which families must adapt. We will consider the developmental stages of the family in Chapters 6 through 9.

In addition to these predictable changes, families sometimes experience unpredicted change. Family members may die unexpectedly. Divorce or marital separation may be a surprise to virtually all but the partner who has left. Injuries and illnesses may be unpredicted changes. These changes—though unexpected—similarly affect the family.

The changes that come from within the family and those that come from outside forces create new challenges for the family seeking satisfaction. Recognizing the centrality of change in family life, the term *adaptation* has been offered to refer to these alterations. Families find that answers to old questions often do not work when new questions are posed. However, being aware that changes will occur to you over the lifetime of your family may be helpful in solving your problems. One woman explained, "It is important to know what changes to expect over time in order to be able to prepare for the future and to cope with it."[24]

Change is not inherently harmful to families or to individuals. Indeed, some people thrive on change and are bored by a life of sameness. Researchers have found that a number of people are *risk takers* who purposely expose themselves to physical, psychological, or relational danger. Ralph Keyes, author of *Chancing It: Why We Take Risks,* observes that for risk takers, the failure to take chances "involves greater risks than taking them—especially the risk of boredom."[25] People may introduce change into their family lives in order to avoid the weariness of sameness.

Change creates new circumstances for the family, however. Change may result in confusion, misunderstandings, stress, and alienation among family members. People may have to learn new behaviors and alternative coping mechanisms. Former expectations are replaced with new predictions. Because family members are inextricably entwined, a change in one person or in one relationship affects the entire family. Change necessarily demands attention; it requires some action, and sometimes, a remedy.

Flexibility is recommended as one response to the changes that are inside and outside the family. Developing a more adaptive approach to family life is certainly recommended. However, all families are not able to demonstrate flexibility on all issues. For instance, a strongly religious family might not choose to accept a divorce among their children. An outspoken advocate of women's rights may be unable to appreciate her own daughter's choice to create a traditional family rather than to combine work and family. Highly *dogmatic* individuals—those who are authoritarian and unyielding about personally held assertions—may rarely show flexibility. Flexibility is theoretically sound, but it is not always chosen by families or the individuals within them.

❖ COMMUNICATION

Communication is vital to a satisfying family life. According to Arthur Bochner, a communication expert, "The most fundamental aspect of family process is communication."[26] An examination of communication within the family setting is important because it is largely through interaction that family units are satisfying or dissatisfying. The geometric changes and the complexity of the family unit in our contemporary culture require each of us to have a thorough understanding of communication if we hope to have satisfying family relationships. Although an understanding of communication may not secure family success, in most cases it will enhance the likelihood of our happiness with family members. Indeed, our understanding of the communicative process may be the most important factor in achieving the kind of family we desire.

■ Definition of Communication

The term *communication* has a variety of different meanings, each of which restricts its usage in particular ways. Communication theorists Dance and Larson found 126 differing definitions of the term in the scholarly books and articles they surveyed.[27] The definition of communication used in this text is based on earlier definitions. One communication author suggests that

> Communication is the process by which we understand others and in turn endeavor to be understood by them. It is dynamic, constantly changing and shifting in response to the total situation.[28]

Blumer offers three premises that guide his understanding of this phenomenon:

> (1) Human beings act toward things on the basis of the meanings that the things have for them; (2) The meaning of such things is derived from, or arises out of, the social interaction that one has with one's fellows; (3) These meanings are handled in, and modified through an interpretive process used by the person in dealing with the things he [she] encounters.[29]

Therefore, *communication* is the interpretive process of understanding and sharing meaning with others. Furthermore, meaning arises out of social interaction and is continually changing and shifting in response to that interaction and to the individual's understanding of it. Given this definition, communication in the family is a topic that is essential to our understanding of human communication in general.

This definition can be clarified by an illustration from a 25-year-old man:

> As two family members communicate with one another, a shared meaning is created. . . . I have perceived for many years that my grandmother is distant, cool, and often unfriendly in terms of her communication style with me. As a result of my perceptions, I have attempted to deal with grandmother in an extremely polite, yet restrained manner. Our communication is superficial, stilted, and unnatural. I believe she has perceived me as talkative, energetic, and impatient. Conversely, I saw her as static, critical, and unfair or biased in her evaluations of others. Others, interestingly enough, probably never considered either one of us in these ways. Yet when we talked, I believe this is how we responded to each other. In sum, I responded to her as a "bitchy, old, and unfair grandmother" and she responded to me as a "loquacious, hyper kid!"[30]

■ Communication Occurs in a Setting

Communication does not occur in a vacuum. Communication occurs in a *setting*, a set of circumstances, or a situation. Sometimes this setting is unobtrusive and almost irrelevant; at other times, the setting is highly apparent and has strong impact. The number of people involved in communication affects the kind of communication that occurs. Similarly, we may communicate in social or work-related situations. We may communicate in a variety of different organizational settings including human services agencies, multinational corporations, church groups, hospitals, civic groups, and small family businesses. The differences among these situations affect the verbal and nonverbal messages we choose to share with others. Similarly, communication with our family members is affected by the nature of the family unit. The family context imposes unique constraints on our interactions. In order to better understand this setting, let us examine the nature of the family.

❖ FAMILIES

USA Today celebrated its fifth birthday by reporting on the issues that Americans cared most about. One of those issues was the family. People from across the country explained the importance of the family in their lives. Earl Green, 42, of Rapid City, South Dakota, noted:

> I've seen a lot of people divorced and separated. In their older years, they're awful lonely. How do they live without people around? I don't see it. You've got to care for somebody.[31]

Vickie Dorman, 26, of Indianapolis, Indiana, is married to Steve Dorman, 32, who works at two jobs. She explained:

> I see him maybe two hours out of the day. Love, understanding and communication (hold us together). That's what we do for two hours—talk.[32]

Bob Loomis, 37, from Hamburg, New York, remains close to his mother:

> I've been helping my Mom, she lives about six miles away. My dad passed away three years ago. She's moving down into Hamburg, probably a half-mile away. It'll be easier. We'll see more of each other.[33]

Families have changed in geometric proportions in the last two decades. Jane Howard, author of *Families,* writes:

> They're saying that families are dying, and soon. They're saying it loud, but we'll see that they're wrong. Families aren't dying. The trouble we take to arrange ourselves in some semblance or other of families is one of the most imperishable habits of the human race. What families are doing, in flamboyant and dumbfounding ways, is changing their size and their shape and their purpose. . . which are often so noisy that the clamor resulting is easily mistaken for a death rattle.[34]

Howard suggests that families vary in definition and that our past conceptions of families, still depicted to a great extent in the media, are outdated.

■ Definition of "Family"

Definitions of the family have been reflective of the times in which they have been offered. Families were defined narrowly in the past. For instance, Murdock's 1949 definition of the family is frequently quoted:

> The family is a social group characterized by common residence, economic cooperation and reproduction. It includes adults of both sexes, at least two of whom maintain a socially approved sexual relationship, and one or more children, of one's own or adopted, of the sexually cohabiting adults.[35]

In 1980, the United States Census Bureau defined the family as a "group of two persons or more related by birth, marriage, or adoption and residing together."[36]

Researchers Klee, Schmidt, and Johnson recently asked children from blended families for their definitions of the family. The children's definitions fell into five groups from a more limited, household definition to a broad definition that included biological, legal, and nonkin members. The authors conclude, "Children's use of criteria beyond biology or law to define their reconstituted families after divorce of their parents illustrates the voluntary nature of U.S. kinship systems."[37]

The differing configurations of contemporary families require that we adopt a broader definition than either of these, which will include the variety of families in which we will find ourselves during our lifetimes. Communication researcher Arthur Bochner offers the beginning point of such a definition. He writes that a family is "an organized, naturally occurring relational interaction system, usually occupying a common living space over an extended time period, and possessing a confluence of interpersonal images which evolve through the exchange of messages over time."[38] We will define the family as "an organized, relational transactional group, usually occupying a common living space over an extended time period, and possessing a confluence of interpersonal images that evolve through the exchange of meaning over time." Let us examine each of the components of this definition.

■ Components of the Definition

Families Are Organized   Individual family members play particular roles within the unit. You may play the role of mother, sister, daughter, aunt, or grandmother or that of father, brother, son, uncle, or grandfather. In Chapter 5, the changing nature of roles in the family will be discussed. Families are also organized, as the behavior among individuals does not occur in a random or unpredictable fashion. We generally can predict, within a range of possibilities, how family members will act and react to each other. For example, when a 6-year-old son and a 12-year-old daughter are watching television together, we can predict they will get into a disagreement about which show to view.

One 30-year-old woman considered the organization of her original family:

> Initially, I didn't think my family could ever be considered organized. From my point of view chaos permeated the family. My family started out with four members living together; then Dad left, leaving three members together. This living arrangement didn't last long; soon it was Mom alone and three members together. This arrangement didn't last as long as the last one. The next living combination was me with another family, Dad alone and two members together. Would you believe it changed again? It ended in two dyads: Dad and I, and Mom and my sister. Where was the organization in this?
>
> If, however, we say that family organization refers to the roles each individual member plays, then my family was full of great actors. Each partici-

pant played their appropriate role, adapted their character to the set and created the scene. For example, when the four of us were together, Mom played
Mom. Whenever Mom wasn't with the rest of us, I covered the role, I adapted my character to the set in order to create the scene.[39]

In some families, when one spouse attempts to control the behavior of the
other spouse, the second person may respond with humor, but he or she may
still behave independently of the first spouse's wishes, as in this example:

> HUSBAND: (in a harsh voice) You're not going back to work again tonight,
> are you?
> WIFE: (with a quizzical look while she puts on her coat) Does a
> duck have feathers?

In other families such a statement on the part of the husband would be expected to be viewed as an order. Nonetheless, the generalization remains that family behavior does not occur in a random or unpredictable way. The behavior
of particular family members can be predicted within a range of possibilities.

Bochner states the family "naturally occurs," which means it is not an
artificially created group. He is attempting to contrast the family with other
communicative groups that might be thought of as "artificially occurring,"
such as small group discussions, classroom situations, and business or organizational groups. We do not choose our parents and we do not choose our
families of origin; however we generally do choose at least one member or
more of our current families. For instance, if you are married, you probably
chose your spouse. If you have adopted children, you chose them. If you have
dissolved a previous marriage, you may have made choices about who would
be in your current family, too. Bochner is correct in saying that we do not
choose everyone in our families; however, some choice is possible and
inevitable. Consequently, we delete his definitional phrase that a family "naturally occurs" from our definition. We also observe that the limited choice
about who is defined as a member of our family affects our interactions with
them.

Families Are a "Relational Transactional Group"   Relationships may be
defined simply as associations or connections. However, relationships are far
more complex than such a definition suggests. The research team of Silverman
and Silverman explains:

> Consider for a moment a passenger ship in New York harbor, whose destina-
> tion is Southampton. It is a "ship," of course, because we choose to call it "a
> ship," and an entity because we define it as one.
>   It is also, among other things, engines, cabins, decks, and dinner-gongs—
> these are some of its parts or components. If we were to rearrange the compo-
> nents, or lay them out side by side, the entity would no longer be a ship, but
> perhaps look more like a junk-yard. The "parts," then, may be said to "make

up" the whole, but the whole is defined by these parts *in a particular relationship*, each one not only to those attached to it, but also to the whole itself.[40]

Similarly, families are relationships that include individual members, their associations with each other, and their connection with the whole unit.

For instance, one family is comprised of two parents who are in their mid-50s, their youngest child who is 18, their child's husband who is 19, and their child's newborn baby. The family includes the five individual members. It also includes the relationship between the two parents, between each parent and the child, between the child and her husband, between each parent and the grandchild, between each parent and the son-in-law, between the child and

Figure 1.2

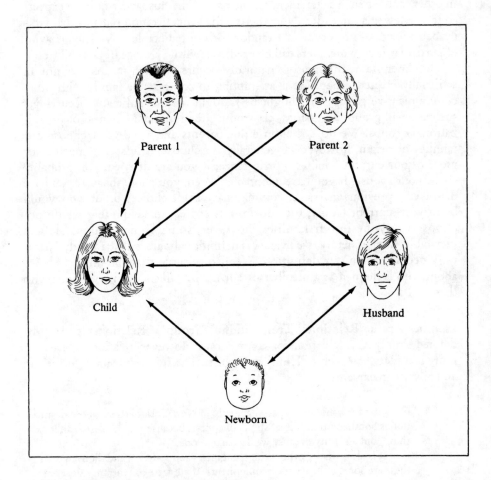

Families include the relationships among the members.

her newborn, and between the child's husband and the newborn. These relationships are depicted in Figure 1.2. The family also consists of the connection of the entire unit. The complexity of the family is evident.

Families Are Transactional   Members share with each other; all participants are actively engaged in the communicative process. When we state that families are transactional, we mean that we see them including a dynamic process that includes communicators who are mutually dependent upon each other. We do not view one family member as the sender of messages while others are merely receivers of them. All family members participate in the give-and-take of interaction. Together, they mutually come to understand and share common meaning.

A family consisting of a mother, a stepfather, a child by the mother's first marriage, and two children by the current marriage provides an example. Marilyn and Ted were married for ten years and had two biological children, Alex and Zeke. Their family also included Samantha from Marilyn's first marriage. Samantha was 15 years old and had been an even-tempered, loving child as she grew and developed. When she reached adolescence, her personality seemed to change. On visitation with her biological father, she called her mother and refused to come home. Samantha's behavior required the response of her family. Although the other family members thought that Samantha was generally satisfied with her family life, her behavior suggested otherwise. While her behavior was extreme, it demonstrates that each family member can exert an influence on the manner in which the family is defined.

In many ways children teach their parents just as parents teach their children. Children contribute to the meaningfulness of events just as certainly as parents do.[41] Lewis and Rosenblum summarized the influence of the child on the parents in their book *The Effect of the Infant on Its Caregiver*.[42] In *Families and Survivors*, Adams provides an example:

> From birth, Maude Wasserman, the daughter of Louisa and Michael, has been a startling child. She refused to be breast-fed (which did not help Louisa's own feelings about her breasts); she would not go to sleep without music playing in her room. By the time she was one, she had begun to talk, and she wanted to be read to all the time; she demanded new Little Golden Books on every trip to the market. She memorized her favorites, *Crispin's Crispian* ("Crispin was a dog who belonged to himself . . . ") and *The Sailor Dog* ("Born in the teeth of a gale, Scupper was a sailor . . . "). But at two she still did not walk. Michael, who had great faith in tests, had her tested with every available battery of psychological-neurological-muscular tests, all of which revealed nothing, except that she was unusually bright. She was a remarkably fast crawler. She had a great many inexplicable and alarming chest infections. She was very blond.[43]

More recently, Bill Cosby provided a humorous example of this phenomenon, as he discussed his first daughter when she was 18 months old:

Every time I went into her room, she would take some round plastic thing from her crib and throw it on the floor. Then I would pick it up, wipe it off, and hand it back to her so she could throw it back to the floor.

"Don't throw that on the floor, honey," I'd tell her. "Do you understand Daddy? Don't throw that on the floor." Then I would give it back to her and she would throw it again. Picking it up once more, wiping it off, and returning it to her, I again would say, "Look, I just *told* you not to throw this on the floor, didn't I?"

And, of course, she would listen carefully to me and then throw it again. . . . Sometimes a father needs ten or fifteen droppings before he begins to understand that he should *leave* the thing on the floor—or maybe put the child down here too.

During this little game, the child has been thinking: *This person is a lot of fun. He's not too bright, but a lot of fun.*[44]

Families Usually Occupy a Common Living Space over an Extended Time Period   Whether the dwelling is a tenement, a large old farmhouse, a contemporary suburban home, an eight-bedroom "mansion" complete with swimming pool and tennis courts, university married students' housing, a furnished apartment, an attic in someone else's home, or a cabin, families generally share a common living space. However, the dual-career couple is frequently seeking other living arrangements.[45] Many dual-career marriage partners have adopted the commuter marriage, which includes two separate living quarters.[46] Two researchers referred to individuals in such living arrangements as "married singles."[47] Although historically families generally shared a common living space, they do not do so with the same frequency today.

Families Possess a Mixture of Interpersonal Images That Evolve Through the Exchange of Meaning over Time   Each of us gains an understanding of the world by interacting with others. We learn to stereotype others because people we trust or respect stereotype them. We learn to be open and to share our feelings with others because our family members behave in such a manner. We view such matters as appropriate levels of intimacy, amount of ambition we should exhibit, earnings that are desirable, and kind of future to expect based largely on our interactions with our family members. Just as sociologist George Herbert Mead observed that one cannot separate the person from his or her society,[48] we observe that we cannot separate the individual from his or her family.

The exchange of meaning may be implicit, rather than explicit. For example, one student wrote:

I can remember only two physical boundaries in my family-of-origin. There were no boundaries the children were told about verbally, and no big issue was made if we crossed these boundaries by mistake. The children just "sensed" that these were boundaries and were to be treated as such.[49]

Messages are provided to family members over time, and through them, images flow and merge.

❖ COMMUNICATION IN THE FAMILY

■ Characteristics of Communication in the Family

Communication in the Family Is Symbolic How do you communicate with other family members? You do so with words and you do so with nonverbal cues. The words we use to communicate with family members are *verbal symbols,* and the gestures, bodily movements, clothing and artifacts, space, vocal sounds, touch, smells, eye contact, facial expression, and so on are *nonverbal symbols.* Our communicative behavior is comprised of these verbal and nonverbal symbols and therefore may be said to be symbolic. In general, the symbols we use to communicate derive their meaning from agreement among the family members, by conventional association, or by some resemblance to the object or thing they represent. In Chapters 3 and 4 we will consider further the verbal and nonverbal codes within the family.

Communication in the Family Begins with Ourselves and How We Believe Other Family Members View Us Our communication exchanges with our family are based on our perceptions. The words we select to use and the nonverbal cues we offer to others as well as our interpretation of others' use of verbal and nonverbal cues are tied to our particular background, experience, and values.

The following dialogue between a newly married couple serves as an example.

PAUL: Would you like to go out with Mac and MaryLou over the weekend?

PATTI: I don't know—what do you want to do?

PAUL: If I didn't want to go out with them I wouldn't have brought it up!

PATTI: Well, why didn't you just order me to go?

PAUL: I can never talk to you about anything!

PATTI: That's how I feel, too!

Paul grew up in a family where plans were initiated by his father, and his mother generally acquiesced to his dad's preferences. When he asked Patti about the weekend, he felt he was simply informing her about what they would be doing. Patti grew up in a family where her parents discussed plans together. Furthermore, her parents were very careful to consider each other's feelings. When Paul asked her about the weekend, she believed he genuinely wanted her opinion; nonetheless, she was attempting to be polite by asking him about his opinion first. She was more than a little surprised that her interest in his preferences was received with such a negative response. Each of them accurately stated they had difficulty in communicating with the other. Each of them, like each of us, is a product of their backgrounds, experience, and values. We view communication from our own vantage points.

We also view our interactions from our interpretations of other people's perceptions. Other people may want to be viewed as intellectual, but we view them as average in intelligence. Partners may see themselves as highly approachable, but we see them as somewhat distant. Similarly, we make judgments about how other people view us. We may think our children view us as contemporary, but they see us as old-fashioned and out-of-date. The columnist Russell Baker explained:

> My mother. . . . When she was young, with life ahead of her, I had been her future and resented it. Instinctively. I wanted to break free, cease being a creature defined by her time, consign her future to the past, and create my own. Well, I had finally done that, and then with my own children I had seen my exciting future become their boring past.[50]

Our assessments of other people's perceptions may be fairly accurate or far from the mark.

Barnlund suggested that each two-person conversation includes at least "six people":

1. How you view yourself

2. How you view the other person

3. How you believe the other person views you

4. How the other person views himself or herself

5. How the other person views you

6. How the other person believes you view him or her[51]

This model illustrates that we tend to "construct" both ourselves and others in our interactions with them.

When we view interactions from our own perspectives, we have a *direct perspective;* when we attempt to perceive interactions from others' perspectives, we gain a *metaperspective.* For instance, we may perceive ourselves to be caring and nurturing toward the other members of our family, but we perceive that a spouse sees us as uncaring and cold. In this instance our direct perspective and metaperspective are in conflict. Relationships are highly complex as a result of the different perspectives we bring to each relationship. Each time we interact with another person, we bring our own perspective and metaperspective and the other person brings his or her own perspective and metaperspective.

Communication in the Family Is Irreversible and Unrepeatable.   At any point in a conversation an infinite number of messages are being understood and shared by the interactants. The variety of verbal and nonverbal symbols and the communicators' interpretation of them are staggering. We cannot reverse this process nor can we repeat it.

Let us consider the irreversibility of communication. Suppose you carefully planned an evening with someone you love. You spent a great deal of time deciding where you would go, what you would do, and probably some of the things that you would say. When the big evening arrives, you experience a series of misfortunes and you are in a terrible mood. You meet your loved one and, because of your foul mood and self-preoccupation, you pay no attention to a request he or she makes. As the evening progresses, your mood lightens, but your partner becomes increasingly distant. Finally, you ask about the problem. However, you are too late and your friend demands to go home. A few days later the two of you talk about the unsuccessful evening. You suggest that you try it again in order to erase the bad memories. Can you forget the first evening? Will you conclude that the evening never existed? No; even if your second evening is all that you had hoped for the first one, you will both recall the events of the unsuccessful interaction. We cannot reverse our interactions with others.

Communication is similarly unrepeatable. If your carefully planned evening was even more of a success than you had hoped it might be, you might want to "do it again." Could you repeat the evening? Again, the answer is no. The complexity of the large number of symbols that are exchanged and the relationship among those symbols cannot be completely duplicated. Romantic couples will sometimes have an especially pleasant evening that they link to a particular place, time, or event. Often they try to re-create the situation by visiting the place again or participating in the event on another occasion. In general, they are disappointed that the second time was not as outstanding as the first. We can have similarly good times with another person, but we cannot duplicate an earlier experience.

Communication in the Family Includes Both Content and Relationship Dimensions.   When we communicate with others, we offer them specific content and we suggest our perception of the relationship between us. For example, if you are a parent and you tell one of your children he must clean his room, you are offering two messages. The content message is the imperative, "Clean your room!" The relational message is that you have the authority or power to tell the child how he should behave.

The content and relationship dimensions of communication are fundamentally linked to each other. For instance, when you tell your child to clean his room, you are using a specific situation to comment on the relationship between the two of you and you are using your perception of the relationship in order to comment on the content or situation that is perceived. If you did not feel that you had the right to tell the child what to do, you would not be able to make the statement; similarly, if you did not offer the content, you would not be able to express your perceptions of the relationship between the two of you. The content of the message and the relationship it suggests are inextricably bound.

The content and relationship dimensions are always present, but they may be implicit rather than explicit. They may be implied or understood even though they are not directly expressed. Sometimes the content dimension is explicit and the relationship dimension is only implied. For example, if you tell your child to clean his room, you will probably not begin your request by an explanation that you are the child's parent and have the right to ask the child to do particular jobs. If the child refuses to act, and thus does not seem to understand the relationship between you as you view it, you might make the relationship dimension explicit: "I'm your mother, and when I ask you for some help, I expect to get it."

Similarly, we sometimes do not explicitly state the content dimension of a message. Our nonverbal responses to others generally have a relational, but not a content, dimension. For instance, we may only cuddle to the touch of our partner rather than state, "I feel very affectionate toward you. Furthermore, when you initiate a behavior that could potentially lead to sexual activity, I tend to respond to you." Such a verbalized response would be construed as humorous or bizarre. Erica Jong's character Isadora describes the verbalizations of one of her young lovers in the book *Parachutes and Kisses.* As we will determine in the excerpt below, Roland overemphasizes the content dimension in a situation in which the relationship dimension is more important:

> "Are you relaxed?" Roland asks, getting up to put on a record. "Would early Beatles be appropriate?"
> "Most appropriate," Isadora says.
> "Then you're getting relaxed?" he repeats.
> "Mmm," says Isadora.
> "Shall we commence something erotic?"
> Whereupon Isadora commences a fit of the giggles.
> "Yes," says Isadora between giggles, "let us commence something erotic."
> "A kiss?" asks Roland.
> "*Do* it, Roland, don't *say* it."[52]

We will observe that misunderstanding can occur on either the content or dimension level of the conversation in Chapter 12.

Communication in the Family Serves Expressive and Instrumental Purposes   Communication is used to express feelings and to relate to people and it is used to accomplish tasks or goals. When you are cuddling a baby, your purpose may be purely expressive; when you are asking a child to get the newspaper from outside, you are primarily task-oriented. Often, your communicative behavior combines the expressive and instrumental purposes.

Other domains of behavior have been similarly divided into expressive and instrumental areas. The most widely known area today may be the research on sex roles. A number of researchers reconceptualized our understanding of gender by moving the variable from one of biology to one of personal endorsement.[53] The Bem Sex Role Inventory and the Personal Attributes Questionnaire both suggest that femininity is primarily expressive, masculinity is principally instrumental, and that androgyny (combining masculine and feminine psychological traits) is most desirable.

Leadership behavior also relies on the instrumental and expressive dimensions. Authors Hersey and Blanchard referred to them as the task and relationship dimensions and defined them in this way:

> Task behavior—The extent to which leaders are likely to organize and define the roles of the members of their organization (group); to explain what activities each is to do and when, where and how tasks are to be accomplished; characterized by endeavoring to establish well-defined patterns of organization, channels of communication and ways of getting jobs accomplished.
>
> Relationship behavior—The extent to which leaders are likely to maintain personal relationships between themselves and members of their organization (group) by opening up channels of communication; providing socio-emotional support, "psychological strokes," and facilitating behaviors.[54]

These authors, too, recommend that successful leaders are able to combine the task and relational aspects of leadership. If we can generalize from such recommendations, family members may also be well advised to recognize both the content and relational aspects of communication within the family.

Families desire satisfying relationships, but internal and external changes disrupt their lives. The thesis of this text is that communication can mediate these seemingly conflicting forces. Communication is not a universal bromide that can be prescribed for all of the world's ills nor is it a simplistic prescription. In the next section, we will consider some of the reasons that effective and appropriate communication will not always result in family satisfaction.

■ Communication Does Not Guarantee Family Satisfaction

While understanding the process of communication and practicing communication skills may help increase satisfaction with the family, there are no guarantees. First, communication is not a simple phenomenon that can be quickly understood and practiced effectively. Communication researcher J. K. Alberts observes:

> In romantic relationships talk must accomplish many purposes—signal interest, declare love, join couples in marriage. However, it must also function in other, less pleasant ways, such as arguing and complaining. Using talk to express negative emotions and dissatisfaction can be uncomfortable and/or unsuccessful for many couples.[55]

In addition, as you have determined in this chapter, communication is far more than simply talking. It includes sending and receiving messages and together interpreting the meaningfulness of those events.

Communication serves expressive as well as instrumental purposes (© 1991, Ulrike Welsch).

Second, the intent of our message may be different than the effect it has on the listener. You may try to communicate your commitment to the family relationship by working extra hours to earn money for family vacations or other luxuries. Your partner may view your work as selfish and feel that it erodes the relationship between you. Your partner may attempt to communicate affection by servicing your automobile, but you may view the rare kiss or touch as the only sign of affection offered. Author Sven Wahlroos observes, "In the vast majority of families troubled by conflict the main reason for the discord is simply that the consciously felt love and the good intentions harbored by the family members are not *communicated* in such a way that they are recognized."[56]

Third, no universal laws about communication behavior in the family have been determined. We cannot offer a list of specific communication skills that will automatically result in highly satisfying relationships. Although some generalizations are possible, they are fairly abstract, rather than concrete.

Families are capable of achieving similar goals or ends through a variety of different ways and with alternative starting points. Theorists refer to this idea as *equifinality.*[57] Equifinality suggests that a childless couple living in the desert may be equally happy as a religious family of eight living in the mountains in Colorado. A dual-career couple may find as much satisfaction in their family life and their children as do a traditional couple in which the mother stays home each day with her children. Similarly, problems of alcoholism, drug abuse, incest, and spousal abuse do not follow any economic or social lines. Families may be functional or dysfunctional regardless of their starting points and regardless of their methods of interacting. Similarly, the communicative patterns of satisfied families may vary greatly.

Fourth, family communication necessarily requires other people with whom to interact and those other people may have differing motives, goals, and attitudes that do not allow a satisfying relationship for you as you define it. A college senior announced to his parents that he was gay, expecting unconditional acceptance. His parents, who were unable to accept their son's disclosure, immediately stopped all contact with their son.

Part of the difficulty with a common interpretation lies in the qualities and characteristics of family members. People understand communication differently based on their age, biological sex, cultural background, and original family background. The difficulties of marital communication lie in the notion that the two people are generally of the opposite sex and thus speak different languages. Lillian Rubin, in her classic book *Intimate Strangers,* sees marriage partners standing with a wide gulf of misunderstanding between them.[58] Deborah Tannen, in her widely heralded book *You Just Don't Understand,* suggests that it sometimes seems to women and men who try to understand each other that the opposite sex is "speaking in tongues."[59]

Changes in one person's behavior may require alterations in other family members' behavior if they are to mutually define the relationship as satisfactory. For example, if one spouse has submissively responded to a domineering partner, alterations in the submissive behavior will necessitate changes in the domineering behavior. One individual cannot be domineering unless he or she has a submissive partner.

Fifth, communication can be used for good or ill. We persuade people to hate and distrust others with the same sets of verbal and nonverbal cues we use when we teach them to love and trust the individuals with whom they interact. Your motives may be pure, but others may hold ill will. You can use your communicative skills to exert coercive power, as we shall determine in Chapter 13, or to show understanding of other family members, as we will discuss in Chapter 11.

Sixth, each of us has sets of expectations about family life from our original families that impact upon our own perceptions and behaviors. Most of us

BLONDIE reprinted with special permission of King Features Syndicate, Inc.

have an *original family*, a family-of-origin, or a family in which we were raised. Many of us go on to create a new or *current family.* You may be surprised by the similarity in your two families or by the similarity of your behavior in your current family with another member of your original family.

A woman who had just begun a current family agreed: "When you begin your own family, your family-of-origin's patterns, rules, and ways in general will inevitably affect your new family."[60] Although you may have vowed never to repeat phrases and words that your parents used, you may find that you automatically repeat the same warnings, threats, and even praise to your new family members. You may find that it is not easy to learn new communicative behaviors. The continuing nature of certain family practices are illustrated in the "Blondie" cartoon.

One woman in her early 20s observed that an understanding of family communication was useful, however. She explained, "An awareness of ourselves and our past histories gives us the control to make choices and to change patterns in our current families."[61] Even though communication will not solve all family problems, a thoughtful understanding of communication theory and a sensitive application to the family setting can result in more satisfying family relationships.

■ Seeking Family Satisfaction Through Communication: An Overview

Communication in the Family: Seeking Satisfaction in Changing Times can be summarized in the visual model presented in Figure 1.3. Change can result in lack of understanding and support; in loss of feelings of autonomy and intimacy; and in conflict, power struggles, stress, and decisions to be made. Communication allows us to demonstrate our understanding and support to other family members, to establish autonomy, to manage power and stress, and to make decisions. These important tasks are likely to result in increased satisfaction within the family unit.

Communicative behaviors provide one avenue to satisfying family relationships. Some authors have given communication strong recommendations. For example, the communication researchers Gerald Phillips and Buddy Goodall write:

Figure 1.3

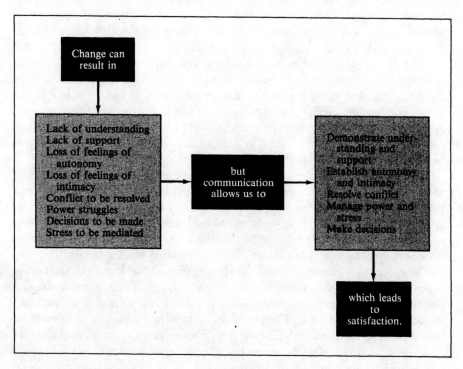

Communication allows us to seek satisfaction in changing times.

Talk is the substance of a loving relationship. Talk enables lovers to exchange feelings and make agreements about their day-to-day life. In this way each couple develops their own unwritten constitutions, agreements about how decisions are to be made and carried out, how disputes are to be settled, how rituals and ceremonies will be conducted, and how they will deal with each other and everyone else.[62]

Family therapists and practitioners often recommend communication to troubled families. Sven Wahlroos, author of *Family Communication*, is unequivocal: "In my two decades of practice as a clinical psychologist I have become convinced that the key to improvement of family relationships—and thereby to emotional health in general—lies in communication."[63] Therapist and hotline volunteer Jane Taylor explained in an interview that communication makes a healthy family:

Healthy families really talk to each other. Not at, over or around each other. Talking makes you vulnerable, but you've got to take the risk. And the other people in your family have to be willing to listen and hear.[64]

Sixth-grade students at Hanes Middle School in Winston-Salem, North Carolina, understand the importance of communication within the family as well. They were asked when they felt bad and when they felt good in their families. Not surprisingly, many of their responses focused on communicative behaviors. Che McPherson explained, "I feel good when my mom gives me helpful advice. I feel good when a family crisis works out. When my mom appreciates what I do, I look in the mirror and say, 'Boy, am I lucky.'" Jamie Grubbs disclosed, "Sometimes we get into arguments, but we always seem to solve them." Gina Facciolo revealed, "My mom makes me feel good when she discusses with me about my day-to-day problems." Aleeta Lofland reported, "I feel good when we talk about problems. I feel bad when my family doesn't get along. I feel bad when my family ignores each other." Stephanie Greer concluded, "The most fun time is talking about our problems because we can be like detectives and solve them."[65]

Popular authors, too, recommend communication. Best-selling books such as Shere Hite's *Women and Love: A Cultural Revolution in Progress* and Warren Farrell's *Why Men Are the Way They Are* discuss the problems in maintaining satisfying relationships. These authors and others identify communication as an essential predictor of satisfaction. In this book you will have the advantage of understanding the topic as a student of communication and the family.

This text is organized around the themes of communication in the family, changing times, and our interest in seeking satisfaction. The first five chapters consider basic information about communication in the family. This chapter introduced us to the topic. Chapter 2 will consider the variety of contemporary American families, and Chapter 3 will consider subsequent role changes. Chapter 4 focuses on verbal rules in family communication, and Chapter 5 will consider nonverbal rules.

The next four chapters deal with changing times. Chapters 6 through 9 detail the developmental changes that occur within families. Chapter 6 begins with the meeting of the couple and concludes with mating or marriage. Chapter 7 traces the family from the time a child is added until he or she is in school. Chapter 8 focuses on the family with an adolescent child. Chapter 9 traces the family from the empty next to the marital couple in retirement and to the demise of the marriage through death or divorce.

The third set of chapters suggests how we might seek satisfaction through our communicative behavior within our families. Family members may report higher levels of satisfaction to the extent that (1) they perceive the communication behavior of others within the family favorably, (2) they interact with each other, (3) they are able to demonstrate their understanding of others, (4) they are able to provide supportive and positive comments to each other, (5) they are able to resolve differences, reach consensus, and minimize conflict, and (6) they demonstrate flexibility. Chapter 10 discusses autonomy and intimacy. Chapter 11 considers understanding and support. Chapter 12 focuses on resolving conflict. Chapter 13 features the management of power and the making of decisions. Chapter 14 concludes the book with a discussion of relieving stress in families.

The purpose of this text is to help people learn more about marriages and family life with an emphasis on communication behaviors. Jeffrey H. Larson, certified family life educator and associate clinical professor in the Counseling and Development Center at Brigham Young University, observed that "students who complete a course in mariage and the family are less likely to believe in marital myths than students who do not complete such a course."[66] Larson proved his point by giving students who had taken marriage and family courses and those who had not a marriage quiz. Those in the first group did far better than those in the second group. Larson's quiz is reproduced here. You may wish to take this quiz before you take this course and then repeat it at the end of the course to determine how many myths have been dispelled during the course of the term.

The Marriage Quiz*

1. A husband's marital satisfaction is usually lower if his wife is employed full time than if she is a full-time homemaker.

2. Today most young, single, never-married people will eventually get married.

3. In most marriages having a child improves marital satisfaction for both spouses.

4. The best single predictor of overall marital satisfaction is the quality of a couple's sex life.

5. The divorce rate in America increased from 1960 to 1980.

6. A greater percentage of wives are in the work force today than in 1970.

7. Marital satisfaction for a wife is usually lower if she is employed full time than if she is a full-time homemaker.

8. If my spouse loves me, he/she should instinctively know what I want and need to be happy.

9. In a marriage in which the wife is employed full time, the husband usually assumes an equal share of the housekeeping.

10. For most couples marital satisfaction gradually increases from the first year of marriage through the child-bearing years, the teen years, the empty nest period, and retirement.

11. No matter how I behave, my spouse should love me simply because he/she *is* my spouse.

12. One of the most frequent marital problems is poor communication.

13. Husbands usually make more life style adjustments in marriage than wives.

---

*Items 1, 3, 4, 7, 8, 9, 10, 11, 13, 14, 15, 17, 18, 19, and 20 are false and are marital myths. The other items are true and are included as filler items for the marital myths.

14. Couples who cohabitated before marriage usually report greater marital satisfaction than couples who did not.

15. I can change my spouse by pointing out his/her inadequacies, errors, etc.

16. Couples who marry when one or both partners are under the age of 18 have more chance of eventually divorcing than those who marry when they are older.

17. Either my spouse loves me or does not love me; nothing I do will affect the way my spouse feels about me.

18. The more a spouse discloses positive and negative information to his/her partner, the greater the marital satisfaction of both partners.

19. I must feel better about my partner before I can change my behavior toward him/her.

20. Maintaining romantic love is *the key* to marital happiness over the life span for most couples.

SUMMARY

You understand the importance of families and you desire a personally satisfying family life. The purpose of this text is to help you to achieve your goal in these times of change. Communication is identified as the mediator. The term was defined as the interpretive process of understanding and sharing meaning with others. We stated that meaning arises out of social interaction and is continually shifting in response to that interaction and to the individual's understanding of it.

The family provides a unique communication setting. We observed in this chapter that families are organized, are relational transactional groups, usually occupy a common living space over an extended time period, and possess a mixture of interpersonal images that evolves through the exchange of meaning over time.

Communication within the family was characterized as symbolic, beginning with ourselves and how we believe others view us, as irreversible and unrepeatable, as including both content and relationship dimensions, and as serving both expressive and instrumental purposes. Communication will not solve all of our problems nor is it simple to understand. However, a thoughtful understanding of communication theory and a sensitive application to the family setting can be beneficial to family members. Communication allows us to demonstrate our understanding and support to other family members, to establish autonomy and intimacy, to resolve conflict, to manage power and stress, and to make decisions. These important tasks are likely to result in increased satisfaction within the family unit.

KEY TERMS

1. *Family satisfaction* is our positive or negative assessment of marriage and family life.

2. *Family stability* is the endurance, or likelihood of endurance, of the family unit.

3. *Relationship awareness* refers to people thinking and talking about their interaction patterns, comparing and contrasting themselves with others in their personal and familial relationships.

4. *Homogamy* means similarity between the two members of the couple concerning such areas as values, beliefs, and background.

5. *Community embeddedness* describes whether the union of the couple was approved by friends and neighbors.

6. *Dogmatic* individuals are authoritative and unyielding about personally held assertions.

7. *Communication* is the interpretive process of understanding and sharing meaning with others.

8. *Family* is an organized, relational transactional group, usually occupying a common living space over an extended time period, and possessing a confluence of interpersonal images that evolve through the exchange of meaning over time.

9. *Family communication* is symbolic, begins with ourselves and how we believe other family members view us, is irreversible and unrepeatable, includes both content and relationship dimensions, and serves both expressive and instrumental purposes.

10. *Equifinality* means families are capable of achieving similar goals or ends through a variety of different ways and with alternative starting points.

11. *Family-of-origin* is the family in which we were raised versus a current family which is the new family we go on to create. Often referred to in the textbook as the original family.

CHAPTER 2

THE CONTEMPORARY AMERICAN FAMILY

How glorious it is ... and also how painful ... to be an exception.

ALFRED DE MUSSET

After you have read this chapter, you will be able to

1. Define the following family types: cohabiting, couples with no children, nuclear, single-parent, blended, dual-worker, and extended.

2. Describe the kinds of pressures families experience within a particular family type.

3. Consider the physical, emotional, and social stressors that may result from different family types.

4. Identify factors that would explain why the blended family type is reported to be the most stressful family type.

5. Explain how communication patterns are affected by family type.

6. List the eight characteristics that distinguish the blended family from the nuclear family.

7. Differentiate among the categories of dual-worker marriages.

8. Identify advantages and disadvantages of a dual-career marriage for the wife, the husband, and the couple.

9. Discuss the unique problems faced by the extended family type.

You will probably be involved in a variety of different families throughout your life. The family in which you were raised, your original family, may be far different from that family, or those families, that you will initiate and create. You are as likely to be divorced, if you marry, as you are to remain in your marriage. You may marry a woman with a full-time career or a man with children from an earlier marriage. You will probably cohabit with another adult for some time period. The variety of family types in which you will engage is limited only by your imagination.

You may find these possibilities difficult to believe. Adolescents and young adults generally feel that they will be married only once and that they will be parents.[1] One study surveyed about 1,600 adolescents and found that 75 percent of the males and 80 percent of the females predicted that they would be married in the future. Of those people who believed that they would marry, 80 percent of the males and 87 percent of the females felt they would be married to only one person in their lifetime. Finally, 89 percent of the males and 80 percent of the females reported they would have children.[2] Although young adults do not predict divorce in their future, they do feel they might be single, widowed, or in nuclear families.[3]

These expectations of younger, never married adults are probably unrealistic given the changing nature of the family. One researcher writes:

> During this century, our society has undergone profound demographic change. Declining mortality and fertility have not only led to a graying of the population, they have also changed the complexion of family life. Families have become more "top heavy," intergenerational ties have become fewer and more homogeneous, intergenerational relations have become more complex and varied, and family bonds have an unprecedented duration. . . . Many aging societies are, like the United States, also divorcing societies.[4]

Some writers have correctly concluded that one American family no longer exists. One author in a special edition of *Newsweek* on "The 21st Century Family," concluded:

> The American family does not exist. Rather we are creating many American families, of diverse styles and shapes. In unprecedented numbers, our families are unalike: We have fathers working while mothers keep house; fathers and mothers both working away from home; single parents; second marriages bringing children together from unrelated backgrounds; childless couples; unmarried couples, with or without children; gay and lesbian parents. We are living through a period of historic change in American life.[5]

John Scanzoni, a family researcher at the University of Florida, acknowledges the changes in family life, but notes, "Although the family is changing in certain peripheral respects, it maintains a great deal of fundamental or core continuity as well."[6]

Contemporary American families are evolving and have problems associated with them, but families in the past were not without difficulties either.

Critics of the family have sometimes idealized the past. Historian Mary Stovall writes:

> A commonly heard cry, which often rises to a shriek, is that the American family is falling apart. Somehow, according to this scenario, the family has fallen from grace—from the stability of a two-parent household, in which the husband is the breadwinner and the wife the homemaker, who devotes herself to home and her numerous children, all of whom are invariably neat, polite, and well behaved. Under the rosy glow of nostalgia, we picture this nuclear group in a snug, comfortable home surrounded by the homes of loving grandparents and other kin, upon whom one could call for aid at any time and who gather for dinner every Sunday and holiday. Contrast this, say the contemporary critics with the present situation: a rising divorce rate, increasing incidence of child and wife abuse, the growing frequency and society acceptance of extramarital sexual relationships and a resultant rise in the rate of illegitimate births, and an increase in the number of unconventional and unsanctioned unions, both heterosexual and homosexual. Further, families in our mobile society are now often widely scattered from Maine to California and have few opportunities of interaction other than by telephone or letter. These are, without doubt, serious problems for American families that should not be minimized. Yet few of them are unique to the present.[7]

Stovall concludes that "No period has been a 'golden age' of the family, but each era has had its own challenges and trials; and yet the family has endured."[8] Felix Berardo agrees and adds that family researchers have been studying and chronicling these evolving family changes for decades.[9] He notes, "The expanding range of alternative marriage and family forms bring with it not only new freedoms and responsibilities but also associated problems. The emerging panorama of modern marriage and family types provokes new challenges for their members and the communities in which they are embedded."[10]

Families are evolving and this is reflected in the definition of families provided in the first chapter. The changing nature of the family poses new challenges for the individual seeking satisfaction within his or her family. In this chapter we will examine the most common types of contemporary American families, and we will consider some of the unique communication problems and patterns that exist in these family types.

As we observed, the family cannot be described simply by one family type. We will consider cohabiting couples, couples with no children, nuclear families, single-parent families, blended families, dual-worker families, and extended families. Your knowledge of the special characteristics of each of these family types may help you adjust to the stress you might experience. Changes from one family type to another may be seen as an expected developmental change or an unexpected event. Your satisfaction in the new family type may well depend upon your ability to communicate with other family members and their ability to interact effectively and appropriately with you.

❖ COHABITING COUPLES

When two unrelated and unmarried adults of the opposite sex share living quarters, with or without children, the family unit is defined as a *cohabiting couple.* Nonmarital cohabitation is not a new phenomenon,[11] but it has become more prevalent and more openly practiced by Americans in recent times.[12] The humorist Gerald Nachman observed that "Marriage could catch on again because living together is not quite living and not quite together. Premarital sex slowly evolves into premarital sox." Although his comments are witty, they are not accurate.

In 1990 approximately 2,856,000 cohabiting households were counted in the United States. This figure is more than five times the number that was reported in 1970. The largest proportion of those who were cohabiting in 1990 was from 25 to 34 years of age and the second largest group was those under 25 years of age.[13]

The research on cohabiting couples has been largely limited to college students; however, as the figures indicate, cohabitation is not limited to those in college. About 3 percent of the total United States households consist of cohabiting couples.[14] Family researcher Jesse Bernard observed, "Whether the United States will reach the Swedish figure—15 percent of all couples living together are not married to one another—is not discernible as yet, but the trend is in that direction."[15]

Over ten years ago, Macklin estimated that approximately one-quarter of American undergraduates had had a cohabitation experience;[16] the figures today are probably much higher. Furthermore, Macklin suggested that at least another 50 percent of college undergraduates would cohabit if they could find an appropriate partner. In general, it appears that college students approve of cohabitation outside the marital relationship.

Why do college students cohabit? Many suggest that they initially cohabited because they were in affectionate and monogamous relationships. This rationale has led other authors to conclude that cohabitation has become an additional step in the courtship process.[17]

Cohabitation occurs for a variety of reasons. It is not always a simple matter of an additional stage in courtship. Macklin identified a typology of cohabitation relationships: (1) temporary casual convenience—two people share the same living quarters out of expedience; (2) affectionate dating—going together type of relationship—the couple stays together because they enjoy each other and they will remain in the relationship as long as it is positive for both; (3) trial marriage—the couple may be seen to be "engaged to be engaged" and they are attempting to determine if their idiosyncrasies can be matched and meshed; (4) temporary alternative to marriage—the couple is waiting until they have sufficient money or another event occurs (such as college graduation) to marry, but they are committed to marriage; and (5) permanent alternative to marriage—couples live together as though they are married, but without either religious or legal sanctions. People in this last group may have been married and divorced earlier and are reluctant to enter into another marital arrangement.[18]

In some ways, college students who choose to cohabit are similar to those who do not choose to cohabit. For example, they do not have lower academic grade point averages, they are no more likely to come from dysfunctional homes, and they do not differ on desire to eventually marry.[19] Cohabiting and noncohabiting couples seem to be equally committed to each other.[20]

Some characteristics do distinguish cohabiting college students from non-cohabiting persons. Individuals who have experienced multiple marriages are more likely to choose a cohabiting relationship than are people who have not experienced earlier marriages. People who describe themselves as highly religious are less likely to cohabit than are those who describe themselves as less religious.[21] Women who cohabit view themselves as more competitive, independent, managerial, and aggressive than do women who do not cohabit. Men who cohabit see themselves as more supportive and warmer than do men who do not cohabit.[22] Cohabiting couples tend to describe themselves in less sex-role stereotypic ways than do noncohabiting couples.

Some researchers have expanded our knowledge of the cohabiting relationship beyond the college campus. Newcomb conducted a longitudinal study in which he assessed a variety of characteristics of students in the seventh, eight, and ninth grades in Los Angeles schools. He assessed these same people five and nine years later to determine personality traits, substance use, relationship with others, autonomy attitudes, dependency attitudes, friendship networks, and quality of life responses. Among his findings were that cohabitors display less law abidance, more drug use, and poorer relationships with parents and adults while in high school than do noncohabitors. He found that females cohabitors report less deliberateness, less diligence, more liberalism, less objectivity, and less self-acceptance than female noncohabitors and that male cohabitors report less congeniality and less orderliness than male noncohabitors.[23]

Yelsma included both older and younger cohabiting couples in his sample and his findings were somewhat different from studies conducted earlier. He determined that verbal and sexual communication were related to individuals' ages rather than to their married or cohabiting situation. Older people, whether married or cohabiting, were less likely to discuss a variety of issues including disagreements and personal problems. They were also less likely to discuss their sexual interests and fantasies.[24]

This study, though limited in scope, suggests that chronological age, rather than the type of relationship—cohabitation or marriage—may account for some of the differences we will discover between cohabitation and other family types. As we examine research in this area, we should keep in mind that most investigations on cohabiting couples have been limited to the college population and that we might not be able to extend our generalizations to other age groups.

What are the advantages of cohabitation? They include companionship, sexual activity, and economic gains. The disadvantages of cohabitation include conflict over property and other legal rights. In addition, young couples may face parental disapproval. Another potential negative outcome may be the legal rights or protection of children born to cohabiting couples.[25]

Finally, researchers suggest that violence may mark the young cohabiting group as compared to married couples. During one year, over 43 percent of cohabiting couples who were under the age of 30 experienced violence, whereas only 13 percent of married couples had such experiences.[26] We can only speculate on the difference in the incidence of violence in the cohabiting and married relationship. The lack of role models and the lack of established rules for the cohabiting relationship may contribute to greater ambiguity, increased stress, and more anxiety, which could lead to violence. Cohabiting couples are in less stable relationships and partners are more competitive with each other. Since the cohabiting couple does not have a legally sanctioned relationship, outside forces, including other people, may intrude into their lives. The partners may feel more concern with the potential dissolution of their relationship.

As we observed, many couples cohabit in order to determine if they will be successful in a marital relationship. However, couples might not behave the same in cohabiting relationships as they do in marriage. Sociologists Blumstein and Schwartz conducted an elaborate investigation of couples who were either cohabiting or married. They determined that cohabiting and married couples responded differently to the three variables under investigation: they handled the areas of sex, money, and work in different ways.[27]

In general, cohabiting couples appear to be more egalitarian than are married couples. For example, in cohabiting relationships, women initiate sex more often than do women in married relationships. Cohabitors feel that both partners should engage in wage-earning work and in housework. Cohabiting females are more independent than are married females and they avoid economic and other forms of dependence. Cohabiting women see money as a way to maintain equality in their relationships. Income, rather than biological sex, determines who makes particular decisions for the couple, including recreational activities and vacations.

In addition, cohabiting couples are more independent of each other than are married couples. Cohabitors spend more time alone or with other friends than do married couples. The partners generally have separate checking accounts. Male cohabitors are more competitive with their partners than are married men.

Finally, cohabiting couples appear to be more loving toward each other. Cohabitors engage in sex more often than do married couples. They fight about finances less than do married couples. And, male cohabitors rank their relationship as more important than their jobs more often than do married men.

This research by Blumstein and Schwartz has two important implications for our purposes: (1) Individuals who experience relational satisfaction in the cohabiting setting may or may not experience such satisfaction in the marital setting, and (2) communication patterns may be distinctive from the cohabitation setting to the marital setting. These implications have received some behavioral validation. Whether couples cohabit or have a more traditional courtship does not predict their long-term marital satisfaction.[28] Indeed, researchers have found that after a year of marriage, married women who had cohabited perceived a lower quality of communication than they had had during cohabitation and both married women and married men perceived less relational satisfaction than when they had cohabited.[29]

A current study extended these findings. Family researchers Alan Booth and David Johnson, at the University of Nebraska, compared white hetero-sexual couples who had cohabited with those who had not. They showed that cohabitation is negatively related to marital interaction and positively related to marital disagreement, proneness to divorce, and the probability of divorce. They suggest that people who cohabit may be poorer marriage risks from the start, but their greater likelihood to be in dissatisfying and unstable relation-ships may also be due to the cohabiting experience.[30]

Cohabitors may not really be experiencing a "trial" marriage as many sug-gest. The cultural demands and the role expectations placed on married cou-ples may far outweigh the relational rules that the cohabiting couple has estab-lished. Although a couple may feel that they are creating lifetime relational patterns during cohabitation, they may find these patterns are dramatically altered when they marry. Cohabitation may have its own unique set of char-acteristics and the communication patterns that occur between and among cohabitors may not be generalizable to other family types.

On the other hand, the differences found between cohabiting and married couples may be a function of the length of the relationship, the age of the cou-ples studied, or other developmental issues. We noted above that most research on cohabiting couples has been done on college students. The one exception showed that chronological age, rather than marital status, was a bet-ter predictor of some communicative practices.

In addition, unless researchers like Blumstein and Schwartz controlled for the length of the relationship, the differences they found may be due to changes that occur over time. For instance, cohabitors may be more egalitari-an because they are more likely to be engaged in similar outside activities (attending college classes or working) and have similar resources (same amount of money, same number of alternatives) while married people may be playing distinctive roles (the traditional mother has no other means of finan-cial support, the traditional father relies upon his wife for nurturing the chil-dren). Cohabitors may engage in more sexual activity because of their own relative youthfulness or the youthfulness of their relationship.

In either case, individuals who are contemplating a blissful married life, based on a relatively successful cohabitation experience, may wish to exercise some caution. The two experiences are not the same. As individuals move from cohabitation to marriage, their relationship may change simply because of the different family type. It may also change because the partners are aging and the relationship is developing and changing. We will consider relational development further in Chapters 6 through 9

❖ COUPLES WITH NO CHILDREN

Couples with no children are included within our definition of a family. Families consist of fewer children today than they have in the past. In the early twentieth century American families averaged 4 children; in 1970 the number was 3; by 1980 the average number of children per family was 2.2. Those families that began in the early 1980s are expected to average 2 children.[31] The U.S. Bureau of the Census found in 1988 that the average household included 2.64 people and the average family had 3.17 members. They observed, "These averages have never been lower."[32]

Greater numbers of young adults are choosing to have no children or fewer children than in the past. In 1971, about 45 percent of women aged 20 to 24 years old expected to have two or fewer children; in the early 1980s, the figure was 70 percent. In addition, for women who were in the age range of 40 to 44 in 1986, about 13 percent will have completed their childbearing years without having borne children.[33] When this same age group was asked ten years before, when they were aged 30 to 34, if they would have children, only 9 percent said that they would not.[34]

In addition, couples are waiting longer to have children today than they did in the past. The U.S. Bureau of the Census observes that a continuing increase in childlessness occurs among women 25 to 29 years old, which implies a greater tendency to postpone motherhood. Only 16 percent of women 25 to 29 years old were childless in 1970, compared with 27 percent in 1983. The bureau adds that women who were born after World War II are not as likely to begin their childbearing as soon as women born before this time.[35]

Will women continue this increased tendency to be childless? Researchers and census takers agree that an increased proportion of women will never have children. Perhaps as many as 20 percent of all married women and 29 percent of all women will remain childless.[36] Modern contraceptives, sterilization, and abortion may make childbearing more of a choice than it has been.

Some couples choose voluntary childlessness. Twenty years ago, a researcher suggested that only about 5 percent of all couples voluntarily forego bearing children, although this figure has probably increased within the last two decades.[37] Childless couples sometimes agree before they marry not to have children; others prolong the postponement of childbearing until the desirability of having children has diminished.

The delaying of childbirth and the decision to remain childless result in an increasing proportion of families who are couples without children. While some of these couples will eventually have children, 20 percent or more state that they do not wish to have any children. Researchers Masnick and Bane suggested that if trends continued, by 1990 an estimated 60 million American households would have had no children under the age of 15.[38]

Why do people choose to marry, but forego parenting? A recent article summarized some of these reasons and included

> lifestyle characteristics, personal characteristics such as birth order, family background, values and attitudes, and social factors such as social norms or sanctions, and the women's movement. . . . Many more women are in the labor force today and many are choosing lifetime careers outside the home. The need or lure for full-time employment for married women and the evi-

dence that employed married women usually receive little help with household or childrearing tasks from their husbands are important considerations for contemporary women and may influence their decisions about childbearing.[39]

What is the effect of remaining a childless couple? Some research suggests that the transition to parenthood is a crisis and that child rearing is associated with a decline in marital satisfaction.[40] Other models of the family suggest that couples without children are immature or maladjusted.[41] Debra Umberson at the University of Texas recently summarized the research on parenthood and psychological well-being. She concludes:

> Clearly, parenting is not a uniformly positive or negative experience, and it is not a static experience. At any given time, a parent may be experiencing both positive and negative effects of parenting. The balance of positive and negative effects can easily change—depending on one's economic circumstances, marital status, support networks, and so on.[42]

She adds that parenthood has a social meaning and that the costs of parenting are rising. She cites the rise in divorce, single parenting, stepparenting, female labor force participation, and poverty among women and children as part of these costs. People with economic and occupational resources may experience increased well-being in their parenting roles while those without such advantages may choose not to parent or may find parenting to be stressful and psychologically costly.[43]

Whether a couple chooses to have children or chooses to remain childless has some influence on their social networks. A recent study showed that when couples have children, they are more involved in a variety of social networks. Couples who are childless are the most isolated in the social networks of both neighbors and confidants. At the same time, a higher level of marital support was found among childless people than among the parents of small children. Childlessness seems to lead to weaker relationships with neighbors and others and stronger martial support.[44]

People who wish to have children, but are unable to do so, do not fare so well within their marital unit. Involuntary childlessness, resulting from infertility and related medical problems, has many deleterious effects on the couple. People who are unsuccessful in becoming parents experience a great deal of stress. Couples who find themselves in this marital crisis can cope by maintaining high self-esteem and by retaining their commitment to the marriage and their partner.[45]

❖ NUCLEAR FAMILIES

Nuclear families are conventionally "nuclear," with breadwinning fathers, homemaking mothers, and resident children. The U.S. Census Bureau does not provide precise statistics on the number of American families who

Figure 2.1

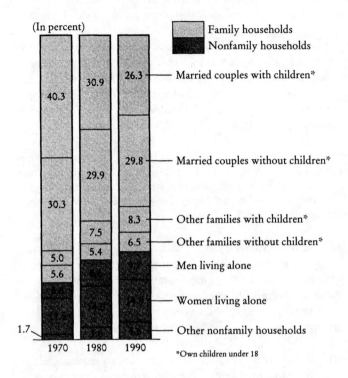

Household composition: 1970, 1980, and 1990 *(in percent)*.

meet these criteria; however, we can infer a decrease in this family type from the statistics that are provided. Figure 2.1, provided by the Census Bureau, illustrates that married couples with children have decreased from over 40 percent in 1970 to approximately 31 percent in 1980 to about 26 percent in 1990. Not all of these families are nuclear, however, since many of the women in these coupled relationships are working. Indeed, the Census Bureau reports that 61.2 percent of mothers with children under 18 years of age were working outside the home in 1990. This suggests that about 28.8 percent of the women who are married and have children are in nuclear families. In other words, approximately 7.5 percent of all American households are composed of nuclear families.[46] Research suggests that the small percentage of American families that are nuclear will decrease even more because this lifestyle does not fulfill the needs of couples in our contemporary world.[47]

Nonetheless, some families remain nuclear. Pressures on individuals in this familial arrangement may include their minority status as a family type. External pressure from friends and other family members may suggest that the family is out of date, that the couple holds ultraconservative values, that the wife is incapable of working, or that the husband is tyrannical.

The mother is often the pivotal person in the nuclear family. One married woman describes her own mother:

> My mother was a housewife, and took care of all of the domestic responsibilities of the household. Our house ran like a top. My mother was so meticulous with her daily routine (and ours) that everything usually came off without a hitch. . . . She reminds me of a general in the army at times. Any information regarding where we would be and what time we'd be home went to Mom. . . . Discussions about meals, shopping, or doctor appointments were with Mom. She played an integral and important role in the communicative practices of the family.[48]

The mother may have more influence on achieving a satisfying family life in the nuclear family than she has in other family types. If she is an effective communicator, the nuclear family may be more satisfied; if she is less effective, lower satisfaction may result.

Women who stay at home appear to be facing particular pressure. Studies that have concerned men's relatively shorter life span have concluded that stress at work accounts for men's earlier heart attacks and other life-threatening diseases. Recent studies that have examined stress in women have determined that women who work do not find their on-the-job role as stressful as they find their homemaking role. Women who have high-powered jobs report that their jobs are the least stressful elements in their lives. Sociologists at the Wellesley Center for Research on Women have demonstrated that homemaking women, particularly those with young children at home, are significantly more anxious and depressed than their working husbands.[49] Such research, which calls into question the notion that the workplace is a jungle of tension and pressure, also demonstrates the difficulty of the role of the stay-at-home woman.

A new reason for pressure on the woman who chooses to stay home is her current minority status. Ellen Rock, a Miami social worker, observes, "Things have been turned upside down. Before, women who went to work were isolated. Today, women who stay at home need support."[50] Working women who sometimes take a year or more off from work in order to have a baby, stay home with young children, or as a transition to a new job find that staying at home can be especially stressful. Marjorie Hansen-Shaevitz, director of the Institute for Family and Work Relationships in La Jolla, California, notes, "Bright, educated women often end up climbing the walls."[51]

Social support is available for women who stay at home. Across the country hundreds of support groups have been started. In many cases these groups consist of social gatherings in which mothers can share their concerns in one room of a home while their children interact in another. Other groups are more task-oriented in tone and discussions focus on infant development, family problems, and when it is appropriate for mothers to return to work.

Formal organizations have been established, too, to meet the needs of homemaking women. They extend across the country from Family Focus, a family center begun in 1976 in Evanston, Illinois; to the Mothers' Center in Hicksville, New York; the Park Bench for Mothers in New York City;

Parents Supporting Parents, Inc., in Grand Rapids, Michigan; and Birth to Three, Inc., in Eugene, Oregon. Such groups provide child care, lectures, discussion groups, and social opportunities to help women who stay at home deal with their sense of isolation; and they also provide a transition for women who wish to go back to work.

❖ SINGLE-PARENT FAMILIES

Just as it is difficult to characterize the contemporary American family as being of a single type, it is difficult to generalize about the single-parent fami-

Single-parent families have increased dramatically in recent times (© 1992, Ulrike Welsch).

ly, which has one adult and may include children who are adopted, natural, step-, or foster children. The single-parent family typically occurs when one parent dies or leaves the family unit; however, some individuals choose to parent by themselves from the start. An increasing number of women are choosing to have children by themselves. This includes women in their thirties who have careers but do not wish to pass up motherhood, as well as teen-agers[52] who may "overestimate the benefits of child-bearing."[53]

Married women with both children and careers may view single parenting as the most reasonable option for themselves if their marriage ends in divorce or the death of their spouse. One woman explains:

> Should my marriage end . . . the type of family I foresee in the future is the single parent family. I would choose this family type because (1) I like being my own person, (2) I don't want my children mistreated, and (3) I want everybody in the family to be comfortable with each other. . . . Having a companion is fine, but I like being my own person. This is not to imply that I can't be myself with a companion. This means, instead, that I believe I can fare far better by myself than I can with another individual. . . . I won't have to be skeptical or worry about getting things I really want when I'm alone. I won't even have to wonder about someone doing something for me when I can do it myself. . . . Being a single parent also means that my children will not be mistreated. . . . I wouldn't want to run the risk of remarrying and discover down the line that the man is a child abuser. This would be a tough pill to swallow. I'm not sure I could ever forgive myself if I end up in a situation like this. To be blamed for psychological maladjustments among my daughters would be something I would not want to experience. . . . In a single-parent family my children and I would be comfortable. We won't have to worry about adjusting to a strange situation with a "new" person or outsider. We can be "real" and at peace with each other.[54]

Single-parent families have increased dramatically in the past few years from 3.8 million family groups in 1970, to 6.9 million in 1980, and 9.7 million in 1990.[55] Table 2.1 summarizes the change in numbers and percentage of single-parent families for all families, as well as white, black, and Hispanic families. A variety of forces affect this change. The rising divorce rate contributes to a greater number of single-parent families. In addition, the larger numbers of mothers without husbands who form separate families increase the numbers of single-parent families. Finally, women's increased labor force participation may allow the dissolution of unhappy marriages and the creation of a single-parent family. (See page 46 for Table 2.1.)

Some single-parent families are families headed by men. An increasing number of fathers seek and receive custody of their minor children.[56] Approximately 17 percent of all divorcing men ask for custody and about two-thirds of those (about 11 percent) receive it. Single-parent fathers have been shown to be highly nurturing. They also show more concern for the nurturing role of the parent than either married mothers or married fathers. The nurturing aspects of the parental role is not dependent upon one's biological sex nor on whether or not one is in a married relationship.[57]

TABLE 2.4   SINGLE-PARENT FAMILIES IN 1970 AND 1990

	1990		1970	
	Number*	Percent	Number*	Percent
All Races	9,749	100	3,808	100
Maintained by Mother	8,398	86.1	3,415	89.7
Maintained by Father	1,351	13.9	398	10.3
White	6,389	100	2,638	100
Maintained by Mother	5,310	83.1	2,330	88.3
Maintained by Father	1,079	16.9	307	11.6
Black	3,081	100	1,148	100
Maintained by Mother	2,860	92.8	1,063	92.6
Maintained by Father	221	7.2	85	7.4
Hispanic	1,140	100	NA	NA
Maintained by Mother	1,003	88	NA	NA
Maintained by Father	138	12.1	NA	NA

*All numbers in thousands.

Nonetheless, most single-parent families are headed by women. While recent evidence suggests that women should not always be the custodial parent of choice,[59] women, men, and the courts still usually conclude that children belong with their mother.[60] Mothers may continue to gain custody of minor children at a far greater rate than do men.

In addition to the approximately 89 percent of women who serve as primary or joint custodial parents are the increasingly large number of women who choose to parent alone. Finally, it is more likely for the husband than the wife to die of illness, injury, or as a result of crime. The majority of single-parent families will probably continue to be headed by women.

Nonetheless, both women and men face difficulties when they serve as heads of single-parent households. Researchers suggest three areas of potential problems: (1) responsibility overload, (2) task overload, and (3) emotional overload.[61] Responsibility overload refers to the decision making concerning home and family that is not shared with another adult. Task overload means that the single parent often has too much to do. She or he must carry a full-time job as well as manage all of the responsibilities of the family and the home. Although we may believe that busy people always find time for everything, and people with leisure find time for nothing, the drain on the single parent is excessive. Emotional overload suggests that the single parent must be able to handle the emotional needs of his or her children even when physically, mentally, or emotionally exhausted from work or from handling other relationships.

The single-parent family is one in which great stress is evident. In essence, one parent must perform the role of two. "Supermoms" and "superdads" are frequently called upon to play three roles—that of mother, father, and economic supporter. Additional stress may result because of the pain of losing a family member. Death of one's spouse, divorce, and marital separation are the three leading causes of life events that cause stress.[62] Finally, many single-parent families, especially those headed by women, live in poverty.[63] The lack of economic resources exacerbates the other problems found in these families. These problems may also be greater or lesser depending upon the developmental stage of the family when the single parenting begins.[64]

Children are found in single-parent families more frequently today than in the past. The U.S. Bureau of the Census observed that one-parent family situations accounted for 28.1 percent of all families with children under the age of 18 in 1990 and contrasted the figure with 22 percent in 1980 and 13 percent in 1970.[65] Figure 2.2 depicts these changes. Stated another way, over one-fourth of

Figure 2.2

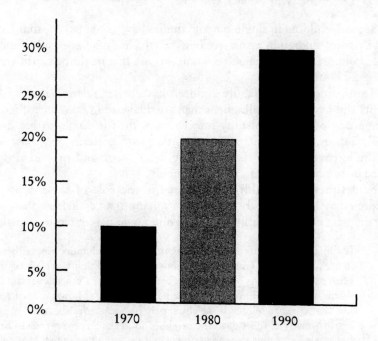

Percentages of single-parent families of all families with children under the age of 18.

all children under the age of 18 lived with only one parent in 1980.[66] If the current trends continue, one-third of all children born in 1970 and nearly one-half of children born in 1980 will live with only one parent at some point before they turn 18 years of age.[67]

A great deal of research and writing has considered the effect of single parenthood on children.[68] For some children, the single-parent family creates problems. For example, only children in single-parent families seem to fare worse than single-parent families in which there are two or more children.[69] Female children evaluate the divorced family situation as more negative than do female children in intact families.[70]

In those instances in which the single-parent family does affect the children adversely, other factors have been identified that account for these problems. Some characteristics of the single-parent mother have been identified that contribute to adolescents' problems. Mothers who are depressed, have lower educational levels, engage in greater rather than lesser conflict with their ex-spouses, and in greater rather than lesser conflict with their children are more likely to have children with academic and other difficulties.[71]

Most of the research in this area has shown that the effect of the single-parent family on the children is not as harmful as we might surmise. First, children adjust faster than adults to new family settings.[72] Although they fantasize about the reconstitution of their previous intact families, they accept their new situations. The children of divorce have a clear-eyed perception of reality, a sense of pragmatism, courage, and muted disappointment and sadness.[73]

Second, children in single-parent families have fewer psychosomatic problems than do children in intact families.[74] Such children have a lower incidence of such illnesses as headaches and stomachaches that might be considered psychological in origin.

Third, single-parent family children have better relationships with their parents and may be less delinquent than are dual-parent family children. More delinquency occurs in unhappy intact homes than in single-parent homes.[75] Family author James Coleman suggests that such patterns may exist because the single-parent family may be more democratic and may exhibit more shared decision making than the intact family.[76]

Sometimes older children are placed in the role of the absent parent. Children may learn more about problem solving at an earlier age than do children in intact homes. The oldest child in one single-parent family explains:

> Living in a single parent home I was attributed much more power than when living in my original dual-career family. I was the oldest and took on the responsibilities of the home. I made breakfast, packed lunches for my sister, Annie, and myself. I even started dinner. After school I took care of Annie. I had the power to tell her if she could play or not. If ever she had any problems with any of the kids in the neighborhood she'd come get me to help her out. I felt like Annie depended on me and I need to be needed. Mom depended on me, too. Mom expected me to take care of Annie and make sure the house was picked up before she got home from work.[77]

Nonetheless we should observe that a classic study on the family has demonstrated that the likelihood of delinquency in children was more a function of maternal supervision than the presence or absence of a man.[78] The single-parent household with a poor woman at its head may deprive the children of maternal supervision. Since the mother may be forced to work, she may deprive the children of her attention, and it is this deprivation that is most critical.[79] Youth in a mother-only family are more likely to exhibit some forms of deviant behavior than are youth in families that include the presence of another adult.[80]

Finally, although children from a single-parent home are more likely to experience congregate care (day care) or informal care (care from a relative or neighbor), we cannot conclude that such care is inferior to care from one's mother. Most children (nine out of ten) spend their time in informal care rather than congregate care and no research has compared this with maternal care. Studies that have compared congregate care to maternal care have not distinguished between adequate and inadequate care, but have nonetheless demonstrated little difference. No differences occur in intellectual development, but some children experience difficulty in emotional and social development.[81] Children whose parents cite others as their major caretakers have the highest self-concept scores, higher than children whose parents (mother only, father only, or both) served as primary caretaker.[82]

While the single-parent situation does not appear to impact negatively on children, its effect on parents can be devastating. In addition, it clearly changes the patterns of communication that exist in the family. Both the external and internal networks change drastically. First, if the single-parent household has occurred as a result of a death, dissolution, or divorce, the absence of one family member creates shifts and changes in the interaction behavior of the remaining members. For example, if one of the children was very close to the noncustodial parent, he or she might have to vie for the attention of a sibling or the custodial parent. Or, if the noncustodial parent created tension and stress in the family, the single-parent family might greatly benefit and interact more smoothly after the absent parent has left.

Second, if the new household has been created because of dissolution or divorce, the family member who has left is generally part of an external network. The noncustodial parent may interact with family members from not at all to every day. Even though the noncustodial parent is no longer living in the same home, he or she may still play an important continuing role in the new family.

Third, new communication patterns between the noncustodial parent and the custodial parent may be created that involve the children. For instance, the children may be used to communicate messages between their parents. Anger, jealousy, and other negative emotions intended for the other parent may be communicated to the child. Conversely, the noncustodial parent may pamper the children in order to hurt or embarrass the custodial parent.

Fourth, external networks that provided social support at earlier times may disappear. The widow often can rely upon her in-laws to share her grief and to provide her with support; the divorced woman cannot. Women often lose their spouses and the spouse's family when their marriage is ended through dissolution or divorce. Friends of a couple may not remain friends of two individuals who are no longer married.[83] Former friends will generally choose one of the members of the couple with which to align, or they may dissolve their relationship with both members of the couple. Rarely do they remain friends with both members of the divorcing or dissolving couple. Individuals who have played key roles in each others' lives may no longer interact.

Roles also shift in the newly created single-parent family. We observed earlier that it is difficult for parents to play the roles of mother, father, and wage earner. Oftentimes one of the children serves as a surrogate parent. An older child may provide the socioemotional comfort that the younger children need. Sometimes an older child serves as the "sounding board" for the single parent and helps to solve problems. Generally, the family members become more democratic; and shared decision making, rather than parental control, becomes the order of the day.[84]

Roles may shift in other ways, too. The custodial parent may not have the authority that the two parents previously held. If the custodial parent is a small woman who rarely punished the children, she may not be able to gain cooperation or compliance from them. If the custodial parent is viewed as lacking in some quality by the children, he or she may not have the respect of older children. If the children blame the custodial parent for the loss of the other parent, new roles may result.

The success or failure of the single-parent family probably rests on the level of flexibility that is present in the family. When the custodial parent is inflexible, he or she is likely to suffer greater loss and be less able to help create a new functioning family. Changing roles, adapting communication patterns, and generally shifting one's conception of the family unit are essential. You may not be in a single-parent family at the current time, but the likelihood that you will be in such a family over the course of your lifetime is very great.

❖ BLENDED FAMILIES

Samuel Johnson and Mark Twain are both credited with the statement that "Remarriage is the triumph of hope over experience." Today's remarriage statistics suggest that people may be exhibiting more hope than experience. This family type has dramatically increased in recent times in our culture.[85]

Before the 1970s most remarriages occurred after the death of a spouse; today most occur after divorce.[86] In the past many remarriages did not include children. The current figures identify more than 1.5 million adults who remarry each year, and in 60 percent of those marriages children are included.[87] The number of remarried families and stepfamilies in the United States has become fairly stable within the last decade. In 1980, 11.2 million American families were remarried families and 4.35 million of those were blended families; in 1987, 11.0 million were in remarried families with 4.3 million of them including children.[88] These figures suggest that in 1987, blended families constituted 17.4 percent of all families with young children.[89]

Although the remarriage and blended family statistics have been fairly stable, demographers believe this family type will predominate by the year 2000 and will actually outnumber first families.[90] Some estimates suggest that over half of today's young people will be stepsons or stepdaughters at the turn of this century.[91] Blended families occur not only after the first divorce, but after subsequent divorces as well. Since the redivorce rate is higher than the divorce rate for first marriages,[92] an increased number of blended families may occur. Today about 49 percent of all women and men divorce after the first marriage, but about 54 percent of women and 61 percent of men who remarry will redivorce.[93]

The blended family, reconstituted family, stepfamily, or remarried family consists of two adults and step-, adoptive, or foster children. One of the difficulties of the blended family is that it is fairly new and that we have neither terminology to discuss it nor do we have research that explains the complex nature of it.

Figure 2.3, which depicts two actual, contemporary men and their spouses, demonstrates the complexity of the increasingly common reconstituted family. David, married five times, has four natural children and two stepchildren (his current wife is Jan). Peter similarly has four biological children and two stepchildren, but he has been married twice. However, Peter's stepchildren are David's biological children and David's stepchildren are not related to Peter at all. Karen (the biological child of David and Jane, but who has lived with Peter and Jane since Karen was 3) was asked in junior high to list the names and ages of her brothers and sisters. She smiled and asked for additional paper. (Karen has one biological full brother, four half-siblings, and four stepbrothers.)

The blended family may resemble the nuclear family and in many ways it is similar.[94] However, some distinctions can be drawn. The blended family experiences three stages of development that the nuclear family does not: (1) the dissolution of the original nuclear family, (2) the reorganization as a single-parent family, and (3) the reconstitution as a remarried family.[95] Prescribable behaviors for remarried families are even more difficult to determine than they are for nuclear families.

Family communication authors Kathleen Galvin and Bernard Brommel summarize eight characteristics that distinguish the blended or stepfamily from the nuclear family that further clarify the uniqueness of this family type:

1. A history of loss emerges for those who were previously in a two-parent system.

2. Some or all members bring past family history from a relationship that has changed or ended.

3. The couple does not begin as a dyad, but rather, parent-child relationships predate the spousal bond.

4. One or two biological parents (living or dead) influence the stepfamily.

5. Children may function as members of two households.

6. The family has a complex extended family network.

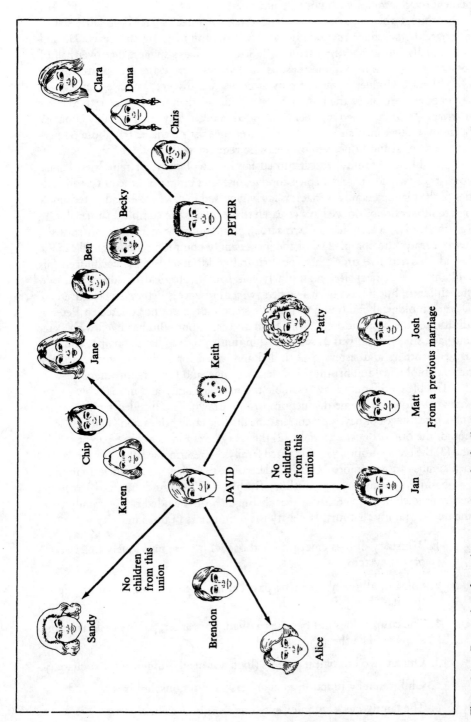

Figure 2.3　Reconstituted marriages create complex family trees.

7. Strong triangles exist, which involve biological parents/former spouses that influence the stepfamily.

8. No legal relationships exist between the stepparent and stepchildren.[96]

The process of blending more than one family is difficult. Similarly, establishing effective and appropriate communication patterns is arduous. In the nuclear family, communication patterns are established with family members, beginning with the marital couple and including children as they are born or adopted. In the blended family, communication patterns have already been established among a group of people or among several groups of people. For example, the spouses may have been a previous childless couple, a nuclear family, a single-parent family, and perhaps even another blended family. The children have been in at least a nuclear and a single-parent family. The family has a complex extended family network that may include far more people than those depicted in Figure 2.3.

Communication patterns in the blended family are often primary between one parent and the child or children from his or her previous marriage. This parent and his or her children may be bonded more deeply than are the parent and his or her new spouse and almost certainly more so than the children and the new stepparent. The new adult needs to become aware of the communication patterns, time commitments, and other constraints that have been established. His or her entry into the family group may be seen as disruptive to the previous relationship. For example, the children may view disclosures between the biological parent and the stepparent as intrusive into their relationship with their biological parent. The time taken away from the children and the biological parent may become a bone of contention.

New patterns are established within the newly reconstituted family, but these are dependent upon previously established patterns.[97] Past family history from the previous relationships is brought forward. The loss of the spouse or parent has created unique memories, and a sense of loss and stress, for the other spouse and children. In addition, former family members may continue to play a role in the life of part or all of the members of the newly created family. The children in the reconstituted family may function as members of two households. Biological parents continue to influence the new family, whether they are still living or whether they are deceased. A divorce or dissolution does not terminate the relationship with former family members; neither does remarriage.

The blended family provides some special problems. Patterns of behavior that might have been part of earlier families may no longer be appropriate. However, individuals may continue to rely upon such behaviors. For example, Karen, the youngest child of David and Jane, found herself in a precarious situation in the blended family created by Peter and Jane when she moved from being the youngest sibling to the middle child (after the birth of Ben and when her brother Chip lived with them), and then to the oldest (when Chip moved to live with David and Alice). Her infantile behavior was no longer appropriate and she was not rewarded for being dependent and helpless.

The woman who described her family life within the single-parent family found herself in a blended family after a period of time. Her role as a caretaker of her younger sister and as the manager of the house became dysfunctional:

> Mom married a man with three children whose ages ranged from a year younger than me to a year older than Annie. We all lived together—yuck!
>
> There was a major difference between his kids and Annie and I. His kids had always had a babysitter, whereas Annie and I had always depended on each other. I was in the position of babysitter, therefore Annie listened to me. When all those kids moved in everything changed. Although it was unspoken, my Mom still expected *me* to make sure the house was clean before she came home. This task was not as easy as it once was. Now when I asked one of his kids to pick up their coat and put it away during the next television commercial, I was met with hostile name calling. They told me I didn't have the right to tell them what to do and they just would not comply with the request. Annie caught on to this real quickly and she too started to see me as the bad guy. Everyone said I was too pushy. Boy, was I in a double bind. When the adults came home, Annie and his kids complained to him about how pushy I was because I was telling them what to do.[98]

Shifting allegiances for marital partners and children create stress. Grandparents may have particular difficulty in dealing with dissolution and remarriage. They may become embroiled in the anger and unhappiness that surrounds the divorce and they may also lose contact with their grandchildren.[99] One of Chip's maternal grandparent's developed a strong dislike for David. He never failed to offer sarcastic remarks about David to Chip. Chip, who felt close to his father, and eventually moved from his mother's home to his father's home, felt alienated by his grandfather's remarks. He chose not to see him after moving to his father's home.

Uncertainty and lack of stability may result in tension and anxiety that interfere with satisfying family interaction. Sandy was David's first wife. When Jane met David, he was married to Sandy. David assured Jane that his marriage to Sandy was "open" and that they could develop their own relationship. After David and Jane became intimate, Sandy learned of their relationship and divorced David. Although Jane married David shortly thereafter she never completely trusted him. She felt that David might behave in a similar manner to her. Indeed, before the couple had been married two years, David had begun another relationship. Alice, David's fourth spouse, confided later to Jane that she felt "nervous" about her relationship to David during the entire three years that she was married to him, too.

Children who enter the blended family may experience more stress than they felt when their parents divorced. As we observed earlier, children often hold the fantasy that their parents will eventually remarry. The marriage of one of their parents to a new partner kills that fantasy. A parent's remarriage may be a way of experiencing the anxiety and loneliness of the divorce again.

The event may call forward past worries concerning marriage and divorce. The children may recognize that the dream of reuniting with their former family is now lost.

In addition, the noncustodial parent, who may have been involved to some extent with the children, may become less involved after the remarriage.[100] In this way, too, children may lose support and understanding. They may feel abandoned by the noncustodial parent a second time. Young children may regress as they experience the remarriage of one of their parents. Adolescents may feel the stress of having two sets of values against which to rebel, two families from which to retreat.[101]

Children who have wanted siblings—the only child who wanted a brother or sister, the young girl who wants an older brother, or the child who wants a same-age, same-sex sibling—may be temporarily pleased with the new family. However, reality is often different from our fantasies. The reality of the new family may not meet their expectations. If children feel that they have suffered many losses, they might be reluctant to develop a closeness or bond with the new family members. For many children, a sense of permanence within the new family does not come about until the remarried couple has a child of their own. At this point, the children of earlier marriages view the remarriage as secure and strong.

Does the inclusion of children from the past marriages enhance or detract from family stability? While many researchers report higher redivorce rates in blended families with children from earlier marriages,[102] others reject the notion that it is the previous children that encourage redivorce.[103] They suggest that while a relationship between having children prior to the marriage may correlate with a higher redivorce rate, the children are not the cause for the redivorce.

Sometimes people in blended marriages rush into having children together in the belief that it will solidify them as a family. Does the marriage benefit by having "our" children as well as "his" and/or "hers"? Having children does not enhance first marriages, even though it is a commonly held belief by laypeople. In the same way, mutual children in blended families do not cement the relationship.[104] In addition, parents perceive differences in the treatment of the three sets of children from the two previous and the current marriage, which can create tension between them and among the children.[105] Couples in blended families may be well advised to delay the addition of more children until their own relationship is stable and satisfying.

Although remarriage is most stressful for mothers, particularly those with young children,[106] it is difficult for both the husbands and wives. If their partner has children, the stepparent may find that he or she is in competition with the biological parent. Special problems may occur if a spouse is being added to a single-parent family that has existed for some time. Legal problems, name changes, and other related matters are difficult for both men and women in remarriage.

Communication researchers Ken Cissna, Dennis Cox, and Arthur Bochner recently studied the dilemmas created within blended families.

They interviewed nine couples who had created blended families and found that the only commonly held problem by the couples was the tension created between the marital and parental relationships. Couples discussed the ambiguity of being both a spouse and a parent and the strain it placed on their multiple relationships. These investigators determined that couples needed first to establish the solidarity and credibility of their marriage, which would then strengthen the stepparent/stepchild relationship. The more solid and strong the marriage, the more freedom the stepparent had to discipline and guide the stepchildren.[107] The primacy of the marital relationship in the blended family seems to underlie the successful functioning of the blended family.

In order to succeed the blended marriage must also develop its own unique communication patterns. As we observed above, these will be built, to some extent, upon past relationships. Nonetheless, each family member must be able to contribute to the new functioning patterns of the family unit if a satisfying family life is a goal.[108] Family members must be able to be open and honest with each other as new patterns are developed.

Other qualities mark the successful blended family. Those families who receive social support report more happiness.[109] Individual qualities such as optimism, expressiveness, and being able to agree with others are related to greater satisfaction within the blended family.[110] Flexibility is essential for all members of the family. We should observe that the newly created blended family will not be static either. Changes will occur throughout the lifetime of this family that will continually require that family members are sensitive to changes and can adapt to them.

The blended family must initially deal with a variety of issues such as *roles*. What does being the mother, father, oldest child, youngest child, stepchild, and others mean in this family? What is the stepmother called? Whom does one call "Dad," "Daddy," or "Paul"?

Who *belongs* to the reconstituted family? Do children who do not regularly live in the home belong to the new family or do only those children who live with the blended couple belong? Can the children change their place of residence if they desire? For whom should family members buy holiday gifts? For whom should they plan a party or entertain? How many places should be set at the dinner table?

Who provides *love*? Do stepsiblings behave as though they care about each other even when they do not? Can a biological mother who lives with her biological children love her stepchildren in the same way? How can biological children feel secure in their parents' love when the family unit is expanding? Do parents who live far away and rarely see their children love them in the same way they did when they shared the same dwelling?

What *subgroups* exist in the family? Do the mother and the children from the first marriage comprise such a subgroup? Does the reconstituted couple form a subgroup? Does the composition of subgroups lead to conflict? To what extent do prior loyalties affect conflict resolution?

Who has *authority or power*? Can the stepparent discipline his or her spouse's children? Does a biological parent who is not living in the home have more authority than a stepparent living in the blended family home? Questions of dependence and independence must be resolved as children gain or lose autonomy over day-to-day decisions.

How are *problems solved*? Should children rely upon biological parents who are not living with them to help them solve their problems? Does the entire family try to solve problems that predate the creation of the newly reconstituted family? Can one of the spouses count on her new spouse to solve problems with the previous spouse?

Similarly, among whom does *decision making* occur? Do members of the extended family network enter the decision-making process? Are critical questions that deal with older children's decisions to enter particular colleges or universities, to get married, to drop out of school, to get a job handled only by the child himself or herself? Do the two biological parents assist in such decisions? Is the stepparent included? Does decision making about such matters change when the stepparent is financially responsible for the child?

How has the *territory* of the home been changed? When stepsiblings visit on the weekends and vacations, do they have access to the bedrooms of the siblings who are in residence? Have rules concerning privacy changed? Can the children still enter the parents' bedroom without knocking? Does the new spouse have a right to claim certain space that previously belonged to someone else? In short, how can a limited amount of space be altered to accommodate everyone's changing needs?

The blended family provides unique problems for individuals who desire effective and appropriate communication patterns. In many ways the blended family is like a Rubik's cube. Alterations on one side of the cube, like changes in one blended family, change the makeup of related blended, single-parent, and childless-couple families. The multiple connections, the different expectations, and the varying past experiences of each of the members create unique and sometimes seemingly insoluble problems. One researcher asserts, "We have no set of beliefs, no language, and no rules for a family form that has 'more than two parents.'"[111] Nonetheless, the blended family is increasing in dramatic proportions in the United States. At some point in your life you are likely to be involved, as a child or as a spouse, in the emerging blended family.

❖ DUAL-WORKER FAMILIES

The dual-worker family, which includes two working adults, has also increased in our recent history. One observer noted that norms concerning the appropriateness of wives working out of the home were reversed within a single generation.[112] Recent statistics suggest a radical shift in the working patterns of American families.[113] Over three-fifths of the women 18 to 64 years of age were in the labor force in 1982.[114] Fifty-one percent of all wives were in that group.[115] Many women who work are also mothers: Fifty percent of working women have children under 6 years of age; 66 percent have children who are 6–17 years old.[116] In 1987, over half of all American families were dealing with the competing demands of marriage, children, and two jobs.[117]

The increasing number of women in colleges, graduate schools, and professional schools suggest that more women will be seeking jobs in the future. After persevering in the academic setting in order to earn coveted degrees, many women are unwilling to forego careers. One woman expresses these thoughts:

> I anticipate the dual-career family in my future for the simple fact that I
> have devoted a great deal of time acquiring an education. As a result of my
> toils, I could not fathom the idea of not being highly committed to work.
> Since I am ambitious, goal-oriented, and future-oriented, I would like to be
> married to someone with similar characteristics, if and when that happens. It
> would be highly likely that this individual would be highly committed to
> work as well.[118]

The new marital arrangements that include two working partners may be divided into conventional dual-worker marriages, unconventional dual-worker marriages, and dual-career marriages. Conventional dual-worker marriages are those in which the husband is viewed to be primarily interested in a career and the wife is primarily associated with the home and family. Unconventional dual-worker marriages place the wife as the one with the major career interest and the husband has the major family interest; such marriages are extremely rare. The dual-career marriage includes two partners who are committed to both their careers and their families. Although this marital arrangement is not experienced by a majority of people, it is steadily increasing. Most dual-worker marriages are also conventional dual-worker families.

The dual-worker couple is a marital arrangement that may be based on economics, egalitarianism, and technology, among other factors. There can be no doubt that it is different from the nuclear family since one's paid employment affects his or her homelife and one's homelife affects his or her work.[119] This new family form calls into question basic assumptions concerning one's sex role and one's function within the family unit. Traditional stereotypes are challenged. Let us examine the conventional dual-worker family and the dual-career family.

■ Conventional Dual-Worker Families

Conventional dual-worker families have not been studied to a great extent. Perhaps they are viewed as closer to nuclear families, or maybe they are seen as less attractive than dual-career families. Dual-worker families can be distinguished in a number of ways. First, their standard of living does not allow services such as day care, housekeeping, or extended babysitting. Second, their social class does not provide support for such choices. Third, their own attitudes do not include the wife in the breadwinning role.

Dual-worker couples, unlike dual-career couples, have relatively little money at their disposal. As a consequence, such forms of assistance as day-care centers, daily or weekly housekeepers, and regular daytime babysitters are beyond the means of most dual-worker couples. Nonetheless, such services are of great help when both members of the couple work.

Dual-worker couples are primarily from blue-collar or middle-income families. They did not experience dual jobs in the past generation and have difficulty supporting it in the current one. The parents of the dual-career couple are more likely to disapprove than approve of their children's lifestyle. In such cases, grandparents are less likely to babysit on a routine basis. Dual-working women feel compelled to maintain the same standards of cleanliness in their homes and to provide the same kinds of meals as they had prepared before they joined the work force.

The dual-worker couples themselves do not accept new sex roles that allow the husband to share in housekeeping and child-rearing tasks. Often, the couples diminish the wife's financial contribution to the family unit. Instead, her salary is viewed as "helping out." In this way, the dual-working couple denies the alteration in their lifestyle and continue to behave as though they are in a nuclear family with a breadwinning father and a homemaking mother. This denial is significant since denial is viewed as a classic stage in family crisis.[120]

Additional problems arise for these families. Women in dual-worker marriages lose both earnings and job prestige when they begin to have children. A Rand Corporation study showed that both average earnings and job prestige declines when working mothers have their first child. Part of the differential may be attributed to women switching from more highly paid work to more flexible, but lower-paid, jobs. In addition, some women leave the work force temporarily after the first birth. However, 22 percent of women continue to work throughout their pregnancies and immediately after the birth of their children. Men in dual-worker marriages do not face such loss upon the birth of the first child.[121]

The stress in the conventional dual-worker family is obvious. Two people are attempting to do the work of three with little external or internal support. In addition, the couple often denies the reality of their situation. Finally, the children in such families may receive inadequate care and insufficient interaction time with other members of their families.

■ Dual-Career Marriages

Dual-career marriages include a husband and wife who are both committed to their careers and to their families. Dual-career couples generally make more money than those involved in conventional dual-worker marriages. The individuals who choose the dual-career marriage are different from those who choose more traditional marital forms.

Women who choose the dual-career marriage are often the oldest child in their families or were the only child. Many had work-oriented mothers; experienced some form of tension with their fathers; had a prolonged separation from parents during childhood or had some other disturbing experience; many had no other adult relative living within their family settings, and were often members of a relatively high social class.[122]

Working women tend to be less traditional in their philosophical beliefs while nonworking women tend to be more stereotypically feminine.[123] Women who work outside the home see themselves as more aggressive, ambitious, and intelligent than do women who are homemakers. Homemaking women see themselves holding more conservative values, having a more traditional view of women's roles, perceiving a more supportive family life, expressing lower self-esteem, and being less dissatisfied than women who work outside the home.[124]

The husbands in dual-career marriages are similarly less traditional in philosophical orientation and behavior, while men who are sole wage earners are the most traditional in orientation and in their actual behavior.[125] Men with working wives make fewer long-distance moves than do men whose wives do not work. Although the two-career family does not move as often for economic opportunities, they are compensated by a higher standard of living in the same geographical area.

Many couples initially choose the dual-career marriage in order to approximate their desired standard of living and, indeed, this marital choice is relatively economically prosperous. Often, dual-career couples limit the number of children to only one or two. Women with high career commitments tend to have fewer children than others.[126]

How do dual-worker couples behave after they are married? They can be distinguished from traditional couples in a number of ways. Wives appear to participate more in financial and socioeconomic decisions in dual worker marriages than in traditional marriages. However, research shows that even though educated, professional women have made financial gains, the control of financial matters in the dual-earner family still lies largely in the husband's hands. More equal sharing of financial decisions occurs only when the wife's income approaches her husband's income.[127]

Their husbands provide more child care than do traditional husbands, but the wives believe they should perform more tasks.[128] Women in two-career relationships still bear the major responsibility for housework and child care; thus working women are simply lengthening their workday.[129]

Dual-career marriages are distinct from traditional marriages, but not in as many ways as one might speculate. Sex roles are not discrepant in the dual-career marriage. Sex roles are not discrete in traditional marriages and sex-role blur does not always occur in the dual-career marriage to the extent that might be suggested. The sanctified sex-role division of work and power continues to dominate. However, the dual-career marriage challenges traditional stereotypes, and power conflicts are common occurrences.[130]

Wives may be limited in their own occupational achievement by their husband's achievement. The higher the husband's occupational attainment, the more likely she is to benefit from her education.[131] While a woman may have the education necessary for job success, she may not be allowed to achieve that goal unless her husband has comparable or higher achievements.

Marital instability distinguishes the dual-career marriage from a conventional marriage. One researcher suggests that for every $1,000 increase in a wife's salary, the possibility that she will divorce increases by 2 percent.[132] More recent studies demonstrate that the relationship between the wife's salary and the likelihood of divorce or dissolution is not so simplistic.[133] In addition, marital stability cannot be equated with marital satisfaction, and we should not conclude that marital satisfaction differentiates the dual-career marriage from the more traditional marriage.

How Do Children Perceive the Dual-Career Family?   The children of dual-career couples perceive both benefits and costs associated with this family type. Dual-career children generally give their family high marks. Adolescents rate the dual-career family high in family strength, especially in the areas of supportiveness and concern. One man in his middle twenties recalled his dual-career original family fondly:

> Both my parents work, and at the same time, are highly concerned for our family of five kids. My mother is a high school teacher as well as the primary person responsible for the duties in the home. Being a teacher was an ideal job for my mom as it enabled her to conveniently attend to her home and family responsibilities. She was home in the mornings sending us kids off to school as well as in the afternoon soon after we arrived from school. In addition, she was home during the summer months while we were home from summer vacation. I never really though of my mom as having a career, just a job she really enjoys. The family was of most importance to her.
> My father works at a federal nuclear power plant. He has worked there for over twenty years. Dad is usually gone by 6:00 A.M., catching a bus to work, and he returns home in the evening around 6:00 P.M. I rarely saw my dad in the morning, but I usually saw him in the evenings. Dad was very committed to the family. I'm not sure if I would consider dad's job as a career either. It seems to be a means to an end: earning money to provide for and be with the family.[134]

A young woman believes that her dual-career parents taught her versatility and flexibility. She explains:

> My original family type was dual-career for the majority of the time at home. . . . My mother and father . . . are able to adapt to the role which is most appropriate for the situation.
> The communication patterns of the family as a whole forced each member of the family to be versatile. This is probably one of the most valuable skills that I am consciously aware of learning throughout childhood. Along with versatility of communicative style comes flexibility in life in general. This is one of the words which was always stressed in family activities. I believe this prepared us for accepting change, differences in others, and the many inconsistencies of life.[135]

However, the children in these families, like their parents, see the primary problem as one of time constraints. The children correctly perceive the enormous time demands on all family members.[136]

The children within the dual-earner families are provided with fewer stereotypic expectations than are those in traditional homes. In a study that examined the family chores assigned to adolescents in the homes of nuclear and dual-earner families, the adolescents in dual-earner families were less likely to be assigned stereotypic male or female chores than were adolescents in traditional families. However, the male adolescents in the dual-earner families spent only one-third the time on chores as did the male adolescents in traditional families, but the daughters in dual-earner families spent 25 percent more.[137] Dual-earner families appear to rely on their female children more than their male children to help with extra household duties.

How Do Wives Perceive This Family Type?   The husbands and wives in the dual-career family also reap both advantages and disadvantages. Wives benefit by being both physically and psychologically healthier,[138] by being more physically active,[139] by having higher self-esteem, and by having less feeling of isolation.[140] Dual-career wives have a sense of financial independence that homemakers do not enjoy. Similarly, they are less apt to gain their identities from husbands and children.

The picture of the dual-career marriage is not completely rosy, however. Wives report a number of disadvantages to this lifestyle. Their primary concern is that of stress,[141] although this is not a universal issue.[142] Internal stress includes worker overload. Even in the dual-career marriage, where both spouses state that they have equal commitments to home and work, the wives carry far more than their equal share at home and they report more overload.[143] One national survey showed that husbands of employed women (those working 30 hours per week or more) spent an average of 3.8 hours per day on housework or child care compared to their wives, who spent 6.9 hours per day on such duties.[144] Having a wife working outside the home is not a sufficient condition in the acceptance by her husband of typically female household responsibilities and roles.[145] The "Hi and Lois" cartoon illustrates the work that waits for the working woman.

A second source of internal stress for women is role conflict and identity confusion, sometimes referred to as "role blur."[146] These wives have particular problems if they are also mothers.[147] Mothers' concerns about their children's development is related to a diminished sense of well-being.[148] Early socialization, a lack of female role models, insufficient networks of supportive individuals, and the attitudes of her current family, particularly her husband, often exacerbate such stress.

Recent research suggest that a "backlash" may be occurring in dual-career marriages and that husbands are less supportive and accepting of their successful dual-career wives than they have been in the past. The report suggests that husbands may, initially, be supportive of their wives' professional development, but then reach a limit. This limit appears to be due to the husbands' perception that the wife is "too successful," that she has changed, or that she is not sufficiently supportive of her husband's career.[149]

External stress comes in two forms for women. First, the culture still

HI AND LOIS reprinted with special permission of King Features Syndicate, Inc.

suggests that a woman's place is in the home. More than three-fourths of the population believe that women should place their husbands and children ahead of their careers, while well over half of the people surveyed state that it is more important for women to support their husbands' careers than for them to have careers of their own.[150] A majority of high school students who were surveyed suggest that the mother of preschool children should stay at home.[151]

Second, jobs in business and industry tend to be inflexible and require geographical mobility and extracurricular responsibilities. Maternity and paternity leaves, on-site child care, job sharing, flex time, and quality part-time positions are promising ideas that are rarely implemented in many occupations. As a consequence, women who are attempting to adequately cope with two jobs—that of homemaking and parenting along with their paid employment—suffer from stress. For women, the primary disadvantage of the dual-career marriage is having too much to do.

Social support is available for the dual-career woman. The term "superwoman" has been coined to describe women who not only balance all of the demands of work and home but appear to do so with a high level of competence. In recent times some women have rebelled against this role. In San Francisco, a self-help group called Superwomen Anonymous was created in 1985. The group's motto is "Enough is Enough" and it provides support for women who want to reduce the stress in their lives created by balancing work at home and the office.[152]

Other resistance to the Superwoman role is demonstrated in popular humor. *Mother Murphy* provides two observations:

The Superwoman Myth

1. Women want to have it all: a successful career, a happy marriage, and loving children.
2. What they get is work, housework, and homework.[153]

How Do the Husbands Perceive This Family Type?   The advantages for husbands have not been as clearly identified as they have for wives, but husbands, too, profit from this marriage choice. The decreased pressure on husbands to earn the family's living allows them more freedom to spend time with their families.[154] Husbands also may feel satisfied that their wives are pursuing experiences that result in fulfillment and happiness. Finally, men in less traditional roles appear to find satisfaction in their careers in different ways than do men in more traditional situations.[155] Men with flexible schedules report lower levels of stress and distress.[156]

Men also face disadvantages in the dual-career marriage. They may experience internal stress as their identity is threatened. Less than full-time employment by husbands is viewed as unacceptable by many.[157] Men's participation in traditionally feminine roles may call their masculinity into question.[158] *The Working Woman Book* humorously, but perhaps accurately, advises women:

> There is hardly anything more critical than having a good understanding with your husband or boyfriend about the importance of your job, about sharing responsibilities, about give and take. Of course, even if he tries his best to be open-minded, he is facing two thousand years of opposite tradition and he will be called a "wimp" at the office.[159]

Men's self-esteem may suffer if their wives earn more money than they do. One wit notes, "Men think it's great that women have careers . . . until a woman's paycheck exceeds their own."[160] Men may feel deprived by their wives' focus on their own jobs and their neglect of traditional supportiveness. Men report some overload problems, even though their wives are primarily responsible for the home and children. Their concerns, like their wives', about their children's development are also related to lower levels of well-being in dual-career husbands. Unlike their wives, men in dual-career marriages are less physically active.[161] The most important disadvantage dual-career men report is not having enough time with their wives.[162]

How Does the Couple Fare in This Family Type?   The couple also reaps benefits in the dual-career marriage. For both husbands and wives in the dual-career marriage, increased income is often listed as an advantage of this marital form. Dual-career status increases relationship satisfaction.[163] The marital researchers Rapoport and Rapoport studied five dual-career couples over a two-year period and found that they enjoyed intellectual companionship, mutual empathy of both work and home obligations, and high feelings of self-fulfillment and contentment.[164] Hall and Hall added the benefits of a more egalitarian distribution of resources and influence power in the relationship, and greater opportunities for both spouses to achieve a meaningful work role as well as a meaningful relationship.[165]

Unique problems are also created for the couple. One such problem is that women and men are now more likely to both work and live together. In the past, corporations, universities, and other employers disallowed married or cohabiting couples to work in the same organization. The rationale for such policies included nepotism, or favoritism, which would create tension for co-workers. Recently, however, organizations have relented on this policy in order to attract qualified personnel. Although the previous policy probably discriminated against women more frequently than it did against men, and the revised policy is more humanistic, new problems can arise when married couples work in the same organizations.

Married couples who work together may feel increased stress because of their tension rather than the reactions of others. Daryll Bem, professor of psychology at Cornell, observes that couples who are highly competitive with each other are particularly at risk. When one spouse reports to the other, additional problems occur. If the personal relationship deteriorates the couple may find it particularly difficult to work successfully together.[166]

Is the dual-career couple more or less relationally satisfied than the single-worker couple? Unfortunately, the data do not clearly support either conclusion. Marital satisfaction suffers when either member of the couple becomes highly involved in his or her job.[167] John Dos Passos remarked, "People don't choose their careers; they are engulfed by them." For the dual-career couple such an occurrence is likely to result in decreasing marital satisfaction.

Marital satisfaction for the dual-career couple remains related to traditional expectations about spouses. One marital investigator showed that couples expressed more satisfaction when the husband was perceived to be superior to the wife.[168] Wives were more satisfied when they perceived themselves to be lower on the dimensions of intelligence, competence, professional success, and income as compared with their husbands. Husbands expressed more satisfaction when they perceived themselves to be higher than their wives on income and professional success. Other research has similarly shown that dual-career couples prefer the husband to earn more money than the wife.[169] However, husbands are also more satisfied when they perceive themselves as less intelligent than their wives.[170] The stereotypes may be more salient for the wives than for the husbands.

Both partners are less happy when the wife works because of economic necessity rather than by choice. Marital strain also exists in dual-career marriages when preschool children are present.[171] In general, dual-career couples are satisfied when the couple shares similar values about working women. Both spouses express more marital satisfaction when the wife is not more interested in her career than the husband is interested in his career, and, in general, when the spouses fit sex-role stereotypes.[172]

Dual-career marriages are increasing at the rate of 7 percent per year.[173] As young women continue their education and enter professional fields, these figures may climb even higher. Recent findings suggest that high school girls are aspiring to higher-level careers compared to boys and that high school boys agree that they will share parenting and career role responsibilities equally with their future spouses.[174] Dual-career marriages are an emerging marital choice that can be made more satisfying.

How do couples cope with the challenges of the dual-earner marriage? Women use the coping strategies of delegating some of their work to others, of limiting their avocational or social activities, and using social support more often than men. Social support in the form of relationships with other people relieves the stress in dual-income couple for women, but it does not have the same effect for men.[175]

Not only does one's biological sex impact one's coping mechanisms, but the presence, and age, of resident children may also make a difference. When the couple has children at home, they compartmentalize their work and family obligations. Couples who have children under the age of 6 cannot, and do not, delegate as much as couples with older children. On the other hand, couples with older children appear to limit their avocational activities more often.[176]

Husbands and wives can both contribute to the success of the dual-career marriage. Husbands who identify with their wives' career goals, who derive satisfaction from their wives' accomplishments, and who do not feel threatened by their wives contribute to more successful marriages.[177] Wives can contribute to more successful marriages by defining their own notions of "the full life" rather than accepting societal expectations and norms.[178] Women may also find some assistance in separating their professional lives from their home lives in the way that men have traditionally done. They might isolate their more expressive, emotional selves at home and demonstrate their instrumental, rational selves at work. Women may also find it useful to establish priorities for domestic roles; spend time with children focusing on them, rather than on other matters; and consider domestic problems that arise on an immediate basis rather than putting them off.[179] Flexibility tends to provide a feeling of deep satisfaction for couples.[180]

Couples who find themselves working together as well as living together may increase their opportunities for success by separating their roles at home from their roles at work. Ivan Lansberg, organizational behavior professor at Yale, observed that couples who were most successful "create boundaries in their minds and treat the same person differently at the office than at home."[181] Some married couples have developed different areas of expertise in order to differentiate themselves from each other. Some have used different last names to symbolize their individuality rather than their marital status.

The dual-career couple may be able to enhance their relationship through communication. Rapoport and Rapoport suggest the couple must deal with five dilemmas in their attempts to maintain their relationship.[182] These include dilemmas that occur from differences between social norms and personal norms, dilemmas concerning their identity and self-esteem, dilemmas associated with the social environment and other relationships, dilemmas concerning the choices and demands at various life stages, and dilemmas relating to the overload of handling both work and family duties. These dilemmas may be resolved through thoughtful and caring interaction.

Research on the relationship between satisfying dual-career marriages and communication has begun,[183] although in general we know little about the interaction patterns of dual-career couples.[184] Communication researcher Julia Wood recommends communication for dual-career relational maintenance. She explains, "Maintenance of a relationship entails unique communication responsibilities for dual-career spouses because of the lack of an externally supplied structure for the dual career family and the consequent necessity to generate a viable structure internally."[185]

❖ EXTENDED FAMILIES

Extended families include families in which not only parents and children are part of the family unit but in which grandparents, aunts, uncles, cousins, and other relatives are included. The longer life span would suggest that extended families are increasingly common;[186] however, extended families, like nuclear families, are relatively rare. Increased mobility encourages second and third generations to live in separate homes, even in separate states. Recent studies have shown that parents and their married children have less contact today than they did in the past.[187]

Statistics on the living arrangements of the elderly demonstrate changes in the extended family. For persons who are aged 75 and older, the proportion living with relatives (in families) declined from 64 percent in 1970 to 59 percent in 1983. Furthermore, 7 out of 10 of the 5.8 million persons 75 and older who were living in families in 1983 were husbands and wives who maintained their own families compared to 6 out of 10 in 1970.[188]

The decreasing number of elderly people who live with their younger relatives may be explained, in part, by the increasing number of working women. Traditionally, caring for elderly relatives has been viewed as an extension of the homemaker role and thus fell to women. Today, a larger number of women work outside the home and thus cannot care for individuals who require supervision or nursing.

The need for care of the elderly has not decreased, however. Consequently many women find themselves faced with the dilemma of choosing between their careers and caretaking. This conflict is exacerbated for many women who have already given up many of their productive years at a career because they chose to care for their own children. Just at the point when middle-aged women feel they have the opportunity to explore career options, they are faced with the needs of an elderly relative.[189]

One man detailed his original family, which most recently became an extended family:

> For the majority of my life, my family was considered nuclear. . . . Yet the status quo changed after my parents felt that they had completed their parental roles. After they felt my sister and I had matured and were more independent, mom felt it was time to complete her college education. After she completed her schooling she also worked as a social worker. . . . In August, my grandmother, mom's mother, had a series of strokes. She never completely recovered. As a result, she was forced to give up her independence. She left her apartment and moved in with us. Thus, we became an extended family. . . . Grandma's arrival forced mom back into the home-

maker/caretaker role once again. Mom's interest in social work was needed at home, not in the context of some nursing home. She became completely involved with grandmother's care. Her recent education and budding career were put on hold. Yet mom did not resent grandma for this role stagnation. . . . However the rest of the family was put on hold. The relationship between mom and dad suffered. Just when my parents were at the point when they were free to explore their mutual interests, mom was tied up with grandmother.[190]

The extended family has unique problems. The caretaking family member may feel isolated or may resent the elderly individual, which can lead to verbal or physical abuse. If the older person is ill, financial and emotional strain may result. Changes in relationships and increased stress occur in homes that include a chronically ill person. Different values, attitudes, and experiences between the older individual and other family members may cause increased conflict and other difficulties.

Although the extended family has problems, many older parents, especially older women, fully expect their adult children to care for them.[191] In addition, the adult children believe they should care for their parents,[192] and are prepared to provide that care.[193] Most adult daughters and most elderly mothers report satisfaction with the caregiver/care receiver roles.[194]

Why do some caregivers feel resentment toward their new role? Daughters who care for their adult parents—generally the mother—may do so out of feelings of obligation rather than at their own discretion.[195] When older mothers believe their daughters are caring for them because they choose to, rather than feel an obligation to do so, they generally report more intimacy in their relationships and are more satisfied.[196] Daughters are similarly more satisfied under these circumstances.[197] Caregiver burden is more likely to occur when the elderly are provided care out of a sense of obligation. Conflict between the older parent and the adult daughter may also result in caregiver resentment and anger.[198]

An interesting and growing phenomenon may alter the decreasing nature of the extended family. In larger numbers than ever before, adult children are returning to their parental homes. In 1984, the Census Bureau reported that 54 percent of 18- to 24-year-old Americans were living at home, which was an increase from 47.3 percent who were living at home in 1970.[199] In addition, 10.4 percent of those between 25 and 34 were still at home, compared to 8 percent in 1970.

Why are an increasing number of children returning home or "refilling the empty nest"? The high divorce rate accounts for some of the returnees.[200] Many of the returning young adults are women with children of their own. The high cost of housing also contributes to young adults returning to the parental home. Many grew up with relative affluence and will not accept living in less acceptable circumstances. Increasing levels of cohabitation, which may result in young adults living together without the legal sanction of marriage, encourages more frequent changes in address and occasional extended visits at the parental home. Finally, the exodus of the "baby boomers" from their family homes has left vacant rooms for themselves and other siblings to which to return.[201]

Just as the addition of an older family member to the family creates special problems, the return of a child whom the parents believed had left causes unique difficulties. External stress may occur because of the societal expectation that young adults leave home rather than return to it. Young adults sometimes retard their maturation by remaining as children in their parents' home. Tension results among the family members, too. The young adult may be treated as a child and/or may behave as a child. Differing role expectations may further complicate relationships. Given these potential problems, a surprisingly low amount of conflict is reported between adult children and their parents.[202]

The minority status of extended families has resulted in few social supports. However, the problems are real and they may result in psychological and physical abuse. Individuals in such families must be able to communicate their needs openly. Adjustments must be made by all family members, rather than requiring one person to make all of the accommodations. The consideration of alternative modes of living—placing the elderly relative in a supervised caretaking facility or hiring a part-time or full-time caretaker—is essential. Establishing new rules for returning family members, including household duties and financial contributions, is important. The extended family may provide new opportunities for relationships among family members; however, such opportunities can be eroded away if communication is not open and honest.

Extended families may be very satisfying to adult children as well as to the grandchildren in the family. Because many grandparents live far from their grandchildren, the grandparent–grandchild relationship is not as prevalent nor as close today as it has been in the past. Robert and Shirley Strom describe a program that provides opportunities for grandparents to share feelings, listen to children's feelings, improve family communication, learn about life-span development, and consider self-evaluation.[203] Such educational opportunities hold great promise. Similarly, programs that link grandparents with younger people of their grandchildren's ages when the two cannot be in regular and personal contact have been received very positively.[204]

The demise of the extended family is surely a product of current sociological and economic circumstances. It may be a family type that holds a great deal of potential for loving and caring relationships. The extended family does provide challenges, but most people in extended families report low levels of stress and conflict. A variety of educational programs and other social interventions today allow opportunities for alternative intergenerational communication.

SUMMARY

Contemporary America offers us a variety of family forms from which to choose. You are living in a challenging time in our nation's history. Remarkable social changes have occurred and even more sweeping changes will be occurring in your lifetime. Prognosticator John Naisbitt observes:

> Although the time between eras is uncertain, it is a great and yeasty time, filled with opportunity. If we can learn to make uncertainty our friend, we can achieve much more than in stable eras.[205]

In this chapter we examined contemporary American families. Cohabiting couples are two unrelated, unmarried adults of the opposite sex who share living quarters, with or without children. We studied couples without children and observed their increase. We noted that one cause for the larger proportion of childless couples is that couples are waiting longer to have their children now than in the past. Many women are putting off having the first child until they are in their mid- or late 30s.

Nuclear families, which have greatly decreased in recent times, have breadwinning fathers, homemaking mothers, and resident children. Single-parent families, conversely, are increasing. Such families have one parent and may include adopted, natural, step-, or foster children. Although the single-parent family typically occurs when one parent dies or leaves the family unit, some individuals choose to parent by themselves from the start.

Blended families, sometimes known as reconstituted or remarried families, consist of two adults and step-, adoptive, or foster children. This family type, like the couples without children and the single-parent family, is increasing in our culture. Dual-worker families, which include two working adults, have also increased in recent history. Extended families, like nuclear families, no longer occur with the frequency that they once did. They include families in which not only parents and children are part of the family unit but in which grandparents, aunts, uncles, cousins, and others are included. However, the new phenomenon, or increased likelihood, that adult children will return home, after completing their educations and sometimes with children of their own, may find the extended family increasing in the future.

KEY TERMS

1. *Family type* refers to the particular combination of family members. The phrase usually refers to cohabiting couples; couples with no children; nuclear; single-parent; blended; dual-worker marriages; and extended families.

2. *Cohabiting* couples are two unrelated and unmarried adults of the opposite sex who share living quarters, with or without children.

3. *Nuclear* families are conventionally "nuclear," with breadwinning fathers, homemaking mothers, and resident children.

4. *Single-parent* families include one adult and may include children who are adopted, natural, step-, or foster children.

5. *Blended* families, reconstituted, stepfamilies, or remarried families consist of two adults and step-, adoptive, or foster children.

6. *Conventional dual-worker* marriages are those in which the husband is

viewed to be primarily interested in career and the wife is primarily associated with the home and family.

7. *Unconventional dual-worker* marriages place the wife as the one with the major career interest and the husband with the major family interest.

8. *Dual-career* marriages include two partners who are committed to both their careers and their families.

9. *Superwoman* has been coined to describe women who not only balance all of the demands of work and home but appear to do so with a high level of competence.

10. *Extended* families include parents and children as part of the family unit but also include grandparents, aunts, uncles, cousins, and/or other relatives.

**CHAPTER
3**

CHANGING ROLES
WITHIN FAMILIES

Denis Thatcher, British businessperson and husband of former British prime minister Margaret Thatcher, was asked by a reporter who wore the pants in the family. "I do, and I also wash and iron them."

After you have read this chapter, you will be able to

1. List three reasons why it is important to study role behavior in families.

2. Differentiate among complementary, symmetrical, and reciprocal roles.

3. Define the term *role* and describe the five functions that require specific family roles.

4. Identify factors that explain why some women choose to serve in a breadwinning capacity.

5. Explain the factors that affect the role of women as providers of nurturance and support.

6. Describe how self-worth, self-acceptance, relationship satisfaction, and the couple's beliefs in equality affect couple sexual satisfaction.

7. Define androgyny and undifferentiated sex types.

8. Explain how sex-role development affects role assignment within a family.

9. List and explain the five subfunctions used in maintaining and managing the family unity.

10. Provide examples of role confusion, multiple role demands, role changes, and conflict.

11. Distinguish among role congruence, role accountability, role alloca
    tion, role expectations, and role performance.

The contemporary American family, as we discovered in Chapter 2, cannot be captured easily. In the past when a majority of American families were traditionally nuclear, roles within the family were clear. "Leave It to Beaver" and "Father Knows Best" provided us with unmistakable models. The women in early television programs were homemakers and their husbands were breadwinners. Today, people play a variety of roles and their biological sex is less predictive of their roles. Women and men both serve as breadwinners and homemakers.

✦ IMPORTANCE OF ROLES

Role behavior is an essential topic in a text dealing with seeking satisfaction in changing times through our communicative behavior. First, roles within our contemporary society and within the developmental stages of the family are changing. Within one generation, the majority of women have moved from the home to the workplace. We have no clear direction about what the next generation of people will bring. Perhaps we will see both women and men competing at work with few people staying within the home. Conversely, both women and men may learn to play multiple roles.

In addition, the developmental stages of the family create changes that call different role behaviors into play. The woman who desires to be a nurturing homemaker and mother may feel frustrated if she is a member of a childless couple or when her last child leaves what she perceives to be an "empty nest." The breadwinning man might be discouraged if he cannot find work, but his wife holds a prestigious position. The couple involved in an age-discrepant marriage might find unique problems as one member of the couple retires and the other person has 15 or 20 years of active employment ahead.

Second, both women and men are expected to play an increasing number of roles in many current families. Both may be expected to be wage earners, loving marital partners, nurturing parents, household workers, and civic-minded community members. Marital couples may feel overburdened by the large number of roles they must play or confused by the contradictory demands they have placed upon them. These multiple role demands, part of our changing times, may result in stress that can be alleviated through communication.

Third, communicating role expectations is related to family satisfaction. The roles family members will play and the accompanying expectations that these roles hold must be determined within families. Couples must consider if they wish to play traditional or newly evolving roles and they must come to some level of agreement. Moreover, they must continue to discuss their changing roles as the family moves through both predictable and unpredictable changes.

Understanding family roles is very important for the individual contemplating beginning a new family or for people involved in developing families. In this chapter we emphasize the changing roles in the American family. Some individuals are going through radical role changes and these personal choices strongly impact the nature of the family and the interaction that occurs therein.

❖ ROLE THEORY

In Chapter 3 we discuss role theory. A number of additional theories have advanced our understanding of family communication. Role theory is rooted in sociology and is based on a dramatic model.[1] The term "role" comes from the theater, and the verbal and nonverbal behaviors that accompany a role are based on the "script." Roles are prescribed by society, and the behaviors that are associated with certain roles tend to remain constant regardless of the specific actor playing the role. Thus "role expectations" are developed that may remain in people's perceptions long after they have become useful in people's behaviors. For instance, the role of a nurturing female partner may exist in our expectations of a wife even though a couple does not have children.

Within the family setting, roles are designated that facilitate interpersonal interaction and the development of relationships and that lead to the overall functioning of the individuals and the group. Individual families may determine unique roles that are necessary for their functioning, and they may dispense with some more traditional roles. Nonetheless, each family determines roles that are essential for the development of the families and the individuals within them.

Roles may be complementary, symmetrical, or reciprocal. *Complementary roles* are those in which each partner carries out the role expectations not enacted by his or her partner. For example, one member of the couple enacts the breadwinning role while the other member carries out the homemaking role. Communicatively, one person may be highly talkative while the other serves as a good listener.

Symmetrical roles occur when the two members of a couple carry out similar roles. Using our example, both members of the couple might serve as the breadwinner and the homemaker. Both people might serve as assertive communicators, considering their own needs and rights as well as the needs and rights of their partner. One married woman describes her relationship with her husband as symmetrical:

> In my current family sex roles are . . . symmetrical. Though we have verbally never decided who should do what, we often play things by ear. This is primarily because we are busy people often going in separate directions. For one thing, my husband does not sit around all day and wait for me to feed him. He realized that with my schedule as demanding as his, if he chose this route, he would merely starve. Many times, even if I'm home, he'll get up and prepare our meals.[2]

Reciprocal roles occur when the members of the couple are more interactive and roles are played based on mutual give and take. For instance, husbands may serve as the breadwinners, but when they lose their jobs, the wives assume this role, relinquishing the homemaking role to their husbands. The partners may share listening and speaking roles—sometimes one person is more talkative, while at other times the other member of the couple is loquacious.

At the beginning of this chapter we observed that changes in our culture and the developmental stages of the family both require that individuals change their roles over the life span, that family members appear to be called upon to play more roles than they formerly were asked to play, and that family members are no longer playing the same roles that they have traditionally played. At the same time, the family appears to hold some roles that are generally necessary for the functioning of the unit and for the development of the individuals within it. Later in this chapter we will consider some of the roles that arise from the functions of the family. Before we do so, we must consider the changing conceptualizations of gender that are relevant in our understanding of current roles in the contemporary American families.

❖ GENDER ROLES

No discussion of family roles would be complete without some prior knowledge of gender roles. At the beginning of this chapter we observed that the roles of family members are in a state of flux. A great deal of this change is a result of more basic changes in the way women and men are perceived and the roles that are deemed appropriate for them. Traditionally, women and men were each perceived to enact specific, unique behaviors. Women were generally perceived to be nurturing, emotional, sensitive, sentimental, submissive, and warm. Men, for the most part, were perceived to be aggressive, confident, dominant, forceful, industrious, and strong.[3] Feminine characteristics were identified as expressive, affiliative, or emotional; and masculine characteristics were determined to be instrumental, logical, or goal-oriented.

The underlying assumption was that women and men each had characteristics that were necessary for a complete life and that the two complemented each other. Thus marriages were based on the notion that a man and a woman would both be necessary in order to fulfill the essential role functions. Women would manage the affective roles within the family, such as nurturing the children, while men would handle the instrumental roles, such as earning a living.

Sex roles have undergone some change. Sandra Bem operationalized a notion that reflected these changes.[4] Bem suggested that older conceptions of masculinity that were equated to the absence of femininity, and femininity as the absence of masculinity were incorrect. Instead, she suggested masculinity and femininity were two independent qualities and one could be highly masculine and highly feminine at the same time or one could be low on both of these dimensions simultaneously.

Bem asserted that individuals should not be categorized into feminine and masculine categories exclusively, but that two other groupings should be added. She relied upon the word *androgynous,* coined by the ancient Greeks to refer to individuals who were both high in masculinity and high in femininity. She introduced the term *undifferentiated* to refer to people who subscribed to neither feminine nor masculine descriptors.

In addition, Bem's theorizing and conceptualizing led individuals to the notion that one's sex role is not dependent upon one's biological sex. In other words, women could be masculine, or androgynous, just as men could. Similarly, men could be feminine, or androgynous, too. Such a notion was liberating to individuals who felt their personality traits were somehow more appropriately linked to the opposite sex. The implications of the newly developed sex roles have importance for family roles, as we shall determine in the next section of this chapter.

❖ SPECIFIC FAMILY ROLES

Family roles may be determined on the basis of identifying necessary family functions and how the family allocates resources to deal with them.[5] Family roles are "the repetitive patterns of behavior by which family members fulfill family functions."[6]

Families must serve five functions that require specific family roles. The five functions are provision of resources such as food, housing, clothing, and money; nurturance and support; adult sexual gratification; personal development, including physical, emotional, educational, and social development for the children and career, avocational, and social development for the adults; maintenance and management of the family, including decision-making functions, boundary and membership functions, behavior control functions, household finance functions, and health-related functions. The family functions are summarized by the authors as serving instrumental (providing necessary resources), affective (adult sexual needs, nurturing, and support needs), and mixed (individual development and family unit management) needs. We will now consider each of the five functions.

■ Providing Resources

This role behavior includes tasks resulting in the provision of money, food, clothing, and shelter. Traditionally, men were primarily responsible for providing the financial needs of the family, which in turn provided necessary physical supplies such as food, clothing, and shelter. Today, many women serve as breadwinners within the family unit.

Why do some women choose to serve in the breadwinning roles of the family while others do not? The most frequently cited reason for wives to work is economic need.[7] However, other reasons also account for their decision to work. For example, a woman's sex role has an impact on her decision.[8] Women who score high on traditionally masculine characteristics such as ambition, task orientation, and aggressiveness may be more satisfied in the workplace than at home. One married 30-year-old woman explained:

> I am so goal- and career-motivated. I want so badly to do all the things that my Mother did not do and I want to have an impact on my environment—to really make a difference. . . . I have so strongly resisted the traditional female sex role. . . . I see myself as more motivated to find a good job and to make it in a career and I resist making babies.[9]

Women who are highly feminine have more traditional feminine expectations. When they do work, they tend to choose occupations in which women predominate, such as teaching or nursing, and they choose jobs that are perceived as including more feminine tasks, such as caring for children, the elderly, or the ill.[10]

In addition, the husband's attitudes affect the wife's decision to work. The husbands of working women tend to be more profeminist than are the husbands of nonworking women.[11] Women who work outside the home are more likely to have supportive husbands who encourage their work-related opportunities than are women who work at home.

Although many women both work and raise children, a number of other women choose between these two roles. Young women's role preferences for work or parenting can be predicted on the basis of their perceptions of parenting. Women who choose parenting rather than work have a perception of parenting as rewarding. Women who choose work over parenting have a perception of parenting as not rewarding.[12]

In other words, a young woman's attitude about work and careers is not salient in determining her choice to parent or work. The relevant factor in choosing between work and parenting is the woman's attitude about parenting. If her attitude is positive, she parents; if her attitude is negative, she works. The current research suggests that work is an alternative for women who have negative perceptions of parenting. Thus for some women, the traditional role of parenting remains intact.

All women do not work from the beginning of their marriages throughout their married life. Some work before the children are born and then return to work after the children have reached a particular stage. The developmental stages of the family encourage and discourage participation in the work force by women. In addition, women's motivation to achieve and to nurture fluctuates depending on their own individual life stages.[13] In many cases, these individual changes coincide with family developmental stages. Thus, women with small children appear to have a lower motivation to achieve, while older women who do not have small children have a higher achievement motivation.

Also, some of the contemporary American families discussed in Chapter 2 deal with the breadwinning role differently. Women who are single parents may have to provide resources, while their children assist with more traditional feminine roles. A young woman explained that she was born when her own mother was 18 years old and unwed. A year later she married, but the marriage ended in divorce in less than two years. Although this young woman has a half-brother who is two years younger than she, she can never remember a time when her mother was not a single parent. She explains the roles in her family:

> The role that is solely my mother's role is that of breadwinner. Since she is head of the household, and has always been such, she is the one who handles the finances. . . . The role handled by me has been that of cook and house-keeper, especially since we moved away from my mom's family of origin. I cook dinner and clean house regularly as well as any other tasks that may be required around the house. Although my brother doesn't really need a baby-sitter, you could say that I'm a sort of "stand-in" mother until our mother gets home from work.[14]

Another single-parent family placed the mother in virtually all of the family roles:

> Coming from a single-parent family (for half of my life) most family roles were primarily enacted by my mother. My mother provided the resources which afforded us the necessities of food, clothing and shelter. She also pro-vided the majority of nurturance and support.[15]

Other contemporary family types may deal with roles differently.

Are women who engage in multiple roles—for instance, being a wife and mother as well as a paid worker—perceived as favorably in the workplace as women who engage in fewer roles? Indeed, they are. Two researchers exam-ined others' perceptions of women who were never married, divorced, or wid-owed, and who were employed either full or part time or were unemployed. They found that both the personal traits and the professional competencies of employed women were viewed as more favorable than those of unemployed women. Further, the personality traits of married women were perceived more positively than those of unmarried women. Finally, unmarried and mar-ried women were perceived as equally competent.[16] Working married women should feel some comfort in that they will be perceived as performing as effec-tively in the workplace as their unmarried female counterparts.

As more women enter the work force, the relationships between women and men change at home. Women and men shift power, change their decision-making strategies, and have more room for potential conflict. Women who work may perceive that they have additional power within the home setting and that they ought to be consulted on more decisions. When the spouses dis-agree on such matters, conflict can erupt. We will cover these salient topics in Chapters 12 and 13. Later in this chapter we will consider other problems associated with contemporary family roles.

Does marital satisfaction depend on success in the workplace? A variety of factors in the marital roles affect marital satisfaction. Among the factors is the wife's perception of her husband's fulfillment of task roles outside the home.[17] This recent study is similar to older investigations that suggest marital satisfaction is dependent on the wife's perception of the adequacy of her husband's salary.[18] In the past, happily married women were those who perceived their husbands' salaries as adequate; today, happily married women perceive their husband's fulfillment of task roles outside the home as satisfactory.

Other factors currently affect marital satisfaction. An increasing number of women work and some women's work is slowly becoming highly paid. As a result, women occasionally make more money than their spouses. However, when the wife's salary becomes greater than her husband's, marital satisfaction decreases.[19]

In general, marital satisfaction is related to work satisfaction. When women and men are satisfied with their jobs, including such features as salary, security, friendships with coworkers, work setting and hours, and organizational policies, they tend to be satisfied with their marriages.[20]

▉ Nurturance and Support

Providing Nurturing and Support   This role involves those tasks and functions associated with the provision of comfort, care, and warmth for the family members. Child care and housework are included. Epstein and his associates grouped this set of needs within the affective area.

Women have been more likely than men to provide nurturance and support within the family.[21] Women averaged 7 hours of housework per day while all other family members (including husbands and children) averaged 3 hours per day in 1977.[22] Indeed, studies from the past 60 years show that women consistently do more housework than men and today average about 2.5 more hours per day.[23] In a national survey that included over 2,000 households, respondents indicated that 75 percent of the women usually did the shopping, compared to 5 percent of the men and 20 percent of the couples who shared the shopping.[24] Husbands report more leisure time per day than do their wives.[25]

After summarizing research conducted over the past six decades, one researcher concludes, "Regardless of employment status, women contribute significantly more time to housework and child care than their spouses or children."[26] One woman shared a typical example:

> My Mom's role is caretaker. And let me tell you there is no better place in the world, than my Mom's, to go if you're sick. She's great at pampering. I know whenever Annie or I are sick we move home for a couple days.
>   My Mom also plays the role of peacemaker. She can't stand it if anyone is fighting. She always told us if we don't have anything nice to say, don't say anything at all. Mom also believes we should turn the other cheek. It is for this reason that it takes a lot to get her mad enough to fight back. Maybe this is why Annie and I are so protective of her.[27]

Marilyn French depicts one mother in the late 1930s and early 1940s through the eyes of her main character:

> My mother always did the cooking for the family. I cannot recall a night she didn't even when she was sick and had spent the day in her darkened room with cloths on her head. Even when I was twelve and she went to work and had to stand all day in high heels, she would come home and cook. She never asked me to do it, although she allowed me to help. I watched her as she had watched her mother, learning without knowing I was. She'd have me string the beans or remove peas from their pods, or peel potatoes, making sure to get every tiny bit of skin and eye.
>
> Putting dinner on the table was the high point of my mother's day. She didn't say or do anything in particular, but you could feel it. She was always hot and tired and her face was always pink, and she was a little cross from all the work, but she laid the bowls of food, the plates, on the table the same way the priest put the host in your mouth—as if she were laying out something sacred. It was her gift to us, her gift of love.[28]

However, these norms have changed modestly. Younger, more highly educated couples are more likely to share household responsibilities than are older, less educated couples.[29] A father in his 30s recalled that his own father rarely provided nurturance and support, although he sees this role in his own behavior:

> In the few cases where my father would be in charge of supervising his children he seemed unable to cope with even the smallest problem. . . . When my younger brother fell off of his bicycle at about age 9 or 10 he received a cut to his head that was not too serious, but required two stitches. My father drove like a madman to the emergency room and when I got home from playing ball that afternoon, he screamed at me for not being around to help when something happened. . . . In my current family . . . childcare is equally shared between my wife and me. I am just as likely to fix our son's lunch or to kiss a minor injury as is his mother.[30]

Poussaint, in Bill Cosby's book *Fatherhood*, observes:

> A new movement has been spawned that has been pushing American men and women closer to the acceptance of androgynous fatherhood—men who take a significant share of nurturing responsibilities for children and the home, tasks that were previously assigned exclusively to women. . . . Recent evidence suggests that the fathering role, or the ability of fathers to support their children's healthy growth, is equivalent to mothers if men develop the attitudes and skills to be good parents. This often requires that they give up old-fashioned ideas about so-called manliness, "who wears the pants in the family," and what constitutes "women's work" as opposed to "men's work."[31]

In the "Dennis the Menace" cartoon, Dennis has neither mother nor father providing this role, and he must rely on a neighbor for nurturance on Saturday mornings.

DENNIS THE MENACE

"IF IT WASN'T FOR GOOD OL' MIZ WILSON, I'D *STARVE* ON SATURDAY MORNINGS!"

DENNIS THE MENACE® used by permission of Hank Ketcham and © by North America Syndicate.

The newly emerging families may place another person in the role of nurturer. One extended family included a grandmother in this role:

> There has been an interesting change in our family in the last five years. We have become an extended family. After the death of my grandfather, my mother's mom moved down from Nebraska to live with my family. This has had a large effect on the roles in the family. Grandma seems to have taken over a large part of the traditional homemaking roles. Some of the activities that she is involved with were taken from the roles of other family members, but some of her role was not present in our family before.[32]

What factors affect the role of women as providers of nurturance and support? A number have been identified, including sex roles, family type, income differential between the spouses, role salience, and developmental stages. Let us consider each of these.

Sex Roles   Sex roles affect the nurturing and support one offers family members.[33] For example, women who are voluntarily childless tend to be less traditional than women who choose to have children.[34]

However, a complete picture of the nurturing and support provided in the family unit can only be assessed when both the wife's and the husband's sex roles are considered concurrently.[35] Families in which women provide less nurturing and support and men provide more are those in which women and men both tend to have less traditional role behaviors.[36]

In general, individuals who exhibit an androgynous preference (they score high on masculinity and on femininity) appear to manage their nurturing opportunities more effectively. Androgynous new mothers are better able to cope with their nurturing responsibilities than are feminine, masculine, or undifferentiated new mothers.[37] Individuals who score high on masculinity (they subscribe to traditionally masculine characteristics) or androgyny cope better with infertility than do individuals who score high on femininity (they subscribe to traditionally feminine characteristics) or who are undifferentiated (they score low on both masculinity and femininity).[38]

Although sex roles—one's endorsement of feminine or masculine traits—affect one's supportive or nurturing tendencies, biological sex is nonetheless more influential than psychological sex role in predicting this behavior. Women continue to provide more nurturing and support in the family than do men.[39]

Family Type   Work outside the home affects the woman's role. Employed wives spend less time engaged in child care and housework than do nonemployed wives.[40] Also, the children and husbands of employed wives spend more time engaged in such activities than do the families of nonemployed women.[41] However, a great deal of variability exists in the distribution of child care and household tasks among family members in families in which both spouses are paid workers.[42] Women who work outside the home are often simply extending their workday. One woman writes:

> Mom is in charge of the housekeeping tasks. Although Mom is at work most of the day, the time she spends at home is quality work time. She will usually have made beds and washed at least a load of clothes before my brother is out of bed in the morning for school. To help Mom we all have our special chores to do plus grandma is home all day and she usually does all of the cooking. Mom is also the child care person. When we do not feel well Mom is always the one to complain to. She was always up in the night with us.[43]

Family type has been specifically studied in a number of investigations. In one-career families, wives describe their roles to be almost exclusively nurturing and supportive.[44] In families in which the husband has a career and the wife has a job (a career, as opposed to a job, is characterized as having a great deal of personal commitment, more education, and a continuous developmental character or promotional cycle), the wife has the main responsibility for caring for the children and the home.[45] In two-career homes a great deal of variability exists, but the husband's participation in child care and household tasks tends generally to increase over the other family types.[46]

Income   As we have observed, income is related to family type and to the relative contributions of child care and household work. As the wife's income increases and her husband's income decreases, men are more likely to engage in child care and housework.[47] However, the husband's and wife's income must be considered conjointly since it is the income differential between the spouses rather than the amount of their individual incomes that determines nurturing roles.[48] Most important is the wife's relative economic contribution within the household, rather than her absolute contribution, that increases her domestic power and lowers her probability of sharing household work.

An elementary school teacher father who is married to a high school teacher mother provides an example of shared nurturing. The father in the family, who is 37 years old, writes:

> The role of nurturance and support is shared. I take care of our son when my wife is in school, when she is working summers, and anytime at night when he is sick or needs something. Since I am off school at the same time my son is, I feel I have spent more time with him than most fathers have the opportunity to do. Last year he and I were in the same school building so we even rode to school together.[49]

Role Salience   The term *role salience* means the relative importance or value people place on the enactment of particular family, employment, or community roles.[50] People vary in the extent of their *career motivation,* or the degree to which they viewed their occupation as being a source of satisfaction, and in the relative importance or priority they ascribed to their occupational roles relative to other roles.[51] Family roles can be assessed in the same way.[52]

More recent investigations have examined the integration of career and family roles. Individuals who have more career salience appear to have less family role salience.[53] However, many people are equally committed to work and family.[54] In Chapter 2, dual-career couples were defined as being highly committed to both work and their family.

A recent investigation examined the relative impact of sex-role orientation, role salience, income, and family type on husbands' and wives' perceptions of family task sharing. The researchers found that women and men identified different factors encouraging the sharing of family tasks. For wives, income and family type translated into increased task-sharing behavior. For husbands, it was sex-role orientation, family type, and role salience.[55]

Women felt that responsibilities around the home should vary when the couple's income differential varied and when their family type was discrepant. Men felt that the work responsibilities should change on the basis of the couple's sex-role orientation, their interest in their jobs and their family life, and their family type. Women were more likely to use relatively objective criteria, while men were more likely to use one's attitudes or predispositions to determine appropriate levels of contribution to child care and housework.

Developmental Stages   The family's developmental stage and the individual's developmental stage affect one's interest in providing nurturing and support. Teenagers may not be as interested in, or willing to provide, nurturance for a baby as are women who are in their 20s. Similarly, older women and men might be less willing to provide nurturance. Individuals' motivation to play particular role changes throughout the developmental stages of the family and throughout their own individual life stages. Nonetheless, women have been shown to provide more nurturance and support at all life stages than do men.[56]

Receiving Nurturing and Support   Nurturing and support are essential for all family members. Indeed, we will discuss the importance of understanding and support in Chapter 11. Sometimes we mistakenly assume this role behavior is intended only for the children in the family. Adults, like children, need to be supported and to be provided with love, reassurance, and admiration. Throughout our lives, our feelings of self-worth arise from positive interactions with one another. Adults need such positive interactions just as their children do. The developmental stage of the family is important to consider in terms of how much nurturing one can provide, but it is also important as we consider how much nurturing a family member may need.

We can identify some points in the family developmental cycle in which people are particularly needy of support. For instance, when couples begin a new family and have cut off ties with their orienting families, they may be in need of more warmth from their partner than they will later when their relationship is more established.[57] Women who have just given birth and couples in the transition to parenthood fare better when they are given support from their families.[58] Persons who are experiencing unexpected events including death, dissolution, or divorce may need more care and concern than they do at times of relative tranquility and calm.[59]

Marital researcher John Gottman suggests that negative interactions occur when husbands are not emotionally responsive to their wives.[60] He determined that husbands who were emotionally responsive to their wives are less likely than unresponsive husbands to have negative, escalating interactions. He calls the positive, relationship-enhancing aspects of a marriage "friendship" and writes that it builds attachment and the affective bond that allows couples to go through the difficult processes of relationship repair. Further, he hypothesizes that the mechanism that allows closeness in marriage is similarity in emotional responsiveness, especially in activities like sharing the events of the day.

Women should similarly offer support to their spouses. Communication investigators Mary Anne Fitzpatrick and Julie Indvik show that when the wife does not perform her relationship maintenance functions, marital satisfaction is much lower.[61] We may conclude that the provision of nurturing and support from both spouses to each other may result in greater family satisfaction.

Some family members may be left out of the nurturing and support that is provided. For instance, some studies suggest children receive differential amounts of nurturing, depending upon their biological sex.[62]

Boys may receive less interaction than girls from the time that they are infants. However, recent investigations have questioned these findings.[63] Younger children often receive more nurturing than older children and birth order may similarly affect interaction. Children may receive differential treatment, as well, because of physical handicaps or psychological or developmental impairment.

■ Adult Sexual Gratification

The authors of the McMaster Model of family functioning observe:

> Both husbands and wives must personally find satisfaction within the sexual relationship and also feel that they can satisfy their partners sexually. . . . A reasonable level of sexual activity is generally required. It has been our experience that in some instances, however, both partners may express satisfaction with little or no activity.[64]

Sexual satisfaction within the marital setting is related to factors other than frequency. Relationship satisfaction predicts sexual satisfaction.[65] Married couples who are satisfied with their relationship are less likely to engage in extramarital sex than couples who are not satisfied with their relationship.[66]

Similarly, our sex roles predict our sexual satisfaction. Women and men who endorse equality between the sexes are more likely to report sexual satisfaction than people who believe the sexes are more dissimilar than similar.[67]

Egalitarian beliefs affect other aspects of the couple's sex life as well. Men who endorse equality for women and men are more likely to share responsibility for birth control than are men who perceive women and men to be unequal.[68] Less stereotypic couples appear to share responsibility for their sexual activity.

Although men tend to initiate sex more often than women, some women behave nontraditionally. Women who initiate sex tend to use direct verbal statements, be more assertive, and less conventional. Their partners are generally more accepting of women, hold more egalitarian beliefs, and are more respecting of the rights of women.[69] Male views of equality appear to result in greater role flexibility and an acceptance of a larger repertoire of behavior on the part of women.

Sexual satisfaction within the marital setting is highly dependent upon how partners feel about themselves.[70] In order that individuals may relate intimately to others, they must think highly of themselves or have high self-esteem.

Sexual satisfaction is related to three primary factors, then. One's feeling of self-worth and self-acceptance is essential. In addition, the couple's relationship satisfaction is important. Finally, the couple's beliefs in equality and their positive perceptions of women and men affect their satisfaction and their role flexibility.

■ Personal Development

Just as we observed that support and nurturance are important for all of the family members, personal development is relevant to each person, too. Personal development includes physical, emotional, educational, and social development for the children and career, avocational, and social development for the adults. Children must move from being totally dependent beings to becoming relatively independent adults. They must change from becoming part of the family of orientation to moving on to creating families of their own. Adults, too, develop within family units. Gail Sheehy popularized the notion that adults continue to grow and develop personally just as children do.[71]

Just as women, as compared to men, have been more involved in the nurturance and support of other family members, they appear to be more invested in the personal development of their family as well. Women take more responsibility for the behavior of their children than men do. For example, two researchers examined parenting success and parenting failure.[72] Women had a tendency to perceive parenting as requiring a great deal of deliberation and skill, while men had a tendency to perceive children's failures as the child's own fault. Mothers might feel guilty about one of their children's problems or failures; fathers might place the blame on the child. Such differences suggest that parents perceive responsibility for children's personal development differentially.

Gender roles are developed within the family (© Crews, Stock, Boston).

Sex-Role Development   Although all personal development topics are not equally salient in a text on family communication, one topic that is relevant to role development within the family and to communicative behavior is sex-role development. One's biological sex, the sex of siblings, and the order of the children affect one's gender stereotypes. For example, younger girls with older brothers as well as younger boys who have older sisters show less gender stereotyping.[73] The older sibling of the opposite sex may model opposite-sex behaviors and may serve to teach younger siblings about alternative behaviors.

Children's interactions with their parents also affect their sex-role development. Children who interact more extensively with their father are more likely to develop androgynous sex roles than are children who interact less extensively with their fathers.[74] Fathers may play an essential role in the development of androgynous persons. Furthermore, our communicative behavior serves as the vehicle by which sex roles are transmitted.

Role models affect children's notions of sex roles, too. For example, children of nonworking mothers are more likely than the children of working mothers to provide more sex-role stereotyped answers when asked about the appropriateness of certain adult and child activities.[75] Children who grow up in dual-career families are more likely to have less traditional sex-role attitudes, relative to adolescents from traditional single-earner families.[76] The newly emerging family forms assist people in socializing children to be less traditional.

Another factor that may affect the sex-typing of children is the jobs they are asked to perform within the original family. In general, daughters are asked to perform far more household jobs than sons are.[77] In this way, parents may be encouraging traditional roles for their female children.

The nature of the jobs that need to be done may affect the role that children play. For example, in farm families, children are expected to participate in the workload from fairly early ages. While all of the adolescents participated in the farm chores in one study, a smaller percentage helped with the household jobs.[78]

The pattern of job assignment may change depending upon the sex composition of the family. As the number of sons in the family increases (holding constant the number of daughters), the sex-typing of traditionally female tasks decreases. In sibling groups with no sons, increases in the number of daughters reduce the sex-typing of male tasks.[79]

This study suggests that even when girls are present, boys may be asked to engage in traditionally female household chores, such as meal preparation and dish washing. The study also states girls are not asked to engage in traditionally male behaviors, such as fixing the car or mowing the lawn, unless they have no brothers. Although our culture is more accepting of women who behave like men than of men who behave like women, these researchers demonstrate that female household tasks are more readily distributed to opposite-sex children than male household tasks. The greater number of female household tasks may be one explanation for this finding.

All households do not abide by the findings in this investigation. One woman who grew up in a large family with six girls and three boys explains a different pattern of job distribution:

Mom always did all of the managing of the household and the children during the daytime. We girls were expected to do the same. We could even be expected to do jobs for the boys—like mow the lawn, clean the rabbit pens, and so on—but God forbid the boys could never be asked to do a "girl's job." Thus it was, the boys never could and still cannot manage for themselves when it comes to household tasks. Don't even expect them to change a diaper! Fry an egg? Do a load of laundry? Never![80]

What factors affect children's desires to play traditional or nontraditional family roles in their newly created families? The children's orienting family exerts an influence. One woman explained:

In my family, both of my parents assume traditional roles and responsibilities.... I believe my family has been a great influence on my own behavior and that when I am married, I will value those same traditional roles and responsibilities.[81]

Children who grow up in dual-career families are more likely than adolescents from traditional single-earner families to prefer a dual-work family structure.[82] However, an extensive study suggests that when children are raised by a single parent, in a blended family, or in an intact home, their marriage-role expectations are not necessarily affected.[83] Children who grow up in a family in which a divorce has occurred are no more likely to perceive they will similarly be divorced than are children who grow up in an intact family. These conclusions are encouraging to people from less than desirable original families.

Should parents socialize children to be egalitarian and androgynous? These traits are related to psychological health.[84] In general, traditional sex roles, particularly for women, tend to be dysfunctional. For example, adolescent women who enacted traditional feminine sex roles were far more likely to become pregnant during their adolescence than were women who did not hold traditional sex roles.[85] Traditional conceptions of sex roles are also moderately related to attitudes favoring the use of physical force in the marital relationship.[86]

Alvin F. Poussaint, writing in the introduction to Bill Cosby's book *Fatherhood*, urges parents to change their behavior with their sons and daughters:

There is a need to eliminate sexism and sex-role typing in child rearing and strive for a more balanced, androgynous approach that maximizes the opportunities and options for both boys and girls. Children brought up with a mix of "masculine" and "feminine" qualities will be better suited to adapt to demands of both the new fatherhood and motherhood.[87]

Parents are increasingly raising their children to be free of sex-role stereotypes. One researcher compared contemporary fathers with fathers from 30 years ago on their goals, beliefs, aspirations, and expectations for their children. She found that some expectations were gender stereotypic and had not changed over the 30-year period. However, a number of striking changes were noted. She concluded that the contemporary father's expectations tended to be more similar than dissimilar for male and female children.[88]

Other alterations in family life also encourage egalitarian roles. For example, as we observed in Chapter 2 an increasing number of people are waiting until they are older to marry. Couples who are older when they marry tend to assume a more egalitarian role structure than do people who marry at a more normative time.[89]

■ Maintaining and Managing the Family Unit

Epstein and his colleagues state that maintaining and managing the family unit consists of five subfunctions: decision-making functions, boundary and membership functions, behavior control functions, household finance functions, and health-related functions.[90]

Let us consider each of these briefly.

Decision-Making Functions   Leadership, power, conflict resolution, and final decision making when family members cannot agree comprise decision-making functions. Because of its importance, we will further devote Chapter 12 to conflict and Chapter 13 to power and decision making.

Men have traditionally held the most power within the family and have been the principal decision makers. One's power within the family is dependent upon one's resources. As women gain in resources, they gain in power. Although egalitarianism has not replaced husband-dominated family power models, many people view it as the ideal model. Some marital couples, particularly women, prefer egalitarianism in their decision making.[91]

One couple is exchanging its paternalistic original family for a more egalitarian style. The man, who is engaged to a woman named Kim, writes:

> My original family is run much like a formal business organization. Dad is the chief executive officer. All policy decisions are implemented at this level. Mom acts as vice-president. Her chief duty is to be the liaison between the children (employees) and the top. Mom has the authority to handle day to day situations. But when a problem arises, the employees have to deal with the C. E. O. ... The family I will create with Kim will be very different. The two of us will make joint decisions as we do now. We interact on an equal basis.[92]

Boundary and Membership Functions   This function involves relationships among extended family members, friends, and neighbors; family size; and interaction with external groups, institutions, and other agencies. A relatively new word, *kinkeeping,* describes the function of maintaining contact with one's extended family and keeping other family members in touch with one another.[93] While the term is new, the function of maintaining family ties is not.

A recent investigation furnishes detailed information about "kinkeepers."[94] and determined that of the families examined, well over half had kinkeepers within their family. These individuals used a variety of activities including visiting, telephoning, letter writing, and mutual aid to keep family members in touch.[95] Families who have kinkeepers have greater extended family interaction and greater emphasis on family rituals within the extended family and within the historical development of the family.

Family celebrations provide one opportunity for interaction among extended family members. In some families, birthdays, holidays, and other events are celebrated with special meals or other rituals. Family members may routinely travel great distances to be part of these events. In other families, no birthday passes without telephone calls, greeting cards, and gifts, but families rarely are in each other's physical presence. Routinized patterns of interaction may be established, in which some family members telephone each other on a regular night each week or in which they write each other once during a designated period of time, such as each week.

Some families use the exchange of money, goods, or services as one method of "keeping the family together." Parents may routinely provide money to their children to purchase homes, businesses, or other material goods. Siblings may purchase property together. Younger family members may provide nursing or other physical assistance to older family members.

Kinkeepers provide important information to other family members. For example, one family always provided the oldest daughter in each family with the same middle name. From 1642 in Holland, each oldest daughter gave her oldest daughter the same name. In addition, the family had a strong sense of womanhood in their family. Many of the oldest women were pioneers in their time. Most had large families, many earned salaries, and some made important discoveries. Each woman who shared the family middle name felt an obligation to be as good or better than her female ancestors before her. The extended family learned of this practice and the significance of it from other family members.

Kinkeepers are more often women than men; grandmothers and mothers are more frequently placed in these roles than are grandfathers and fathers. Further, grandmothers are more likely to keep close contact with their female children and their children than they are with their male children and their children. No differences were shown in this study between Anglo and Hispanic grandchildren, nor were differences shown in grandmothers' closeness to male or female grandchildren.[96] Similarly, daughters are more likely to interact with their mothers than are sons.[97] Men sometimes participate in the kinship role function by providing economic aid, although women are more likely to be involved in communication activities and overall kinkeeping.[98] Normatively, family members define kinkeeping activities as "women's work." The position of kinkeeper is frequently passed from mother to daughter, and the position persists over time.[99]

The need for interaction among extended family members changes throughout the family and individual life cycle. Individuals who are widowed or divorced may be in more need of support and interaction with extended family members than are persons in intact families.[100] Older people may have greater interest in kinkeeping than younger people have. A variety of factors including urban or rural residence, race, migration, proximity of kin, occupation, age, and education affect the frequency of interaction with members of the extended family.[101]

The new family forms in contemporary America place distinctive requirements on kinkeeping. Adults in single-parent households may be required to assist young children in maintaining contact with parents who are not within the family home. Blended families can have particularly confusing networks of interacting family members. Previous in-laws may be maintained within the extended family long after the marital couple has divorced and remarried. Dual-worker families may have little time to interact with extended family members.

Behavior Control Functions   This area deals with disciplining the children as well as maintaining the standards and rules for the adult family members. Each family has boundaries or "limits for how members may act."[102] These boundaries are more or less permanent. In some families, the boundaries appear to change routinely; in other families the boundaries are inviolate.

The disciplining of children changes throughout history and among families. Children may be provided with physical punishment, feedback in the form of "time out," or limits on participating in some favorite activities for wrongdoing.

Adults have certain guidelines for their behavior, too. What happens if one of the adult members becomes intoxicated, has a sexual relationship with another person, or becomes addicted to drugs or work? Adults in the family must assist one another with such behaviors and determine the limits that will be tolerated surrounding such choices.

Household Finance Functions   This function considers the payment of bills, completing tax forms, banking, and other household money handling. The husband and wife may share these functions or one spouse may be generally responsible for financial matters. The individual who makes the most money may have the opportunity to determine how it will be spent. Single-earner families have interesting patterns that include a household allowance for the homemaker, separate accounts for the home and for the earner, or one account from which both the earner and the individuals who do not earn money are allowed to draw money.

Many couples argue about money. One study of 265 Indiana families showed that 25 percent of all couples reported "intense disagreement" about financial matters. Men were more likely to report disagreements over money when they were married shorter, rather than longer, times. They were also more likely to report problems when their wives worked part time rather than not at all or full time. Women reported less disagreement if they perceived that they were openly communicating about money with their spouses when they worked full time, and if they felt they were financially secure.[103] The new family forms create interesting responses to the management of the finances. Some cohabitors and dual-worker families maintain totally separate checking and savings accounts. Decisions about large family purchases or investments are made independently or on some shared basis. Blended families may pay bills for some members but not for others.

Single-parent families may be dependent upon individuals outside the family to manage certain aspects of their financial life. The busy lifestyles of many families encourage people to maintain enough money in their accounts so that they do not need to "balance their books," or else these families allow the bank to keep track of their records.

Dual-earner families may be generally satisfied with financial handling, but they can improve their satisfaction further. Dual-earner families who are smaller in size have been able to save more money, and have little or no credit-card debt report greater happiness than do dual-earner families that are larger, have little money saved, and have considerable credit-card debt.[104]

Do satisfied couples differ from dissatisfied couples in their handling of finances? One research team looked at couples over time. They found that happily married wives were more involved with financial decisions than were unhappy wives. Happily married husbands were less dominant in family finances. Happily married couples generally engaged in more joint financial decision making. Happily married couples also spent more money on household appliances, home purchases, and recreation vehicles while couples who eventually divorced spent more money on stereos, color televisions, and living-room furniture.[105] Other studies document that more satisfied couples generally have learned financial management skills.[106]

Health-Related Functions   These functions involve all relationships with physicians and other health personnel as well as identifying health problems and complying with health prescriptions. Important activities include observing signs of illness such as a flushed face, a lowered appetite, or increased distress. The person fulfilling these functions similarly dispenses prescription and over-the-counter drugs within the family. Gaining compliance on wearing appropriate clothing for the weather, drinking juices and water, and eating balanced meals is also important.

Who leaves work if a child becomes ill during the workday? Dual-worker couples often have to negotiate such a decision. Alternating the person of choice, having a neighbor or friend care for the child, or selecting one parent as the regular caretaker are all patterns that may be selected. The single parent does not have the same luxury, and parents in blended families may not choose to leave work if the children who are ill are not their own biological offspring.

❖ COPING WITH CHANGING FAMILY ROLES

■ Problems Created for the Family Unit

The variety of family roles that must be played within the family have become greater in number and more complex. The family must cope with changing roles. New family roles have both created problems and have provided solutions to older problems. Let us consider some of the problems that have been created in the contemporary family.

Role Confusion Family members may have always felt some role confusion. As dating couples become engaged and married, they experience changes in the roles they play. Similarly, as they add a child to their family unit, new roles are added. One fictional character in the late 1950s discussed the dissatisfaction she felt with her husband's new role and the expected change in behavior for her:

> I knew that Brad had loved me once, genuinely; and that what had changed was that he had adopted a role for himself, and wanted me to adopt the complementary role, and I wouldn't. I *was* being stubborn and rebellious and intractable; and even though I told myself regularly that I had the right to be the person and live the life I wanted, I only occasionally believed it. After all, no other woman I knew felt they had such a right. Whatever they'd been, or their husbands had been when they first married, all their husbands had adopted the role Brad had chosen, too; and their wives had gone along and been complements. Who was I to stand out against the whole world? Or what seemed like the whole world.
>
> Brad didn't want a divorce because he no longer loved or liked me; he couldn't even see me, so how could he know who I was? He wanted a divorce because I was not playing the role he wanted his wife to play. He wanted a wife who cared about the same things he did. His friends' wives all acted as if they cared about the same things their men did, whether or not they felt that way. And none of those men really saw their wives as people, any more than the wives saw the husbands as people. They each saw each other as roles.[107]

Today, even more than the past, women and men are not clear about their roles. A conversation between two children in elementary school illustrates the confusion that people feel. A neighborhood boy came over to play with his best friend, a 7-year-old female classmate.

KIRK: Hi, Kate, can you play this afternoon?

KATE: Sure, Kirk, what do you want to do?

KIRK: Well, it rained last night and I've got a big mud puddle behind my house. Do you want to make mudpies?

KATE: No, Kirk, I'd get all dirty.

KIRK: Well, I've got some new guns, do you want to play war?

KATE: You know that girls don't like to play war, Kirk!

KIRK How about if we run around the block. I know you like to race.

KATE: Kirk, you know that when girls compete with boys they are not allowed to win. If we raced around the block, I'd have to let you win.

KIRK: Well, you decide what we should play.

KATE: All right, let's play house.

KIRK: Okay.

KATE: Good—you be the mother!

This story admittedly exaggerates sex-role stereotypes, and the original conversation implies that even *little* girls recognize that the role of mother may be less desirable than other roles within the family. It also suggests the ambiguity children may perceive in family roles.

The family researchers Rapoport and Rapoport discuss the role-identity dilemma that confronts many contemporary couples.[108] Many people are unclear about their career and family roles and how appropriate their own definitions are, particularly in light of their partner's definitions. Ambiguity, rather than prescriptive clarity, marks family role behavior. Women are unsure if they are to be both breadwinners and homemakers; men are uncertain of the expected extent of their homemaking skills. When dating, engaged, or cohabiting couples do not discuss their role expectations for themselves and their intended spouse, conflict may arise. Role behaviors must be carefully and sensitively negotiated today, unlike the past when both women and men could take particular role behaviors for granted.

Role confusion appears to be particularly traumatic for women who are attempting to deal with careers and parenting. An intriguing study examined the differences between the dreams of women who were working mothers and compared them with the dreams of women who were exclusively homemakers. The researchers found that working mothers experienced more unpleasant emotions, more male characters, and fewer dreams that occurred in residential settings than homemakers did. However, homemakers had more overt hostility in their dreams.[109] Working women may be dealing with more tension among their various roles, and the settings for their dreams seem to reflect their work settings. Homemakers may not be satisfied with their roles either.

This role confusion extends to the children in the family as well as to the marital couple. Children can no longer be provided with the simplistic socialization patterns previously available. Messages that suggest that "boys don't cry" and "girls don't shout" are viewed as outdated. Today, both options are possible. However, all families are not changing at the same rate. In some families, traditional role expectations are being taught and required. In others, role flexibility is offered as the panacea for relational problems. Parenting in these times becomes increasingly complex and difficult.

Multiple Role Demands   Both women and men are expected to serve in multiple roles. They may both be expected to parent, keep house, earn a salary, manage the family unit, and play other roles. Such expectations are difficult for the most energetic and flexible person. Rapoport and Rapoport discuss overload dilemmas that face many married couples when spouses attempt to share many necessary family roles.[110]

Related to overload dilemmas are role-cycle dilemmas, which Rapoport and Rapoport explain are those role involvements that carry with them different demands at various stages of the life cycle.[111] Sometimes working women are expected to quit working when they have children. However, many women who parent do not wish to quit their jobs or to put their careers on hold. One researcher determined that "paid employment has psychological importance for many mothers of infants and . . . work involvement should be considered as an individual difference variable in research on new motherhood."[112] In other words, people should not assume mothers of newborns all wish to adjourn from the workplace.

Women may feel real conflict about their infants' needs and their own need to work outside the home. An investigation of mothers of newborns showed the women held traditional views about the importance of exclusive maternal care for infants, but they also stated that they planned to return to work before the infant's first birthday.[113] Such incongruity may exist among the attitudes, values, and behaviors of both the women and men who attempt to play multiple roles.

Women have been the traditional providers of support and confirmation in the family. They may still behave in a more nurturing manner than men do. However, these roles, too, are shifting. Today, both women and men may show warmth, comfort, reassurance, support, and affection for the children and for each other.

Few men have relinquished the provider role, however. Instead, men have engaged in role sharing, in which they spend part of each day (or each week) engaged in child care and nurturance of the children. Humorous events like those depicted in "The Family Circus" cartoon occur as both women and men must quickly shift from their nurturing roles to their professional interactions.

Role Changes   Role changes suggest two related problems for family members. First, roles are changing quickly, and it is difficult for us to be adaptable enough to manage the changes. Second, some of our roles should change in

THE FAMILY CIRCUS reprinted with special permission of Cowles Syndicate, Inc.

order that family members may have satisfying family lives, but they do not change. In other words, some of us are as rigid as the ancient dinosaur in our unwillingness to change and, like the dinosaur, we face extinction.

Not only are women and men expected to play a variety of roles and to negotiate their roles in their own situations, but roles change more rapidly and radically today than in the past. One cartoon depicts a husband and wife interacting about their changing roles. The husband remarks that he is willing to do half of the housework. The wife responds, "Fine, I did the last eight years; you do the next eight."

Unmarried people resolve to alter the role behaviors that they viewed in their own homes. A college sophomore explains:

> I live in a very old-fashioned family role environment. My father does the traditional "male" chores and my mother does all of the chores considered "feminine." . . . I expect my future husband and I to have a totally 50–50 relationship in every respect, including family roles. My ideal of a perfect marriage would be to share the roles of provider, supporter, sexual gratification, sex role development of our children, decision-making, handling finances, providing discipline for our children (including changing diapers, feeding, bathing, and so on). In other words, sharing every family role with my husband 50–50. Are there any men left who would consent to this arrangement?[114]

Family developmental changes may affect one's role. A childless couple that suddenly expects and has a child may have to renegotiate roles. The commuter marriage, the blended family, and the higher incidence of divorce in contemporary times require that people be flexible and adaptable in their role behaviors. For instance, a dual-career couple in which both husband and wife are professionals with high incomes may be jarred when the husband is offered a large pay increase and promotion across the country. The wife may have to choose between a commuter marriage, in which either she or her husband will do most of the child rearing alone, or the role of homemaker.

Sometimes our unwillingness to change roles creates problems within the family. Gail Sheehy has pointed out that we must change if we want to grow. She writes:

> We must be willing to change chairs if we want to grow. There is no permanent compatibility between a chair and a person. And there is no one right chair. What is right at one stage may be restricting at another or too soft.[115]

However, change is often difficult for us to manage. Nonetheless, we are continually called upon to make major changes in our role behavior. Changes, like that to parenthood, create major upheaval in the life of the family.[116]

After her children were in school, one mother decided to complete her college education. Although she enjoyed the change in her role, other family members were not as flexible. Her son explains:

> When Mom decided to complete her college education, roles were changed. Mom understood her maternal role in the family, yet her primary focus

became her studies. . . . Consequently, Dad was thrust into performing functions that were unfamiliar to him. When this happened, the structure of our family was altered.

These role changes upset the previous status quo. Mom could only enact the supermom role for so long. . . . What was the result?

Dad became frustrated. Mom was no longer free at night to share a dinner, walk, talk, or take a short trip. If Mom became free, she was tired. Dad was left to fend for himself.

Mom wanted to actively pursue her newly founded social work career, while Dad was considering how to best spend free time in pleasurable ways. Dad maintained a traditional, static view of role enactment, while Mom preferred to adopt a liberal, dynamic view of their roles.[117]

Men seem to have particular problems with role rigidity. For instance, in a study of different couple types, the women perceived their instrumental and expressive roles differently depending upon their couple type. The men perceived their roles as instrumental and traditional regardless of their couple type.[118] Men still appear to engage in more controlling behavior than is desirable, according to their wives.[119] Finally, fathers are still perceived as less expressive of all emotions, with the exception of anger.[120]

Role Conflict   The problems with role confusion, multiple role demands, and changing roles create conflicts within people and between family members. Let us consider each of these potential areas of conflict.

Role Conflict Within Individuals   Sometimes people do not feel comfortable about the roles that society or family has provided them.[121] Rapoport and Rapoport discuss dilemmas that occur between one's personal norms and social norms.[122] Contemporary women may resent traditional roles. A man in a particular family may disagree that he should be sharing the supporting and nurturing role. The spouses in dual-worker families may feel they are playing more management and maintenance roles than their partners and that this distribution of roles is unfair and inequitable.

Role Conflicts Between People   Family members may disagree with one another over the roles they should play. A husband may feel that his wife should provide support and nurturance to the children, but the wife wishes to play a provider role. No one in the family may wish to be charged with the health needs of the family or with the financial aspects of running the home. Both spouses may vie for the decision-making functions.

Conflicts may occur among family members because of the manner in which individuals conduct themselves within a particular role. The sculptor who is in the provider role may feel that it is reasonable the family is on welfare for much of the year while she is completing a large piece which will eventually be sold. The individual who is managing the household finances may feel an occasional "bad check" is nothing about which to be alarmed. The guidance provided to the children may be viewed by the children as inadequate.

Family members may perceive some roles to be more essential than other roles. For example, a woman may see her provider role as more relevant than her nurturing role. When she has additional work at the office, she tends to stay late regardless of the personal needs of her children or spouse. Her husband may disagree about the relative importance she ascribes to these two roles that she plays.

■ Solutions for the Family Unit

Solutions Provided by the New Sex-Role Conceptions   The recent developments in the conceptualization of sex roles carry attendant solutions as well as problems. First of all, these recent developments suggest women and men may be fully functioning without the assistance of a partner. In other words, if women and men can each be both masculine and feminine, they can independently provide all of the needs of the family or can play all of the necessary roles. Single parents, then, can be both mothers and fathers to their children as they serve both the provider of goods function and the support and nurturance function.

This suggestion is encouraging to the countless number of people who are serving in the roles of single parents. It allows them to reevaluate the need to remarry in a situation that does not require a spouse to be "whole." Nonetheless, many people still perceive the adult single state to be one of incompleteness.

In addition, the new theorizing suggests that women and men are not necessarily tied to traditional functions. The marriage that includes a cross-sexed female (a woman who exhibits masculine characteristics) and a cross-sexed male (a man who exhibits feminine characteristics) might be better served if they reverse traditional roles. A voluntarily childless couple may consist of two masculine people (a woman and a man) who both choose to emphasize the provider role over the nurturing role. Similarly, a couple composed of two feminine people may choose jobs that are people-oriented, may choose to work only part time in order to spend more time with their own children, or may choose another arrangement that allows them to engage in more supportive and nurturing roles.

Children who are being socialized in these times of change may have an improved situation over their ancestors. Children generally do better when they are provided with flexible and numerous role models. They may come to learn through lesson or experience that a large behavioral repertoire with many options is necessary in order to succeed. The little boy growing up as a person may learn that he can cry at home but not on the school playground. The adolescent girl may find that she can be aggressive with her siblings but not with her peers.

People who travel internationally find it highly useful to know several languages so that they can speak to people in different countries. In some ways, being male or female provides us with different ways of communicating. *Code switching,* or changing one's verbal and nonverbal behaviors from masculine to feminine as the circumstances warrant and the context varies, may be as important to the person who wishes to manage within our own culture as being multilingual is to the international traveler. In addition, it is useful to learn communicative behavior that is appropriate for both women and men, rather than use restricted codes that are idiosyncratic to either women or men. In any case, children must be made aware of the changing conceptions of women and men and be provided with the opportunity to choose their own sex role, whether it is consistent or inconsistent with their biological sex. Adults, like children, may benefit from code switching. Flexibility in our communicative behavior as well as our role behavior may be useful as we attempt to have full and satisfying lives.

Another way that adults are increasingly choosing to deal with their diverse roles is through role cycling. *Role cycling* refers to the pattern of first playing one role and then playing another. For example, a woman who wishes to have a career and children might work from the time she graduates from college until she is in her late 30s and then stop to have her family. Conversely, a person might parent early and then begin a career after the children are in school.

Solutions Provided Through Communication   The couple must communicate with each other in order to establish satisfying roles for themselves and for each other. They must have some procedure of allocating roles, of determining role accountability, of achieving role congruence, and of gaining a goodness of fit between role expectations and role performance. Some empirical backing is available for this advice.[123] Studies have shown, in general, that when partners are competent in carrying out their roles, family satisfaction is increased. However, family members need not be competent in all of their roles. Let us consider role allocation, role accountability, role congruence, role expectations, and role performance.

Role Allocation   Role allocation refers to "the family's pattern in assigning roles."[124] The family must determine if the person who is to fulfill a particular role has the ability to do so. It must determine how roles are designated and how they are redesignated. In addition, family members must be satisfied with the roles they play and with the roles other family members play.

Role Accountability   Role accountability deals with the procedures implemented ensuring necessary family functions are fulfilled. Individual family members must be responsible within the roles they play, and a mechanism must exist that allows the monitoring of roles and appropriate feedback. In other words, responses to individual's ability to provide necessary family functions must be offered. Both positive and negative evaluations are useful in helping family members to determine their success within a particular role.

Role Congruence   Role congruence refers to the agreement among family members about the roles each will play. When family members agree, we say they have congruence; when they disagree, we say that they have role incongruity. Newly created families may be more likely to agree about their multiple roles when they come from similar backgrounds. They may be most likely to disagree when their orienting families have been highly discrepant from each other.

Couples who contemplate creating a new family need not despair if they are from highly different backgrounds. Indeed, recognizing they have been involved in unique families with distinctive roles may help the couple to identify a variety of patterns of interrelated behavior. They may select a pattern similar to either original family or may choose an entirely new way of interacting. The key to successful coping, however, is recognizing the differences and determining acceptable standards.

Even when a couple comes from similar backgrounds, they may have difficulty achieving role congruence. They may believe their partner knows and understands which roles they wish to enact and which they do not. However, without sharing role expectations, partners may be totally in the dark. They may enact roles that do not allow other people to perform expected roles. Partners might behave this way not out of malice but out of ignorance. Unhappy couples may spend years enacting unsatisfactory roles simply because they do not talk to each other about their role expectations and preferences. The importance of communication in solving role difficulties cannot be overemphasized.

Another difficulty in achieving role congruence is reaching agreement on the roles each person will play. Perhaps the couple has discussed their satisfaction and dissatisfaction with the roles they play. However, the family members do not agree with accepting and rejecting particular roles. For example, the husband understands clearly that his wife is dissatisfied with her role as primary caretaker of the children, but he is unwilling to exchange roles with her. In this case, methods of conflict resolution or decision making may be appropriate. You may read more about these topics in Chapters 12 and 13.

Role Expectations and Role Performance Role expectations are our own idealized set of projections about the functions that we will serve. A couple contemplating marriage may view themselves in expected roles that are quite different from the roles they will eventually play. Our role expectations originate in our orienting family and in our role models.

Role performance, by contrast, is the way we actually behave within a particular role. The way we behave is at least partly dependent on the way our spouses behave in their roles. For instance, women who perceive themselves as people high in affective skills such as nurturing, supporting, and kinkeeping, who have spouses and families who act as though they need no support and relatively little interaction, may have their role performance curtailed. The performance of our roles is interrelated to the role performance of other family members.

When our role expectations and our role performance are similar, we feel in balance. When our role expectations are far different from our role performance, we feel dissonance. The couple anticipating marriage may consider discussing how they view particular roles in the family and who they each believe will be enacting them. Although a heterosexual couple may have no problem agreeing upon who will be the wife and who will be the husband, they may disagree about what roles each will play.

Similarly, married individuals may believe that they will feel a particular way during a certain stage in the life cycle of the family, but when they reach that stage, they do not. For example, a woman who puts off having a child until after she has developed her career may predict she will desire to stay home with the baby when the child arrives. However, once she has delivered the baby she may be eager to go back to work and even resent staying at home.[125] In such a case, it is essential that she share her perceptions with her spouse and that the two are able to bring role expectations in line with role performance.

Both men and women are becoming more sensitive to the changing roles of women. Adolescent women and men recognize that factors like sex role; background of the person; the attitudes, values, and beliefs of the significant other; and achievement variables all influence the woman's choice to parent, have a career, or engage in both activities.[126] Such a recognition will allow women and men to make reasonable choices that will allow role performance to approximate role expectations.

Solutions Provided Through the Passage of Time   Both changing sex roles and communication will assist us in becoming more effective in the family setting. Our family lives will become more satisfying as we adopt more flexible sex roles and as we interact openly with each other. In addition, time itself will allow change. Although women and men tend to be more rigid than we would sometimes hope, each generation brings new change.

Women are particularly eager to adopt new roles and their attitudes toward family-related tasks are changing dramatically.[127] Younger women tend to be more profeminist than their mothers and in general are more liberal.[128] Men may profit from the example women have provided.

However, we may not want to adopt wholesale all of the changes that are occurring within our culture. A survey of college students suggested some positive and negative areas of change. Among the kinds of changes that are applauded by college students are the awareness of unmarried people about what is involved in becoming parents, increased sex education, sex counseling, flexible sex roles, this generation marrying at an older age than their parents, fathers participating in the births of their children, women pursuing careers, reduced pressure to get married, and fathers getting custody of their children. However, college students do not approve of single parenting, commuter marriages, parents choosing the sex of their children, and teenagers having premarital sex.[129]

SUMMARY

This chapter considered the changing roles in contemporary American families. Role theory originates in the theater and relies on dramatic language, including "script" and "role." Roles originate in society and tend to remain constant, causing role expectations to last long after they are useful for people. Roles may be complementary, symmetrical, or reciprocal.

Since the mid-1970s, gender roles have been sharply altered. A variety of social and economic factors have contributed to this change. Changes in gender roles are basic to changing family roles.

A number of functions must be fulfilled within the family; therefore, a number of roles are necessary. Epstein and colleagues have suggested five major family roles. They include provision of resources, nurturance and support, adult sexual gratification, personal development for both children and adults, and maintenance and management of the family unit. Five functions subsumed under the maintenance and management category are decision-making functions, boundary and membership functions, behavior control functions, household finance functions, and health-related functions.

As we discussed these various family functions and roles, we noted that traditional prescriptions for each have changed with the changing conceptualizations of gender roles. We also observed that individuals in contemporary family types may fulfill these functions in unique ways. Other variables that contribute to each role were also discussed.

American families must cope with role confusion, multiple role demands, and changing roles that lead to conflict within persons as well as between persons. However, new views on women and men assist us in dealing with these problems. The new conceptualizations suggest that women or men can be fully functioning alone; that women and men can play any role they choose, regardless of biological sex; and that children increasingly see individuals playing flexible and different roles than in the past. Marital couples can use role cycling to solve their multiple role demands. Families must communicate with one another about their roles. They need to establish a clear method of role allocation and role accountability as they attempt to achieve role congruence and as they bring their own role expectations in line with their role performance.

KEY TERMS

1. *Family roles* are the repetitive patterns of behavior by which family members fulfill family functions.

2. *Complementary roles* are those in which each partner carries out the role expec tations not enacted by his or her partner.

3. *Symmetrical roles* are when two members of a couple carry out a similar role.

4. *Reciprocal roles* occur when the members of the couple are more interactive and roles are played based on mutual give and take.

5. *Sex roles* describe one's endorsement of feminine or masculine traits.

6. *Androgyny* refers to individuals who are high in masculinity and high in femininity.

7. *Undifferentiated* refers to people who are neither feminine nor masculine.

8. *Role salience* means the relative importance or value people place on the enact ment of particular family, employment, or community roles.

9. *Kinkeeping* describes the function of maintaining contact with one's extended family and keeping other family members in touch with each other.

10. *Code switching* refers to being able to change verbal and nonverbal behaviors from masculine to feminine, for example, as the circumstances warrant and the context varies.

11. *Role allocation* describes the family's pattern in assigning roles.

12. *Role accountability* deals with procedures implemented to assure that roles are being fulfilled.

13. *Role congruence* is the agreement among family members about the roles each will play.

14. *Role expectations* are our own idealized set of projections about the functions that we will serve.

15. *Role performance* is the way we actually behave within a particular role.

RULES IN FAMILY COMMUNICATION

If you're going to play the game properly you'd better know every rule.

BARBARA JORDAN

After you have read this chapter, you will be able to

1. Describe rules theory and explain the four key components used to define a rule.

2. Define and provide examples for rules, patterns, images, themes, and rituals.

3. Discuss the implicit and explicit nature of rules.

4. Explain how the original family, the current family, and one's roles impact upon rule development in the family.

5. List and describe the six functions of verbal communication rules.

6. Describe how family size and one's relative age in the family influence the functions of communication rules.

7. Diagram the most common family networks.

8. Differentiate between selective attention and selective retention.

9. Identify topics that may or may not be appropriate to discuss in certain families.

10. Explain the expression of emotions that may be face-honoring, face-compensating, face-neutral, or face-threatening.

Rules are important to people who play games, to legislative bodies, and to members of other groups. Rules about verbal and nonverbal behavior are central to our understanding of communication in the family. In this chapter we will identify the functions rules serve in our verbal interaction. Communication scholar Julia Wood affirms, "It is through talk that persons define themselves and their relationships and through talk that definitions once entered into are revised over the life of a relationship."[1] Minuchin explains, "A family is a system that operates through transactional patterns. Repeated transactions establish patterns of how, when, and to whom to relate, and these patterns underpin the system."[2]

❖ THE RULES PERSPECTIVE

A consideration of rules is important in social and personal relationships.[3] Family communication authors Kathleen Galvin and Bernard Brommel define family rules as "relationship agreements that prescribe and limit a family's behavior over time."[4] These authors explain that because families are governed by rules, their interaction is patterned and predictable. Another author defines family rules as metaphors "coined by the observer to cover the redundancy he [she] observes."[5] Researcher Ford adds that rules can be "inferred from any repetitive family behavior."[6] Communication scholar Susan Shimanoff identifies rules as the guiding principle which gives our interactions meaning.[7] In addition, she provides an integrative view of rules theory. Rules theory is not easy to understand and Shimanoff's assistance is of value.

■ Definition of a Rule

Shimanoff defines a *rule* as a prescription that can be followed and that suggests the behavior that is obligated, preferred, or prohibited in particular contexts. The four key concepts in this definition are that rules must be capable of being followed, are prescriptive, are contextual, and must specify appropriate behavior.

Let us consider each of these ideas. To state that a rule must be *capable of being followed* means that other individuals can determine if they wish to follow the rule or if they wish to ignore it. A person is not following a rule if he or she is not voluntarily responding to it. A child who is forced to sit at the dinner table until he or she "finishes everything on the plate" is not following a rule. In addition, an individual must have the ability to follow it. We cannot ask children in our families to behave in ways that their level of maturity and development disallow.

Shimanoff states that rules are *prescriptive*. This suggests that rules are sanctioned or authorized. They provide direction to others. Rules are not descriptive; they do not merely state what *does* occur. They go further as they suggest what *should* occur. Children may argue with each other at the dinner table, and we may describe their behavior. However, such conflict is not a rule; it is not behavior that is required or recommended. The children would not receive negative sanctions if they avoided conflict through an entire meal. On the other hand, eating with a knife and fork may be a rule, and the child who began to eat his vegetables and potato with his bare hands might soon learn of the rule involved. Negative responses frequently follow when an individual "breaks" a rule.

Stating that rules are *contextual* suggests that rules do not generalize over all situations. Some rules are particular to a few situations, while others have more generalizability. For instance, families develop rules to guide interactions that are sometimes unique to their own families. Rituals to put children to bed serve as an example. Parents may have routines that include such activities as brushing one's teeth, bathing, reading a story, telling a story, getting a drink of water, listening to prayers or personal thoughts, arranging dolls and stuffed animals on the bed in a certain pattern, chanting a favorite verse or nursery rhyme, putting on a night light, shutting a closet door, opening the bedroom door to a certain angle, or finding a favorite blanket when putting small children to bed. These routinized behaviors become rules to be followed, and ignoring part of the procedure can result in a great deal of disturbance on the part of the child.

Other rules in the family may be more generalizable and apply in additional contexts. For example, siblings may be able to borrow items from each other, but they must return what they borrow in the same shape and state of cleanliness in which it was when they took it. Such a rule would probably also be true with friends or coworkers.

Shimanoff writes that rules *specify an appropriate behavior.* Her emphasis here is on the notion of behavior as opposed to attitude, value, or feeling. She is suggesting that rules deal with the observable rather than with internal states. We can ask one of our children to be home at a certain hour, but we cannot ask him or her to appreciate coming home at that time. We can require children to attend church or synagogue, but we cannot require that they share our faith.

This notion also suggests that the behavior can be specified. It cannot be abstract, ambiguous, or lacking in clarity. One format that has been used by rules theorists, including Shimanoff, to state rules is the "if-then" format which specifies behavior. Examples for the family might be:

If the house has just been cleaned, and it is raining outside, you remove your shoes before entering.

If your father displays a bad mood, you do not ask him if you can borrow the car.

If your sister has the door to her room shut, you do not walk in without knocking.

This format clarifies the relationship of the conditions under which the rule should be followed.

In order to determine the rules that exist in interactions among people, we must look at the "actor's" behavior. Sometimes rules are easy to determine because they are *explicit;* that is, they are stated as clearly and succinctly as those above. More often, however, the rules are *implicit,* or simply understood by those involved. You may be unaware of some of your family's rules because so many of them are not stated; instead they are assumed or absorbed through the practice of family living. One writer considers the implicit nature of family rules:

> To the extent that family rules are implicit they have the attributes of secrets, i.e., they give power over others and induce guilt. In addition, they allow for modulation of energy so as to control or limit relationships as well to allow intimacy.[8]

The implicit nature of many rules leads to confusion for those involved. One person's understanding of the rules may be very different from another person's understanding. For instance, the wife in one couple might feel that it is perfectly appropriate to flirt with the husband in the couple they call their best friends. However, the other wife may view such behavior as questionable, even bordering on the immoral.

Oftentimes family rules are implicit, until someone breaks one of them. One 23-year-old woman explains:

> It seems that if you grow up with your family, the rules are more likely to be implicit. Many statements do not need to be made because the children have grown up with their parents as examples. If the parents follow the rules, the children may not know the options of disobeying them—at least for awhile.
>
> I remember stomping my foot in reaction to my mother when I was about seven. At that point I learned from Mom's explicit verbalization that "you will *not* stomp your foot at your mother!" The tone of voice and facial expression were more than enough to give me conscious knowledge of the rule![9]

■ Importance of Rules

Rules theory emphasizes the notion that interaction and meaning are uniquely related in human experience. *Rules* are prescriptions that can be followed and that suggest obligated, preferred, or prohibited behavior for particular contexts. We determine the specific rules existing in interactions among people by looking at their behavior. Sometimes they are explicit, but more often they are implicit, or simply understood by those involved.

The term "patterns" refers to a similar concept. *Patterns* are the predictable and manageable sets of behaviors that are unique to the family and that are distinctive from any one family member's own actions. For instance, Kristina is the youngest child in a family of six children. Her parents have determined that they will have no additional offspring and they view Kristina as the "baby." Kristina thrives on being treated as the stereotypical youngest child. She basks in the attention that she receives from her older siblings and from her parents. She enjoyed her bottle until she was two; stayed in her crib until she was three; and was sometimes carried by her father or an older sibling until she was nearly five. Kristina's favorite game is, "Let's pretend—you be the Mommy and I'll be the baby." Kristina's "baby talk" is met with positive reinforcement. The pattern of behavior in this family encourages Kristina to be a baby rather than to develop as an individual.

■ Rules Allow Us to Define Our Families

Rules are important to the family unit because they help the family to establish their identity. Through our interaction and the creation of rules in our family we are able to provide family images, family themes, and family rituals. *Family images* are the verbal and nonverbal pictures we use to describe our family and its members. *Family themes* are underlying family perspectives or points of view. In some ways, family themes suggest the relationship of the family to the rest of the world. *Family rituals* are "symbolic forms of communication acted out in systematic fashion over time because of the satisfaction that family members experience through their repetition."[10] Family members are probably more satisfied with their families when they agree upon family images, themes, and rituals and when they feel they are appropriate.

Family images are created through our interactions with other family members. They are word pictures of how we see our family. We often use metaphors, analogies, similes, and other figurative language in the construction of our family images. We might visualize the interaction in the family that was described with this image:

> My family image is that of 4 natives living on an island with an ever demanding volcano to appease. The 4 natives are myself, my father, and my two younger brothers. The volcano is my mother.[11]

A more complicated, but perhaps more satisfied, family is described by a college student who was attending a university far from her family home:

> When I think of my family image I visualize a football team. My father's position is the quarterback who calls his own plays. He decides what strategy to take and then implements it. My mother could be considered my dad's right arm and therefore is placed in the position of running back, the star running back. She is the consistent one who will always get at least four yards. My "little" brother resembles the entire front line. Not only by his physical size, but by his concern for our family. He would never let anyone penetrate through the line to get to any of us. My sister holds the position of second string quarterback. She's a lot like my father as far as attitudes and values. She is very independent and believes "her way" is always best. My position on the team would be on the sidelines. I am the biggest fan, the loudest cheerleader and, at times, the head referee. I am not as involved in the play-by-play because of geographical barriers. However, when I am able to be with my

family I play an active role. Regardless of victory or defeat my family remains strong and united, our spirit never faltering. Together we are definitely a winning team![12]

Family images may change as other changes occur in the family unit. A mother in an adolescent family described her family image that occurred with the onset of her daughter's adolescence:

Our family is like a swarm of bees living in a beehive. All five of us are busy doing both what we like to do, what we must do, in order to keep the hive functioning. Most recently, we had a Queen Bee emerge among us. She is our adolescent daughter. Depending on her mood, the Queen Bee can be kind and affectionate, usually when wanting something from us. Or, she can be cool and aloof spending most of her time in her chambers. Most of the time the remaining four of us find ourselves flying around our hive unassumingly so as not to disturb the Queen. We look forward to the day when the Queen Bee either leaves our hive or by some miracle transforms into a fellow worker. I have heard there is hope for a transformation and that it usually occurs toward the end of adolescence.[13]

The new family types similarly require new family images. One 21-year-old woman wrote:

My parents were divorced and remarried when I was quite young and I think my families represent an equally weighted scale. The scale is perfectly balanced, but with different substances. On my mother's side of the scale is an apple pie, on my father's side is a gin and tonic.[14]

A man in a childless couple explained that his family image was a house with four rooms:

The first room is a battlefield, where my wife, Jean, and I argue, challenge each other, spite one another, and act out our vindictive impulses prompted by our selfish emotions. The second room is a hospital where we soothe, relieve and nurture each other. This is where we recover from a hard day's exhaustion, a hurtful experience or a robust argument. Forgiveness, reassurance, empathy and encouragement occur here. The third room is an office, where Jean and I attend to the details of maintaining a home. We discuss finances, future plans, relations with the outside world and day-to-day housekeeping activity in this room. The fourth room is a playroom, where we freely enjoy ourselves and each other. We talk, we laugh, we watch TV, entertain friends or do whatever our spirits inspire. At times we "play" together, as in lovemaking or sharing a good meal. And sometimes we act together "individually," as when we are reading separate periodicals, yet silently involved in the process of jointly establishing and maintaining a peaceful and happy home.[15]

One's family image may be different in the original family than in the current family. One 30-year-old married woman distinguishes the two images for her families:

My original family is like a clean sparkling window on a warm sunny day. Everyone is smiling and happy to be one of the five shining panes that make up the unit. Unfortunately, at times, the window becomes spotted and streaked. My role has always been that of the window cleaner once I see a spot. . . . I come along with a bucket of sudsy water and clean, clean, clean to ensure that clear, bright outlook and an overwhelming sense of exhaustion and satisfaction.

My current family image, which includes Andrew and I, is like a can and a can opener. Of course, I am the can opener, often attempting to pry open the can. This can is at times extremely stubborn and difficult to open. It is then that the opener may give up, putting the task aside for awhile. Being a persistent opener, though, I'll always return when the can looks ready (or even eager) to be opened.[16]

Although these images are different, they both place the role of the woman as the nurturer or initiator of action.

Family themes are oftentimes stated more briefly than are family images. They may take the form of a well-known slogan or cliché or they may be highly unique. Some of the family themes that are offered by family members include the following.

1. You can attain all of your goals with a little work.[17]

2. You always go to the family first when you need help.[18]

3. All people are created equal.[19]

4. Whenever possible, help the family.[20]

5. The family is always first.[21]

6. The family that keeps their struggles well hidden and concealed appears stable and satisfied.[22]

7. Family appearances are more important than openness, intimacy, and honesty.[23]

8. You're in this life alone.[24]

9. You can depend on mom and dad.[25]

10. Be careful where you walk, the world is full of banana peels, and no one will pay your hospital bill, and while you are on your back, you will lose your job and your house and of course if you lose those you will also lose your wife. . . .[26]

These themes instruct family members on how they are to view their family and how they are to view people outside the family. They also provide behavioral expectations. The work ethic is clearly evident in the first theme, while a focus on support is more evident in the fourth and ninth entries. The tenth entry, from the contemporary book *Her Mother's Daughter*, depicts a depressing and threatening future. The family theme may be passed from one generation to the next. Like the family image, the family theme may change due to other alterations in the culture or within the family unit.

Family rituals may be a more obvious concept to you than are family images or family themes. Family rituals include routinized behaviors that families come to expect over time. Many family rituals center on holidays or celebrations. They may include certain food choices for particular parties, a certain time to celebrate a holiday, or precise clothing or costumes that accompany an event. They include the lamb on Passover, the turkey at Thanksgiving, the Christmas Eve church service, and the red, white, and blue worn on the Fourth of July. Rituals lead to family strength and satisfaction and are more important to women than to men and more important to grandparents and parents than they are to grandchildren.[27]

■ How Rules Are Developed

Rules are essential in developing and satisfying family relationships. Rules emerge from the interactions of the family members. The primary contributors to the development of rules include the original family, the current family, our roles, our peers, the media, and education. Although the influence of our peers, the media, and education are unmistakable,[28] these areas are beyond the scope of this text. In this section we will consider the influence of the original family, the current family, and our roles.

Original Family   Columnist Russell Baker, in his autobiography *Growing Up*, emphasizes the importance of our history in understanding our present:

> We all come from the past, and children ought to know what it was that went into their making, to know that life is a braided cord of humanity stretching up from time long gone, and that it cannot be defined by the span of a single journey from diaper to shroud.[29]

Our lives do not begin when we are born and our original families contribute to the rules in our created families.

Many of our attitudes, values, and behaviors are passed from one generation to the next.[30] Bill Cosby humorously remarks, "Raising children is an incredibly hard and risky business in which no cumulative wisdom is gained: Each generation repeats the mistakes the previous one made."[31] He adds that parents often place a curse on their children, asking that when they marry, they will have children who behave similarly to how their children behaved. Cosby parenthetically notes, "(And, of course, the curse always works, proving that God has a sense of humor)."[32]

Our *original family*—the family in which we grew up and were socialized—taught us a variety of lessons. Among our understandings was how we would view communication. We might be fearful of interacting with strangers, with large groups, or when the outcome is unknown. We might enjoy interacting with others and seek out opportunities to talk with new acquaintances. You might say "hello" or smile at virtually everyone you see on the street or you may rarely initiate interaction with others. You may have learned these reactions to communication opportunities because of your orienting family.

Children acquire conversational competence in the family. Communication researcher Beth Haslett explored the conversational abilities that children acquire in early interactions with their primary caretaker. She found that children develop in four areas. First, they begin to *understand the value of communication.* Children learn both the instrumental, task-related purpose of communication as well as the value of communication as a means for expressing oneself and for developing relationships.

Second, they *develop their ability to communicate* using conventional or agreed-upon signs. Children gain some understanding of the consensual nature of interaction. They learn, through trial and error, that some sounds have communicative value while others do not.

Third, they *develop an appreciation of the requirements of dialogue.* They learn the intricacies of subject-verb agreement and the placement of subjects and verbs within sentences as well as rules about interrupting and overlapping others.

Last, they *develop particular communicative styles* because of the interactional opportunities provided by the caretaker. They may learn to be highly expressive, responsive, relaxed, or noncommunicative.[33]

Language acquisition and communicative competence are widely studied. However, little agreement about the process has been reached by theorists.[34] The "Doonesbury" cartoon (p. 114) is humorous because it suggests that children acquire language in a nonintegrative way. The child appears to be acquiring prepositions and conjunctions at random.

Beth Haslett suggests that the caretaker has the opportunity of facilitating children's communicative development by (1) interpreting their children's statements, (2) modeling appropriate communicative behavior, (3) extending their children's responses, (4) providing opportunities for interaction, and (5) demonstrating positive attitudes toward communication.[35] Caretakers can limit children's communicative development if they do not listen to children, if they fail to understand what children are attempting to say, if they do not model appropriate behavior, if they interrupt or negate their children's responses, if they disallow opportunities for the children to interact, and if they demonstrate negative feelings about communication opportunities. We will consider children's communication development further in Chapters 7 and 8.

Haslett's advice is well taken as we observe that a variety of specific communicative behaviors appear to originate in our family of orientation. For example, young adults who report having been raised by parents who encouraged open expression of feelings and opinions provide more self-disclosure (sharing of personal information) to both of their parents and to their best same-sex friend. Furthermore, they are more honest and they exhibit greater awareness when they are providing personal disclosures.[36] Children who are

rewarded for being frank in the statement of their opinions and feelings may learn to reveal a great deal.

Assertive parents may raise assertive children. The couple building the house in the nonfiction book *House* decided to build their home on the wife's parents' property in order to have three generations of their family within close proximity. The only concern they had was the woman's relationship with her father. The author explains:

> Actually, the only obvious problem was that Judith sometimes bickers with her father, Jules Wiener. She remembers Jules closing out disputes, when she was still a child, by saying to her, "My house, my rules." Now when he visits her house and takes out a cigar, she says, "My house, my rules. No cigars." She smiles when she says her lines, but the joke sometimes leads to sharper words. "I'm pretty direct with my father, and he's pretty direct with me," she explains. "As they say, I come by it honest."[37]

The father's assertive behavior, as well as his specific verbalization, were learned by the daughter.

Similarly, marital aggression is transmitted intergenerationally. One study showed that children who observed physical hitting between their parents were more likely to be involved in severe marital aggression as adults than if *they* were physically struck when they were teenagers by their parents.[38] The modeling of marital aggression was not sex specific. Sons and daughters who observed their fathers striking their mothers increased in likelihood as both the victims and the perpetrators of physical violence.

Intergenerational continuity may be questioned because most information on the similarity in values, beliefs, attitudes, and behavior between parents and their adult children is reported by the adult children. The similarities may be exclusively within the adult children's perceptions. An investigation attempted to determine the agreement between adult children and their parents about intergenerational similarity. The researchers found the children perceived less similarity than the parents did. The similarities between the parents and the adult children may be conservatively reported.[39] Children may more closely resemble their parents than they report.

Current Family   Our original family contributes to the development of the communicative rules we individually hold. When we begin a new family, these rules are only one set of the possible sets of rules we will establish in our created families. The newly created family may have rules that do not resemble the rules we bring from our original families. However, family researcher Minuchin underscores the importance of the original families in creating new rules for the current family:

> When partners join, each expects the transactions of the spouse unit to take the forms with which he [she] is familiar. Each spouse will try to organize the spouse unit along lines that are familiar or preferred, and will press the other to accommodate. A number of arrangements are possible. Each spouse will have areas in which he [she] cannot permit flexibility. In other areas, alterna-

tive ways of relating can be chosen in response to the other's preferences. Each spouse will confirm the other in some situations and disqualify him [her] in others. Some behaviors are reinforced and others are shed as the spouses accommodate to and assimilate each other's preferences. In this way, a new family system is formed.[40]

Each of us begins the development of new families with a sense of reality, somewhat dependent upon the sense of reality created by our orienting family. The set of rules from our original family must in some way merge with the set of rules from our partner's original family. One theorist explains the development of rules:

> Rules implement themselves and each other; paradoxically they oppose, contradict, or totally negate each other at the same time. These contradictions and paradoxes are possible because rules appear as straight-line forces opposing each other but are in fact arcs on a circle, sphere, or helix. Each discrete rule system is not only discrete but also circular, with no particular beginning or end. When distant rule systems come in contact, they may impinge upon each other in a variety of ways. They may connect at only one point, as does the tangent to a circle (and tangents are arcs, too), or they may have the relationship of spheres with many points in common and may oppose or reinforce or both oppose and reinforce. Two clusters of rules may also be as the intersection of two spheres with many points of contact and the generation of new circular configurations. This latter pattern is the one that is seen in marriages of two autonomous people; giving up personal autonomy to the relationship allows for the merger, union, or fusion of parts of two systems without loss of integrity for either. Naturally there will be enhancing and disrupting effects from the conjointure of the two rule-family-systems.[41]

Marilyn French's book *Her Mother's Daughter* shows the many repetitive patterns that have been passed down from the women in her main character's family. One particularly poignant example from the book follows. Anastasia, the central character, recalls:

> There was a particularly cruel story that I mulled over night after night in bed, vowing to get revenge when I grew up. In it, my mother was assigned in fifth grade to copy some maps from her geography textbook. Unsure of herself, she made many trials, and did painstaking sketches and finally produced maps she thought might pass. She handed them in the next day, and when the teacher saw them, she cried out, "You traced these!" and tore them into shreds. My timid mother was unable to protest, and was merely heartbroken. . . .
> I never told my children the story about the maps: by the time they were born, it had faded from my mind. But when my first volume of photographs was published, some man gave it a brief and especially nasty review in a photographic magazine. Arden [her older daughter] was about fourteen, and we were not getting along well. Yet without my knowing it, she wrote a letter to the editor complaining about the critic's blindness and stupidity, and for unnecessary viciousness. I never saw her letter and wouldn't have known

about it had he not replied, rather sweetly, explaining to her that no one wanted to harm her mother, but that was the way things were done in the public world. She wasn't satisfied, tossed the letter down in a huff, and cried out. I held her close to me, I tried to console her. I couldn't, any more than I could console my mother. Children do not understand that nothing they do can repair the past.[42]

Although patterns of alcoholism, physical abuse, incest, and other social problems recur in families, such patterns can be altered. Similarly, if you grew up in a home where negative communicative behaviors such as *verbal aggression*—spoken attacks or hostile comments—or *communication apprehension*—the extreme fear of communicating with another person or group of people—were common, you need not perpetuate those behaviors. Being aware of underlying communicative rules, talking about your communicative patterns, and purposefully changing ineffective communicative habits can help you to have a more satisfying family life.

On the other hand, children may learn positive behaviors from their original families. You may be encouraged to know that parents who exhibit high levels of competence in their interaction often have children who exhibit similarly high levels of skill. Researchers Filsinger and Lamke examined marital adjustment and interpersonal communication competence. They concluded that marital adjustment is not transmitted from parent to child, but general interpersonal competence is.[43] Competence in our interactions with others, in turn, encourages marital adjustment.

Families develop rules because of events in their current families, too. Salvador Minuchin reports a dialogue he had with a family in therapy. The Wagners divided their weekends so Mrs. Wagner planned the activities for Saturday and Mr. Wagner planned Sunday's events. In probing, Minuchin discovered the rationale for this division:

MINUCHIN: It just happens. How did that happen? That's interesting historically; how did you come to this kind of division of decision making? Do you remember?

MR. WAGNER: I will hazard to venture a guess. I used to work Mondays through Saturdays, in the hospital business; Saturday was sort of bataround. I felt Sunday was my day off, as far as I was concerned. So as soon as Saturday was available, she jumped at it, so to speak. I wouldn't let her have her preference on Sunday, because Sunday was sort of my day.

MINUCHIN: So, you evolved that kind of implicit rule without ever having it stated that this was the way you function.

MRS. WAGNER: As a rule, on Sunday he goes fishing or something, and I go my way. It's always been that way; well, it's been that way for about a year.

MINUCHIN: He goes fishing Sunday. Saturday is the day on which both of you do things together, and you are the one that decides.

MR. WAGNER: It's not, it's not that hard and fast, really. I would say that on Saturday there is a better chance that my wife would decide what we are going to do.

MRS. WAGNER: I usually have something planned, you know, that I want to do, and we usually do it.[44]

Roles   The roles that we play in the family similarly affect our communicative rules. Individuals who cohabit are sometimes surprised to find that their partners behave differently after marriage than they did when they were living together. One reason that people may behave differently in a cohabiting situation than in a married situation is because of the roles they perceive they are enacting. The cohabiting partner may view the couple in an egalitarian relationship with both partners contributing to the economic well-being of the household. The married partner may have far different expectations for someone who is a "wife" or "husband" largely because of his or her own original family.

Our sex roles may affect our communicative behavior in the family. For instance, the right to determine the communicative rules themselves may be viewed as more appropriate for men than for women. Communication researchers Hopper, Knapp, and Scott demonstrated that men originate the majority of idioms or unique terms used by the couple as they develop their relationship.[45]

Further, fathers and mothers communicate differently to their children. For instance, two investigators showed that fathers produced more directives than mothers and they tended to phrase them as imperatives (e.g., "Put the plate on the table") or as highly indirect "hints" (e. g., "You're going to drop the plate") more often than mothers. Mothers were more likely to use relatively transparent indirect forms (e. g., "Can you put the plate on the table?") The parents did not alter their verbalizations for their male or female children.[46] We will consider the importance of roles further in Chapter 5.

❖ VERBAL COMMUNICATION RULES

Communication rules in the family fulfill a number of functions. They tell family members to whom they can speak, who can speak to them, what they can speak about, when they can speak, where they can speak, and why people speak. Let us consider each of these areas.

■ To Whom Can You Speak and to Whom Can You Listen?

Young children are advised in televised messages, from programmed learning packets, and in informal ways, that they should avoid speaking to strangers. Children as young as 2 and 3 years old who formerly showed uninhibited delight with interacting with others in public places such as the park, the grocery store, and restaurants, now shy away from the friendly stranger who begins to interact with them. Increased problems with child molesting, child abduction, and child custody have led parents and social agencies to support national efforts to discourage children from speaking to individuals not known to the family.

The motivation of such groups to discourage children from interacting with strangers is understandable, but the effect on the child's interest in initiating conversations and relationships as he or she continues to develop is unclear. Children who are taught from their earliest memories to avoid initiating conversations with unknown people may be inhibited in beginning friendships and acquaintanceships later in life. At the same time, we may not encourage our own children to seek out new people with whom to interact for fear they will become part of a growing statistic of missing children.

■ To Whom Do You Speak?

Families teach children and other family members rules about the persons to whom they can speak. Not only do families teach their members about the appropriateness of speaking to individuals outside the family, they also provide rules about to whom they may speak within the family. Sometimes we are told not to speak to family members about certain topics because they are too young to understand an issue. At other times we do not talk to a family member because of his or her attitudes or values. Sometimes we do not talk to others in a certain way. Let us consider these possibilities.

The other person's age, attitudes, mental state, or other characteristics may cause family members to engage in less communication with one of their kin. Topics are screened for children in the family. Young children generally do not hear discussions that deal with sexual matters or with physical violence. Children in elementary school and junior high might not be let in on the family finances. High school age children are generally not privy to serious problems between the marital couple. An ill relative might not be told distressing news. A deeply religious or moral member of the family might be spared information about teenage problems with drugs, alcohol, or sex. An emotional member of the family may rarely learn of any of the problems that the family is facing. A person who responds with hurt and disappointment at every suggestion of conflict might never know about the problems within his or her own family.

To whom do family members speak? Many people, reflecting on their childhoods, identify their mothers as the person to whom they spoke the most. A 34-year-old male elementary teacher is typical:

> While growing up, I would speak most often to my mother who was much more available. My father was usually busy with his job and hobbies (horse racing) and did not take much interest in my school activities or sports. Most

communication was one-way from my father and any questioning of his direction or attempt at discussion was viewed as insubordination and was countered with much anger.[47]

A 22-year-old nurse agreed:

The center of communication in my family revolves around our mother. I talk with her most often and in the greatest depth.[48]

A 37-year old teacher offered an exception:

As I think back it was my father who was easiest to talk to. When Mom and I communicated it was more her doing the talking and me listening.[49]

With some exceptions, availability and approachability have made mothers the communication partner of choice by children in many families.

The patterns of interaction in families may be changing as fathers become more involved with their children and mothers become more involved with work. In addition, some current studies suggest that previous research may have evidenced a bias toward studying mothers and grandmothers to the exclusion of fathers and grandfathers.[50] These older studies may thus be positively distorting the amount of time mothers and grandmothers spend engaged in interaction with children and grandchildren and ignoring the interactions of adult males with children. In any case, as roles continue to change in American families, we will want to consider the interaction patterns between both mothers and fathers with their children.

Changing family types, too, may encourage different communicative coupling in the future. Divorce has already altered the rules about the family members to whom we speak the most. One woman wrote, "My father and mother divorced when I was 18 months old; I do not remember my father at all."[51] A male college student explained that his parents were divorced and that he had lived most of the time with his mother and stepfather. Within the last two years, he moved to his father's and stepmother's home. He describes the communication within the new home:

I communicate with my dad in a fairly formal manner. He is the one financing my education; as it turns out, I end up mostly telling him good news and refrain from the bad. His wife doesn't communicate with me at all (except for essential communication). It is a difficult situation that the entire family recognizes.[52]

On the other hand, divorce need not disrupt open communication:

I speak and listen to every person in my family. My parents divorced when I was nine. Both remarried and my family, consisting of both sides, equals twelve people. I talk and listen to my stepfather and mother, and to all my stepbrothers and -sisters. To me, communication with kin is necessary. We all get along very well with one another; it would be foolish not to communicate.[53]

The relatively smaller families that occur today, as opposed to the larger families of the past, also affect interaction patterns. One man wrote:

> In my family there are only 3 members: my mother, father, and myself. Communication is very open. We are close knit because of the small number in the house. My mom and dad aren't just my family, they are my closest friends.[54]

Contrast this experience with that of a woman who came from a family of nine children. This 47-year-old woman writes:

> Just because of the large number of persons under one roof, who spoke and when one spoke was often determined by the one in authority. During the daytime there was no doubt in our minds that Mom was boss and when Daddy came home he was the boss.[55]

One's relative age in the family also affects communicative patterns. One person explained, "Since my mother is so much older than me and my father is deceased, I speak and listen mostly to my brother and sister."[56] A man in his late 30s reflected:

> My sister was born when I was twelve and my youngest brother when I was eighteen. Therefore, I think there wasn't as much communication with them because of the age differences.[57]

Many families have networks of individuals through whom information regularly travels. Some teenagers might almost always ask their mothers for favors, but generally tell their fathers about something that has gone wrong. If they want to use one of the family cars, their mother is asked. If they have an accident with the car, their father is informed.

Communication researchers who have studied small groups have determined various predictable patterns of interaction that occur among people. They have labeled these patterns networks; *networks* refer to the patterned channels through which information normally flows. Networks describe who normally talks to whom in what order. The most common networks are the chain pattern, the Y-network, the wheel pattern, and the all-channel network. These networks have application in the family setting.

The Chain Network   The chain network, depicted in Figure 4.1, occurs when each family member communicates to only one or two others in a linear fashion. In the depicted example, Dad talks to Mom, who talks to the oldest daughter, who talks to the youngest daughter. The example illustrates the communication pattern that sometimes exists in a traditional patriarchal family. Dad makes the decisions, passes them on to Mom, who shares them with the oldest child who, in turn, shares them with the youngest child. The process can be reversed. If the younger daughter wants something from her parents, she might talk with her older sister, who asks Mom, who asks Dad.

Figure 4.1

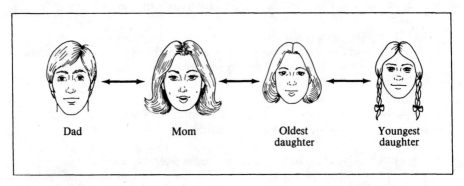

Dad   Mom   Oldest   Youngest
daughter   daughter

The chain network.

The chain network was present in one woman's family when she was a child. Virtually no communication occurred between her parents, and the family seemed almost divided into two "camps." Her parents divorced soon after this period:

> As I recall, I always spoke to Dad. They say we were inseparable. Annie, in turn, learned to speak to Mom. It seemed that there was a real dichotomy in our family: Mom and Annie, and Missy and Dad. Mom and Dad rarely spoke except through their pawns, Annie and I.[58]

The chain network has both advantages and disadvantages in the family. The advantage of the chain network is that it allows busy families who may not be in physical proximity for very long to communicate with each other. For instance, if an older child works after school and does not return home until his siblings are asleep, he can still communicate with them by providing his parents with a message to share with them. If one of the parents leaves for work before the children are awake, the other parent can pass on messages to them from the absent parent.

The disadvantage is that information can be misinterpreted or misunderstood as the message travels from one person to another. Family members may add or subtract information from the originally intended message. They can embellish the story or add nuances of meaning through their nonverbal gestures, facial expressions, or vocal tones. They can suggest to the family member receiving the message how they should respond by the way they provide the message. Families who rely on the chain network extensively may find that their interaction is less than satisfying and that other family members do not really understand them or their messages.

Y-Network This communication pattern is similar to the chain network, but two people or two sets of people send or receive messages from another set. The Y-network is depicted in Figure 4.2. This is an example of a blended fami-

Figure 4.2

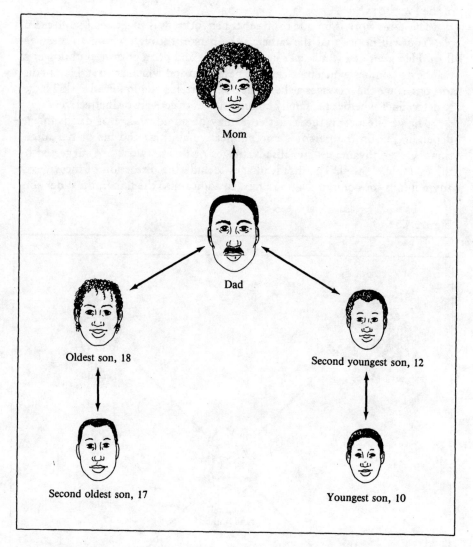

The Y-network.

ly in which the mother is the stepmother to the two older boys and the bio-logical mother of the two younger boys. The pattern of communicating to Dad, who in turn communicated to the children, began when the family consisted of the stepmother, father, and two older boys. Later when the family added two sons of their marriage, the pattern did not change. In this particular family, the mother does not have the stereotypical close relationship with her children. She works far more hours per week than does her husband; and her husband, although professionally employed, has served as the primary parent of the four boys.

The Y-network is unique from other networks, as is suggested by the example. You will notice that the father is the person through whom all messages flow. He serves as a *gatekeeper* in this instance and has a great deal of power in that he determines which messages are passed on and which are not. He can distort or change the messages as he wishes. In short, his communicative skill largely determines whether the family communicates effectively or ineffectively.

The gatekeeper in the Y-network may be an advantage or disadvantage, depending upon the person's communicative abilities and his or her intentions. Other advantages and disadvantages of this network are suggested by the example, as well. The disadvantages include the distortion of messages at any point in the communication links. In addition to the father, the older sons

Figure 4.3

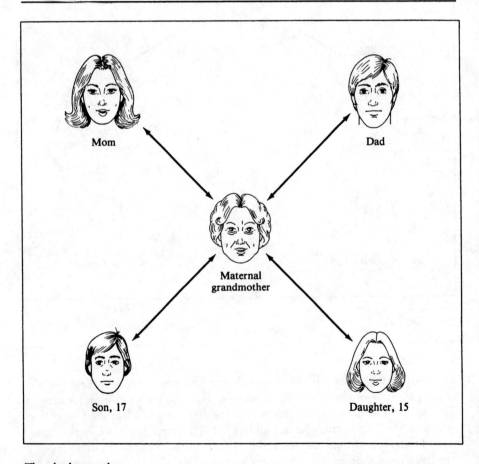

The wheel network.

in the two pairs of boys can change the message that is shared with their younger brothers. The primary advantage of this model is that everyone can communicate with each other in some fashion even though the family is busy or is less than willing to listen to some members of the family. In this example, the stepmother did not believe her husband's sons respected her and she relied upon the Y-network in order to have her perceptions shared with the boys.

Wheel Network The wheel network is illustrated in Figure 4.3. The wheel network, even more than the Y-network, has one central gatekeeper. The family pictured in the illustration is an extended family. The maternal grandmother, who is in her late 50s, essentially is in charge of communication in the family home. Both of the parents are professionals who work long hours each day. The children are gone from home for most of the day, too, either at school or in extracurricular activities. Both children are actively involved in athletics, student government, and their church. The grandmother, who is highly active, essentially lost her reason for living when her husband died unexpectedly of a heart attack. Her daughter (the mother in this family) invited her to live with her family. The arrangement has generally worked out very satisfactorily.

In traditional terms, the grandmother serves as the "wife" in this family. During the week, many days go by when members of the original four-member family do not see all of the others; however, each person always sees and communicates with the grandmother. The grandmother rises early to provide breakfast first to the parents and later to the children. She is at home when the children return from school to change clothes and to leave for after-school activities. She has dinner waiting first for the children and later for their parents.

One mother of two children identified her family's network as a wheel and suggests it is her own mother's communicative skills that place her in the center of the wheel:

> Communication evolves around my mother, "the guiding light.". . . The sunrise of yesterday, today and tomorrow, "mama" knows how to cause the roaring lion in Sarah Mead to purr like a kitten. She can tame the beast in a James Brown ("daddy") when he goes on a tantrum to what appears to be a "world of no return." She can speak to her sons-in-law and her daughter-in-law who'll listen to her without questioning her motives. "Mama" stops the ship from rocking when strong winds are raging at sea. Yes, she calms the nerves of her children when they seemingly can't get themselves together in their restless search for "truth." It goes without saying that her grandchildren prefer her over their own parents, for she has a special knack that none of their parents possess.
>
> Having the horoscope sign of "Taurus the Bull," "mama" is persistent enough to iron out conflicts that her loved ones may encounter. Not one to give up, she knows there is an answer somewhere to such problems. So she keeps working at solving them through patience and diligence.
>
> What I *really* like about "mama" is the fact that she does not "pry" in our business. If we seek her advice, she'll try to help us.... Maintaining self-respect and cordiality with us, "The Big Wheel" (as daddy calls her) knows how to draw the line.... We all know ... that "mama" has our interests at heart.[59]

The advantages outweigh the disadvantages of the wheel network for this family. The advantages include the efficiency of communication, and, since the gatekeeper is an effective communicator, accurate communication. The grandmother cares for each family member and typically neither adds nor subtracts essential elements from the messages that she transmits. She has no hurtful intentions toward her family that would encourage her to embellish or add her own point of view to their messages. Her nurturing nature causes her to help family members empathize with each other when messages are not understood.

For instance, the mother had a large project at work recently, which required her attention on weekends as well as during the week. The children felt angry at their mother for spending so much time at work. The grandmother was quick to point out how difficult it was for the mother, too, since she loved her family and would prefer being with them.

Disadvantages can exist for the wheel network. If gatekeepers are poor communicators (do not listen effectively or are unable to express themselves adequately) or have bad intentions (desire to hurt family members, selfishness,

Figure 4.4

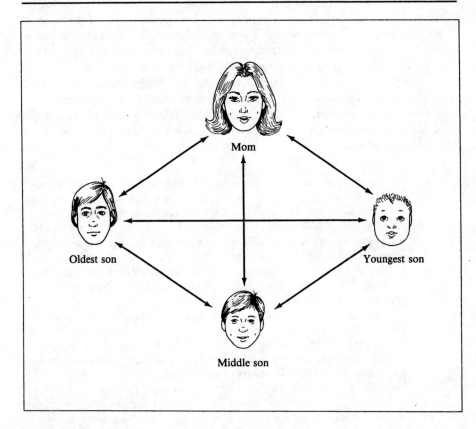

The all-channel network.

or an interest in creating conflict), this network can result in disaster. Also, family members sometimes wish to communicate more with others in the family. The mother in the family in the example sometimes longs for the days when she and her daughter shared more time and more talk. The father states that he would like to spend more time alone with his wife.

All-Channel Network The final network that we will consider in this chapter is the all-channel network, which is depicted in Figure 4.4. The all-channel network, as you can determine, allows communication from all members to all members. No one is a gatekeeper in this arrangement. The particular example that is depicted is a single-parent household headed up by the mother. Although the mother works and the children are all in school, the family network ensures they all interact with each other each day. The family normally eats breakfast and dinner with each other where they share the events of the day. In addition, the boys spend time together after school without their mother before she returns from work. During the evening hours, the mother may interact with one or more of her sons and two or more of them might spend time together watching television, doing homework, or relaxing.

One new father in his mid-20s reports that the all-channel network is used when he calls his parents and brothers and sisters on the holidays. However on other occasions, he speaks only with one of his parents:

> If mom answers the phone I often only talk to her. She relays any messages on to dad and the family. . . . For instance, when Janice and I had Allison, I only spoke with mom. . . . On the other hand, the all-channel network is used . . . on most holidays when I call home. This is a time when I speak with all members of the family. When I speak with each family member I usually talk about what's happening in my life to each one. As the all-channel network suggests, it does take more time to repeat the same story to each family member. However, talking to each family member results in better family relationships.[60]

The all-channel network has the advantage of allowing open interaction among all of the members; no one can control or distort messages from one person to another. The disadvantage of this pattern of communication is that it is time-consuming, and it requires that people sometimes repeat their messages two or three times before everyone has heard them. Busy families or families who do not have overlapping time at home often cannot take advantage of this network. Nonetheless, the all-channel network often results in the most satisfaction among family members. The pattern is inefficient, but accurate messages are transmitted by satisfied communicators.

We have discussed the various communication networks as though they are only methods of describing communication patterns. Sometimes they provide an effective means of describing decision making in the family as well. For instance, the chain network, the Y-network, and the wheel network all have individual decisions makers who provide their decisions to others. The all-channel network has shared decision making among the family members. You may wish to apply these networks as models of decision making when you read Chapter 14.

By placing communication patterns into four separate networks, we have suggested these are the only, or primary, ways that families interact. We may have also suggested that families rely exclusively upon one of these patterns. Neither conclusion should be drawn. First, families can communicate through a variety of channels. For instance, without too much imagination, we could depict a form of communication in which the linear depiction of the chain network is pulled around into a circle. In our example, Dad and the youngest daughter would interact as well as Dad and Mom. Or, perhaps most family members engage in two-way communication as illustrated in the all-channel network, but an older child refuses to talk with a younger sibling. A number of additional networks are possible. The four that are discussed in this chapter merely serve as some of the more common patterns.

Second, most families do not rely on only one of these patterns. We noted that the extended family that served as an example of the Y-network had previously communicated differently. Changes in the family may affect the networks that exist. In Chapter 8, we will note how the family interaction patterns change with the addition of children to the family unit. Too, family members may alter their patterns of interaction each day. Seemingly insignificant events like arriving home earlier or later than normal may alter the entire network. Nonetheless, as we have seen, family members often interact most frequently in patterned ways that can be depicted along some common dimensions resulting in routinized networks of communication.

■ To Whom Do You Listen?

This discussion of networks suggests that we not only do not speak to all of family members equally, but we also do not listen to them all equally. In our communicative behavior with family members we engage in both *selective attention* and *selective retention*. Selective attention means we focus on some people and ignore others. Selective retention refers to our retrieving and recalling information from some people, but discarding information from others.

Although many children recall that they spoke most often with their mothers as they were growing and developing, they are about equally divided between the parents to whom they listened. Some report that they listened most to their mother, since they spoke more often with her. One stated, "I listen mainly to my mother. We are exact carbon copies and we think and feel the same way."[61] Others explain that they listened more often to their father since he was viewed as the authority within the home. For instance, one college student wrote:

> I listen to Dad. He has the last word in what goes down. I may hear Mom speaking but I pay little attention to her. Father gets all my attention.[62]

We actually close ourselves off from hearing some people. The small child that we discussed above, who is taught to be wary of strangers, is not allowed to "hear" the stranger who is attempting to captivate him or her into a conversation. You may not be allowed to listen to one of your aunts or uncles who your parents believe is "immoral."

In other instances, we hear the messages that others send us, but we do not offer the other person a full and complete hearing. We may judge their credibility to be low and dismiss them as unworthy of our time. For instance, the blended family that served as an example in the depiction of the Y-network included a stepmother who had low credibility with her stepsons. We may stereotype the other person and hold certain attitudes about them before they begin to speak. For example, you may have the idea that older people are overly conservative and you may not heed the warnings offered by your grandparents.

You might not listen to other family members because of your own characteristics. Perhaps you are preoccupied with yourself, you feel defensive, you feel superior, or you are egocentric. One college student reported that she could not truly listen to her mother because of her own self-focus during her adolescence. A man in his 20s reported that he and his father always seemed to compete with each other's achievements and he was therefore unable to take advice from his father. A mother of school-age children revealed that she seldom listened to her children's opinions because they were "only children."

The way other people in your family communicate might similarly provide a barrier to your ability to listen to them. Family members may habitually exaggerate or they may use language that is unique or specialized. One family of Irish descent included members who loved to tell stories and to be entertaining. The family members regularly embellished the retelling of incidents that occurred to them. For instance, one of the adult women in the family appeared on a local televised talk show. When she told about the experience to her family members, the show grew from being a local production to a regional and finally a nationally syndicated program. The program grew in length, as well. The woman had actually appeared for about 15 minutes of airtime on a 30-minute program. Before the young woman was finished telling about her experience, it had become an hour-long format in which she was the only guest. No one in this family considered such behavior to be inappropriate, but they did take the family characteristic into account when they listened to her. In short, no one believed fully what the others told them. They assumed that details had been added and minutiae had been enlarged.

Perhaps your family includes members who use language in unique or specialized ways. Children may adopt the slang of their peer groups. Adults may use the jargon that is associated with their professions. Adolescents may use provocative or unusual language in their efforts to assert their independence from the family. Using language in unconventional or idiosyncratic ways may cause other family members to be unable to understand you, and, over time, they may stop listening.

The way you are perceived may similarly affect your selective listening. If family members perceive you as "too busy," "impatient," or "short-tempered," they may be less likely to offer you opportunities to listen to them. On the other hand, if you exhibit concern for others, you may be the popular target for family members' messages. One 30-year-old woman disclosed:

> I've been known as the "listener" in the family of origin, so in answering the question, to whom do you listen, I'd have to say everyone. Some more than others. My older sister is a demanding and domineering person who has always requested a open ear. I usually comply, and am probably overly accommodating.[63]

We do not speak with the same frequency to all other family members and we do not listen to all family members in the same way. Our patterns of speaking and listening are determined by our own characteristics, by the characteristics of the other family member, by messages that are offered, and by the varying situations in which we find ourselves. As we will determine in the next section, we not only have communicative rules about to whom we speak and to whom we listen, we also have rules about the topics of our family conversations.

■ What Can You Speak About?

Can you talk about any topic in your family? Probably not. Most families have rules about topics that are generally taboo or are "unspeakable" at certain times. For example, you might never be able to talk about sexual matters or financial matters in your home. Or, you might not be able to speak about these topics under certain situations—for example, at the dinner table, with younger siblings, or in front of your grandparents.

One young man from a very proper family in Cincinnati, Ohio, met a young woman from an ethnic family in Cleveland. The couple dated during college, but neither family had met the person their child was dating. During the couple's senior year, the young man brought his then-fiancée home to meet his parents. The result was disastrous. At dinner (served at 8 P.M., by servants, to the family who was "dressed for dinner"), the young woman, who was somewhat nervous, began to relate humorous stories about the engaged couple's sex life. Her parents-in-law-to-be were mortified. One of the family rules was that people never discussed sex, they certainly did not discuss premarital sex, and under no circumstances would such a topic be appropriate at the dinner table. The young woman was almost removed from the room. Although the couple survived and are now married, their entire relationship was nearly unsalvageable because the young woman did not play by her in-laws' rules.

The columnist Russell Baker recalls a humorous incident from his childhood that illustrates that sex was a taboo topic in his family, but that the family members would not admit that it was out of bounds:

> I made the mistake of saying something that indicated I was curious about where babies came from. Uncle Jack looked at my mother.
> "Doesn't he know about *that* yet?" he asked.

No, she said, she had not gotten around to *that* yet.

"Why don't I take him upstairs and tell him?" he suggested.

She must have felt an immense sense of relief. "I think it's about time somebody did," she said.

Uncle Jack looked at me gravely. "Go upstairs," he said. "There's something I want to talk to you about alone."

Uncle Jack was slow in arriving, and, when he finally did come up, he didn't seen to be too easy in his own mind. He looked at me and then walked across the room and looked out the window. Then he paced silently for a minute or two.

Finally: "You think the Giants can win the pennant this year?" he asked.

"Well, they've got Carl Hubbell, who's the best pitcher in the League, and if Mel Ott hits .350, and if. . . ."

And on and on I went in a happy torrent of arcane baseball speculation.

"Yeah," Uncle Jack said, "but it don't make any difference who wins in the National League because nobody's going to beat the Yankees in the World Series."

"Don't be so sure. Who've the Yankees got as good as Mel Ott?"

"They've got Lou Gehrig, they've got Bill Dickey, they've got this kid DiMaggio, they've got. . . ."

We were slowly exhausting baseball. Uncle Jack went back to the window and looked out again, then turned to face me.

"Look here," he said, "you know how babies are made, don't you?"

"Sure," I said.

"Well that's all there is to it," he said.

"I know that," I said.

"I thought you did," he said.

"Sure," I said.

"Let's go on back downstairs," he said.

We went downstairs together.

"Did you tell him?" my mother asked.

"Everything," Uncle Jack said.[64]

One man in his mid-20s disclosed that his family included many taboo topics including death or serious health issues, sex, income, personal finances, and age:

Death is an area that is acknowledged and understood but not considered something we want to accept nor something we want to talk about in our family, particularly while dining. . . . Similarly, serious health issues or diseases are not socially sanctioned topics within the context of our family environment. If this topic arises, my dad will indicate through nonverbal communication (facial frown, eye squint, general look of disdain, etc.) that enough has already been said.

Rules have also dictated a tacit agreement regarding the avoidance of sex discussion. Any allusion or reference to this area is avoided at all costs. However, if I attempt to talk about sex, even in generic terms, my parents will utilize euphemisms or other avoidance strategies, particularly the evil eye from mom, or dad who will completely remove himself from the context of the communication. Dad will actually leave the room in embarrassment and mom may emit a nervous, adaptive laugh. The interesting aspect about the topic of sex is that on the surface we all feign that we are open and that sex is a viable topic; however, in reality it isn't. Also, homosexuality is a forbidden fruit never to be granted air time. Homosexual friends, their lifestyles, including personal habits and problems are not dealt with. If I choose to mention a friend who happens to be gay they will either disregard the statement or demand I not speak with the person! To my parents homosexuality, like poison ivy, strep throat, or AIDS, is very contagious.

I've grown up learning that we don't talk about personal finances, particularly dad's, either inside or outside familiar boundaries. Topics such as yearly income, life insurance, values of antiques, retirement plans, and wills are rendered as restricted topics.

Ages has been dealt with in a less than open and direct manner. For years, mom claimed she was 39 years old. I was too young to know the difference. Until one day I proudly announced to my best friend and his mother, "My

THE FAMILY CIRCUS®   **By Bil Keane**

"Mommy didn't think it was that funny when I
said it this afternoon. I had to
go to my room."

THE FAMILY CIRCUS reprinted with special permission of Cowles Syndicate, Inc.

mom's only 39." They regarded me in disbelief and exclaimed: "how could that be, she was 39 last year, and the year before that, and the year before that." From that day on I realized two things: 1. Mom's over 39—but let her believe she is 39. 2. My parent's ages are not a good topic. To this day I am unable to determine their exact ages—though I'm not all that interested either.[65]

Developmental changes in the family may impact on topic appropriateness. As we observed above, small children rarely discuss the family's finances. Similarly, the "Family Circus" cartoon illustrates this idea. The children in this cartoon are gaining an understanding of one of the rules that is common in many families: Topics that are appropriate for the adults in the family are not necessarily appropriate for the children. We will note in Chapter 8 that adolescents have clear ideas about those topics which are appropriate to discuss with their parents. They tend to talk about summer jobs, foods, sports, classes, and grades, but they do not talk about parties, alcohol, drugs, and their boyfriend or girlfriend.[66]

Should parents discuss sexual matters with their adolescent children? Recent research suggests that this topic is increasingly important. Two communication professors write, "The high teenage sexual activity and pregnancy rates in America are generally attributed to ineffective communication of sexual information."[67] Indeed, studies have shown that parents do not provide sufficient information about the menstrual cycle, sex, and contraception.[68] This is one topic that should be discussed in families with adolescents.

The relationship that has been established between the marital couple might affect topic choices. A team of marital communication researchers determined that traditional couples (couples who hold a conventional set of beliefs about marriage, emphasize togetherness, seek regularity in their use of time, prefer stability in the relationship over uncertainty and change, and confront conflicts with tactful restraint) were more likely than other spouses to focus their discussion of marital conflicts on matters of family togetherness and they were less likely to discuss individual personality characteristics. The most satisfied traditional couples were especially likely to discuss stoic themes (themes that recognized that conflicts and problems were inherent in marriage) rather than role obligations or personalities.[69] The authors conclude, "The results support prior characterizations of traditional family members as emphasizing social harmony and stability over explicit verbal negotiation of relationship issues."[70]

Certain categories of topics might be out of bounds for some families. One group of communication investigators categorize messages according to whether they are topics dealing with external events, ideas, or places; topics dealing with oneself; topics dealing with the other person; and topics dealing with the relationship between the two people.[71] This categorization schema allows us to provide some conclusions. Most families allow discussions of general topics, but they might not be equally liberal about allowing people to talk about themselves, each other, or their relationships. For instance, a young nurse provided this information:

My family is very open about most of the traditionally taboo subjects such as sex, birth control, VD, opposing opinions, religious beliefs, politics, and so on. The thing we cannot do is talk about Dad's parents in front of him, Mom's parents in front of her, or my fiancee in front of me.[72]

A college student agreed that her family allowed the discussion of sex, drugs, and alcohol, but she said that a taboo topic was "to speak of other individuals in a derogatory or critical manner."[73]

Some families believe that speaking about the overall relationships among them is not right, or that speaking about specific relationships is taboo. For example, one family included an aunt and uncle who had an unusual relationship. The aunt was a regional salesperson who was gone from home far more than she was at home. She was a fun-loving, effusive person who worked in a job that was dominated by men. The uncle was very quiet and the two rarely appeared even to talk to each other. The nieces and nephews may have speculated about their aunt's activities when she was away from home, but no one ever breathed a word. The family had a rule that no one ever talked about Aunt Irene or Uncle Alex.

Some families teach their members that speaking about one's own needs, desires, or interests is "selfish" and inappropriate. Others talk about themselves to the exclusion of other family members. The culture itself may influence whether family members speak about themselves as individuals or view themselves as part of a larger group. Western, industrialized societies, for example, are often individualistic, while Asian countries are more often viewed as collectivistic. As a consequence, family members in America may be more likely to discuss "I" while Japanese family members may be more apt to consider "we." Some research suggests that focusing on "we" may be an important element to family satisfaction.[74]

Another way to categorize topics is according to their cognitive, intellectual, or factual nature as opposed to their affective, emotional, or feeling nature. In some families, members are allowed to discuss facts and ideas, but they are not allowed to express their feelings. In other families, particular feelings are outlawed. For instance, you might not be allowed to show anger—particularly when it is directed toward one of your parents. You might not be allowed to show extreme enthusiastic excitement—especially if it involves knocking into furniture and breakable objects in the home. Maybe your family has taught you that you cannot express love for each other in overt ways. You do not ever say, "I love you" to family members, nor do you kiss or hold each other.

Communication researcher Susan Shimanoff determined that married couples prefer some emotions to be expressed over others. She explained that people seek to maintain a positive sense of self known as "face" and that the expression of emotions may be face-honoring, face-compensating, face-neutral, or face-threatening. Face-honoring expressions express pleasant emotions; face-compensating expressions offer apologies for transgressions; face-neutral expressions deal with people other than the listener; and face-threatening expressions include any disapproving statements about the listener. Not surprisingly, Shimanoff determined that married couples preferred face-honoring, face-compensating, or face-neutral statements over face-threatening ones.[75] More recently, Shimanoff also showed that relational partners responded with positive messages when they were told about their partners' vulnerabilities, and hostilities toward people other than themselves.[76]

Specific words may also be out of bounds. You might not be able to use particular words or certain sets of words in your family. The most common category of words that people are required to avoid are traditional "four-letter" words or "swear" words.

An elementary school teacher recalled her own childhood:

> Mother was the most immediate source of advice and directives. Very few restrictions were made as to topics that were unacceptable for discussion. Profanity was forbidden and conversations concerning sex and sexual behaviors were not discussed openly and completely.
>
> I remember one incident relating to this. It concerned a word I heard expressed by a neighbor boy who I was playing with one summer morning. I did not understand the word, so when I went home I decided to ask Mother what it meant.
>
> I recall standing at the top of the basement steps and yelling down to Mother as she was doing the family washing what the word "bitch" meant. For the next few minutes time stood still as Mother stomped up the basement steps reprimanding me all the way. She said, "Where did you hear that word? Don't you ever say it again! How dare you bring profanity into this house!"
>
> I was severely admonished in this manner for quite a while for what I thought to be an innocent question. Mother never did tell me what it meant. All she did was bawl me out.[77]

■ When and Where Can You Speak?

Does everyone at your dinner table have an equal opportunity to talk? Do some members of the family take more "turns" than other members? Can some people interrupt and overlap other family members while others cannot? Can you argue with your parents in public? The answers to such questions should demonstrate that everyone cannot speak at any time. Families have rules about when its members are allowed to speak.

One family was very talkative and had determined an actual turn-taking sequence in which to communicate. The five-person blended family included two daughters and one son. At the dinner table each night, the following pattern generally was followed: the youngest daughter was allowed the first opportunity to talk, followed by the son, followed by the oldest daughter, followed by the father, and then the mother. Each person was allowed one "turn" before anyone else had a second turn. The young son, who was 5 years old, was particularly cognizant of the communication rules in his family.

The paternal grandparents lived some distance away and had not visited the family for two years. The grandparents, like their offspring, were also enthusiastic communicators. During dinner, the first night, the grandmother

Family members sometimes create opportunities to communicate with each other
(© Whitmer, Stock, Boston).

dominated the conversation. The 5 year old, who could take it no longer, finally blurted out, "Grandma, you've had five turns and no one else has had a chance to talk!" The grandmother thought the child was somewhat rude, until the parents explained the rule about talk-turns. She and her husband were incorporated into the system during the remainder of their visit. However, the young son kept his ears open for possible infractions of the rule.

Families establish rules for when its members can speak within conversations, as we have seen from the example above. Although some families have a fairly egalitarian turn-taking system, such as that described, other families have clearly dominant members. For example, the parents may be allowed to interrupt the children or to talk for longer periods of time than their children. Younger children may be humored by the family and are allowed to dominate interaction at mealtime. Older siblings may disallow younger children to talk frequently or for very long periods of time.

Families also determine, in a larger sense, when and where the members may speak. For instance, the family may be very clear about not speaking at all after they have entered church or synagogue. Other families are almost noisy in such contexts. Some families have rules about when—during the course of a day—the members may speak. For example, the family may jabber at dinner, but no one is allowed to speak to anyone else during breakfast. Instead, each family member reads the newspaper, a book, or magazine, or the family watches the morning news. If the parents work at home, the children may learn that they are not allowed to speak to them when they are in their office, or during the daytime working hours.

Mealtime remains a favorite time for families to talk to each other. One woman reports:

> In my family, most meals are eaten together. At the breakfast table the general game plan for the day is discussed and orders for chores are given. At the supper table the day's activities are reported, experiences are shared, and work schedules outside the home are discussed.[78]

However, busy schedules sometimes interfere even with the family sharing the evening meal.

The evening hours, after dinner, provide time to talk, though many families prefer to watch television or to read. However, in some homes, families use television viewing as a time to interact. However, one young man cautions, "If a good TV program is on, then you had better be quiet!"[79]

Other families recognize the importance of talking with each other and make time to share thoughts and ideas in spite of hectic days. Such families are more likely to be satisfied than are families in which little communication occurs. While it was commonly believed that couples who "play" together, or enjoy mutual leisure time, were happier than couples who do not engage in mutual social events, current research adds a new interpretation. Sharing leisure time is predictive of marital satisfaction only when that time provides opportunities for increased levels of communication. When couples engage in low levels of interaction during mutual leisure time, they do not report increased marital satisfaction.[80] Communication, rather than leisure time, predicts happiness within families.

Family members who become aware of where and when people are allowed to talk may learn to use this information strategically. For example, you probably know that you do not disclose negative information to your parents when they are already upset about another matter. One man from the Middle East explained:

Most of the time I try to choose the most suitable time to communicate with my family. If it's my father, then I wait until he takes his nap and drinks his tea. It also depends on the topic I want to discuss.[81]

■ Why Do You Speak?

What is the function or purpose of speaking within the family context? Is the purpose to share information, to persuade each other to behave in certain ways, to learn more about oneself, to develop and maintain relationships, to play with each other, or to achieve other goals? The answer, of course, is that we interact with our family members to fulfill all of these purposes.[82] One college student summed it up when she wrote:

We communicate in my family because of our needs ("I need a hundred dollars, Mom"), to express our opinions ("I don't feel that's fair"), and to express our feelings ("Mom, I'm happy because I got an 'A'" or "Mom, I'm happy because you're my Mom").[83]

Some families speak to express their emotions while others have difficulty expressing themselves. One woman explained, "My family understands that when someone is yelling at you, they are mainly just relieving their own tension."[84] However, most family members may not be that understanding. Indeed, many people report having difficulty expressing their feelings within their families. One woman recalls her father's behavior:

I can remember my father getting angry and being very angry but never verbalizing the emotion of anger. Likewise, he was a happy man I am sure, but he never verbalized or openly gestured or expressed happiness. I truly believe his "strict Catholic religion" wouldn't allow him to do otherwise.[85]

In Chapter 1 we observed that communication serves both expressive and instrumental purposes. Sometimes busy families combine these purposes; others determine that they will communicate in a primarily expressive way at some times, but in an exclusively instrumental manner at others.

One couple, comprised of two college professors who wrote and taught together, provides an example of communicating to fulfill both expressive and instrumental goals. The couple had a full life, with three children and two full-time careers. They found that the bulk of their day was made up of interacting with students or with their children, and they had very little time to spend with each other. Since they were also both long-distance runners, they settled on a format that worked well for them. Before their children rose for the day, the couple went for a long morning run. Since the children were old enough to care for themselves if they awoke before the couple returned, no danger was involved. During their run the couple would plan their day, including such trivial matters as who was going to provide rides for children who had activities after school and who was going to be home for dinner. They would then spend their day talking with their children and fulfilling their professional responsibilities.

When the children were in bed for the night, the couple made a point of talking again for about 30 minutes. This time was devoted to talking about their feelings and other more affective matters. Although this particular couple sometimes could not have their two daily talks, they generally found the arrangement to be both satisfying and satisfactorily fulfilling their needs. In addition, we see that they used the two talk-times quite differently. The morning talk was instrumental in purpose—devoted to planning and task-related matters—while the evening talk was expressive—focused on their feelings and their relationship.

Of course, family life is not always so idyllic. Sometimes one person will desire more expressive talk while the other prefers instrumental expression. One married woman illustrates this point:

> Andrew and I seem to be able to talk and listen to each other in very recipro-cal ways. I *do* talk more than he does, especially about feelings, conflict, and relationships. . . . I try to communicate encouragement and support so that he will open up when he feels the need or desire. And then I'll listen for as long as he talks. I crave this kind of interaction with him. I really want him to talk with me like my women friends do. He does that pretty well when we're dis-cussing other people. It's more difficult for him to talk about himself and our relationship.[86]

Other families communicate for different reasons. You will read about conflict in Chapter 12 and determine that as strange as it might seem, some families appear to require a certain level of conflict in order to function.[87] Some families use communication to create the conflict that is necessary for them to function. These families have a moderate to high need for tension in their relationships and they are able to fulfill this need through their interactions with their family members.

SUMMARY

In this chapter we considered the development of communicative patterns or rules in family communication. Rules theory helps us understand our interactions. A rule is defined as a prescription that can be followed and that suggests which behavior is obligated, preferred, or prohibited in particular contexts.

We considered the importance of rules and how rules develop. We noted that the original family is instrumental in providing a baseline for rules for the newly created family. Although the original family is important, the newly created family and the family roles within it may similarly affect the rules.

We also considered the function of rules in verbal interaction in the family. As we determined, rules provide a number of functions. They tell us to whom we may speak and to whom we may listen. Family rules suggest the topics we may discuss. Family rules identify when and where we may communicate. Finally, family rules suggest the rationale for why family members interact. Understanding the role of communicative patterns within the family unit may encourage more satisfying family relationships.

KEY TERMS

1. *Rules* are the guiding principles that give our interactions meaning. A rule is a prescription that can be followed and that suggests the behavior that is obligated, preferred, or prohibited in particular contexts.

2. *Patterns* are the predictable and manageable sets of behaviors that are unique to the family and that are distinctive from any one family member's own actions.

3. *Implicit* rules are unstated agreements whereas *explicit* rules are stated.

4. *Family images* are the verbal and nonverbal pictures we use to describe the family and its members; an example could be a picture of a football team.

5. *Family themes* are underlying family perspectives or points of view; an example could be "the family is the first priority."

6. *Verbal aggression* includes attacks or hostile comments.

7. *Communication apprehension* is the extreme fear of communicating with another person or group of people.

8. *Networks* refer to the patterned channels through which information normally flows.

9. The *chain network* occurs when each family member communicates to only one or two others in a linear fashion.

10. The *Y-network* refers to two people or two sets of people sending or receiving messages from another set through a gatekeeper.

11. The *gatekeeper* is the person through whom all messages flow: he/she has a great deal of power in that he/she determines whether the family communicates effectively or ineffectively.

12. *Wheel networks* have one central gatekeeper with whom family members communicate on a regular basis.

13. *All-channel networks* allow communication from all members to all members. The all-channel network often results in the most satisfaction among family members.

14. *Selective attention* means we focus on some people and ignore others.

15. *Selective retention* refers to our retrieving and recalling information from some people, but discarding information from others.

16. *Face-honoring* expressions express pleasant emotions; *face-compensating* expressions offer apologies for transgressions; *face-neutral* expressions deal with people other than the listener; and *face-threatening* expressions include any disapproving statements about the listener.

CHAPTER 5

RULES ABOUT NONVERBAL CUES IN THE FAMILY

A smile is the shortest distance between two people.

VICTOR BORGE

After you have read this chapter, you will be able to

1. Define nonverbal communication.

2. List and explain the various kinds of nonverbal communication.

3. Describe how gender and the size of the interacting group affect what gestures and other bodily movements are used by family members.

4. List and describe three kinds of space and explain how each type of space establishes boundaries.

5. Distinguish among four types of space that people use when they interact.

6. Describe how touch can be positive or negative within the family.

7. Identify factors that affect the amount of touch that children receive from their parents.

8. Explain how artifactual communication allows families to develop a sense of uniqueness.

9. Differentiate among past-oriented, time-line, present-type, and future-type families.

10. List the four functions of nonverbal communication in our interactions with others.

11. List the set of nonverbal cues communicators use to regulate inter action when they have the floor, when they wish to yield the floor to another, and when they wish to acquire the floor.

In the last chapter we considered the rules about verbal communication within the family. But communication includes *both* verbal and nonverbal elements. While verbal language is important, family communication involves far more than the words we speak. In this chapter we will consider the nonverbal contribution to communication.

The relative importance of nonverbal cues on the impact of our messages varies from one situation to another.[1] Indeed, in some situations in which verbal communication decreases among family members, nonverbal communication increases.[2] Regardless of alterations in the specific proportion of the message that is nonverbal, the results of studies show the overall significance of nonverbal cues.[3] Most of our interactions with family members involve complex sets of verbal and nonverbal signs.

When verbal and nonverbal cues conflict, what do we believe? This question may be answered differently depending upon one's development. Young children between the ages of 6 and 12 years of age rely on the verbal component of the message.[4] Adults rely upon the nonverbal elements.[5]

Why do adults view the nonverbal rather than the verbal message as more truthful? Anaïs Nin observes, "When one is pretending the entire body revolts!" We may understand intuitively that other people have less control over their nonverbal cues and are therefore more honest in this realm. Nonverbal behavior is less easily "faked" than is verbal behavior.[6] We may view nonverbal messages as more basic, or innate, than verbal messages. Whatever the reason, adults who receive contradictory messages will generally believe the nonverbal, rather than the verbal.

Conflicting verbal and nonverbal cues are a critical issue for the healthy development of children. Bateson, Jackson, Haley, and Weakland hypothesized over 30 years ago that verbal and nonverbal inconsistencies could encourage emotional problems.[7] While the development of emotional disorders is beyond the scope of this text, we should note the importance of consistent verbal and nonverbal cues within the family.

An understanding of nonverbal communication is especially important to students of family communication. First, understanding is important to achieving satisfying family lives, as we will determine in Chapter 11. The potentiality for misunderstanding is greater within the nonverbal realm than within the verbal world. Family researcher Patricia Noller explains, "Although nonverbal communication is crucial in interaction, it may be more open to error since the rules that govern it are neither stated so explicitly nor taught so formally as are the rules governing verbal communication."[8]

Second, nonverbal communication is critical to marital satisfaction. Indeed, Professor John Gottman concluded that nonverbal codes were more discriminating between distressed and nondistressed couples than were verbal codes. He observed satisfied couples developing a private message system that permits efficient, telegraphic nonverbal communication; dissatisfied couples do not demonstrate a similar system. The satisfied couples generate sets of agreed-upon meanings for specific nonverbal signals through their history of interaction.[9]

Third, nonverbal cues are learned, often unintentionally, within the family. Our style of communicating—including both verbal and nonverbal elements—is initially developed within the family home. Children observe their parents' eye contact, facial expression, posture, bodily movement, gestures, use of touch, space, movement, clothing, and other nonverbal cues and adopt similar behaviors. It is highly common for fathers and sons to walk the same way and for mothers and daughters to use similar gestures and facial expression.

This chapter parallels the last chapter, which focused on verbal communication. In this chapter we will consider the role of nonverbal communication within the family. We will ask questions about how families use gestures and other bodily movements, how they view space, how touch is used, what artifacts are used, and how families view time. We will also consider why we use nonverbal cues in the family.

❖ WHAT GESTURES AND OTHER BODILY MOVEMENTS ARE USED BY FAMILY MEMBERS?

Kinesics is the study of bodily activity and is known popularly as body language. Kinesics includes such nonverbal behaviors as eye contact, facial expression, posture, bodily movement, and gestures. Family members use these behaviors in different ways.

When the smiling behavior of mothers and fathers are compared, it is evident that fathers smile at their children less than mothers smile at their children.[10] Do fathers smile at their children less because of their gender or because they are generally not in the caretaking role of their children? Mothers were more likely to smile at their infants than were fathers, regardless of who was the primary caretaker.[11]

Children, including very young children, are aware of the differences in the facial expression and smiling behavior of their parents. When young children were questioned about the emotion their parents were expressing, the children used the facial cue of the smile to determine that their fathers were offering positive sentiment. However, they were unable to determine if their mothers were offering positive or negative feelings, even when they were smiling. The researchers concluded mothers smile so frequently, their mood cannot be determined by their smile alone.[12]

Family members use facial expression differently depending upon a variety of factors. For instance, when a mother, father, and child interact, they decrease some signs of nonverbal closeness but they appear to compensate for this decrease in intimacy by increasing their positive facial expressions.[13] Facial expressiveness seems to interact with nonverbal cues such as the use of touch and the use of space. We will consider these nonverbal cues in the next sections of this chapter.

❖ HOW IS SPACE VIEWED WITHIN THE FAMILY?

Proxemics is the human use of space and was first discussed in author Edward Hall's books *Silent Language* and *The Hidden Dimension.* Hall identified three kinds of space. He defined *fixed feature space* as the unmovable structural arrangements around us, such as walls and rooms in traditional homes. *Semifixed feature space* includes objects, such as furniture, that can be moved but tend to be in the same place. *Informal space,* or personal space, is the area that surrounds a person and that moves with him or her.

Fixed feature space is relevant in the family context in the form of the family home. The family home has as many forms as there are families. The home provides a place for communication to occur or for it to be avoided. The plans for the three floors of a new home in a small midwestern community are provided in Figure 5.1. What can you conclude about the family that resides in the home?

Although families do not normally alter the fixed feature space of their home, sometimes walls are knocked down, rooms are added, or partitions are used to divide spaces. One woman whose parents divorced when she was a child writes:

> My Dad and I lived together in a two bedroom house, a rather small house. Originally, the fixed feature space in this house consisted of three bedrooms, but the walls of one of the bedrooms was knocked out in order to enlarge the living room area, thus creating a formal dining room. Well, Dad had different ideas for this enlarged living area; he turned it into a studio (my Dad is a professional photographer). So rather than living in a house with a normal entertaining area like the rest of my friends, I lived in a video and photographic studio.[14]

Sometimes the family home is off limits to its own family members, their friends, or to others. The wife of a well-known musician was quoted as saying that she decided to terminate her marriage on the day she returned home to find her children locked out of their home by their eccentric father, who was inside composing music. Although this occurrence may be relatively rare, families frequently limit the use of the house to outsiders. For example, one woman wrote:

> One boundary in my family was that no one besides family members were allowed in the house when my parents were gone. This fulfilled a safety need within my parents. They felt if they weren't home to supervise that some friend of ours would steal something or fall and hurt themselves or something. The children hated this boundary.[15]

Figure 5.1

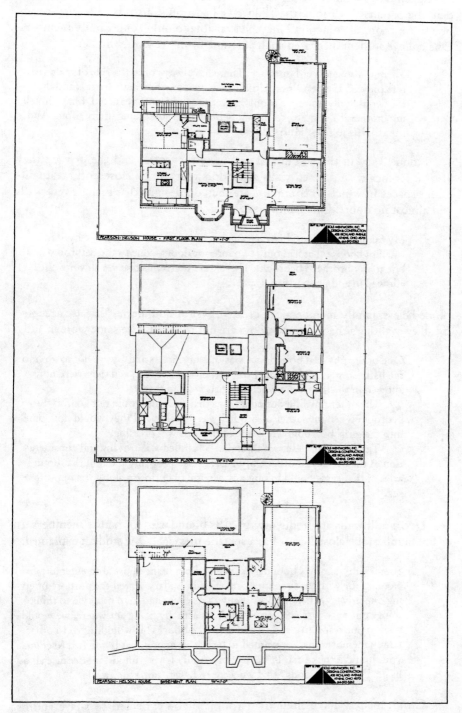

The family home affects the communication that can occur.

Specific rooms may be off limits to family members, too. The traditional den, the parents' bedroom, the children's bedrooms, a study, a sewing room, or a work room of some kind may be available to only some family members. One college student discussed such a boundary in her family home:

> There is also another boundary. There has always been the rule of male visitors only on the first floor. Unless they were my brother's friends and then they could only go to his room. Even though I am 21 years old, I have to tell my mother if I'm going to show my boyfriend something in my room. And she still has to say, "Hurry down!"[16]

Homes vary in the amount of openness they offer and the privacy they afford. Homes with defined walls and doors that can be closed off create different spaces in which to communicate than do designs that include few walls and almost no doors. One woman explains:

> My family of origin did not have many physical boundaries. We lived in a small old house that had only two interior doors—one to the bathroom and one to my brother's bedroom. There were no rooms that we all were not allowed in and privacy was scarce.[17]

Nonetheless, family members can create physical boundaries that are accepted by all even though the walls and doors are not changed. The same woman adds:

> One of the physical boundaries was that my sisters and I were not to go into the bathroom when my father or brother was in there, and they were not allowed in the bathroom when the girls were in there.
> The other physical boundary was that the girls would not go into the bedroom when my father or brother was dressing and they would not come into the girls' bedroom when one of the girls was dressing.
> The function these two boundaries fulfilled was privacy and consideration of the privacy of others. My parents also probably thought that boundaries of that type would inhibit any arousal of curiosity about the opposite sex.[18]

Doors and walls are frequently used as boundaries for family members. In many families, the closed door has a specific message. One student explained:

> Some of my family's boundaries included not being allowed to enter any closed door without first knocking. This boundary served the purpose of giving one privacy when needed. If any of us ever wanted to be alone to think things out or to just "get away" without actually going anywhere, we would go into our respective rooms and close the door. This would signal to other family members that we wanted to be left alone and that if you had to come, you should knock first. Privacy in my family is very important because all of us get into our "moods" that we want to be left alone for awhile.[19]

Children may have their own rooms or be expected to share rooms. Although we may think that having a room of one's own is a luxury that everyone would enjoy, some children, particularly younger ones, prefer to share a room. One woman recalled her childhood:

> When my sister was two and a half and I was just born we each had our own rooms. Every night, Karen, my sister, would come into my room and pull my bed into her room. Mom and Dad finally got the hint and we shared a room for years.[20]

Other children may simply slip into their sibling's beds after the parents are asleep or occupied.

As children we may enjoy the company of a sibling or parent to share our bed or room. As we grow and develop, many of us desire more space. The same woman who wrote about her sister continues;

> It was interesting after awhile because Karen never wanted to stop sharing a room. I *desperately* wanted my own room. When I finally convinced Mom, Dad, and Karen that it was a good idea, I was ecstatic. I love my sister, but I needed my own space. Karen never really got into having her own room, but I loved it. There must be a difference in personal space needs between us.[21]

A 30-year-old married woman felt the same difference in space needs between herself and her husband:

> When I first met Andrew, I was struck by what a large person he was, but such a child at heart. He would come to class (where we first met) with his backpack slung over his shoulder. The pack was always open with several papers, books and other items hanging out. He struck me as extremely disorganized. This notion has proven to be quite accurate. . . . The first time I saw his house, it was difficult to see the floor. It looked as though he had just moved in, but actually he had clothes strewn everywhere and the closet was empty. This should have been a sign to me, but I saw it as somehow charming. . . . Obviously by now, you've gathered that Andrew takes up lots of space, but yet says he really doesn't need space for himself at all. No—he doesn't need space; he just forces his intimates into demanding more space for themselves. . . . My need for space, *lots of it,* only emerged recently.[22]

Semifixed feature space includes objects, such as furniture, that can be moved but tend to be in the same place. Furniture is arranged for a variety of purposes, not the least of which is the degree to which it encourages or discourages interactions among the family members. Although we may occasionally "move the furniture," it generally provides the same levels of interaction possibilities. Chairs and couches may be placed at angles that encourage small-group interactions or that simply put the occupants on display. One or more conversational groupings can be put together in a single room.

Sometimes people use furniture to "solve" some problem their living space affords. A married couple consisting of a graduate student and a home-making mother learned how to use their furniture in this way:

> First of all there is no front door. Our house is structured so that you have to drive to the back of the house into a carport and then walk in. . . . As you walk into our home from the back you step right into the living room. We have positioned our couch so that the back is facing the door of the house. What this does is gives living room an extra wall. As you walk in the house the couch serves as a divider which gives the room a little hallway going to the kitchen as well as a sectioned off space for the living room area. This gives more privacy to the living room and it feels more comfortable.[23]

Small items such as tables, lamps, and other objects can interfere with conversations. Similarly, piles of books, papers, or other personal belongings can literally or figuratively "get in the way." The same graduate student writes:

> Janice and I have habits of leaving a few piles of paper around the house. We both don't mind a couple of piles for a while, but as soon as there are more than a few then we feel a need to clean up the piles of paper and put them where they belong. There are two places I don't like piles, or anything for that matter, lying on them. One is the kitchen table and the other is the couch in the living room. When I want to sit down on the couch I want to be able to do so. And if I want to use the kitchen table, I want to be able to do so. If I find piles on either of these items, I simply put them on the floor.[24]

The woman whose childhood included growing up in a "video and photographic studio" tried to solve her dilemma by changing the semifixed feature space:

> It really upset me to have friends visit my home because it didn't fit my picture of a home. It was a studio and there was nothing "homey" about that. My need to have a more traditional home environment led me to play with the semifixed feature space. I would move the 19th century chairs into strategic positions in front of tripods and flood lamps, hoping the chairs would hide these monstrosities. I would remove the industrial prints off the walls, leaving only portraits up if I had friends coming over. It's interesting to note that I was the only one that was bothered about my living area; all my friends thought it would be great to live with so many props.[25]

Examine the three living room arrangements in Figures 5.2, 5.3, and 5.4. You can easily determine which of the three allows little interaction among family members, but excellent television viewing; which allows substantial interaction possibilities among one group of people; and which allows several smaller subunits to interact.

Informal space, or personal space, is the area that surrounds a person and that moves with him or her. Informal space tends to be affected by a variety of factors including the purpose of our interaction, our gender, our age, our degree of attraction, and our interest in interacting with others. The purpose of the interaction affects our use of space.

Hall distinguished among four types of space that people use when they interact. *Intimate distance* extends from touch to about 18 inches and is used with people to whom we feel close. You may use this distance when you are showing affection to a family member, when you are offering comfort to a younger sibling, or when you are offering support to an older member of your

Figure 5.2

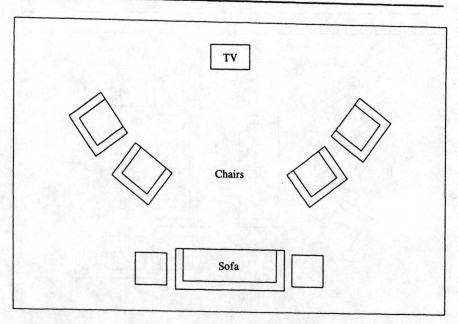

Living Room 1.

Figure 5.3

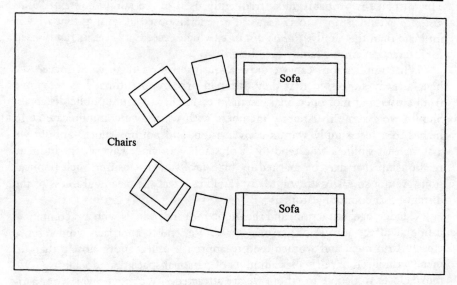

Living Room 2.

Figure 5.4

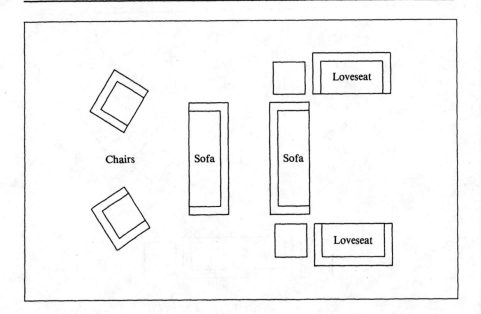

Living Room 3.

family. *Personal distance* ranges from approximately 18 inches to about 4 feet. This distance is probably most frequently used in the family context. *Social distance* extends from 4 to 12 feet and is generally used in settings that are less intimate than the family. *Public distance,* which exceeds 12 feet, is rarely used for interaction among family members.

What implications can we draw about the four categories of space? We have already suggested that they differ in privacy or intimacy as we move from closer and more personal distances to further or more public distances. Should we assume that family members with whom we communicate at 18 inches to 4 feet simply want a conversation, and nothing more? Should we assume that siblings who tend to sit or stand very close have a very intimate relationship that may be marked by high levels of disclosure? Such implications are not so easily drawn. Many variables affect the meaningfulness of the distance that communicators use.

Gender, age, attraction, and the number of individuals who are communicating all affect our use of personal space. We tend to approach women more closely than men; and women tend to approach others more closely than do men.[26] Children have smaller amounts of personal space than do adults.[27] We move closer to people to whom we are attracted.[28] We move away from people when we do not wish to communicate with them and toward them when we wish to interact.

Family members use space differently depending upon the number of family members interacting, the gender of the children involved, and the gender of the parent. One investigation compared differences in the use of space in the triadic (father, mother, and child) and dyadic (father and child or mother and child) settings. When a mother, father, and child interact, they establish more space between themselves than when just one parent and one child interact. However, they appear to compensate for this decrease in intimacy through other nonverbal cues that suggest more intimacy.

Spatial distances between mothers and children are smaller than the spatial distances between fathers and children when mother, father, and child interact. Nonetheless, these distances are not different when mothers interact alone with a child or when fathers interact alone with a child. Under these circumstances, fathers and mothers use similar amounts of space. In addition, both fathers and mothers interact in smaller amounts of space with daughters than with sons.[29]

❖ HOW IS TOUCH USED IN YOUR FAMILY?

Tactile communication is the use of touch in human interactions. Touch is generally construed as a positive behavior within the context of the family. Touch is viewed positively when you comfort family members by holding them close, when you express love for siblings by hugging them, when you hold a new baby in your arms, or when you tenderly kiss your partner.

However, touch can also serve as a negative behavior in the family context. Spanking, beating, incest, or physically abusing family members are also classified within the framework of tactile communication. Bill Cosby provides a humorous example of the negative use of touch:

> It is also possible to get tired of a small person who yells to another, "Will you stop *touching* me!"
> "What's going on?" you say.
> "She's *touching* me!"
> "Look, don't touch her anymore, okay?"
> "But she touched me *first.*"
> And then you resolve the dispute with wisdom worthy of Solomon: "I don't want anyone in this house to touch another person as long as you live."[30]

When we consider the positive aspects of touch, we find that touch is essential to the healthy growth and development of individuals. Numerous investigations have substantiated that people who receive an insufficient amount of touching may develop disorders including allergies, eczema, speech problems, and delayed symbolic recognition. When babies' physical needs are satisfied but their need to be held and touched is not, they become ill and may die.[31]

People learn about touching behavior in the family setting. Families do not share the same level of touching. People learn both to avoid and approach opportunities for touching.[32] One man discussed his original family:

> We just don't touch one another frequently. Mom and Dad didn't; nor do Jenna and I. To kiss or hug my parents or sister is a rarity, reserved only for very rare, extreme or structured situations. . . . I believe our love is effectively expressed in other ways, i.e., thoughtfulness, concern, or verbal expressions of affection. For example, I often bring home small, inexpensive but meaning-ful gifts, often for no special reason. I may bring home some chocolate nut fudge for Mom or a small package of dad's favorite pipe tobacco.[33]

Parents model touching behavior for their children and they teach them how they should view it. Male and female parents provide different amounts of touch to their male and female children. Mothers begin to touch their female children more than their male children when the children are as young as 6 months of age.[34] Fathers touch their children less than mothers do and they touch their daughters more than their sons. The family members between whom the least amount of touch occurs is between fathers and sons.[35] Lewis observed that fami-lies teach women to be dependent and to learn to view themselves as the objects of manipulation rather than as the manipulators of their environments.[36]

Patterns of touching behavior are also different for boys and girls when physical play between parents and their children are considered. Fathers engage in more physical play than mothers; girls participate more often in nonstrenu-ous physical games; and boys are more likely to engage in strenuous physical games such as wrestling and ball playing.[37] To the extent that children are treat-ed differently by their parents, different relational messages are provided.

When the touch behavior of mothers and fathers are compared, two con-clusions are consistent: (1) Fathers touch their children less than mothers touch their children;[38] and (2) When mothers touch their children, it is usually for caretaking, whereas when fathers touch their children, it is generally for play.[39] Theorists are unable to conclude from these studies whether they pro-vide distinctive parent–infant interaction patterns based on biological sex or based on the caretaking roles generally assumed by mothers.

A more recent study explored this unknown area by comparing caretak-ing mothers and caretaking fathers with noncaretaking mothers and noncare-taking fathers. A team of researchers determined that mothers were more like-ly to hold and tend to their infants than were fathers, regardless of who was the primary caretaker.[40] In other words, the greater amount of touch behavior between mother and child over the lesser amount of touch behavior that is exhibited between father and child appears to be a function of biological dif-ferences rather than the assumption of the caretaker role in the family setting.

Some additional factors affect the amount of touching that children receive from their parents. One study showed that mothers and fathers did not touch their children to a significantly differing degree when each parent was interacting alone with the child. Nonetheless, the mothers did touch their children more than did fathers when they were interacting with the children in the presence of their fathers.[41] Mothers may be attempting to compensate for the smaller amount of touching that they perceive the father is providing or they may be touching the child because they feel that it is a societal expecta-tion of being a "good mother."

Parents use touch differently in another way when they are interacting together with a child than when they are interacting alone with one of their children. When a mother, father, and child interact, they touch each other less than when just one parent and one child interact. However, they appear to compensate for this decrease in intimacy in other ways. For instance, they use more positive facial expression when interacting in the triad rather than the dyad.[42]

Parents also teach their children about touch to the extent that they touch each other. Many people find it difficult to believe that their own parents enjoy a sexual relationship. This comment is typical:

> It is very difficult for me to envision a physical intimacy between my parents. I never really focused on that aspect of their relationship. In fact, for many years I was naive to the point that I didn't believe they had a sexual relationship. When I finally opened my eyes and thought about it, it was still hard to envision.[43]

Nonetheless, parents appear to touch each other in front of their children. For example:

> . . . my parents' . . . day to day physical relationship around the house is a warm and open one. When passing each other it is common to reach and touch the other. My dad always receives a kiss before leaving for work and my mom always gets a hug at the end of a day's work. They find reassurance and comfort in the physical relationship.[44]

Intimacy is demonstrated in other ways, as well:

> My parents' physical relationship is still very close. My father has a need to be with other people almost all of his waking hours. He does not like to work alone, or even watch television alone. You don't have to be participating in the same activity, you just have to be in the same room. Even though my mother likes a large amount of time to herself, she is sensitive to my father's needs, and tries to accommodate him as much as possible. My parents own a business together, and participate in many activities together outside the home. They often take separate cars to work, or my mother will stay home to take care of household duties. When they separate, they always kiss before parting, and my father will often show his affection when he comes in for supper.
>
> For the past five years, they have been taking a two week vacation to Florida. Every other year they take at least my younger sister, and sometimes my grandmother. On the odd years, however, the vacation is almost a honeymoon all over again. They go to romantic places, and watch the sun set on the beach. This is an indication of their intimacy.[45]

Not all relationships are so idyllic, however. Another college student differentiated between her father's need for touch and her mother's needs, but the couple had not appeared to have been able to adjust to each other:

> My father is an extremely loving person and is at times very "huggy" toward my mother. My mother usually acts as though he is interrupting her with the

> hug. . . . I, on the other hand, have always been a very affectionate person. My
> father responds to me very well, but my mother always gives the impression
> that there is something else she would rather do than give me a hug. I don't
> know how much their relationship has affected me, but I do know that . . .
> affection is very important to me.[46]

This woman suggested that touch became increasingly important to her
because of what she had viewed in her family. A 21-year-old man concurred
with her conclusions and offered additional reasons for the importance of
touch in family relationships:

> In my own relationships and in my future family, I want to show more inti-
> macy in my family. I think my parents' lack of intimacy has made me work
> harder to keep an intimate relationship. I show people my emotions and my
> girlfriend and I are very intimate. We enjoy walking together, holding hands,
> talking and sitting together.
>
> I believe that parents should show their intimacy with each other.
> Children need to see their parents show their love. Many times I wondered
> about the future of my parents' relationship. I think showing intimacy estab-
> lishes security for children. If I saw my parents closer in a physical relation-
> ship, then I would have been more secure in my family. I often thought my
> parents would get divorced because they never showed their intimacy. But
> now, I realize that they showed intimacy together when they were alone.
> They just never showed their intimacy in front of the rest of the family.
>
> In my future family, I want to show a closer physical relationship. I
> think it's important to keep intimacy in the family relationship. Parents need
> to show their love and affection for their own benefit and the benefit of their
> children's security, too.[47]

✦ WHAT ARTIFACTS ARE USED BY FAMILY MEMBERS?

Artifactual communication includes the messages that are provided by our display of material items such as our clothing, hairstyles, jewelry, cosmetics,
automobiles, smoking paraphernalia, umbrellas, expensive pens, briefcases,
glasses, and other adornments. Artifacts provide information to others about
us and they extend the image we have of ourselves. Our status, age, roles, values, lifestyle, socioeconomic class, group memberships, and personality are
communicated by our clothing and material items. The cartoon that appears
below gains its humor from the slovenly dress of the husband, which is not
generally associated with someone who is a surgeon.

Artifacts help each of us clarify the sort of person we believe we are.[48]
Our clothing permits personal expression[49] and it satisfies our need for cre-
ative self-expression.[50] People use clothing to enhance their self-concepts.[51]
An interest in clothing predicts a high level of self-actualization.

As children grow and develop, they may exchange children's clothing for
more mature styles. Sometimes certain clothing signals a major developmental

GUINDON 2-9

© 1980 L.A. Times Synd.

"Somehow, I thought things would be different, being married to a surgeon."

GUINDON. Copyright © 1980 by the Los Angles Times Syndicate. Reprinted by permission of the author.

change. Columnist Russell Baker recalls his own childhood and his mother's behavior sometime after his father's death:

> She began telling me I was "the man of the family," and insisting that I play the role. She took me to a Newark department store and bought me a suit with knickers, a herringbone pattern that must have represented a large fortune on her meager resources. But a suit and a necktie and a white shirt weren't enough; she also insisted on buying me a hat, a junior-scale model of the gray fedora Uncle Allen wore.
> "You're the man of the family now," she said. "You have to dress like a gentleman."[53]

Oftentimes adolescents dress in a manner that is distinctive from other family members to illustrate their independence from them, as the woman in this excerpt discloses:

In my family's opinion, I've never been a "true" girl since I've been in my teens. I've always been content with jeans and a sweatshirt and they've always wanted me to wear a dress or at least carry a purse. I've always considered purses to be in the way and unnecessary. I figure that as long as you have pockets, you don't need a purse. This view of mine has always "upset" my family so they had a tendency to buy me purses and dresses and other "cutesy" things that I would hardly wear. During high school, my mother even told me that if I didn't carry a purse and wear dresses at least once in a while "people would start to wonder about me." This remark didn't get to me at all; I continued to wear my jeans, sweatshirt, and my gym shoes. For some reason I don't feel it necessary to dress up unless I'm going somewhere important (an interview, wedding, church, etc.) but until then I just "cool out."

The past two or three years my family hasn't been too concerned with the way I dress, but there is still an occasional, "I'll be glad when you realize that you're a young lady" statement heard. Of course this doesn't bother me much either because I feel comfortable with what I wear. Lately with the new fads and with girls wearing men's clothes (which I often did) and baggy clothes—with or without purses—they don't say much.

There was a time, however, when they dropped hints toward me about the way I dressed. They would take me shopping and pick out a dress and say, "Don't you like this?" or "I bet this would look nice on you." My grandmother even stopped buying me anything unless it was a dress. This tactic stopped once I had accumulated five or six dresses and had outgrown them before I had worn them. My mother tried a similar technique of buying me purses all the time. If she went shopping and they had purses on sale, she would almost always buy me one, saying, "I thought you'd like this one." (As if I liked any of them!) Like my grandmother, however, she also stopped when the purses began to build up in the top of my closet. They have since learned to save their money and let me dress the way I like and if they do buy me something then they make sure that it's something that I'll make use of in some way.[54]

On the other hand, we might dress similarly to other family members to establish that we belong with them. Our clothing and artifacts allow us to express group affiliation and commitment to the values and standards of particular groups such as the family. Families sometimes go to extreme measures to demonstrate their commitment to each other by wearing identical clothing. Dating couples will wear matching sweaters or shirts; square dancers wear outfits that have been made from the same material; children—especially twins—are sometimes dressed in similar outfits; and holiday catalogs are filled with matching sleepwear for all ages.

Families establish their own unique ways of dressing and dealing with the display of material objects. Some families are very "showy" and attempt to draw attention to themselves by driving expensive or sporty automobiles, decorating their homes in elegant and attractive ways, and wearing clothing that is brightly colored or provocative. The children in these homes may be regularly "dressed up" in miniature suits and ties and colorful and highly decorated dresses. Other families are modest by comparison and drive mid-priced sedans, decorate their homes in bland colors, and wear clothing that is designed for warmth and comfort. Children in these families may wear slacks, shirts, and sweaters for formal occasions.

❖ HOW DOES YOUR FAMILY VIEW TIME?

Chronemics refers to the influence of time on our interactions. Different cultures treat time differently; families teach children unique ways of viewing time within particular cultures. Some families appear to believe that "time is money" and that each moment must "count" in some real sense. Other families are very relaxed and casual about time. Some families are late for every event while others are always "on time." The wife in one family was so fastidious about time that she would throw an entire meal in the garbage if her husband was so much as five minutes late in arriving home. Few families are so exacting about time, but all families develop ways of perceiving time.

Four distinctive ways of viewing time have been determined. *Past-oriented* people view events as circular. They view common events as occurring over and over and use the past to solve problems in the present. They like to take photographs, collect souvenirs, and record memorable events in a journal or diary. Past-oriented people are viewed as emotional and sentimental. *Time-line* people are systematic and methodical. They view time proceeding from the past to the present to the future in a linear way. Sometimes they are viewed as cold, detached, or even uncaring. *Present*-type people view life as a spontaneous occurrence that does not need to be integrated with the past. They are quick to respond and do not wait for others to act in situations. *Future*-type individuals focus on the future and consider the possible worlds rather than the present one. They spend their time "dashing around the next bend." These ways of viewing time may characterize individuals within families or may identify entire families.

Family members may view time differently. They may view time alternatively at different points in development, or they may view time differently during prescribed periods. Children may be indifferent to time, while their parents are highly clock-conscious. If you are attempting to juggle a career and a family, you may find that you must be very aware of wasted time and that you have little time to spare, while other members of your family who have fewer responsibilities may have a more relaxed attitude toward time. Retrieving a child from a day-care center or a babysitter may cause you to be very aware of the time toward the end of the workday, but you may not be so conscious of the time after dinner.

The determination of how a family will view time may result in power struggles among family members. The wife who turned her dinner into garbage when her husband was tardy demonstrated her control of how the family would view time. Spouses who are "never ready on time" foil their partners' attempts to arrive on time. Children who take excessive time eating a meal, dressing, or preparing for school disallow their parents' desire for promptness to be imposed on them. Some of these power struggles become routinized into family life.

❖ WHY DO YOU USE NONVERBAL CUES IN THE FAMILY?

Nonverbal cues serve a variety of functions in our interactions with others. Judee K. Burgoon and Thomas Saine suggest that among the functions that nonverbal communication serve are to suggest first impressions, to provide relational messages, to allow us to communicate affect, to regulate interaction, to present ourselves, and to manipulate others.[55] Some of these are highly relevant to the family context and others are less important. We will consider these functions proportionate to their importance in family communication.

■ First Impressions

Families are not intact units that never admit new members. Families expand as babies are born, people marry, children are adopted, preexisting families are blended, and others are added. Nonverbal cues provide our first information about these new family members. We make many judgments about other people based on our observations of them. Adoptive parents may draw conclusions about a new child to be added to their family at first sight. The children in a single-parent family may closely examine a potential new stepparent. The parents of a young adult will be careful to "look over" the men or women that she or he is dating. Every new mother tells the story of how she carefully and completely examined her newborn in the privacy of her hospital room to "make sure all of the fingers and toes were there."

One 3-year-old girl understood intuitively the role of first impressions when she met the man her mother wanted to marry. Both her mother and her stepfather-to-be were eager to establish a good relationship among the members of the new family. When the man was presented to the 3-year-old, her mother asked her, "What do you think?" Kate, the 3-year-old, replied, "I don't know—take off your hat and coat." The man willingly removed these articles of clothing. The little girl, amused by the power she possessed, then replied, "Take off your shirt." Again, the man was willing to oblige. Before the game was over, the little girl had managed to convince her soon-to-be stepfather to remove all of his clothing except for his undershorts. At this point, she smiled, turned to her mother, and said, "He looks okay." Everyone was delighted and repeated the introduction of the two throughout the years of their long relationship.

■ Relational Messages

What are some of the relational messages that nonverbal cues provide? They tell others when we are attracted to them or when we like them. They communicate one's status and power. They allow others to determine our credibility, including our honesty, trustworthiness, enthusiasm, and competence.

We communicate we are attracted to others or we like them as we extend our gaze and establish lengthy eye contact with them, as we sit closer to them, as we move toward them, as we lean toward them and orient our bodies in their direction, and as we use an increased amount of touch. When people like each other, they frequently mirror the behavior of the other person.[56] For instance, if one person crosses his legs, the other may cross her legs; if one person slumps down in a relaxed position, the other might similarly slump down.

THE FAMILY CIRCUS®   **By Bil Keane**

"Don't kiss me yet, Daddy. I don't
have my lips out."

THE FAMILY CIRCUS reprinted with special permission of Cowles Syndicate, Inc.

Family members demonstrate their positive regard for each other through these nonverbal means. Parents hold their children and each other; they may routinely kiss each other. They sit and stand closer to those family members they like and they avoid or move away from family members whom they like less. Even small children have a sense of "Mom likes him better than me" and "I'm Dad's favorite," probably as a result of nonverbal cues.

Nonverbal cues also suggest our status, power, and credibility. People who are looked at more frequently are viewed to be higher in status and power than are people who are less frequently offered our gaze. Similarly, people with lower status position their bodies toward those with higher status. People with higher status use more relaxed body positions. They are free to stare at others and they expect others to look away rather than to engage in sustained eye contact.

Credibility involves one's honesty and trustworthiness. Such characteristics are attributed to individuals who use direct eye contact and open bodily postures. Competence is another part of credibility and is exhibited by people who use appropriate posture and gestures and avoid nervous habits.

Dynamism or enthusiasm is suggested by the person whose walk is character-ized by a long stride and who engages in animated behavior, including lively gestures and bodily movement. Credible communicators have calm but responsive voices.

Who demonstrates more power, status, and credibility in your family? Does your mother avert her gaze, or look away, when your father looks at her? Do the children engage in "staring contests" to see who will look away first? Does your mealtime behavior suggest one member of the family has more power than others? Are any members of your family viewed as lacking in credibility—not honest, trustworthy, competent, or dynamic? What non-verbal cues lead you to this conclusion?

■ Communicate Affect

We use nonverbal cues to communicate our emotional feelings. Nonverbal researchers Ekman and Friesen defined *affect displays* as nonverbal movements of the face and body that hold emotional meaning.[57] They provide information to others about how we feel, they frequently influence the behav-ior of others, and only occasionally are they used deliberately to convey meaning. When you feel hurt, anger, surprise, excitement, sorrow, or pleasure you probably express it through your face and body. You might use your face as you smile, frown, narrow your eyes, or open your eyes wide. You might use other parts of your body as you bang your hand down on a table, when you jump up and down, when you relax the muscles in part of your body, or when you raise your arms.

Affect displays are important in family interactions. We may feel more freedom in expressing our feelings and emotions with family members than when we are with strangers, acquaintances, or even friends. However, family members may use affect displays in different ways. For instance, some research has suggested women tend to smile more and use more facial expres-sion than men.[58] Similarly, mothers smile more than do fathers. However, smiling may have a social motivation. Mothers in lower-class families were shown to smile less than their middle-class counterparts. The middle-class mothers may have been motivated to smile by the societal expectations of being a "good mother."[59]

The societal expectations theory about smiling was confirmed in a second investigation. Men were found to smile much less often and less noticeably at babies and puppies that were presented in a videotape if there was another man present in the viewing room. When no other men were present, the male subjects smiled significantly more. One of the researchers concluded, "We think there are certain cultural rules among men that inhibit some emotional responses in men, especially a response of tenderness or affection."[60]

Although we have not answered the question concerning whether the communication of affect is learned or innate, developmental stages of demon-strating such an ability have been offered. Wolff states children use nonverbal cues to communicate affect from the time they are born and divides their use of nonverbal cues into three developmental stages.[61]

The *instinctive phase* begins at birth and includes unlearned, instinctual behaviors. Crying, smiling, being startled, and using gestures in order to maintain balance while sitting or standing are included in this stage. This phase overlaps with the next phase in the learning and displaying of emotions.

The *emotional phase* involves the use of nonverbal cues to display emotions. This phase may start, in rudimentary form, as early as the second or third week of life and continues until the child is 5 or 6 years old. Children slowly add additional emotions to their repertoires as they develop. Some emotions, such as rage and disgust, are exhibited before they are 6 months old; other emotions, such as jealousy and affection, may not appear until after 2 years of age or more.

The *objective phase* completes Wolff's stages and begins at about 5 or 6 years old. Although children in the emotional phase learn to display emotions such as fear, joy, rage, jealousy, affection, and disgust, they are not relating these displays to thought. During the objective phase, emotions are related to thought.

Wolff's developmental stages demonstrate that children begin to learn how to display emotions at a very early age. However, they are not as successful in interpreting and understanding the emotional cues offered by others. Her stages also suggest the display of emotion may be critical in human interaction since it is part of us from birth.

The family context provides an important setting for the display of affect. We may only display extremes of emotions to our family members. For instance, we may only show anger, fear, jealousy, love, or disgust around our family. Because of our emotional ties to members of our families, our affect display may be highly salient in this setting.

■ Regulate Interaction

Nonverbal cues are used to initiate interaction, to take turns in conversations, and to end interactions. Ekman and Friesen categorized some kinesic behaviors as *regulators,* which are those nonverbal behaviors that are used to regulate, control, coordinate, or monitor our interactions.[62] We demonstrate our interest in another person's message by shaking our head, establishing eye contact, smiling, and making a variety of sounds. We suggest our interest in changing from the role of the listener to the role of the speaker by changes in eye contact, by opening our mouth, by moving forward, and through gestures. Similarly, you may feel encouraged to talk when others offer you eye contact, positive facial expression, smiles, physical movement toward you, a physical body lean toward you, and changes in facial expression. You may feel discouraged from interacting when you are offered neutral or negative facial expression, physical movement away from you, looking away, and no responsiveness.

People who use regulators to a great extent tend to be the "architects" of conversations. They determine when new topics are introduced, when old

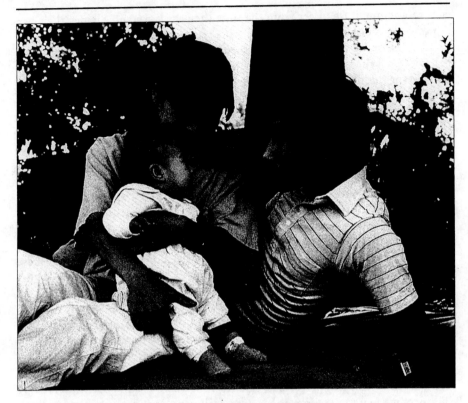

Nonverbal cues allow us to regulate our interactions (© Crews/The Image Works).

topics are discarded, who is allowed to speak, and how long each person is allowed to speak. In general, people with more status or power are allowed the opportunity to use regulators to a greater extent than are those with less status or power. In the family, parents may use more regulators than children; older siblings may use more regulators than younger brothers and sisters; and grandparents or members of the extended family may be allowed to provide more regulation of the interactions than anyone else.

Let us consider some specific ways in which we regulate interaction with our nonverbal behavior. We initiate interaction, or suggest having a conversation, with nonverbal cues. When we wish to interact with others, we tend to look at them and offer such positive cues as smiling and gesturing toward them. When we do not wish to interact with someone, we may look away and provide no reinforcing cues.

Turn-taking in conversations is bound by our cultural norms. In general, people exchange turns in conversations in our culture rather than talk and listen simultaneously. These "talk turns" generally do not last more than six to eight seconds in duration. When we "have the floor," we engage in speaking; when we do not have the "speaking turn," we are to engage in listening.

A complex set of nonverbal cues is used to regulate interactions in a smooth and functioning way. We can examine the cues we use when we have the floor and we wish to maintain it, the cues we use when we wish to yield the floor to another speaker, and the cues we use to acquire the floor when someone else has it. When others want to gain the floor and we are unwilling to yield, we may engage in five behaviors:

1. An audible inhalation

2. A continuation of gesture

3. A diverting of the eyes from the listener

4. A sustained intonation pattern, or similar pitch level

5. Fillers, including vocalized pauses or filled pauses[63]

By inhaling, we suggest we are getting some air so we can continue. When we continue to use a gesture or an intonation pattern, we are suggesting there is no change or termination of our message. When we look away from listeners, we make it more difficult for them to gain our attention and to encourage us to yield the floor. Fillers such as "ah," "um," and "mmmh" suggest we want to maintain our "talk time" and we are thinking about our next word or idea.

What behaviors do we use to yield the floor to others? We may use audible exhalation, we may terminate our gestures, we may look at the listener at the end of our sentence, we may use a downward or upward inflection to suggest we are at the end of a declarative or interrogative sentence, and we may fall silent. Such behaviors move the focus from the speaker to the listener and suggest that the speaker has completed his or her thought.

Sometimes, as listeners, we want to gain the floor from someone else. Again, we can rely on nonverbal cues to communicate our interest in talking to others. We can use a direct eye gaze, we can use positive head nods, we might lean forward, we may begin to gesture, and we may use audible inhalation. Such cues signal our desire to talk as they suggest we understand the speaker's message and he or she need not continue (positive head nod), we are literally trying to "get their eye," and we are preparing to talk (forward lean, gesture, and audible inhalation).

The wife of a minister explains her use of nonverbal cues to gain the floor:

> At home or among friends (or acquaintances), particularly if I'm surrounded by members of the church and I want to break away from a conversation, one that is going on too long, I'm often guilty of leaning forward, conveying the impression that I'm now ready to express myself. I might even gesture to continue to convey that I'm already concurring with the message. Nodding the head might not work, though. If it does not, then I resort to audible inhalation. If one is observant, this usually says, "It's time to let her speak." If there is no luck, then I might have to twist and turn to keep from screaming.[64]

We terminate our interactions with others through nonverbal cues as well. Mark Knapp and his colleagues identified the most frequently occurring nonverbal behaviors individuals use when they are attempting to end a conversation with another person. They include (in order of frequency):

1. Breaking of eye contact

2. Left positioning, which refers to pointing one's hands or feet toward the proposed exit

3. Forward lean (leaning toward the partner)

4. Nodding behavior

5. Major leg movement

6. Smiling

7. Sweeping hand movement

8. Explosive foot movement (the striking of the foot against the floor)

9. Leveraging (using one's hands to raise oneself up from a chair)

10. Trunk movement (including straightening one's posture and leaning backward)

11. Handshake

12. Explosive hand contact (striking one's hands on an object or on other parts of the body)[65]

In the same way we initiate interactions and manage turn-taking, we similarly terminate interactions with others through our nonverbal behavior.

Families may develop unique patterns by which they initiate a conversation, by which they terminate a conversation, and by which they manage their interactions. These patterns may originate on the basis of one's role. For instance, the father of the family may simply walk out of the room when he is done talking to a family member rather than exhibit some of the termination behaviors cited above. In still other homes, the initiation of a conversation may only come from one or two members, and the attempts of some family members to start a conversation literally "fall on deaf ears."

Different patterns sometimes develop, too, because of cultural or ethnic background. Some families do not endorse the norm of only one speaker at a time and several members may talk simultaneously, thus eroding the usefulness of the turn-taking strategies. In other families, communication is not valued and family members are encouraged to be relatively quiet, particularly when the entire family is gathered, as at meal time.

At specific times, these patterns of initiation, management, and termination may be inappropriate in the family setting. The baby's needs or wishes of a young sibling may override all of the nonverbal attempts an older sibling offers in order to be in a conversation with one of his or her parents. Fatigue, grief, or pressures of various kinds can erase the usefulness of using nonverbal cues to regulate interaction.

Not only do gestures, bodily movements, and touch allow us to regulate our interactions with others, but our use of space and artifacts may make conversations more likely to occur or less likely. You may dress in a way that suggests you are superior to others and uninterested in interacting with them. You might choose casual clothing that is more inviting to potential interactants. Your home, too, can encourage interaction. As the author of *House* explains:

> For Judith, living in her new house is like a treasure hunt. . . . When daylight-savings time ends, New England's afternoons turn into evenings. That is when a cozy house needs to feel coziest. Around dusk Bill [the architect and friend of the couple who built the house] drives up to the white house at the edge of the trees, and the windows are all lighted. He walks inside, and sees his friends really are living there. At a time that seems long ago, Judith and Jonathan told Bill that they did not want a formal living room from which everyone would shy away until company arrived. So Bill drew his vision of coziness, but a drawing stands only a small step away from an abstraction. . . . Now Bill watches. When they come downstairs, bound for the kitchen, both children and adults often turn left, eschewing the hallway to the kitchen. Instead, they often go the long way around, just in order, it seems, to pass through the living room. And when Jonathan comes home that evening from a meeting, he and Judith head right for the living room for the day's summary. So does Bill, feeling, as he says later, "thankful."[66]

A variety of nonverbal cues serve to regulate interaction within the family.

■ Persuading Others

We learn to alter the behaviors of others through nonverbal cues. We positively and negatively reinforce their behavior and we punish them when they behave in unacceptable ways. The role of nonverbal cues in persuasion is particularly salient in the family setting. Parents continually teach their children through these methods. Five- to 7-year-old children learn how to ride a bike through a series of verbal and nonverbal responses from parents and older siblings. If you want to teach a teenager how to drive a car, you may offer both positive and negative nonverbal behaviors as they successfully and unsuccessfully master starting, shifting gears, signaling for a turn, turning, parking, and stopping. Husbands and wives encourage each other to share tasks, display more affection, and care for the children in particular ways through nonverbal means. The wink, the smile, the friendly nod, and the playful beckoning gesture are familiar positive reinforcers. Similarly, the squinted eyes, the frown, and placing one's hands on one's hips reinforce negatively.

One mother explained how she was able to communicate to her 9-year-old daughter in front of company:

> Sometimes it is extremely difficult for us to communicate with each other when visitors call on us. If there is something that needs to be done and I'm

pressed to do it (for example, set the table), then I often have to get Pat's assistance. Because we might be too far apart to mumble, I might have to subtly "eye" Pat to beckon for her to come help me. Should she fail to get my message, it sometimes becomes essential for me to try to position myself so Pat can see me. I sometimes extend one of my arms in some kind of way (without giving myself away to others). Believe me, this is *not* easy to do at times. Beckoning for Pat by moving my head to the side usually works, though.[67]

SUMMARY

In this chapter we have considered the rules that families establish concerning nonverbal communication. We began the chapter with a discussion of the importance of nonverbal communication and its role within families. We considered the gestures and other bodily movements that are used by family members. We noted that both parental role and size of the family affect the use of smiling and other facial expressions.

How is space viewed within the family? Families use fixed feature space (unmovable structural arrangements such as walls and rooms), semifixed feature space (objects such as furniture), and informal space (or personal space) differently. Sometimes the entire home may be off limits to family members; more often the use of only specific rooms is limited. While some contemporary living spaces are relatively open compared to more traditional homes, family members can create their own boundaries.

Families use their informal or personal space differently, too. The intimate distance, which extends from touch to about 18 inches, is often used among family members who are in deep conversation, showing affection, or demonstrating comfort. Personal distance ranges from 18 inches to 2 feet and may be most often used among family members. Social distance and public distance are generally reserved for people who are not family members or for more formal communication exchanges.

How is touch used in the family? We know that family members teach each other different meanings about touch. Also, touch can be a negative or a positive behavior. Fathers and mothers do not touch their children to the same extent or for the same purpose. They also use touch differently depending upon the composition of the group that is interacting.

What artifacts are used by family members? Families establish their uniqueness through their clothing and their display of material objects. Sometimes families deliberately show their unity through matching or similar clothing and other adornments. At other times, family members show their independence from their family by choosing styles that are decidedly different. Clothing styles change as one moves from childhood to adulthood and specific clothing may signal the beginning of a new stage of development.

Families teach their members how they should view time. Some families are past-oriented and see events as cyclical. Others are time-line people, who are systematic and view time proceeding in a linear way. Present-oriented people sense that life is a spontaneous occurrence and do not require that it be integrated with the past or the future. Future-oriented families focus on the future and are continually wondering what will occur next. Some families are always early for events while others are perpetually late.

Why do we use nonverbal cues in the family? In our discussion, we, determined that we use nonverbal cues, to offer first impressions to others, to send and receive relational messages; to communicate affect or emotion; to regulate interaction including the initiation, management, and termination of conversations; and to persuade other people. Some of these are particularly important for families, and we have considered them in more detail.

Nonverbal communication may be more important than the verbal messages we offer and receive. It is an especially important topic in the family context. In Chapters 10 through 13 we will see that nonverbal cues help families demonstrate understanding and support, develop autonomy and intimacy, resolve conflicts, relieve stress, and manage power. This chapter should therefore help you understand the role of nonverbal communication within the family context and should assist you in seeking a satisfied family life.

KEY TERMS

1. *Kinesics* is the study of bodily activity and is known popularly as body language. Kinesics includes eye contact, facial expression, posture, bodily movement, and gestures.

2. *Proxemics* is the human use of space.

3. *Fixed feature space* is the unmovable structural arrangements around us such as walls and rooms.

4. *Semifixed feature space* includes objects, such as furniture, which are movable.

5. *Informal space* or personal space is the area that surrounds a person.

6. *Intimate distance* extends from touch to about 18 inches.

7. *Personal distance* ranges from approximately 18 inches to about 4 feet.

8. *Social distance* extends from 4 to 12 feet.

9. *Public distance* exceeds 12 feet.

10. *Tactile communication* is the use of touch in human interactions. The study of touch is sometimes referred to as haptics.

11. *Artifactual communication* includes the messages that we provide by the display of material items such as clothing, jewelry, glasses, and other adornments.

12. *Chronemics* is the study of how time affects human interactions.

13. *Past-oriented* people view events as circular.

14. *Time-line* people view time proceeding from the past to the present to the future.

15. *Future types* focus on the future and consider the possible worlds rather than the present one.

16. *Affect displays* are nonverbal movements of the face and body that hold emotional information.

17. The *instinctive phase* is the first of Wolff's (1972) developmental stages of demonstrating affect; it begins at birth and includes unlearned, instinctual behaviors.

18. The *emotional phase* begins at the second or third week of life and continues until the child is 5 or 6. It involves the use of nonverbal cues to display emotions.

19. The *objective phase* begins at about 5 or 6, and during this phase emotions are related to thought.

20. *Regulators* are nonverbal behaviors that are used to regulate, control, coordinate, or monitor our interactions.

PART TWO

CHANGING TIMES

CHAPTER 6

THE DEVELOPMENT OF THE FAMILY: FROM MEETING TO MATING

It begins in delight and ends in wisdom.

ROBERT FROST

After you have read this chapter, you will be able to

1. Explain the Altman and Taylor social penetration model with the four stages: orientation, exploratory affective exchange, affective exchange, and stability.

2. Define the eight overlapping characteristics of communication that individuals move from in the nonintimate to the intimate relationship (richness, efficiency, uniqueness, substitutability, pacing, openness, spontaneity, and evaluation).

3. Describe Knapp's ten stages of interaction that reflect the escalation and deescalation of interpersonal relationships—initiating, experimenting, intensifying, integrating, bonding, differentiating, circumscribing, stagnating, avoiding, and terminating.

4. Differentiate among social exchange, similarity, need complementarity, competence, mutual liking, physical attraction, and propinquity as factors relevant to relationship development.

5. List topics that close relational partners consider taboo.

6. Determine why these topics are not discussed by couples.

7. Identify the eight-stage categorization system that describes family developmental stages.

8. Define uncertainty reduction and affinity seeking.

9. Outline and briefly discuss how public commitment affects relational development.

10. Summarize findings on dating, serious dating, engagement, and the wedding.

11. Differentiate among the honeymoon phase, the disillusionment and regrets stage, and the stage of accommodation.

Most people accept the basic tenets of developmental psychology; that is, we take it for granted that what occurs in a person's early childhood affects his or her later experiences. We tend to agree that general stages of development occur for the child, and more recently we have expanded the notion that developmental changes occur for the adult as well. Popular books such as *Passages* and *Seasons of a Man's Life* have encouraged us to consider the alterations that occur as people develop from birth to death.

In the same way, relationships develop through identifiable stages. The family, one kind of interpersonal relationship, can be examined as it develops from an individual seeking a partner through death, divorce, or dissolution. We should observe that just as all individuals do not experience developmental stages in exactly the same way, all families do not experience the family developmental stages discussed in this chapter in an identical manner. Changes occur in the family unit as a result of emerging family types discussed in the last chapter; similarly, changes occur because of the development of the individual family.

Researchers have used the family development perspective for over 40 years. Sociologists originally adopted this point of view in order to understand poverty within families. They determined that families were more susceptible to poverty both when they were engaged in childbearing and when they were in their later years.[1] The developmental perspective was given additional credence recently with the new interest in the life-course perspective or life-span analysis.[2]

Most of the developmental stages discussed in this chapter will occur in most families. We can note some obvious exceptions. Cohabiting couples will not experience the wedding and early marital life in the same way as do people who are legally married. Couples without children will not experience the various stages associated with preschool, school-age, and adolescent children, nor will they experience the phenomenon of the "empty nest." Blended families may not enjoy the period of marriage that precedes having children since children are part of the initial marital package. Some couples who have already launched their children may find that the children return after a divorce or a failed love relationship. Nonetheless, virtually all families begin with two individuals meeting each other and deciding to develop their relationship.

Similarly, if the couple remains married, they will become older and will experience the effects of marriage in the middle and later years, whether they have chosen to have children or not.

A variety of individual developmental theories has been posited. Such theories are examined from such viewpoints as biological, learning, psychoanalytic, cognitive developmental, and role theory. Similarly, interpersonal communication scholars have provided theories that describe and explain the alterations that occur in our relationships with others.

❖ RELATIONSHIP DEVELOPMENT

■ Social Penetration

Relationship development may be viewed generally to consist of initiation, maintenance, and termination.[3] Relational researchers Altman and Taylor suggested that relationship development fit a model of social penetration. They viewed interpersonal interactions moving from the superficial and nonintimate to the deeper, more intimate levels as people assessed the costs and rewards related to the relationship.[4] Their model includes four stages: orientation, exploratory affective exchange, affective exchange, and stability and is depicted in Figure 6.1.

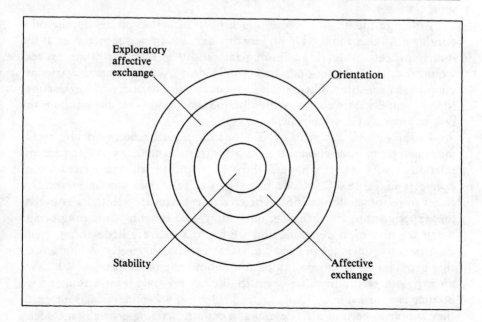

Figure 6.1 Altman and Taylor's social penetration model.

The orientation stage occurs in initial interactions when you are gaining superficial, nonintimate information from another person and when you are providing similar disclosure. In the exploratory affective exchange stage, people share some opinions or feelings, but they tend to be of a general nature rather than highly personal. The affective exchange stage consists of personal information and usually does not occur until people have established close friendships, have dated for some period of time, or are family members. The stage of stability represents the most intimate stage of disclosure and sharing of information and is generally associated with long-lasting or committed relationships.

Altman and Taylor suggest that differences occur along eight somewhat overlapping characteristics of communication as individuals move from the nonintimate to the intimate levels of communication. Specifically, individuals find that their interaction increases in richness, efficiency, uniqueness, substitutability, pacing, openness, spontaneity, and evaluation. *Richness* means that individuals who are close can share the same message in a number of ways. *Efficiency* means that messages are transmitted and received accurately and quickly. *Uniqueness* refers to the idea that individuals who are close often develop idiosyncratic modes of communicating. *Substitutability* means that the same message can be conveyed in different ways as necessary. *Pacing* is synonymous with synchronization and refers to the coordination of interpersonal behaviors. *Openness* suggests verbal and nonverbal accessibility. *Spontaneity* refers to informality, unpredictability, and flexibility. *Evaluation* suggests that both positive and negative assessments are part of close relationships.[5]

Although this theory focuses much of its attention on developing relationships, Altman and Taylor suggest that dissolution or depenetration is the reverse process of development or penetration. The depenetration process would result in interaction, which would decrease in richness, efficiency, uniqueness, substitutability, pacing, openness, spontaneity, and evaluation. More recent evidence calls into question the assumption that dissolution is the reverse process of development.[6]

Knapp expanded Altman and Taylor's social penetration model by detailing ten stages of interaction that reflect the growth and decay of interpersonal relationships. These ten stages, which are depicted with associated verbal examples in Table 6.1, include five stages of relational escalation and five stages of relational deescalation. The escalating stages are identified as initiating, experimenting, intensifying, integrating, and bonding. *Initiating* occurs when we first meet someone and we know relatively little about them. *Experimenting* includes the small talk that occurs fairly early in interactions that provides us with safe information about the other person. When we *intensify* our relationship we begin to disclose personal information and we become less formal in our language and behavior. When individuals *integrate,* they appear to become a single unit as a couple. *Bonding* generally includes a public announcement that a commitment has been made by the partners.

TABLE 6.1	Stages of Relational Development and Deterioration
STAGE	VERBAL EXAMPLE

	Relational Development
Initiating	"How are you tonight?"
Experimenting	"How long have you been running—you're really good!"
Intensifying	"I really feel good about our relationship."
Integrating	"Sometimes I feel like we are one person—your experiences become my own."
Bonding	"I'd like to marry you."
	Relational Deterioration
Differentiating	"You want to go skiing every weekend, I want to stay home!"
Circumscribing	"Are you going back to work tonight?"
Stagnating	"Nothing ever changes—I ask you a question and you bite my head off!"
Avoiding	"I won't be home for dinner tonight, and it will probably be late enough that you should just go to bed."
Terminating	"I'm moving my things out—this just didn't work."

The deescalating stages are called differentiation, circumscribing, stagnating, avoiding, and terminating. When couples *differentiate*, they begin to disengage from each other. *Circumscribing* suggests that communication becomes limited or constricted. *Stagnating* occurs when the relationship is relatively inactive. When partners *avoid* each other, they attempt to be in different physical and communicative environments. *Termination,* the death of the relationship, is the final stage in relationship deescalation.[7] These stages of relational development and deterioration are summarized in Table 6.1 with verbal examples.

In a manner similar to Altman and Taylor, Knapp writes that communication in developing relationships becomes broader, smoother, more unique, efficient, flexible, personal, spontaneous, and evaluative. In deteriorating relationships, he suggests that communication becomes narrower, more stylized, difficult, rigid, awkward, public, and hesitant. Cline demonstrated that relational development is not quite so linear.[8]

Close relationships are marked by a number of behaviors. The researcher Maxwell showed that these include separation distress, disclosure, naturalness, similarity, following, giving and receiving help, and communicating about important issues. *Separation distress* refers to the feelings of loss or sadness when two people cannot be together for lengths of time. *Disclosure,* which we will discuss further in Chapter 10, means that two people tell each other information that is important and personal. *Naturalness* refers to honesty and truthfulness in both feelings and behavior. *Similarity* suggests the two have common interests, attitudes, and values. When people are engaged in *following,* they seek out the other person or spend time actually looking for them. When couples *give and receive help,* they may do so in a way that is normally done with others. *Communicating about important issues* means that the two do not limit their talk to trivial matters. These behaviors appear to hold for married couples, in the early stages of marriage and after 20 years; for close same-sex friendships; and for mothers and their young adult children.[9]

■ Social Exchange

Social exchange theory also helps us understand relational development. This theory, which is consistent with the work of Altman and Taylor and Knapp, states that relationships deepen when the needs of the persons involved are met. Individuals assess both the rewards and the costs of their relationship. The *rewards* of the relationship include any positive consequences that a person gains and the *costs* are any negative consequences that are incurred. Examples of rewards are social status, money, feelings of belongingness, understanding, and approval; examples of costs are loss of freedom, time spent, conflict, harassment, and disapproval. Rewards and costs are not static quantities: they vary over time and they are differentially evaluated by individuals.

Each person compares the rewards and costs of a relationship. If the rewards outweigh the costs, they claim a profit; if the rewards are less than the costs, they declare a loss. Unlike other endeavors, the goal in relational development is not to gain the largest profit with the smallest loss, but rather to balance the books. Individuals generally seek relationships that include both rewards and costs and they tend to remain in relationships that sometimes show a profit and sometimes show a loss. Two theorists explain that people feel uncomfortable when their losses are excessive, but they are also uneasy when their profit is too great.[10]

Although it may sound mercenary, a discussion of profit and loss can be extended to one's market value. Our *market value* is determined by adding together all of our positive interpersonal attributes and subtracting our negative qualities from them and then comparing ourselves with others. We can also refer to this concept as our social desirability. Individuals who are high in social desirability have far more positive attributes than negative ones compared with other people. They have more opportunities to enter into relationships with others with similar high market value. People low in social desirability have fewer opportunities.

Our market value changes throughout our lifetimes. The adolescent female who enjoys woodworking, is highly competitive in sports, and is an "A" student may have low market value in junior high; as an ambitious, creative, and financially successful adult, her market value may have a sharp upward swing. The physically attractive teenager who puts all of her effort into being attractive, by contrast, may have higher market value at this age than when she ages and finds that physical beauty is ephemeral. Health, social status, age, income potential, and fame all affect one's social desirability.

Most of us have a fairly accurate view of our market value and the market value of others. Relationships sometimes change because of changes in the desirability of the people involved. For instance, one homemaking mother with no professional aspirations began to attend college when her three children were enrolled in elementary school. Before the children had graduated from high school, she had a business and economics degree and began to work in one of her city's major investment firms. Meanwhile, her husband's real estate business floundered and he increasingly found solace in alcohol. Before the children were through college, she was an important vice-president in her company with a six-figure income. By the time the wife's career was peaking, her husband was an alcoholic who refused treatment and found sport in embarrassing his wife in public. After more than 20 years of marriage, the couple divorced. The market value of the two dramatically altered during that time.

Disclosure of personal information may be viewed as part of the social exchange that occurs between people. Two communication researchers explain, "Disclosure intimacy is one of many possible relational investments."[11] People may share information with each other in order to maximize rewards. Indeed, disclosure of personal information is highly related to liking and loving relational partners.[12] The anticipated length of the relationship, sex roles, and disclosure intimacy affect one's personal revelations, which suggests that self-disclosure fits the social exchange model.[13] In addition, the perception of the degree of disclosure *offered* by the other partner is more highly related to liking and loving for the partner than is the degree of disclosure *provided* to him or her.[14]

Relationship commitment can be explained on the basis of social exchange theory. Our commitment to our relational partner varies depending upon relationship outcomes, outcomes relative to the attractiveness of alternatives, relationship satisfaction, and duration.[15] When the outcomes of the relationship are positive, and when they exceed the likely outcomes from alternative relationships, we feel more commitment to our partner. When we are satisfied with our relationship, we feel more commitment to it. Finally, the longer people are together, the more committed they become.

Although individuals in close relationships spend a good bit of time disclosing personal information, some topics are off limits. Communication researchers Leslie Baxter and Bill Wilmot determined those topics considered taboo by close relational partners. Couples tend to avoid discussing the state of their own relationship, relationships beyond their own relationship, the norms or rules of their relationship, prior relationships, conflict-inducing topics, and topics that damage one's own image or are unpleasant to consider.[16]

Why don't they talk about their own relationship? Many feared such a discussion would destroy their relationship because the partners might determine that they had different commitment levels and they would have to deal with this discrepancy. Second, they felt they would be vulnerable as individuals if they shared how they viewed the relationship. Third, couples felt that they both understood the meaningfulness of the relationship and that words were a "weak substitute" for this level of understanding. Fourth, partners felt the relationship was beyond their control and that talking about it would be futile. Last, some couples felt that talking about their relationship would suggest that it was even closer than it already was.

Why don't partners talk about relationships with other people? First, many feared anger or jealousy on the part of their partner. Second, some felt that they had a "right to privacy" and did not have an obligation to share everything about themselves. Finally, some thought that it would create problems with their partners and others; awkwardness or choosing of sides might be necessary.

Relational norms are not discussed by close relational partners for two reasons. First, couples thought such a discussion would hold negative implications for the relationship. Disagreement might result from such a talk. Second, the relational partners expressed that they would be embarrassed to bring up the norms or rules of the relationship.

Prior relationships are not discussed by many relational partners. Many people view such a discussion as a relational threat. Others viewed the past as irrelevant. Some did not discuss the past because they wanted to present a positive image of themselves and discussing information from the past might place them in a negative light.

Conflict-inducing topics were avoided because relational partners perceive similarity to be important in the developing relationship. If their focus is on dissimilarity rather than on similarity, the relationship would have a lessened chance of survival and growth. Negative self-disclosures were not provided because individuals felt their partners would perceive them less favorably.

❖ FAMILY DEVELOPMENTAL STAGES

Family researchers have built upon such interpersonal theories to further describe and explain the stages of interpersonal relationships in the family context. Family roles change systematically over one's lifetime; the nature of the family unit changes as well. Researchers have suggested specific family life-cycle changes.[17] Based on their writing, we will present an eight-stage categorization system. The eight stages include:

1. *Selecting a mate and developing the unmarried relationship:* Two individuals meet, choose each other to establish a marital relationship, and further develop their relationship.

2. *Beginning marriage:* These couples have been married fewer than seven years and have no children.

3. *Childbearing and preschool stage:* These couples have children, the oldest of whom is between birth and 6 years of age, and younger siblings may be present.

4. *School age:* The children range in age from birth to 12 years of age.

5. *Adolescent age:* The oldest child is between 13 and 19 years of age and younger siblings may be present.

6. *Launching stage:* The children in the family are between the ages of 13 and 24.

7. *Families in middle years:* The children have all left home and the couple is in preretirement years.

8. *Families in older years:* The couple is in retirement.

As we shall determine, marital satisfaction, overall life satisfaction, and other factors fluctuate in a consistent way throughout the adult's family life cycle. Let us begin to examine the development of the family by considering the essential first step—meeting another person.

■ **Selecting a Mate and Developing the Unmarried Relationship**

All relationships and marriages begin with the unmarried relationship and with communication. Why do couples in initial interactions talk with each other? A variety of explanations may be offered but two motives that have gained some popularity are uncertainty reduction and affinity seeking.

■ **Motives for Initial Interactions**

Uncertainty Reduction Communication theorists Berger and Calabrese hypothesized that couples in initial interactions talk with each other to reduce uncertainty.[18] Partners wish to diminish the unknown about the other. Although individuals may vary in their disclosures based on their awareness of how they will be perceived,[19] uncertainty reduction theory is a good explanation of initial talk in relational development. In general, researchers have found that Berger and Calabrese's theorizing is accurate. Interaction results in a lowering of uncertainty between partners. As people learn about each other, they ask fewer questions and provide more self-disclosure, or personal information. And, as uncertainty is reduced, the two people become increasingly attracted to each other.[20]

Although relational partners may ask questions to reduce uncertainty, they may regulate this impulse in order to avoid negative conversational outcomes.[21] When information is inconsistent or discrepant from other information, communicating with another individual can actually increase uncertainty.[22] Uncertainty reduction does not only occur with the relational partner. Individuals can decrease uncertainty when they talk with their partner's friends and acquaintances and gain support from them.[23]

Affinity Development Communication researchers James McCroskey and Lawrence Wheeless identified affinity development as one of the main goals of interpersonal communication.[24] Robert Bell and John Daly define affinity seeking as "the active social-communicative process by which individuals attempt to get others to like and feel positive toward them."[25] Affinity development may be highly relevant when people interact in social situations.

Relational partners use affinity testing and affinity seeking in their early interactions. William Douglas, from the University of Houston, discussed the idea that people test how much their new partner likes them. He suggests that although uncertainty reduction techniques such as self-disclosure and question asking may provide some information, it does not provide this kind of affective information.[26] Among the strategies that couples use to test the liking of their partner are confronting, withdrawing, sustaining, hazing, diminishing, approaching, offering, and networking.

Confronting includes "actions that required a partner to provide immediate and generally public evidence of his or her liking" such as "I asked him/her if she/he liked me."[27] *Withdrawing* suggests that one partner engages in "actions that required a partner to sustain the interaction."[28] One example would be for one partner to fall silent to see if the other person would resume the conversation. *Sustaining* involves "actions designed to maintain the interaction without affecting its apparent intimacy."[29] An individual might ask his or her partner questions about himself or herself; similarly, the individual might self-disclose information about himself or herself. *Hazing* means that the person has taken "actions that required a partner to provide a commodity or service to the actor at some cost to him or herself."[30] The person may create a difficult situation for the other relational partner. For example, he or she might suggest that he or she needs a ride, and that he or she lives far away.

When the relational partner offers to provide a ride, an additional barrier might be erected. *Diminishing* occurs when an individual uses "actions that lowered the value of self; either directly by self-deprecation or indirectly by identifying alternative reward sources for a partner."[31] He or she might suggest that other people are more attractive, interesting, or better in some way. *Approaching* involves "actions that implied increased intimacy to which the only disconfirming partner response is compensatory action."[32] The relational partner might move closer to the other person or actually touch him or her. When *offering* is used, the person provides "actions that generated conditions favorable for approach by a partner."[33] One person might wait for the other until everyone else is gone and the second person can speak more freely or the first person might accompany the second person to a more secluded place. *Networking* involves "actions that included third parties, either to acquire or transmit information."[34] An individual might ask his or her friends about the potential relational partner.

These strategies are similar to those identified by communication researchers Leslie Baxter and Bill Wilmot. They identified seven "secret tests" that relational partners use to determine how the other person views them. They include directness, endurance, indirect suggestion, public presentation, separation, third-party tests, and triangle tests. *Directness* occurs when one person asks the other about his or her feelings or else self-discloses his or her feelings, hoping the partner will reciprocate. *Endurance* is the strategy used when the first partner increases the costs of the relationship to the other partner and if the partner tolerates the negative behaviors, the first person concludes that he or she is serious about the relationship. An *indirect suggestion* is used when a person uses jokes, hints, and the increased intimacy of touch to suggest implicitly that one is serious.

When *public presentation* is used the first person introduces the partner as one's "boyfriend," "partner," or in another intimate role to determine if the second person is comfortable with the role. *Separation* occurs when people temporarily separate to determine if the relationship is serious enough to withstand the test of being apart; it is based on the idea that absence makes the heart grow fonder. *Third-party tests* involve asking the partner's friends, colleagues, or family members questions to obtain information about the partner's feelings. Finally, *triangle tests* involve the manipulation of three-person triangles to obtain information—attempts to make the partner jealous.[35]

Communication investigators Robert Bell and Nancy Buerkel-Rothfuss examined how these strategies are related to other relationship characteristics. They found that using these tests are inversely related to courtship progress; in other words, they are associated with early stages of courtship. They also found that, in general, they are positively related to jealousy. Specifically, people who are jealous tend to use them more.

Bell and Buerkel-Rothfuss also determined which strategies are more likely to be used by particular relational partners. For example, endurance tests were more likely to be used if the relational partner felt that the other person was highly committed to the relationship. Separation tests were more likely to be used when commitment by both self and partner was low, when the relationship had not advanced much, and when the information seeker was jealous. Triangle tests were especially likely when the first person showed high levels of jealousy.[36]

The communication research team including Richmond, Gorham, and Furio showed that college females and males reported they would use a variety of affinity-seeking communication in their cross-sexed interactions. Women and men reported that they would use strategies that were different from each other. College men were more likely to complement women and to tell others how terrific they were, to initiate interactions with women, to present themselves in an interesting manner, to offer favors or rewards, to suggest how similar they are, to help the other person, and to assume control of conversations or other activities. College women were more likely to ask questions and encourage the other person to talk, listen to their partner, show empathy and sensitivity to the other person, emphasize their consistency and trustworthiness, include the other interactant within their group, assume equality rather than pretending to be a superior or a subordinate, look physically attractive, and let the other person maintain control both of conversations and other activities.[37]

■ Factors Relevant to Relationship Development

People are generally more aware of the factors that lead to initiating and developing a relationship than they realize. For instance, in a study of video dating, individuals were shown to give a great deal of thought to selecting pictures and writing a biographical statement that would specifically appeal to a particular kind of person. They appeared to understand, almost intuitively, how they should compose messages and how they should present themselves for the most positive outcome.[38]

As couples begin to interact, they make decisions concerning the future of their relationship. When the benefits appear to outweigh the costs, the relationship may be further developed. A number of factors are relevant as the relationship proceeds. While these factors all hold some explanatory value about why people choose their partners, no single theory or explanation has provided the complete answer about mate selection.

Physical Appearance   We draw conclusions about others on the basis of relatively little information and in a very limited period of time. It is not surprising, then, that appearance plays a key role in our judgments. Physically attractive people are generally viewed more positively than are less attractive people.[39] This generalization appears to be true from the time one is born.[40] One exception to the rule may be highly attractive women, who are sometimes not viewed to be as high in achievement or as competent as are less attractive women.[41] Physical attraction is highly relevant in our early interactions with others, particularly with the opposite sex.[42] Physically attractive men, for example, engage in more mutually initiated initial interactions with the opposite sex than do less physically unattractive men. Attractive men spend more time conversing in their interactions with others and less time engaged in activities. Attractive women also report that their interactions are less task-related and more social.[43]

Physical attractiveness continues to affect our relationship development. People who are more physically attractive have a higher likelihood of being asked for a date and they are seen to be more desirable dating partners.[44] However, people can be too attractive. The most likely person to be asked out on a date may be someone of moderate attractiveness.[45] The highly attractive person might not be asked out because of the likelihood that he or she would refuse.

Another factor that affects the attractiveness of one's partner is one's own attractiveness. Persons who rate themselves as unattractive are more likely to date others who they perceive as unattractive than they are to consider attractive people.[46] We will observe that similarity in attractiveness is a good predictor of whom one marries, as well. In general, we select people to marry who are about equal in attractiveness to ourselves[47] or whom we feel are slightly more attractive.[48]

Marital researchers Walster and Walster demonstrate that people feel uncomfortable when they perceive their partners to be more attractive than they are.[49] This conclusion is consistent with the notion of social exchange discussed earlier in this chapter. We tend to seek a balance in the costs and benefits of our relationships; when a partner is far more attractive, the relationship appears to be out of balance. We may also be concerned because a far more attractive person may be likely to investigate attractive alternatives in the interpersonal marketplace. We may thus accurately feel a threat of competition and ultimate rejection.

One man explained how similar physical appearance affected one of his relationships:

> According to the matching hypothesis, individuals are more likely to choose others who they perceive are about as good looking as they are. We don't pick them much better or much worse looking through our perceptions. If I perceive someone to be better looking than me I will stay away because I'm afraid they could do better than me. Likewise, if I perceive someone to be much worse looking than me I will similarly stay away but this time because I figure I can do better in the "dating marketplace."
>
> I saw Lydia as my type regarding her physical appearance. She was cute; not too pretty, nor too attractive or made up. . . . She was innocent looking, but had an air of elitism or sophistication that made her seem all the more attractive. I did not see her as too threatening. Since I perceive myself as average looking I assumed Lydia and I were fairly matched in terms of physical appearance. I was choosing someone whom I perceived to be slightly better looking than myself. Choosing someone whom we perceive to be just slightly better looking than ourselves is quite common and often considered getting your optimal value in the market![50]

Physical attractiveness may be a more important characteristic for women than for men to be selected as a marital partner. Stated another way, men are more concerned with marrying an attractive woman than women are concerned with marrying an attractive man.[51] Men may feel more pressure to marry an attractive partner than are women since men are evaluated more favorably when their partners are attractive than when they are intelligent.[52]

What attributions are offered when an unattractive man marries an attractive woman? He is believed to possess a variety of positive qualities including high status, income, and intellect.[53] This conclusion fits traditional beliefs that encourage a man to marry an attractive woman and a woman to marry a successful man. The social exchange theory would posit that, in such a case, women were exchanging or trading their physical attractiveness for social status, income, and security.

Traditionally, men exchanged their career status and income for the physical attributes of women. A provocative recent study of profiles or self-advertisements from a magazine for singles attempted to determine if women and men are currently willing to exchange such traditional commodities. This study found that men emphasized attractiveness and other traditional feminine, expressive qualities of potential female respondents in exchange for their career status and attractiveness.

Women, however, did not rely upon traditional social exchanges. They asked for men who were attractive, "sincere, intelligent, sensitive, honest, and able to genuinely accept and respect her competence, and who share her interests."[54] Women advertised themselves as educated, and they emphasized their personality traits and their career over any physical characteristics or degree of physical attractiveness.

Our interest in physical attractiveness may change over time. One woman, who had been married and divorced, explained:

> I find that my views of what is important have changed with age. When I was younger the absolute most important factor was physical appearance. Did he look good? More than that, would everyone else think he was good looking? Initially, it didn't matter if we shared similar beliefs and attitudes, it didn't even matter if there was mutual liking. My early relationships were always based on physical attractiveness.
>
> Today looks aren't as important as they used to be. I still say that it is someone's physical appearance that attracts me to them, but I've learned to include more than the G.Q. image into what I think is attractive. I've gotten to the point where I think those G.Q. guys are more trouble than they're worth.[55]

Similarity   A second predictor of our interest in initiating and continuing a relationship with another person is our perception of their *similarity* to us. We generally prefer people who are similar to us. We are drawn to those who have similar beliefs, attitudes, values, interests, and social backgrounds. If the value or belief is highly important to us, similarity becomes even more important. For instance, a woman who believes strongly in egalitarianism between women and men will be attracted to a man who holds a similar belief.[56]

Similarity may be important in early relationships for a number of reasons. First, when we meet someone who shares interests and hobbies, we have an immediate conversational topic that we can share. Second, finding another person who is similar to us in values and beliefs is satisfying because it reinforces our own ideas. Third, common goals may provide us with a shared purpose in a continuing relationship. Finally, similarity on some dimensions will probably result in less conflict and fewer misunderstandings.

We discovered earlier that people tend to select marital partners who are similar to themselves in attractiveness. In addition, couples often resemble each other.[57] A recent study shows that this tendency for couples to look alike occurs with both engaged and married couples. It also demonstrated that because people have repeated exposure to their own face and to the faces of others such as family members who look similar to themselves, they are attracted to people who look like themselves.[58]

People also choose partners on the basis of other similarities. We tend to select spouses who are similar in intelligence, dependability, warmth, honesty, and mental health.[59] Just as mentally healthy people tend to marry others who are mentally healthy, maladjusted people tend to marry others who are similarly maladjusted.[60] The woman who had been married and divorced observed:

> I think the most important factor in beginning to develop a relationship is similarity of values and beliefs or at least acceptance of the other's values and beliefs. I believe it is the level of this similarity or acceptance that will serve as an indicator of how long you will remain with this person. If the level is low the life of the relationship will be short. On the other hand, if the level of acceptance of agreement is high, the life of the relationship will be high. I am not saying this is a guarantee that the relationship will move to marriage, but I feel that if it doesn't become a committed love relationship it will become a deep friendship.[61]

A man in his 20s also felt that similarity was important to his developing relationship:

> Lydia and I shared common interests, values, and backgrounds. . . . We shared common backgrounds. We both were rather conservative, traditional, preppy, moralistic, and enjoyed the benefits of suburbia. For example, I believe our similar styles of dress served to cue us both that we may have similar outlooks and viewpoints. We assumed conservative dress meant conservative values, beliefs, etc. Also we both had very close and nurturing families who had a propensity for spoiling offspring![62]

Sometimes unknown to us, we seek people with similar psychological or relational deficits. People who are addicted to alcohol or drugs are often drawn to others with addictions. One author suggests that because women are socialized to be relational, nurturing, and caring, they may become addicted to love relationships. She labels such people "women who love too much" and describes their self-defeating behaviors and destructive relationships with men. Norwood explains that these women's addictions sometimes also include food, alcohol, or drugs.[63] Most important for our purposes, however, is the finding that even those women who are addicted only to men, and not to more traditional substances, are frequently drawn to men with alcohol or drug addictions. Thus a person with one kind of addiction may be drawn to another with a different kind of addiction.

Similarity continues to be important in the more developed relationship. Spouses tend to be similar on dominating and communicating behaviors.[64] Couples tend to be similar, too, on directing, or decision making. They were also similar in their willingness and ability to share essential information about their lives to each other.

Need Complementarity   Sometimes researchers who are frustrated in their attempts to explain and predict factors that account for successful relationships or satisfying marriages state that the popular maxims "birds of a feather flock together" and "opposites attract" are both accurate. In other words, they are suggesting that people are attracted to each other because of similarity, which we discussed above, and because of differences, which we will discuss in this section. Even though we all know people who are similar and interpersonally satisfied, and others who are very different from each other, yet happy in their relationship, we should not conclude that prediction is not possible.

We tend to choose people with whom to interact who are similar to us in basic attitudes, values, and beliefs. We tend to choose people who are different from us who complement our needs. For example, a person who is very unorganized might choose another who is organized because the second person compensates for his or her weakness. Someone who is shy and anxious about communicating with others might be attracted to a person who is talkative and friendly. If you are a high risk taker you might choose to interact with someone who appears to be a little more cautious. Mutual attraction results when people perceive that another's strengths might compensate for their weakness.[65]

Mutual Liking   One somewhat egocentric young woman commented that the feature she found most attractive in others was the extent to which they demonstrated their attraction to her. In other words, she found another person's admiration of her to be highly attractive. She was more likely to approach a man and initiate a conversation after she was confident that he was impressed or intrigued by her.

Although we all may not conclude that this is the most important feature in initiating a conversation with another person, mutual liking influences with whom we choose to interact. All of us enjoy hearing positive evaluations of ourselves and we do not even seem to mind flattery.[66] We are most attracted to others who initially appear to be neutral to us, but then seem to grow to like us more over time.[67]

Just as similarity is very satisfying to us as it reinforces our beliefs and attitudes, mutual liking is satisfying. When we like ourselves and others agree, we avoid the dissonance of resolving two different perceptions of the same person. Our agreement in assessment is another area of similarity. When we engage in mutual liking, conflict may be reduced, too. Individuals who like each other are less likely to be distrustful or suspicious of each other. They are more likely to cooperate and to build a relationship built on trust and openness.

One man explained the role of mutual liking in his initial interactions with a woman with whom he would have a relationship:

> My arrival for Lord & Taylor's orientation/training session for new employees was met with surprised, inquisitive looks. Both from the woman charged with providing the training and from the participants. More specifically, one

cute woman seemed to take note of my tardiness—but in a seemingly empathic manner. I noted her noting me and soon I found myself noting her—examining her clothes, physical appearance, her attention level to the class, and other information which I could glean from merely watching her from afar.

This is a direct application of the mutual liking factor. Mutual attraction or liking suggests we are attracted to people who are attracted to us. Essentially, we had the basis for a mutual admiration society—all without any verbal interaction yet! Later in our relationship, mutual liking continued to play an integral role in the maintenance of our relationship. For example, since she liked me so much and paid much attention to me I likewise did the same to her. The result being I found myself liking her more.[68]

Mutual liking may be difficult to discern. One woman in her 20s observed:

Mutual liking is a tricky factor because of the many games that we all play with each other. It is difficult to decipher whether a person is actually attracted to you and is trying not to be obvious about it, or whether they truly are not interested. This is easy for me to understand since I am not immune to these types of acts. If I like someone more than I believe I should, or more than I believe they like me, it is difficult not to act as though I am totally disinterested. I have realized the downfalls and missed opportunities of this attitude in the past few years and am working on finding a happy medium.[69]

A circular effect occurs with mutual liking. Not only do people like others who like them, but people also provide others they like with more positive attributions. Attributions are qualities or features assigned to others. People in satisfying relationships provide more positive attributes to their partners while people in dissatisfying relationships provide more negative attributes.[70] Mutual liking thus seems to gain a positive momentum; however, mutual disliking may also have a spiraling effect.

Competence We observed that we make judgments about the interpersonal attraction of other people on the basis of physical, social, and task attractiveness. This last dimension suggests that we are also interested in another person's ability to be effective outside the social arena. We are interested in their capabilities of problem solving, decision making, and task completion. We tend to prefer people who are intelligent, organized, sensitive, believable, poised, interesting, and of good character.[71] This area is somewhat important for early interactions, and it becomes increasingly important as the relationship develops. One woman explained the importance of competence in her relationships:

Competence has become very important to me. In fact, I seem to have a prejudice against incompetent people. That doesn't sound very good. I am attracted to people who know what they want and are capable of finding a way to get it. Competence may have become more important to me as a function of my perceiving myself as more competent.[72]

Another agreed that competence was important. She maintained:

> Competence is one of the most important factors in the development of my relationships. If either person feels that the other is incompetent the relationship will never be successful in my mind. Competence, whether it is interpersonal, academic, or logical, is one of the factors that attracts me to another person and enhances the development of the relationship. Throughout the relationship each person hopefully feels some sort of admiration for the competencies of the other person. Although each should possess their own qualities which they believe are of great value, there will be certain skills that they admire in the other person.[73]

Propinquity Another factor that affects relationship initiation and development is propinquity, or closeness. Simply stated, we tend to interact more with people we are physically close to than we do with people who are farther away. Studies show, for example, that college students who live closer to each other are more likely to begin relationships than are those whose housing is farther away from each other.[74]

In some ways propinquity seems to be an obvious feature of relationship development. You cannot interact with someone who is not close to you. However, propinquity is more than physical closeness. Consider how often you begin a relationship with someone who was in your office, your class, your university, or dormitory. You may have known the person for some time, but did not consider the possibility of a personal relationship until after you had seen him or her day after day. Your physical closeness and personal contact with the individual created familiarity and that familiarity affected your attraction to him or her. Thus it is not merely closeness that affects your relationship, but the effect that closeness has on our awareness and knowledge of another person that influences interpersonal attraction.

Interacting with another person on a regular basis also allows you to gain information about your similarities and complementary features in a nonthreatening way. If you work with someone, for example, you are likely to engage in the levels of communication known as orientation and exploratory affective exchange according to Altman and Taylor or in Knapp's initiating and experimenting stages.[75] However, you can interpret such behavior to be consistent with your work roles rather than as the beginning stages of personal relationship development. If you determine high levels of similarity and need complementarity, you might be encouraged to deepen the personal relationship.

The "Yuppies" (young, upwardly mobile baby boomers) are among the first generation of people in which over half of the working-age women work rather than stay at home. These young Americans who are large in number and influential in creating changing mores within the culture have added a new dimension to personal relational development. Just as we have observed that we might begin a personal relationship with a coworker because of the relatively safe conditions under which such a relationship may begin, the Yuppies have institutionalized such a move. Their workaholic lifestyles leave little time for play. As a consequence, work environments have replaced the singles bar and fitness center as a place to "meet and mate." Courtship occurs over a stockholders' report, in the board room, or in an executive office. This new feature of American life underlines the importance of propinquity in affecting relationship development.

The factors that we have been discussing in this section all hold some explanatory value about why people choose their partners. However, no single theory nor explanation has provided the complete answer about mate selection. Currently, family theorists are providing alternative theoretical approaches[76] and they are carefully testing existing theories.[77] Perhaps it is not possible to identify a single theory nor a single variable that explains the diversity in people's selections of their partners.

■ Public Commitment Associated with Relational Development

Personal relationships move through Altman and Taylor's stages of exploratory affective exchange to affective exchange or Knapp's intensifying and integrating stages as the couple interacts as an unmarried couple. They may even move to a stable stage (using Altman and Taylor's terminology) and to bonding (using Knapp's category system). However, these stages are not necessarily apparent to others. Most of the couple's communication is private and reserved for each other.

Why do couples move from one stage in their relationship to another? Couples' reasons for the major changes in their relationship development are called "turning points."[78] Catherine Surra, at the University of Arizona, has conducted a great deal of research attempting to understand these relational changes. With another researcher, she identified four categories of turning points. *Individual reasons* are those that originate in one person's beliefs or values, such as "I decided I was ready for a committed relationship." *Dyadic reasons* represented an event in the interaction between the two partners, such as "We never disagreed about anything of any importance so we thought we could make it as a married couple." *Circumstantial reasons* originated in random events, such as "We got stuck at a ski resort in a snowstorm and ended up sharing a room." *Social network reasons* occur when third parties intervene, such as "I really fell for her kid brother."[79]

As a result of such events, courtships may follow at least four patterns. Surra identified these as follows:

1. The Accelerated Type, in which partners' relationships moved smoothly and rapidly to the certainty of marriage.

2. The Accelerated-Arrested Type, in which relationships initially moved most rapidly to a high chance of marriage, but then lost momentum.

3. The Intermediate Type, where relationships fell about midway between the two accelerated and prolonged types in terms of average length of courtship and the rapidity of movement to marriage.

4. The Prolonged Type, which included unusually long courtships and seriously dating stages of involvement.[80]

In a later study, Surra showed that these four types of relationships are marked by different reasons for upturns and downturns in their relational development.[81] More recently, Surra and her colleagues demonstrated that some relationships and commitments are event-driven (a person is hired or fired, has an accident, uses the calendar) and some are relationship-driven (are based on the feelings between the two people). They further showed that people who rely on events to govern their relationships may find that they have made less suitable marriage choices than those who rely on their feelings.[82]

As couples reach positive turning points they begin to show public commitment. Although "mate selection" may be used broadly to include all premarital relationships, regardless of the outcome, oftentimes people reserve the term for those relationships that ultimately result in marriage.[83] Recognizable steps generally occur for most couples who eventually marry. These include dating, serious dating, and the engagement. Let us briefly consider these three signs of public commitment.

Dating   Traditionally, dating referred to young men initiating social experiences with young women. The purpose of the date was to learn about the opposite sex, to improve one's social skills in intimate settings, to engage in sexual exploration, and to determine one's compatibility with others in order to choose a marital partner.

Popular advice on dating is abundant. For example, "Mother Murphy" has some observations on dating that are humorous because of their closeness to reality. She offers "The Law of Date Distribution":

1. The more dates you have, the more dates you'll get.

2. The fewer dates you have, the fewer dates you'll get.

Corollary: The best way to get a date is to already have a date.[84]

These laws and the corollary suggest that people who have an abundance of dates will have more and people who have few will continue to have few. A similar issue that has gained research interest is how available one should be. Early studies suggested that people were well advised to "play hard to get."[85] Other investigations suggested that such advice was limited and should either be modified or rejected.[86]

Recent research suggests that individuals are well advised to be moderately selective if they wish to be perceived as an attractive dating partner. People who are viewed as nonselective or extremely selective are seen to be less desirable than those who are moderately selective.[87] "Mother Murphy's" law might be revised to suggest that to the extent that you are viewed as moderately selective, the more dates you will get!

"Dating" may be a term that is itself dated. Changes in courtship patterns and the ages of individuals who engage in premarital relational development suggest that a new term might be appropriate. Persons in their middle or later years suggest that the term "dating" does not adequately describe their behavior. Cohabitors similarly find the term to be inaccurate.

Not only is the term "dating" problematic, but the activity of dating has been criticized for a variety of reasons. First, it is clearly a sexist institution. Men generally serve as the initiators and women typically serve only as respondents; further, the date encourages men to exchange money for sexual favors. Second, the date may be seen as an artificial game in which people with different goals attempt to conceal their real purpose. (Some writers suggest that women may desire security and commitment, while men may simply desire sexual activity.) Finally, the date is highly anxiety-producing for both women and men because of the uncertainties that are involved.

Dating has an additional dark side. Family violence has been documented for some time. More recently, investigations have uncovered significant amounts of violence in dating relationships. Two researchers examined past experiences with violence, attitudes, personality factors, the nature of the relationship, and socioeconomic status with 410 college and university students. They found that nearly half of the respondents had experienced dating violence. Most of these experiences were reciprocal, with both partners becoming violent at one time or another.[88] Nonetheless, women are more likely to be the principal victims.[89] The best predictor of violent experiences in current dating relationships was violence in past relationships. The social profile of the offender includes social stress, isolation, a disrupted home, distant-harsh parenting, early dating, and school, employment, and alcohol problems.[90]

Some couples engage in more casual social interactions rather than in formal dating. Women and men may meet at an agreed-upon location rather than have the man "pick up" the woman. The couple may share the expenses of the evening or of a number of evenings rather than relying upon the man to be financially responsible. The couple may have common goals, or, when their goals differ, they may be more direct and assertive about their expectations. Women may be as likely to suggest an activity as are men.

A married woman began dating her husband by seeing him socially with a large group of students from a graduate class in which they were both enrolled:

> Andrew and I started spending time together along with other students from class. We'd usually go to a restaurant after class and have drinks and talk. Usually Andrew and I were the last to leave, as we would sit and talk for hours. We'd have so much to share and discuss. I remember these days with such fondness.
>
> Eventually, we began to go out on our own (without people from the class) and soon our relationship became more and more intimate.[91]

One married man observed that he and his wife never actually dated. He describes the beginning of their relationship:

> At BYU, Janice and I lived fairly close to one another. We began spending a lot of time together when she and my best friend and roommate stopped dating. Janice would come to me and talk about her "broken heart." Because of this, we spent much time together and began to have fun as friends. We would go to movies, dances, simply "bum" around together. We were great friends with no romantic feelings apparent for several months. We thought we would never marry each other because we were too good of friends and because we thought we were too much alike (crazy reasons, huh?). In fact, we spent hours talking about each other's love lives.
>
> It was in the spring of our senior year at BYU that we began to think that maybe there was more to our relationship than just good friendship. Janice was the first with romantic feelings. I "kicked" against the notion for awhile, but finally realized that this relationship was indeed a good thing.
>
> We never really formally dated. Although we did many things together, neither of us formally asked each other out on a date. We always did things on the spur of the moment, just like good friends would do.[92]

Other couples find themselves in long-distance relationships. Because of college locations, job opportunities, and family relocations, many partners must rely on travel and telephoning to interact with each other. These "fax affairs" may provide safe sex, but they provide limited opportunities for interaction. Communication researchers Laura Stafford and James Reske, at Ohio State University, showed that long-distance couples have more restricted communication and more idealized views of each other than do other couples.[93] These authors suggest that people in long-distance relationships postpone realistic assessments of their partners until they are allowed to be in closer physical proximity.

Another development that has increased rapidly in the past decade is the use of self-advertisement in order to make a date.[94] The use of personals, profiles, or companion advertisements, just like video dating and computer matching, facilitates the dating process. While some researchers view such developments as indicative of loneliness and alienation, these services may be viewed as a reasonable and systematic response to rapid social changes.[95] They allow the increasing number of single people an efficient and effective way to meet each other and to begin a dating relationship.

Serious Dating   Serious dating, for lack of a better term, occurs when the couple begins to pair off exclusively with each other. They frequently began spending most of their leisure time together. They might not choose to engage in social activities that do not include their partner. During this period of time, the couple begins to discuss the possibility of living together or becoming married. They are viewed as a couple by others.

Although couples become sexually intimate at a variety of different stages ranging from the first date to when they are engaged or married, many are sexually intimate at this stage.[96] The sexual aspect of dating was investigated recently. Two communication researchers found that people use four strategies to engage in sexual behavior with their partners. They include antisocial acts that include imposing one's own sexual wishes on a dating partner in socially unacceptable ways. For instance, the person desiring sexual activity may insult or ridicule the partner, use physical force, cry, plead, or verbally or physically threaten the partner. Emotional and physical closeness is a strategy in which an individual tells the partner how much he or she likes him or her or loves him or her. The individual using this approach might sit or stand physically closer to the other person. Logic and reason are used when attempts to influence occur through presentation of an authoritative argument. The person might try to assert his or her authority, use logic, or claim to be knowledgable about how sexual the couple should be. Finally, pressure and manipulation occurs when alcohol or drugs are used to influence the partner, when one person manipulates the partner's mood, when one individual is persistent, or when the person either talked fast or used white lies.

Although some of these strategies seem unethical, it is encouraging to learn from this research that only emotional and physical closeness and logic and reason were related to actual sexual behavior. However, males were more likely than females to use pressure and manipulation. Further, people who wanted more sex than they currently had, compared to people who had enough sex or wanted less sex, used pressure and manipulation more. Finally, people who wanted less sex than had occurred were more likely to use logic and reason. The authors suggest that these individuals might be attempting to cool the flames of passion through reason.[97]

Regardless of when the couple becomes sexually intimate, conflict is often present during the period of time surrounding sexual intimacy. Couples who become sexually active early in their relationship identify this period as the most conflictual while couples who become sexually active later in their relationship name this later period as the most conflict-filled.[98] We will consider conflict further in Chapter 12.

The couple experience Knapp's intensifying and integrating stage. They tell each other about their feelings toward each other, which generally include disclosures of loving the other person. They talk about their feelings of closeness and "oneness" with the other person. They may change their language from talking about "I," "my," and "me" to "we" and "us." They discuss a future that includes the two of them together as opposed to each person seeking independent goals or as members of their original family.

For example, Tracy Alp and Walter Green are engaged to be married, but not with their parents' blessing. They are an interracial couple and their families are concerned that the marriage has too many strikes against it. However, their love for each other is more important than their families' opinions. Tracy explains, "I have to live my own life and do what is right for me and him. I would rather hurt my parents and my family than hurt Walter."[99] Tracy has already moved from seeing her primary role as a daughter to seeing her role as Walter's partner.

A great deal has been written on love and the romantic relationship in this stage. Some of the more humorous comments include the following:

> Love is the crocodile on the river of desire—Bhartrihari
>
> Love is what happens to men and women who don't know each other—W. Somerset Maugham
>
> A relationship is what happens between two people who are waiting for something better to come along—Unknown
>
> A man always remembers his first love with special tenderness, but after that he begins to bunch them—H. L. Mencken
>
> Love is the ideal; marriage is the reality—"Mother Murphy"

You may wish to try to capture your own understanding of love by defining it in terms that are consistent with your experience.

At this stage in the relationship, a couple may decide to live together. In Chapter 2 we discussed cohabitation, which has increased dramatically in recent times. For some couples, cohabitation becomes an intermediate step before they become engaged and marry; for others, it becomes an alternative to marriage. A recent survey demonstrated that a majority of college students indicated they had, or would, engage in cohabitation, but nearly three-fourths of those interviewed felt that it was not acceptable to experience sexual intercourse without love of one's partner.[100]

Engagement   The last stage of public commitment that the couple makes before their wedding and marriage is the period of engagement. At this stage, the couple have reached Knapp's final stage in relationship development—bonding. Generally, some public announcement is made of this event. The couple may choose the media to announce their intentions to marry, signal their impending wedding with the exchange of an engagement ring or other symbols, or simply report their plans to friends and family. Although the announcement of the engagement may appear to be more important than the couple's transition from casual to serious dating, two researchers have determined that the transition is less pronounced for the couple.[101]

The engagement period allows couples to test their relationship for compatibility, if they have not already done so. Some relationships end at this point before the couples marry. Conflict may occur during the engagement period and researchers have determined that premarital conflict predicts marital conflict and marital satisfaction.[102] Couples in the premarital stages who engage in high levels of conflict are likely to engage in more conflict after they have been married for some time and they are more likely to be less satisfied.

During the engagement period, the couple plans their wedding and, more important, plans their marriage. They consider such issues as where they will live, who will work and where, how they will spend their income, whether or not they will have children, how they will deal with their parents and in-laws,

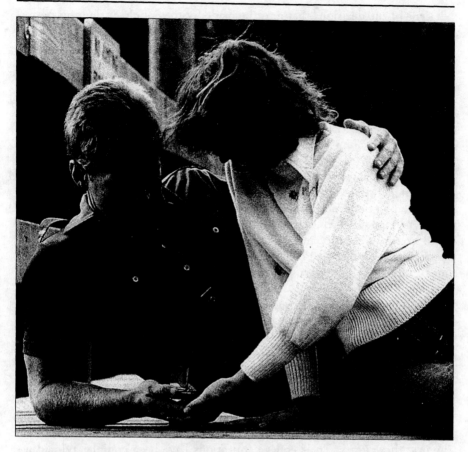

The engaged couple makes their commitment public through a variety of artifacts (© Hill, Jr./The Image Works).

what their sexual needs and expectations are, and how they will achieve their short-term and long-term goals. One married woman recalls her own engagement period:

> Our engagement stage was full of up and downs. Fortunately, this only lasted for six months and our families lived in other states. We planned and carried out all of our own wedding arrangements, based on what we wanted. Some of it was fun, but most of it was a lot of work. . . . Andrew and I spent some time discussing our marriage and what we expected, including hopes, dreams and goals. At the time, I thought we really covered all the important topics, but once we were married, we had lots more to discuss.[103]

Because of the number of decisions that must be made and because of their seriousness, we should not be surprised to observe that for many couples the engagement is a "rather turbulent and traumatic period."[104]

One of the decisions that must be made by the couple during this period is whether either person will change his or her surname. Will the couple use hyphenated names? What is the effect of name changes on credit ratings? Why do some women change their names while others use their original names or a combination of their husbands' names and their own? Communication researchers Karen Foss and Belle Edson found that married women who did not change their surname value themselves first, followed by their relationship and cultural concerns. Women who adopted their husbands' names placed more importance on their relationships, followed by cultural concerns and issues of self. Women who hyphenated their original names with their husbands' names valued themselves and their relationships equally.[105]

Premarital anxiety may show itself during the engagement period. Premarital anxiety includes concern about security, excitement, and fulfillment.[106] Individuals' concern about security and excitement focus on one's ability to have both security and excitement within the same relationship. Concerns about fulfillment included having close rapport, equality with one's mate, emotional fulfillment, and staying romantic. Premarital anxiety is not related to a person's interaction style, relationship orientation, or past experiences.

Many couples anticipating marriage have unrealistic notions about the nature of marriage.[107] For example, Janet Polk and Bob Dennis are still college students. They are both exceedingly good-looking. Janet is about 5'9" tall and very slender. She typically wears name-brand clothes and always looks very neat. Bob is tall, dark, and handsome. At 6'2", he is physically fit and muscular. Bob's eyes are light green, which contrasts with his dark hair and tanned skin. Bob looks as if he could model for L. L. Bean or Lands' End.

Janet and Bob are part of the "Greek" system—Janet is an Alpha Phi and Bob is a Sigma Chi. They have lived in their sorority and fraternity houses for the past three years. Their college educations have been completely paid for by their parents. How ready will they be to manage a home, families, and jobs?[108]

Although many engaged couples may acknowledge they understand that problems often arise in marital relationships, they often have not assessed their own particular situation. A recent survey found that over 75 percent of college students surveyed felt that their parents' marriage was happy, that over 90 percent saw marriage as a lifelong commitment, that close to 80 percent believed they had the skills necessary for a good marriage, but that they were evenly divided about whether or not they were specifically prepared for marriage.[109]

What can couples do to help prepare themselves for marriage? Over 75 percent of those college students who were interviewed expressed a need to learn better ways to communicate.[110] A variety of programs have been developed that assist couples who anticipate marriage to prepare more carefully and personally for a satisfying married life.[111] The success of such programs is encouraging and the engaged couple may benefit by exploring such options.

■ **Beginning Marriage**

After you have developed your unmarried relationship through the stages of dating, serious dating, perhaps cohabitation, and engagement, the next step in the development of the family unit is the beginning marriage. Everyone does not get married; indeed, everyone who is engaged to be married does not marry, but many do. In this section of the chapter we will consider the early marriage, beginning with the wedding and extending through the first few years, stopping when the first child arrives.

The Wedding   The first event of the marriage (or just preceding it) is the wedding. The wedding is the clearest public statement that a couple makes about their commitment to each other. The wedding involves a legal-contractual agreement between two parties that changes their rights, privileges, and, to a large extent, their roles. The ceremony may be highly traditional or very contemporary; vows may be timeless or unique to the particular couple. Nearly three-fourths of all couples marrying for the first time choose a religious ceremony.

The wedding may be a particularly stressful time for the couple. One woman reported writing a check out to her husband-to-be on their wedding day because he accused her of spending too much money on the flowers for the reception. (Perhaps one reason they have been married so long is that he never cashed the check!) A man about to be married for the first time sought counseling because although he and his wife-to-be had never fought in their five-year courtship, they were continually bickering in the month preceding their wedding.

One college professor from Mississippi in her 30s explains that her wedding was particularly traumatic:

> Since I was marrying a minister who chose me out of the congregation in which I grew up, I decided to have a private wedding ceremony with a few relatives and close friends. I wanted people to be present who I felt were genuine and had my husband's and my best interests at heart. My husband agreed to this, and we had the wedding at my oldest sister's and brother-in-law's home.
>
> It seemed an eternity for Reverend Powell to complete his performance of the ceremony. I recall perspiring heavily and breaking down in tears once Reverend Powell finished his job. There were so many things running through my mind. . . . "Am I doing the right thing?" "Why won't Reverend Powell speed up the pace?" "Will I be a good wife?" "Can I get along with my mother-in-law?" These were just a few concerns at the time. . . .
>
> In the midst of all the crying were the hugs I received from my loved ones who kept telling me everything would be all right. I should be happy. Feelings of ambivalence did not allow me to actually listen to them, though I knew they meant well.[112]

FOR BETTER OR FOR WORSE reprinted by permission of Universal Press Syndicate copyright © 1987. All rights reserved.

Kathy Moore and Terry Black are seniors at a midwestern university. They have been engaged for the past six months. As they have planned for their wedding, they have begun to argue. Kathy shares:

> I wanted to have the bridesmaids carry candles down the aisle, but Terry thought it might be dangerous and may cause a fire. To prove he was wrong, I marched around his apartment holding a lit candle. I proved my point and he agreed that it would be safe![113]

The wedding may be stressful because the two original families may have entirely different ideas about the nature of the wedding. Rick Pinto and Jackie Herschel have been planning their wedding for the past few months. They dated for eight months before Rick proposed to Jackie. They have been engaged for five months and will be married in about three months from now. Their families are very happy about their children's marriage. Indeed, they have been "helping" to plan the wedding. Rick's family has rented a reception hall with a polka band. Jackie's parents have planned a simple party at their family lodge which is near a pond. The details and the planning associated with the wedding can be overwhelming, but, like the young woman in "For Better or For Worse," most of us look forward to our weddings.

Alan and Karen Simms have been married for three weeks. They have just moved into a new apartment and are busy painting their new home. During the wedding preparations, Karen lamented, "This should be the happiest time of my life, so why isn't it?"[114] She and her husband agreed that the two weeks before their wedding was the most difficult period in their entire relationship.

Did their difficulties ensue throughout the wedding and their early married days? Indeed, the conflict ended during the wedding ceremony, as Alan related:

> All of a sudden, I turned around and saw the most beautiful woman in the world coming down the aisle to marry *me*. The last two weeks just didn't seem to matter. I can hardly remember them now.[115]

The Honeymoon   Although honeymoons have been less popular in recent times, today about 85 percent of all couples who marry go on a honeymoon. (see note 109). This transition period allows the couple privacy to achieve or improve a satisfying sexual relationship and time to discuss their future more thoroughly. In addition, it provides time for rest and relaxation after the hectic events leading up to the wedding. Last, it allows the couple a time to interact without the pressures of work, school, or everyday interruptions.

Marital Stages   Marriages move through three stages: the "happy honeymoon" phase, the disillusionment and regrets stage, and the stage of accommodation.[116] Let us consider these stages.

The "happy honeymoon" phase begins with the wedding and extends through the actual honeymoon. For some couples, the period is brief and may end before the actual honeymoon is over; for others, the honeymoon appears to go on indefinitely.[117] During this period, the couple is filled with optimism about the future and their union. Romantic love, which generally marks the premarital courtship and engagement periods, extends through the "happy honeymoon."[118] Miss Piggy, the cartoon character, offered her view of this period: "When you are in love with someone you want to be near him all the time, except when you are out buying things and charging them to him."

The marital couple Clyde Hendrick and Susan Hendrick, who have contributed a great deal to our understanding of love, describe how people feel when they are in this stage. They recall Lee's taxonomy of love attitudes:

Eros—romantic, passionate love

Ludus—game-playing love

Storge—friendship love

Pragma—logical, shopping-list love

Mania—possessive, dependent love

Agape—selfless love[119]

They found that people who were "in love" tended to be more erotic and agapic and less ludic in their love attitudes than were people who were not in love.[120]

For some couples, the "happy honeymoon" stage seems to extend throughout their married life. U.S. General Mark W. Clark, for example, was asked what was the best advice he had ever been given. "To marry the woman I did," he replied.

"And who gave you that advice?" was the next question.

"She did," responded the general.

Some time later, the couple may realize that the "honeymoon is over" and they move into a phase of disillusionment and regrets. In essence, reality collides with the dreams of the earlier romantic period. One member of the couple, or both, feels as though they have made a serious error by getting married. Presumably the couple discussed such matters as where they would live, who would work and where, how they would spend their income, whether or not they would have children, how they would deal with their in-laws, what their sexual needs and expectations were, and how they would achieve their short-term and long-term goals before they were married. If they have not, differences in outlook on such issues might contribute to the disillusionment phase.

The focus is on the differences between the two rather than the similarities that originally brought them together. Just as some couples never move beyond the "happy honeymoon" phase, others never move beyond this period of disillusionment. This phase of marital life may have been responsible for the philosopher Friedrich Nietzsche's observation, "One should never know too precisely whom one has married," and Peter DeVries's, "We fall in love with a personality, but we must live with a character."

When couples do not move beyond the disillusionment stage, their marriage may end in divorce or dissolution. Some other factors that negatively impact marital success include a premarital pregnancy, a remarried family, a stepfamily, lower income, lower educational levels, younger ages, and a shorter period of courtship. Some personality factors are also negative precursors of marital happiness. They include people who are less attached, women who are lower in instrumentality (or a task orientation), people who are higher in belief structure, and men who are lower in social support.[121]

Many couples move beyond this stage, but they recognize how difficult it may be for their partners. For example, Charles Laughton, the British character actor, was married to actress Elsa Lanchester. When he was asked if he would ever marry again, he immediately responded in the negative. After citing several reasons, he elaborated, "During courtship, a man reveals only his better qualities. After marriage, however, his real self gradually begins to emerge, and there is very little his wife can do about it." After a moment he added, "I don't believe I would ever put a woman through that again!"

Most couples, however, move on to the third phase of accommodation. In the classic pattern of thesis, antithesis, and synthesis, these couples incorporate their highest hopes and their worst fears into a realistic picture of their marriage. They recognize their partner's positive attributes as well as his or her negative characteristics. They come to recognize that the married state is distinctive from singlehood.

Conjugal love replaces, or accompanies, the romantic love felt earlier. Two researchers distinguish conjugal love from romantic love:

> Conjugal love . . . grows as the marriage progresses, thrives on companionship, common experiences, and the number of happy episodes which are scattered throughout a rich marriage. Conjugal love . . . waxes stronger with each additional year of marriage. Unlike romantic love, conjugal love is impossible for newly acquainted young people, since it takes time to form and grows from continuous association. Romantic love is greatest where each party knows least about the other—reality gets in the way of romance.[122]

Communication is critical in the accommodation phase. The members of the couple must use communication both in an expressive and an instrumental way. They must share their feelings with each other, which involves trusting the other person as well as themselves. They must use communication, too, to solve problems and to make decisions about a variety of issues.

Expressive communication is that which is relational in nature. Traditionally, women have viewed communication to serve a relational purpose. They perceive interaction as something that builds interpersonal relationships and allows us to demonstrate our concern and interest in the welfare of others. Women have thus perceived communication as something that is enjoyable in and of itself. Expressive communication allows the couple to share their feelings.

Expressive communication can play an essential role in the development of a happy and successful marriage. Husbands and wives demonstrate their interest and concern for each other through their affective and expressive interactions. Feelings of love and belonging can be shared in this way.

Expressive communication can allow couples to deal with subtle issues that may arise. Each member of the couple learned about family life in his or her family of orientation. He or she learned how husbands and wives interacted by observing his or her own parents. Although the couple is likely to come from a similar socioeconomic background, it is probable that their two sets of parents are distinctive from each other in their communicative patterns. For instance, if the husband's father was unemotional and analytic, he may question his wife's need for expressions of love and affection. Sharing one's feelings can allow the airing of such differences in perception.

Instrumental communication is also important. The couple must use communication to solve problems and to make decisions about a variety of issues. The couple's disillusionment, in the previous phase, may have been partly a function of inadequate discussion of such issues as how they would spend their income, whether or not they would have children, and how they would deal with their in-laws. Or, the couple may no longer agree about where and how they should live, what their sexual needs are, or how they can achieve their short-term and long-term goals. Open and full discussion of such issues may be the only way they can identify and resolve differences between them.

Again, the prior learning of the roles of husband and wife come from the family of orientation. To the extent that the members of the married couple learned different roles in decision making, they may have difficulty in solving their problems. For instance, if the wife learned by example that women are strong and independent and that men generally do not intrude on decisions concerning the home, she may resent her husband's demands to be consulted on furniture purchases and redecorating. Both expressive and instrumental talk can assist the married couple as they accommodate themselves to their married life.

The theoretical advantages of both expressive and instrumental communication patterns in the marital relationship have received empirical support. Expressiveness is similar to femininity on measures of sex roles while instrumentality can be equated with masculinity. Patricia Parmelee showed that feminine (expressive) men and masculine (instrumental) women are more satisfied with their relationships than are others. In addition, men expressed greater satisfaction when they were married to masculine (instrumental) women than if they were married to noninstrumental women.[123]

SUMMARY

In this chapter we began our consideration of the development of the family from meeting to mating. We examined both the social penetration theory and the social exchange theory. Although all of our first meetings with others do not begin the trajectory toward intimacy and family development, all families begin with two people meeting each other.

Selecting a mate and developing an unmarried relationship are very complicated. No single factor nor any single theory explains this phenomenon completely. However, some factors do appear to predict the likelihood of relationship development. Among these characteristics are the physical appearance of the other person and ourselves, the similarity between ourselves and the other person, the need complementarity that may exist between us, mutual liking, competence of the couple, and propinquity or physical closeness. As we develop the unmarried relationship we typically move through the stages of dating, serious dating, and engagement. However, as we noted early in this chapter, all couples do not go though all of these stages and some couples add other stages such as cohabitation.

If we have moved through the stages that lead to an engagement or some form of public commitment associated with relationship development, marriage may occur next. The early married stage extends from the wedding through about the first seven years of marriage and includes no children. Typical marital stages are the "happy honeymoon" stage, the disillusionment and regrets stage, and finally accommodation. In the next chapter we will continue our discussion of family development.

KEY TERMS

1. *Social penetration* refers to interpersonal interactions moving from the superficial and nonintimate to the deeper, more intimate levels as people assess the costs and rewards related to the relationship.

2. *Orientation stage* occurs in initial interactions when you are gaining superficial, nonintimate information from another person.

3. *Exploratory affective exchange* occurs when people share some opinions or feelings, but they are of a general nature.

4. The *affective exchange stage* consists of personal information and does not occur until people establish a close relationship.

5. The *stage of stability* represents the most intimate stage of disclosure and is associated with enduring relationships (Altman and Taylor's Social Penetration Model).

6. Knapp's stages of relational development consists of *initiating*—when we first meet someone; *experimenting*—small talk and safe information; *intensifying*—begin to disclose personal information and we appear less formal; *integrating* the couple forms; *bonding*—describes public commitment by partners. The *deescalating stages* include *differentiating*—couple disengages; *circumscribing* communication becomes limited or constricted; *stagnating*—relatively inactive relationship; *avoiding*—couples have different physical and communicative environments; and *terminating*—the death of the relationship.

7. *Social exchange theory* states that relationships deepen when the needs of the persons involved are met.

8. *Market value* is determined by adding together all of our positive interpersonal attributes and subtracting our negative qualities from them and then comparing ourselves with others.

9. *Affinity seeking* is the active social-communicative process by which individuals attempt to get others to like and feel positive toward them.

10. *Need complementarity* suggests that we tend to choose people who are different from us who complement our needs.

11. *Mutual liking* suggests we are attracted to people who are attracted to us.

12. *Propinquity* claims that we tend to interact more with people we are physically close to than people who are farther away.

13. *Accommodation* occurs when married couples incorporate their highest hopes and their worst fears into a realistic picture of their marriage.

14. *Conjugal love* refers to a deep love that replaces romantic love. It is the type of love that takes time to form and grows from continuous association.

CHAPTER 7

THE DEVELOPMENT OF THE FAMILY: FROM THE CRADLE TO THE CLASSROOM

A mother's pride, a father's joy.

SIR WALTER SCOTT

After you have read this chapter, you will be able to

1. Describe the positive and negative aspects of pregnancy and parenting.

2. List the four family-related issues that are reported by pregnant couples.

3. Define the crisis, event, and relational stages of pregnancy.

4. Explain the five parental role responsibilities that contribute to the healthy development of children.

5. Identify the six stages of parenthood.

6. Discuss the changes that occur in the interactional group when a couple becomes parents.

7. List specific strategies that women and men can use to cope with the demands of work and home.

8. Describe the communication development of infants.

9. Explain communication development; mass media consumption; formation of attitudes, values, and beliefs; development of self-esteem; and sex roles of preschoolers.

10. Discuss the parent–child interaction and other interactions of school-age children.

In the last chapter we began our exploration of the development of the family from the first interaction to the early stages of marriage. In this chapter we will continue to examine family developmental stages. The chapter opens with a consideration of adding children to the family unit and examines families with preschool and school-age children. All families do not include children, but many do. Let us begin our discussion in this chapter with the impact of adding children to the family unit.

❖ ADDING CHILDREN

A larger number of couples are remaining childless today than in the past and many couples are postponing childbearing until the woman's mid- or late 30s. Many women are facing traumatic decision making about whether to parent or not. These women were raised with traditional values and sex-role stereotypes concerning parenting, but they are experiencing a conflict in the emergent cultural values and lifestyle pressures.[1] Nonetheless, the majority of married couples eventually have children.

The motivations for having a child range from social, cultural, family, and peer pressure to the desire to give and receive love. Young adult college students identified a strong interest in establishing an identity and social network as the most common reasons for having children. They named financial, marital, and emotional stability as the variables that influenced the timing of their becoming parents.[2] Bill Cosby adds, "Having a child is surely the most beautifully irrational act that two people in love can commit" and notes, "The decision to have such a thing is made by the heart, not the brain."[3] Both conscious and unconscious reasons contribute to the decision to become pregnant and produce offspring. In addition, many people become parents by accident. One observer noted that "sex is a formula by which 1 + 1 = 3," and that "familiarity breeds children."[4]

Children are no longer born into nuclear families, as we discussed in Chapter 2. Researchers have specified the circumstances that mark the childhood experience. They observe that of each 100 children born today,

Twelve are born out of wedlock

Forty-one are born to parents who divorce before the child is 18

Five are born to parents who separate

Two will experience the death of a parent before they reach age 18

Forty-one will reach age 18 without such incidents[5]

GROUP	NUMBER OF CHILDREN PER FEMALES
Cubans	1.3
Whites	1.7
Blacks	2.4
Mexican-Americans	2.9

TABLE 7.1 NUMBER OF CHILDREN PER FEMALES FOR VARIOUS ETHNIC GROUPS

Another demographic trend concerns the differential fertility that occurs among various races. While 2.1 children per mother are required to maintain our current population, racial groups reproduce differentially. Table 7.1 summarizes the current figures.[6]

These different birth rates will continue to lead to a very different ethnic composition in our country. For example, the state of California has a majority of minorities within its elementary schools. The same is true of the 25 largest city-school systems in the nation.[7] It is predicted that 265 million people will populate the United States in 2020, that 91 million of these people will be minorities, and most of them will be children.[8]

A final demographic trend concerns the feminization and youthfulness of poverty.[9] Half of all children who live in families headed by women live in poverty, as compared with 12 percent of children who live in families that have a male present. Too, 25 percent of our country's poor are preschool children and 21 percent are school-age. This compares with 14 percent of the nation's poor who are elderly, and 12 percent who are adults but not elderly.[10] These differential rates of poverty will continue to be of concern to sociologists and people in social service agencies.

■ Effects of Pregnancy

Pregnancy affects both parents. The effects of pregnancy on the mother are well-known. She gains weight, may experience nausea and vomiting in the early stages of pregnancy, may experience mood swings, and will probably feel somewhat anxious and stressed. The husbands of pregnant women often experience these same symptoms during their wives' pregnancy.[11] Recently Glazer, a nursing professor at Case Western Reserve University, replicated these findings. In a study of 108 couples taking childbirth education classes in the Cleveland area, he found that 9 of the men reported nausea and vomiting, 44 experienced mood changes, and some gained as much as 25 pounds.[12]

Men, women, and couples experience "significant shifts in their beliefs and attitudes from the prenatal to the postpartum period."[13] These changes may be positive or negative. One factor that affects how a woman views her pregnancy and postpartum period is whether she is in a partnered relationship. Women need greater social support during pregnancy and those without partners fare far worse than do those who have husbands or boyfriends.[14]

People in married relationships similarly experience change over the pregnancy and postpartum period. Two researchers concluded, "Both husbands and wives were found to peak in their reported marital adjustment at one month postpartum, and both spouses showed a significant decline in marital adjustment at six months postpartum."[15] At one month after the birth of their baby, the parents may be experiencing a kind of "honeymoon stage" with their new child; at six months, the extra responsibilities and stress may have become apparent.

Why do some couples adjust more positively to the birth of a baby than do others? The researchers noted:

> For wives, the best single predictor of postpartum marital adjustment was their level of marital adjustment during pregnancy; perceived parenting stress was the only other significant predictor. For husbands, marital adjustment at six months was also predicted by their prenatal level of marital adjustment and their perceived parenting stress. In addition, wives' prenatal marital adjustment was found to contribute to the prediction of husbands' marital adjustment at six months postpartum.[16]

Husbands and wives who report happiness during their pregnancy are more likely to report marital satisfaction after their child is born. In addition, the added stress created by the child's needs and demands may affect marital satisfaction.

Another research team determined similar findings. They examined four different patterns of marital change that they labeled accelerating decline, linear decline, no change, and modest positive increase. They found that people who experienced a declining relationship exhibited marital problems during the pregnancy period, as well. They also determined that the infant's temperament added to their stress during postpartum.[17] Both of these studies suggest that pregnancy and the addition of a child to a family may be stressors that exacerbate marital difficulties. If the child is particularly demanding, marital satisfaction is in even greater jeopardy.

One new father in a highly satisfying marriage recalled the effects of pregnancy on his relatively new relationship:

> During the nine months that Janice was pregnant, we experienced many changes. These nine months covered the majority of our first year of marriage, so not only were we adjusting to a new relationship, but we were also adjusting to the many changes that pregnancy brings.
> The first thing that comes to my mind is the first five or six months of pregnancy. Although we knew Janice was pregnant, it wasn't something I

thought about often. At the time, I was relatively busy with a highly stressful job and therefore had my mind on other things. Whereas Janice was constantly aware of the physical and emotional changes that were occurring to her. Because of this, I was not as sensitive to her mood changes, nor did I understand them as well as I ought to have.

It took me a few months to finally realize that big changes were headed our way. Still then, it was hard for me to realize we were really having a baby. It wasn't until Janice started getting bigger and the baby started kicking that I partly understood what was happening. Typical male![18]

Although this man did not focus on the pregnancy during the first two trimesters, he became increasingly involved throughout the last three months.

Couples report a number of changes during the pregnancy. Four family-related issues that are reported by a high percentage of pregnant couples are the transition from being a couple to a family, changes in closeness (usually increased) with the spouse, a changing involvement with the extended family, and the male partner's positive involvement with fathering.[19] The researchers conclude, "First pregnancy is associated with an increased focus on family issues for both women and men, and represents a developmental process not only in the individual parents but in the family itself."[20]

One method of dealing with pregnancy is for the relational partners to talk with each other about the experience. Friends and other family members can similarly provide support to the couple. Three themes emerge in communication about pregnancy. The first is *crisis*, in which people view the pregnancy as a change, and is exemplified in statements such as, "Your life is going to change in more ways than you know," "You've been a long-distance runner all of your life—don't stop running now," and "Make sure you keep your feet up so you don't experience swelling in your ankles."

The second attempts to erode the negative features of the crisis theme by replacing it with a focus on the *event*. Pregnancy as an event is most familiar in the Lamaze method of childbirth. When viewed as an event, the couple plans and prepares during the pregnancy for the birth of their child. The parents-to-be may encourage each other to exercise, to learn breathing techniques, and to engage in other training activities.

Third, pregnancy is considered in *relation* to other experiences. The pregnant woman views herself in relationship to her own mother, who has previously experienced pregnancy. Women may view themselves as part of a linear progression of women becoming pregnant and delivering babies. The couple may achieve some group identity as they experience a phenomenon that others have experienced before them.[21]

Communication about the pregnancy may be important for the couple as well as for other family members. Each of the themes may serve different functions. The crisis model may increase the couple's fears and concerns; the event model may help to focus the couple's attention on the need to prepare for a specific task; and the relation model may assist the couple in viewing themselves as part of a larger family or culture.

TABLE 7.2   PARENTAL ROLE RESPONSIBILITIES[27]

ROLE	EXAMPLE
Teaching cognitive development	Help child develop reading skills
Teaching handling of emotions	Teach child how to be affectionate
Teaching social skills	Teach child how to compromise
Teaching norms and social values	Help child develop values to live by
Teaching physical health	Engage in athletic play with child
Teaching personal hygiene	Make sure child bathes regularly
Teaching survival skills	Show child what to do in case of fire
Basic needs—health care	Arrange for child to see dentist regularly
Basic needs—material (food, clothing and shelter)	Provide adequate shelter for the child
Basic needs—meeting the emotional needs of the child	Express affection toward child
Basic needs—child care	Provide care for child after school
Interface role between child and social institutions	Encourage child to have a sense of civic responsibility
Interface role between child and family	Facilitate the relationship between child and grandparents

Source: Gilbert and Hanson, 1983.

The pregnancy and postpartum period may be disastrous for the couple. In most marriages, marital satisfaction declines after the birth of the baby. However, both communication and social support have been shown to ameliorate these outcomes. Satisfaction with the marital and new child–parent relationships may be improved with understanding and support in this predictable changing time.

■ Parental Role Responsibilities

Changes occur during pregnancy for the mother and sometimes for the father. These changes do not approach the numbers or kinds of changes that occur after the baby is born. Parental role responsibilities are major. We might commonly believe that the only responsibilities a parent has are to provide for the needs and socialization of the child. However, working adults felt that the parental role responsibilities included 13 distinct components.[22] They are provided in Table 7.2 with representative items to illustrate each role.

Coleman, a marriage and family author, summarizes the role responsibilities contributing toward the healthy development of children.[23] He includes providing love and acceptance, supplying structure and discipline, encouraging competence and self-confidence, presenting appropriate role models, and creating a stimulating and responsive environment. Let us consider each of these activities.

Love and acceptance are essential for healthy child development. Such an atmosphere leads the child to feelings of self-esteem and self-worth. Three researchers, for instance, demonstrated that love and warmth expressed by parents were the most crucial of all of the influences provided in the home.[24] Children who feel loved and accepted develop such traits as self-reliance, independence, and self-control.[25]

Further, the mother's patterns of providing support to the child are related to his or her security of attachment.[26] A sense of trust is established that assists the child in dealing with fear and anxiety. The negative impact of problems such as poverty, physical handicaps, and unemployment may be overcome when the child feels that he or she is loved and accepted by his or her family.

How is love and acceptance communicated in the family? First, parents provide time for the children to communicate their experiences and needs. Second, a higher proportion of positive, rather than negative, comments is provided. Third, warmth and affection are offered nonverbally through touch and movement toward, rather than away from, the child.

When parents do not communicate love and acceptance, they may do so by ignoring or avoiding the children, by abusing the children physically or mentally, by providing negative or critical comments in a higher proportion than positive comments, or by physical distance from the child. Such interaction results in low self-esteem, feelings of inadequacy or insecurity, increased aggression, loneliness, generalized fear or anxiety, and difficulties in both the giving and receiving of love on the part of the child.[28]

Structure and discipline are a second set of factors that foster the healthy development of children. Order and consistency are important qualities of a healthy family environment. Children need to understand standards and limits of behavior, clearly defined roles for the members of the family, and the methods of discipline commensurate with misbehavior. In order to understand the standards and limits of their behavior, children must know what goals and conduct are approved. In order to understand the roles for the members of the family, the expectations of family members' behavior must be clearly delineated and it must be consistent. In order to understand discipline that is appropriate for various forms of misbehavior, the parents must define misbehavior and they must deal with infractions of the rules as they occur.

These requirements underline the importance of open and complete communication with children. Basic definitions and assumptions must be offered.

The overall values, attitudes, and feelings of the parents must be explained in language that is appropriate for the child. Consistency in behavior is similarly important so the child learns to trust the messages his or her parents present.

Competence and self-confidence are encouraged in the family that encourages the healthy development of children. How do parents encourage such qualities in their young children? Advice and counsel provide the basis for competence. Parents who guide their children through varied experiences are behaving in a manner that should encourage competence. Such guidance should include both cognitive matters such as reading, writing, and speaking as well as affective issues such as caring about others, dealing with one's feelings, and responding to stress.

In addition, parents need to be responsive to the messages that their children provide. Children who are rewarded with praise and positive nonverbal behaviors when they are successful and are given constructive and helpful explanations when they fail will probably learn to become competent and self-confident. Placing excessively high standards on children, trying to achieve one's own ambitions or dreams through one's children, or suggesting that individual failures doom one to a dissatisfying life may lead to one's ability to perform satisfactorily and to related feelings of inadequacy or low esteem.

Parents also serve as *role models* for their children. They have opportunities to present both positive and negative models for children to learn. People learn best through the observation and imitation of others. For instance, many educators point to mentors or former teachers they have had as the explanation for their own teaching style rather than the extensive curricula of teacher training and methods courses.

Similarly, children learn how to be parents and how to behave from their own parents. Parents sometimes mistakenly believe that they can teach their children to "do as I say, not as I do." Unfortunately, the alcohol-abusing parent often has children who use drugs or alcohol to excess; the teenage mother finds her own teenage daughter pregnant; and the abusive father frequently lives to see his own sons verbally or physically abuse their children. Harry Chapin's song "Cat's in the Cradle," with its familiar refrain "My boy is just like me," illustrates this point.

A caveat should be offered at this point. All children do not model their parents completely. If you have a parent who is alcoholic, sexually abusive, or dysfunctional in some other way, you should not assume that you are doomed to similar behavior. Indeed, a study of famous people determined that fewer than 15 percent of them came from loving and supportive families.[29] Your parents may serve as negative examples or one parent or another significant adult may serve as a positive role model.

A *stimulating and responsive environment* is essential if children are to develop in a healthy manner. How can parents create such an environment? Parents' communication must include sensitive listening and empathic understanding. Parents must provide feedback or appropriate responses to children's questions and their statements. Parents must listen not only to children's comments, but also try to decipher the intent of their remarks. For instance, when the preschooler who attends a day-care center states that she does not like the new male teacher in her classroom, the parents must be careful to discern if the child's dislike is based on more trivial matters or on a significant problem. The child may be responding to sex-role stereotypes that suggest that adult men seem out of place in the preschool classroom or she may be an early victim of sexual, physical, or verbal abuse.

■ Parental Development Stages

Chapters 6, 7, 8, and 9 trace the developmental stages of the family from the meeting couple through the final stages. Some of these stages are based on the age of the children in the family. We know that children develop through various stages. The researcher Galinsky argues that parents similarly go through developmental stages as their children grow and develop. She writes of her then 2-year-old son:

> He was figuring out how to be the child in our family. I was figuring out how to be the adult. . . . Now as a parent, I was learning it all over again. He was going through something. So was I.[30]

The six stages of parenthood that Galinsky identifies are the image-making stage, the nurturing stage, the authority stage, the interpretive stage, the interdependent stage, and the departure stage. The *image-making stage* occurs while the couple is expecting the baby and ends with the birth. Based on previous memories as well as the current circumstances and culture, parents rehearse parenting by imagining themselves in the parenting role.

The *nurturing stage* begins with the baby's birth. The previous images the parents held must be brought into line with the reality of their situation. During this period of time, the baby and the parents form a bond. The feelings of attachment result in questions including whether the child is actually that of the parents, if the parents will be able to care for the child, and who the baby is as well as who the parents are. Relationships between the parents and their own parents (the baby's grandparents) often change. Similarly, relationships with other relatives and friends are altered.

The *authority stage* occurs in response to the child's increasing exploration and managing of his or her world. The child begins to use language and to communicate with others. He or she becomes increasingly mobile and expands his or her abilities. Parents recognize that they must limit some of the child's behavior for safety and for the proper development of the child. Galinsky notes that parents must recognize that some images are illusory, including the image of never feeling anger, the image that parents can provide unconditional love, the image that they are different from their own parents, the image that children are always nice and always do the right thing, and the image that the child will remain the same over time.[31]

The *interpretive stage* may begin at different times, but generally the entrance to school marks the beginning of this stage. The child is becoming increasingly independent and begins to leave the family home by himself or herself. Galinsky explains the parents' role in this stage:

Their major task is to interpret the world to their children, and that entails not only interpreting themselves to their children and interpreting and developing their children's self-concepts, but also answering their questions, providing them access to the skills and information they need, and helping them form values. As such, parents also continue to define the separateness/connectedness of their relationships and to figure out how involved they want to be in their children's lives.[32]

Parents' interpretations are based on their images, comparisons with others, the judgments of others, and their children's self-evaluations.

The *interdependent stage* begins when children reach the teenage years. Adolescence is a difficult period for many parents. Parents have less control over the child than they had in the past. Nonetheless, parents must set limits and provide guidance to the child. They must understand themselves as well as understand their teenager. They must accept the teenager's identity, which may be very different form their own identity. New bonds are formed with a person who is almost an adult.

The *departure stage* begins as the parents contemplate their child's leaving the home. Galinsky writes:

> Parents take stock of the whole experience of parenthood. They have the related tasks of preparing for the departure, then adjusting their images of this event with what actually happens, redefining their identities as parents with grown-up children, and measuring out their accomplishments and failures.[33]

During this stage, parents often spend more time reflecting back on the past and projecting ahead to the future than considering the present. Parents must prepare for the child's eventual departure and then adapt to it. They must loosen their control over their child since he or she, as an adult, must have a separate identity. Galinsky's stages of parenthood are additive to our understanding of the role of adding a child to the family unit. Let us consider next the changes in the interactional group that occur when a baby is added.

■ Changes in the Interactional Group

Children change the nature of the family unit in many ways. Indeed, some couples do not believe that they are a family until they have a child. For the first time, subgroups of two people can form and exclude a third family member. Before the baby was born, the interacting unit included only the husband and the wife. Now four interacting units are possible:

1. The husband and wife

2. The husband and child

3. The wife and child

4. The husband, wife, and child

Figure 7.1

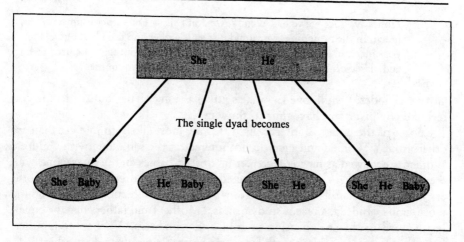

Adding a child to the family unit changes the number of interacting dyads from one to four.

This distinction is illustrated in Figure 7.1. This is one situation in which 2 + 1 = 4. Thus communication becomes more complex simply because additional interacting groups are possible.

The new father describes his interaction patterns with his wife and 3-month-old daughter:

> Now that we have Allison, quite a bit of our attention and communication focuses on her. Janice and I find ourselves having to make a special effort to find time to have meaningful talks together. Because we're having to put more effort into communicating with each other, these times seem to be more meaningful than when we were always together.
>
> When I enter a room where Allison and Janice are, it is natural to respond to Allison and play with her. However, I've learned to try and give equal time to Janice. During these times I try to make a special effort to communicate specifically with Janice rather than just acknowledge her presence. It's so easy to have Allison be the center of attention; therefore, Janice and I need to continue to meet each other's needs and communicate specifically with each other.[34]

Another couple, Lyntha and Cory, have been married for five years and they have a 2-year-old child, Wendy. Cory reports that they have to limit a lot of their conversations to night time:

> Before we go to sleep. . . . That's the best conversation we have. In fact, there are times when I'm not sleepy and I'll want to talk and we'll go to bed. There are no distractions: no TV, no telephone, and no Wendy. We just lie in the darkness. It's a good time to talk.[35]

Lyntha is not quite so positive as she adds:

> Honestly, since we've had Wendy, we don't show each other intimacy very much. In the beginning, we would just sit together and hold her, but as she got older and more demanding, we've gotten away from that. We used to hug and kiss a lot. Now I'm too tired, she takes so much out of me.[36]

Cory concludes, "I still love Lyntha as much as I ever have, but the fact is you feel like you just don't have time to show it."[37]

Some of the potential interacting dyads are more likely to interact than are other groups. Women and men do not interact at the same rate with children. Women are viewed as having a greater interest in babies and in interacting with them more.[38] Fathers have not interacted with their children as much as mothers have, but as family types change, we may see interaction time becoming more similar. Indeed, a recent study claims, "Mothers and fathers may be equally involved in the socialization of sons and daughters."[39] In some families, fathers may interact with their children to a greater extent than do mothers.

Both mothers and fathers adjust their interaction with their children when both parents are present rather than just themselves and their child. For example, when the father is present in the hospital room, the mother interacts less with the infant than when she is alone with the infant.[40] Similarly, Belsky demonstrated that both parents interact with the infant less when the other parent is present than when they are alone with the infant.[41] Most of these differences in interactional rates are accounted for by spousal communication. The couple communicates with each other rather than with the infant.

While we may assume that the parents are responsible for differences in interaction among the subgroups in the family, even the child exerts an influence on interaction in dyadic (two-person) versus triadic (three-person) group settings. Infants adapt their behavior to the size of the group.[42] Toddlers are more likely to move toward, to show or offer things to do, and to vocalize to each parent when only one is present rather than when both are present.[43] The child's behavior accommodates the parents' needs to communicate with each other as well as with the child.

The formation of subgroups or coalitions may be an accidental, rather than a planned, feature of the family. The husband may have a difficult time focusing on two people simultaneously and find that he prefers to interact with just the child or just his wife, but not both at once. The wife, particularly if she is the primary caretaker of the child, may find that her relationship with the child is closer than the husband's relationship with the child. Such alterations can create tension, stress, and fear of rejection for all of the family members.

■ Other Major Changes

Many people view parenting as an idyllic time in which the couple truly becomes a family with the advent of an infant to call their own. The birth of a baby is a miracle and the beauty, poetry, and romance of the occasion should not be ignored. At the same time, it is essential for people contemplating parenthood to be aware of some of the documented, behavioral, day-to-day changes that occur that might impact on their lives in a negative way.

The new father who described the recent pregnancy of his wife discussed the changes that occurred when his daughter arrived:

> Undoubtedly, our lives changed when our daughter finally arrived. Spontaneity decreased dramatically. We now had to consider a third person in all we did. Plus, that third person was totally dependent on us. When it was just Janice and I we would do almost everything together outside of work. When shopping needed to be done we both went. When we washed the cars we did it together. When we wanted to get an ice cream cone on the spur of the moment, we did it. But now that Allison is here, these simple things we once did together suddenly become complicated. We have to plan out when we're going shopping. Will Allison stay with one of us or will she go with the person buying the groceries? Will she stay asleep or will she wake up and start crying in the middle of the store? When Janice needs some personal time to get her hair done, shop, just take a break, etc., we have to plan for me to stay home with Allison.[44]

What factors are particularly problematic for people becoming parents? A recent study suggests that both mothers are fathers are distressed by the inconvenience of parenting and the lack of privacy in the home. Fathers are also pressured by financial stress. The size of the family and the developmental stage of the family seem to affect mothers more than they affect fathers in feelings of parenting difficulty.[45]

Adding children to the family unit increases the family's needs for such resources as money, time, and energy. Estimates on raising a child vary, but most sources suggest that at least $700,000 is required to raise a child from birth through college. Of even greater importance, particularly for today's busy working couple, are the needs for time and energy. Many young couples feel they are already operating at their limits when the new baby arrives. The addition of a child increases the demands on both husband and wife.

When a couple has a child, they generally retain all of their former roles and add the roles of mother and father. This additional role may be burdensome or confusing, particularly if each member of the couple is already playing a variety of roles both at home and at work. In addition, parenthood may encourage more traditional sex-linked behavior. The young female professional may feel role confusion as she must incorporate traditional parenting into her repertoire. The sensitive and flexible male may be uncertain about his new role as the less involved father.

The role responsibilities for both parents are overwhelming. They are most traumatic for the mother if she provides the majority of nurturing, and most mothers still do. New mothers report that they experience role conflict with new parenthood in four domains: work, social life, marriage, and housekeeping.[46] Mothers find that parenting conflicts with their work, their social life, their time with their spouse, and their housework.

Confusion about roles is exacerbated by the changes in sex roles that occur when couples become parents. Systematic changes in one's sex roles occur with developmental changes in the family. Masculine and feminine roles are most discrepant in the stage of the family cycle after the first child is born. The first child creates major role upheaval[47] and polarizes the sex roles in the family.[48] The demands of parenthood may be primarily responsible for traditional sex-role behavior in younger adults while the end of parental responsibility shifts such behavior.[49]

We observed that women interact more with babies than do men. The researchers Feldman and Nash have examined the interactions of women and men with babies and have determined that sex differences do occur in early parenthood and early grandparenthood, but that college students who are not parents do not exhibit sex differences. They suggest that early parenthood and early grandparenthood might include certain demand characteristics for sex-linked behavior.[50] Women and men may feel it is more appropriate to behave in a traditional sex-linked way as parents and grandparents, but may not feel similar constraints at other periods of their lives. Expected role behavior might thus alter our behavior.

One study, however, found results that dispute, to some extent, the notion advanced by Feldman and Nash that interest in babies and interaction with them fluctuates during the adult years as one's circumstances change. Sex differences among nonparent college students were determined. In addition, feminist and traditional female and male college students were compared and no differences were found between the students' attitudes (feminist or non-feminist) and their behavior toward a baby, but sex differences were found.[51] Women interacted with the baby more than men did.[52]

These somewhat discrepant findings can be summarized. Women probably interact more with babies than do men in general. This difference might be even more marked at a time when traditional sex-linked behavior is salient. For instance, parents or grandparents of new babies may be more likely to exhibit sex differences in their behavior toward the child. This conclusion is relevant for our understanding of changes that occur as a family moves from a couple to a family that includes a child.

Marital satisfaction also changes when the couple has a child. The transition to parenthood appears to be particularly traumatic for marital satisfaction.[53] Lowered satisfaction during the child-rearing period may occur because of the large number of different roles a person is to play.[54] Another explanation may be the couple's relatively lower income and high job pressure at this stage. Both of these explanations gain support in examinations of dual-career couples. Stress and conflict are even higher at this stage if the couple is in a dual-career marriage rather than a traditional marriage.[55] Parenthood presents greater problems for the wife than the husband.[56] Finally, couples who recall their own parents having a dissatisfying marital relationship and who were reared in a cold and rejecting home rather than a warm and supportive home tend to disagree more over time about their own marital satisfaction.[57]

The motivations for having a child are many. Both conscious and unconscious reasons contribute to the decision to become pregnant and produce offspring. In addition, many people become parents by accident. The addition of a child to a family is often romanticized; people considering becoming parents must also be aware of the personal, social, and economic costs.

■ Coping with the Changes

Parents can cope with family changes. The specific coping strategies chosen will affect one's coping effectiveness.[58] Coping effectiveness may also be influenced by personality and situational variables. For example, one's self-esteem and one's interest in a career may affect how well one can cope with multiple roles and changes that occur as a result of adding a child to the family.[59] Most research on coping strategies has focused on working mothers. However, you may be able to generalize these findings to working fathers or to homemaking mothers.

Younger and older working mothers use different strategies to cope with their situations. Younger working mothers tend to use a strategy that involves increasing their role behavior.[60] In other words, they try to work more efficiently, plan their time more carefully, and generally try to fit all of their demands into their day. Older working mothers tend to redefine their structural role or they redefine their personal role. By redefining their structural role, they may bargain with their employer for time to do parenting during normal work hours; they may arrange for additional child care; they may negotiate schedules with their spouses; or they may work on a flex-time basis. They may choose between their two major roles or they may change either their career or parenting aspirations. These coping strategies are probably realistic given the differences in the realities of the younger and older women's work worlds.[61]

Four specific strategies, which overlap somewhat with the strategies we have been discussing, have been developed that assist women in coping with the role strain they experience in parenting. First is a favorable definition of the situation that includes an absence of guilt and the belief that conflicts can be overcome. Second is the establishment of a salient role, which means that a woman must decide which role she will typically enact when two roles conflict. She may determine that her parenting comes first or that another role is most salient for her.

Third is compartmentalization, which involves the ability to separate the roles and to forget one while enacting another. For example, women are encouraged not to worry about work when they are with their children, and not to worry about their children when they are at work. Fourth is a compromise of standards, which means that a woman should judge herself less harshly in any of the multiple roles in which she is engaged. She does not have to be a "superwoman" at work, with the children, with her housework, with her husband, and in social settings.[62]

Both women and men need assistance in coping with the multiple roles required by family and work relationships. The strategies outlined here may be useful starting points in developing one's own coping mechanisms. In addition, it may be refreshing for the person struggling with both personal and professional obligations to simply recognize that an increasing number of people have similar situations and must learn to adjust to a continually changing world.

❖ FAMILIES WITH PRESCHOOL CHILDREN

We may divide families with children into three groups: families with preschool children (families in which the oldest child is between 3 and 6 years of age and he or she may have younger siblings); families with school-age children (the children range in age from birth to 12 years old); and families with adolescent children (the oldest child ranges in age from 13 to 19 and younger siblings may be present). Although many families cut across these boundaries, particularly the blended family in which children may range in age from birth to their 20s or 30s, these groups will be useful as we distinguish among special features of families in each stage of development.

Families with preschool children may have children that range in age from birth to 6 years of age. In addition, the parents in this stage may range from teenagers to couples in their late 30s and early 40s. The tendency for women to marry older men added to the increased number of blended families that exist in the United States today means that some fathers may be in midlife or retirement.

What is the effect of the age of parents on their children? We will consider some aspects of middle-aged and older couples in the next two chapters and you will be able to infer information about individuals in these age groups as you read that material. For example, you will find that people tend to reverse their sex roles as they get older; this means that men become more nurturing, empathic, and sensitive and women become increasingly independent and task-oriented. You might infer that fathers in their middle or later years may thus be more involved with their children than they were in their younger years when their sex role was more traditionally oriented and when their career aspirations may have been more salient. Older mothers may be more interested in their careers than parenthood. Since parenting in one's middle or retirement years is relatively rare, we will not provide a thorough description here. However, we will consider the differences in parenting between teenagers and older parents since childbearing in one's teenage years still occurs at historically high levels.[63]

More teenage mothers are keeping their children today than in the past.[64] In general, children born to teenage mothers suffer from behavioral, social, intellectual, and even physical deficits compared to children born of older mothers (mothers who are at least 20 years old when they deliver their first child).[65] The retarded development of these children is primarily a function of lower socioeconomic status.[66] Teenage mothers and their children often live in the mother's parental home, in conditions that are more crowded, and with less financial security than older mothers and their children.

Teenage mothers not only provide a less optimal home environment for their children, they also provide less verbal stimulation, and less responsiveness to their children than do older mothers.[67] Teenage mothers tend to be less educated than are older mothers, may have less knowledge about child care and individual developmental states, and may have less positive attitudes toward parenting.[68]

Studies that have compared teenagers with older parents have generalized about the two groups. However, great diversity exists among teenage mothers and these differences should be examined. Two researchers speculate that identifying differences in the parenting of teenage mothers may lead to predictions about competent, as opposed to less competent, parenting among teenage mothers.[69] Furthermore, such a discovery may suggest educational experiences that would assist the young mother in providing quality care and in promoting a positive attitude toward parenting.

Our consideration of family developmental stages is primarily based on the age of the children rather than the age of the parents, however. As we consider families with preschool children, we are considering families with parents of a variety of ages who have children that range from birth to 6 years of age. We will begin our consideration of these families with the infant and move through some relevant material on children as they develop from birth to school age.

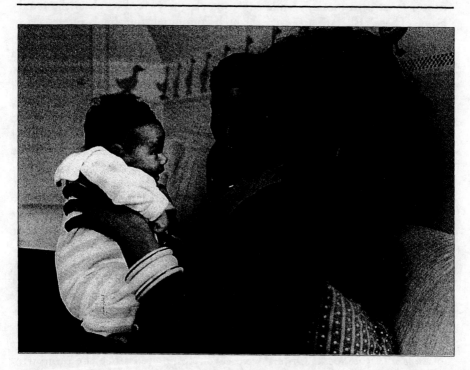

The infant's communicative development is affected by interaction with parents and significant others (© Crews, Stock, Boston).

■ Infancy

In order to understand the communication behaviors of families with children and with the development of communication in children, we must first review symbolic interactionism. This theory originated in sociology. The originator of work on symbolic interactionism was George Herbert Mead, whose theory included three essential components: society, self, and mind. Mead did not view these three as separate categories, but as different aspects of the same general process, which he labeled the social act.

Society was defined as a "cluster of cooperative behaviors on the part of society's members."[70] Mead believed that in order for humans to cooperate with each other, they must understand the intentions of others. He further contended that in order to explain and understand these intentions, symbols are necessary. Symbols include both words and nonverbal cues such as pointing to oneself or smiling. The symbols that are provided are interpreted by receivers. In this way, society is composed of cooperative, symbol-using interactions. Society is not defined as people, but their symbolic interactions. People communicate in order to understand each others' intentions, which is a prerequisite for cooperation.

Applying the idea of "society" to a family, family members must cooperate in order to fulfill their needs. For instance, someone must prepare food, others must earn money, while someone else may need to clean the family home. These tasks are achieved through communicating one's intentions to the other family members through verbal and nonverbal symbols. Nonverbally, an older child demonstrates her willingness to cook by making a meal. The marital couple may discuss their common interests in working to provide sufficient income for the family. Another person is assigned the task of housekeeping.

Implicit to Mead's notion of *self* was the idea that people could act toward their "selfs" just as they could behave toward others. People could like their "selfs," dislike their "selfs," or have other perspectives about how they viewed themselves. How do we come to see ourselves in a certain way?

Mead theorized that individuals move through stages of self-development. These included the *play stage,* in which children play the roles of significant others in their world (parents, *postal carrier*, siblings, teacher). During the *game stage* an individual responds in a generalized and simultaneous way to the expectations of those around him or her. The individual develops a composite role of all others' definitions of self. This generalized other is the vantage point from which one views the self. It is, in effect, our perception of the overall, holistic way that others see us. Our understanding of who we are occurs through our symbolic exchanges with others. Communication, therefore, allows one to gain a sense of self.

C. H. Cooley also contributed to these ideas in his seminal book *Human Nature and the Social Order.*[71] Research completed since the pioneering efforts of Mead and Cooley has identified parents and peers as significant others in one's development of self.[72] Both of these groups contribute to a child's self-esteem, or conception of worthiness. The importance of either parents or peers varies over time and situations. During some developmental ages, parents are more important; later, peers might replace parents as significant others. Teachers, siblings, and role models from sports, television, and other fields can also serve in these roles.

Children learn who they are from a variety of people significant in their environment. The family members and others can sometimes place limitations on the children by labeling them in particular ways. An example from *Her Mother's Daughter* illustrates this idea. Marilyn French, the author, explains Joy's perceptions (Joy is Anastasia's younger sister):

> Anastasia says Mother thinks Joy is pretty and popular and Anastasia is smart and talented. Joy knows this is what Mother thinks. And Anastasia said Mother had made her believe that she was ugly, and Joy that she was stupid. And she said it wasn't true, that Joy was really smart. Anastasia was mad at Mother for making them think that. But Joy feels that Anastasia was mad at Mother for making her feel ugly, but not for making Joy think she was stupid because Anastasia thinks Joy is stupid too. She just had to say that to be polite.[73]

Mead divides the self into two components. The "I" is the unorganized, unguided, impulsive part of the person. It is the part of you that would prefer to be eating pizza, drinking beer, or be out dancing rather than reading a textbook. The "me" is the generalized other, is made up of consistent patterns held in common with others, and is a more organized way of viewing oneself. The "me" keeps you studying when you would rather be doing almost anything else. Mead suggests that every act begins with the "I" and is moderated quickly by the "me." For instance, a married person who is monogamous may notice attractive and interesting people of the opposite sex, but hastily recalls his or her marital state and does not initiate a romantic encounter. He states that the "I" is the force that moves one to act, and that the "me" provides necessary guidance and direction.

The final component of Mead's model is the *mind*, which he defines as "the process of interacting with oneself."[74] Mead's definition of the mind is similar to *intrapersonal communication*, or interaction within an individual. Mead suggests that we "mind" when we hesitate to consciously assign some meaning to a particular stimulus. "Minding" generally occurs when individuals find themselves in a problem situation in which they must consider future actions. The individual considers various outcomes, selects and tests possible alternatives, and makes a decision among the alternatives. Suppose a person is considering terminating his marriage. He might consider possible alternatives. For instance, he may think about other people to whom he could be married. He might also consider being single. He may imagine how his wife would fare if she were no longer married to him and how his children would react to his leaving the family unit. Based on this "minding," he makes a decision to stay or to leave.

As people develop, they are better able to engage in "minding." Annie Dillard discusses the exhilaration of this developmental process in her book,

An American Childhood:

> Who could ever tire of this heart-stopping transition, of this breakthrough shift between seeing and knowing you see, between being and knowing you be? It drives you to a life of concentration, it does, a life in which effort draws you down so very deep that when you surface you twist up exhilarated with a yelp and a gasp.
>   Who could ever tire of this radiant transition, this surfacing to awareness and this deliberate plunging to oblivion—the theater curtain rising and falling? Who could tire of it when the sum of those moments at the edge—the conscious life we so dread losing—is all we have, the gift at the moment of opening it?[75]

The notion of mind is essential to symbolic interactionism because it illustrates that people are actors, not reactors, which is a basic tenet of this theory. Symbolic interactionism views people as actors having the freedom to make choices and decisions. When people are viewed as reactors, they merely respond to events beyond their control.

In summary, Mead views people as beings capable of rational thoughts. He feels that through role taking, we become objects unto ourselves. In other words, we come to see ourselves as others see us. We internalize the generalized self-view and we behave in a manner which is consistent with it. "Minding" allows us to rehearse symbolic behavior for our interactions with others. Symbolic interactionism is important in family studies because it suggests that parents and significant others impact upon children's definitions of themselves.

Figure 7.2

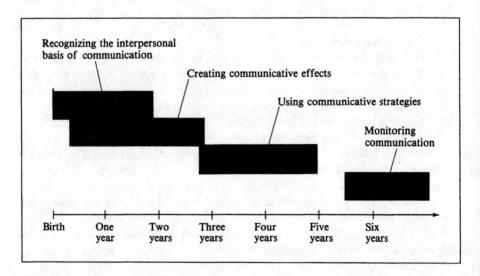

Time line of children's pragmatic communication development.

Communication Development The communication development of children has been widely studied and researchers have identified the developmental ages of many communicative abilities.[76] Communication researcher Beth Haslett summarized the research in this area and showed that children develop pragmatic communication and social knowledge about communication. Four stages are involved in pragmatic communication skills. They include recognizing the interpersonal basis of communication, creating communicative effects, using communicative strategies, and monitoring communication. The first stage extends from birth to about 2 years of age. The second stage begins at about 4 months and extends to 3 years. The third stage begins at about age 3 and ends at about age 5. The fourth stage begins when the child is around 5 years old and continues to middle childhood.[77] These stages are depicted on the time line in Figure 7.2. We will consider the first two stages in this section and the second two in the section on preschool children. We will similarly consider the development of social knowledge about communication in the section on preschool-age children.

Beth Haslett explains that people recognize the interpersonal basis of communication when they demonstrate a motivation to communicate.[78] Shortly after birth, exchanges begin to occur between the infant and the caregiver. By 9 months, the infant shows evidence of conceiving of others as "having interests, purposes, and helpful powers."[79] Nonlinguistic communication may help us to understand language acquisition. When the infant is 15 months of age, symbols are used to represent objects.[80]

The second stage, creating communicative effects, includes three substages according to Haslett's classification. *Preverbal routines* include a variety of routinized social exchanges. Infants learn about turn-taking through feeding, bathing, and playing games. *Communicative intentionality* occurs when a communicator considers before the sending of a message the likely effect it will have on a listener. Infants use the sounds that they can make to elicit food, cuddling, and more comfortable surroundings. After some experimentation, the infant begins to use particular cries to gain particular ends. *Linguistic communication* includes single words as well as phrases.[81] Children from 2 to 4 years of age understand both direct and indirect speech acts,[82] and they use both direct and indirect requests for action between the ages of 3 and 5.[83]

Infant–Caregiver Interaction The role of the caregiver in the development of communication is established. Laura Stafford observes that the most important variable in the learning of language is "the adult who acts as a guide in the language learning process."[84] Researchers have demonstrated that adults use unique communication patterns with children. These patterns, which include short sentences, simple syntax, clear enunciation, and few grammatical errors, have been termed "motherese," reflecting the traditional, primary role of mothers in teaching language to children.[85]

Because of their traditional importance, mothers have been specifically studied to determine their role in interaction. Mothers use routinized games and other traditional formats to encourage their infants to acquire language.[86]

Many researchers have observed the turn-taking or dialogue-like nature of mother–infant interaction.[87] Turn-taking in preverbal interaction may be essential to language development.[88]

Adults can enhance infant language development by being responsive and by encouraging the infant to interact. Infants of responsive mothers develop language more quickly than do infants of unresponsive mothers.[89] Laura Stafford found that mothers use five strategies in encouraging their infants to take their turn: questions, tag questions, repetition, upward intonation, and eye gaze.[90]

These interactional strategies may be useful in increasing the infant's communicative competence. However, we must remember that infants, like their caregivers, are human persons who may have their own agendas in interaction. As active agents of discourse, they cannot be viewed as robots that will respond in an absolutely predictable way to specific stimuli.[91] Julie Yingling, a professor of communication, observes that "Infants are now viewed as competent—although physically dependent, communicatively adept."[92]

Although most studies have focused on mother–infant interaction rather than father–infant interaction, fathers are increasingly serving as primary caretakers of their infants.[93] Parents who have exchanged the traditional nurturing role have been described as better educated, with more prestigious occupations (particularly the mothers), and with fewer children. The fathers tend to be androgynous (they hold instrumental characteristics such as independence, assertiveness, and self-confidence and expressive characteristics such as warmth, sensitivity, and empathy). Both parents placed less importance on conformity to social norms and more emphasis on interpersonal sensitivity, expressiveness, and independence. Both choice (the mother was strongly committed to her career; the couple held egalitarian beliefs) and economic necessity (the father had no job, but the mother did) were offered as reasons for entering this nontraditional arrangement. Couples who adopt a traditional arrangement are likely to consist of fathers who value work more than parenthood as compared to their wives. Couples who adopt a nontraditional arrangement are likely to be just the opposite, as the wives value work more than parenthood as compared to their husbands.[94]

What similarities and what differences exist in the behaviors of mothers and fathers with their infants? The behaviors of mothers and fathers may be more similar than different.[95] Both parents may be equally adept at providing the security that inhibits distress over separation from another attachment figure.[96] Children protest their mother's and their father's leaving almost equally.[97] Between the period of birth and 3 months of age, some of the parents' behavior with their infant converges.[98] Apparently, each parent adopts some of his or her partner's behaviors.

What differences occur? Mothers verbalize and smile more than fathers.[99] Mothers are more likely to engage in social play while fathers are more likely to engage in play that includes a great deal of movement and vigorous action.[100] Mothers tend to be more verbal and didactic, or instructive, in their play while fathers are more physical and arousing.[101] Mothers are more likely to hold their infants in routine care while fathers are more likely to hold their infants in play.[102]

MARVIN reprinted with special permission of NAS, Inc.

■ Preschool Age

As children move from infancy to preschool age, they become increasingly independent, which places less pressure on the parents and less stress on the family unit. Children who range in age from 3 to 6 years of age are able to fulfill many personal needs. They can generally dress themselves, feed themselves, and take care of personal needs such as going to the bathroom.

Communication Development Preschool children continue to become increasingly competent in their communicative abilities. Three- to 6-year-old children have an increasing vocabulary, which allows them to communicate their needs to others. Children use single words at first, which are replaced with simple, two-word sentences between 18 and 24 months of age. By the time children are 2 years old, they usually have a vocabulary of about 300 words. The increase in the next year is great; typical 3-year-old children can use or understand approximately 1000 words. During the next two years, they add about 50 words to their vocabularies every month.[103] Many humorous stories are shared about children who have gained an inaccurate or limited understanding of a new word in their working vocabulary. The infant in "Marvin" provides an example.

Preschool-age children move through Haslett's third and fourth stages of pragmatic development.[104] As you will recall, the third stage extends from 3 to 5 years of age and involves using communicative strategies. The fourth stage, monitoring communication, begins when the child is around 5 years old and continues to middle childhood.

Using communicative strategies allows children to engage in enduring conversations. Children in this stage begin to use reasoning and arguments[105] and they engage in role playing with their peers.[106] They adapt their messages to others[107] and they adapt noncontent aspects of their speech (vocal behaviors that regulate the intensity, duration, timing, tempo, and the quality of communication in interpersonal interactions) to adults.[108] Children develop prepared and well-learned sequences with which to interact.[109] They learn how to provide reasons, a type of interpersonal persuasion, between early and middle childhood.[110]

The fourth stage of pragmatic development is monitoring communication. Beth Haslett summarizes the research on the monitoring of communication by children:

> Children begin to evaluate message adequacy, to alter messages when needed, to adapt their messages when conflict with others' goals are recognized, to discuss the communication process explicitly, and to utilize knowledge of others in constructing their communicative strategies. . . . Through monitoring communication, children become increasingly adept at sending socially appropriate messages in a variety of contexts.[111]

An example of the development of monitoring communication was shown by two researchers. They found that third-grade listeners who were asked to perform a task were more likely to ask for additional information than were kindergarten listeners. Similarly, third-grade speakers were more likely than kindergarten speakers to provide additional and new information in response to these requests. This process extends from about 5 years of age until middle childhood.[112]

Children's social knowledge about communication develops in three general stages, according to Haslett's taxonomy. The first stage involves the child distinguishing between self and others. The stage begins during the first year and extends through early childhood. Barbara O'Keefe and Jesse Delia have shown that 5-year-old children have internalized ideas of the interpersonal characteristics of others.[113]

Knowledge of others, a second stage, develops at the same time as the third stage, knowledge of social context. These stages begin in the preschool age but continue to develop through middle childhood. Interaction is more effective when we understand that other communicators are independent persons with unique characteristics. Children respond differentially to other children with whom they interact, based on the children's relative ages.[114] When older children interact with younger friends, they provide instruction and engage in leadership behavior. They may also engage in some types of prosocial behavior, such as helping and nurturance, which will not occur as frequently with children their own age. When they interact with children of approximately the same age, they rely upon behaviors that show fairness and morality.

Similarly, it is more appropriate when we acknowledge both the social relationships and the social situations in which we are involved, which together form the social context. Children develop an understanding of both the feelings and intentions of other family members and they begin to understand the social rules within the family as early as between 18 months and 2 years of age.[115]

Parents can enhance their children's communicative development in a variety of ways. Most parents spend very little time interacting with their children, but those who spend more time have the greatest impact on their development. A child's self-confidence can be increased when the parent practices active listening and clear verbal feedback. Similarly, the child's self-worth may be enhanced by offering him or her problem-solving opportunities and praise for the child's suggestions. Parents are encouraged to discuss the child's daily activities and to focus on positive aspects of the child's behavior.[116] A recent study demonstrated the potential value of engaging in activities such as sharing past photographs and collections of family snapshots.[117] Although interaction with children is not always possible, the benefits are evident.

Mass Media Consumption Preschool-age children typically cannot read, but they do consume mass media through television viewing. Some researchers have suggested that television viewing is a social event that family members use as a focal point for interaction.[118] The programs that children view change as the child matures and develops; however, the amount of viewing remains relatively stable from ages 2 to 12.[119] The children of working mothers view television less than do the children of homemaking mothers.[120]

Children's abilities to understand and organize programs on television are related to family rules governing the use and control of television viewing.[121] Children who are in homes in which low viewing, family control of television, and positive communication with the mother are present are better able to comprehend television programs than are children who watch a great deal of television, who have parents who demonstrate little control over the programs the children watch, and who use psychological methods of discipline such as love withdrawal.

Problems may surround the television viewing of children. For example, television programs such as "The Cosby Show" and "Growing Pains" were examined for their realistic portrayal of family life. Mary Strom Larson, a professor of communication at Northern Illinois University, determined that such programs were unrealistic.[122] Children who view such popular programs may have a distorted view of family life or may evaluate their own families as less positive because of the idealistic depiction of the family.

Other recent technological advancements may similarly be used for good or ill. For example, while VCR units currently augment and extend the opportunities family have to view television, they can also lead to family conflict.[123] Each family needs to assess the role of mass media within its own framework.

Understanding of Values, Attitudes, and Beliefs Children begin to demonstrate the lessons of their socialization during this period. They may demonstrate an understanding of cultural values or the family's attitudes or beliefs. Children frequently ask questions about a supreme being during this period. Rebekah, a 5-year-old girl, went fishing with her father one evening. She looked in wonder at the large lake and surrounding green hills. Finally, she turned to her dad and asked, "Mom said God is everywhere; where is He *really*?" Children also come to have rudimentary understandings of such values as honesty and fairness.

Development of Self-Esteem Although the developing child's self-esteem begins forming before the preschool age and continues after the preschool age, interaction with the parents is critical during this time. Family therapist

Virginia Satir asserts that children do not develop positive esteem unless at least one of the parents provides validation of his or her growth.[124] Validation by either mothers or fathers results in enhanced self-esteem. The parental support of children seems to have an even greater effect for female children than for male children.[125]

Parents can provide validation to their children by being aware of changes within each child, by communicating their awareness of it to the child, and by allowing the child additional opportunities to demonstrate their newly learned behaviors. Parents should hold reasonable expectations for a child's behavior and not expect older children to behave as younger ones nor younger children to act like their older siblings.

At the same time, parents are not expected to accept all behavior in an uncritical or approving manner. They must provide rules, restrictions, and guidelines for the child's behavior. They must help the child to recognize that other people are in the world with them and must be taken into consideration. The child must understand the importance of the situation and circumstances in determining appropriate behavior.

Virginia Satir concludes:

> If parents consistently show that they consider their child a masterful, sexual person, and if they also demonstrate a gratifying, functional male–female relationship, the child acquires self-esteem and becomes increasingly independent of his parents. . . . The close relationship between parental validation, self-esteem, independence, and uniqueness shows up when one observes how a dysfunctional person (an unvalidated child who is now an adult) still clings to his parents, or substitute parent figures, or relates to his sexual partner as if that partner were, in fact, a parent.[126]

The importance of parent–child communication is evident in the development of a healthy sense of self.

Development of Sex Roles   Related to one's self-esteem is one's conception of self as a male or female. Between the ages of 3 and 5 sex roles develop[127] and children sex type others.[128] Between the ages of 5 and 7 children develop gender constancy, or the ability to see themselves consistently as male or female.[129] The parent's, particularly the mother's, reinforcement of different sex-typed play positively affects gender constancy.[130]

Although children may not see play as a task, it does become a primary way that they learn about themselves, others, and their world. Play may promote children's language development as well as their social, intellectual, physical, and emotional development. Play is instrumental in the development of sex roles.

Most research on play and sex roles divides toys into masculine toys, feminine toys, and sex-neutral toys. Masculine toys include toys that encourage construction and manipulation, while feminine toys are strongly oriented to domestic pursuits.[131] Neutral toys include dress-up clothes, modeling compound, and kitchen equipment.[132] Children from 0 to 2 years of age show little sex-role preference for toys, but preschool-age children begin to select toys based on their biological sex.[133] While children may play with toys that are viewed as sex-role inappropriate, they are less likely to do so when they are playing with children of the opposite sex.[134] Boys show an earlier and stronger preference for sex-appropriate toys than do girls.[135]

Children's sex-role stereotypes are critical. They serve to organize information that children receive. They also affect their assumptions about sex-typed abilities. Finally, they influence their recall and recognition of both stereotyped and discrepant information.[136]

Development of Unique Characteristics The child in this age range may begin to develop his or her own characteristics, which may be distinctive from those of other family members. This is particularly true if the child attends a day-care center or is cared for by persons other than the biological parents. The "significant other" from whom children learn about themselves and their world was equated to one's biological parents in the past. Today one's significant other may be other relatives, friends, or day-care workers. As an increasing number of children are cared for in formal or informal arrangements, children may be developing in diverse emotional, intellectual, and physical ways.

❖ FAMILIES WITH SCHOOL-AGE CHILDREN

Increasing Independence When families move from early parenthood (when the oldest child is less than 3 years old), to becoming a family with preschool children, they experience less stress and tension. Similarly, as families move from the preschool age to the time when the oldest child is in school, a reduction of stress and tension is evident. This change is due to children's increasing independence and their increased skills and abilities. The child is gone for at least part of each day, during the school year, to an academic setting away from the home. Many mothers who felt obligated to stay home during the preschool years now return to work. Children can do more for themselves and may be helpful in accomplishing family work. For instance, many school-age children are able to come home alone after school and manage the house until their parents return. They may have jobs, which include cleaning their own room, setting the table, preparing simple meals, or caring for a pet.

School-age children are less dependent upon the family and they begin to make far more contacts with others. In school, children interact with both peers and adults. They may join clubs or organizations such as the YWCA, YMCA, Cub Scouts, Brownies, athletic teams, and play groups. The parents may enroll children in swimming, dancing, skiing, or skating lessons. Children may attend church, synagogue, or related child-oriented religious classes.

Children who did not attend a formal day-care center before kindergarten may now have a greater proportion of time with others than with the parents as compared to the preschool years. These outside influences may affect chil-

Figure 7.3

More accepting

| Parents are warm, affectionate, and loving. Parents are controlling and restricting. | Parents are warm, affectionate, and loving. Parents allow freedom and independent decisions. |
| Parents are aloof, hostile, and disapproving. Parents are controlling, and restricting. | Parents are aloof, hostile, and disapproving. Parents allow freedom and independent decisions. |

More controlling

Less controlling

Less accepting

Acceptance-control dimensions of parent–child interaction

dren's growth and development in a variety of ways. At the same time, the parents' interaction with the child continues to hold importance.

Parents who wish to encourage independence in their children as well as cooperation may wish to consider cooperative learning approaches within the family. A recent article suggests that parents consider participative rule making, planning special events, assisting with chores, and playing cooperative (rather than competitive) games.[137] School-age children need to learn both independent and cooperative behaviors. Although their peer group begins to gain in importance as they progress through school, parents remain as important role models for them.

Parent–Child Interaction   Two dimensions of parent–child interaction are especially relevant. The first dimension is represented by the parents' acceptance or rejection of the child and the second is the control–autonomy dimension. These dimensions are depicted in Figure 7.3.

The acceptance–rejection dimension suggests that parents can be warm, affectionate, and loving at one end of the continuum, or aloof, hostile, and disapproving at the other. Severe problems result for the child whose relationship with his or her parents is characterized by hostility. Among the problems that may result are poor self-esteem,[138] academic difficulties,[139] poor peer relationships,[140] poor health,[141] delinquency, and neurotic disorders.[142]

The child who is rejected is frequently aggressive toward his or her parents, as well as his peers and siblings, although such aggressiveness may be

FOR BETTER OR FOR WORSE reprinted by permission of Universal Press Syndicate copyright © 1987. All rights reserved.

unconscious.[143] An example of acceptance is provided in the cartoon, "For Better or For Worse."

The other dimension of parent–child interaction concerns the level of control that parents provide to their children. They may be high or low in the control of the child's behavior and the rules for behavior, and in their restriction of his or her development of autonomy and individuality. They may be highly controlling on one of these aspects and less controlling on the other. For instance, some parents have clear sets of standards for their children, but they allow them more leeway in developing as autonomous individuals. Or, the day-to-day rules may be fairly relaxed, but one parent, or both, allows the children to know that they "must" attend college, marry someone of a particular religious affiliation, participate in certain civic or social groups when they become adults, or engage in a specified profession. When parents do not allow their children the freedom to develop as independent people, the children often respond with dependent, infantile behavior. Furthermore, they have difficulty in identifying life goals and in forming positive relationships with peers.[144]

One young woman, who was the youngest child and the only girl in a family of three children, had a mother who was overly protective and who attempted to control her daughter's day-to-day behavior as well as her lifetime goals. At the age of 35, the daughter regularly received letters and phone calls from her mother in which the mother coerced the daughter into attending church, cutting her hair in a particular style, voting for a particular political candidate, and dating only men whom she found to be "acceptable." The daughter either complied with her mother's wishes or she avoided the topic. Not only were the interactions between the mother and daughter strained, but the daughter appeared to be a child at the age of 35. She continued to receive financial support from her parents, she attended college on an occasional basis, and she worked at part-time jobs. Although she had a small group of friends and dated a few men, her relationships with peers were generally shallow and short-lived.

On the other hand, John was the oldest child in a blended family. His parents both remarried when he was in the third grade. He lived with his mother and her husband until he was 13 and then asked to live with his father and his wife. John was allowed to move because both biological parents felt that he should have the final say in his place of residence. Both parents allowed John maximum freedom and were very flexible in their behavior toward him. Unfortunately, John interpreted his parents' behavior as a lack of interest. As a teenager, he experimented with alcohol and drugs. Although he was extremely bright, he barely graduated from high school. Now in his 20s, John works at dead-end jobs that allow him to quit when he is motivated to move to another part of the country. John has no plans to attend college, to marry, or to work toward any long-term goal. He allows whims to control his behavior.

Parents should find some middle ground between being overly controlling and being totally permissive. When parents provide excessive rules, their children become inhibited; when few rules exist, children may be overly impulsive. Furthermore, the rules for behavior should be carefully specified. The child's response, "I didn't know," may be an accurate reflection of his or her perceptions as well as a convenient way to sidestep responsibility for misbehavior. The positive benefits of conforming to necessary rules and the negative repercussions for violating the rules must be similarly clear to the child. Both rewards and costs must be clear, tangible, and immediate.

For example, one 7-year-old child had some problems staying dry at night. He sometimes drank too much before bedtime and at other times he simply did not exercise proper control. After ensuring that his problem was not physiological, his parents explained to him that wetting his bed occasionally was not a desirable behavior and that he would receive a small plastic farm animal each night that he stayed dry. The boy wet his bed only once during the entire next year. The rule was clear, the "reward" was motivating, and the behavior changed. Another child loved to draw, but she did not like to keep her room tidy. Her reward was a drawing pad or art materials on each Saturday that followed an entire week of a clean room.

Special problems with the dimension of control may occur in stepfamilies. One man, who came from a very strict family, wrestled with this issue as he attempted to help raise his stepchildren. He reported:

> Disciplining the kids sometimes gets very stressful. In the back of my head I can hear my father's voice and it is very strict and what he says goes. If I try that with Josh and Jen, though, I feel like they're going to say, "You're not my dad!" At the same time, I can't stand by and not get involved in the things that come up. I guess I am trying to be something between a friend and a dad to these kids. I want to get their respect and have them listen to me, yet I don't think I can do the things my dad did as far as disciplining them. It gets confusing.[145]

What does the literature suggest for parental communicative behavior? One implication is that supportive rather than evaluative messages may lead to lower levels of aggressiveness, fewer antisocial behaviors, greater independency, and higher self-esteem. Mary Anne Fitzpatrick and Diane Badzinski observe, "There is little doubt that making a child feel loved, supported, and comfortable in the presence of a parent leads to the development of a large range of socially valued behaviors in the child."[146] Another implication is that avoiding overly controlling communicative statements may lead to less aggression and to a higher level of internalization of moral standards in children. Children's social, intellectual, and even physical growth may be enhanced by parental messages that are marked by love, acceptance, and support; their growth in these same areas may be retarded by messages that are characterized as hostile, indifferent, evaluative, and overly controlling of the child's behavior or his independence.

We observed at the beginning of this section that the school-age child is influenced to an increasing extent by his or her peers and by adults outside the family. Thus far we have considered the role of the family in his or her development. Let us consider now the role of others on the school-age child.

Interaction with Others   The most important new adults in school-age children's lives are, of course, their teachers. The teachers' attitudes toward school, themselves, and children may greatly influence a child. Most elementary teachers are women and thus the atmosphere that pervades most elementary school buildings is a feminized one. In other words, children in the elementary school are likely to be encouraged to be compliant, quiet, responsive, empathic, and caring. Children who are boisterous, rowdy, loud, aggressive, talkative, assertive, and independent may be penalized excessively.

In some ways, the school-age child is oblivious to the perspectives of those around him or her. Annie Dillard, in *An American Childhood*, describes the young school-age child:

> Young children have no sense of wonder. They bewilder well, but few things surprise them. All of it is new to young children, after all, and equally gratuitous. Their parents pause at the unnecessary beauty of an ice storm coating the trees; the children look for something to throw. The children who tape colorful fall leaves to the school room windows and walls are humoring the teacher. The busy teacher halts on her walk to school and stoops to pick up fine bright leaves "to show the children"—but it is she, now in her sixties, who is increasingly stunned by the leaves, their brightness all so much trash that litters the gutter.[147]

Peer approval becomes more important to the school-age child than to the preschool child. Children venture out into new environments where they learn about their own skills and personalities as well as the abilities and temperaments of others. They have firsthand opportunities to learn about leadership, cooperation, competition, and group behavior. They begin to see themselves as other peers see them. Children's conversations change in content as they develop friendships with peers.[148] They learn to alter their communication behavior as they deal with older, younger, and same-age peers.[149]

Why are some children popular while others are rejected by their peers or neglected? A recent study suggests that differences in communicative abilities may place children in these categories. The investigation determined that children rejected by their peers had less developed communicative skills than those children who were accepted by their peers. Neglected children, however, did not show similar communication-skill deficits. The authors suggest that communication skills may differentiate the accepted children from the rejected children, but that neglected children may have particular personality traits or may have little interest in social interaction with their peers that explains their neglect. They recommend, "It is quite possible that training rejected children in appropriate communication skills would result in enhanced peer acceptance."[150]

Can children be trained in communicative skills? While most communication training occurs in the high school, collegiate, or adult settings, children can be taught to be more effective communicators. Communication researchers Clark, Willihnganz, and O'Dell showed that "even very limited instruction can produce improvements in some forms of children's communicative performance."[151] Fourth-grade children showed an ability to understand and apply compromising strategies, but they were unable to show similar understanding and application of persuasive strategies. The authors suggest that the persuasive strategies may have been more complicated to understand, given the variety of contingencies in the situation.

Parents may help children develop their social and communicative skills albeit indirectly. A recent investigation shows that to the extent that parents possess dependable friends, children rated themselves as happier, being more adjusted to school, and having greater social skills. The researchers suggest that when parents have good friends they provide models to their children and they also create access routes to people within the community for their children.[152]

The school helps children grow intellectually in the period from age 6 to age 12. Children also make important advances in the development of moral reasoning. Their conscience develops and they no longer follow rules simply because they have been told to do so. Children begin to behave in a manner that is consistent with their own internalized sense of right and wrong during this period. Miss Manners (Judith Martin) may have been speaking tongue-in-cheek when she observed, "We are all born charming, fresh, and spontaneous and must be civilized before we are fit to participate in society."

SUMMARY

In the last two chapters we have considered the various stages of family development. In this chapter we began with the addition of a baby to the family unit and we concluded with the child in preschool years. Adding children to the family creates major changes. These differences occur as early as the pregnancy. Both women and men may experience physical and psychological symptoms related to pregnancy.

After the child is born, the couple may feel overwhelmed with the variety and number of roles they must play. Family author Coleman summarized the factors that contribute toward the healthy development of children including providing love and acceptance, supplying structure and discipline, encouraging competence and self-confidence, presenting appropriate role models, and creating a stimulating and responsive environment.[153]

Adding children to the family may be especially stressful if both parents work. Major difficulties occur for the couple, but coping mechanisms are possible. People can work to have a favorable definition of the situation, which includes an absence of guilt and the belief that conflicts can be overcome. They can establish a salient role, which means that they can decide, in advance, which role they will enact when two roles conflict. They can compartmentalize their lives and separate their roles. They can also compromise their standards.

Families with preschool children face a great deal of stress. The newborn is helpless and requires constant care and supervision. As the child grows and develops, he or she becomes increasingly independent. Most research on infant–parent interaction has considered the mother, but some studies have allowed us to make comparisons between mother–infant and father–infant interactions. You may wish to review some of those distinctions.

As the family moves from the preschool age to the school age, less stress is present. School-age children can do a great deal for themselves and they spend some part of every school day away from home. Peer groups begin to influence their behavior and the family becomes less important in forming attitudes, values, and beliefs.

Two dimensions of parent–child interaction are relevant during this stage. They are the parents' acceptance or rejection of their children and their control or lack of control of them. Empirical evidence encourages parents to be accepting and supportive on the first dimension and to provide their children with some autonomy in the direction of their lives but with some control in the day-to-day rules for behavior.

KEY TERMS

1. In the *crisis* stage couples view pregnancy as a major change. In the *event* stage they see it as something that requires planning and preparation. In the *relation* stage the couple begins to relate more with their mothers and with other people who have had children.

2. *Imaging-making* refers to couples rehearsing parenting by imagining themselves in a parenting role.

3. Creating communicative effects includes *preverbal routines* (routinized social exchanges), *communication intentionality* (considering what effect a message may have on the receiver), and *linguistic communication* (single words as well as phrases).

4. *Monitoring of communication* refers to children evaluating message adequacy to adapt their message when needed. This stage of communication development begins around 5 years old and continues to middle childhood.

5. *Gender constancy* refers to children's abilities to consistently see themselves as male or female. Usually children develop gender constancy between the ages of 5 and 7.

CHAPTER
8

THE DEVELOPMENT OF
THE FAMILY :
ADOLESCENCE

. . . not quite children and certainly not adults, in many ways privileged, wielding unprecedented economic power as consumers of clothing, entertainment, and other amenities, the object of a peculiar blend of tenderness, indulgence, distrust, hostility, moving through a seemingly endless course of "preparation for life". . . not quite children and certainly not adults.[1]

A. K. COHEN

After you have read this chapter, you will be able to

1. Define adolescence.

2. Explain the physical changes that occur during this stage of development.

3. Distinguish between the physical changes that occur in female and male adolescents.

4. Describe the psychological changes that occur in adolescence.

5. Discuss how individuals establish a clearer identity during adolescence.

6. Identify ways that adolescents become increasingly autonomous and independent.

7. Describe how adolescents have both greater freedom and increased responsibilities.

8. Explain the communication patterns that emerge among adolescents and their parents.

9. Discuss the communication that occurs between adolescents and their peers.

10. Name some communication behaviors that are further developed during adolescence.

11. Discuss the effect of the physical, psychological, and communication needs of the adolescent on the family unit.

In the last chapter we explored the development of the family from the child's birth to his or her entrance into formal education. In this chapter we will continue to examine family developmental stages. Because so many people seek information on talking with teenagers, we will devote an entire chapter to the turbulent teen years. Every family does not have teenagers, but most who add children to their family experience this time of great change.

❖ FAMILIES WITH ADOLESCENT CHILDREN

"Little children have little problems; big children have big problems." Adolescents are big children; they do, indeed, have big problems. As children develop from infancy into later preschool age and then school age, parents may be misled into believing children's growth and development are consistent and uniform. Parents may believe that adolescents will become increasingly independent and will make fewer and fewer demands upon the parents and the family unit. Instead, the adolescent's behavior causes parents to yearn for the period of infancy when the child was totally dependent on the caretaker. One jaded parent of four adolescents observed that this period was God's joke on parents. Robert Byrne added, "Learning to dislike children at an early age saves a lot of expense and aggravation later in life."

The adolescent is an interesting person to observe. Dressed up for a middle school or high school dance, the 13- to 16-year-old young woman looks like an adult. Her figure has begun to develop and she wears clothing that is associated with older women. However, she may alter her adult look as she adds a large piece of bubble gum to her mouth, as she giggles with her friends, as she trips her "date," or as she hits her younger brother on the way out of the house. No middle school or junior high dance is complete without several young women running out of the gymnasium crying while another group engages in petting behavior on the dance floor. As an unknown source suggested, "Adolescence is the stage between infancy and adultery."

Changes in behavior from the school-age child to the adolescent become the rule. The child who was polite and eager to please learns improper behavior and does nothing to please. The even-tempered, loving little girl becomes an angry, crying young woman who slams her door and screams, "No one understands me." The attractive and popular elementary school boy begins to avoid people, preferring to lie on his bed, alone in his room. Physical and psychological changes place the adolescent in turmoil; the adolescent's behavior places everyone else in the family in limbo.

Adolescence represents a time of change for the person and for his or her family. (© 1991, Gelles, Stock, Boston).

Adolescence is defined in many ways. Rogers observes that the term is "variously treated as a specific span of years, a stage in development, a subculture, a state of mind, or a combination of these concepts."[2] As we shall determine, adolescents (typically persons in their teenage years), experience significant physical, psychological, and communicative changes. Adolescents encounter growth spurts and changes in their primary and secondary sex characteristics. They gain a sense of identity and become increasingly independent. As communicators, they use distinctive language, but they also become more communicatively competent.

▪ Physical Changes

The physical changes experienced by adolescents are significant. One only has to visit a middle school or a junior high to understand that young teenagers come in all sizes and shapes. Dramatic growth occurs in height, weight, reproductive functions, and hormonal functions. Concern about these physiological changes are of real concern to adolescents. Bill Cosby observes, "My eleven year old daughter mopes around the house all day waiting for her breasts to grow."

Growth curves for size, as well as for reproductive and hormonal functioning for adolescents, include a dramatic change that is commonly referred to as the adolescent growth spurt. For height and weight, the female growth spurt begins at about 10½ and continues for two years. This two-year period of rapid growth shows females adding about three and one-half inches each year. Male growth spurt starts at about 12½ and also lasts for about two years. During their growth spurt, males gain about four inches each year. The growth rate for adolescents' weight follows essentially the same timetable as that for height. Nonetheless, the growth spurts can vary widely, beginning as early as 7½ for girls or 10½ for boys or as late as 11½ for girls or 16 for boys.[3]

Sexual maturation in adolescent males and females follows fairly predictable patterns. For the males these patterns include penile growth, testicular development, the growth of pubic and axillary hair, and voice changes. For the females, the changes include breast growth, the addition of pubic and axillary hair, and menarche—their first menstruation. The age of first menstruation may occur as early as age 9 or as late as age 17, but the average female experiences menarche at age 12 or 13. Although these patterns of change are fairly predictable, great variations may occur as to the timing of the onset and the completion of growth for each development. Needless to say, these variations create great uneasiness for the early, or late, developing adolescent.[4]

■ Psychological Changes

Although some cultures have rites of passage, most Americans do not practice such a tradition. Such ceremonies, which generally occur at puberty, serve the purpose of announcing a child has become an adult. Because we do not celebrate the occasion, it is often unclear when we identify a girl as a "woman" and a boy as a "man." Although legal definitions exist, these vary for such activities as serving in the armed forces, drinking alcoholic beverages, driving a car, staying out after curfew, seeing pornographic movies, marrying, voting, or owning property. It is no wonder adolescents are unsure about how to establish their independence. Such a move may depend upon the laws in their state, and may be "void where prohibited by law."

Some of the psychological changes adolescents experience occur because of these new opportunities and responsibilities. Others occur because of the physical growth and development discussed above. During the adolescent period individuals establish a clearer identity; they deal with issues of self-concept and self-esteem; they become increasingly autonomous and independent; and they grapple with greater freedom and increased responsibilities.

Symbolic interactionism, which was introduced in Chapter 7, is relevant to these changes. Adolescents no longer depend so exclusively on their parents as significant others. Now, peers play a more important role. The adolescent identity is dependent on an ability to separate from the family and to become integrated as an independent individual. At the same time, adolescents need to feel accepted by their parents even as they begin to move psychologically away from them.

Adolescents come to develop a sense of identity during the teenage years. Their identity development, like their physical changes, shows great variation; some teenagers are highly reflective while others spend less time in self-reflection.[5] Eventually, they come to see themselves as distinctive individuals and as people with self-consistency. Adolescents struggle to identify themselves as unique from others, but also as people who have integrated their needs, goals, values, attitudes, and capabilities in a coherent way that is consistent through time. These struggles can be easier or more difficult, depending on the quality of the family relationships. When families adapt to the changing adolescent, the adolescent shows greater psychosocial competence and higher self-esteem.[6] Adolescents develop their sense of identity by relating to folk heroes, media figures, rock stars, and role models as well as peers and parents. Charles Schulz's comic character, Lucy, observes, "If you're not beguiling by age twelve, forget it!"

Sex-role identity forms one part of an adolescent's identity. Adolescent males and females continue to view traditional sex roles as salient. Traditional masculinity, equated with aggressive, independent, unemotional, objective, dominant, active, logical, worldly and direct qualities, clashes with stereotypical femininity, which includes dependence, tactfulness, gentleness, sensitive, religious, emotional, submissive, passive, and illogical traits.

While masculine traits are more culturally rewarded than are feminine ones, adolescents expect each other to behave within traditionally sex-typed roles. Young women who enjoy athletics, woodworking, and competing for high grades may find that they have little social support, while young men who spend their leisure time cooking and their wage-earning time babysitting may feel they have no one with whom to discuss their interests. One eighth-grade female who enjoyed masculine activities said in dismay, "The boys no longer treat me as their friend and the girls say I am a boy." Her problem may become increasingly widespread as fewer adolescents identify with traditional female roles.[7]

A variety of models have been proposed that explain sex-role identity in adolescents. To date, no single model adequately covers the variations that occur in sex-role acquisition, continuity, and change. One limitation of sex-role identity models is that they focus on children, rather than adolescents. Another problem is that they fail to include the new adolescent–adult relationships that result from the newly emerging family forms.[8]

Just as sex-role identity is difficult for the adolescent to internalize and the researcher to explain, adolescent self-concept and self-esteem are complicated. As we observed in the last chapter, our self-concept and our self-esteem are determined, at least in part, by our interactions with parents and primary caretakers. Although it is not completely confirmed, our self-concept becomes somewhat less related to these significant others as we mature.[9] Adolescents' significant others become their peers, coaches, and teachers rather than their parents and primary caretakers.

A number of factors affect the adolescents' self-esteem. Both age and biological sex show an impact. Adolescent females have more positive self-esteem than older adolescents.[10] Age and biological sex are interesting variables, but little can be done to alter them.

Other factors in the adolescents' world that can be altered and that either positively or negatively impact self-esteem include the nature of the family unit, stressful events, residential mobility, sports competition, and one's career goals. Children who grow up in homes without fathers, where the father left the family home after the child had entered the third grade, tend to have lower academic self-concepts, but they do not have lower academic achievements. If the father left home at an earlier period, no effect is evidenced on either academic self-concept or academic achievement.[11]

Stressful events impact most people's self-esteem, and adolescents are no exceptions. While both negative and positive stressful events can cause changes in one's self-perceptions and behavior, only negative stressful events decrease the self-esteem of the adolescent. Positive stressful occurrences have no effect on self-esteem.[12]

Families are moving across the country, and even around the world; they are changing their residence at a greater rate today than in the past. These changes can cause stress for all family members. For adolescents, such moves can result in major losses in self-esteem, but the negative impact may be attenuated by social support. If such residential changes are necessary in the family that includes an adolescent, parents are encouraged to find socially supportive people and agencies to offset potential long-term damage. Moving is difficult for adolescents and many will show symptoms of depression, which may include feeling lonely, crying, and becoming generally upset. Typically, such behaviors will only be shown for a few months after the residential move.[13]

While sports competition may build character and may help adolescents learn the value of playing on a team, it can also have deleterious effects. Consequently, many youth athletic programs have deemphasized the competitive nature of their events. Current research demonstrates that peers and parents can offset the negative aspects of sports competition on adolescents' self-esteem by providing support to them. Of even greater importance is the role of the coach in building self-esteem. The "coach's assessments of ability and intention of participation" was shown to be key in helping adolescents develop positive self-esteem.[14]

A final factor that impacts adolescents' self-esteem is one's career goals. One theory suggests that young people fulfill their sense of self, at least in part, by selecting or considering potential, future occupations. This theory was given credence in a study of over 200 high school sophomore and junior high school students. Those adolescents who had career goals had significantly higher self-esteem than did those who had no career goals.[15] One writer suggests, "Adolescents need to identify, at least generally, what occupational role they expect to play as adults and to determine some alternative paths toward these goals."[16]

In addition to self-esteem, the adolescent's independence is relevant to his or her psychological growth. Typically, adolescents gain increasing independence. Three types of independence and autonomy are particularly relevant: emotional autonomy, behavioral autonomy, and value autonomy.[17] *Emotional autonomy* suggests that adolescents are no longer as dependent upon others for their emotional states. *Behavioral autonomy* shows itself in independent action. *Value autonomy* refers to adolescents' commitment to values and beliefs that may be discrepant from family and friends. Parents of adolescents and the adolescents both recognize the importance of the task of gaining independence in this period.[18] However, at the same time that adolescents are struggling for autonomy, they still wish to have the security of knowing their parents are oriented toward the family.[19]

Successful separation-individuation, which results in a strong sense of self and also a feeling of family membership, is the goal for adolescents. Those who are unable to achieve this goal may show disruptive behaviors, a rejection of societal or family norms, and potential suicide. Conflict within the family, parental relationship, parenting styles, family interactions, and other factors may affect whether an adolescent is successful or unsuccessful in accomplishing this developmental task. Parents who believe their adolescent children are at risk should consider therapeutic intervention from professionals that incorporates all of the members of the family. In addition, community support can be invaluable in helping the adolescent gain healthy individuation.[20]

Appropriately socialized adolescents begin to move away from their family of orientation. They spend less time with their parents.[21] They begin to see themselves as individuals apart from their family. They begin to practice separating from their families through a variety of activities. They may take trips with others; they spend more time away from home or on the telephone; they spend more time in their room either alone or with friends. One woman recalls her adolescence:

> Going through adolescence I spent a lot of time alone. I'd shut myself off from the seemingly demanding world, by closing my bedroom door and blaring the sounds of Led Zeppelin and Emerson, Lake, & Palmer through my headphones while I curled myself up like a cat under my desk. There were many times when I would get angry if someone walked into the family room if I was in there. When this occurred I would exhale very loudly, roll my eyes, and storm out of the room. I also distanced myself from family members by pretending they weren't there. I would outright ignore people, pretend I couldn't hear them. This did not go over too well. During the years I was going through adolescence there was a song called "Music Man." A line from that song, "It's so nice to be insane, no one asks you to explain," helped me. I'd just act a little crazy so everyone would leave me alone.[22]

The adolescent needs to separate not only from his or her parents, but from other family members, as well. One woman explains her need to separate from her older sister:

> Because there was not a period of rebellion toward my parents, I did not give adolescence much thought. After analyzing the actual process I can see that autonomy and independence were sought, but not from my parents. The person that I probably needed to become independent from was my older sister.
> My parents were always very careful to make sure that each child was unique in their eyes and in ours. My sister and I were always very close and

enjoyed being friends. As I grew into adolescence I remember choosing actions and activities that were more and more distinct from my sister's.

My sister and I are close enough in age that she went through the rebellious stage near the time that I might have. Seeing her go through all of that made me become more of what my parents would want instead of what they would not. It was as if, if she was going to cause tension, then I was going to relieve it. I chose the positive attention instead of the negative.

Now that I think about it, this probably prolonged her adolescent stage and shortened mine. She probably felt opposition from all sides while I only felt it from her during those years. Whatever I did seemed to upset her—whether it had anything to do with her or not. I suppose that this hurt my feelings enough that I decided to at least get positive strokes from others. I did not want to go through what she went through.[23]

The time of increased separation from the family may vary widely from one family to another. Important factors affecting the timing of separation include whether one is in a rural or urban family, the biological sex of the adolescent, the closeness of the adolescents to the parents, relationships with peers, and the desirability of creating a new family.[24] Current social trends encourage children to individuate both earlier and later than in the past. Clearly, no "right" time exists for all families.

Adolescents gain greater freedom during this period of their life and they are provided with increased responsibilities. Adolescents are typically allowed more freedom than younger children in the family. They may be encouraged to make their own decisions in an increasing large number of spheres. However, some of the messages sent to adolescents by their parents may have two levels of meaning. On the one hand, they suggest freedom to choose; on the other, they require conformity to family rules. The "Hi and Lois" cartoon illustrates this idea.

In general, adolescents who feel that they have control over their lives and who have high feelings of responsibility show greater life satisfaction.[25] Similarly, feelings of trust for oneself and for others leads to greater confidence, popularity, and less loneliness.[26] Parents should consider how they can encourage both freedom and responsibility in their adolescent children.

HI AND LOIS reprinted with special permission of King Features Syndicate, Inc.

■ Communicative Changes

Communication patterns change during this time, too. A child's mother may have been the first person with whom he or she shared information in the past. The adolescent may now disclose more to a best friend, usually of the same sex. The adolescent may have spent a great deal of time talking with siblings and parents previously. Now a large proportion of talk time is with peers or with a favorite teacher or other role model. One article notes that "the peer group emerges as an emotional anchorage, an experiential educator of socialized attitudes and behaviors."[27]

The move from communicating more to peers and less to parents is not a simple linear change. Indeed, a recent article suggests that "two dialectic principles" inform teenagers about which audience is more appropriate for their conversations. The authors write:

> The dialectic of historical perspective and contemporary experience regards opposing temporal orientations by parents and friends towards adolescent activities. The dialectic of judgement and acceptance involves polar evaluative tendencies demonstrated by parents and friends that were mediated by perceptions of caring.[28]

If the adolescent wants an historical insight, he or she is more likely to talk with parents; if a contemporary view is in order, peers are consulted. When judgments are called for, parents are the target of talk, but acceptance makes peers more relevant.

Adolescents distinguish between the time they spend with their parents as "task time" and with their peers as "leisure time."[29] What topics do adolescents feel are appropriate to discuss with their parents? Most adolescents feel it is appropriate to discuss summer jobs, foods, sports, classes, grades, plans for the future, homework, family news, feelings toward school, views on religion, and appreciation for their parents' contributions. Topics that adolescents feel are taboo in discussions with their parents are sex, the secrets of friends, parties, alcohol, drugs, their boyfriend or girlfriend, and their feelings of insecurity.[30]

A number of studies have shown that viewing sexuality as a taboo topic for parent–adolescent conversations creates serious problems. Teenagers are often not provided with enough information about sexual matters and the family appears to be an excellent source for such education. To the extent that parents do not talk to their teenagers about sexual matters, the teenagers experience more sexual problems, including premarital pregnancy and sexual diseases.[31]

Can families that do discuss sexual matters be distinguished from those that do not? Indeed, two researchers showed that when adolescents viewed their family interaction as satisfying and classified their communication as open, they also reported more sex education within the family. Similarly, fathers who reported the healthiest family interactions also stated that they were most involved in sex education. Interestingly, mothers' reports of sex education were not correlated with their perceptions of family communication or interaction.[32] This difference between adolescents, fathers, and mothers leads to interesting speculation.

Parents may be playing a different role in sex education than are other sources of influence. Researchers recently revealed that while parents were rated the highest of all sources as an influence on sexual opinions, beliefs, and attitudes, they were rated lower than friends, schools, and books as sources of information. Adolescents gave their parents higher marks if the parents had exhibited a positive reaction to sex education in the past, if they were sexually permissive, and if they had already provided an influential role on sexual matters. However, the sexual knowledge held by the adolescents was not related to any of these family variables.[33] Parents may serve less as a source of information and more as a source of values and attitudes.

Relationships change in the family. A mother and daughter who have been very close may find a gulf separating them. The daughter who is very much like her mother may emphasize differences and may take on new characteristics in order to separate herself from her mother. Fathers and daughters may grow distant as the teenager physically becomes a woman. Fathers may feel some sexual attraction to their daughters who look so much like their wives at an earlier age and feel guilty over such observations and sensations. Fathers may overcompensate for their feelings and feel reluctant to hold their daughters on their lap, to kiss them good night, or to hug them. The daughters, not understanding their fathers' motivation, may feel unloved or unaccepted.

Another factor that contributes to the diminished relationship between parents and adolescents is the adolescents' perceptions of their parents. Two researchers found adolescents felt their parents did not understand them, did not help them, and did not spend enough time with them. Further, these researchers determined that adolescents perceived their parents as being too involved in their own activities and evaluated their parents' expectations of the adolescents as far too high. Consequently, the adolescents rated their parents as the least influential group on their attitudes and feelings of loneliness.[34]

The negative picture of the parent provided by these studies of adolescents' perceptions may be due in part to the differences in values that adolescents and parents exhibit. An investigation of about 1000 people, approximately the same number of adolescents and their guardians, showed a marked difference in values between the two groups. The authors conclude that there is a "great gap" between teenagers and the adults in their families.[35]

Decreasing parent–child communication coupled with increasing peer communication is normative during the adolescent period. Exhibiting extremes on these dimensions is not normal and may indicate problems. Two investigators found that families who perceived that they held positive parent–adolescent communication patterns also perceived themselves as higher on family cohesion, adaptability, and satisfaction.[36]

A recent investigation suggests that at least some of these perceptions could be validated in actual behavior. Family members related to adolescents who were successful in public schools were compared with family members related to adolescents who required alternative school programs. The two groups reported relatively the same amount of adaptability; however, the difference between the two groups on cohesion was striking. Three-fourths of the alternative school families described themselves as disengaged while fewer than one-fifth of the public school families described themselves this way. Public school families generally showed more balanced functioning and they had more positive communication.[37] The author notes that there was far less discrepancy between the real and the ideal for the public school families than for the alternative school families.[38]

Anastasia, in *Her Mother's Daughter,* illustrates the importance of people other than her parents for her role models during adolescence:

> Having no model for the new person I intended to become, I drew from the culture around me, which in my day contained figures like June Allyson and Doris Day. I would be cheerful, "Relentlessly cheerful," full of jokes and light of heart. I would be my mother's opposite: I would not care about the things that mattered to her, I would be sexual, open, full of laughter. I would also be intellectual and imaginative, I would give every part of myself full expression. I would allow nothing to depress me.[39]

Peers play a far more important role in adolescents' lives than they do in children's lives. Younger adolescents have particularly strong needs to conform to peer pressure. One survey of adolescents demonstrated that socioeconomic differences among adolescents could be used to predict other differences; however, it clearly showed that regardless of one's socioeconomic status, adolescents were united in their need for popularity and their tendency to conform to their peer group.[40] Parents of adolescents identify communication and peer pressure as their greatest concerns about their children.[41]

Many adolescents experiment with drugs, drinking, and sex in their attempts to be independent from their families and to be closer to their peers. One 30-year-old woman writes:

> I was a real pain in the neck as an adolescent. . . . Many of my friends had a lot of freedom and a lot of money to spend. I was a true follower at the time and very curious about the world and what it had to offer me. Unfortunately, I was easily pulled into a scene that was very available to me. I started experimenting with drugs and alcohol when I was in the 8th grade. . . . This period of experimentation had a profound effect on my relationships at home, as well as my communicative behaviors. I thought my parents were pretty square and I closed myself off from them as much as they would allow. They were very busy with their lives, so this wasn't much of a problem. Every chance I got, I would be out with my friends.[42]

Adolescent breaks with the family need not be so traumatic. One woman in her mid-20s recalls:

> As an adolescent, I was basically a bookworm. I was really concerned about grades and doing well in school. This attitude was pretty consistent until I was about 16 or 17. At this point I became a social butterfly. I never neglected school work; however, I became more committed to attending social functions with my girlfriends. For awhile I had a commitment for every Friday,

Saturday and Sunday evening. Looking back I find that for some reason it
was imperative to always be out with my friends. I guess this was my way of
establishing independence. . . . My mother felt I should relinquish some of
my social activity . . . because it interfered with family time. I no longer spent
much time with my family. [43]

Adolescents use their communication patterns to distance themselves
from their parents and to establish close peer relationships. For example, adolescents demonstrate their psychological and emotional distance from their
parents with physical distance when they communicate. A study that included
younger and older adolescents showed that as adolescents become older, the
physical spacing between themselves and other family members increases. The
authors suggest that such spatial distancing is an indication of the older adolescents' need for more autonomy.[44]

Self-disclosure, the revelation of personal information to others, is an indicator of close relationships. As adolescents mature, they change the target of
their self-disclosure. While younger adolescents are more likely to provide
emotional self-disclosure to their parents, older adolescents are more likely to
reserve such behavior for their peers. Further, emotional self-disclosure to peers
is related to high self-esteem in the peer context and to identity development.[45]

At the same time, communication strategies are used to become closer to
peers. Adolescents' personal relationships are affected by their communication
networks.[46] They create a unique world with unique language[47] and they use
specialized peer group symbols to establish their identity.[48] Adolescent speech
serves they purposes of rebelling against parents and authority as well as
demonstrating their independence and development.[49]

One woman explained:

I spoke like all the other kids that were trying to gain autonomy. We seemed
to have a language uniquely our own. It was a time when "bad" meant good,
which to our sense of satisfaction, confused our parents. We had a way of
talking that allowed us to talk about "the adults" in front of them without
them knowing, or at least they never acted like they knew what was going on.
It gave me great pleasure, or at least a good laugh, to use terminology that
was, as I thought, over my parent's heads.[50]

Similarly, clothing is used to symbolize the adolescent subculture. The same
woman recalled:

Clothing was great. If either of my parents hated it, it was the thing to wear. I
lived in extra-wide bell bottom jeans pulled low on my hips. The hem had to
drag so the bottoms would fray. I never wore shoes—just to irritate my
Mom. I wore three necklaces at once, each with a St. Christopher medallion.
My Mom thought they made me look cheap, I thought they would save me
from sin.[51]

Although communicative behaviors are changing, communication is key
to parent–adolescent relationships. Adolescents' perceptions of disagreeing

with their parents are inversely related to their satisfaction within the family; however, whether the difference of opinion was expressed in a calm or heated argument had no effect on level of satisfaction.[52] When adolescents perceive their parents to be engaged in a great deal of conflict, feel their relationships with their parents are poor, and see one of their parents as either angry or depressed frequently, they may engage in negative behaviors and consider suicide.[53] The importance of positive communication patterns and of agreement among family members will be discussed further in Chapter 11.

Adolescents, like their younger counterparts, interact with their environment, including the people within it, to become increasingly communicatively competent. Interpersonal understanding increases in a sequential way from childhood to preadolescence to adolescence.[54] Adolescents use their peer relations to develop better interactional skills.[55] They become more adept at interpersonal relationships and more sophisticated in their choice of friends.[56] They also learn about intimate relationships and become increasingly able to develop and maintain intimacy.[57]

At the same time, adolescents become more proficient in their persuasive and decision-making skills. They become increasingly able to adapt to specific people in their persuasive efforts.[58] They establish larger repertoires of strategies to avoid complying with requests from their parents.[59] They become increasingly successful at persuading their parents and other adults to change their attitudes and behaviors in areas including sports, leisure, minority groups, youth, drug use, and sexuality.[60] Finally, they are viewed as participating in family decisions.[61]

■ Effects of These Changes

The changes that occur in adolescence may affect both adolescents and their parents. However, the changes that occur in adolescents may be overstated by parents and others experiencing the phenomenon.[62] The difficulty of raising children was observed as long ago as Socrates, who wrote, "Children today are tyrants. They contradict their parents, gobble their food, and tyrannize their teachers." Humorists, too, have used adolescence as the basis of their jokes. Robert Orben laments, "I take my children everywhere, but they always find their way back home." Evelyn Waugh asks, "What is youth except a man or woman before it is fit to be seen?"

Some evidence suggests the agitation identified with adolescence is exaggerated.[63] Mark Twain recalled, "My mother had a great deal of trouble with me, but I think she enjoyed it." Two researchers, for instance, state that only about 20 percent of adolescents experience a time of general confusion; 33 percent have occasional periods of upset, but they are equally likely to feel calm and undistressed; and 20 percent are confident and free of anxiety and depression.[64] The others fall between these extremes.

Adolescents move from being children and dependent to becoming adults and independent. This movement is fairly smooth and even-moving for some people. For others, the period seems to jerk along like an amusement park ride that is letting people off and on in increments. Finally, some people experience a totally disorienting ride.

For those teenagers who are disoriented during this period of their life, a number of problems may arise. Loneliness is a qualifying characteristic of adolescents and young adults,[65] which may lead to feelings of anxiety, depression, and alienation.[66] Adolescents may commit suicide, run away from home, drop out of school, or turn to drugs or alcohol for solace. Their levels of stress should not be underestimated.

Conflict may arise within the family, particularly if family members do not understand the developmental changes that are occurring and if they fail to communicate with each other about these changes. Conflict may similarly occur if parents attempt to exercise too much control at a time when adolescents need increased autonomy and freedom. Both parents and adolescents need to recognize that adolescents are preparing to separate themselves from the original family unit.

In addition, both parents and children are wise to remember that conflict is not limited to the family context. Adolescents experience conflict in both their familial and their peer relationships.[67] This conflict may simply be a result of learning new communicative skills and the "bumps and grinds" that accompany the learning of any new skill. Adolescents need the opportunity to experiment with a variety of communicative strategies to separate the more effective from the less effective.

Young adolescents focus on themselves and believe they know everything. Thirteen-year-olds can only view the world from their own perspective. Dinner conversation that centers on others may be quickly changed in order that adolescents can put themselves in the spotlight. Oscar Wilde may have been thinking of younger adolescents when he commented, "I am not young enough to know everything." The older adolescent moves from a self-focus to an other-focus. Many changes occur within the individual as he or she moves from early adolescence to older adolescence.[68] While younger adolescent females are more likely to define group boundaries and to differentiate themselves from others, older adolescent females are more inclined to validate their friends as group members in their communicative behavior.[69] Older adolescents develop a true sense of identity and can view the world from the perspective of another person. They begin to recognize the wisdom or knowledge that others possess.

SUMMARY

In this chapter we considered families with adolescent children. We determined that a variety of changes make this stage unique and filled with challenges. Communicating openly and honestly is important in the family as it grows and develops. Supporting other family members who may be in very different stages is essential. Sensitivity to the alterations that are occurring within individuals and among the interactants is necessary.

Although adolescence is a tumultuous time for many families, it is not a difficult period for all. Furthermore, an understanding of the physical and psychological change that is occurring in the adolescent can assist parents in being more sensitive and supportive to their teenaged children. Adolescence is the period when individuals move from being dependent children to becoming independent adults.

The communicative changes that occur in the family with adolescent children provide opportunities for continued development of the adolescent as well as other members. Communication patterns change as adolescents begin to interact more with peers and less with parents and other family members. Relationships between the adolescent and his or her parents change, too. Nonetheless, communication is still the key to successful parent–adult relationships.

KEY TERMS

1. *Emotional autonomy* suggests that the adolescent is no longer dependent upon others for his or her emotional development.

2. *Behavioral autonomy* shows itself in independent action.

3. *Value autonomy* refers to the adolescent's commitment to values and beliefs, which may be discrepant from family and friends.

4. *Task time* refers to the time adolescents have to spend with parents and family.

5. *Leisure time* is the time they spend with peers.

CHAPTER 9

THE DEVELOPMENT OF THE FAMILY: THE MIDDLE AND RETIREMENT YEARS

When I was young there was no respect for the young, and now that I am old there is no respect for the old. I missed out coming and going.

J. B. PRIESTLEY

After you have read this chapter, you will be able to

1. Describe the launching stage of family development and explain why it may be a confusing time for the family.

2. List communicative changes that occur during the launching stage.

3. Differentiate between families in middle years and families in older years.

4. Discuss couple communication during the launching stage, and during the last two stages of development.

5. Explain parent–child interaction with adolescents and adult children during the middle and older family life stages, and grandchildren.

6. Identify factors that affect grandparent–grandchildren interaction.

7. Describe the impact the "empty nest" and retirement may have on marital satisfaction.

8. Consider the impact the increasingly aged population will have on family life.

In the last chapter we explored the family during the adolescent child stage. In this chapter we will continue to examine family developmental stages. The chapter opens with a consideration of families that are launching children, and discusses the family in middle years and in older years. All families do not go through the stages outlined in this chapter, but many do. In addition, some families add stages to this process as they cohabit or blend their family with another family. Let us begin our discussion in this chapter with the impact of launching children from the family unit.

❖ LAUNCHING CHILDREN

The family moves from the stage when children are present to the time when the children have left home. The period of time when the children leave home is usually between 18 and 22 years of age, which is roughly when children graduate from high school or college. The family development stage of launching children is defined as when the children in the family range in age from 13 to 24. The underlying assumption is that the oldest child may have already left and the younger children are preparing to follow the oldest sibling's example.

■ Confusing Developments

This period may be somewhat confusing to family members, since some children may still be going through adolescence while others are relatively independent, beginning careers and families of their own. Too, parents may feel somewhat distressed over their "emptying nest" or they may feel relieved as the pressures of a larger family begin to let up and they are left with fewer residential children. Parents who have exhibited considerable control over their children may feel distressed that they are no longer able to monitor their older children's behavior. Parents who have allowed their children autonomy may see minimal differences in their interactions with their children now than they did earlier.

Part of the confusion may be due to the variety of alternative patterns of leaving home. Not only do some residential children return to the family home after they have left, as we shall discuss later, but children leave at a variety of times. Children in rural families may leave later than those in urban homes. Children from single-parent and stepfamilies often leave earlier than do children from nuclear families.[1] Although many children leave home for college, others commute and remain at home.[2] These different patterns can cause increased stress for family members and may change the communicative patterns within the family from those normally associated with the emptying nest.[3]

Confusion may also exist since an increasing number of homes appear to have a "swinging door," with children leaving and returning home. In general, parents report positive relationships with their returning adult children.

SMALL SOCIETY reprinted with special permission of King Features Syndicate, Inc.

However, conflict, financial dependency, unemployment on the part of the child, being divorced or separated on the part of the child, and bringing home grandchildren all create tension and a lowering of parental satisfaction.[4]

We observed in Chapter 2 that a larger number of children in their 20s and 30s are returning home after they have completed college, been married, or had children. One man in his 20s describes his family and his older sister's departure from the family of origin:

> My sister was the first to sever the ropes. Her leave-taking behavior was met with resistance, to say the least. The day she moved out was turbulent. She left to live in an apartment in the adjacent state of New Hampshire. However, she was to return home within a few years.
>
> Problems resurfaced. My parents treated her as a child in terms of their communicative behaviors. My sister thus reacted as a child. They had reverted to previous roles which had not been used in years. Their repertoire of behaviors were limited to problematic and antagonistic communication. They were never able to successfully renegotiate their new roles of adult-to-adult. Neither was willing or able to relinquish their previous, familiar roles. Unfortunately, I don't believe my parents are able to forget their parental roles.[5]

Youth unemployment is a major reason for children to return home. In general, parents are less distressed by their daughter's lack of employment than their son's and they are more tolerant of younger children's unemployment than they are of older children's unemployment.[6] The frustration felt by the father in the cartoon "Small Society" may be shared by an increasing number of parents who believed they were in the "launching nest" stage of family development.

At the same time, the parents may now be dealing with other problems of aging. Specifically, they may be confronting difficulties that exist because their own parents are in their older years. They may be managing their own parents' affairs, they may be incorporating the reality of their own parents' illness or mortality, and they may be considering moving their own parents into their home. Many women who have postponed their careers while they are rearing their children find that just when their children are leaving home, their parents return to their home and require constant supervision or care.

The parents may also be confronting their own mortality and be experiencing a "midlife crisis." The medical doctor Alvin F. Poussaint notes, "Women at this stage worry about the approach of menopause, men about declining sexual performance, and both bemoan lives that could have been richer, fuller, or more successful."[7] The likelihood of many life-threatening diseases, including cancer, heart attacks, and stroke, increases as one gets older. Bad habits, including smoking, excessive drinking, overeating, and a lack of regular aerobic exercise, begin to show their effects at this time. Both women and men recognize that they should be nearing some sort of peak in their career and they may be depressed over their lack of success. Similarly, they may take an accounting of their interpersonal relationships and find that they are shallow or limited as well.

■ Communicative Changes

Communication patterns change between the parents and their children. The older children now reside in another home, city, state, or even country. Spontaneous, immediate, and frequent interactions are no longer possible. Conversations may be limited to phone calls that occur once a week. Routine, day-to-day matters may not be discussed with children who are living elsewhere as they once were.

The older child's physical move affects the communication that occurs between the parents and the absent children and it also changes the communication between the residential and absent children. Close relationships between siblings are changed. Younger siblings may feel left behind and the children who have moved may feel that younger brothers and sisters cannot understand their new experiences. Two siblings may no longer share a room, or other physical space. They may similarly let go of psychological or emotional closeness.

On the other hand, siblings may come to appreciate each other more when they are no longer competing for the resources of the family. They may perceive qualities in each other they have never had the perspective to observe previously. Older siblings may enjoy their role as leaders venturing into the outside, unexplored world. They may enjoy telling brothers and sisters about the workplace, graduate school, the military, or married life. The younger siblings may be fascinated by these new experiences.

The parents may find they have neglected their relationship with each other during their child-rearing years. As the children begin to leave home, they observe the big holes that are left in relationships and in everyday conversation. An investigation that compared families in which adult children left home for college and those in which the children remained at home and commuted to college sheds some interesting light on the parental relationship in this stage of the family. Both mothers and fathers reported less stress after their child went to college than before, regardless of whether the child actually departed or commuted. However, mothers reported more stress when their child commuted than if they departed. At the same time, mothers reported more talk with their spouse when the child commuted than when he or she departed. Fathers felt emotionally better when the child commuted than when he or she departed. Fathers appear to feel worse and mothers report less talk but less stress, as well, with departing rather than commuting college children.[8] The absent child may negatively impact communication between the parents while at the same time decreasing stress for at least one parent.

The dinner table that was once noisy with chatter about the day's events may now be far quieter with some of the children missing. Bonds of love and affection that always appeared strong in the family unit may have been between resident children and their parents, but not between the parents themselves. For instance, the oldest daughter who always reminded her father to buy her mother a birthday, Christmas, or anniversary gift may no longer be providing reminders.

Alternatively, the parents of the absent child may become closer to each other or to their residential children. The parents may find more time to spend together and may enjoy the additional time they have with each other. They may also be able to focus on a child who was previously overshadowed by an older sibling. The oldest residential child may now have more time to interact with his or her parents than he or she did when an older sibling was in residence. The parents may value the time with younger children more because they now recognize how quickly the children are gone from home.

❖ FAMILIES IN MIDDLE YEARS

Although humorist Herb Caen suggests that "Middle age begins with the first mortgage and ends when you drop dead," family researchers classify this period more precisely. When the children have all left home but the couple has not yet retired, the family is classified as being in the middle years. Folklore suggests that the period of time after the last child leaves home is particularly stressful, especially for the wife. However, behavioral evidence does not bear out this commonly held view.[9] Overall marital satisfaction is high, sexual activity is high, and women do not have an increase in either physical or emotional illness.[10]

A crossover in sex roles appears in midlife.[11] Two researchers state that aging women become more accommodative of their aggressive and egocentric impulses, while men become more accepting of their nurturing and affiliative impulses.[12] Another writer concludes that later life includes a pattern of "normal unisex."[13] Behavioral manifestations of these changes include the husband's increased involvement in housework in the later stages of the family cycle[14] and an increasing number of women in their 40s and 50s joining the work force.

Another myth operates during this period, too. The notion that the children have all left home suggests that the couple is left completely alone. Instead, behavioral evidence demonstrates that the couple has frequent interactions with the children. Over 80 percent of couples live within close proximity of their children and see them at least once each week.[15]

Most couples are not isolated and they may, indeed, find an increase in the number of people in their family and the amount of interaction they have with them. Many couples take on new roles as grandparents during these middle years of family development. Although we speculate and show interest in the grandparenting role, little empirical research has shown how this role affects the couple in middle years and how grandparenting may have important social value. The limited findings do suggest that interactions between grandparents and their grandchildren are generally positive.[16]

Some of the factors that affect how frequently grandparents interact with their grandchildren include residential propinquity, or how close they live to each other; social class; education; and the grandchildren's sense of responsibility to the older generation.[17] In general, when grandparents and their grandchildren live in close proximity, they interact more frequently. The higher the social class and the higher the education of the grandparents, the less likely they are to interact frequently with their grandchildren. To the extent that the grandchildren feel a sense of responsibility to their grandparents, interaction will increase.

Our culture encourages warm relationships between grandparents and their grandchildren, with minimal responsibilities on either side. Some helping behavior flows from the grandchildren to the grandparents, but it is dependent upon how close the grandchildren feel to the grandparents, the responsibility felt by the grandchildren, and the dependency needs of the grandparents. Grandparents have few obligations; they serve as the bearers of family history and they may engage in some gift giving. Since the grandparent role is not marked by economic power nor does it carry social prestige, the grandparents have the opportunity to relax and simply enjoy the interaction with younger family members.

The changing roles of the couple from parents to grandparents and of their offspring from children to parents may require negotiation. Problems may erupt if some of the family members have different views about their roles than do other members. For example, if the grandmother wants to serve as an important, if not primary, caretaker of the newborn grandchild, the mother may be dismayed. Or, if the child's mother works and she finds it convenient and helpful to assume that the grandmother will care on a regular basis for the youngster, the grandmother may find it necessary to explain her own understanding of her more limited, new role. The single mother who lives at home may have particular problems resolving the conflicting roles that may be created by this situation.

Other issues may necessitate clear and open communication during this period of a couple's life, including changes in economic needs and goals; alteration in interaction patterns that no longer include children on a day-to-day basis; future plans, particularly for retirement; and the effects of aging on their bodies and their life choices.

Communication between women and men is always difficult because of differences in socialization and how women and men view communication. It is marked by special problems at this time. Both women and men may be facing midlife crisis, but they may be dealing with different issues.[18] Job success and satisfaction may be paramount in the husband's mind, while the emptied nest and questions about her role may dominate the wife's concerns. Menopause, which has been largely unstudied, may create physical and psychological changes for the wife that unsettle her and may create barriers to communicating with her husband since he has no basis for understanding the phenomenon. Concerns about disease may influence the decision making of both the husband and the wife.

Some couples cannot resolve the difficulties they face during their middle years. Couples in unhappy marriages may have waited until the children were gone to dissolve their marriage. Other couples, who felt that they were reasonably happy, may find that the absence of the children points up that they have little in common to keep them together. The divorce rate for couples in their middle years is not nonexistent, as can be determined from the figures supplied by the National Center for Health Statistics, provided in Table 9.1.[19] Nearly 14 percent of couples married 20 to 24 years divorce each year.

Nonetheless, we remain optimistic about the middle years when we are relatively free of such worries as rearing the children and earning enough money to meet all of the demands placed upon the family. Increased time is available that can be used for recreational purposes. In addition, the possibility of increased sexuality if the couple is healthy is encouraging. The crossover in sex roles suggests that greater understanding is potentially possible for women and men. Finally, the possibility of new relationships with grandchildren, with whom grandparents can enjoy maximum affection with minimum stress, is a pleasant prospect.

In general, people report greater marital satisfaction after the children have left home than they did before.[20] Although the empty nest does result in improvements in marital happiness, it does not affect other features of life satisfaction. Adults who are experiencing this stage of family life are encouraged to maintain frequent contact with their children, which helps to continue the parental role identity. The maintenance of this role may also enhance marital satisfaction.[21]

Frank and Mary Jean Cain provide an example. This couple has known each other since grade school. Growing up in West Virginia, they attended the same schools and the same church. Their three children are grown and have left home. Together, the couple manage a dentistry business. When asked about their happiest time, Mary Jean responded easily:

> Now that the kids are gone. Just don't tell our kids! Our youngest son who is 21 just left for the Air Force and our daughter called us, and asked me, "Are you all right?" I said, "What do you mean, 'Am I all right?'" She said, "Well

TABLE 9.1   CHANCES OF DIVORCE

LENGTH OF MARRIAGE	RATE OF DIVORCE
1 year	50.9%
5 years	41.9%
10 years	30.0%
15 – 19 years	21.0%
20 – 24 years	13.8%
30 – 34 years	3.8%
40 – 44 years	0.9%
50 – 54 years	0.2%

you haven't been by yourselves for years." I told her, "Yes, we're all right. Your daddy and I really like each other!"[22]

❖ FAMILIES IN RETIREMENT

This final stage of family development begins when the couple is in retirement and ends when the couple divorce or when one member dies. Commentators have viewed this stage with humor. A number of people are credited with "Old age is not for sissies." George Burns explains, "I smoke cigars because at my age if I don't have something to hold onto I might fall down." Garrison Keillor laments, "They say such nice things about people at their funerals that it makes me sad to realize that I'm going to miss mine by just a few days."

A greater number of families continue into the later years than they have in the past simply because people are generally living longer today. One set of figures illustrates this phenomenon:

The approximately 28 million people in the United States who are currently over sixty-five represent about 12 percent of the population. By the year 2030, more than 64 million Americans will be over sixty-five, comprising a staggering 20 percent of the population. Contrary to the popular misconception that most of the elderly are consigned to institutions, 95 percent live in the community, and most manage their own households.[23]

Although all of these older Americans are not married, many are.

The couple may be happier at this point than at any other time, except for the beginning of their marriage. Marital satisfaction and overall life satisfaction fluctuate in a consistent way throughout the adult's family life cycle. The relationship is curvilinear: Couples report the greatest happiness at the beginning of their marriage and during their retirement years.[24]

Many retired couples, when asked when the most rewarding time of their marriage occurred, name the present. Christian Kloos was quick to answer:

> We are now to the point where we can do the things we want to do, things we have looked forward to all these years, things we have planned for. We can travel when we want to and do crazy things when we want to. Like last night we went to a wine bar and had caviar and a drink. Then we came home and grilled hamburgers. It is fun to be able to do these things now.[25]

Linda Robertson, too, talked about the advantages of the retirement years:

> This time in life is really rewarding because we have the time to do so many things that we didn't have. We have a little more money to spend because we are not feeding and clothing our kids, or educating them. This time is the best.[26]

Retirement, like other stages, provides both positive and negative aspects. Arthur Schopenhauer noted, "The closing years of life are like the end of a masquerade party, when the masks are dropped." As we know, some of us look better without our masks while others look worse. Men may question their identity or be unsure of how they are to spend their days after they retire. Women may find it disconcerting to have their husbands home all day. As one wife of a newly retired man quipped, "I married you for better or worse, but not for lunch." Clearly, the relationship between the couple changes as they have more time to spend with each other.

Men sometimes participate in a greater amount of household tasks as one way to cope with retirement.[27] Even for rural couples, who may have tended to have a more traditional, gender-differentiated division of work earlier, the housework becomes less role segregated.[28] The impact of the husband's increased participation in housework on the wife is generally positive.[29] Little research has examined the impact of the wife's retirement on marital satisfaction or on specific alterations in behavior.[30]

The crossover in sex roles that begins in midlife that we noted above continues during this period. Both husbands and wives tend toward a pattern of "unisex" in which their behaviors can not be distinguished on a sex-role continuum. Men are likely to be nurturing of small children and to participate in homemaking. Women are likely to be independent and assertive. Greater understanding between women and men becomes possible.

The cross-sexed activities in which women and men participate may contribute to their health and satisfaction, as well. An investigation that compared older people in rural and urban environments found that for both men in the city and in the country, cross-sexed work such as volunteer work and cross-sexed leisure activities such as hobbies, reading, and television viewing contributed to the men's happiness and satisfaction.[31]

Another factor that contributes to the successful management of one's older years is changing one's identity from one based on effectiveness to one based on affectiveness. Elizabeth Mutran, of the University of North Carolina, investigated identity in old age and determined that self-meaning came from feeling and emotion (affectiveness) rather than action (effectiveness). She found that older people did not define affectiveness as ineffectiveness, but as a separate quality. She noted, "Although differences in the environment, including poor health and role losses, are related to differences in the self meaning of the elderly, the meaning is not necessarily a negative or pathological one."[32]

The implication of these studies is that change is necessary in order to maintain happiness over the life cycle. Similarly, the marital unit must adapt in order to achieve marital satisfaction. Joyce Baumgard, in a long-term marriage, noted, "Both of the people in the relationship are going to change over time and you have to adjust to those differences or it will never work."[33]

■ Ill Health May Affect Satisfaction

One problem that may disrupt the satisfaction with this family stage is ill health. Dr. Alvin Poussaint observes:

> Unlike the earlier stages of development, growing old can be an especially poignant time, full of rewarding but difficult tasks. The "best years of our lives" are frequently marred by a slow but inevitable decline in our physical and, occasionally, mental abilities.[34]

We observed that the couple in the older years is the final stage of family development and we might note that this stage generally ends with the death of one or the other spouses. As a consequence, ill health often occurs. Many diseases are relatively slow moving and yet seriously debilitating. Alzheimer's disease, a variety of forms of cancer, and heart disease may be detected in persons years before they prove fatal. However, the insidious nature of such diseases can kill an individual's personality and his or her relationships with others long before it kills the physical body.

The loss of memory that may occur as an accompaniment to a disease or without any diagnosed ailment is the source of humor in Bill Cosby's book, *Time Flies.* Cosby explains his own loss of memory:

> The most embarrassing trick your mind can play: forgetting what you have been talking about.... The moment happens to you like this. You and another friend in his fifties are sitting together, perhaps at a party where none of the younger people will talk to you because you still read books, or perhaps in the waiting room of a doctor who specialized in the treatment of people who have begun to click. You have started talking to this man about a subject in which you always have been deeply interested: the history of hot chocolate. You can see that your friend is listening with attention.... And so, you are merrily spinning these unforgetable thoughts, while your friend is responding with continuous support....
>
> But suddenly another person approaches you and says, "Would either of you gentlemen like some coffee?"

Older couples frequently report great marital satisfaction (© Cleo, The Picture Cube).

"No, thank you," you reply.
"No coffee for me," says your friend.
"Some tea or prune juice, perhaps?"
"No, thanks."
"None for me."
"Perhaps a mint or a Tootsie Roll?"
"No, nothing thanks."
"Right, nothing for me either."
And then you speak the chilling words: "Now where was I?

You are trying to return to your train of thought and discover that you can't even find the station. And neither can your *friend*, who has been listening with such attention. . . . The only good thing about the decline of my memory is that it has brought me closer to my mother, for she and I now forget everything at the same time.[35]

The "inevitable decline" of the body causes some older couples to worry about the death of their spouse. One man in his retirement years described himself as highly independent earlier. When asked how he would feel if he lost his wife, he revealed, "I would be a lost soul. It is frightening and I wouldn't want to think about being alone."[36] Another older man added, "I would feel lost, I need a companion. It's an emotional dependency."[37] The husbands appear to be more concerned about losing their spouses than do the wives in the older marriages. Both traditional sex roles and the new sex-role crossovers may render the men more vulnerable.

■ Importance of Communication

Communication is very important during this stage of family development. The couple must attempt to communicate openly and honestly with each other about the changing nature of their relationship and of their unique individual experiences. Bill Cosby observes that

> the essential ingredients for a fulfilling life are the same for young and old. Older people need not undergo a prescribed disengagement from life. Love, friendship, a feeling of connectedness with others, and a sense of humor remain critical to our sense of well-being.[38]

One advantage that older couples have is that they know each other so well that they can "mind read." Often one member of the couple knows what the other is thinking even before he or she utters a word. Michelle and Victor Beaumont live in a small town in central Ohio. The two are very traditional in their beliefs and behaviors. Michelle discusses their relationship, "We aren't very verbal people and even our friends ask us, 'How do you stay together, you never talk!'"[39] Burt takes up the explanation:

> We know the answer to each other before we even ask. We know what the other one is thinking. We do have a lot of quiet times but we never feel uncomfortable.[40]

The relationship between other family members and the elderly couple is essential. One author notes that

> the kinship network continues to be the most important support to older Americans. It serves as one of the few relatively stable forces in their lives and provides the stage for most of the limited roles available to them.[41]

Grandchildren are important interactants in the grandparent's life. Nearly half of the grandparents who are 65 years old or older see their grandchildren within every day or so; 28 percent see them within every week or so.[42]

"Interactional and subjective relationships" between grandparents and grandchildren have been shown to be "extremely strong."[43] About 43 percent of undergraduate college women reported they felt "quite close" or "extremely close" to their grandparents.[44] Other young adults have explained that the motive for their visits with their grandparents are not based on ritual, but on quality time.[45]

What do grandchildren talk about with their grandparents? An investigator identified seven topics that were reported being discussed by at least 30 percent of the grandchildren. These topic areas included (in order of likelihood of being discussed) family, school and education, health (usually the grandparent's), dating and marriage, work (of both the grandchild and the grandparent), travel, and food.[46]

Older couples also need to interact with their children. The importance and nature of interaction between women and men and their children is different. Older women have higher life satisfaction when they are closer to their family and when their children agree with them about such issues as child rearing and valuation of money. Although they have higher self-esteem when their children provide them with psychological support and emotional security, it was lower when the number of letters or gifts increased. Older men are benefited by being able to provide their children with financial aid. Their satisfaction also is higher when they agree with their children about how decision making occurred, and about the valuation of the parental role.[47]

Whether one is living in a rural or urban environment also affects the nature of the relationship with older parents and their adult children. Rural parents view having their children live close to them as a major contributor to a high quality of relationship, while urban parents do not view close proximity as essential.[48]

What kinds of expectations do older adults hold for their adult children? When older adults were asked about their expectations, they identified affection, assistance, respect, responsibility, and open communication as important. The desired relationships they hoped to have with their adult children were marked by warmth, sharing, affection, and avoidance of direct interference in each others' lives.[49]

The older couple and their family members can each contribute to satisfying relationships. Unless one of the elderly members is seriously ill, they can provide as much support to younger members as they receive. For many families, the elderly play essential roles in the family and provide a variety of kinds of support to their children.[50]

SUMMARY

In the last four chapters we have considered the various stages of family development. In this chapter we began with families launching children and we concluded with the couple in their older years. We determined that a variety of changes make each of these stages unique and filled with challenges.

Communicating openly and honestly is important in the family as it grows and develops. Supporting other family members who may be in very different stages is essential. Sensitivity to the alterations that are occurring within individuals and among the interactants is necessary.

The family with adolescent children, discussed in the last chapter, soon becomes the family that is launching children. Children may leave home as early as 18, when they have completed high school, or they may leave far later. Some children never leave home while others leave home only to return a short time later. The mother may dread this stage if she has built her world around her children. Differences in interaction patterns occur within the family that is still in residence and with the child or children who have left home.

Families in their middle years and their older years have unique problems. They must cope with changes in their body, their lifestyle, and their health. They may find that such changes outweigh their ability to cope and they may dissolve their marriage after 30 or 40 years. More couples find these periods to be relaxing and refreshing as they are free of many responsibilities and they have economic and interpersonal security.

You have already gone through some of these family stages; you will continue to go through others. Being part of a family is inevitable. Whether you will be satisfied in your family relationships or not is largely dependent upon your ability to communicate successfully with other family members and upon their skill in communicating with you. The last four chapters should be instructive as they provide specific information on the variety of family stages that occur and as they help us to understand differences in the communication demands that each stage provides.

KEY TERMS

1. The family development stage of *launching* children is defined as when the children in the family range in age from 13 to 24.

2. The *"empty nest"* phase usually begins during the launching stage. This is a time when children begin to leave the household and parents reflect about the many changes that will take place or have taken place without the children.

3. The families in the *middle years* stage of development begins when all the children have left home but the couple has not yet retired.

4. The families in the *older years* stage of development begins when the couple is in retirement and ends when the couple divorce or when one member dies.

PART THREE

SEEKING SATISFACTION

CHAPTER 10

ACHIEVING AUTONOMY AND INTIMACY

It's co-existence or no-existence.

BERTRAND RUSSELL

After you have read this chapter, you will be able to

1. Differentiate between autonomy and intimacy.

2. Discuss how relational currencies and unexpressed expectations affect intimacy.

3. Identify the four levels of cohesion, including disengaged, separate, connected, and enmeshed families.

4. Explain the importance of self-concept in gaining autonomy and intimacy.

5. Identify factors that affect individual needs for autonomy and intimacy.

6. Describe the couple typology that includes traditionals, separates, and independents.

7. Define self-disclosure and explain how it allows us to regulate our needs for autonomy and intimacy.

8. Differentiate among the breadth, depth, duration, valence, and target person in self-disclosure.

9. Describe two theories that explain how self-disclosure operates in communication.

10. Identify factors that affect self-disclosure.

11. Explain patterns of self-disclosure in families.

12. Consider the most current research on the relationship of self-disclosure to marital satisfaction.

Each of us needs to establish our autonomy, or independence, and at the same time each of us desires intimacy with other people. We wish to be self-governing and independent individuals, but we also have a need to be part of a group, to belong, to be needed by others, and to need them. We desire relational development and increased intimacy, but we are sometimes afraid of relationships developing too quickly. These seemingly conflicting goals exist in each of us. The establishment of both autonomy and intimacy are important in the family context.

❖ THE NATURE OF AUTONOMY AND INTIMACY

▤ Definitions of the Terms

What is the nature of autonomy and intimacy? *Autonomy* means the state of being self-governing, self-determining, and independent. *Intimacy* refers to close relationships, associations, affiliations, or acquaintances with other people. Intimacy suggests two (or more) people share personal, private, informal, or secret information.

Autonomy and intimacy may be viewed as opposites or as separate dimensions. As you become increasingly intimate with another person, you may feel you have less autonomy. As you become more autonomous, you may feel less intimacy. On the other hand, you may find that you are sometimes highly autonomous and on other occasions you are extremely intimate. Although the relationships between autonomy and intimacy have not been fully determined, we do know that individuals have need for both.

Recent research suggests that since "relationships are dynamic social processes,"[1] couples in lasting relationships continue to negotiate matters such as independence and interdependence. Leslie Baxter, from the University of California at Davis, and Kathryn Dindia, from the University of Wisconsin in Milwaukee, have contributed a great deal to our understanding of relational maintenance. In a current article, they explain that relational partners face many dialectical tensions in their maintenance of a relationship over time. They include "the tension between the need for the parties to have independence and separation from the relationship, combined with the connectedness and interdependence of relating"[2] and "the tension between the need for open disclosure coupled with the need for information discretion."[3]

In other words, partners may each hold contrary needs—the needs for both independence and interdependence, for example—or each partner may have one need that contradicts the other: One person wants total disclosure while the other wants a great deal of discretion. These opposing needs act to continually change the relationship.

This sentiment was similarly expressed by philosophers of love. For example, in *The Art of Loving,* Erich Fromm writes:

> Love is an active power in man; a power which breaks through the walls which separate man from his fellow man, which unites him with others; love makes him overcome the sense of isolation and separateness, yet it permits him to be himself, to retain his integrity. In love the paradox occurs that two beings become one and remain two.[4]

Similarly Kahlil Gibran, in his masterpiece *The Prophet,* writes:

> But let there be spaces in your togetherness, and let the winds of the heavens dance between you. Love one another, but make not a bond of love: Let it rather be a moving sea between the shores of your souls. Fill each other's cup but drink not from one cup. Give one another of your bread but eat not from the same loaf. Sing and dance together and be joyous, but let each one of you be alone, even as the strings of a lute are alone though they quiver with the same music. Give your hearts, but not into each other's keeping. For only the hand of Life can contain your hearts. And stand together yet not too near together: for the pillars of the temple stand apart, and the oak tree and the cypress grow not in each other's shadow.[5]

Couples in satisfying marriages reflect the paradox between the desire to be simultaneously independent and interdependent. The Turks have been married nearly 30 years and are a very traditional couple. Henry Turk observed:

> I feel as though we gave up our independence when we got married, and partly our individuality. I think when you get married you take a vow to become one, and you spend the rest of your married life becoming one, and you can't become one if you hang on to your individuality and your independence. I depend on her as much as she depends on me.[6]

His wife, Sandra, was less positive in her understanding of their relationship:

> Through the years I think that I really lost my individuality, cause I think when we were young and I worked at the bank I felt secure in making my own money and I liked my job—but then Billy was born and it seems like I spent the rest of my life just raising (as bad as it sounds) HIS kids. But now because they are all gone, I am scared because I have to learn to be myself.[7]

Contrast the Turks with the Kloos, who have also already celebrated a silver anniversary. Christian Kloos began, "We have an agreement—she doesn't play golf and I don't quilt."[8] This couple agreed that they engaged in few activities apart from each other, but Tina Kloos asserted, "Both of us are very independent people, it is part of our personalities. So that helps us be part of a team and still have our own identities."[9]

Another couple, married only three years, shows similar independence. Sherry and Chad Ehrlich both have graduate degrees in psychology. They worked as professionals in social service agencies until a year ago when they quit their jobs to move back to Chad's family's farm. The couple appear to have achieved an ideal relationship as they rise at 4:30 each morning to work side by side in the calf barn. They share chores outside the house and within the older home on his parents' property, which was vacated by the older couple when they built a new home. The two are inseparable, rarely spending even an hour apart during a day. Yet Sherry stated:

> The whole reason our relationship stays together is because we are not dependent on each other and we are happy with ourselves. This way of life makes things much easier, because when you don't need somebody, you're free. It's a paradox.[10]

Couples do not only vacillate between their needs for independence and interdependence, they also vary in whether they view each other as best friends or not. Arnold Lazarus, a marital researcher, posits that the belief that husband and wife should be best friends is a myth. He argues:

> While it's true that a marriage is like a friendship in some ways, the two relationships are far from the same. Friends don't usually live under the same roof year in and year out. Spouses share more daily events in which the feelings of one partner have a direct effect on the other. What's more, friendship emphasizes the needs and interests of two different people, while the focus of marriage is often on the family.
>
> A best friend is, by definition, your most intimate confidant. There are no emotional taboos, no unmentionable subjects. Yet in marriage, the continuous physical closeness, the shared burdens and responsibilities, and the special kind of intimacy all dictate the need for more emotional privacy. Whereas best friends may exchange information from A–Z, the ideal couple should probably proceed no further than from A–W.[11]

Phil DeLong, engaged to Debra Fogle, is aware of Lazarus's advice, but maintains that his engaged relationship is highly satisfying because "we are good friends as well as lovers."[12] His advice to others includes, "You have to like each other—to be friends."[13] Similarly Christian Kloos, in a long-term happy relationship, explained, "She's my best friend and it's nice when you live with your best friend, and I feel more strongly about her now than I did 30 years ago."[14]

Friendship may be critical to some couples, while requiring the partner to be one's "best" friend may place unrealistic expectations on the relationship. One couple described their friendship with others, which served to summarize their autonomy and intimacy. Janeen Nickerson, who sings in the Cleveland Opera, explained, "I have my friends, Gene [her husband] has his friends, and we have our friends."[15]

Clearly, family members negotiate autonomy and intimacy. Communicative rules are created that allow certain levels of autonomy and intimacy for each individual and each subgroup within the family. Sometimes we are not very clear about our needs and consequently are unable to gain the levels of intimacy and autonomy that are comfortable for us. Misunderstandings and differences in needs for autonomy and intimacy may be no laughing matter, but they sometimes form the basis of humor.

We noted in Chapter 6 that as relationships develop, couples begin to use idiosyncratic communication. In other words, they develop specialized language and ways of talking understood to the two of them but not necessarily understood by others. This personalized communication has been examined by social scientists. They have found that couples use idiomatic expressions, including playful nicknames for each other and their activities, in order to know each other in ways that others do not know them.[16]

The research team of Hopper, Knapp, and Scott examined idiom use of cohabiting and married couples and determined that couples' idioms could be classified as partner nicknames, expressions of affection, labels for others outside the relationship, confrontations, request and routines, sexual references and euphemisms, sexual invitations, and teasing insults.[17] In a second study, these researchers found that couples had both public idioms—those used in public places; those used by others, and/or words other people would not recognize as unique; and private idioms, which were those used in private circumstances, were used only by the couple, and were not used by others.[18] Another research team including Bell, Burkel-Rothfuss, and Gore found that that to the extent that couples used private language, the couples reported more love, commitment, and closeness.[19]

One couple provided an example of idiosyncratics. Lori Strauss and Joel Woods are an engaged couple who related this conversation:

LORI: "When we had been dating for awhile, we had a code for when he wanted to tell me that he loved me, he would go 1-4-3 with his fingers. It meant 1 for I, 4 for love, and 3 for you.

JOEL: And then I'd go 1-4-3-4-4-3-4-2.

LORI: And then I would say 2. And he would say 3.

JOEL: Meaning, I love you more than you love me. She'd say no and I'd say yes. That's one of the things that we have between the two of us.[20]

Intimacy may increase as people exchange particular behaviors with each other. Kathleen Galvin and Bernard Brommel label *relational currencies* as behaviors that demonstrate the affective dimension of a particular relationship and thus encourage or discourage intimacy. They write: "All relationships involve: (1) an investment of time and/or money, (2) a trading of currencies, and (3) a degree of risk taking."[21] We exchange relational currencies with others in order to move toward (or away from) increased intimacy.

You may show your affection for another family member in a variety of ways. You might make popcorn for the entire family while they are watching television together. You might repair another person's clothing. If family members arrive home at night after everyone is sleeping, you might leave notes telling them how much you care about them. You might say, "I love you," or you may rub someone's back.

Others may show you affection in a variety of ways, too. They might change the oil in your car or wash your car every week for you. They might compliment your cooking or send you flowers. They may purchase low-calorie food when you are dieting or identify exercise classes that you can take together. They may go on long walks with you so that you have an opportunity to share your feelings.

Bess Pittman, married nearly 30 years, explained an important relational currency in her marriage:

> After so many years, there is a lot that can go unspoken with us. I know his needs, his looks, his moods, etc., but even though I know (he loves me) it is really nice to hear it every once in a while. The best part about hearing it this late in our relationship, is that it comes at the most surprising moments and it means more than it ever did before.[22]

Frequently, husbands and wives desire relational currencies that are different from each other. Curt and Donna Emde have been married for two years, have no children, and work together in a full-time ministry on staff with Campus Crusade for Christ. Curt discussed their differences. "I'm more physically oriented, but I know Donna likes to be romanced and she likes to talk."[23] Donna responded by saying she realizes that Curt feels intimate through physical touch, "Curt likes his face kissed, even in the car, I'll kiss him on the cheek, or on the neck. I also put my hand on his leg at church."[24] For this couple, both verbal and nonverbal communication help them to maintain intimacy in their relationship.

Because we have so many ways to show our affection for other family members and because of the ambiguity of these cues, you may find your family sometimes disagrees about the nature of the relational currencies you exchange. For example, a woman may prefer being held by her husband, while he shows his affection by repairing her car. A man may prefer to have time alone each night to watch television or to read a book, while his wife insists on a greater amount of companionship.

One woman reported her husband never purchased or prepared a birthday cake for her, which made her feel he cared less about her. When asked, the husband explained the absence of a cake was a sign of his love because he knew she tried to avoid sugar in her normal eating and was highly weight conscious. The wife explained that from her childhood experiences she viewed the birthday cake as a sign of affection.

Unexpressed expectations are our unstated requirements for other people. Just as we observed in Chapter 3 that rules may be explicit (stated) or implicit (understood), our expectations may be clearly verbalized or may be unstated.

Family members may need to communicate clearly to each other both the nature of the relational currencies they prefer to provide to others and of those they prefer to receive. Sometimes people meet each other's needs, but at other times they are unaware of the needs of the other person. The negotiation of relational currencies occurs whether we attend to the process or not. If your needs are not being met, you may discover that they are not understood by your partner or other family member.

One couple failed to discuss their differing needs for intimacy. The husband preferred to be alone, but was married to a woman who preferred total companionate time in the evening. He was surprised to come home one evening to no television and no new books. The television set had broken and his wife refused to call a repair person. Furthermore, unknown to him, she had cancelled his book-club subscription without his knowledge two months earlier. If the couple had expressed their needs to each other and negotiated their relational currencies, they might have found they had time for both time alone and time together.

By contrast, Alan and Karen Simms are newlyweds who reported a problem in their relationship that occurred about a month after their engagement. Karen recalled:

> I felt as if Alan was taking me and how much I care for him for granted. I would say that I loved him and instead of saying it back, I would get a kiss on the cheek or "I'm glad," anything but what I wanted to hear. It was not that I thought by any means that he didn't love me, but any type of verbal support was absent. So we fought about it, and it was a big fight.
>
> It was also a dumb fight, but I made a big enough stink about it. Now he is very good about saying things like "good job," "everything is going to be fine," the little things that mean so much. But best of all, I don't even have to work at getting an "I love you" out of him.[25]

By raising the issue early in the relationship, Karen did not have to live with unexpressed expectations.

Just as you may encourage intimacy by exchanging relational currencies, you may encourage autonomy by allowing other people freedom and independence. Adolescents, for instance, develop stronger needs for autonomy as they prepare to leave the original family.[26] In response, a parent might allow the adolescent child to establish his or her own bedtime, curfews, or study times. Marital couples may have different needs for autonomy, too. One partner might not ask his or her partner to vote the same way in an election. You may avoid encouraging your partner to have the same sexual fantasies you have. Individuals in the family develop differently and a parent might allow the children to show anger in a variety of ways. They may encourage rather than discourage idiosyncratic behavior.

How much autonomy or intimacy is appropriate in a family? No standards exist, but some balance is probably in order. Although closeness is important in family life, remaining separate individuals is essential, too. A woman in one successful 23-year marriage stated she hoped her four children, ranging in age from 13 to 20, learned about autonomy and intimacy from their parents' marriage. She explained, "I hope they've picked up that marriage is a most important commitment, but not suffocating."[27]

Families must find their way to a space between commitment and suffocation. One well-known model of family functioning incorporates three aspects of behavior: cohesion, adaptability, and communication.[28] The dimension of cohesion is similar to the autonomy-intimacy continuum. The authors define family cohesion as "the emotional bonding that family members have toward one another."[29] They identify four levels of cohesion: the disengaged family with very low levels of bonding, the separated family with low to moderate levels, the connected family with moderate to high levels, and the enmeshed family with very high levels. They hypothesize that satisfied families probably fall within the two mid-levels of cohesion (separated or connected). They explain:

> When cohesion levels are high (enmeshed systems), there is overidentification so that loyalty to and consensus within the family prevent individuation of family members. At the other extremes (disengaged systems), high levels of autonomy are encouraged and family members "do their own thing," with limited attachment or commitment to their family.[30]

This theoretical work and its empirical validation support the importance of balance on the continuum of autonomy and intimacy.[31]

How do you feel about autonomy and intimacy? Do you allow other family members their idiosyncrasies and expect them to allow your unique behaviors? Do you talk honestly and openly about all topics with everyone in the family or do you limit your discussions? Does anyone know as much about yourself as you do? Do you respect your partner's emotional needs even when they differ from your own? Do you sacrifice your individuality for the relationship? Does your family agree on all major values? Do you engage in behaviors you feel other family members have no right to know or should not know? Your answers to such questions may help you assess the level of autonomy and intimacy you desire.

■ The Role of Self-Concept

In order to establish autonomy and intimacy within the family, we must have a positive self-concept. Our own inner security will largely affect our willingness to allow others to maintain autonomy and subgroups to gain intimacy. If we do not feel self-love, we will have difficulty in loving others. Virginia Satir explains:

> A person with low self-esteem has a great sense of anxiety and uncertainty about himself. His self-esteem is based to an extreme extent on what he thinks others think of him. His dependence on others for his self-esteem cripples his autonomy and individuality. . . . His low self-esteem comes from his growing-up experiences which never led him to feel that it is good to be a person of one sex in relation to a person of the other. . . . A person with low self-esteem has high hopes about what to expect from others, but he also has great fears; he is only too ready to expect disappointment and to distrust people.[32]

How does one gain a positive self-concept? In Chapter 7 we discussed symbolic interactionism, which posits that we gain a sense of who we are through our interactions with others. One critical element is our sense of attachment to a parent or caretaker. One author explains:

> A few babies never become attached. For the most part, they are the babies in foundling homes or institutions who have no permanent caring adults around. Even though they are receiving adequate physical attention, they become withered, apathetic, withdrawn, or they die. . . . Furthermore they don't form a sense of self or ego. . . . Babies need people to care passionately about them in order to survive and grow well.[33]

The bonding that occurs during the nurturing stage of parenthood is critical to the psychological health of the individual. Children who do not develop feelings of attachment may have different needs for autonomy and intimacy as children and adults. Their communicative behavior may be affected. For example, children who are not securely attached by the first year interact more slowly and less smoothly with strangers when they are 3 years old.[34] In Chapter 7 we discussed the relationship between self-esteem and validation from the parent or caretaker that was provided by Satir.[35]

While our self-concept originates early in childhood, it is not a static entity. The development of self has been there through childhood, adolescence, and adulthood.[36] Our self-concept changes as a result of developmental stages and because of differing interactions we have with others as we grow and mature. In addition, we do not hold the same self-concept with all people, under all circumstances, and at all times. For instance the way you see yourself vis-à-vis your father may be very different from the way you see yourself in terms of your own child. One author notes that "Parents interpret their children to their children," but she adds:

> Books, articles, and papers about child development may make it seem as if parents hand the child a self-concept like a paper-doll cutout, ready-made. This is not the case, as parents know. Children form their own self-concepts, taking into account their parents' opinions, the opinions of their brothers and sisters, friends, relatives, teachers, and grandparents, and their own assessment of themselves.[37]

As children grow, they reflect on the appraisals of themselves offered by others to form a consistent, integrated, unified sense of self.

Some discrepancies may occur between our own knowledge of who we are and the knowledge others have of us. We do not know all that is to be known about ourselves and we do not share with others all we do know; similarly, others may possess information about us they do not share with us. This situation allows us to distinguish among four different sets of information: information we know and share with others (e.g., our nickname, age, political affiliation); information we know but we do not share with others (e.g., something about which you are embarrassed or something of which you are proud);

Figure 10.1

	Known to self	Not known to self
Known to others	Open self	Blind self
Not known to others	Hidden self	Unknown self

The Johari Window.

information we do not know but others do (e.g., you bite your lip when you are nervous, you are adopted); and information neither we nor others know (e.g., you are alcoholic, you are in the first month of pregnancy, or you have recently contracted AIDS). These four possibilities were presented in a visual model known as the *Johari Window,* which is shown in Figure 10.1.[38]

The complexity of self-concept is apparent in this discussion. Our self-concept emerges from our interactions with others. However, lack of information or understanding may occur on several levels. Significant others may be responding to us on the basis of their own general response pattern. First, they may have learned to confirm, reject, or disconfirm most other individuals. They may suffer from poor self-concept and treat others in a dysfunctional way. Second, they may have information about us we do not have. A parent may know one of his children has an incurable disease, but the child does not possess this information. Third, we may not be aware of how they are treating us. An adolescent daughter who is fighting for independence may ignore all of the loving behavior her mother provides. Fourth, we may misinterpret their behavior. A wife may allow her husband, who is also a college student, time alone to study out of love for him; the husband may interpret his wife's behavior as a sign of lack of caring about him.

An understanding of our self-concept is complicated by misunderstanding and lack of information. It is rendered additionally complex because it is continually in flux and it changes over time, with different individuals, and in different situations. Nonetheless, it forms the basis for our interactions that allow us to gain autonomy and intimacy.

■ Factors That Affect Our Needs

Our developmental stage, the characteristics of other family members, our relationship with our family, and our current circumstances may alter the relative proportions of our need for autonomy and our need for intimacy.[39] We observed in Chapter 7, for instance, that people in some developmental stages have more need for autonomy than individuals in other stages. For example, both the 2- to 3-year-old and the teenager have a greater need for independence.[40] On the other hand, individuals between the ages of 19 and 25 have a need to form at least one intimate relationship and to become interdependent with that person.

Persons who are in different relational development stages may similarly have different needs for autonomy and intimacy. Engaged couples and newlyweds may be more desirous of close contact. Couples in the child-rearing stages of the family may either not desire as much intimacy, or may not be able to manage it with the multiple roles they must play. Retired couples, with a greater opportunity for time together, frequently find their "new togetherness" stifling and find ways to gain autonomy. One retired couple from a rural Ohio community discussed their new pattern of behavior:

> HE: "We try not to spend too much time—"
> SHE: "We give each other a lot of space."
> HE: "It seems to me that when you retire you don't want each other underfoot every moment. And so we try to get involved in activities that are separate and then we come back together again."[41]

The characteristics of other family members may also affect the relative proportions of autonomy and independence one desires. Children who live in an overprotective family may resist the push for interdependence and feel greater needs to be self-determining. Suppose both members of the married couple are very independent and rarely rely on others. Also, they do not ask for help or support from others. How will their children grow up? They may develop a stronger need for belonging to a group or may reflect their family's behavior and become very independent family members. Nonetheless, their parents' characteristics affected their needs.

Our relationships with other family members may similarly affect our relative needs for independence and togetherness. Mary Ann Fitzpatrick's typology of couple relationships is relevant. She observed that couples relate to each other in three distinctive ways, and she labeled the three types *independents, separates,* and *traditionals.* Fitzpatrick's couples can be distinguished by their relative needs for independence and interdependence. For instance, the independent couples desired great autonomy but would negotiate the amount of sharing that would occur. The separate couples experienced little togetherness and engaged in little sharing. By contrast, the traditional couples evidenced high interdependence and low autonomy.[42]

Our current circumstances may also affect our needs for autonomy and intimacy. For instance, families on vacation with one another feel stress because of the pressured togetherness that is often experienced.[43] On a vacation the family may be required to interact in a physical space that is far smaller than their home, may not be allowed to eat any of their meals alone, and may be expected to spend virtually every waking moment with other family members.

A family of five traveled from their spacious home in the Midwest to Orlando, Florida, to visit the numerous attractions in the area. Since they were busy sightseeing each day, they shared one room in a motel. On the second night, the little boy, who was 5 years old, pulled a blanket and pillow off his bed and departed into the closet. When he was asked what he was doing, he explained that he was going to sleep in the closet because "I've got to get away from everybody." He was asserting his needs for autonomy.

❖ SELF-DISCLOSURE REGULATES OUR NEEDS FOR AUTONOMY AND INTIMACY

Self-disclosure can be used to assert our autonomy and independence in the family or to encourage intimacy and interdependence. Although we will be advised of some evidence to the contrary in the following pages, self-disclosure frequently results in more intimate relationships. As we tell others about ourselves and they tell us about themselves, we feel closer. Self-disclosure may help us separate ourselves from family members. As we identify and articulate personal thoughts about ourselves, we may be engaged in the act of differentiating ourselves from the family.[44]

Self-disclosure is the process of offering verbal revelations about oneself to others.[45] It is sometimes called openness, verbal accessibility, and social penetration[46] and it occurs when we voluntarily and intentionally tell another person accurate information about ourselves that the other person is unlikely to know or find out from another source. Self-disclosure requires the discloser to risk sharing his or her personal thoughts and private feelings to another person. Self-disclosure thus renders one vulnerable to another.

Self-disclosure messages are not all similar. Researchers have suggested that self-disclosure can be analyzed for its *breadth,* or total amount of information disclosed; *depth,* or intimacy of the information disclosed; *duration,* or the time spent engaged in disclosure; *valence,* or its positive or negative impact; *timing,* or when it occurs in a relationship; and *target person,* or individual who receives the disclosure.[47]

We will determine that these dimensions are important considerations in prescribing self-disclosure within the family.

■ Theories About Self-Disclosure

How does self-disclosure operate in communication? A number of theories have been advanced. Two of them seem particularly appropriate to our understanding of family communication. The *social exchange theory*, discussed in Chapter 6, suggests behaviors are valued to the extent they result in positive outcomes. The relative benefits must outweigh the potential costs. Two researchers observe: "Whatever the nature of the early exchanges between [two individuals], they will voluntarily continue their association only if the experienced outcomes (or inferred but as yet unexperienced outcomes) are found to be adequate."[48]

Self-disclosure, or personal information, is generally viewed as a valuable commodity. The social exchange theory suggests that self-disclosure will operate in a linear manner in family satisfaction. In other words, as individuals provide personal information to each other, they view the relationship as providing positive outcomes. Thus the social exchange theory would suggest that high levels of self-disclosure will result in increased family satisfaction.

Equity theory suggests people feel an obligation to exchange comparable behaviors in order to maintain balance in their relationships. Individuals feel equity is achieved when one person discloses information and the other person reciprocates. A lack of equity occurs when one person discloses and the other does not. Equity theory predicts that

> when individuals find themselves participating in inequitable relationships, they will become distressed. The more inequitable the relationships, the more distress individuals will feel.[49]

This theory suggests that the same sense of imbalance that occurs when someone unexpectedly gives us an expensive gift on a holiday when we have no gift to reciprocate likewise occurs when someone provides us with intimate self-disclosure and we are unwilling, or unable, to self-disclose. Truman Capote used this notion to entice Marlon Brando to disclose to him in an interview:

> One evening Marlon broke his seclusion and submitted to the widely quoted interview by Truman Capote published in *The New Yorker*. To ensnare his quarry, Capote resorted to the only psychological finesse that could succeed: "I made up stories about what lushes my family were," he admitted, "and, believe me, I made them lurid, until he began to feel sorry for me and told me his to make me feel better. Fair exchange."[50]

While the social exchange theory suggests a linear relationship between self-disclosure and family satisfaction, the equity model suggests a curvilinear model. Family members will be distressed if their levels of disclosure are not comparable or approximately the same, but they will be satisfied if their levels of self-disclosure are relatively the same. The more discrepant, or different, the self-disclosure levels of individuals, the more inequity and distress they will feel; the more similar the levels of self-revelation, the more equity and satisfaction they will feel. According to this theory, dissatisfaction emerges when imbalances occur in the exchange.

Family members may feel dissatisfied when they learn self-disclosure has not been reciprocated. For instance, if adolescents and adult children have routinely shared their secrets with their parents, they may feel distressed to learn the parents have not been similarly disclosive. One female college student explained:

> [My parents] always encouraged me to disclose. I don't think they realize the importance of reciprocity. For instance, I found out much later, in my adolescent years that my mother and father eloped. When I learned this by accident, through another family member I recall being extremely hurt.[51]

Reciprocated self-disclosure between family members can lead to increased intimacy and closeness. Another female college student adds:

> ... between me and my mother. It was during a time when I thought that I was pregnant and I shared this information with her. She then went on to explain to me the feelings and experiences she went through when she was pregnant with me. (She was still in high school at that time.) She also told me something that shocked me: she told me that she had an abortion at one time in her life. This was the deepest disclosure of herself that I have ever received.[52]

■ Self-Disclosure Affected by a Number of Factors

Individuals do not self-disclose to the same extent. Some of us provide a great deal of information about ourselves early in relationship development, while others are hesitant to provide any information—even after we have a long-established relationship. Furthermore, some people self-disclose to a similar extent regardless of the development of the relationship, while others are highly sensitive to the contextual constraints upon self-disclosure.

Why do individuals disclose differentially? As we observed in Chapter 3, our families of origin teach us a great deal about communication. The patterns of communication we develop can be traced back to our earliest interactions with other family members.

While people vary in their styles of disclosure, subsets of individuals appear to have similar styles of disclosure.[53] Socialization in particular families may account for differences in styles of disclosure. Young adults who report having been raised by parents who encouraged open expression of feelings and opinions are higher in the amount of disclosure they provide to both parents and best same-sex friend. They are more honest and exhibit greater awareness when disclosing. Children who are rewarded for the frank and open statement of their opinions and feelings may develop a general response of revealing information about themselves.

Socialization differences occur for women and men in our culture, too. In general, women appear to self-disclose more than men do;[54] they disclose more negative information than men do;[55] they provide others with less honest information than men do;[56] and they disclose more intimate information than men do.[57] While both women and men report greater self-disclosure to people of the same sex, women actually disclose more intimate information to men.

Women and men avoid self-disclosure for apparently different reasons. Men avoid self-disclosure in order to maintain control over their relationships. They tend to perceive relationships as battles in which others are adversaries who must be controlled. Women avoid self-disclosure in order to avoid problems with their interpersonal relationships and to avoid personal hurt, including threats to their physical well-being.[58] In addition, men control the intimacy of their disclosures more than women do.[59] These differences between women and men are important to consider in the context of the family.

■ Patterns of Self-Disclosure Among Family Members

Self-disclosure does not flow equally from all family members to all other members. For example, wives are more likely to disclose information than their husbands, and they do so on the basis of liking. Husbands' disclosures are based on their trust of their spouse.[60]

Wives often complain about the lack of disclosure on the part of their husbands. In Alice Adams's *Families and Other Survivors*, one of the female characters considers the paradox of the importance of talking and not talking between husbands and wives:

> At times (as even "happily married" women will) Louisa has a lonely sense that she and John don't *talk*. How she yearns for more conversation, for in fact the sort of conversation that she often has with Kate. Can one have personal conversations only with women? And she thinks then of a succession of men who wouldn't talk with her (Michael talked *at*). Instead of talking (perhaps) she works, alone, and she and John make love.
>
> In other moods she romanticizes their relationship, and she tells herself that their lengthy frame of reference makes talk unnecessary—simply to be together is to communicate.
>
> (Perhaps both are true?)[61]

College students do not disclose to the same extent to their same-sex best friends and their parents. Recent evidence suggests that they disclose more to their best same-sex friend than to either their mother or father. They also provide more negative disclosures to their best same-sex friends than to either of their parents. However, the communication climate between college students and their parents is more defensive than is the climate between themselves and their peers.[62] College students are more honest and accurate in their disclosures to their best same-sex friend than to either of their parents.[63] Finally, college student's disclosures to their friends of the same sex are more negative, honest, intimate, and frequent than are their disclosures to their parents.[64] The results of these studies suggest communication with friends serves a different function than does communication with family members. Changes in the social and economic characteristics of the college population in the past 20 years may account for such findings.

Family members do not self-disclose to the same extent to all other members of the family. In general, children of either sex tend to self-disclose more to their mothers than to their fathers.[65] Mothers also receive more intimate information than fathers do.[66] Fathers tend to be the recipients of more inaccurate information, while mothers are the recipients of more accurate disclosure.[67] Mothers receive relatively the same amount of information about social topics (dating, friendship) as they do about task-related topics (academic progress, grades), but fathers receive less information on social topics than they do on task topics.[68] In general, mothers receive a greater amount of information, more intimate information, more accurate information, and more information about a child's social life than fathers do. One male student validated these findings as he wrote:

> The nature and extent of disclosure in my family of origin has always been very limited. . . . Dad rarely disclosed with anyone about anything, unless it was in fits of rage. My brothers and I did not have a really good relationship with our father. He never showed affection or disclosed with us. However, my oldest brother did get closer to him than the rest of us. With my father, we rarely disclosed any intimate or positive information. . . .
>
> Everyone disclosed with Mom and rarely with anyone else. My mother and I would disclose most to each other. We penetrated some intimate areas, but never reached the core of each other's personality. I am closer to my Mom than anyone else in my family. I talk to her about a lot of topics but there are still some boundaries. Now that I am out of the home, I disclose more with Mom. We do some risk taking disclosure when I discuss my girlfriend and when she gives me her opinions on matters. Generally, though, our disclosure is moderately intimate and positive. Mom and I understand each other and have a really good relationship.[69]

Another male similarly wrote:

> I have a strong bond with my mother. I could never talk to my father like I did with my mother. It seems as though she understands my positions and attitudes better than anyone I know. . . . My father and I get along best when we are working. In fact, that is how I mainly interact with my father. . . . In an interpersonal setting with my brother, my older sister or my mother, I might disclose more important information. For example, I would disclose personal information about personal relationships with girlfriends and other personal subjects. I can only talk to my father about work related subjects and my occupational hopes. Other subjects seem to be too difficult to talk about with him. My younger sister has few similar experiences with me and therefore hears very little personal disclosure.[70]

How do family members select a target person to whom to disclose? Factors such as trust, ability to keep a secret, and the target person's overall interest in communication appear to be factors if these college students' experiences can be generalized:

My brother and I probably self-disclose the most to each other, probably because we're closest in age and temperament, and trust each other. I disclose to my parents as little as possible because of lack of trust. . . . Gordon [her brother] and I probably talk the most, about the most personal subjects. I think this has a lot to do with mutual trust. Despite the fact that we didn't get along very well until I went to school, we never betrayed each other to our parents. If one of us broke the rules, the other one never told the folks about it, and on occasion, we've lied to them for each other. . . . I try to avoid telling my father as much as I can, because he tends to use information against me. For instance, John [her boyfriend] came home from school one weekend over Winter Break, and instead of going home, he stayed with us. Because Dad knew for a fact we'd be at the house all day, he canceled a trip he and Mom had planned; whereas, if he hadn't known John was going to be there, he would have gone ahead and gone. To me, that is the greatest kind of hypocrisy, as well as abusing information freely given. For that reason, I don't freely give information to him very often; or at least, not sensitive information.

My mother is a slightly different matter. There is an element of trust with her because she's known several "deep, dark secrets" about me for several years that she never told Dad. The knowledge itself was not really freely given—she asked a question point-blank, which I answered honestly—and I regretted the disclosure for a couple of years because she, too, seemed to hold the knowledge against me, though in no overt way, like Dad does. Recently, however, the mutual knowledge has become a bond of trust, so that I am willing to discuss more personal things about John with her, and tell her about some of the things I do at school, and some health problems that Dad isn't privy to. I don't think she and I will ever be best friend close, but as I get older, and especially after I'm married, I think we'll develop a more equal, sharing relationship.[71]

A married woman reflected on her childhood and noted she disclosed more to her mother, even though she was "not as open-minded and understanding as she could have been." She explains her choice of a target for disclosure in the family: "We children seemed to disclose more to our mother than father because she was more talkative and liked to discuss matters."[72]

The availability of mothers, the higher trust between children and their mothers, and mothers' higher interest in interaction may account for some of the differences in the patterns of self-disclosure among family members. Men can alter this situation if they consider the motivations for disclosure. Fathers can be increasingly available to their children, they can work to increase trust, and they can demonstrate an interest in interacting with their offspring about relational and social topics as well as those that are task- or job-related.

Self-disclosure generally occurs in a dyad, even within the family setting. A child may talk to a sibling or a parent, but rarely would he or she disclose to the entire family on a regular basis. One young man explained:

Disclosure takes place . . . in our family. Many times during a dinner conversation, someone might bring up a subject that he or she wants to disclose about so a comment will be made to indicate that "I need to talk about this." The subject will very seldom be discussed in detail at that point but later an older brother or sister or my mother would pursue the subject in a more interpersonal setting. Many trivial things can be discussed at the dinner table but personal disclosure ends when the entire family can no longer relate to the situation rationally. For example, if we were discussing accidents that happened on our way home that evening, old stories that happened years before might be brought up and I might tell the family (for the first time) about the time I put my car over the hill on the way to high school one day. This disclosure would be the extent of the risk that I would take in disclosing to the entire family.[73]

Similarly, a female college student explained, "The nature and extent of disclosure is usually one on one in my family."[74]

❖ AUTONOMY AND INTIMACY RELATED TO FAMILY SATISFACTION

The importance of autonomy and intimacy within the family setting has been emphasized by writers in the area. The need for autonomy is clarified by one recent author:

> The family unit is composed of individuals. Each of the individuals has a need for independence and autonomy which precedes his or her need for the group. When we become a member of a family, we do not lose our essential self. Families that smother members or do not allow individuals to grow and develop in independent ways may be doomed. We need to establish our need for autonomy, even in our family.[75]

Women may have more difficulty than men in achieving autonomy in their marriages. One woman explains:

> My husband sometimes doesn't see me as an individual—someone who has separate ideas and thoughts from him. He thinks I should think and act like him. This causes me to strive even harder for autonomy and in the process of proving I'm "me," we overlook some of the better aspects of our relationship.[76]

Children, too, may have some difficulty in gaining autonomy within the family.
Intimacy is similarly important in satisfying families. Sullivan, in his classic work *The Interpersonal Theory of Psychiatry,* discusses the importance of intimacy. He observes intimacy is central to the growth and fulfillment of each of us and we all hold "the need for intimacy—that is, for collaboration with at least one other person."[77] Sven Wahlroos concurs: "An emotionally healthy person is able to give of himself fully in deep and lasting emotional relationships."[78] Wahlroos contrasts the emotionally healthy person with the narcissist:

Both autonomy and intimacy are important in satisfied families (© Crews, Stock, Boston).

The opposite of an emotionally healthy person . . . would be the narcissist, the one who sees other people only in terms of whether they could be of use to him or not. To a narcissist, other people possess no intrinsic worth, they exist only as pleasure-providers or obstacle-placers. A narcissist is often an injustice collector, he is unable to live his life without being outraged over the minor injustices, unfairnesses, and rejections which befall us frequently for the simple reason that people are not perfect. He is imbued with the importance of his own minor "rights" and he flaunts these at any opportunity . . . a narcissist creates his own tragedy: he can never experience a satisfying emotional relationship with another human being, unless he is willing to see his narcissism as the problem it is.[79]

People surveyed by *USA Today* agree with the experts.[80] Couples identified those factors most important to maintaining a good relationship with their mate. Among the most important factors were honesty (96 percent of those polled), discussing feelings (95 percent), sharing financial goals (65 percent), sharing religious values (52 percent), and sharing career goals (42 percent). These behaviors are related to talking to family members and to providing self-disclosure, which allow the achievement of autonomy and intimacy. As we shall determine, such behaviors encourage family satisfaction.

■ **Satisfaction Related to Family Members' Abilities to Provide Both Verbal and Nonverbal Messages**

In other words, communication, in and of itself, is related to satisfying relationships. Couples who talk to each other tend to be more satisfied than couples who do not talk to each other.[81] Open and interactive communication affects the quality of the marital relationship.[82] Overall marital satisfaction is highly related to the couple's ability to discuss problems effectively and to share their feelings.[83] Wives who rate high on communication competence state they have high levels of marital satisfaction.[84]

Greg and Sharon Brennan are an example of a couple who show high levels of marital satisfaction and who are highly communicative with each other. Greg met Sharon 26 years ago at an elementary school where he was the principal and she was a teacher. Although the two are 15 years apart in age, they married less than a year after they met. Sharon stopped teaching to raise the couple's three children, who have now all left home. Seven years ago, Greg retired; three years later, when the youngest child left for college, Sharon resumed her duties in a local elementary school. What do they talk about? "Everything but Bangladesh and the homeless," they quipped. Although they admitted later that the only topic of discussion that causes strain, and sometimes conflict, is their adult children; they find their high levels of talk and disclosures a factor in their happiness. Sharon concluded, "We know each other so well that I can anticipate what he is going to say."[85]

Marital couples may talk to each other far less than they realize. Of the 10,080 minutes in a week, the average couple spends about 17 minutes talking to each other.[86] Often the contemporary couple is rarely at home at the same time, and often they have spent a great deal of their busy day interacting with others, so additional time spent in communication is not necessarily seen as inviting. Nonetheless, as we have observed, satisfied families tend to interact more than do dissatisfied families.

■ **Self-Disclosure and Increased Family Satisfaction**

Early Research Recommended Self-Disclosure Unequivocally   Sidney Jourard provided the earliest research on self-disclosure and implied it was related to a "healthy interpersonal relationship" in which people were willing and able to communicate all of their real selves to others.[87] He suggested that open communication promoted growth in relationships. Other theorists in the next two decades similarly prescribed self-disclosure and suggested that it was related to personal growth, interpersonal competence, attraction, liking, trust, and facilitative conditions.[88]

One popular author writes:

> Being truthful is, in my opinion, the only choice in a relationship that means to be long-lasting, intimate, and committed. Lies are the single most corrosive influence upon relationships.[89]

In the area of family communication, theorists were similarly positive about the role of self-disclosure. Earlier investigators viewed self-disclosure as the "lifeblood" of the marital relationship.[90] Two researchers add: "Communicating about fears, problems, self-doubts, feelings of anger or depression, and aspects of marriage perceived to be bothersome to one or both partners, as well as openly sharing positive feelings about the self and other, are of central importance in fulfilling the therapeutic function of marriage."[91]

Furthermore, current research has shown that a couple's ability to openly express their feelings and to discuss problems effectively predicts their marital satisfaction.[92] The willingness to disclose is one predictor of close relationships.[93] Self-disclosure and marital satisfaction have been shown to have a strong and positive relationship.[94]

The social exchange theory has been supported in some investigations, as these studies have suggested self-disclosure leads to positive outcomes.[95] Higher levels of self-disclosure are associated with increased family satisfaction; lower levels of self-disclosure are related to decreased family satisfaction.

College students sometimes express regrets about the low levels of disclosure available in their original families. One man writes:

> I really regret the disclosure process that occurred in my family. I have friends whose families are so close that they tell each other everything.... I always wanted my family to be close like that.... In my future family, I am going to work very hard to keep a close family who talk to each other and show their feelings. I believe that there is something missing in a family that does not disclose or show their affection. I hope that my family-of-origin can someday change and experience more disclosure and closeness, and I will strive very hard to establish a future family that is open, intimate and rewarding.[96]

More Recent Studies Are Cautious in Recommending Self-Disclosure
Current theorists and researchers are less enthusiastic about prescribing self-disclosure as a vehicle to insure relational satisfaction and growth. For example, two investigators write that "the communication of intimacies is a behavior which has positive effects only in limited, appropriate circumstances ... 'the transparent self' is not, perhaps, the ideal model for all people."[97] Similarly, other authors have identified potential problems of disclosure.[98]

A research team explains that simply increasing the quantity of one's disclosive behavior will not result in increased marital satisfaction. Instead, they recommend selective disclosure.[99] Others similarly recommended selective disclosure. They determine that couples who disclosed information that dealt with communal and interpersonal conversational themes were more satisfied than couples who disclosed information that was more individually based.[100]

Privacy, secrecy, and deception play an essential role in relationships.[101] Such techniques provide relief when contact becomes too intense or involved. In addition, privacy and secrecy serve to maintain relationships, as they allow individuals to hide their inadequacies and errors, thus making them appear to be more attractive to their partners. Indeed, recent research suggests that privacy violations are expected from spouses; however, less satisfied couples are more

DENNIS THE MENACE

"IF ANYONE ASKS ABOUT ME, CHANGE THE SUBJECT."

DENNIS THE MENACE® used by permission of Hank Ketcham and © by North America Syndicate.

likely to need to restore privacy after a privacy violation has occurred than are more satisfied couples.[102] There is no real empirical backing for the prescription of complete openness and honesty in interpersonal relationships.[103]

A certain amount of deception, privacy, and secrecy may be more accurate descriptors of many intimate relationships. Deception can promote intimacy in three ways: It allows us to protect others, it helps to maintain a focus in conversations, and it aids in avoiding tension and conflict.[104]

Finally, Arthur Bochner concludes, "Liking inhibits self-disclosure."[105] He explains discriminating disclosers are more satisfied and more likely to remain attractive to their partners than are indiscriminating disclosers. In addition, he asserts that people in long-term relationships cannot afford to be totally disclosive because they have too much to lose. If they believe a particular disclosure will threaten their relationship, they are likely to withhold it.

Two other researchers also recommended the importance of privacy, secrecy, and deception, but in a totally different manner than the previous theorists. These researchers advise individuals to be open and disclosive within the relationship, but to exercise secrecy and privacy with the outside world.[106]

This same advice is provided in the "Dennis the Menace" cartoon shown here.

This recommendation underlines the importance of avoiding relationships with individuals outside the marital relationship, including separate activities and separate identities that have the potential of becoming more important than the family or marital relationship. Two investigators validate this advice in a study that considers emotional and sexual extramarital involvement. Not surprisingly, they found both women and men who experienced extramarital involvement report the greatest amount of marital dissatisfaction.[107]

Expectation Levels Affect the Appropriateness of Self-Disclosure The equivocal findings on the simple, linear relationship between self-disclosure and marital satisfaction may be due to a lack of sophistication of measurement.[108] Investigators tested three different models of marital disclosure and marital satisfaction: the linear model, the curvilinear model, and a social desirability model. They found overall satisfaction with the marriage increased as self-disclosure increased. They observe, however, that their measures did not take into account such factors as individual expectation levels or the perceptions of the appropriateness of disclosing information on specific topics in particular places or at certain times.

They suggest that studies that consider the appropriateness of disclosure may determine that a curvilinear relationship exists between self-disclosure and satisfaction. Thus, medium levels of marital disclosure are associated with satisfaction, while low levels and high levels of disclosure are associated with less satisfaction. Shirley J. Gilbert similarly suggests that while a low level of disclosure is probably related to low marital satisfaction and that as disclosure increases, satisfaction increases, the highest levels of disclosure may not be related to the highest levels of satisfaction.[109] This suggestion is based on the notion that high levels of self-disclosure often include negative information that may be detrimental to the levels of satisfaction.

Two investigators examined marital communication and found that the suggestion concerning expectations about communicative behavior was accurate. They showed that the relationship between verbal communication patterns and marital satisfaction is dependent "on a couple's implicit expectations and standards of communication."[110] Satisfaction, then, may be more a function of the couple's expectations than of the overall quantity of disclosure.

The equity theory, which demonstrates a curvilinear rather than a linear relationship between self-disclosure and satisfaction, has been supported in other research. Couples had similar disclosure levels; that is, husbands and wives stated that they tended to match the disclosure levels of their partners.[111]

Another research team confirmed that the greater the discrepancy in partner's affective self-disclosure, the lower was their marital adjustment. This result held whether the other partner was perceived as disclosing more or less information than the reporting partner.[112]

Factors other than total amount of self-disclosure affect marital satisfaction.[113] The contribution of disclosure to satisfaction lies in the history of the relationship and the goals for the self-disclosing talk. Expectations based on implicit rules developed over the lifetime of the relationship may be key.

Negative Information May Be Best Left Undisclosed   The valence of the disclosure rather than the act of disclosing may encourage relational satisfaction. For instance, dissatisfied couples disclosed more unpleasant feelings than satisfied couples. The researchers conclude that "talking about one's feelings does not necessarily refer to spilling out everything. For the average couple, *selective disclosure* of feelings seems more beneficial to marital harmony than indiscriminate catharsis."[114]

Many studies have shown that more satisfied spouses report less disclosure of negative feelings toward their mates or less negative disclosure, in general.[115] The item on a marital inventory that most discriminated satisfied from dissatisfied married couples was the tendency of the individual's spouse to disclose information that would be better left unstated.[116] Recently, Sprecher recommended, "If the disclosure is negative affect, hostility, nagging, and/or excessive concern about the self, less may be better."[117]

Stella Ting-Toomey found similar results. She examined integrative, disintegrative, and descriptive verbal acts. *Integrative verbal acts* were defined as positive communication that reveals one's inner feelings or ideas and at the same time conveys understanding and empathy with the listener's feelings or ideas. *Disintegrative verbal acts* included communication that discloses one's feelings or ideas and at the same time functions as a threat-inducing strategy in the partner. *Descriptive acts* were communication acts that function primarily as information exchange. Ting-Toomey established that couples who engage in more integrative acts, in more descriptive acts, and in fewer disintegrative acts report a higher degree of marital satisfaction. Couples who engage in more disintegrative acts, in fewer integrative, and in fewer descriptive acts report a lower degree of marital satisfaction.[118]

Unsolicited criticism has harmful effects. One author observes, "Unsolicited criticism in the name of honesty can be like a punch in the stomach for which we are unprepared." He adds, "The great magician Houdini died of such a punch from a fan who didn't allow Houdini time to prepare himself."[119]

Are all negative feelings out of bounds for the couple who desires satisfaction? Shimanoff determined that couples can discuss some unpleasant topics and receive positive responses. When individuals disclose vulnerabilities and hostilities about people *other than* the listener, the spouse who is the target of the discloser is more likely to respond with positive messages and to state that he or she has a more positive attitude toward requests made by the discloser, toward his or her relationship with the disclosing spouse, and toward himself or herself.[120]

The Topic Under Discussion May Affect the Appropriateness of Self-Disclosure   Sandra Petronio examined women's perceptions of their family role satisfaction. When the husband's disclosure exceeded the wife's perceived importance of his disclosure, family satisfaction did not increase. Petronio suggested that too much spousal disclosure can be perceived as an exercise of power.[121] The appropriateness of self-disclosure may be related to the target's assessment of the topic under discussion.

Similarly, marital satisfaction may be more affected by the communicators' attitudes toward the information being disclosed than by the amount of disclosure.[122] Only two of 17 potential disclosure topics were found to be important in predicting marital satisfaction: "shared activities" and "children and careers." Couples surely disclose about a variety of other topics, but the amount of disclosure about them does not appear to affect marital satisfaction.

On the other hand, Leslie Baxter and Bill Wilmot showed that six types of topics are taboo: in order of importance, state of the relationship, extrarelationship activity, relationship norms, prior relationships, conflict-inducing topics, and negatively valenced self-disclosure.[123] These results are consistent with the previously cited studies that suggest that negative disclosures may be less desirable for couples who seek satisfaction.

Marital Satisfaction May Be More Highly Related to the Perception of, Rather Than the Behavior of, Disclosing   Some research suggests that the amount of self-disclosure occurring in a family may be irrelevant to the level of satisfaction expressed by the family. John Gottman holds that the importance of self-disclosure may be overrated. He avers, "Couples in nondistressed marriages are indirect; they mindread rather than directly ask about feelings."[124] Two investigators verified that husbands and wives overestimate how much they disclose to each other. They allege that the knowledge one partner accumulates about the other in long-term relationships is based more on the other's behavior than on his or her self-disclosure.[125]

These conclusions suggest that a couple's perceptions of how much disclosure occurs may be discrepant from the actual amount that does occur. Indeed, the couple's perceptions of disclosure may be more important than the amount of disclosure in which they engage. One research team validated this suggestion. They found that individuals with high levels of marital adjustment were more likely than those with low levels of marital adjustment to distort selectively their perceptions of disclosure received, in an apparent attempt to eliminate distress from their relationships.[126] This finding was corroborated. In a study, nondistressed couples revealed greater discrepancy scores from their actual and perceived communication than distressed couples did. The discrepancy was due to the positive distortion on the part of individuals in nondistressed marriages. The authors hint that positive distortion may be a healthy and useful aspect of a well-functioning marriage.[127] In Chapter 11, on understanding and support, we will discuss this important correlate of family satisfaction.

Finally, marital satisfaction is more highly related to the perceptions of the other person's disclosures than the actual disclosure provided.[128] Our perceptions, then, that a partner is disclosing may be more important than his or her actual behavior.

Self-disclosure is not a one-dimensional trait that can be prescribed for marital satisfaction. More is not necessarily better. We should observe, however, no one recommends the absence, or minimization, of self-disclosure in families.

What factors inform the family member about self-disclosure? First, the family member's expectation levels affect the appropriateness of self-disclosure. The history of the relationship and the goals for the self-disclosing talk must be kept in mind. The implicit and explicit rules developed over the lifetime of the family relationship must be followed.

Second, negative information may be best left undisclosed. Satisfied couples are less likely to disclose negative information and dissatisfied couples are more likely to do so. Vulnerabilities and hostilities toward people other than the listener may be negative areas that do not affect the relationship negatively.

Third, the topic under discussion may affect the appropriateness of self-disclosure. If family members determine that some topics are inappropriate to discuss, family satisfaction may be threatened by the disclosure of information about that area. Topics considered taboo by relational partners may include state of the relationship, extrarelationship activity, relationship norms, prior relationships, conflict-inducing topics, and negatively valenced self-disclosure.

Fourth, satisfaction may be more highly related to the perceptions of, rather than the behavior of, disclosing. Family members may know that disclosure is generally a positive behavior and may distort the amount of disclosure that occurs. Researchers suggest that positive distortion may be a healthy and useful aspect of a well-functioning marriage. We will discuss this notion further in the next chapter.

SUMMARY

This chapter considered our needs for autonomy and intimacy. After defining these terms, we observed families negotiate the role of these needs within the family setting. Some balance between autonomy and intimacy is probably appropriate, but each family may exhibit different levels of these two needs. A number of variables affect our needs for autonomy and intimacy. Our developmental stage, the characteristics of other family members, and our relationship with our family may alter the relative proportions of our needs.

Basic to our needs for autonomy and intimacy, self-concept is our awareness of our total and unique being, which is acquired through our experiences and interactions with others. The notion is elusive. While our self-concept emerges from our interactions with others, problems can occur on a variety of levels. Others may respond to us on the basis of their own general response pattern. They may have information about us we do not have. We may not be aware of how others are treating us. We may misinterpret others' behavior. Self-concept is rendered additionally complex because it is continually in flux and changes over time, with different individuals, and in different situations.

To achieve our needs for autonomy and intimacy, we engage in communicative behavior with our family members. While we do not wish to oversimplify a complex set of motivations, self-disclosure is a means of establishing autonomy and intimacy with our family. Self-disclosure is the process of offering verbal revelations about oneself to others.

Why do individuals disclose differentially? Our families of origin teach us about self-disclosure just as they teach us about other communication behaviors. However, women and men receive different messages. In general, women appear to self-disclose more than men do; they disclose more negative information than men do; they provide others with less honest information than males do; and they disclose more intimate information than males do.

Patterns of disclosure can be examined in the family context. College students disclose more to their best same-sex friend than to either their mother or father. In addition, children of either sex tend to self-disclose more to their mothers than to their fathers. The availability of mothers, the higher trust between children and their mothers, and mothers' higher interest in interaction may account for some of the differences in the patterns of self-disclosure among family members.

Autonomy and intimacy are related to family satisfaction. Families are more satisfied when they talk to one another. Self-disclosure is generally considered a desirable behavior, but some reservations have been offered. Our awareness of the research findings on self-disclosure and our sensitivity to our own family members may allow us to communicate most effectively.

KEY TERMS

1. *Autonomy* means we are self-determining, self-governing, and independent.

2. *Intimacy* refers to our close relationships, associations, affiliations, or acquaintances with other people. Intimacy suggests that two (or more) people share personal, private, informal, or secret information.

3. *Relational currencies* are behaviors that demonstrate the affective dimension of a particular relationship and thus encourage or discourage intimacy.

4. *Unexpressed expectations* are our unstated requirements for other people.

5. *Family cohesion* refers to the emotional bonding that family members have toward one another. Four levels of cohesion exist, including the *disengaged* family, which has a very low level of bonding; the *separated*, which has low to moderate levels of cohesion; the *connected* family, which has moderate to high levels of bonding; and the *enmeshed* family, which has very high levels of bonding.

6. The *Johari Window* explains the *open self* (that which we and others know about ourselves), the *blind self* (that which others know but we do not know), the *hidden self* (that which we know but others do not), and the *unknown self* (that which is not known to others and not known to ourselves).

7. *Independent* couples desire great autonomy, but negotiate the amount of sharing that occurs.

8. The *separates* have little togetherness and engage in little sharing.

9. The *traditional* couples have high interdependence and low autonomy.

10. *Self-disclosure* is the process of offering verbal revelations about oneself to others. Self-disclosive messages are evaluated based upon *breadth* (the total amount of information disclosed), *depth* (the intimacy of the information disclosed), *duration* (time spent engaged in disclosure), *valence* (the positive or negativeness of the disclosure), *timing* (when it occurs in the relationship), and *target person* (the person who receives the disclosure).

11. *Equity* theory suggests people feel an obligation to exchange behaviors in order to maintain balance in their relationships. Individuals believe equity

exists when one person discloses and the other person reciprocates. This theory suggests a curvilinear relationship between self-disclosure and family satisfaction.

CHAPTER 11

UNDERSTANDING AND SUPPORTING OTHERS

. . . incline thine ear unto wisdom, and apply thine heart to understanding.

PROVERBS 1:5

After you have read this chapter, you will be able to

1. Describe understanding and supportive communication.

2. Identify the benefits of understanding and support for families.

3. Define listening, empathy, and nonverbal sensitivity.

4. Explain how biological sex, psychological gender, and the level of intimacy in a relationship affect one's ability to provide understanding and support.

5. Differentiate between understanding and acceptance.

6. Provide examples of statements that express mutuality.

7. Differentiate among confirmation, disconfirmation, and rejection.

8. Identify strategies to use to improve one's abilities to be understanding and supportive.

Understanding and supporting others require us to focus on another person rather than on ourselves. In Chapter 10 we considered autonomy and intimacy, which are both primarily self-related concepts. In this chapter we examine understanding and supporting others, which moves the focus from ourselves to

Calvin and Hobbes   by Bill Watterson

the other person or other people. The greatest distraction in our ability to understand and support others may be ourselves. As the cartoon character Pogo commented, "We have met the enemy eyeball to eyeball and he is us."

Understanding and supporting others is a complex activity. It involves truly hearing what other people have to offer. For example, in the cartoon "Calvin and Hobbes" the two characters are both hearing the words the other is offering, but understanding is not evident. Understanding and supporting others is not a natural, physiological function like hearing, which we are able to do unless we suffer a physiological loss. Understanding others requires sensitivity in the selection of cues we choose to hear, see, smell, touch, or taste, and it necessitates care in our interpretation of those cues.

Understanding and support can break down at several points. First, the sender of a message may provide ambiguous or unclear cues. Second, the receiver of a message may be inept in his or her ability to decode the message provided. Furthermore, senders (or receivers) may not understand that the message they have sent (or received) is not similar to the one understood by other communicators.

The communication theorists Watzlawick, Beavin, and Jackson note that communication may fail on two levels: first, when understanding is inaccurate, and second, when people do not realize their messages are misunderstood.[1] Family members may find particular difficulty in the second level since familiarity increases an individual's confidence in his or her ability to understand others.[2] Because of the length of their relationship, family members may believe they understand others in the family even when they do not.

Sometimes family members believe they understand each other because of their similarity. You will recall that we considered the importance of similarity in relationship development in Chapter 6. Some theorists have held, and some researchers have shown that similarity and sharing those similarities predicts, feelings of being understood;[3] nevertheless, other research is equivocal. One investigator hypothesized that the similarity spouses perceived in each other would be positively related to their understanding of their spouse. However, his results did not confirm this hypothesis.[4] While researchers Bochner, Krueger, and Chmielewski found that similarity predicted satisfaction, their results were only true for some specific issues.[5] The relationship between similarity and understanding may be issue specific. Global perceptions of similarity do not predict understanding among family members.

Understanding and supporting others are not behaviors that simply originate in receivers of messages without regard for the senders. Understanding and support are transactional concepts rather than psychological ones. Gottlieb observes: "Present research on social support can contribute little to an understanding of the processes underlying the conduct of close relationships because it embraces a psychological perspective on social support rather than a transactional perspective."[6] Both family members and the interaction between them must be considered when a lack of understanding or support is evidenced.

Family members may show a lack of understanding or support because of their own experiences in their original families. Anastasia, the central character in Marilyn French's *Her Mother's Daughter,* relates an experience that occurred with her daughter:

> I guess if one has to put up with one's children not recalling the love, one is rewarded by them also forgetting the moments of hate. Or whatever it is. I remember one time, Arden was about thirteen. And she came in from school late, around five, very excited. Some friends were there, I was preparing dinner, Toni [her husband] was helping me peel vegetables. And Arden was glowing, and cried out, "Oh, Mommy! I've found the most wonderful book, it's like poetry it's so beautiful. Have you ever heard of it?" And she held up *The Prophet,* by Kahlil Gibran.
>
> I groaned. "Sentimental slop! I found it in the attic, it had been my mother's, she loved it, and at your age I thought it was wonderful too. But it's trash," I informed her.
>
> Her face fell. "Well, I like it," she mumbled. She left the room.
>
> Toni turned to me. "That was really cruel. She was all excited about that book. Why did you do that?"
>
> I stopped. Why had I? Maintaining high literary standards, regardless of cost? How ridiculous! "I don't know. You're right," I said, puzzled at myself. But it was done, and could not now be remedied. Except that I never again doused her excitement like that. At least I don't think I did. . . .[7]

Later in the book. Anastasia recalls an experience from her own childhood with her mother. Although the author does not connect the two incidents, the similarity seems striking:

> It was a Sunday in January, and I was eight. It was a gray day, cold and bleak, without snow, a depressing winter day. It was even more depressing because Mommy wasn't speaking to us. She often stopped speaking, and I never knew why; but this day was heavier somehow. . . . When my father came through the living room, I went up close to him and whispered.
>
> "What's the matter with Mommy today? She's so *mad.*"

Surprisingly, my father did not deny my charge. He whispered back, "She's mad because we forgot her birthday."

"When is her birthday?"

"Today."

I was appalled. I went back to the porch and just stood there. My heart hurt. How terrible to have your birthday forgotten. . . . I went up to the room Joy and I shared, and examined my few possessions: a scrapbook, a couple of games, and my small library, about eight books. There was nothing there Mommy would want. But I also had a few treasures. I decided Mommy would understand that I didn't have money, and she might cheer up if someone remembered her, and if I gave her something pretty.

I worked for several hours, pasting cotton fabric into an old shoe box. The material was scraps from the slipcovers Mommy had made for the porch chairs. Then, I lay inside the few treasures I owned: a pretty pinecone I'd found in the fall; a picture of a beautiful lady I'd cut out from a magazine; and a necklace made of unpolished stones that my uncle Eddie had made himself and sent me last year. The box looked terribly empty, so I took some hair ribbons whose mates had been lost, and made them into bows, and put them among the treasures. Then I closed the box and tied it up with another ribbon and, my heart beating with nervousness, ran down to give it to Mommy.

She was sitting at the kitchen table, smoking and drinking coffee. A roast was baking, and the kitchen smelled delicious. I ran up to her.

"Happy Birthday, Mommy!"

She turned, surprised, and took the box I held out. Slowly, she untied the ribbon and removed the cover. She peered inside. She looked up at me angrily. "What do I want this junk for?" she cried, thrusting the box back at me.[8]

Showing understanding and support to other family members is not a simple skill that can be easily learned. Our past histories as well as our current interactions may affect our ability to communicate understanding and support.

❖ THE NATURE OF UNDERSTANDING AND SUPPORTING OTHERS

■ Communicative Activities Related to Understanding and Support

How do we show understanding and support to others? Listening, nonverbal sensitivity, and empathy are key interpersonal communication activities in our demonstration of understanding and support of other family members. Let us define each of these terms.

Listening   Listening is a selective activity that involves both the reception and the interpretation of aural stimuli. Current investigators consider the specific skills involved in listening,[9] but even the ancients understood the importance of listening. In some ways, we may view listening as bridging the gap between hearing and understanding. While hearing does not require intention or thoughtfulness, listening demands both our attention and our consideration.

Empathy   Empathy may be defined as one's ability to perceive another person's view of the world as though it were his or her own. One writer elaborates on this definition by stating that it is "the capacity of an individual to feel the needs, the aspirations, the frustrations, the joy, the sorrows, the anxieties, the hurt, indeed the hunger of others as if they were his or her own."[10]

Empathy sometimes takes the form of verbal or nonverbal messages; at other times, silence conveys our understanding. Proverbs 11:12 states, "He who belittles his neighbor lacks sense, but a man of understanding remains silent." Mark Twain remarked, "Good breeding consists of concealing how much we think of ourselves and how little we think of the other person."

Many factors affect our ability to empathize with another person. We may feel defensive, or in need of protecting ourselves. We may exhibit a self-focus, or preoccupation with our own thoughts. Similarly, we may demonstrate experiential superiority, or believe that we know more than another person because of our age, education, or other experiences.

Nonverbal Sensitivity   Nonverbal sensitivity involves our ability to accurately decode the nonverbal cues of others. It may be considered the nonverbal partner of listening. Listening focuses on the aural aspects of communication; nonverbal sensitivity focuses on the sights, smells, touches, and even tastes in our communicative environment. While listening requires us to receive and interpret sounds, nonverbal sensitivity demands our reception and interpretation of sights, smells, touches, and tastes.

Understanding others' nonverbal cues may be more difficult than understanding their verbal cues. Nonverbal cues are more ambiguous than verbal cues; the rules governing nonverbal communication are not as explicit nor as formally taught as are the rules of verbal communication. Both the difficulty of understanding nonverbal cues and the relational nature of family communication suggest that nonverbal sensitivity may be more important than listening for the family member seeking satisfaction.

■ Factors Affecting Understanding and Support

Individuals do not listen or empathize with others with the same skill. Although we cannot be certain of all of the factors affecting one's ability to listen or empathize, some distinctions can be made. One's biological sex, psychological sex type, status, and occupation or training all affect one's ability to demonstrate understanding and support.[11]

Biological Sex   Biological sex affects individuals' sensitivity to nonverbal cues. Women appear to be better judges of nonverbal behavior[12] and more accurate decoders of nonverbal communication.[13] However, men in occupations such as acting, art, and mental health are equal, or superior, to females in decoding nonverbal cues. Women are not superior to men in decoding unintended, uncontrolled, brief, or "leaked" nonverbal cues,[14] and men have been shown to be more accurate in judging deception.[15]

Earlier in the book we discussed the pattern of children disclosing information to their mothers, who, in turn, would talk to the fathers. Similarly, children may perceive their mothers to be more understanding and supportive. Nonetheless, many college-aged men hope to change these trends in the future. One explains: "Most of all, I want my children to think of their father as a friend that they can come to at any time for any reason to communicate with and not fear embarrassment or poor self-image."[16]

Sex Role or Gender   Our biological sex is only one aspect of our makeup that may affect our ability to understand and support others. Our *psychological sex role,* or our internalization of characteristics traditionally linked with masculinity or femininity, may similarly influence our ability to be understanding and supportive. You will recall that we discussed Bem's contribution to psychological sex roles in Chapters 1 and 5. Analytical-logical-objective thinking is associated with masculinity and intuitive-emotional-subjective thinking with femininity. In some instances, one way of viewing the world works best; in others, the other may be preferred. Wahlroos suggests that logic can sometimes be used to avoid emotional reality and can thus block our understanding and support of others:

> In intimate communication it is the emotional, subjective perception that counts, not the logical or objective aspects of the situation. To use the logical aspects in order to hide from or cover up the emotional aspects is a destructive technique which interferes with good communication and prevents a truly intimate relationship from being formed.[17]

Wahlroos's theorizing suggests that feminine individuals might be superior at understanding—at least the understanding of emotions; however, empirical research has not demonstrated this conclusion.

Julie Indvik and Mary Anne Fitzpatrick tested the effect of psychological sex role on the level of understanding that occurs among members of marital dyads. They first examined individuals' sex roles and found *androgynous individuals*—persons who have internalized both femininity and masculinity—showed more understanding of their mates than did *undifferentiated people*—persons who have internalized neither femininity or masculinity—but not as much as *sex-typed individuals*—persons who have internalized either femininity or masculinity.

Next, they examined both members of the couple and they determined understanding was related not only to the perceiver's psychological gender but also to the target's sex role. Sex-typed spouses were the easiest to understand, while undifferentiated mates were the least understood by their partners.[18] In other words, to the extent an individual conforms to convention, he or she is more predictable. Although undifferentiated individuals have the most difficulty in being understood by their spouses and in understanding them, androgyny does not result in optimum levels of understanding, either. People with traditional sex roles (masculine men and feminine women) were both more understanding and more understood.

Intimacy of the Relationship The closeness of the interactants may also affect their ability to understand and support each other. Nonverbal sensitivity was examined between intimate couples. Similar to other nonverbal research, Mark Comadena validated females as more adept at decoding nonverbal cues. He also showed intimates were better detectors of deception than friends were. Intimates were significantly more accurate in judging deceptions about emotional information than in judging deceptions about factual information.[19] Familiarity with another person may enhance judgmental accuracy in deciphering deceptive and accurate information.

The converse of this finding may also be true; that is, when a member of a couple demonstrates little nonverbal sensitivity, the other member may feel the relationship is not intimate or close. This suggestion was given credence in an investigation that confirmed that the husband's inability to accurately read his wife's nonverbal messages seemed to be highly important in predicting marital dissatisfaction. In distressed marriages, a wife has trouble nonverbally communicating with her husband, but not with other married strangers, but the husband's receptive difficulties are confined to his interactions with his wife.[20] When a wife is not understood by her husband, she appears to feel the relationship is less intimate and less satisfying.

■ Providing Understanding and Support Does Not Mean You Accept All Behavior

When we engage in understanding and supporting other family members, we do not become doormats for unacceptable or hurtful behavior from others. Sven Wahlroos encourages family members to accept the feelings of others and to try to understand them, but not to accept all actions, even though they do try to understand them. He explains:

> Children often complain that their parents don't understand them. When you question these children a little more closely, it often turns out that they simply demand that their parents let them do whatever they want. A prohibition is interpreted by these children as a lack of "understanding." And then both parents and children, instead of differentiating between understanding feelings and accepting actions, begin to hide behind the current universal excuse for poor or destructive communication called "generation gap."[21]

He suggests parents need to teach their children the difference between understanding another person and accepting all of their actions. We can understand other's feelings while we disapprove of their behavior. He offers two examples:

> When a child demands a toy, for example, the parent who says no can sympathize with the child's desire and discuss ways in which the child can earn and save up the money for the toy. When a teen-ager demands to be allowed to go to an unsupervised party, the parent who says no can discuss various ways in which the teen-ager could meet the same friends and have just as much fun, including the possibility of his throwing a party himself.[22]

Other researchers have similarly stressed understanding, rather than absolute approval of all behavior. *Mutuality,* defined as "showing sensitivity and respect for others' views," is essential for the family.[23] Included within this behavioral index are indirect suggestions, initiation of compromise, statement of the others' feelings, and answers to requests for information. Mutuality has been shown to be important in parent–child interactions.[24]

Understanding and supporting others does not mean family members live a life of pretense or suppress their feelings. Understanding and support suggest a generosity of spirit. When we understand and support other people, we give them the benefit of the doubt rather than assume they have performed some misdeed. We attempt to avoid false pride or egocentrism. We strive to see ourselves and other family members in the same imperfect sea of humanity.

■ Importance of Understanding and Supporting Others

Understanding others is critical to the family. Of the total amount of time we spend engaged in communication with others, more of it is engaged in listening than in any other activity.[25] William S. Howell, a professor at the University of Minnesota, observes that "empathic skills are central to competence in human interaction."[26] He adds, "Empathy enables us to engage in true joint ventures, giving weight to the interests of others as well as promoting our own."[27]

Understanding and supporting family members are important for at least four reasons. They lead to more harmonious interactions, convey a sense of regard for the other person, allow us to become a family unit, and encourage us to feel better about ourselves. Let us consider each of these in more detail.

Harmonious Interactions   First, understanding and support allow family members to predict another's response and thus lead to harmonious interactions. As we carefully listen to a family member, we are more accurate in our

For Better or For Worse®   **by Lynn Johnston**

FOR BETTER OR FOR WORSE reprinted by permission of Universal Press Syndicate copyright © 1987. All rights reserved.

perceptions of his or her attitudes, feelings, and behaviors. With more accurate perceptions, we should be able to adjust more readily to them. As a consequence, we should profit from increased family adjustment and satisfaction.[28]

Understanding and support also lead to harmony as they avoid creating discord. Sometimes, understanding and support are more important than one's personal observations. For example, in the cartoon "For Better or For Worse," the husband may not have preferred his wife's costume, but he responded in a manner consistent with her need to be supported. On other occasions, this husband may find complete honesty is more important than offering support.

Conveying a Sense of Regard   Second, understanding and support convey a sense of regard, confirmation, or self-validation to the other person.[29] Marital adjustment or satisfaction may be more related to the perception of basic regard than to such factors as perceptual accuracy, empathy, or congruence. To fully capture the positive nature of this benefit, we need to contrast confirmation with rejection and disconfirmation. Communication theorists originated this three-part classification schema and suggest that we respond to others in one of three distinctive ways.[30]

Confirmation occurs when we treat others in a manner consistent with their presentation of themselves. For example, if your oldest child sees herself as independent and nurturing, she is confirmed when you depend on her to handle the younger children after school while you are at work. She is confirmed when you compliment her for her ability to handle small emergencies that arise and for the loving responses she provides to her siblings. Confirmation is satisfying to others and strengthens their established self-concept.

This example illustrates the role of confirmation in one man's relationship with his father and an employee in the family business:

> The one thing that I liked the most about growing up in my family is the interaction that I enjoyed. My father was always accepting of my ideas. He worked at home for many of the years that I remember. I also remember an employee (Rick) who has worked for my father for the last fifteen years. He could almost be considered family; nonetheless, he played a big part in my growing up. Rick is about ten years older than I am and he was my "Big Brother." He is a Black Belt in Karate and he would show me how to do different moves during his break. We would also work together, he had a lot of patience.[31]

Rejection occurs when we treat others in a manner inconsistent with their self-definition. Suppose you perceive your spouse to be inflexible and domineering, while he perceives himself to be adaptable and cooperative. The following conversation exemplifies your rejection of his self-definition:

HUSBAND: Why don't we go out for dinner tonight—everybody is too busy to cook.
WIFE: Where do you want to go?
HUSBAND: I don't care—any place is great with me.

WIFE:	Okay, but you choose the place. You complained a lot the last time we went out.
HUSBAND:	Who me? I'm easy to please.
WIFE:	I don't want to go out to eat if we're going to end up fighting before the meal is over.
HUSBAND:	Normally, I'm easygoing. The place we went last week was terrible—the food tasted rancid.
WIFE:	You never like any restaurant except for the place down town.
HUSBAND:	What do you mean? I'm easy to get along with!
WIFE:	Why don't you choose where we'll eat and I'll go tell the kids to get ready to go.
HUSBAND:	Why me?

Rejection results in one's questioning of self-concept. However, in the example that follows, the son in the family shows amazing independence and perseverance.

> My dad argues about my future plans, friends, my drinking behavior and almost every issue or idea which I have. Dad always think I'm crazy, but now he knows that all he can do is think I'm crazy and tell me about it. His power and influence is not as strong, and I, being a very independent person, am going to make my own decision, live by my own ideas and philosophies, and Dad may disagree, but I'm going to choose my own path and walk on it with or without my family's understanding or agreement.[32]

Disconfirmation occurs when we fail to respond to another person's view of self or when we respond to others in a neutral way. If you have a busy schedule and a full life, it is not difficult to disconfirm one or more of your family members. The middle child in a large family may feel he has to resort to negative behaviors, such as wetting the bed, disobeying family rules, or beginning conflicts with his siblings, because he feels disconfirmed. Grandparents who are recent additions in the family home may feel disconfirmed as they are the recipients of little interaction with other family members.

Disconfirmation may result in loneliness and alienation. One man described his childhood:

> You may consider me a "brat," and in some ways I was, but in general, I just wanted to learn things and try to look at alternatives to everything. My parents are very nice people, but my father was always the one who told us what to do, when, and where. And if we didn't listen, well, we got hell. My dad was a sergeant in the marine corps, and I was the one who didn't like to take orders. So already we had conflict.
>
> Much of the time I had ideas that I thought were good but my old-fashioned father thought that "children should be seen and not heard" so I spent a lot of time trying to be heard.[33]

How to Become a Family   Third, understanding and supportiveness allow family members to come to define themselves as a unit. Individuals become partners rather than simply interacting individuals.[34] Similarly, family members view themselves as part of a group rather than as independent entities. If others do not respond to you verbally or nonverbally, you may feel you are cut off from them rather than part of a single unit.

One woman explained understanding and support was how her family defined itself and was, indeed, a family theme.

> One specific family theme associated with my family is that of "always come to the family first" when you need help. Anytime one of our family members need money, a place to stay, or just help in a troubled situation, they can always depend on the family.... Our family has never, to my knowledge, turned its back on another family member. Even if a member of the family doesn't have the resources capable of helping another, he/she will still help in some way. Whether it involves suggesting a solution or just listening to the problem, it will be done.... We know that no matter how distant we may appear, when there's trouble we can come to one another for help and support.[35]

A man in his 20s explained that his original family had not been so close, but he hoped for such an atmosphere in his pending family: "Everyone will be understood and given the time to explain how they feel. I don't want to be just a father to my children, I want to be their friend, something my parents never found a way to be."[36]

Feeling Better About Ourselves   Understanding and support not only help the recipient, they also have beneficial aspects for the person demonstrating the understanding and support. The reciprocal nature of these essential activities is illustrated in one woman's explanation: "Understanding and support are paramount in a healthy relationship. One must give understanding and support to receive understanding and support."[37] Dale Carnegie similarly noted: "Life is truly a boomerang. What you give, you get." Finally, the playwright James M. Barrie, author of *Peter Pan*, observed: "Those who bring sunshine to the lives of others cannot keep it from themselves."

We might feel better about ourselves as we demonstrate understanding and support for others around us. Wahlroos maintains:

> The first characteristic of emotional health is the most important; all others can be seen as corollaries or derivations: An emotionally healthy person is one who does not, for some conscious or unconscious reason, hurt himself or others through his actions or words; on the contrary, he helps himself and others through his actions and words.[38]

❖ UNDERSTANDING AND SUPPORT ARE RELATED TO FAMILY SATISFACTION

Understanding and support, shown through listening, empathy, and nonverbal sensitivity, result in family satisfaction. The preeminent child psychologist

Bruno Bettelheim prescribed understanding and support to parents in his book, *A Good Enough Parent: A Book on Child-Rearing:*

> I feel that a parent's most important task is to get a feeling for what things may mean to his child, and on this basis handle himself in ways that are most helpful to both; if he does, this will also improve the parent's and child's relation to each other. The best way to get this feeling is to remember what a parallel issue meant to us when we were children and why and how we would have liked our parents to handle it, us, and themselves.[39]

Lay people concur. One woman explains: "I believe there are several factors which contribute to family satisfaction. In my opinion, acceptance, mutual love and support, honest communication, and trust are among the most important factors."[40]

People surveyed in polls agree. *USA Today* identified the top reasons people provided as being key to a good relationship with one's mate. Among those reasons were being good friends (identified by 92 percent of the people polled) and receiving support and encouragement (88 percent of those asked).[41]

Similarly, mothers, fathers, and teenagers were surveyed about the importance of 34 different aspects of family functioning. Some of the aspects were paraphrasing, speaking for self, expressing thoughts, expressing feelings, expressing intentions, spontaneity, metacommunication, emotional attraction, loyalty, reliability, physical caretaking, pleasurable interaction, flexibility, shared leadership, negotiation, and rules. The five most important aspects, as ranked by the family members, in order of importance were:

1. Family identification

2. Attend to the affect and content of another's message

3. Emotional attraction

4. Attentively listen

5. Supportiveness[42]

Three of these aspects directly relate to the topic of this chapter: attentively listening, attending to the affect and content of another's message, and supportiveness.

Family members agree on the importance and role of understanding and supporting each other in the family setting. Their judgments are borne out in the literature examining satisfying and dissatisfying marital relationships. These studies demonstrate one's ability to listen attentively and exhibit empathy to family members predicts satisfaction.[43] For instance, satisfying marital relationships can be distinguished from less satisfying relationships on the basis of spouses' reactions to comments such as "I listen and attend when my spouse expresses a point of view."[44]

Family satisfaction is based on a number of behaviors related to understanding and support. They include the sending of messages that suggest others are understood and the actual understanding of others' messages, providing supportive and positive comments, and perceiving others' communication behavior favorably. Let us consider the research findings in each of these areas.

■ Satisfaction and Accuracy in Message Reception

The more understanding that is conveyed, the more satisfied are family members.[45] For example, Stella Ting-Toomey determined that couples who used more communication acts that incorporated the conveyance of understanding and empathy with the listener's feelings or ideas expressed higher marital satisfaction than couples who used a smaller number of such acts.[46] Other research has demonstrated similar findings.[47]

Understanding one's partner, demonstrating understanding, and perceiving that your partner understands you are all related to marital satisfaction.[48] It is through identification and empathy that marriage partners come to define themselves as a unit. Building such a partnership is not possible without understanding one's partner.[49] We cannot identify with a person or show him or her empathy unless we first understand that person.

Indeed, families mature as they become increasingly sensitive to each other's views and to their own views of other families.[50] Maturing families continue to integrate and reintegrate each individual's view into a common set of understandings and conceptions. Less healthy, less adaptive, or less satisfied families fail to reconcile the varying perceptions and conceptions of their members.

Nonverbal communication is critical to satisfying family lives. John Gottman concluded that nonverbal codes were more discriminating between distressed and nondistressed couples than verbal codes were. He observed satisfied couples developing a private message system permitting efficient, telegraphic nonverbal communication; dissatisfied couples do not demonstrate a similar system.[51] Satisfied couples generate sets of agreed-upon meanings for specific nonverbal signals through their history of interaction.

It may be the wife's inability to communicate nonverbally with her husband or the husband's inability to accurately read his wife's nonverbal messages that seem to be most important in predicting marital dissatisfaction. In distressed marriages, wives have trouble nonverbally communicating with their husband, but not with other married strangers.[52] The husbands' receptive difficulties appear to be confined to their interactions with their wife.

Dissatisfied couples do not understand each other as well as satisfied couples do; in fact, they appear to have a negative bias toward the messages sent by their partners. We will observe in the next section of this chapter that dissatisfied couples tend to send more negative messages than satisfied couples do. At this point we should note that regardless of the intent of the speaker, spouses in distressed marriages tend to evaluate the messages from their partners more negatively than spouses in satisfying marriages.[53]

Why might a member of a dissatisfied couple respond to his or her partner's messages more negatively? A number of suggestions can be made for the greater frequency of negative responses by the receiver of the message in the dissatisfied marriage. First, dissatisfied couples tend to send more inconsistent messages.[54] Second, dissatisfied couples offer more negative nonverbal affect, which emphasizes the negative verbal message.[55] However, we should not ignore the obvious: respondents in dissatisfied marriages may simply tend to react more negatively than respondents in satisfied marriages. They may be like the proverbial soul who walks around with a chip on his or her shoulder, waiting for someone to knock it off. Because of the nature of the marital relationship, the partner may frequently be the person who performs that function.

Understanding may be particularly important in the affective or emotional arenas of family life. For example, blue-collar couples were interviewed. The researcher found that marital stress was created when the husband demonstrated a lack of emotional responsiveness to his wife. She concludes that such couples talk *at, past,* and *through* each other, but rarely *with* or *to* each other.[56]

John Gottman has provided important work on the interactional differences of dissatisfied and satisfied couples. He has demonstrated that marital satisfaction is related to the couple's ability to demonstrate emotional responsiveness. Although couples involved in relatively low levels of conflict do not behave differently, dissatisfied and satisfied couples do behave differently when engaged in higher levels of conflict. Husbands in dissatisfied relationships are less emotionally responsive to their wives than their wives are to them. These husbands fail to respond to gross changes in the mood of their wives, while the wives tend to respond to the most incidental expressive change in their husband's affective communication.[57] Thus we see that neither husbands nor wives in dissatisfied marriages demonstrate understanding of their spouses' emotional tone.

One research team found a relationship between marital satisfaction and the understanding of a partner's desire for change. They tested 75 married couples from Houston and 75 cohabiting or married couples from Los Angeles. Each individual completed an Areas of Change Questionnaire, which listed behaviors common to marriage and assessed desires for more or less of these behaviors in the current marriage. The understanding of desires for change was operationalized as the discrepancy between the partner's scores on the behaviors listed on the questionnaire. Couples who showed less discrepancy had more understanding of desires for changes, and couples who had a greater discrepancy had less understanding. In general, the more accurately individuals can report their partner's desires for changes, the more satisfied they are with their marriage.[58]

We may view understanding as a construct that deals with understanding specific information someone has offered to us, or we may view it in a larger sense of understanding normative communicative behavior. For example, when someone offers an emotional alteration in their behavior, people normally respond to it. People in dissatisfied relationships appear to be more likely to show their lack of understanding of normative communicative behavior as well as their lack of understanding of specific messages provided to them.

Investigators examined the self-disclosure patterns in dissatisfied and satisfied couples. Wives in dissatisfied relationships provided higher percentages of self-disclosure than their husbands as compared to wives in satisfied relationships. Husbands and wives in satisfied relationships tended to provide relatively equal amounts of disclosure.[59] Satisfied couples thus demonstrated an understanding of equity and reciprocal exchange in self-disclosure, while dissatisfied couples did not.

Just as we observed that the negative response provided by the dissatisfied couple may be due to the characteristics of the speaker rather than the listener, lack of understanding on the part of the receiver in the dissatisfied couple may be due to poor sending skills of one's partner. Indeed, Chelune and his colleagues found that members of dissatisfied couples do not communicate as clearly when they disclose information to each other as satisfied couples do.[60] Regardless of the cause, however, we have several pieces of evidence that suggest understanding and a demonstration of understanding are related to marital satisfaction, while a lack of understanding or a lack of demonstration of understanding are related to marital dissatisfaction.

Providing understanding is not only important for marital couples, it is similarly key to parent–child interactions. One woman in her 20s commented:

> If you cannot be supportive of your own family, who can you be? I think encouragement to the children for their ideas, goals, ideals, and dreams needs to also be shown. The children need to know that their parents believe in them, too.[61]

A teacher in his 30s adds:

> The understanding and support given to family members by other family members is needed for some to be successful in life. Sometimes it's a cruel and uncaring world but knowing that you have loved ones who care about you and would support you even if you've made some mistakes is vital. Personal growth requires some risk-taking. I feel those who have strong family support are most likely to succeed and keep growing because in the event of failure the family will get them back on their feet again.[62]

■ Satisfaction and Supportive Communication

In general, satisfied family members provide more positive, supportive, and agreement statements.[63] Satisfied family members also feel or perceive support.[64] When stress occurs, successful and satisfied family members may seek support beyond the family.[65] Positive and supportive responses may be of even more importance in the nonverbal cues provided than in the verbal utterances. Satisfied couples provide fewer negative comments than dissatisfied couples do.[66] Satisfied couples are more likely to reinforce each other positively,[67] and to confirm each other.[68] Stella Ting-Toomey examined the interaction of dissatisfied and satisfied couples and found marital satisfaction is related to sequential patterns of confirming behavior.[69] Satisfied couples also enjoy more humor and laughter.[70]

One method of measuring positive comments has been to compare the ratio of agreement statements with disagreement statements. Researchers who have done this have determined satisfied couples provide relatively more agreement statements than disagreement statements compared to dissatisfied couples.[71] Happy couples tend to be more agreeing and more approving than unhappy couples.[72] In a review of literature on agreement/disagreement, two researchers prescribed that "families should have more agreements than disagreements for healthy functioning."[73]

Thus the communication behavior of satisfied couples is marked by fewer negative comments, more agreement statements, more approval, and more confirmation compared to dissatisfied couples. The communication behavior of dissatisfied couples is characterized by such behaviors as defensiveness;[74] quarreling, nagging, arguing;[75] aversive control and coercion;[76] expressions of hostility;[77] and attempts to humiliate and threaten.[78] Furthermore, dissatisfied couples use even more direct or intense negative communication than satisfied couples do.[79]

Happy couples engage in conflict, but they tend to be more successful at handling differences. Satisfied couples use more positive problem-solving behaviors than dissatisfied couples do.[80] Also, the supportive and positive comments they routinely use are helpful. They are not only more likely to offer generally positive comments, but they are also more apt to provide positive descriptions of their spouse.[81] Since husbands are less likely than wives to express positive feelings, Patricia Noller recommends that counselors and therapists might be well advised to encourage the husbands in distressed marriages to practice expressing positive feeling.[82]

Supportive and positive verbalizations are equally important among parents and children. Families that include a delinquent child use less positive and more negative interactions than families that do not include a delinquent child.[83] Families with delinquent children include three times as many negative statements as families with nondelinquent children. Furthermore, the positive or negative nature of the comments appears to affect delinquency itself, as delinquent behavior decreased when there was a balance of positive and negative statements, but increased when more negative statements were offered.[84]

Nonverbal behaviors are also critical. Couples can be discriminated better on the dimension of satisfaction or dissatisfaction by negative nonverbal behavior than by verbal negative behavior.[85] A greater number of nonverbal positive affect cues (smiling, positive facial expression, movement toward the other person, and an open body position) are provided by satisfied couples relative to dissatisfied couples.[86] Satisfied couples demonstrate their positive response to their partners by sitting closer together and by using more positive, accepting, and open gestures than dissatisfied couples do.[87] Both verbally and nonverbally, satisfied couples tend to use more positive and supportive statements, while dissatisfied couples tend to use a greater number of negative, hostile, and threatening comments.

■ Satisfaction and Perception of Communication

Both the couple's perceptions of their interaction and their interaction behavior contribute to our understanding of marital satisfaction. The contribution made by actual interaction behavior can now be measured using the increasingly sophisticated methodology that has recently been developed. Before we consider such communicative behavior, let us consider the role of a couple's perceptions of their communication in achieving high marital satisfaction scores.

We might hypothesize that couples who have a realistic (objectively verified) perception of their communicative behavior are more satisfied than are those who hold distorted (subjective) views. Just the opposite appears to be true. Couples who positively distort their partner's communicative behavior are generally more satisfied with their marriages than couples who do not distort their partner's behavior.[88] In other words, to the extent couple's perceive their partner's behavior more favorably, they also are more favorably disposed to rating their marital satisfaction.

The conclusions of this study suggest that people who view events more favorably consistently view both their partner's communicative behavior and their marital satisfaction more favorably. Such a result may seem somewhat trivial, since positive people are positively disposed across a variety of measures. However, it may also suggest if we are concerned with increasing couples' self-reports of their marital satisfaction, one tack may be to increase individuals' overall positive outlook. If therapists and practitioners can increase people's perceptions of various aspects of their partners' behavior, they may find them likewise reporting greater marital satisfaction. People who intervene in dissatisfied marriages may need to work on behavioral change, but perhaps more important is the need to work on changing the perceptions of that behavior.

❖ IMPROVING OUR ABILITY TO DEMONSTRATE UNDERSTANDING AND SUPPORT OF FAMILY MEMBERS

Understanding and supporting family members increase family satisfaction; yet many of us are relatively unsuccessful in demonstrating this quality. One woman expressed this sentiment: "I want my future family to be more accepting and confirming than my family-of-origin was, not only of ideas and beliefs, but of individuals as well."[89]

In this section of the chapter we will consider how we might demonstrate our understanding and support to family members and how we can thus improve our family relationships. We need to keep in mind that providing understanding and support is an ideal toward which we can strive; however, no family members behave in these ways all of the time. In addition, understanding and support, like other communicative behaviors, are transactionally defined. Although we may believe we are demonstrating understanding and support, other family members may see our behavior differently.

At the beginning of this chapter we discussed the idea that communication can fail when understanding is inaccurate and when people do not realize their messages are misunderstood. In the first case, the receiver does not understand the sender's message. In the second instance, the sender does not know the receiver does not understand the message accurately. At least six suggestions can be offered for improving understanding in the family context, based on these levels of misunderstanding originally suggested by Watzlawick, Beavin, and Jackson. The recommendations include: (1) take time to communicate, (2) give family members a full hearing, (3) provide messages that convey understanding, (4) accept other family members as they see themselves, (5) show your support of others, and (6) avoid negative behaviors. Let us consider each of these.

■ Take Time to Communicate

Understanding and support cannot be demonstrated if family members fail to communicate with one another. Busy families can sometimes spend days without seeing other family members and may spend far longer than that without really talking to them. Planning schedules and handling routine matters may be discussed, but individuals' feelings, needs, and aspirations are avoided. Simply scheduling time to talk to one member or another of your family or arranging an atmosphere conducive to a personal talk may demonstrate your concern.

Family members may consciously or unconsciously avoid communicating with others. They may use silence in a harmful way by ignoring others and withdrawing from communication with them. Although silence is sometimes appropriate—particularly when we are listening to another person—it can also be used destructively by the family member who routinely engages in sulking or pouting. If you have ever been the victim of the "cold shoulder treatment," you recognize the discomfort created by silence. Silence can be used as a weapon.

Sometimes people fail to communicate with each other because they *assume* they know the other person's opinion or point of view. They may feel it is useless to talk to their spouse or child because they can predict how the other person will respond. For example, one dual-career couple shared mealtime chores; typically, she made the meal and he did the dishes afterwards. Generally, the meal was ready about 6:30 P.M., at the same time as the national news. Since the family had a rule that people did not watch television or read during the evening meal, the family never saw the evening news. The husband was particularly angry that he was ill-informed, but he did not mention his feelings to his wife because he assumed she would not change the mealtime. His wife prepared dinner at 6:30 P.M. because it was the earliest time she could have a complete meal made, and she assumed her husband was ravenous and wanted to eat at the earliest possible time. Both members of the couple assumed they knew the other person's attitude and both were incorrect.

To avoid the error of untested assumptions, we need to talk to one another. Sometimes simply asking family members for their opinions, ideas, or perceptions is all we need to do. At other times, we may need to explain our assumptions about their perspectives to determine if we are fundamentally correct or incorrect. We may need to ask probing questions: "Do you mean. . . ?," "Are you saying. . . ?," or "Let me see if I can restate your idea." Probing questions should not be used to exaggerate the other person's position or to ridicule or humiliate.

In general, asking questions can be a useful way to initiate or maintain a conversation with another person and to demonstrate your understanding and support. Further, you gain important information from a family member. Sven Wahlroos recommends question asking between parents and children. He writes:

> Millions of parents today are concerned with "getting through" to their children. A partial answer to their problem is just this: ASK QUESTIONS! It is through questions and posing problems that we teach children to think for themselves. At the same time we show our interest in what *they* have to say, thus helping them develop a positive self-concept. And we show confidence in their ability to work out problems on their own, a confidence they will eventually adopt and which will help them throughout life.[90]

■ Give Family Members a Full Hearing

In addition to finding opportunities to communicate with our family members, it is essential we give each of them a full hearing. Too often we are considering our next remark rather than listening fully to another person. Sometimes we interrupt or overlap their remarks with comments of our own.

The importance of giving other family members a full hearing was illustrated in a story written by a mother who had throat surgery and was forced to be silent for a number of weeks. She wrote:

> One day during my enforced silence, Dean [a son] came home from school shouting, "I hate my teacher! I'm never going back to school again!"
>
> Before my vocal-cord problems, I would have responded with my own outburst: "Of course you are if I have to drag you there myself." But that afternoon I had to wait to see what would happen next.
>
> In a few moments, my angry son put his head in my lap and poured out his heart. "Oh, Mom," he said. "I had to give a report and I mispronounced a word. The teacher corrected me and all the kids laughed. I was so embarrassed."
>
> I wrapped my arms around him. He was quiet for a few minutes. Then suddenly he sprang out of my arms. "I'm supposed to meet Jimmy in the park. Thanks, Mom."
>
> My silence had made it possible for Dean to confide in me. He didn't need any advice or criticism. He was hurt. He needed someone to listen.
>
> Silence taught me that the listener is the most important person in any conversation. Before I lost my voice, I never really paid attention to what anyone else was saying. I was usually too busy thinking of my response. Often I'd interrupt.[91]

Giving the other person a full hearing requires us to listen with our heart as well as our head. Although you may provide the other person time to talk, avoid interruptions and overlaps, and generally listen to other family members, you will not demonstrate understanding unless you listen to their *intent* as well as their *content.*

When a high school student exclaims, "I hate tennis—I'm going to quit the team," what does she really mean? On a content level, she is declaring her intentions to quit an activity in which she has been involved. But on an intent level, she is saying far more. She may be expressing her frustration with playing tennis for years and still remaining on the reserve team while girls who are younger and less experienced move ahead to the varsity team. She may be demonstrating her vulnerability and hurt. She may be asking for support from other family members.

As we give other family members a full hearing, we must listen to what they are saying and also to what they are not saying. Another person's intent may be far more critical than his or her content. We need to continue to ask why this person is making the statement, what does he or she really mean, what does he or she want or need, and what can I do to help fulfill the want or need. As we observed at the beginning of the chapter, demonstrating understanding and support is far more complicated than simply hearing the words offered by another person.

■ Provide Messages That Convey Understanding

Awareness of the Other Person   How can we provide messages that convey understanding? A first step is to be aware of the other person and to try to understand his or her need for attention. The middle child in a large family and the grandparents that were mentioned earlier in the chapter may not feel anyone is aware of them. How could these situations be turned around?

We could begin by communicating our awareness of them in nonverbal ways. We can use such nonverbal cues as touch, changes in facial expression and bodily movement, movement toward them, and eye contact to demonstrate we are aware of them. Our verbal messages indicate our awareness of family members, too. Phrases such as "I'm glad to see you," "I see you just got home," "I missed you today," "You've been gone a long time," and "I don't get to see you enough" all indicate our awareness of the other person.

It is difficult to indicate our awareness when others are far away. For more and more families, living apart has become a reality. For example, an increasing number of couples have commuter marriages, where most of their time is spent in separate residences. For such families, confirmation of family members through acknowledgment is difficult. Many college couples, too, find themselves living hours or miles away from each other, as in the following example:

My fiancé, John, and I attend different universities that are 6 hours apart and we have had to put a great deal more work and effort into our relationship than most do; however, the fact that we've held together through 1½ years, and plan to continue the relationship indefinitely indicates that the rewards are pretty high.

One of the highest costs in our situation is our emotional health. We take a great deal of emotional support from each other, and long distance is not conducive to this, unfortunately. I can't count the times one of us has called the other, needing the other for support and been frustrated. . . . However, because of our commitment to each other, and the relationship, we've been willing to wait. . . . A great deal of our success is based on a mutual belief in each other. Neither of us has ever dated anyone that gave either of us what we give each other—support, understanding, honesty, and friendship.[92]

Importance of Feedback In Chapter 1 we defined communication, in part, as the interpretive process of understanding and sharing meaning with others. We noted meaning arises out of social interaction and is continually changing and shifting in response to that interaction and to the individual's understanding of it. Finally, we observed we tend to "construct" both ourselves and others in our interactions with them. When we attempt to understand others, then, we engage in a kind of dance in which each of us offers our understanding of who they are.

One of the means by which we offer such information to others is through feedback. *Feedback* is defined as the receiver's verbal and nonverbal responses to the sender's messages. Feedback suggests to the source of a message that he or she might alter, change, reinforce, or embellish the message.

Feedback is an important communicative behavior by which we demonstrate, or fail to demonstrate, our understanding of other people. You may have observed all feedback is not equally useful or equally clear. For feedback to be effective, the other person needs to be able to understand what you mean, accept the information, and act on the information. Let us consider these three steps in more detail.

First, in order to help the other person understand what you mean, you need to consider carefully the words you choose. Is the other person likely to understand the language you have chosen? Will the other person be aware of what you are describing? Can you place your feedback in a context in which the meaning will be more easily understood? Should you preface your feedback with explanations, observations, or other information?

Second, in order to help the other person accept the information you are providing, you need to consider his or her feelings, attitudes, and values. Avoid "loaded" terms that might produce emotional reactions. Attempt to be descriptive rather than evaluative. State your perceptions as opinions and reactions rather than as absolute and indisputable facts. Refer to specific, observable behavior rather than general or global issues. Discuss the relevant behavior rather than the person. Communicate acceptance of the other person and his or her right to view the world in a different manner from your own.

Third, in order to help the other person act on the information, you may need to consider your feedback. Do not provide feedback to individuals about things over which they have no control. Consider how changes may occur once the other individual has received your feedback. Suggest specific outcomes rather than bombard the person with general information. Provide possible means of altering one's behavior, if necessary; provide specific examples of the other person's behavior that you would like to see reinforced.

Six behaviors are associated with appropriate and effective feedback.[93] These behaviors are useful in the family context. They include:

1. Providing clear verbal responses. Responses that are ambiguous, complex, or overly simple do not help other communicators. Family members may feel you are talking down to them or purposefully trying to confuse them. In addition, the feedback will not illumine their understanding of your response.

2. Relying on descriptive statements. Descriptive statements, rather than evaluative statements, are preferred. Rather than telling a child, "You don't know anything about the real world," a parent could offer, "Your experience with business people is relatively short." Evaluation and evaluative statements encourage defensiveness; description and descriptive statements suggest support.

3. Providing reflective statements. Reflective statements are those which "mirror" or "reflect" back to a communicator what he or she has stated. Reflective statements may be paraphrased comments or direct quotations. If a husband states to his wife, "I really like the way your car looks," she could offer the reflective statement, "You always compliment the appearance of my car when it's just been washed." Reflective statements are at the opposite end of the continuum from irrelevant statements or those which have little to do with the other communicator's message.

4. Demonstrating bodily responsiveness. Nonverbally, we can show our understanding of others, too. When we move in a responsive way, we suggest that we are actively listening and concerned about the other person. The individual who never moves and never changes his or her facial expression appears passive and unconcerned. The person who offers random movement appears to be distracted.

5. Using a sincere, warm voice. As we observed in Chapter 4, the tone of our voice can communicate a variety of emotions. A voice marked by harshness, hostility, or aggressiveness will not be viewed as one that offers concern or understanding. A sincere, warm voice tone, on the other hand, suggests support and understanding.

6. Establishing eye contact. When we look at the person who is speaking, we demonstrate interest. When we look away, we may appear to be thinking about other matters.

■ Accept Other Family Members as They See Themselves

Attending to other people and providing them with feedback is not enough if we wish to demonstrate both our understanding and our support. We also need to consider how other people view themselves. Furthermore, we need to accept the other person as he or she views self. We all view the world from our own perspective and other people are part of that world. When we think about our children, we remember them as pregnancies, as tiny infants, as awkward toddlers, as beginning first graders, as rebellious adolescents, and as young adults. We might recall particularly painful or poignant memories of them that alter the way we see them. The child, however, has no memory of his or her earliest existence and does not even remember the incidents we do in the same way. He or she views himself or herself in a manner that is consistent with his or her perceptions and that view can be sharply discrepant from our own.

At the same time, parents frequently impose their reality on their children. They recall particular situations from their own growing-up years and assume their children's experiences are similar. One woman writes:

> Many of my disagreements with my father are based on our differences in belief about my good judgment. I suspect that Dad doesn't trust me to have sound judgment, or perhaps he feels his age and experience make him a *better* judge, regardless of the situation. I think cognitively he realized that my generation is very different from his when they were our age; he doesn't translate that awareness into his dealings with me. I went through high school living with his distrust of my male contemporaries. He dated when he was in high school, and he knows why he took girls out, and he'd be damned if any boy was going to try that with his daughter! Consequently, we had a hard time talking about dating.[94]

It is vital, if we wish to confirm family members, that we accept them as they see themselves. We must figuratively "become" other people in order to accept them in this way. We must be descriptive rather than evaluative and treat family members as our equals rather than as inferior in any way. We need to avoid judgmental statements about other people's perceptions of self and instead try to reflect their statements about who they are. We should avoid behaving in a superior manner to others and avoid statements like "Well, I guess you're finally growing up!" "It's about time you understand that," "When you're older, you'll understand why I have to do this," and "If you had my experience, you'd know what I was talking about." The following discussion provides a negative example of accepting others as they view themselves:

> When my dad is mad at us because we're not living up to his expectations, or do something wrong, he will yell something like, "When I was your age. . . I wasn't allowed to do this or that," or "I had to do without a lot of things." Dad rarely discusses anything with anyone unless it is in fits of rage. My brothers and I do not have a really good relationship with our father. He never shows affection or discloses with us. . . .[95]

Instead of providing judgmental statements, we should offer comments like "We're never too old to learn," "We all have a lot of growing to do," "Everyone makes mistakes; what's important is we recognize them and grow from them," and "No matter how much experience we have had, we are constantly surprised by how things turn out."

We cannot accept other people as they see themselves unless we are involved with them in a personal way. It may seem somewhat strange to remind ourselves we need to treat family members in a personal way; yet we sometimes forget this essential element of confirming family members. When we treat people personally, we not only use their name, use other personal pronouns, and respond to them directly, we also keep in mind past experiences we have shared, their particular personality, attitudes, values, and beliefs. Comments that demonstrate the contrast between personal and impersonal responses are provided below:

Personal Comments	Impersonal Comments
I need to talk to you, John.	People should talk to each other.
Remember when we went to the lake for our summer vacation?	Summer vacations sometimes include going to a lake.
You know just what I like.	Some people know what I like.
Sarah, you are always so sensitive to the feelings of others.	People vary in their sensitivity to others.

■ Show Your Support of Others

Support is essential for family members to grow and develop. Positive behaviors such as encouragement, descriptive rather than evaluative statements, and constructive rather than destructive communication are essential. Nonverbal cues may be more important than verbal cues in our demonstration of support for other people. A touch, a hug, a kiss, a smile, or movement toward another person can all communicate support.[96] One woman explained the role of support in her family:

> I will be the first person in my family-of-origin to get a degree. . . . I receive all the needed affection, nurturance and encouragement from my family-of-origin and my current family now that they can see my mind is made up and my deep determination will get me through the tough times. . . . Since my husband is pursuing a degree also, we can empathize with each other. We both know it isn't easy to work full-time, raise a family, maintain a marriage, pursue a degree and keep our sanity. We listen to each other, console each other and encourage each other. A hug and a smile before a tough exam goes a long way![97]

■ Avoid Negative Behaviors

Negative behaviors decrease family satisfaction.[98] To the extent we can avoid or limit these behaviors, we can increase the satisfaction of all family members. What are some behaviors that may negatively impact upon family satisfaction? They include being critical, evaluative, destructive, humiliating, and sarcastic. These behaviors may cause an individual to feel rejected or disconfirmed as we discussed earlier.

We oftentimes make snap judgments or offer quick retorts to others rather than consider the intent of their messages. If you are a parent and your teenager asks you what you think about cocaine as a recreational drug, how are you likely to respond? If your spouse asks your opinion on extramarital sexual relationships, will you provide a thoughtful answer or a speedy admonition? If a sibling questions your academic major, are you likely to be defensive? Too often we are critical and defensive.

Destructive communication patterns may begin with another person's remark. For instance, suppose your spouse correctly accuses you of forgetting to run an errand and then incorrectly adds you obviously have no concern for others. Your likely response may be a counteraccusation: "You think I have no concern for others? You never even remembered my birthday last year!" Such destructive patterns can escalate far beyond the seriousness of the forgotten errand.

Conflict occurs in all families and individual family members all get angry from time to time. However, conflict can be constructive or destructive as we shall see in Chapter 12. It is important that our communicative patterns—particularly in times of conflict or disagreement—remain constructive rather than destructive.

Humiliation is difficult for both children and adults. When we engage in insults, abuse, name-calling, put-downs, hostilities, and other humiliating behaviors, we all lose.[99] Humiliation may be particularly troublesome for children since their self-concepts are so dependent upon our interactions with them. The child who is called stupid, fat, lazy, or dirty may learn to develop in ways consistent with these labels.

Wahlroos asserts that humiliation results in destructive consequences:

1. The most serious consequence is the destructive influence humiliation has on another person's—especially a child's—self-concept. A child who is subjected to frequent humiliations from his parents will come to feel that he is worthless and thus does not deserve any better treatment.

2. Another destructive consequence is that the humiliated person, adult or child, will feel anger and resentment toward the humiliator and, instead of trying to correct his behavior, may concentrate his energies on how to "get back" at the humiliator.

3. A third destructive consequence is that when you use rude and disrespectful language, you are at the same time—unknowingly, but nevertheless—telling the other person that you are a rude and discourteous person. If the other

person is a child, you are then by example (which is the most effective teaching method) teaching him to be rude and discourteous. Rudeness, disrespect, and sassiness in children's behavior does not come only from the influence of their friends, although that, too, can play a role. Very often you find that rudeness and disrespect are being taught to the child in the home, without the parents realizing it! What happens in these cases is that the parent does not realize that his own behavior is disrespectful and that he is thereby teaching his child to be disrespectful.[100]

Sarcasm is closely related to humiliation and is a similarly negative behavior. Sarcasm is difficult for the receiver because of the double bind created. For example, suppose a woman tells her husband she is going to begin a new diet and she is confident she will lose weight. He responds with a smile, a wink, and the sarcastic comment, "I'll just bet you will!" In essence, he is eroding her confidence in herself and her belief she can lose weight. At the same time, the wife loves her husband and respects his judgment. What choices does she have? She can lose her sense of belief in herself that she is capable of losing weight or she can lose her belief in her husband's love and the strength of their relationship. In either case, she loses. Sarcasm creates a "Damned if you do, and damned if you don't" situation.

SUMMARY

In this chapter we considered the role of understanding and supporting others in the family context. We learned this complex activity includes listening, empathy, and nonverbal sensitivity. Listening is a selective activity that involves both the reception and the interpretation of aural stimuli. Empathy is "the ability to perceive the other person's view of the world as though it were our own." Nonverbal sensitivity involves our ability to accurately decode the nonverbal cues of others.

Several factors interact with our ability to understand others. Among these variables are biological sex, gender, and the intimacy of the relationships. For example, although neither men nor women listen "better" than the other sex, they do listen differently. At the same time, women are more sensitive to subtle nonverbal cues and "extraneous" information that others provide. They therefore appear to be more empathic than men.

Understanding and supporting family members are important for allowing us to have harmonious interactions with family members, conveying a sense of regard to others, allowing us to become a family unit, and making us feel better about ourselves. We convey our sense of positive regard to others through the process of confirmation. Confirmation may be contrasted with rejection and disconfirmation. Confirmation occurs when we treat others in a manner that is consistent with their presentation of themselves. Rejection occurs when we treat others in a manner that is inconsistent with their self-

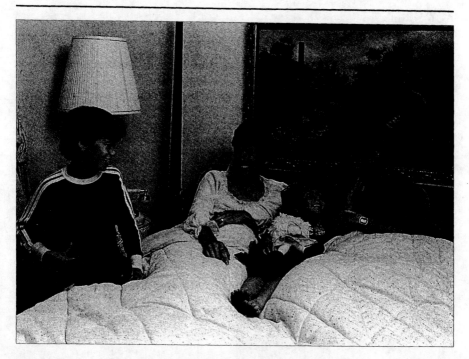

Family satisfaction increases as family members feel understood and supported (© Myers, Stock, Boston).

definition. Disconfirmation occurs when we fail to respond to another person's view of self or when we respond to others in a neutral way.

Understanding family members is key to family satisfaction. Researchers have found that satisfying marital relationships can be distinguished from less satisfying relationships on the basis of spouses' reactions to how well they listen and attend to their spouses. In general, the more accurately individuals can report their partner's desires, the more satisfied they are with their marriage.

Family satisfaction is based on a number of behaviors related to understanding and support: the sending of messages that suggest others are understood and the actual understanding of others' messages, providing supportive and positive comments, and perceiving others' communication behavior favorably.

We can improve our ability to demonstrate understanding and support to other family members. Among the recommendations offered in this chapter are (1) to take time to communicate, (2) to give family members a full hearing, (3) to provide messages that convey understanding, (4) to accept other family members as they see themselves, (5) to show your support of others, and (6) to avoid negative behaviors. To the extent we are able to practice these behaviors, we may be more satisfied as family members.

KEY TERMS

1. *Listening* is a selective activity that involves both the reception and the interpretation of aural stimuli.

2. *Empathy* may be defined as one's ability to perceive another person's view of the world as though it were his or her own.

3. *Nonverbal sensitivity* involves our ability to accurately decode the nonverbal cues of others.

4. *Psychological sex role* refers to our internalization of characteristics traditionally linked with masculinity or femininity.

5. *Mutuality* simply shows sensitivity and respect for other's views.

6. *Confirmation* occurs when we treat others in a manner consistent with their presentation of themselves.

7. *Disconfirmation* occurs when we fail to respond to another person's view of self or when we respond to others in a neutral way.

8. *Rejection* occurs when we treat others in a manner that is inconsistent with their self-definition.

9. *Feedback* is defined as the receiver's verbal and nonverbal responses to the sender's messages.

CHAPTER 12

MANAGING CONFLICT AMONG FAMILY MEMBERS

Sometimes it's worse to win a fight than to lose.

BILLIE HOLLIDAY

After you have read this chapter, you will be able to:

1. Define conflict.

2. Identify the five stages of conflict.

3. Discuss disagreements or differences in understanding of the content and relationship dimensions of interaction.

4. Explain Feldman's model of repetitive cycles of nonproductive marital conflict.

5. List and describe the five types of intimacy anxiety.

6. Differentiate between constructive and destructive conflict.

7. Identify six common patterns of conflict resolution.

8. Apply guidelines for conflict resolution.

9. Discuss how conflict affects family satisfaction.

Conflict is inevitable among family members. Nikki Giovanni observed, "Mistakes are a fact of life. It is the response to error that counts." One humorist suggests, "The last time married couples agree about anything is when they both say, 'I do.'"[1] Conflict occurs because individuals in families do not always share the same meanings for the things or events in their lives. They may interpret such events differently because of differing values, perceptions, needs, beliefs, feelings, opinions, or attitudes.

Conflict is viewed differently by different families. In some families, conflict is avoided; in others, it is a common occurrence. Conflict may lead to the destruction of one family unit; it may be the manner by which problems are solved in another, and is thus viewed as essential for the continuation of a satisfying family life.

In this chapter we will consider the role of conflict within the family. Conflict is not static over the development and deterioration of intimate relationships. As couples change in their level of commitment to each other, their attributions about the causes of the conflict change.[2] Before partners are married they may explain conflict as situational, but after their marriage, they may view the causes to be a result of their partner's personality.[3] Two researchers showed that conflict increased greatly as couples moved from casual to serious dating, but that it leveled off from serious dating through marriage. Nonetheless, no relationship was shown between love and conflict levels during the premarital relationship.[4] Another research team similarly showed that conflict levels change in the dissolution of relationships.[5]

"Stop banging on the door...we're trying to attain serenity!"

MARMADUKE. Reprinted by permission of UFS, Inc.

❖ THE NATURE OF CONFLICT

■ Definition of Interpersonal Conflict

Conflict occurs for many reasons among family members and it may be either constructive or destructive. Interpersonal conflict has been defined by communication researchers Joyce Frost and Bill Wilmot as "an expressed struggle between at least two interdependent parties who perceive incompatible goals, scarce rewards, and interference from the other parties in achieving their goals."[6] The phrase "an expressed struggle" suggests that conflict is not present in the interpersonal setting when one person is aware of a problem but tells no one about it. Both (or all) of the communicators must be aware a conflict exists.

"Perceived incompatible goals" suggests the individuals involved in the conflict believe if one of them achieves his or her goals the other (or others) cannot. The "Marmaduke" cartoon illustrates perceived incompatible goals—Marmaduke's banging on the door interferes with the serenity and solitude sought by the women who are meditating.

Another example would be if two siblings are arguing over who will play with a particular truck, they may believe only one of them can win and the other will lose. If a young couple is looking for a home and the husband wants to live in a low-maintenance apartment and the wife wants to live in an older home that will require a great deal of work, they may perceive incompatible goals. In the first case, the goals might not be truly incompatible. The two siblings could each play with the truck for one-half of the play time. However, as long as the people involved believe the goals are incompatible, this criterion for interpersonal conflict is met. Businessperson David Sarnoff remarked, "Competition brings out the best in products and the worst in people."

"Perceived scarce rewards" means interactants believe there is a limited and small number of rewards to be distributed between, or among, them. Two children may perceive too little candy to share; the dual-career couple may see too little time available for relaxation and enjoyment; and the dating couple may feel they have too little money to do all of the things they would choose to do.

Interpersonal conflict requires "interference from the other parties in achieving one's goals." Individuals feel others are intervening in the path to their goals. The medical student may feel his spouse is sabotaging his career by making entertainment plans during times he needs to study. The older brother may feel his younger sibling is intruding when she is always in the room when he brings home a date. Mark Twain observed, "Nothing so needs reforming as other people's habits."

Linda Robertson, who is in a long-term marriage, recalls the couple's early days together. The example of conflict she remembers illustrates the concepts of incompatible goals, scarce rewards, and interference from other parties. Linda relates:

On Sunday we would go to his Mother's house. I loved their family. So I really enjoyed that. We would go over there on Sunday and we would be doing the dishes, all of us women would be doing the dishes. Then here would come this string of guys in there, each one would say to his wife, "I think we're going to go to the races or go to the ball game, or something else." They would just leave us sitting there. That didn't set too well.[7]

■ Stages of Conflict

Although conflict may seem to simply erupt from time to time in the family, conflict actually goes through some recognizable stages. The communication authors Kathleen Galvin and Bernard Brommel identify five stages:

1. Prior conditions stage

2. Frustration awareness stage

3. Active conflict stage

4. Solution stage

5. Follow-up stage[8]

Let us consider what occurs in each of these.

The *prior conditions stage* includes the situation and circumstances preceding the actual conflict. Among the prior conditions producing conflict are ambiguity about one's responsibilities and roles; excessive dependency of one individual upon another; competition over a limited resource such as affection, time, or money; the recollection of a previously unresolved conflict; prior negative experiences with decision making; or the necessity for agreement by everyone.[9]

Let us provide examples for each of these potential prior conditions. Ambiguity about one's responsibilities and roles can occur because of external changes in the family or because of internal or psychological changes in the individuals in the family. For instance, we may feel some ambiguity about our responsibilities if one person's role changes in the family. Lila remained at home during the preschool period of her children, but decided to attend some classes at the local college once they were all in school. Do her partner's responsibilities change? Do the children's responsibilities change? To what extent or degree? We can clearly see that some conflict may arise over new responsibilities and newly defined roles.

Similarly, the feelings of one person may create ambiguity in the roles of others. After working with a number of competent females, Bill began to see his own wife in a different light. He began to feel she was sheltered or limited in her traditional lifestyle, even though they originally agreed it was appropriate for her to stay at home. He began to urge her to consider a career that resulted in ambiguous role expectations for his spouse and conflict for the couple.

A second prior condition for conflict is the excessive dependency of one individual upon another. A department chair in a fine arts college was viewed by his faculty as weak, powerless, and insipid. They were very surprised to find that his wife was strong, tough, and assertive. The faculty negatively evaluated the chair the first year he served in his office. During the second year, the man began to make decisions in a very tough-minded manner. The second year the faculty negatively evaluated their chair, too. The reason? They believed his wife, who was trained in the same field as he was, was making all of the decisions and writing all of the memos. During the third year of the chair's tenure, he and his wife divorced. Although the public reason offered for the dissolution was the wife's new position in a remote area, the husband privately disclosed that his reliance upon her for day-to-day decision making in his new job had provided more conflict than the couple could handle.

A third prior condition for conflict is competition over a limited resource, such as affection, time, or money. The dual-career couple, with or without children, may find this prior condition to be the most relevant. Although the dual-career couple report marital satisfaction on many dimensions, they state that the lack of time they have for themselves and for others in the family is one of their greatest problems.[10]

When two siblings are born close together, the oldest may feel a lack of affection or time from the parents. One woman reported that she tried to kill her baby brother with a tin can lid she found in the garbage when she was 3 years old because she could not deal with the amount of time and affection he was provided. Although most of us have not gone this far, we may have felt hurt or angry because of the amount of time someone else in the family was afforded.

Marriages face particular problems when the children in the family have special physiological or psychological problems.[11] The excessive amount of time one parent or another member of the family must spend with the child pulls time and affection away from others. As a result, conflict erupts.

The recollection of a previously unresolved conflict can also serve as the prior condition for new conflict. If a family includes four drivers and two cars, conflict may be a regular occurrence. Suppose the father in a family dislikes conflict and tries to suppress or "smooth over" every potential conflict without actually resolving it. On Friday night, the newest driver in the house, 16-year-old Jason, reminds everyone this is the night he and his friends are going to a dance at the high school. The mother asks which car he is taking since she and the boy's dad are going to a party. Nick pipes up that he's not taking Dad's car because he asked Dad for it two weeks ago. Dad quietly responds that both of the boys can go out and he and Mom will be happy to stay at home. Although the mother in this situation is not pleased with the situation, she says nothing. For her, the conflict is unresolved and may serve as a prior condition for conflict later on.

Prior negative experiences with decision making also serve as a condition that sets the stage for conflict. If you grew up in a home in which decisions were not handled well, you may feel some anxiety about decision making. For instance, one man reported his parents never had a fight. He explained whenever his father disagreed with his mother, she would sniffle and act very hurt. Sometimes she would cry outright. When she began to weep, her husband became very protective and apologized for hurting her. He also did what she had suggested. Her strategy of tears in times of disagreement left her children with fairly negative responses to decision making. They felt badly for their parents and they had no model of how decisions are made within the family. As a consequence, the man said he and his wife had frequent arguments and experienced a high level of conflict. Why? He suggested his early negative experience with decision making created a level of anxiety in him that made him ready to do battle over the most insignificant differences.

Finally, the necessity for agreement by everyone can create a prior condition for conflict. One large family included a 17-year-old son, a 15-year-old daughter, a 12-year-old son, a 3-year-old daughter, a father who was an engineer, and a mother who was a librarian. Each year the family would plan a four-week family vacation. Actually, the family never spent the entire four weeks away because the conflict became so intense they would return home before their vacation period was over. However, the interesting part of their story was their description of the period of time in which a decision was made. Since the family could not manage to take six separate vacations, everyone had to agree upon where they would travel. Needless to say, each person always had a different idea. Even when coalitions of two or three people would agree on a vacation spot, the others would disagree. One of the members of the family reported that even before it became time to consider the family vacation, the tension in the house began to be felt. The necessity for everyone agreeing to the decision created a prior condition for conflict.

The second stage in the conflict process is the *frustration awareness stage*. At this point, family members become frustrated or upset with the others in their family. They may feel others are stopping them from doing something they desire to do, forcing them to do something they do not want to do, or providing confusion or ambiguity about what they might do. For instance, the woman who wishes to diet may feel frustrated in her attempts as her husband brings her ice cream, candy, and other "treats" when he comes home from work. The teenager may feel frustrated when he wants to go out with his friends, but his parents increase the number of chores he must do before he leaves. The husband of a complex woman may feel frustrated because he is not provided with clear and unambiguous signals about his wife's expectations of him.

These suggestions often precede the active conflict stage of conflict, which we will consider next. The *active conflict stage* brings the conflict into the open between the participants. In this stage, the conflict is discussed verbally and nonverbally. Individuals attempt to negotiate or bargain and it is apparent to the interactants an active conflict exists. Some families are vociferous in this stage while others are fairly subdued.

The active conflict stage is illustrated in a story that is told about Molnar, a Hungarian dramatist and novelist, who frequently argued violently with his wife. On one occasion, an old friend listened as they disagreed over some trivial matter. Both shouted at each other at the same time and neither listened. As the argument abated, the friend asked if they routinely communicated in this way. "Of course," replied Molnar, "it saves time. Now that we've both unburdened ourselves we can enjoy some delicious silences."

Most couples are not so dramatic. However, most couples do have routine ways of engaging in conflict. She may cry and he may storm out of the house. He may shout and she might become quiet. She may want to talk about all of the issues while he wants to retreat. Each couple enacts patterns that become fairly commonplace as they struggle to resolve conflicts.

The *solution stage* evolves when potential solutions are offered to deal with the conflict. During the earlier stages, people focus on the problem; they now turn their attention to the solution for the problem. Sally Kempton remarked, "To discover that something is wrong is not necessarily to make it right." During the solution stage, the family members begin to try to "make it right."

Ron and Jeannie Hamm have been married for two years and five months. They have a lifetime commitment to each other, but they still find they engage in conflict from time to time. During the active conflict stage, they place blame and express anger. Ron states that they come to the solution stage fairly quickly:

> And we get to the point that we try to trace things back. We end up tracing back to how it began. We find out that at some point we were accusing the other person of something.[12]

Jeannie adds:

> We both admit that we were wrong. Usually, we do that. We literally ask, "Will you forgive me?"[13]

Ron concludes:

> We almost always do that. We ask specifically, "What are you asking me to forgive you for?" We make sure that we are really forgiven for everything that was involved in making us upset."[14]

Other couples do not move to the solution stage so quickly. Norma Rogalski, in a long-term marriage, explains:

> Al's very good about saying he's sorry. We usually just come to some kind of an agreement. Sometimes, too, he'll say he sees it my way. Or, I'll say I see it his way. We agree finally on everything. I mean, he doesn't go his way and I don't go my way. We don't always reach an agreement right way. It may take several days, and we won't even talk about it. But each of us will think about it.[15]

The solution may be one all endorse or it may be one with which only one person agrees. Family members may view the answer suggested as constructive and helpful or as destructive and hurtful. Later in the chapter we will discuss methods of resolving conflict that can result in more satisfying solutions.

The *follow-up stage* is the final stage in the conflict process. This denouement, or unraveling of the conflict, occurs after the conflict has been solved. It may include positive outcomes such as increased understanding of the other family members or negative responses such as angry acceptance of the pro-

posed solution. The follow-up stage may be relatively short or it may last for
several days. The follow-up stage leads once more to the prior conditions
stage and the conflict cycle has come full circle. Another conflict may not
erupt immediately or for a long period afterward. Nonetheless, the reactions
in the follow-up stage become part of the past history of the family, which
goes into the prior conditions stage.

A college student from the Middle East explained the relationship of the
follow-up stage to the prior conditions stage and the importance in follow-up:

> From my experience, I think there are certain rules that should be followed
> when both parties are trying to settle a conflict. One of the most important and
> essential factors is to discuss all sides of the conflict and deal with it no matter
> how simple it may seem, because such things may be the basis of a more com-
> plicated conflict in the future. Another thing that should be considered is that
> both parties of the conflict should try to control themselves, and not talk about
> other things that are bothering them. These may affect how they feel about
> each other in the future, particularly if they are a married couple.[16]

As we shall see in a later section that provides guidelines for conflict resolution, this advice is well taken.

Family therapist Sven Wahlroos offers advice on the follow-up stage:

> Once an agreement has been reached, however, it is useful to keep in mind
> that agreements are sometimes perceived and/or remembered quite different-
> ly by the parties to the agreement. Thus, arguments can arise as to what the
> agreement actually was. If this happens frequently, it is best to start an
> "agreement book" into which agreements are entered and initialed by each
> party. Many agreements should, in any case, be time-limited and renegotiable,
> and the book would then serve as a useful reminder of when such renegotia-
> tions are due.[17]

This complete set of conflict stages, like this last stage, may occur in quick
succession or it may extend over a long period of time. An elementary school
teacher who worked in her husband's florist business discussed a conflict that
extended over a number of years:

> I wanted to help with our florist business. I loved buying for the shop and
> bringing in merchandise that I knew women would like. I did not realize that
> my husband did not share my enthusiasm or ideas. He did not tell me of his
> disapproval directly. This was done indirectly over a period of years. Last
> year the final incident occurred.
>
> I like working with dried materials and have been very successful in
> making arrangements and wreaths that sell quickly. Last summer I told my
> husband that if he would purchase some materials I would be happy to make
> arrangements at home as it would give me something to do. The summer
> passed and every time I asked for the materials, I was given varying excuses:
> there is no money right now to buy supplies, we have to go to the wholesaler
> on Tuesday because only then can we get a 10% discount, or we don't need
> anything in the shop right now. In time, I quit asking.
>
> I have stopped participating in the business because of the frustration I

felt. The satisfaction I once received from working with my husband is no longer there. I had unintentionally stepped on my husband's toes. I now know what his feelings are and I abide by them.[18]

❖ CAUSES OF CONFLICT

Why does conflict arise? A variety of causes have been proposed. Let us examine some of the most frequently discussed suggestions.

■ Differences Among the Interactants

The reason for conflict in the family setting may be rather straightforward. For instance, one set of investigations suggests conflict arises because of differences among the interactants. For instance, when self-contained, internal husbands are married to external wives, the wives report high marital dissatisfaction. Similarly, when marital partners provide significantly different amounts of affective or emotional disclosure to each other, their marital adjustment is lower.[19] Others concur that differences and dissimilarities have a negative impact on marital bliss and are positively related to conflict in the family setting.[20]

In *Everything to Gain, Making the Most of the Rest of Your Life,* former president Jimmy Carter provides an example of a long-term difference between him and his wife, Rosalynn:

> There was one aggravation that had persisted during our marriage. Perhaps because of my Navy training, punctuality had been almost an obsession. It is difficult for me to wait for someone who is late for an appointment, and even more painful if I cause others to wait. Even during the hurly-burly of political campaigns I rarely deviated from my schedule, and staff members had to go out of their way to ensure that these demands of mine were met. I was difficult on this issue and I know it.
>
> Rosalynn has always been adequately punctual, except as measured by my perhaps unreasonable standards. All too frequently, a deviation of five minutes or less in our departure time would cause a bitter exchange, and we would arrive at church or a friend's house still angry with each other. For thirty-eight years, it has been the most persistent cause of dissension between us.
>
> On August 18, 1984, I went into my study early in the morning to work on a speech and turned on the radio for the news. When I heard what the date was, I realized it was Rosalynn's birthday and I hadn't bought her a present. What could I do that would be special for her without a gift? I hurriedly wrote a note that was long overdue: "Happy Birthday! As proof of my love, I will never again make an unpleasant comment about tardiness." I signed it, and delivered it in an envelope, with a kiss. Now, more than two years later, I am still keeping my promise and it has turned out to be one of the nicest birthday presents in our family's history—for Rosalynn and for me![21]

■ Disagreement or Differences in Understanding of the Content and Relationship Dimensions of the Interaction

The differences existing among family members may be more complex. In Chapter 1, we observed that communication always includes a content and relationship level that are inextricably bound to each other. For instance, when a husband tells a wife, "You're not going to take three classes next term—it's too hard on the whole family!" he is providing two messages. First, he is sending a content message about the wife's college coursework and the effect he perceives it has on the family. Second, he is offering a relational message that suggests he has the right to tell the wife how she can behave. The content of the message and the relationship it suggests are fundamentally linked. The husband is using a specific situation to comment on the relationship between the two, and he uses his perception of the relationship in order to comment on the content, or situation he perceives.

The content and relationship dimensions are always present, but they may be implicit rather than explicit. Sometimes the content dimension is explicit and the relationship dimension is only implied. For example, if you tell a child to bring a pair of scissors to you, you will probably not begin your request by explaining you are the child's parent and have the right to ask the child to assist you occasionally. Similarly, we sometimes do not explicitly state the content dimension of a message. Our nonverbal responses to others generally have a relational but not a content dimension. As we observed in the first chapter, we generally respond lovingly and warmly to others through nonverbal means rather than by offering verbal statements about our feelings.

We also observed in Chapter 1 that individuals view interactions from the perspective of the other person as well as from their own perspective. Our perceptions of our own interactions are not always the same as our perceptions of the other person's interactions. Our direct perspective and our metaperspective may be discrepant.

As we noted, relationships are highly complex as a result of the different perspectives we bring to each relationship. Each time we interact with another person, we bring our own perspective and metaperspective and the other person is bringing a unique perspective and metaperspective. For example, if you are engaged to be married, you may have to consider religious affiliation. Suppose you are Catholic and your partner is Jewish. Your regular church attendance is known to your partner. His commitment to Judaism is clear to you. Both of you are strong-willed individuals who wish to dominate the other person. What is likely to occur?

We can analyze this situation by considering both the content and relationship dimensions and the levels of perspectives and metaperspectives. Figure 12.1 illustrates the possibilities on the content dimension. Figure 12.2 suggests the same possibilities on the relationship dimension. In this situation we find disagreement on the content level (the direct perspectives differ between yourself and your partner) and on the relationship level (again, the

Figure 12.1

	You	Your partner
Direct perspective	I want him/her to become Catholic.	I want her/him to become Jewish.
Metaperspective	He/she wants me to become Jewish.	She/he wants me to become Catholic.

Direct perspectives and metaperspectives of two people on the content dimension.

Figure 12.2

	You	Your partner
Direct perspective	I want to dominate him/her.	I want to dominate him/her.
Metaperspective	He/she wants to dominate me.	He/she wants to dominate me.

Direct perspectives and metaperspectives of two people on the relationship dimension.

direct perspectives differ between yourself and your partner). However, understanding occurs between the two of you on the content level (your metaperspective matches your partner's direct perspective and your partner's metaperspective matches your direct perspective) and on the relationship level (again, your metaperspective matches your partner's direct perspective and your partner's metaperspective matches your direct perspective). Although you understand each other, conflict is inevitable because of the disagreement that exists on both levels. To some extent, individuals can determine the content and relationship levels of conflict.[22]

Bill Wilmot suggests there are innumerable combinations of degrees of agreement and degrees of understanding within any dyad. He recommends we limit our consideration to the basic cases of agreement or disagreement and understanding or misunderstanding. Based on this recommendation, he generates eight possible causes of conflict between two people. The causes include the following:

1. They agree and mutually understand each other on the content issue but still have a relationship conflict.

2. They agree on the content issue but one or both participants misunderstands the other's position.

3. They disagree on the content issue and understand they do.

4. They disagree on the content issue and, on top of that, one or both misunderstands the other's position.

5. They agree and mutually understand each other on the relationship definition, but still have a content conflict.

6. They are in relational agreement but misunderstand they are. For instance, they may misperceive each other's relational stance.

7. They disagree relationally (both wish to control the relationship) and understand they do.

8. They disagree relationally and, in addition, misperceive the other's relational stance.[23]

These categories may be criticized on a number of grounds. First, they are not all-inclusive; other categories could be determined. Second, conflicts are sometimes difficult to analyze in terms of their relational or content base. At the same time, these eight possibilities are representative of the causes of conflict. Let us examine each of them.

1. *They agree and mutually understand each other on the content issue but still have a relationship conflict.* Suppose you and your spouse come from very different backgrounds. Your partner's father was a very quiet man, but the person who made all decisions. Even though he rarely spoke, when he did,

"everyone listened." You come from a home where the mother was both talk-ative and dominant. Your partner imitates his father's behavior and you mimic your mother. When you needed to make major decisions about political party affiliation, the amount of income each of you should bring to the relationship, and the kind of neighborhood in which you chose to live, you found you understood each other and you agreed. However, the way you made the deci-sions involved your spouse's relative silence and your talkativeness. Your partner perceives your gregariousness as "idle chatter" that contributes little to the decisions or as attempts to unsuccessfully dominate the decision. You perceive your verbalizations as clear and direct evidence of your contribution to the decisions. You perceive your partner's reticence as a sign of his lack of involvement and submissiveness while he sees the behavior as consistent with the father's "strong but silent" approach. The two of you agree and under-stand each other on several content issues, but misunderstand each other on the relational level.

An elementary school teacher married to a florist explained how just such a problem nearly resulted in divorce:

> A major on-going conflict in our lives has been my husband's unwillingness to engage in everyday chitchat and to talk about inner concerns and prob-lems. For years I've been carrying on a one-sided conversation. Not until my husband stopped answering all together did I realize how far our communica-tion with one another had deteriorated. I started asking him to give at least a grunt or a groan to let me know he had at least heard me. When I asked him why he did not respond to what I was saying he only replied that he had nothing to say.
>
> Only when our marriage was on the brink of ending did my husband begin to make an effort to communicate with me. The threat of divorce has forced him to become accountable and responsive. We have engaged in some lengthy discussions about his reluctance to talk and are now considering counseling.[24]

2. *They agree on the content issue but one or both participants misunder-stands the other's position.* Jackie is a 21-year-old college senior who plans on attending law school. She has taken the LSAT and surprised everyone with a very high score. Because she also has a high grade point average and good rec-ommendations, many top-rated law schools have offered her scholarships and have invited her to visit their campuses. Jackie's parents live in Michigan and Jackie has attended undergraduate school in a liberal arts college in the East. Her parents feel they have not seen enough of her during her undergraduate education, while Jackie feels the distance between herself and her parents has been just about right. Jackie has been offered a scholarship at the University of Michigan. She wants to attend the school because of its high academic ranking. Her parents want her to attend the school, too, since she will be closer to home. However, they have been somewhat vague in their responses to poten-tial law schools since they are afraid if they encourage her to attend Michigan, she will go somewhere else in order to demonstrate her independence. Jackie

misperceives their ambiguity as lack of concern about her and as discouragement from attending a law school within driving distance of her parents' home. While she and her parents agree on the content issue, Jackie misunderstands her parents' position.

3. *They disagree on the content issue and understand that they do.* As children mature, they begin consciously and unconsciously to separate themselves from their parents. One method of separation is to identify themselves with groups, values, or beliefs sharply discrepant from their parents. The individual who grows up in a politically conservative family may support liberal or radical candidates. The young woman who grows up in a family in which her mother wore no make-up and feels strongly about others not wearing cosmetics may use excessive amounts of lipstick, mascara, and eyeliner. The young man who grows up as an "army brat" and is expected to dress and behave in certain prescribed ways may grow his hair long or shave his head, may wear an earring or other jewelry, may be truant from high school, may engage in vandalism, and may simultaneously dress in camouflage fatigue uniforms to show his disdain for the military. In all of these cases, the parents and the child probably understand they disagree on a content issue.

4. *They disagree on the content issue and, on top of that, one or both misunderstands the other's position.* Married couples make differing decisions about monogamy. Some couples view faithfulness as a cornerstone of their marriage, without which there would be no marriage. Others view fidelity as irrelevant; they may generally support monogamy, but they would not be destroyed if their partner had an occasional relationship with someone else. Still others endorse multiple sexual relationships within their married life. Suppose a couple is in the early years of their marriage. The husband feels monogamy is essential to a successful married relationship. The wife feels faithfulness is a relative matter and while it is important to be faithful to one's spouse in a psychological way, it is not imperative to be physically monogamous. Because the husband believes his position is universally understood, he sees no reason to discuss fidelity. Because the wife believes sexual activity with others is irrelevant to the success of a marriage, she sees no reason to discuss it with her husband. The two individuals disagree on the content level and they do not understand the other's position.

5. *They agree and mutually understand each other on the relationship definition, but still have a content conflict.* Paula and Joe have been married for a few years. They both have successful careers and they have two children. Both individuals in the couple are ambitious and love their work. They agree that both careers are important and they have made every attempt to share the responsibilities in the home and with the family. Their youngest child, Jeannie, has developed chronic bladder infections. As a result, her day care teacher has called her parents four times in the past three months with the news that Jeannie was ill and had to be taken home. The first and third times, Paula picked up Jeannie and stayed home with her for two or three days. The second time, Joe did. Today is the fourth time the teacher has called. Joe is in the middle of an important meeting and he knows Paula's work is relatively

slack right now. He calls Paula to determine if she can take off another two or three days to care for Jeannie. Paula does not believe it is her turn. The couple disagrees on the content issue, but they fundamentally agree on shared responsibilities and roles.

6. *They are in relational agreement but misunderstand that they are. For instance, they may misperceive each other's relational stance.* Julie and Ed have a nontraditional relationship. Julie and Ed began their marriage as a typical couple with two jobs and every reason to believe they would be among the most successful in their graduating class from the state university. Julie worked long and hard hours in a middle-management position at an older corporation. Ed began work in a more entrepreneurial computer-support company. Ed rose quickly in his company while Julie's promotions were slow but steady. Ed learned three days before it was announced his company had gone bankrupt. Through overextensions and poor management, the company went out of business with less than a week's warning. Ed was devastated by the loss of his job, but even more overwhelmed when he found he could not gain a similar job at other companies. Meanwhile, Julie's career improved and she was made a vice president in the company. Julie and Ed decided they did not need two incomes and Ed would be in charge of the home and would also be free to develop software products independently.

As the new relationship became permanent, Julie became more assertive and domineering while Ed became more responsive and submissive. Both Julie and Ed felt satisfied with the changes in their roles and the changes in their behavior. However, neither set of in-laws felt comfortable with the new arrangement and Julie and Ed were both encouraged to "rethink" their decision. Julie and Ed began to believe the other person in the marriage was dissatisfied with the new relationship, yet neither of them was unhappy with it. They were in relationship agreement, but misunderstood that they were.

7. *They disagree relationally (both wish to control the relationship) and understand that they do.* A contemporary family provides an example: Kate and Ben are siblings. Kate is 12 and in middle school; Ben is 6 and is in the first grade. The two children are part of a blended family. Chris and Kate Larson are two children from the mother's first marriage. Ben and Becky Johnson are two children from the mother's second marriage. Chris Larson lives with his father in another state so Kate is the oldest child in her family unit. Kate visits her father and his new family for about one to two months each year. During that time, Ben is the oldest child in the family unit. Because of their position in the family, because of the role modeling provided by two strong-willed parents, and perhaps because of their individual personalities, both Kate and Ben wish to dominate the other. When Kate is home, she believes she should be the boss because she's the oldest. When she has been gone for an extended period of time, Ben delights in "taking over." When Kate returns, a high level of conflict ensues. Both Kate and Ben know they disagree on their definition of the relationship; nonetheless, they still disagree.

8. *They disagree relationally and, in addition, misperceive the other's relational stance.* Rita is the second wife of Bill, who is 20 years her senior. Bill is a

highly successful businessperson who has three children from a previous marriage. His first wife died of cancer a short time before he met Rita. Although
Rita had not been married before, she did have a number of close relationships
with men and lived with two different men for extended periods of time. Bill's
children range in age from 30 to 19; Rita is 33. The oldest child, Willy
(William Jr.), is in his father's company and maintains close ties to the family.
He is somewhat uncertain of the relationship between his stepmother and
himself—particularly since she dated a friend of his from college.

Rita has been very warm and friendly to all of Bill's children because she
loves him and wants to develop the same kind of family atmosphere that existed in Bill's first marriage. Willy perceives her behavior toward him as inappropriate and believes she must be interested in developing a sexual relationship.
Willy has still not accepted his mother's death and believes his father and Rita
got married far too soon. Rita and Willy disagree relationally and they misperceive the other's relational stance.

■ A Buffer to Intimacy

Conflict may arise among family members for more complex and perhaps
dysfunctional reasons. Current theorists suggest one of the purposes of conflict is that it serves as a buffer to intimacy. As such, conflict serves the purpose of disallowing a relationship to become more intimate. Some families
experience conflict in regulating their interpersonal distance because they are
afraid of separation and intimacy.[25] You will recall we considered the relationship between autonomy and intimacy in Chapter 10.

Feldman offers a model of repetitive cycles of nonproductive marital conflict.[26] He offers the caveat that his model is not all-inclusive, but it is clearly
relevant for our understanding of conflict as a mechanism to avoid intimacy.
His model is based on three premises. First, he believes that repetitive, nonproductive marital conflict behavior has a purpose or goal and it is maintained
by reinforcement and negative feedback. Second, he believes that for the individual, a goal of conflict is to prevent intense unconscious anxiety to emerge
into the consciousness. For the interactants, a major goal is to decrease real or
anticipated intimacy. Third, he posits that once conflict is triggered, its
destructiveness escalates until conflict-generated anxiety or one's fundamental
need for intimacy become stronger. His model is presented in Figure 12.3.

In order to understand Feldman's model, let us consider an example. We
will begin at the rectangle at the top of the depiction, even though we could
begin at any point in the cycle. Margaret and Al have been married for four
years. Each of them has a successful career. The couple has talked of having
children in an abstract way, but they have never talked about the prospect as a
serious or real topic.

One Monday night, Al initiates a discussion about having a baby. Margaret,
fearing such a change would result in more permanence in their relationship and
greater intimacy, feels Al has deviated from their rule-governed homeostasis—

Figure 12.3

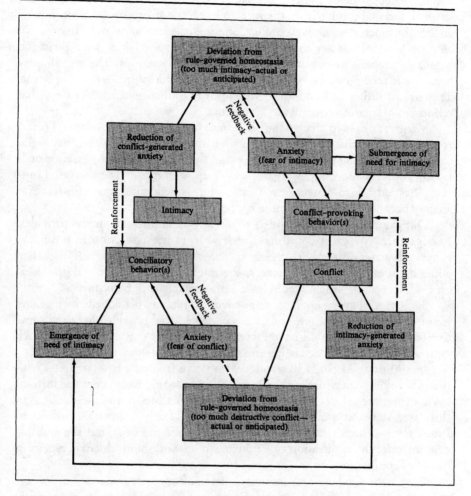

Feldman's intimacy-conflict cycle. The major components of the cycle are connected by solid lines, with arrows indicating the direction of movement around the circle. The broken lines are the pathways of reinforcement and negative feedback. (Feldman, 1979; adapted with permission.)

she anticipates too much intimacy. This perception leads to anxiety and a submergence of need for intimacy because of Margaret's fear of intimacy.

Margaret's anxiety leads to conflict-provoking behaviors and she begins to start arguments over meaningless details throughout the week. She and Al end up shouting at each other over trivia. Margaret feels some reduction in her intimacy-generated anxiety and is therefore reinforced for her behavior. As a consequence, she continues to provide conflict-provoking behavior and on Friday evening, without telling Al, she goes to a "Happy Hour" with some of her coworkers. Al is asleep when she stumbles in on Saturday morning.

Margaret awakens at noon on Saturday with a hangover and the feeling she had deviated too far from the rule-governed homeostasis—she has experienced too much destructive conflict. She then feels anxiety over her fear of conflict, which leads her to conciliatory behaviors. She takes two aspirin and begins to prepare an elaborate meal Al particularly enjoys. The conciliatory behavior is recognized by Al and the couple spend a loving evening at home. This rise in intimacy leads to a reduction of conflict-generated anxiety that reinforces Margaret's conciliatory behaviors.

Margaret offers to change the oil in both of their cars on Sunday. Al reciprocates and does the weekly shopping. When the couple go to bed that night, they feel very loving toward each other and their feelings are expressed sexually. On Monday morning, Margaret wakes up with dread. The increased intimacy has led her to observe the relationship is becoming too intimate. Her anxiety because of her fear of intimacy returns.

Our example has not provided all of the possibilities the model provides. For instance, Margaret could have moved from her reduction in intimacy-generated anxiety directly to an emergence of need for intimacy. Rather than going drinking with her coworkers, she might have made a wonderful meal on Friday evening, which would have led to conciliatory behaviors.

Similarly, Al might not have responded favorably to her conciliatory behavior of making an elegant meal on Saturday, but instead provided her with negative feedback. This would have increased Margaret's concern that too much destructive conflict was occurring and she would have felt increased anxiety.

In addition, Al could have offered negative feedback to Margaret's conflict-provoking behaviors in the first place. This would have taken the form of his ignoring her efforts to start a fight or his refusal to join in the conflict. In this case, Margaret would have felt even more clearly the couple had established too much intimacy. Certainly other possibilities exist, but the example demonstrates the application of Feldman's model of nonproductive, repetitive cycles of conflict.

Why do individuals fear intimacy? Feldman suggests five types of intimacy anxiety. They include the fear of merger, fear of exposure, fear of attack, fear of abandonment, and the fear of one's own destructive impulses. Let us examine each of them.

Fear of Merger   When couples become increasing intimate, their self-boundaries become relatively weaker. In essence, they "become one." When people are secure, this feeling of merging is both stimulating and gratifying. When they are insecure, such a merger is perceived as dangerous and the person feels anxiety.

Fear of Exposure   As relationships develop, individuals disclose greater amounts of information about themselves and more intimate details about who they are. People with high self-acceptance and self-esteem view disclosure as enhancing their intimacy and as relatively nonthreatening. For those who do not enjoy self-acceptance, such disclosure is highly risky. They are concerned the negative qualities they believe they hold will be seen by others. Thus they wish to deescalate the relationship.

Fear of Attack   This fear rests on more of a psychological basis than the others. It is related to one or both of two developmental periods. They include the period in which the child develops trust as opposed to mistrust and the Oedipus/Electra period. If children learn mistrust in the first period, they gain an overwhelming frustration which stimulates aggressive impulses projected onto others. When children do not resolve the major conflicts of the Oedipus/Electra period, they have anxiety about the fear of danger from the same-sex parent. Such associations result in anxiety when intimacy exceeds prescribed limits.

Fear of Abandonment   When children have experienced extremely upsetting or extended separations, an unconscious relationship between intimacy and loss is created. One fears intimacy because it is associated with being abandoned or being left. Anxiety results in intimacy development because of this projected, certain, eventual development.

Fear of One's Own Destructive Impulses   During one period of development, children view their parents as "whole objects" who can be both gratifying and frustrating. When children experience their parents as frustrating, intensely hostile feelings develop that may lead to destructive, damaging fantasies about injuring or destroying them. This feeling leads to concern about losing the gratifying parent. When such anxiety has not been resolved, it creates a fear of one's own destructive impulses. These individuals feel anxiety about increasingly intimate relationships because they believe eventual hurt or destruction will be provided to the partner.

Conflict may exist for many reasons. Among the most common reasons in the family context are those detailed above: because of differences among the interactants, because of disagreement or differences in understanding of the content and/or relationship dimensions of the interaction, and to avoid increased intimacy. With these explanations in mind, let us consider two outgrowths of conflict.

❖ OUTGROWTHS OF CONFLICT

Conflict may be constructive or destructive in the family. Let us consider both of these alternatives more fully.

■ Conflict May Be Destructive

Conflict may be destructive to relationships.[27] To the extent family members feel a struggle, and perceive incompatible goals, scarce rewards, and interference from other family members in achieving their goals, they may feel less satisfied and they may be more inclined to terminate the relationship. However, some families thrive on conflict; others use conflict constructively; and still others view conflict as a necessary evil. The question remains: Why is conflict destructive to some family units?

Conflict is destructive when family members do not recognize the inevitability of it. Perhaps our "instant" culture with its "band-aid" cures suggests conflict is dispensable. If we can have breakfast by simply adding hot water to instant coffee and instant oatmeal; if we can have a new muffler installed on our car after a short wait; and if we can have new eyeglasses in less than an hour; surely, we can resolve a conflict before it even erupts.

Conflict is similarly destructive when family members view it as unpleasant, dangerous, or undesirable. Again, our culture may be largely accountable for teaching us conflict is to be avoided. Popular messages suggest people who "talk back," "argue," or "bicker" are not as desirable as are those who "always have something nice to say about everyone." When people overhear an argument, they feel embarrassment; when they eavesdrop on a compliment or positive evaluation, they do not. Why? Primarily because we view conflict as an undesirable state.

Family author Sven Wahlroos explains that when people state they do not like to argue, they are intimating a communication problem. He asserts that the phrase "I don't like to argue" is used for one of three reasons:

Couples' conflict may be constructive or destructive (© Barnes, Stock, Boston).

A. The basic purpose is common but almost always unconscious and involves a middle form of the defense mechanism called denial of feeling. It appears to be an almost universal human tendency to wish to deny the existence of an alter ego. Rare is the person who admits that there is a "devil" within him (and those who do admit it usually do it for the purpose of excusing their destructive actions).. . .

B. Another purpose, very common and often conscious, is to convince yourself and the world not only that you are innocent and lily white, but that it is the *other* person who *forces* you to be destructive when the discussion turns into an argument. The processes involved are blaming (conscious) and projection (unconscious). The statement "I don't want to argue" implies "*but you do*" and thus involves the pretense "I am the innocent victim of my communication partner's cruelty.". . .

C. A third purpose, also very common and sometimes conscious, is to avoid a discussion. The reason for such avoidance is usually some fear, perhaps of embarrassment, of being found out, of losing, etc. The avoidance may be conscious or it may involve various degrees of the unconscious defense mechanism avoidance.[28]

Conflict can also be dangerous or undesirable when it results in physical or verbal attacks. Physical aggression occurs in up to 70 percent of families in disputes between parents and children and up to 30 percent of the conflicts between husbands and wives.[29] Physical violence and verbal aggression are detrimental to family relationships. They corroborate the conclusion that conflict is dangerous and to be avoided.

Conflict is similarly destructive when family members view the conflict as personal, as opposed to issue-oriented. If family members provide negative attributions or misattributions about others, rather than seeing the conflict about a difference in perception, attitudes, beliefs, or needs, the conflict can be destructive. For instance, suppose you have an argument with one of your parents about the amount of time you spend studying each day. Your parents feel you spend too little time studying and you feel you spend an adequate amount of time preparing for your classes. This conflict is destructive if your conclusion is that your parent is naive, stodgy, or pompous. Attributing negative attitudes and intentions to others may result in additional conflict.[30]

Conflict is destructive when family members view communication as unilateral rather than as shared. When we view communication as a unilateral behavior, we see communication originating in one person while the second person is dependent upon the first. When we view communication as a shared activity, we view both interactants as simultaneous senders and receivers of messages. The first view suggests one person is responsible for the successes and failures occurring in interaction; the second view gives both individuals the responsibility for potential successes and failures that occur.

How we view communication is related to marital satisfaction and marital distress. As we observed above, couples who blame each other more have less marital satisfaction[31] and attributing responsibility to one person, rather than sharing the responsibility for the conflict, is related to more distress in relationships.[32]

Finally, conflict is destructive when it is not resolved. We observed earlier the recollection of an unresolved conflict can be the impetus for another conflict cycle. We generally view the conflict process as one that includes both conflict and conflict resolution. The eventual resolution is viewed as a necessary part of the process. However, sometimes the conflict is not resolved. The individuals involved might not reach an alternative, agreed-upon level of understanding. In this case, no agreement is reached and the conflict ensues. Sometimes the conflict leads to increased disagreement and the conflict escalates.

■ Conflict May Be Constructive

Conflict need not be destructive, however. Conflict apparently has a driving or energizing force that is not unlike the motivation created by our physical needs such as hunger, thirst, and pain. Conflict may result in physical arousal, just as our physiological needs do. Thus, conflict may produce a sharpening of our faculties, more efficient learning, and increased motivation to act. Some attitudes and behaviors encourage the constructive use of conflict within the family setting.

First we must understand that conflict is inevitable in human communication. Each of us views our interactions from our own viewpoints, which include distinctively different attitudes, values, needs, opinions, and behaviors. Our goals are not identical to other family members; sometimes we must compete with siblings for rewards, and occasionally others in our family interfere with our achievement of our goals. We experience cyclical changes in our health, in the weather, and in time. We must accept conflict, too, as part of an inevitable cycle.

Second, we must disavow conflict as unpleasant, dangerous, or undesirable. We have observed that conflict, by itself, is neither positive nor negative. We need to appreciate the positive values associated with conflict and learn to manage it successfully and effectively. Verbal and physical attacks must be replaced with constructive strategies. We deflate the cultural myth that conflict is a negative behavior when we see conflict as an inevitable, natural part of interaction.

Third, we must view conflict as issue-oriented rather than as person-oriented. When we move the source of conflict from the person to the issue, we often find we can disagree without damaging the other individual. Haim Ginott popularized this notion as he wrote in the 1960s and 1970s about parent–child interactions.[33] He recommended parents clarify that their anger was focused on behaviors and on circumstances in the environment rather than on the child. For instance, he humorously stated that when a small child spilled indelible ink on a new carpet we should insure the child "we are mad at the ink and not at him or her." Ginott observed, "People are not for hurting. People are for respecting."[34]

Fourth, we need to move the responsibility for the conflict from one individual to the interactions between or among the family members. Communication is transactional, and both interactants serve as simultaneous senders and receivers of messages. We should not blame ourselves or the other person when a conflict occurs; instead, we must share the responsibility.

Fifth, we must view conflict within a cycle of conflict leading to conflict resolution. Conflict may be destructive when it is not resolved, rather than when it is. The constructive use of conflict requires that it be resolved. In the next section of this chapter we will examine methods of resolving conflict.

❖ CONFLICT RESOLUTION

We have observed that conflict affects families in different ways and families do not view conflict in the same manner. For example, Judith, the female main character in the book *House,* explains her attitude about conflict:

> My idea is you yell, you scream. . . . What could be better? . . . If you grow up with a lot of yelling and screaming, yelling and screaming doesn't scare ya. In fact, you kind of like it.[35]

Similarly, families do not resolve conflicts in the same ways.

Conflict resolution is essential to successful family functioning, however. Children learn fairly early on how to resolve conflicts in a way that is neither unpleasant for them nor difficult to do.[36] Marital couples who report high scores for conflict management also report high marital satisfaction.[37] As we shall determine, a variety of methods exist for the resolution of conflict. The method of conflict resolution that is most satisfying may be a function of the characteristics of the family member.[38]

■ Conflict Resolution Methods

Although many techniques are used to resolve conflicts, we will consider six common patterns: denial, suppression, authority, majority rule, compromise, and collaboration.

Denial When family members withdraw from the conflict and do not acknowledge that a problem exists, they are engaged in denial. Denied problems do not evaporate, however. Wahlroos explains, "To leave a significant problem or concern undiscussed is similar to leaving a festering infection untreated. The problem will not go away; on the contrary, like a spreading infection, it will get worse."[39] The cause of the conflict remains, and members may feel increasingly uncomfortable. The problem may become unmanageable.

A woman in her 40s who came from an original family of nine children recalled her mother's long illness and death:

> Two siblings were very psychologically dependent on Mom and denied her illness and coming death. Rather than enjoy her life, they created a monster for everyone to deal with. The other seven of us children requested a session with Hospice, but these two flat out denied they had a problem or that any problem existed. This happened repeatedly. Knowing a problem existed, my sister would in all honesty, make a statement such as, "I told my children

how wonderful and beautiful it is that we all get along so well together at a time like this. You know our brother just takes care of everything for us. Like seeing there is enough grocery money." The truth was that to have power over those who were caring for Mom, he would refuse to cooperate by not signing checks for groceries or he would make remarks like, "How can Mom eat that much if you say she is dying?"[40]

A recent study suggests that when dating couples do not resolve their differences, their relationship may not last. Sally Lloyd studied dating couples and then contacted them three years later. Females in relationships that had ended reported less conflict resolution than did those females in enduring relationships. Interestingly, the males in discontinued and continuing relationships reported no differences in the amount of conflict resolved.[41] Men may be less aware of conflict or they may not be as troubled by the lack of conflict resolution.

Suppression   Smoothing over the problem and minimizing differences occur when people practice suppression as a conflict-resolution technique. When they are engaged in denial, they do not acknowledge a problem exists; when they are involved in suppression, they know a problem exists but they choose to minimize it.

A recent study showed that suppression is more likely to be used by blue-collar wives than white-collar wives.[42] The study is reminiscent of the "All in the Family," in which Archie Bunker complains to his wife and storms around the house. His wife, Edith, by contrast, rarely raises her voice and virtually never complains. When she offers the mildest disagreement, she is ordered to "stifle." "Rocking the boat" may be reserved for men in the blue-collar family.

In general, women may be more likely to engage in suppression than men. Mothers may readily use suppression, as in this example:

> My family's usual mode of settling conflict is by suppressing it, by smoothing over problems and minimizing differences. . . . My Mom usually acts as the mediator between all those involved, trying to smooth things over or forget them altogether. . . . Getting our minds on something else; changing the subject.[43]

Sometimes people engage in suppression because they feel the relationship is more important than a seemingly trivial difference. Leah Fraley's children have left home, but she and her husband are not yet retired. Her marriage, long and strong, includes a lot of humor. In discussing conflict, she wisely observed, "We talk about the big deals and we overlook the small ones."[44]

Suppression is appropriate under such circumstances, but some people routinely rely on suppression in all potential conflict situations. Individuals who always use suppression may feel that people should not argue, fight, or engage in conflict. They may misunderstand the positive aspects of conflict and conflict resolution. The complete reliance on suppression to resolve conflicts is not appropriate, although it may result in increased family satisfaction as we shall determine later in this chapter. Wahlroos discusses suppression:

Accommodating to the other person's wishes may be courteous and nice and lead to smoothness in living and to "getting along." But to accommodate or acquiesce when important issues are at stake, or when you yourself feel strongly against the other person's position, can be costly and dangerous. It can be costly because the price of accommodation is often chronic inner resentment and a feeling of being a "second class citizen." It can be dangerous because the bottled-up resentment may take pathological forms of expression.[45]

The destructive nature of relying on suppression was offered by one 20-year-old man. Although an outsider may believe the family's fighting suggests they are resolving their differences, as we shall determine, their arguments merely suppress the conflicts they feel:

A typical Christmas dinner at the Garrison household. We eat at 11:00 P.M. Everyone is tired, but we eat anyway. We drink and nobody is tired anymore. Then, we fight. We argue all the time when we get together and nothing ever gets resolved. I think it is because the fights are so trivial that there really is no reason to resolve them. We are all so stubborn, too, and nobody will admit when he is wrong.

The way we settle conflict? We forget about it. I know that's horrible, but it's reality in my house. How can my brother, sister and I be expected to resolve our conflicts when our parents still have not settled a conflict of eleven years ago?[46]

Authority When people use the power vested in their position, they are relying on authority as a conflict resolution technique. The father in a family might act as an authority. One man explains:

Whenever there is a conflict in our family, my father acts as the judge. There is no jury. If we are out past the hour of 4 A.M. for more than 3 consecutive days, my father rules. I have no lawyer. My father's ruling would be, "Under my house rules, this type of behavior will not be tolerated. If it continues, you will be asked to leave!" The general rule in my house is that my father has his way or no way at all! If I am in the wrong and mother knows about it, she will not input her opinion. But if my father is not making a strict enough penalty for me, she will add her opinion.[47]

Another discloses:

In our family, my father is like a referee. It is usually whatever he says that goes. My mother and I respect what he says because he is the man of the house. When he solves a problem, it is usually the right solution. But no one is perfect.[48]

Janice and Steven Rohrbach are in their retirement years. They account, in part, for their long marriage on viewing the husband as the authority figure. When asked how they resolve the conflicts that occur, Janice asked her husband, "I usually have to give in, don't I?"[49] Steven answered directly, "Yeah, when you hush up it's all settled. That's the only way we resolve it."[50]

The authority figure may be people other than the father. One educator detailed the various authorities in his original family, his current family, and the family of his in-laws:

> We try to reach some mutually acceptable compromise. As I think about some of our conflicts, though I have a "gut feeling" that many times the compromise is me giving in. For example, she [my wife] does not feel my parents or brother and sister-in-law have ever treated her "right." Therefore they are not welcome in "our" home.
>
> In my childhood family, I feel my mother usually got her way when she felt strongly about something. And in my in-law family, I think all of the members would agree that my father-in-law almost always has his way concerning the outcome of the conflict resolution.[51]

In another family, too, the mother was the authority figure. The Gregori couple have been married for over 40 years. When asked about their conflict resolution techniques, Tony began tentatively, "We usually do what she wants."[52] His wife, Cookie, looked disapproving. Tony quickly added, "No? Well, okay, we come to a decision together."[53] This interaction was humorous because it illustrated that his first answer was probably more accurate.

Majority Rule   When the family relies upon a majority agreement, they are engaging in another form of power within conflict resolution. The rule of the majority may appear to be democratic, but it can also backfire on the group who always uses this method. The children in a family can gang up on an unsuspecting parent and determine how the parent should spend a free weekend. A number of family members can make a decision that really does not affect them, but affects someone in the minority. For example, the father and children may decide they would like some gourmet cooking, but the mother is responsible for spending the hours in the kitchen. Or, the parents and some of the children may agree that another child is responsible for cleaning up a pet's area on a regular basis.

Although majority rule works well frequently, it does have some drawbacks. This technique creates winners and losers. If a discussion results in two possible solutions and the majority supports one solution, those supporting the alternative may feel as though they were completely disenfranchised. Those who have been "outvoted" may feel no commitment to the solution proposed by the majority and may work to interfere with the decision. Similarly, the losers may begin to resent the people who were able to achieve a majority opinion.

Compromise   Compromise occurs when family members state their opinion, and then some middle ground is determined. Like the other methods of conflict resolution, compromise can be used for good or ill. Sometimes it is highly effective, but it can be misused, too. If people know they are going to use compromise, they might state highly inflated opinions at first. For instance, if a family decides they are going out for dinner, one member might cite a five-star restaurant as her choice in order to compromise on a more moderately priced cafe that she really prefers.

Sometimes the compromise does not embody the desires of anyone. For example, one family was building a new home. The children wanted a swimming pool to be included in the plans and the parents wanted a large exercise room complete with the latest exercise equipment. The family compromised and built a sauna. Today, the sauna sits empty.

Collaboration   The hallmark of collaboration is communication. Interaction is used to resolve a conflict when people collaborate. Each family member recognizes the abilities and expertise of the others. The emphasis is on the problem, rather than on defending one's individual position. The family members act as though the group's decision is better than that of any one individual, or even the majority. This orientation leads to a supportive climate in which each member can voice his or her opinion.

Although collaboration may sound ideal, it, too, has inherent problems. If solutions to the conflict are offered as "either-or" statements, negotiation may break down. If the family does not have sufficient resources to resolve the conflict, problems can occur. For instance, the children in a dual-career family insisted their mother spend time driving them to various school-related activities each afternoon. The mother, who was an attorney, simply could not arrange her schedule to meet their demands. The resource of time was not available so negotiation did not work. The family's lack of money, understanding, or other resources can similarly negate the positive effects of collaboration.

Although the methods of conflict resolution presented can sometimes be exclusively identified within the family, most families use a combination of techniques to resolve conflict. This more complicated pattern is illustrated by an adult woman who continues to live with her parents:

> Excluding Dad, when there is conflict we battle it out verbally until an understanding is reached, or when it gets out of hand, it is mutually nonverbally understood when to stop and that it will be finished at some other place and time. The specific ways we solve problems would be compromise and collaboration. If no understanding can be reached, Mom usually will pull rank or intervene.
>
> Dad just tells everyone how it's going to be. If someone speaks up to protest that it is unfair, or to defend their point, it is considered "bad mouthing" or "sassing." When my brother and I were younger, we got our mouths washed out with soap for "talking back."[54]

Former president Jimmy Carter, too, explains that he and his wife, Rosalynn, solve problems by being direct sometimes and at other times by suppressing the situation, at least temporarily:

> ... we have learned to address ... disagreements more directly instead of letting them fester. If direct conversation results in repetitions of arguments, we

have learned the beneficial effects of backing off for a while. A good solution, we have found, is for one of us to describe the problem in writing. It is surprising how ridiculous some of the arguments seem when set down in black and white, and it is much easier to make the small concessions that can end the disagreement.

But what is life if not adjustment—to different times, to our changing circumstances, to shifting health habits as we educate ourselves, and to each other? Jimmy Townsend says it well: "Marriage teaches you loyalty, forbearance, self-restraint, meekness, and a great many other things you wouldn't need if you had stayed single."[55]

Each of the methods of conflict resolution holds some usefulness. As we will determine in the next section, individual and family differences affect our methods of conflict resolution.

■ Individual and Family Differences

Differences occur in conflict resolution because of individual differences and because of differences in family types. An example of an individual difference that affects conflict resolution is one's focus on self-uniqueness. To the extent individuals are concerned with their own uniqueness, they appear to become less concerned with their partner's uniqueness, which leads to the dysfunctional management of conflict. Positive feelings about oneself, on the other hand, impact positively on conflict management. High task energy, too, correlates positively with the motivation to resolve conflict and to select appropriate communicative strategies.[56]

Educational achievement is another individual variable that affects one's ability to resolve family conflicts. Education accomplishes many changes in individuals, especially the facilitation of verbal and conflict resolution skills that enhance marital adjustment and further companionability.[57] Thus one may become more proficient at resolving conflicts through further education.

One's biological sex may affect conflict-resolution strategies. Men report that they use a competing style that includes assertive and uncooperative behavior. Women assert they use a compromising style that is intermediate in assertiveness and cooperativeness. Both men and women state they use accommodating behavior that is unassertive and cooperative when the person with whom they are interacting is female.[58]

Differences also occur in conflict resolution because of differences in family types. Mary Anne Fitzpatrick distinguished among traditionals, separates, and independents in her examination of couples. Traditionals held a conventional belief system and resisted change since it was threatening to their routine existence. They maintain both physical and psychological closeness and sharing with each other.

Fitzpatrick describes separates as those couples who shared little with each other, maintained fairly regular schedules, established distances from others and their problems, and had little sense of togetherness with their spouses. Separates were both physically and psychologically differentiated from their partners and are described by Fitzpatrick as the "emotionally divorced."

Independents paid little attention to traditional values and while relatively autonomous, they still shared with each other and they negotiated autonomy. They accepted uncertainty, change, and flexibility.[59]

These different family types establish different methods of resolving conflict.[60] Separates maintain a neutral emotional climate and keep their discussion of conflict to a minimum. They also express the lowest satisfaction. Independents expressed negative emotions frequently; more satisfied independents provided more informational acts, self-disclosure, description, qualification of conflict, and questions eliciting disclosure. More satisfied traditionals were more positive and less negative. This investigation verifies different couple types establish different patterns of conflict and conflict resolution.[61]

■ Guidelines for Conflict Resolution

Since couples and families do not resolve conflict similarly, we must be hesitant in prescribing appropriate methods of conflict resolution for all. Indeed, we should be wary of adopting the advice of another. Others may have a very different conception of what is appropriate for themselves, which may not be correct for you. With this warning in mind, let us suggest some general guidelines to be used to resolve conflicts in the family.

Perhaps the most critical element in effective conflict resolution is the right of each family member to have a complete hearing. Family members should have the opportunity to state their feelings, needs, attitudes, beliefs, and goals openly and to the extent they wish. They should be provided with enough time to complete their thoughts and to orally outline their point of view. Although individuals should not be forced to disclose beyond their desired limits, every opportunity should be provided for them to state their position. The thoughts and feelings of a family member should not be suppressed by others. Others should not control or limit the disclosure.

One woman, who was an only child, expressed the importance of openness in her family:

> The most unusual aspect of our conflicts would probably be that even as a teenager I was able to express my opinions, however loudly, and it is not always me who gives in to my elders. Everyone's opinion counts and we all know that it takes all three of us to make up our family. This may sound storybookish but it is true. I grew up mostly surrounded by adults and therefore had a mature outlook early in life and fortunately, since my parents always encouraged maturity, I was able to express my adult feelings even if I do so in the childish form of yelling at my parents.[62]

Just as each family member has the right to a complete hearing, others in the family must provide active listening, respect, and empathy. Active listening is demonstrated by verbal and nonverbal responsiveness. Respect is shown by a lack of interruptions and overlaps. Empathy is exhibited when family members paraphrase the content and intent of the original speaker. These verbal and nonverbal skills will encourage the speaker to communicate fully. Family therapist Sven Wahlroos writes, "A discussion of problems between intimates, especially, requires that the other person's self-concept, feelings, desires, and goals be viewed with compassion and understanding by each participant and that such variables be seen as important elements in the discussion."[63]

Family members should demonstrate a sense of equality rather than a sense of power or control over others. We may have a tendency to make quick judgments or to offer evaluative comments, but these should be avoided if conflict resolution is to be effective. Long ago Washington Irving wrote, "A sharp tongue is the only edge tool that grows keener with constant use."

We might seek out family members who provide us with consideration and concern. One man observed:

> I believe we [my two older sisters and I] settle our conflicts with Mom easier than Dad. She's more willing to listen to our problems and work them out. Dad hears what he wants to hear and blocks the rest of the information out creating a major communication barrier. Resolving problems with him is difficult for all of us due to this barrier.[64]

Individual family members have the right to a full hearing and the obligation to provide honest information. Accompanying the right of openness is the responsibility of honesty. Behaving truthfully and in a trustworthy way is essential to effective resolution of differences. Wahlroos advises, "Be open and honest about your feelings. . . . Do not walk on eggs."[65] Dan Canary and Brian Sptizberg found that people who use cooperative behavior and offer disclosure are viewed as being more appropriate (avoid the violations of relational and situational rules) and effective (manage to accomplish their goals) than are people who do not engage in these behaviors.[66]

Secrecy, hidden agendas, and misrepresentation will result in less than effective resolution in the long run. We should strive to accurately represent our own needs, plans, and goals rather than disguising them. Similarly, we should avoid threats and bluffs.

The conflict must remain on the issue at hand and not be extended into unrelated and irrelevant matters. We observed earlier that unresolved conflicts from earlier disagreements may precipitate another argument. Family members may have several such unresolved matters in their history. The practice of storing such disagreements and then using them as ammunition in a later argument is known as "gunnysacking" and tends to have a disastrous effect on conflict resolution. Instead of resolving conflicts, it exacerbates them.

It is tempting to extend an argument beyond the matter at hand to other areas of disagreement. For example, if a woman is angry about her husband's tendency to leave his clothing and personal effects scattered around the house, she might be lured into broadening the argument. She might add he rarely tends to the children when they awaken at night or he never writes the grocery list. However, these issues are separate from the disagreement for which she seeks some resolution. The result of adding other grievances to the conflict under discussion is that none of the problems are likely to be resolved.

The discussion should focus on specific, concrete behaviors rather than on general, abstract ideas. Sometimes we focus on the unresolvable rather than on the resolvable problems we face. One of the most productive ways to resolve conflict is first to agree about what the disagreement is about and then look for the specific problem. Family disagreement on the problem may occur because we oftentimes deal with the abstract rather than the concrete.[67]

A specific example may clarify Whitehouse's suggestion. If we follow her advice, we will discuss who will complete specific household chores rather than who will fulfill certain roles or display personality traits. For example, one spouse may ask another, "Will you do the dishes on the three nights when I have class?" rather than, "Will you be more considerate in the future?" Instead of complaining about lack of parental understanding, children might ask they not be interrupted when sharing an idea or disclosing a past event.

Emphasize agreement rather than disagreement. A communication educator observed that argumentation is the art of finding differences and persuasion is the art of finding similarities. Using this contrast, we might observe conflict is the act of finding differences among people and conflict resolution is the act of finding common ground or similarities. Conflict resolution is dependent upon our identification and establishment of areas of agreement. We should strive for such commonality rather than emphasize minor or irrelevant differences. Sometimes the relationship is more important than less significant content disagreements.

Conflict resolution is more effective if planning has occurred. Planning for conflict and its resolution may appear to be somewhat bizarre. However, if we view conflict as inevitable, the idea becomes more reasonable. In the same way that we plan an escape route from our homes in case of fire, we write wills to plan for the inheritance of our worldly goods, we determine where we will seek shelter in the case of a tornado or hurricane, we have health insurance in the case of serious illness or injury, and we write an outline or organizational plan when we are asked to deliver a public speech, it is useful to plan methods of effectively resolving conflicts with our family members.

When we plan for conflict and its resolution, we sometimes use our past experience. When we recall those features of conflict resolution that worked well for us, we can attempt to duplicate them. When we remember events that were disastrous, we can try to avoid them.

One couple routinely dealt with conflict in an unproductive manner. Whenever the wife raised an issue of disagreement, her husband became defensive and stormed out of the house. He usually did not return until several hours later when both members of the couple were unwilling or unable to continue the fight. As a consequence, the two never resolved their differences. When they realized they could plan how to more effectively interact over disagreements, they changed their behavior. Their plans included more descriptive statements and less evaluative ones, a recognition that disagreements were neither person's fault or responsibility, and an agreement that talking about problems could be viewed as a healthy rather than as an unhealthy way to relate to each other.

Another couple who had a similar pattern of the wife wanting to "fight" and the husband wanting to take to "flight," planned their subsequent arguments differently. In their case, the wife would follow her husband down the street after he had left the house. He marched down the street with his wife a few feet behind. The two did not solve their problems because the husband had no opportunity to cool down and the wife felt her husband was not listening nor responding in an adequate way. After they planned more effective methods of resolving their differences, the wife let the husband leave for a short time to calm down. He would return after fifteen minutes or so and the two could calmly discuss their problems.

No specific method is appropriate for all couples. In these two examples, two different procedures were adopted. But, both couples took time to plan more effective methods to resolve their differences. Preplanning conflict and its resolution can mitigate against personal disaster and relationship deterioration. Such planning is not possible if family members do not understand conflict is inevitable and resolution of those conflicts can result in the growth and development of the family unit. As we will determine in the next section, conflict and its resolution are related to family satisfaction.

❖ CONFLICT AFFECTS FAMILY LIFE AND SATISFACTION

Agreement is key to successful marriages. One area in which agreement may be essential is the couple's agreement about their relationship itself. Fitzpatrick and Best demonstrated couples who share a similar definition of their relationship are likely to agree on more relational issues and to be more cohesive than are couples who do not share relational definitions.[68] A couple's ability to reach consensus is highly related to marital satisfaction.

John Gottman suggests marital satisfaction may be more highly related to the couple's ability to resolve their differences or to achieve consensus than any other communicative behavior. He writes:

> . . . of all the relationship variables that could be selected for understanding marital satisfaction, the couple's ability to arrive at consensus in resolving differences may be of central importance. There are two ways in which a couple could arrive at consensus. One possibility is that they share normative conflict resolution rules transmitted culturally or from parental models. The other possibility is that they are able to construct their own decision rules.[69]

Specific research studies add credence to Gottman's conclusion. For example, one researcher provided a longitudinal study and showed happily married husbands and wives could be distinguished from unhappily married husbands and wives. This investigation showed the values of happy couples tended to merge after 18 years of marriage with the wives' values becoming closer to the husbands' values. The values of unhappy couples tended to become more disparate with the husband moving away from the values of the wife.[70] This study suggests that happy couples resolve their differences over time whereas unhappy couples increase their differences.

Conflict affects one's family life and the satisfaction one feels within a particular family. It similarly affects family stability. One man explained:

> As my parents are divorced, I should note that their inability to resolve their dynamic conflict was a result of neither side giving in, especially my father. When my mother realized this she began to adopt his philosophy and also refused to give in.[71]

Marital conflict can also be devastating for the children in the family. An investigation showed that as marital conflict increased within a family, primary school girls' self-esteem decreased.[72] Another study similarly showed that adolescents who perceived their parents as having many conflicts were more likely to consider suicide than were adolescents who did not perceive their parents to engage in a great deal of conflict.[73]

Conflict, in and of itself, does not lead to marital dissatisfaction or dissolution, however. Indeed, one author observes some people welcome crisis or conflict while others react dysfunctionally.[74] Conflict does interact with marital satisfaction, however, and both attribution and specific communicative skills separate the satisfied family from the dissatisfied family.

Attributions When we draw attributions, we assign qualities or characteristics to people. A family communication researcher observes that attributions not only influence individuals' perceptions and interpretations of messages, but they also influence responses individuals have as they enter into the development of conflict.[75] Our assignment of characteristics to family members affects how we understand their messages and how we respond in turn.

What are some differences in attributions among marital couples? First, we tend to attribute more positive qualities to ourselves than do our spouses. In general, spouses perceive their own conflict behavior more favorably than it is perceived by their partner.[76] Second, we tend to project our feelings onto our partners. People in intimate relationships offer attributions for their partner's behavior at times when they themselves experience negative emotional reactions.[77]

Attributions and misattributions might serve to maintain relationship conflict and communication problems. One author notes that to the extent the attributions we make point to negative attitudes and intentions, our cognitive processes may be contributing to the creation of relationship conflict.[78] For example, the man who believes his wife would have an affair if she were given the opportunity might be creating conflict in the relationship for no reason other than his own attribution.

Dissatisfied marital couples make different attributions than do satisfied marital couples. Less satisfied married couples tend to blame each other more than do more satisfied couples.[79] Dissatisfied couples more often attribute responsibility to partner or self, but satisfied couples share the responsibility for the way they interact on issues in which there were differences.[80]

The authors of this investigation suggest a model of conflict in which five levels of interaction are possible. They observed that dissatisfied couples tended to remain in a particular level and had little movement among them. Satisfied couples established greater flexibility among the various levels. This study suggests that dissatisfied couples are more personal in their blaming behavior in conflict situations and they are less flexible as well. Rather than rely upon other causes for the conflict, they rely upon dispositional factors routinely. We will consider the role of flexibility later in this section.

Some couples do not believe they can resolve the conflicts they will encounter, while others have an optimistic viewpoint. A couple's belief in their ability to resolve conflicts is more predictive of marital satisfaction than other predictors.[81] Couples who positively construct their abilities to handle conflict are more satisfied than are couples who hold a negative perspective. This is similar to the observation in Chapter 10 concerning self-disclosure that positive distortion may be a healthy and useful part of a satisfying marriage.

Communication Behaviors   While conflict varies in intensity and in frequency among satisfied and dissatisfied married couples,[82] some communication patterns distinguish people with satisfying marriages from those with dissatisfying marriages. By and large, these tend to be general as opposed to specific conclusions. As we noted above, satisfied couples do engage in conflict and they do disagree, but their methods of doing so are different than are those of dissatisfied couples. Satisfied couples avoid conflict by accepting the other's ideas, using humor, and changing the subject.[83] They also avoid disagreement by using supportive behaviors such as positive description of the partner, paraphrasing, and outcome and process agreement.[84]

Couples who are interested in assessing their own conflict were recently provided with such a measure. Sally Lloyd, at the University of Utah, reported a behavioral self-report technique that can be used to measure conflict in everyday life. Her measure "assesses information such as the length of the disagreement, who initiated the disagreement and time of day as well as assessments of the intensity, resolution and stability of the conflict."[85] Lloyd has shown that her self-report measure can be used to examine both relationship satisfaction as well as stability.

A research team categorized couples who engaged in conflict and those who avoided conflict. Surprisingly, they found that conflict avoiders were neither less compatible with their spouses nor less comfortable in their marriages than were the conflict engagers.[86] Avoiding conflict does not have a necessary negative effect on the marital relationship.

More recently, Pike and Sillars showed that more satisfied couples used more conflict avoidance than did less satisfied couples.[87] Just as we cautioned in Chapter 10 against total and complete self-disclosure, these studies do not allow us to encourage family members to engage in conflict at all times and under all circumstances. Total honesty and directness without regard for the history of the relationship and the type of marriage cannot be recommended.

Why would avoiding conflict be appropriate? Sometimes couples do not have the resources to deal with conflict. They may be short of patience, time, or energy. Avoiding conflict in the short term may be useful in order to be prepared to better deal with a difficult matter.

Some couples may avoid conflict altogether. Fitzpatrick and Best[88] distinguished between Fitzpatrick's couple types[89] on satisfaction. They found that traditional couples report the greatest satisfaction and suggest they might experience less ambiguity or possible dispute since they adopt conventional roles. Separates relate the least amount of satisfaction, probably because they engage in so little communication or because their marital satisfaction is not relevant to an overall assessment of their life. Independent couples fall between these two couple types in satisfaction. These hypotheses were proven in a more recent study.

Pike and Sillars classified couples into the traditional, separate, and independent groups and determined differences in conflict strategies. They found that satisfied independent couples whom they described as both "change-oriented and communication-sensitive" engaged in more informational acts, including questions that elicited disclosure, self-disclosure, and descriptions and qualifications of the disclosure. Satisfied separate couples denied that conflict existed and they were more likely to change the conversation to avoid the conflict issues. The communicative behavior of the satisfied and dissatisfied traditionals could not be distinguished. The authors conclude, "Satisfaction was associated with open, direct communication [for the independent couples]. . . . Avoidance may be a satisfying style of communication for separates. . . . Communication is not a critical mediator of marital satisfaction for traditional couples."[90]

Another factor that appears to affect the avoidance of conflict is the length of the marriage. Paul Zietlow, at Ohio State University, and Alan Sillars, from the University of Montana, examined the conversations of couples who were in young, middle-aged, and retired marriages. He found that older couples reported few marital problems and they did not engage in conflict. Middle-aged couples were also nonconflictive, but they saw problems as more salient. Younger couples had a more intense style of interaction.[91] Couples may avoid conflict as their marriage matures.

Avoiding conflict may be an appropriate strategy for some married couples, but not for all. Further, avoiding conflict for either the short term or the long term probably needs to be a mutual decision rather than a decision of one of the partners if marital satisfaction is a goal. Fitzpatrick and her colleagues explain:

> Distinctions have to be drawn between avoidance as a joint decision in a couple to leave certain issues alone in a given conversation and avoidance deci-

sions made individually. Individual conflict avoidance moves serve a competitive function in an interaction in that they tend to limit the options of the marital partner. Joint avoidance moves in an interaction function prosocially in the dyad in that they help to dampen a conflict.[92]

While some couples avoid conflict, others seem to thrive on argument. Dominic Infante, at Kent State University, has developed an argumentativeness construct that is helpful in understanding couples who use arguments successfully.[93] Infante defines argumentativeness as "a generally stable trait which predisposes the individual to advocate positions on controversial issues and to attempt refutation of positions which other people take on such issues."[94] He explained that people who are high in argumentativeness see arguing as an exciting intellectual challenge, a competitive situation which entails defending a position in order to win. Feelings of excitement and anticipation preceded an argument and after the argument, the person felt "invigorated, satisfied, and experienced a sense of accomplishment."[95] Low-argumentative people feel just the opposite—defeated and with unpleasant feelings before, during, and after the argument.

In general, Infante and his colleagues have shown that an ability to argue effectively is a positive quality in a person and that it relates to an improved self-concept, improved learning, greater creativity, and enhanced problem solving.[96] More recently Infante has shown that people who do not have argumentative skill may be the very people who are involved in interspousal violence. With Teresa Chandler and Jill Rudd, Infante demonstrates that people who rely on violence generally engage in verbal aggression and use physical violence as a backup behavior when they are aroused. He also shows that these same individuals have an inability to argue effectively.[97] In other words, argumentative skill is more likely to be held by those in nonviolent marriages than by those in violent ones.

John Gottman examined communicative behavior during conflict and found different interactions for dissatisfied and satisfied couples. He showed in the early phases of a conflict, satisfied couples use more validation sequences and fewer cross-complaining sequences than do dissatisfied couples. Further, satisfied couples engage in less metacommunication (communication about communication) than do dissatisfied couples in the negotiation stage of conflict and they are more likely to reach agreement after they have engaged in their interactions about communication than are dissatisfied couples. By contrast, dissatisfied couples are more likely to provide negative comments which leads to the reciprocation of negative comments and to mind-reading (or second guessing) the other person, but with negative affect.[98]

J. K. Alberts similarly examined communication behavior during conflict. She studied complaint behavior and found that couples engage in five types of complaints:

1. Behavioral complaints—about actions done or not done.

2. Performance complaints—about how the action was done.

3. Personal characteristic complaint—about dispositional, attitude, emotional, or belief system.

4. Personal appearance complaint—about the physical characteristics.

5. Complaint complaint—about complaint behavior.

Alberts had observers rate couples' complaint sequences. She learned that while both satisfied and dissatisfied couples used effective and ineffective complaint sequences, happy couples were more likely to use effective sequences.[99]

The reciprocity of negative comments has been associated with dissatisfaction in a number of studies.[100] Dissatisfied couples are more likely to reciprocate hostile-dominant remarks than are satisfied couples.[101] Stella Ting-Toomey determined that individuals who expressed low marital adjustment used the specific reciprocal patterns of confront-confront, confront-defend, complain-defend, and defend-complain, which were not used to the same extent by individuals with high marital adjustment.[102] Even when dissatisfied couples code their own interactions from tape recordings, they perceive more negative reciprocity than do satisfied couples.[103] The pattern suggested by such studies is that dissatisfied couples tend to reciprocate negative remarks in an escalation of conflict.

Pike and Sillars qualified these findings. Although they showed that reciprocity was "a basic rule for all couples,"[104] the importance of the topic interacted with satisfaction and reciprocity. When the topic was highly salient, dissatisfied coupled had greater negative reciprocity than did satisfied couples. When the topic was only moderately important, the dissatisfied couples showed less negative reciprocity than did those who reported they were satisfied. Satisfied couples, by contrast, were more consistent in their negative reciprocity, not dramatically increasing or decreasing the amount because of topic salience. Dissatisfied couples escalated the conflict on important topics, but did not evidence this pattern when the topic was less important. Negative reciprocity may be a more complicated phenomenon than we have yet discovered.

Dissatisfied couples engage in a communicative practice that may actually increase conflict and decrease agreement. While satisfied couples send messages to each other that are consistent when the verbal and nonverbal cues are considered simultaneously, the dissatisfied couples send conflicting messages.[105] Since nonverbal affective behaviors are more difficult to alter than are verbal behaviors,[106] the dissatisfied couple is more likely to "leak" their actual feelings through this channel. In other words, the dissatisfied couple may verbally make a positive statement while nonverbally providing an evaluative or negative comment. One study showed that dissatisfied wives tended to use a positive facial expression (specifically, a smile) while using a negative vocal tone.[107]

SUMMARY

Conflict is inevitable among family members. However, families deal with conflict very differently. It leads to the destruction of some families, but it is essential for the continuation of satisfying family lives. In this chapter we considered the nature of conflict in the family. We defined conflict as "an expressed struggle between at least two interdependent parties who perceive incompatible goals, scarce rewards, and interference from the other parties in achieving their goals." Conflict appears to go through specific recognizable stages in families and these were outlined and discussed.

Conflict exists for many reasons in the family context. Among the most common reasons are because of differences among the interactants, because of disagreement or differences in the understanding of the content and/or relationship dimensions of the interaction, and to avoid increased intimacy. Conflict may be destructive or constructive.

Conflict resolution varies as a result of individual and family differences. Nonetheless, we can offer some general guidelines for resolving family conflicts. None of the suggestions are always appropriate, although some of them are more likely to result in satisfaction than are others.

Both satisfied and dissatisfied families engage in conflict and conflict resolution. Satisfied couples are distinctive from dissatisfied couples in both their attributions and their communicative behaviors, however. The management of conflict in the family unit may make the difference between a vital, satisfying unit and a dysfunctional or deteriorating group. As William McFee remarked, "The world is not interested in the storms you encountered, but did you bring the ship in."

KEY TERMS

1. *Conflict* is defined as an expressed struggle that involves at least two people who feel that they have incompatible goals, scarce rewards, and problems in achieving goals because of the other person's interference.

2. The *prior condition stage* includes the situation and circumstances preceding the actual conflict.

3. The *frustration awareness stage* occurs when the person becomes upset with or frustrated with the other party.

4. The *active conflict stage* brings the conflict into the open between the participants.

5. The *solution stage* evolves when potential solutions are offered to deal with the conflict.

6. The *follow-up stage* is the final stage and refers to the outcome of the conflict after it has been solved.

7. *Fear of merger* refers to people not wanting to be too intimate for fear of losing identity.

8. *Fear of exposure* occurs when people fear disclosing because they do not want others to know their inadequacies.

9. *Fear of attack* refers to anxiety about the fear of danger from the same-sex parent.

10. *Fear of abandonment* occurs when people do not want to be intimate because they fear being abandoned or separated.

11. *Fear of one's own destructive intentions* refers to the anxiety individuals feel because they believe eventual hurt or destruction will be provided to the partner.

12. *Denial* refers to a conflict resolution method where people decide not to acknowledge the existence of conflict.

13. *Suppression* is a strategy the people use to smooth things over and to minimize the problem.

14. *Authority* refers to people using the power vested in their position to resolve questions.

15. *Majority rule* occurs when the family relies on majority agreement to resolve the conflict.

16. *Compromise* occurs when family members state their opinions and some middle ground is determined.

17. *Collaboration* considers each person's expertise and focuses on the problem rather than individuals.

18. *Gunnysacking* is the practice of storing up disagreements and then using them as ammunition in a later argument.

19. *Avoidance* is a strategy used by couples who do not want to deal with conflict.

CHAPTER 13

MANAGING POWER

Power is the great aphrodisiac.

HENRY KISSINGER

After you have read this chapter, you will be able to

1. List and define the six categories of power.

2. Identify factors that affect the usage of power strategies.

3. Define compliance gaining and compliance resistance.

4. Describe factors that affect the selection of compliance gaining and resistance strategies.

5. Differentiate between wife-dominant, husband-dominant, and egalitarian patterns of power.

6. Explain complementary and symmetrical patterns of power.

7. Define dominance and domineeringness.

8. List ways in which family members can increase power.

This chapter focuses on power. This topic may seem more relevant to communication in public or business settings, but we will determine that it is an important topic for the family context as well. We will consider managing power in the family context. Let us begin by considering the nature of power in the family.

❖ MANAGING POWER

How is power relevant to family communication? An unknown source quipped that marriage is the only war in which you sleep with the enemy, but are all marriages battlefields on which enemy lines are clearly drawn? Does power come into play in all of our interactions with family members? We learned in Chapter 12 that conflict is inevitable in family communication. In this chapter you will see that power is an underlying force that affects the relationships in a family.

■ Definition of Power

Before we consider the role of power in family interaction, let us define the term and classify some forms of power. A general definition of *power* is the ability to influence others or to achieve one's ends. Rogers-Millar and Millar refine this definition for the family context:

> . . . the potential to define, influence, or modify the behavior of others. It refers to the system members' joint perceptions of what the other members "have" as resources, and/or are believed to be able to do.[1]

This definition has two essential features we should note. First, it shifts power from serving as the property of a person to being the property of a relationship among people. Individuals do not hold similar power across all situations and with everyone with whom they interact; instead, power is relative and is based on the relationship between or among people. This feature of the definition has important implications. We cannot simply total up the amount of power each person has available and make a comparison in all circumstances.

Second, power is a perceptual variable. It is not a quantifiable property that can be objectively measured. Instead, it exists in the eyes of the beholders. An outsider's observations of a family member's power might result in a very different conclusion than would the family's own perceptions. Whom should we believe? Rogers-Millar and Millar suggest we should rely upon the family members' perceptions. Further, the interactions among the family members might provide even more information than would the family members' perceptions regarding the amount of power each person displays.

■ Categories of Power

Power has been categorized by many researchers. One of the most frequently cited categorization schemas has been provided by French and Raven.[2] Their typology includes six types: reward power, coercive power, expert power, position power, referent power, and information power. Let us consider the role of each within the family.

1. *Reward power* occurs when you have something of value to offer another person. When a parent offers one of his or her children money for completing a task, the parent is said to have reward power. One father offered his college-aged daughter a trip to Florida over spring break if she quit smoking,[3] while a mother of a high school student promised her daughter a trip to France if she received an A in French. Similarly, siblings can "trade" toys or other commodities for the services or goods of brothers and sisters. One 18-year-old woman with a 4-year-old brother reported she would do almost anything for him because of the rewarding nature of the relationship. In addition, he routinely offered her "rewards" for doing things for him. A typical conversation:

> BROTHER: Will you buy me some Raspberry Rambo gum?
> SISTER: No, Mom didn't put that on the grocery list.
> BROTHER: Please, it's only 30 cents and you're my big sister. I'll help you pick up my toys when we get home.
> SISTER: Okay, I guess.[4]

If you are attempting to change someone's behavior, you might extend such rewards in an effort to provide positive reinforcement. A nurse in her 20s who still lives with her original family explains:

> One thing that used to be common would be if I waxed the wood cabinets, Mom would give me money or take me somewhere or buy me something. Now that I am older, I am expected to do it without any type of reward, but because I want to help Mom. Most of the time that's enough of a reward.[5]

2. *Coercive power* is the power to punish other people if they do not comply with your wishes. Sexual favors may be withheld from a spouse who behaves in a way the other spouse determines to be inappropriate. Dessert may not be forthcoming to children who do not "clean their plate." Siblings may threaten each other with bodily harm.

Parents frequently use coercive power with children. One woman explained:

> My father usually uses punishment or coercive power. I think this is because he seems to have difficulty communicating with me. This usually is in the form of just threatening. I rarely remember him actually going through with his threats.[6]

Another added:

> My mother is the primary disciplinarian. She holds coercive power with her ability to punish me. If I am late I will not be allowed out as late the next

time. If I don't keep my grades up in school, I will have to quit my job and devote more time to studying.[7]

More complex patterns of coercive power are sometimes evident in families. A woman in her 40s recalls her mother's use of coercive power:

> My mother's power over my father, sister, and me was done through coercion. She would become angry, play the martyr, threaten to leave (once or twice she did walk out), or she would have an asthma attack. We knew we had better do what we were told because Mother upset easily, and when that occurred we all suffered in that hostile atmosphere. When either my sister or I misbehaved Mother would either spank us, take away privileges, or send us to our room.[8]

Although children in many families are often threatened and punishment frequently follows, coercive power does not appear to be as effective as reward power.

3. *Expert power* is based on knowledge or experience. If a husband can convince his wife he knows far more about automobile mechanics than she does, he may be relied upon for decisions about when to change the oil, when to have the family cars tuned up, and when a new car is needed. Parents may use expert power with their children. One woman reported:

> My Mom also used *knowledge* as power. She was very insightful to many issues concerning teenagers. This is because she taught at the same high school I attended. It was impossible to pull anything over her—she was too informed on the issues.[9]

Another said, "My mother tells me she knows that school and studying can seem like a lot of work, with little reward, but that I must hang in there and I will reap the benefits in the future."[10] One woman stated that her father relied upon expert power:

> Explaining and discussing were his tools for keeping control. In college he majored in English and minored in math so he has information and skills that my sister and I were able to tap into during our years of school.[11]

One's ability to communicate with others may place that person in the role of an expert. One son explained his father's power base:

> His (my father's) greatest power source is the respect we have for him. He is fair, understanding, strict when needed, and even-tempered. He deals with us; he does not order us. He gives reasons why he rules the way he does. My father has more control than my mother.[12]

4. *Position power* results from the roles one plays. If the family perceives the father as the head of the household, they may allow him to make many family decisions simply because of his "position." In organizations, such

"legitimate power" belongs to the superiors relative to the subordinates. In universities, university presidents have legitimate power in running the entire university, while deans have legitimate power in managing the affairs of the individual colleges or schools.

Parents frequently use their position as a source of power with their children. One woman recalls her childhood and her mother's position power: "I can remember her often resorting to that ancient phrase, 'You'll do it because I'm your mother and I say so.'"[13] Another revealed, "My mother reminds me that one day I will be a mother and I will understand her motives for worrying and being protective,"[14] One man reported that his father frequently resorted to the line, "You'll do what I say in my house or you'll move out,"[15] to his children who ranged in age from 13 to 26.

Older siblings may also be cast in the role of an authority, particularly in single-parent households. One woman in her 20s who currently lives with her mother and a younger sister felt that she and her mother shared position power:

> Position power is used by both my mother and myself, her because she is the mother and me, because I am the eldest sibling. A lot of responsibility has come with that position in the past years, and probably will all of my life, especially in our family situation, where I was often the oldest person at home, even at a very young age.[16]

5. *Referent power* is granted to the person who identifies with another. In the university example above, the president's spouse and the dean's spouse each have certain spheres of power because of their marital choice. In the family, a younger sister may team up with her older sister in order to have more power than the middle child in the family. Under other circumstances the younger sister may be the low person in the "pecking order."

In a relatively large family, the youngest son proved to be an excellent athlete. None of the older children had shown any interest or ability in high school or college sports. The father, however, was very interested in sports of all kinds. As he began to recognize the youngest son's potential, the child gained significant power:

> Steven is the youngest, and as a result has little power. His one power base is referent power with my dad. Steven is a great athlete and my dad is trying to live out his dreams of glory through his son. An example would be Steven saying, "If you let me do this, I may raise my batting average." It works every time.[17]

6. *Information power* occurs when people respond to the persuasive arguments of others. A Persian proverb suggests "With a sweet tongue and kindness, you can drag an elephant by the hair." Both personal appeals and carefully structured and fact-filled arguments may persuade some family members to allow another to make a decision for them. For instance, the person who manages the family finances may be able to make a coherent argument about why the family should consider a more modest vacation one year in order to enjoy a more extravagant trip the next year.

The difficulty in determining who possesses power in a family based on such classification systems is apparent. First, individuals do not always agree on the kind of power another person is using. While people may believe they are relying upon legitimate power, others may believe they are attempting to use expertise power, but are using it unsuccessfully. For instance, suppose Mom believes she has the right to tell her adolescent children with whom they can interact, doing so on the principle of "other people judge you by the company you keep." Her adolescent children may disregard her attempt at changing their behavior because such an argument seems superficial or unrealistic to them.

Second, individuals do not always use the same kinds of power in all situations. People who normally use coercive power may be misunderstood when they try to use reward power. Suppose a 3-year-old boy regularly finds excuses to get out of bed several times each night. His father tries to discourage this by threatening to shut his door, to shut off his night light, and to take away some privileges. After numerous unsuccessful attempts, the father decides to try reward power. However, the boy has been conditioned to expect hollow threats and may not understand he is being offered a reward.

Third, the relevance of the kind of power one is using may vary. The person who uses coercive power may find that reward power is called for. Suppose a relatively bright child regularly receives low grades. Each time the child receives a grade below a C, the parents require that he or she complete an additional hour of homework per week. After several such occasions the child is completing an enormous amount of homework, but the tactic may have lost its effectiveness and a new approach may be more appropriate.

Finally, the effectiveness of a particular form of power may vary. The person who tries to use referent power may find expert power will be more effective with other family members. If the wife in a family is away on a business trip and she normally does most of the cooking, her husband may attempt to use referent power as he encourages his children to eat what he has made. However, the questionable-looking dish will not be more desirable if he explains that his wife assured him he would be able to prepare it. He needs to assure the family that he is capable of making a tasty meal.

The problems inherent in measuring power cause difficulty in assessing which family members hold more power. All decisions are not equal in importance. Too, we cannot easily determine who possesses a particular kind of power in a family, since the kind of power held is dependent upon others' perceptions of it. Furthermore, people alter their use of power because different situations call for different approaches. In the next section of this chapter we will consider some of the variables that affect power strategies within the family.

■ Power Strategies

Persuasion occurs routinely in the family. One research team asked college students to identify who they persuade and who persuades them. They found that a clear majority (61 percent) of persuasive activity in which they were involved occurs within the family setting.[18] Family members use a wide variety of strategies, as we shall determine. We will determine, too, that the strategies chosen by family members vary on the basis of gender, age, and family role.

Two other investigators examined power strategies within interpersonal relationships and identified two dimensions: directness-indirectness, referring to the explicit or inexplicit nature of the strategy, and unilaterality-bilaterality, referring to a one-sided or two-sided approach. They found gender differences, as heterosexual men were more likely to use direct bilateral strategies (bargaining, reasoning, persistence, and talking), while heterosexual women were more likely to use indirect unilateral strategies (negative affect, withdrawal, and laissez faire). Homosexual men and women did not differ in their strategy use. The authors concluded that men see themselves as having greater power than their intimate partner and thus influence them from a position of strength. Women, operating from a subordinate position, anticipate noncompliance and therefore use more unilateral strategies. They observe, "Unilateral strategies do not require the partner's cooperation."[19]

One study demonstrated that psychological sex had an impact on power strategies as well. Androgynous individuals were more likely to use bilateral strategies, while undifferentiated persons were more likely to employ unilateral strategies. Masculine types tended to use primarily direct and somewhat bilateral strategies, while feminine individuals used indirect and unilateral strategies.[20] One's endorsement of masculinity—which occurs in both masculine and androgynous individuals—may coincide with the self-perception of power or strength. Just as men may engage in bilateral strategies because of their sense of strength, persons who perceive themselves as masculine may similarly believe they can gain their partner's cooperation.

Compliance Gaining   Traditionally, communication researchers examined persuasion as an act most likely to occur in a public setting, particularly in public speaking. In the last decade, persuasion has been examined within the interpersonal communication arena. The expanded view of persuasion is evident in the new literature on compliance gaining.

Marwell and Schmitt devised one of the first taxonomies of compliance-gaining strategies. They identified 16 strategies that fit into five major clusters: rewarding activity, punishing activity, expertise, activation of impersonal commitment, and personal commitment.[21] Other researchers have refined and altered these original strategies.[22]

Researchers have determined that strategies may vary as a function of the setting or social context. Fitzpatrick and Winke examined compliance gaining in the interpersonal setting and identified five strategies:

> *Strategy of Manipulation:* Being particularly helpful or pleasant before the subject of disagreement is raised; encouraging the other person to believe they are doing the first person a favor if they agree.

> *Strategy of Nonnegotiation:* Refusing to discuss with, or listen to, the other person until he or she gives in; repeating one's own position or arguing until the other person agrees.

Strategy of Emotional Appeal: Appealing to the other person's affection for the persuader; promising more love in the future; becoming angry and requiring that the other person give in.

Strategy of Personal Rejection: Withholding love and affection until the other person gives in; making the other person jealous by pretending to lose interest in him or her.

Strategy of Empathic Understanding: Discussing what would happen if the two accepted the other person's point of view; talking about why they disagree; having mutual talks without arguing.[23]

Compliance gaining use varies as a result of a wide variety of situational and personal factors.[24] Compliance-gaining strategies may change as a result of perceived long-term and short-term consequences[25] self-interest,[26] desire for liking,[27] Machiavellianism,[28] dogmatism,[29] perceived consequences,[30] communication competence,[31] and other variables,[32]

An important consideration in the use of compliance-gaining strategies is the risk involved. Michael Cody and his associates observed that individuals chose strategies based on their perceived risk in implementation. They explained that people engaged in compliance gaining choose strategies on the basis of three considerations:

> (1) whether strategy implementation would lead to successful compliance; (2) whether strategy implementation would result in relational harm; and, (3) whether strategy implementation would result in poor management of the agent's image.[33]

Others, too, have discussed the potential for relational harm in the selection of compliance-gaining strategies. Mark de Turck noted that individuals who are in attractive interpersonal relationships must select a message strategy that will allow them to maximize their opportunity for achieving their goal while minimizing potential relational damage.[34] Antisocial messages decrease relational satisfaction.

Margaret McLaughlin and her fellow researchers suggested that some strategies, including refusal to negotiate, may carry high risk and may negatively affect relational maintenance.[35] Leslie Baxter similarly found that females, people in close relationships, and less powerful people are all more likely to rely on politeness than are males, people in less involved relationships, and more powerful people.[36]

A research team compared individuals who were casually involved with those who were married. They found that those who are casually involved with each other frequently use either manipulation or nonnegotiation strategies in interpersonal situations. Those committed to the relationship, or married, use more emotional appeals and more personal rejections than any other relational group.[37] The potential relational harm of the compliance-gaining strategies may be viewed differently by those in less committed relationships than by those who have made a marital commitment.

Marital couples do not all use compliance gaining similarly. We have discussed the usefulness of Fitzpatrick's typology of couples in earlier chapters. Her classification schema is useful as we consider compliance gaining, too. You will recall that traditional couples are those who hold conventional values, emphasize stability in their relationship, are interdependent, and engage in conflict. Separate couples are those who are not interdependent, are ambivalent about their relationship, and avoid conflict. Independent couples are not conventional in their values and they do engage in conflict. They are psychologically interdependent but not physically interdependent.

Witteman and Fitzpatrick suggested that compliance gaining may be founded on three bases: (1) *activity or power messages* focusing on either "negative or positive outcomes that an individual can expect by engaging in specific behaviors" or on "the consequences of compliance or noncompliance;"[38] (2) *relational messages* that encourage compliance on the basis of the importance of the relationship to the interactants; and (3) *value or obligation messages* that consider the values held by the interactants, including how people see themselves, others, and things apart from the relationship.

They found that traditional couples used relational messages in gaining compliance. Separate couples did not use relational messages, but instead relied on "the negative consequences of noncompliance."[39] They note: "The messages of the Separates are blatant attempts to constrain the behavior, and in some cases even the internal states of their spouses."[40] Finally, independent couples use all three bases from which to derive compliance-gaining messages. They thus have a wider range of power bases in their repertoire.

Nonetheless, both Dillard and Fitzpatrick and Witteman and Fitzpatrick observe that the most frequently used compliance-gaining strategies between marital spouses is the direct request.[41] Further, this strategy seems to be effective and satisfying to the relational partners. Witteman and Fitzpatrick suggest that in our attempts to further clarify and better classify the use of compliance gaining between marital partners, we may be ignoring the obvious. Simple and direct requests may be superior to complicated messages relying upon alternative strategies.

Furthermore, even when spouses feel positively about messages being provided, they are not necessarily more likely to comply to their partner's wishes. For example, Susan Shimanoff showed that relational partners responded with positive messages when they were told about their partners' vulnerabilities and hostilities toward people other than themselves. They also had a more positive attitude about requests made by their partners after they had disclosed vulnerabilities and hostilities toward others; however, they were no more willing to comply with the requests that were made.[42]

Although we do not know as much about compliance gaining between parents and their children, some information is available. A recent study investigated compliance gaining on prime-time family programs to determine what children and their parents learn from televised characters. Margaret J. Haefner from Illinois State University and Jamie Comstock at the University of Arizona examined 18 prime-time programs. They found that most of the compliance gaining included simple statements, reasons, and commands.

Parents were more likely to attempt to gain compliance than were children. They were also more successful than unsuccessful, while children were more likely to be unsuccessful than successful.

Haefner and Comstock compared what occurred on family television programs with a naturalistic study of actual parents and children observed in public settings. They found that actual parents generally used more than one attempt to gain the compliance of their children while televised parents rarely did. About one-fifth of the time, actual parents used command while televised parents used command nearly half the time. Actual parents use name saying,

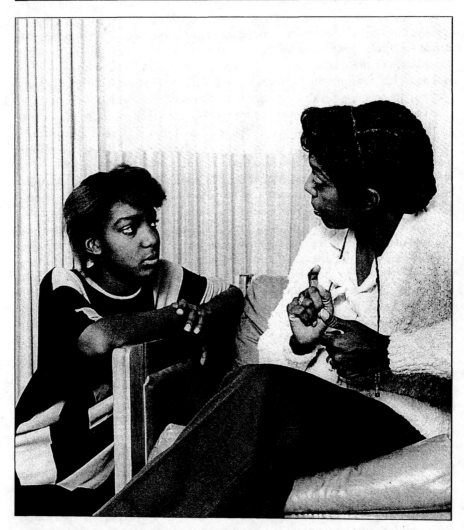

Children learn compliance-gaining strategies as they develop, just as they learn other communicative behaviors (© 1992, Takatsumo, The Picture Cube).

promises, and physical punishment frequently while televised parents used such attempts rarely.[43]

Another study compared dysfunctional and functional families. A team of researchers found that abusive mothers are more likely to use commands and power-assertive compliance attempts and less likely to use positively oriented control strategies than are nonabusive mothers.[44] Dysfunctional parent–child relationships appear to include less negotiation and less positive behavior than functional relationships do.

As children grow and develop, they have an increasing amount of power in the family. As we observed in Chapter 8, adolescent children seek more independence than younger children. One researcher studied high school students and their parents and found that they did not agree on the amount of power they wielded in the family. Both the parents and their adolescents exaggerated the amount of power they held. The researcher concluded that adolescents have increasing decision-making power and control within the family.[45] In general, a child's influence on other family members increases as he or she matures.[46] Furthermore, older children generally have more status and power with younger siblings.[47]

In addition, children learn compliance-gaining messages as they grow and develop. We have discussed the development of children's communication skills in Chapter 7. We shall now consider the specific development of compliance-gaining skills.

Children's compliance-gaining abilities change developmentally. Clark and Delia showed that both cognitive complexity and social perspective taking were related to the communicative effectiveness of children. They concluded that cognitive complexity and social perspective taking are central to the ability to develop adaptive strategies.[48] Similarly, cognitive and social maturation are involved in the development of social perspective taking and thus the development of persuasive communication adaptive skills.[49]

Developmental patterns exist in children's use of direct and indirect requests.[50] Haslett examined the compliance gaining of preschoolers from 2 to 5 years of age. She found clear developmental trends in children's adjustment to each other and in handling conflict when they discovered incompatible goals. As the children increased in age, their compliance-gaining strategies were more adaptive and their conflict episodes increased in complexity.[51]

Other researchers have found similar results. A research team demonstrated a developmental progression of reason giving (a type of compliance gaining) ability in children.[52] Two others examined the use of 5-, 9-, and 13-year-old girls' persuasive tactics. They determined that a greater number of different kinds of appeals were used as age increased and a greater variety of appeals were used with friends than with mothers.[53]

Compliance Resisting   Compliance resistance—verbal attempts by a target to gain the agent's acceptance of the target's unwillingness to comply—has not enjoyed the same attention as has compliance gaining.[54] McLaughlin and her colleagues observe:

To date, research interest in compliance-gaining activity has been one-sided, focusing only on the potential persuader (the agent) as an active element in the interpersonal persuasive attempt; yet the recipient of a particular compliance-gaining message (the target) may, for whatever reason, choose to resist compliance. Our observations of daily transactions suggest that first-attempt compliance-gaining messages are not always successful. Furthermore, the type of strategy selected by the target to resist the compliance-gaining attempt is just as important as the agent's strategy in affecting relational definitions.[55]

In the intervening decade there have been some investigations of compliance resistance.[56]

Compliance resistance results from the incompatibility between the agent's request and the target's unwillingness to comply. Compliance resistance may be viewed as "reflexive persuasion."[57] McLaughlin et al. proposed a four category schema of compliance-resistance strategies,[58] which they determined by synthesizing the work of earlier studies.[59] McQuillen et al. summarize these strategies:

1. *Nonnegotiation:* Inflexible, unapologetic refusal to assent to the agent's request.

2. *Identity Management:* The indirect manipulation of the image of the agent or the target or both, either positively or negatively.

3. *Justifying:* Offering support, based on the projected outcomes of compliance or noncompliance, of one's unwillingness to comply.

4. *Negotiation:* Proposal to engage in mutual talks that will result in maximized goals for both involved parties.[60]

McLaughlin et al. asked college students to rate the likelihood of their use of each of these strategies for eight situations that varied in level of intimacy, consequences of the relationship, and rights of the target person to resist. They found that identity management may be used most frequently among intimates; that negotiation is most likely to be used across all situations; that justification is used in situations with long-term implications for making the motives behind one's resistance evident, all other things being equal; and that nonnegotiation, the least popular of the strategies, may threaten a relationship and is avoided in highly intimate situations in which the relational consequences are long term.[61]

Compliance-resisting skills, like compliance-gaining skills, develop over one's lifetime. A child's compliance also changes as he or she matures. Older children are less compliant than younger children.[62] However, other factors affect compliance. For example, children with abusive mothers are less compliant than children who do not have abusive mothers.[63]

Compliance resistance has been studied among children and adolescents. McQuillen et al. examined compliance resistance with these groups, using McLaughlin, Cody, and Robey's resistance strategies. These authors attempted to determine how children in the first, fourth, and tenth grades resist compliance strategies and different compliance agents. The three strategies were simple request, incentive request (promise), and altruistic request (invocation of normal behavior), and the three agents were mother, best friend, and younger sibling. The authors reported differences between the age of the person and the use of three of the four major resistance strategies. The childrens' and adolescents' reliance on nonnegotiation strategies decreased with age, while the frequency of justification and identity-management strategies increased with age. Furthermore, resistance strategies varied as a function of the type of compliance-gaining strategy.[64]

McQuillen demonstrates that perspective taking increases as a function of age, as well. Further, he shows that adolescents vary their compliance-resistance strategy use based on the person attempting compliance gaining. Tenth-grade students were least adaptive with their best friends or, stated differently, more adaptive with their mothers and younger siblings.[65] McQuillen and Higginbotham show additionally that explaining one's choice of compliance-resistance strategies also progresses developmentally.[66]

Three authors show that adolescents vary their compliance-resistance strategies on the basis of their parent's gender, their own gender, and the parent's compliance-gaining strategy. Female adolescents use identity-management strategies more often than males, while males use nonnegotiation and negotiation strategies more often than females. In general, adolescents use more identity management with their mothers and more justification strategies with their fathers. When the mother uses personal rejection or empathic understanding, the adolescent's resistance strategy is most often nonnegotiation. When the mother uses an emotional appeal, the adolescent counters with identity management. When the father uses manipulation or an emotional appeal, resistance is most often in the form of justification. When the compliance-gaining strategy is nonnegotiation or personal rejection, the most frequent resistance strategy is nonnegotiation. When the father uses empathic understanding, the adolescent responds with identity management.[67]

Family members use persuasion routinely in their day-to-day functioning. Compliance gaining and compliance resisting are used differentially by family members on the basis of their age, gender, and role. Although we are frequently strategic in our persuasive attempts, Luloffs demonstrates that 73 percent of compliance-seeking interactive communication is nonstrategic.[68] Her results are important because we should not conclude that all attempts at compliance are strategically planned and executed. A great deal of spontaneous persuasion occurs, as well. Nonetheless, as we shall determine, family members establish general patterns of power.

■ General Patterns of Power Among Couples

Four patterns of power are possible for marital couples. The husband may be dominant, the wife may be dominant, the couple may engage in relatively equal decision making on nearly all matters, or the couple may split the responsibilities over which they exercise decision-making power.[69] When either the husband or the wife is dominant, that individual makes the decisions for the family in a unilateral way. The workability of this pattern is dependent upon the submission or acquiescence of the other family members.

When couples attempt to share power, they may do so in one of two ways. They may engage in a great deal of interaction or share decision-making power on a wide range of issues, or they may split their responsibilities so that relatively little interaction occurs when a decision needs to be made. Peter and Jane, for instance, engage in decision making based on splitting the areas of responsibility. Peter makes decisions about the outside of the family home, while Jane decides about the inside of the house.

Frequently, such divisions of decision-making power fall along traditional lines. For example, the husband may make decisions about the family's automobiles and the yard, while the wife decides which meals to prepare and which child-rearing philosophy to follow. However, couples may determine that they will split decision making according to their abilities rather than along stereotypical male-female lines. For instance, Sophia and Darrel determined that she would manage the family's finances because of her accounting skills and analytic abilities, and he would determine how the children should be raised because of his training in early childhood development and his special interest in children.

The pattern of power a marital couple chooses may be dependent on a variety of factors. One of the most important may be the relative economic power each person holds.[70] However, recent evidence suggests that economic power is more than a comparison of paychecks. Blumberg and Coleman, from the University of California, San Diego, and the University of Texas at Austin, respectively, suggest there are "discount factors" that operate to create net economic power, which may be discrepant from each person's gross economic power.[71]

Another factor that may affect a couple's pattern of power is their individual backgrounds. People learn about power in their orienting families. A number of factors predict a couple's willingness to share roles. Among those factors were mothers working outside the home, postgraduate liberal arts education, maturing during the 1960s and 1970s, performing some nontraditional sex-typed chores when they were growing up, and a nontraditional child-rearing philosophy.

The present family is a product of the negotiated realities the couple builds. Through communication, the couple creates a shared reality. Thus the pattern of power in this newly created family may be very different from either original family. The created pattern of power may be further complicated by earlier marriages, by children from other marriages, or by members in the extended family.

Cohabiting couples tend to be more egalitarian than married couples. These couples believe in each person's responsibility to contribute an equal share. They use money to achieve equality in decision making. They tend to share decisions in who initiates and who refuses or accepts sexual advances.[72] One's sexuality also affects perceptions of power. Lesbian couples similarly believe in equality, but nearly 40 percent of those surveyed suggested an unequal balance of power in their relationships.[73]

Equality may be difficult to achieve because of the different resources each person brings to the family and the different values placed on those resources. Furthermore, the couple might not agree about the relative value of the resources within the family unit. Finally, our society, which values masculine traits more highly than feminine ones, tends to encourage devaluation of the attributes of women.

The sex-role socialization of women and men may also interfere with a mass movement toward equality among couples. Traditional socialization encourages females to be nurturing and to socialize with others and encourages males to be competitive and domineering. These tendencies have been demonstrated in a variety of spheres, including the interactions between adult men and women with young girls and boys.[74] Thus women may acquiesce more willingly and men may dominate more eagerly as they interact.

Which of the patterns of power—husband-dominated, wife-dominated, or egalitarian—is more desirable? Some evidence suggests the husband-dominated or wife-dominated pattern is probably not most desirable. Violence marks those relationships in which either the husband or the wife has far more power, whereas egalitarian couples are less prone to conflict and violence.[75] In addition, if the couple is in a low socioeconomic class, the husband is likely to use physical violence in order to maintain his dominant power position. Wife abuse occurs in about 20 percent of husband-dominated marriages compared to 5 percent in egalitarian marriages.[76] Marital satisfaction is inversely related to the amount of coercive power exhibited by the spouse.[77]

Inaccuracy in understanding and inflexibility also mark husband-dominated or wife-dominated marriages. Frank Millar, Edna Rogers-Millar, and John Courtright determined that the more dominant one spouse was relative to the other, the less accurately each spouse predicted the partner's responses.[78] In other words, the more rigid the dominance hierarchy, the less each person knew what was expected of them. Researchers suggest this sequence is descriptive: the more equivalent the dominance pattern, the more flexibility exists in the couple's interaction, the more often the couple will discuss who is to do what when, and the more conflict potential will exist in the couple's conversations, but the more up-to-date the dyad's expectations of each other. Others concur that rigidity of the patterning in the structure of conversations is predictive of marital distress.[79] Marriages dominated by either the husband or the wife tend to be inflexible in a variety of areas, including the family's responsiveness to crisis.[80]

Egalitarianism, which is valued in our culture, is the pattern of choice for many families. Marriages in which decision making is shared or split are most highly related to marital satisfaction. The second choice of couples is the husband-dominated pattern, and the distant third choice is the wife-dominated pattern.[81] However, these studies tend to examine couples of higher socioeconomic status; the same findings might not be found with people in all socioeconomic categories. In addition, they may not be determined if couples are differentiated along other lines, such as those suggested by Fitzpatrick.

Studies that have considered sex roles and the status of one's job corroborate these conclusions. For example, two researchers examined couples in which both spouses had traditional sex roles, where both had contemporary views of role behavior, and where both had discrepant sex roles (the husband endorsed a traditional sex role and the wife endorsed a contemporary sex role, or the wife endorsed a traditional sex role and the husband endorsed a contemporary sex role). The researchers found marriages that included a traditional husband and a contemporary wife received the lowest evaluation of marital satisfaction.[82] Similarly, the greater the degree of conflict over sex-role expectations, the greater is the depression of the wife and the more dissatisfied she was with housework.[83] Finally, when wives have more status than their husbands, the marriages are more likely to result in divorce.[84] The greater the incongruity between the spouses, the lower was the couple's marital satisfaction and the greater was the pressure on the wife to change her role or disrupt the relationship.

A study considering the interactive behavior of husbands and wives discovered some provocative findings relevant to the power patterns of couples. Edna Rogers-Millar and Frank Millar distinguished "domineeringness" from dominance in verbal interactions. They defined *domineeringness* as providing a verbal statement to one's partner in which the right to be dominant was exhibited. *Dominance*, by contrast, included such a statement followed by a verbalization from the spouse in which he or she acknowledged and accepted the first person's right to dominate.[85] For example, if a wife told her husband to purchase groceries for the family on his way home from work, and the husband did not respond, domineeringness would be present. If her husband responded, "Sure, I'll be happy to do that," then dominance would be evidenced.

The results of this research determined that marital satisfaction was related to lower levels of domineeringness on the part of the wife and higher levels of dominance on the part of the husband. When wives made unsuccessful attempts to dominate (became domineering) and husbands made successful attempts, marital satisfaction increased. Their study does not allow consideration of more egalitarian verbalizations, but it does suggest husband dominance is preferred over wife domineeringness.

Egalitarian couples seem to be more satisfied than couples where power is unevenly distributed on a number of dimensions. For example, couples who feel they have equal control over how money is spent have a less discordant relationship than couples who feel one person or the other has more control.[86] Such feelings of equality may come from two different patterns. First, couples may discuss each financial decision and come to an agreement. Second, they may divide the areas of responsibility for spending. In addition, equality in sexual initiation and refusal is related to a more positive sex life, while a wife initiating sexual activity and the husband refusing results in dissatisfaction.[87]

Marital satisfaction appears to be somewhat dependent on the equality existing in the relationship or on the traditional power lines of husband-dominant. Marital stability is similarly dependent upon these combinations. Women with income that allows them to support themselves are far more likely than women without such incomes to end an unhappy marriage.[88] Such women may choose to end their relationships because they are able to survive without it. The more power they are afforded because of their income may tip the balance toward a wife-dominated power pattern.

Both women and men desire egalitarian relationships, but women are more desirable of equity than men are.[89] Men express more happiness in a traditional marriage and a significantly greater attraction to the traditional husband's role than women do for the traditional marriage and the traditional wife's role.[90] Equality may be more important for women since they are more likely to gain power if their relationships are equitable. Women are more likely than men to be aware of inequity that is unfair to them.[91] They may also hold more idealized views of relationships than men do.[92] Alternatively, women may have different values that emphasize such ideas as equality and cooperation, and they may develop morally in a different way than men.[93]

The perception that equality exists in a relationship may be more important than the reality of it, however. The communication patterns of dual-career couples have been examined by Dorothy Krueger. She found that decision-making egalitarianism and satisfaction are not related, but that the wife's perception of egalitarian decision making and satisfaction are positively related. Krueger suggests that women may expect a subordinate status and may thus overevaluate their participation in decision making.[94] Women might idealize their relationships and attempt to see them as they wish they were, instead of how they appear to others. Such findings suggest researchers might more profitably study couple's perceptions of their relationships, rather than observe their behaviors, if they wish to advise individuals on how they might seek satisfaction.

These general patterns of power among family members have been augmented by communication research. Communication studies have examined power within actual interactions. Let us consider these findings.

■ Power Defined Within Relational Exchange

Basic to our understanding of power in the family is the notion of *control*. Schutz identified three basic interpersonal needs that each person holds: inclusion, control, and affection. Our *inclusion needs* focus on our requirements to feel that we are part of a group. Our *control needs* are based on our needs for control and power. Our *affection needs* deal with our desire to feel affection and love. According to Schutz, each of us has needs in these three areas.[95] Indvik and Fitzpatrick show that our need to control and our willingness to be controlled mark our intimate relationships.[96]

We demonstrate our need for control through our communicative exchanges. This need may be communicated through either the content or relational aspects of our messages. (You will recall that we discussed the content and relationship aspects of communication in Chapter 1). We may verbally signal our desires to family members or we may nonverbally suggest that we want their agreement.

Researchers have shown that our interactions with familiar people, including family members, become patterned. Furthermore, the examination of these patterns suggests which person maintains control and which acquiesces. Frank Millar and Edna Rogers explain that relational patterns occur on the levels of control, trust, and intimacy.[97] Their research has focused on control within relational patterning.[98]

Millar and Rogers base their theorizing on the work of individuals at the Mental Research Institute at Palo Alto, California.[99] Watzlawick, Beavin, and Jackson first discussed power in two basic types of relational patterns: the symmetrical and the complementary. These authors explain:

> They [the relationships] can be described as relationships based on either equality or difference. In the first case the partners tend to mirror each other's behavior, and thus their interaction can be termed *symmetrical*. . . . In the second case one partner's behavior complements that of the other, forming a different sort of behavioral Gestalt, and is called *complementary*. Symmetrical interaction, then, is characterized by equality and the minimization of difference, while complementary interaction is based on the maximization of difference.
>
> There are two different positions in a complementary relationship. One partner occupies what has been variously described as the superior, primary, or "one-up" position, and the other the corresponding inferior, secondary, or "one-down" position. . . . A complementary relationship may be set by the social or cultural context (as in the cases of mother and infant, doctor and patient, or teacher and student), or it may be the idiosyncratic relationship style of a particular dyad.[100]

Marital partners may engage routinely in symmetrical interactions or in complementary patterns. Fitzpatrick's couple types, discussed earlier in this chapter, are useful as we consider differing patterns. Williamson and Fitzpatrick analyzed conversations among traditional, independent, and separate couple types. Their results showed that traditional couples relied on complementary interactions when they discussed a neutral topic, but they became symmetrical when they engaged in conflict. Traditional couples rely on orders and engaged in little give-and-take. Independent couples used competitive symmetry in their discussions. Challenges and justifications marked the control attempts by independent spouses. Separate couples selected complementarity regardless of the issue under discussion.[101] Although we may be inclined to idealize the symmetrical relationship within families, as we have seen the complementary relationship may be preferred by particular family members.

■ Increasing One's Power in the Family

As you have read the information on power in this chapter, you may have been analyzing your own family. Perhaps you have concluded that you have too little power within that context. Can you increase your power in the fami-

ly? Two authors suggest seven ways people can increase their power in a relationship.[102]

First, individuals can increase their own alternatives. Suppose a woman
feels powerless vis-à-vis her husband because compared to him she holds a job
with little future and small economic gain. She can enroll in courses that will
help prepare her for a potentially more fulfilling work life and certainly more
alternatives than she currently has. This, in turn, may grant her a sense of
increased power within the family.

Second, people can minimize the rewards others give them. One couple
had in-laws who enjoyed both giving them expensive gifts and controlling
their behavior. The husband's parents provided automobiles, furniture, and
luxury items to the struggling young couple, but they expected high degrees
of compliance in return. For example, after giving the younger couple a new
automobile, they expected them to drive across the country to visit. They also
expected them to belong to the same church, to vote the same way in political
elections, and to live their lives as the older couple had done. As the younger
dual-career couple matured, they made increasingly large salaries. After about
15 years in the work force, the young couple were worth more money than
the in-laws. They began to buy more luxury items for themselves and yielded
less to the persuasive efforts of the husband's parents. They had, in effect,
gained power by minimizing the gifts the older couple provided.

Third, people can minimize the hurt of the punishment they have received
from others. Children who are attempting to gain more power in their family
settings may use this approach. Young children who receive "time out" may
state they wanted to be away from their siblings. Older children who are
"grounded" may suggest they had no plans to leave the family home anyway.
In these ways, children minimize the punishment they receive.

Fourth, people can exaggerate the hurt incurred by the punishment.
Children can act as though their parents' punishment has no effect, or they
can exaggerate the hurt that is felt. For example, one child received no physical
punishment such as spanking, but occasionally her mother would push her
through a store, by taking her arm and propelling her forward. The child
resented her mother's action and began to scream whenever her mother
touched her in these circumstances. Others within hearing would glance at the
mother and daughter, which encouraged the mother to extinguish the behavior. Similarly, children who are sometimes spanked may scream and shout far
more than they would if they received the same amount of pain from falling
down or injuring themselves.

Fifth, individuals can build up the value of their behavior in the eyes of
the other person. People who do not work can suggest to their spouses that
they have received compliments on their physical attractiveness or personal
qualities. Couples who both work can suggest their supervisors or coworkers
are impressed with the jobs they have done. Children can share the positive
comments offered by a neighbor or a friend's parents.

Sixth, people can increase their own value by increasing their skills.
Women who have been homemakers may return to college or may enroll in

other courses. Husbands who have played traditional roles may learn to cook, iron, or do the laundry. Children whose parents are unemployed can find part-time jobs to supplement or provide family income.

Last, individuals can increase their power to reward. Husbands and wives can become increasingly sensitive to their spouses and compliment them on their looks, their work, or other qualities. They may ingratiate themselves to the other in order to increase their power in the relationship.

For example, if one of the spouses has behaved in a way his or her partner finds inappropriate, he or she may attempt to gain power by getting in the good graces of the other. If the wife has had too much to drink at a party and behaved in a questionable way, she may later cook her husband's favorite meal. If the husband has insulted his wife in a social situation, he may offer to take her out to dinner.

SUMMARY

In this chapter we have considered managing power. We began our discussion with a definition of power in the family. Power refers to our ability to alter the behavior of others. It is not the property of a person but the property of a relationship among people. Power is a perceptual variable; it does not exist in any "real" sense. We may categorize power into reward power, coercive power, expert power, position power, referent power, and information power.

In recent times, communication researchers have moved the concept of power from the public communication arena to the interpersonal communication sphere. Compliance gaining and compliance resisting are important to our understanding of power strategies within the family. Both compliance gaining and compliance resisting change as a function of a person's sex, age, and role within the family.

A variety of patterns of power exist among couples. They may be husband-dominant, wife-dominant, or egalitarian. Egalitarian couples may make decisions together or each spouse may have his or her separate sphere of influence. Communication researchers have begun to examine power in the interactions between women and men. This research should help us better understand family communication.

KEY TERMS

1. *Power* is the ability to influence others or to achieve one's ends. Power is the property of the relationship, and it is a perceptual variable.

2. Categories of power include: *reward power,* which occurs when you have something of value to offer another person; *position power,* which results from the roles one plays; *expert power,* which is based on knowledge or experience; *referent power,* which is granted to the person who identifies with another; *information power,* which occurs when people respond to the per-

suasive arguments of others; and *coercive power,* which is the power to punish other people if they do not comply with your wishes.

3. *Compliance gaining* refers to communication strategies that people use to get others to do what they want. Examples of compliance-gaining strategies include manipulation, nonnegotiation, emotional appeal, personal rejection, and empathic understanding. *Compliance resistance* refers to strategies people use to resist someone's request. Examples of compliance resistance include nonnegotiation, identity management, justifying, and negotiation.

4. *Domineeringness* is defined as providing a verbal statement to one's partner in which the right to be dominant was exhibited.

5. *Dominance* includes such a statement followed by a verbalization from the spouse in which she or he acknowledged and accepted the first person's right to dominate.

CHAPTER 14

MANAGING STRESS AND MAKING DECISIONS

Charm is a way of getting the answer yes without asking a clear question.

ALBERT CAMUS

After you have read this chapter, you will be able to

1. Define stress and stressors.

2. Describe developmental stress.

3. Identify some of the developmental processes that create stress.

4. Distinguish between predictable and unpredictable stressors.

5. Suggest methods of coping with stress.

6. Describe a model of stress.

7. Differentiate among accommodation, consensus, and de facto decision making.

8. Distinguish between successful and unsuccessful decision making.

9. Explain how decision making is related to a satisfying family life.

This final chapter focuses on managing stress and decision making within the family context. Although these topics may seem to be more relevant to public communication settings such as the workplace or the executive board room, we will determine that an understanding of them is critical between relational partners and family members. We begin by considering a definition of stress and stressors.

❖ MANAGING STRESS

Stress is inevitable within the family, as is conflict (which was discussed in Chapter 12). *Stress* occurs when disruptive or disquieting influences are experienced by family members, and *stressors* are defined as "those life events and related hardships that are of sufficient magnitude to bring about a change in the family system."[1] These events may be viewed objectively as positive (purchase of a new home, building of a new home, addition of a baby to the family) or negative (death of a family member, extended illness of a child, or failure to gain a promotion at work). In a review of family stress and coping, one author lists some of the stressors that have been studied and includes "chronic illness, drug abuse, sudden divorce, death, disaster, war, unemployment, parenthood, captivity, and rape."[2]

A number of researchers have attempted to create measures of life events that result in stress. One of the more popular, the Social Readjustment Scale, consists of items that range in value from 100 to 11, depending upon the severity of the event.[3] At the top of the scale are items such as death of spouse (100 points), divorce (73 points), marital separation (65 points), and death of a close family member (63 points). In the middle of the scale are change to different line of work (36 points), change in number of arguments with spouse (35 points), and foreclosure of mortgage or loan (30 points). Toward the bottom of the scale are vacation (13 points), Christmas (12 points), and minor violations of the law (11 points). Life events scales have been criticized on the basis of individual variability.[4] People simply do not respond to the same stimuli in the same way.

Stress can be harmful to the individual as it is related to a variety of health problems, including cardiovascular problems and cancers,[5] or it can be welcomed by people who enjoy changes in their lives and are bored when events are not in flux.[6] Individuals respond differently to changes that occur within their lives. Three researchers have shown that individuals who learn how to cope with stress early in their lives may be better able to cope with problems later on.[7]

Stress occurs in response to life and family developments, and it also occurs as a result of less predictable events. Most couples experience both kinds of stress. Norma Rogalski and her husband are in their retirement years. When asked about the stress she had encountered in her long marriage, she laughed:

> I think we have had them all. He was in the hospital. He lost his job one time, and we were on the verge of bankruptcy. We lost our home. We had a real time when we had the kids. He was in the army then, he was over in Italy. That was stressful for me, and him, too. When we moved to our current house, we thought all of our troubles were over. After all, we were retired. The kids were married and we thought everything was going to be fine. We

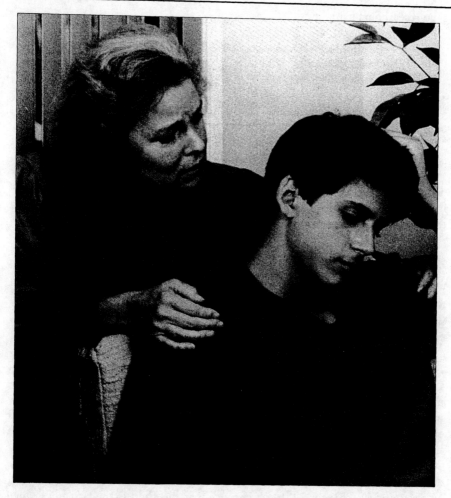

Stress results from both predictable and nonpredictable events (© Bachmann/The Image Works).

don't like to interfere. Shortly after we moved here, our son's wife left him with their little boy. And then our son went to pieces. It has been very stressful trying to get him back on his feet and taking care of our grandson, too.[8]

We will consider developmental stress first and then consider unpredictable stress.

■ Developmental Stress

Stress occurs when changes occur in an individual's life. Some of these changes are fairly predictable and are related to the developmental process.

Two researchers explain:

> ... we must see people as engaged in a life drama with a continuous story line that is best grasped not as a still photo but as a moving picture with a beginning, middle, and end.[9]

One woman in a long-lasting and happy marriage provided a wise answer to the question about the most stressful time in one's marriage. She smiled, "Each period of life has its areas of difficulty—and the period you are living in is always the most difficult time!"[10]

Stress may occur in any developmental stage, but it may be most likely during adolescence, during the early marital years, when a baby is added, during middle age, and in later years. The choice of these stages, like the stages themselves, is fairly arbitrary.

Adolescence   We discussed adolescence in Chapter 8, where we observed that this period of one's life may be filled with great stress for an individual or may be relatively stress-free. Changes in physical size, emotional makeup, and psychological characteristics render the adolescent vulnerable to stress. For many adolescents, the early period (between 12 and 14 years of age) of this stage is most disconcerting.[11]

Early Marriage   The first years of marriage are filled with changes. In Chapter 6 we discussed Coleman's three marital stages: the "happy honeymoon" phase, the disillusionment and regrets stage, and the period of accommodation.[12] These alterations are accompanied by stress. The middle period is especially stressful, as people's ideals collide with reality; however, even the honeymoon and accommodation phases are marked by changes.

Adding a Baby   The addition of a child to a family results in many changes, as we noted in Chapter 7. Stress may occur if the child is the first born since parents must now juggle both spousal and parenting roles. If other children are present, the parents and the siblings must alter their roles to accommodate another person. More mothers work today than in the past; consequently, new mothers may have to accommodate work roles, too. Contemporary parents report four sets of stress: demands of parenting, spousal, and work roles; care for the child; spousal interaction; and interactions with other family members.[13] For most couples, the stress of parenting begins before the child is born, during the pregnancy.[14]

Stress may continue throughout the child-rearing stages of the family. Children's personalities and behavior may add to the stress experienced by parents and siblings. Child-rearing problems may include the child's dishonesty, irresponsibility, emotional swings, hyperactivity, and emotional problems.[15]

Children also are more likely to be born during the first few years of a marriage, when job stress, financial pressures, and other matters may be at an all-time high. Christian Kloos's children have now all left home, but he recalls the time when they were young as the most difficult in his long marriage:

> Everybody said that we would look back on it someday and think of it as the best years of our life. They were four years of hell. The kids were little. I was gone 16 hours a day, six days a week, twelve hours on Sundays. And we had no money. Those were the most stressful times all the way around.[16]

Middle Age Midlife may present an especially stressful time for individuals. Some studies have suggested that midlife may be viewed as a time of relative peace and satisfaction, while others have viewed it as a period of crisis and discontent. Researchers Farrell and Rosenberg conducted a study of 500 men at midlife and suggest that the individual may be more actively involved in defining this period than earlier studies have acknowledged.[17] Individuals do not simply react to the events around them; instead, they are active agents in naming and interpreting their own reality.

Late Adulthood As adults age they may feel increased stress because of physical and psychological problems. The mental health of older adults is a national health problem:

> Since mental handicap makes an individual increasingly dependent on the help and care of others, the cost of these services and perquisites to other members of the family and to the whole of society as well represents a burden which has been estimated at 36.78 billions of dollars per year in the United States. More important, perhaps, is a cost that cannot be measured or tabulated: the loss of human potential and of the affected persons capacity for adaptation and ability to contribute to human welfare.[18]

Depression is a common problem among older adults. Dependency among older adults may cause stress for them and for their families.[19]

In addition to their own failing mental and physical abilities, older people often must concern themselves with their own parents or their adult children. One older woman discussed her stress:

> When our youngest son graduated from high school and joined the Navy, it was very stressful. He was the baby. We also have had stressful times with our daughter because her husband was ill with cancer and then he died. My mother's illness was very stressful, too, because I stayed with her every night for a long time.[20]

Clearly the later years can be filled with stressful circumstances.

■ Less Predictable Stress

Some stress occurs because of fairly predictable developmental changes in families and in individuals. In addition, stress sometimes occurs because of less predictable events. Family researcher Walsh calls these "the slings and arrows of outrageous fortune."[21] Such events may be positive or negative and include both chronic and terminal illnesses, unexpected or untimely deaths, unexpected promotion or demotion at work, surprising windfalls of resources or personal accomplishments, and wars or national events. When families unexpectedly change their form from the more traditional nuclear family to the dual-worker family or from the single-parent family to the blended family, stress accompanies the change. Although the consideration of all unpredictable events is beyond the scope of this text, we will consider some common examples.

Financial Problems   The most common source of conflict among marital couples concerns money.[22] Most often the couple feels they do not have sufficient money to meet their needs. Amassing debts, poor budgeting, and lack of well-paying jobs are often involved. Sudden unemployment, or the unexpected loss of any job, can result in financial problems and immediate and long-term stress.

Job Distress   Related to financial problems is job distress. When one is unhappy at work, the problems often spill over at home. A recent study shows that husbands and wives in blue-collar and white-collar marriages cope differently with job distress. Lowell J. Krokoff, at the University of Wisconsin in Madison, contrasted the companionship model of marriage, which predicted that job distress on the part of the husband would lead to less laughter and humor between the couple with the coping model, which predicted more humor in times of difficulties. He found that husbands in white-collar marriages followed the companionship model more than husbands in blue-collar marriages. The coping model was followed by blue-collar husbands and wives more than white-collar couples.[23]

Building or Buying a Home   While many Americans view their own home as part of the American dream, the building or buying of a new home, particularly a first home, is stressful. One problem associated with the purchase of a new home is relocation. The family must leave familiar neighbors and environs to move to a different location. Another difficulty created in the choice of a particular home is that family members may learn their individual "ideal" is not shared by others in the family and major compromises are in order. Unrealistic ideas about the cost of a family home or additional unexpected expenses may create problems. Finally, the idealization of the purchase of a home portrayed in the media and other popular sources may encourage frustration in family members who must confront the realities of purchasing or building a home.[24]

Living in the Country or the City   A popular television program of over 20 years ago, "Green Acres," is now rebroadcast by some stations. The program depicted a city couple who attempted to cope with country living. The humor in the situation comedy was based on the differences in rural and urban life.

Different stressors are present in these two environments. Urban dwellers complain of pollution, overcrowding, limited resources, and traffic problems. Rural residents are sometimes dissatisfied by their lack of cultural and social stimulation and their inability to buy goods and services locally. Urban and rural dwellers use a variety of coping strategies to deal with their individual problems and these strategies do not differ in kind. However, rural people use more strategies, which suggests they may be attempting to control their lives more actively.[25]

Chronic Illness in Children   Recent figures indicate that more than one in ten children suffer from some kind of chronic illness and of these children, 1 to 2 million have severe chronic illnesses.[26] This illness can create extreme stress within the family unit and often leads to separation or divorce. Frequently intervention by social service agencies or social support systems is in order.[27]

Separation and Divorce   Marital separation and divorce is stressful for both the marital couple and for children within the family.[28] One person writes:

> For the person who goes through a divorce, an entire life is often turned topsy-turvy. Intimate bonds with another person are broken; relationships with children are changed; friendship patterns are disrupted; different living arrangements must be established; employment must often be obtained.[29]

Family members feel increased stress when they lose their social network or when it decreases in size. They may also feel more stress if they experience a lowered income. Finally, the perceived severity of the divorce affects the levels of stress reported.[30]

Husbands and wives sometimes differ on their perception of the relative distressed nature of their relationship. A recent study showed that if the husband is distressed, the couple reports the marriage to be distressed. If wives are distressed, the couple does not report the marriage to be distressed.[31] It appears that the husband's level of distress, rather than the wife's, defines the marital distress level. In this sense, as in others that we discussed in the last chapter, men have more power to define the relationship.

❖ A MODEL OF STRESS

Hill offered the most influential model explaining stress. His ABC-X Model includes four essential variables.

A The event and related changes,

B The resources of the family to meet the crisis, and

C The definition the family places on the event, which results in

X The crisis[32]

Hill's model includes two stages: the development of crisis, explained above, and the adjustment to it, which results in a new organization of the family. Burr modified Hill's model to include both the family's vulnerability and its regenerative power.[33] Some families are more vulnerable to changes because of their lack of, or lessened, resources. Others have regenerative powers as they are more likely to recover from disruptions.

McCubbin and Patterson have further refined Hill's model. They suggest that the event that results in crisis is often not a single event. Appropriately, they label their model the double ABC-X Model. The double A is defined as current and continuing family *hardships* (such as a terminal disease in one family member or the loss of a job by another) and *prior strains* (such as coping with being both a paid worker and a parent) added to the *event* itself.[34] McCubbin and Patterson's contribution lies not in their definition of the A within the model but of their placement of stress within a process orientation. Events do not simply occur to families; instead, they fit into the quilt of the family's past and present.

Families have a limited number of resources and coping mechanisms.[35] When they face many life changes or when they have few available resources, they may fail to adapt to the changing events in their lives. Stressful events are additive. For instance, if the resources of time and money are already depleted because of earlier events, a family might not be able to cope with an additional burden. Negative consequences may occur for individuals within the family (physical or psychological illness) or for the entire family unit (dissatisfaction or instability).

❖ ADJUSTMENT TO STRESS

How do families adjust to the changes and crises occurring in their lives? Irwin Sarason, an important researcher on stress, has explained that coping with stress requires an individual to set aside unproductive concerns and deal with problematic situations.[36] His advice is similar to the often quoted prayer: "Lord give me the courage to change the things I can, the serenity to accept the things I cannot, and the wisdom to know the difference."

Sarason identifies five factors that influence how individuals respond to stress. They include:

1. Nature of the task or the nature of the stress

2. Skills or resources available to perform the task or to achieve the goal

3. Individual personality characteristics

4. Individual's history of stress-arousing experiences

5. Available social support[37]

These factors are similar to those identified by others.[38]

Hill conceived of the "crisis proof family"[39] and Pratt discussed the "energized family,"[40] which was unlikely to become unstable when faced with major changes. Such families were characterized by flexible relationships and a shared sense of power. Family adaptability is viewed as a major consideration in Olson's circumplex model of family functioning.[41] Problem-solving abilities may help families cope with changes. Finally, social networks are of increased importance during times of stress.[42]

Families use both internal and external approaches in coping with stress. The internal strategies include (1) redefining the stressful event so it is more manageable and (2) attempting to view the stressful event as less important by determining a positive response to it. The external approaches were (1) gaining social support from friends and family, (2) finding spiritual support from the clergy, and (3) using community resources, including social service agencies and educational opportunities.[43]

One couple did not realize that they used different means of relieving stress until they were asked about it. James Robertson began:

> I just have to be active and keep my mind off things that are causing the stress. I go out and work with my hands, instead of using my mind or brain. I go out and work. That's the best way to relieve stress.[44]

Linda Robertson added:

> That's interesting. I just realized this is a difference in us. What I do is rely on my religion, my Christian beliefs. I do a lot of reading, scripture and books. That's my way of coping.[45]

Many couples find that humor is important in relieving stress. Patty Woodyard, from Cleveland, Ohio, has been married for nearly 30 years. She observed, "Humor can ease the tension in tense moments, and make intimate ones that much more memorable.[46] Craig Jackson, a salesperson who lives on the same block in Cleveland, also explained, "Humor is a good means of communication between my wife and I because it allows us to make our point gracefully and with less tension. It also allows me to overstate my point so that Jackie [his wife] knows exactly where I am coming from without getting upset."[47]

Few studies have examined family coping skills, but two conclusions seem warranted. First, the family may be better able to cope with a stressful situation if they perceive it as less rather than more severe.[48] The meaning the family attaches to the event is critical in determining how they will experience it and how they will cope with it. Second, discussing the stressful situation in order to gain a shared social meaning may render it more understandable and solvable.[49] Specific coping strategies may vary across different families.[50]

A recent investigation shows that if a family has a sense of coherence, which means they view their world as "comprehensible, manageable, and meaningful," they may be better able to cope with stress than if they do not have this sense. The families that had this sense were better able to adapt and to deal with stressful situations than were families who did not see their world in a coherent, manageable, and meaningful way.[51]

❖ MAKING DECISIONS

Families make decisions about a myriad of items, from the trivial to the essential. They determine which brand of toothpaste to buy, on the one end of the continuum, and whether or not the family should remain together, on the other end. How are decisions made in families? How should decisions be made? These questions form the basis for this section.

All families do not make decisions in the same way. Some appear not to make decisions at all. Others carefully discuss the pros and cons and come up with a decision with which all can agree. Still others allow one person or another to make most of the decisions for the entire family. Not only do couples vary in their decision making, but husbands and wives do as well.[52]

How do families determine patterns of decision making? Certainly our orienting families affect the way we make decisions. Couples recall the way their parents made decisions and enact the same patterns. An individual's own characteristics may similarly affect how he or she solves a problem or makes a decision. A relationship between wives' tendency to attribute other couples' marital problems to undesirable personality traits or negative attitudes and the likelihood of their verbally criticizing their own husbands in problem-solving discussions exists.[53] How we view others may affect how we relate to our own partners.

In addition, when the couple forms, it creates a new joint reality that affects their decision making. Although people may be predisposed to behave in a particular way because of the way their parents behaved or because of their own characteristics, such behavior can be altered. When one spouse demonstrates high levels of trust in his or her partner, the partner is likely to become more trusting, risk taking, and flexible. Since trust breeds trust, greater mutual flexibility results as well.[54] Thus one's treatment within the marital relationship may result in changes in behavior and improved decision-making ability.

■ Kinds of Decision Making

We will consider three basic kinds of family decision making: de facto, accommodation, and consensus. You will observe a relationship between these and some of the six conflict resolution methods presented in Chapter 12.

De Facto Decision Making   *De facto* is a Latin term that literally means in reality, in fact, or from the fact. The term is contrasted with *de jure,* which means according to law or from the right. De facto decision making, then, means people do nothing, but let circumstances and the situation govern them. In the 1960s, news reports were filled with stories about de facto school segregation, meaning that local school districts decided to do nothing about busing students to public schools, which resulted in de facto segregation. The officials did not deliberately segregate the schools, but they simply allowed segregation to occur.

De facto decision making occurs in the family when members either cannot or will not make a decision; instead, they let circumstances prevail. For example, if a family moves into an older home with the idea that they will remodel the house as they can afford to do so, but no one makes a move to contact contractors or interior designers, they are deciding de facto to live in the house as is.

Although de facto decision making is often viewed as making no decision at all, some families rely upon this method. Indeed, some philosophies and religions suggest that things which "should occur, will occur." These perspectives maintain that people often attempt to usurp the authority belonging to nature or God. This point of view suggests that we sometimes go to absurd lengths to attempt to control uncontrollable events in our lives.

Accommodative Decision Making   Accommodation suggests we make adaptations or adjustments to others. Accommodative decision making occurs when family members adapt or adjust to someone else in their families. Such accommodation may be regularly made for one family member. For example, if one of the parents is particularly domineering, the children and the other parent may allow the person to make decisions for the entire family. If the family includes an infant or a very young child, the family may feel their decisions must accommodate the needs of this youngest member.

Accommodation may occur as a routinized form of decision making that takes into consideration those persons who are primarily involved in the decision. For example, if the family is considering the undergraduate education of the oldest child, they may decide they should accommodate the child's choice of a college or university, regardless of the cost or distance from home. If a decision is being made about who may have the family's second car on a weekend night, those individuals who have asked for the car may have their needs accommodated.

Although accommodation is sometimes viewed as a poor way to make decisions in the family because one member may always get his or her way, it is sometimes a useful approach in decision making. Oftentimes the most vocal members are those who are most deeply involved in the decision. Also, families learn that they must continue to adjust as the family develops and changes. Accommodation may be viewed as negative only if some members are never on the receiving end, but are always making sacrifices for others.

Compromising may be viewed as one form of accommodation or as a method to achieve consensus. Although some researchers suggest compromise is not a desirable way to solve problems or to make decisions, others find it can be useful. Compromising is one of the most important indicators of a happy marriage. In other words, happy couples rely upon compromise as a method of making decisions, while unhappy couples did not.[55]

Consensual Decision Making   The term "consensus" refers to a collective decision or general agreement. Consensual decision making occurs when all of the family members mutually agree to a decision. A variety of factors need to be present for the family to reach a mutual decision. They must have sufficient time, knowledge about the decision to be made, common assumptions, good communication skills, and flexibility.

We have observed that compromising may be seen as a method of accommodation or a means to a consensual end. A number of writers have determined that a willingness to compromise and to be flexible in decision making is central to effective bargaining and negotiation.[56] Further, interaction skills are important predictors of effective family problem solving.[57] In these studies effective bargaining and negotiation were equated with consensual decision making.

Although consensual decision making is generally viewed as the best method of reaching a decision, it probably occurs the least frequently in families. Oftentimes, families are missing one of the vital elements necessary for agreement. Perhaps they do not have enough time to discuss the matter because of busy workdays and multiple demands on their waking hours. Sometimes everyone is not fully cognizant of the issues involved in the decision. Maybe family members disagree about the goals of the family and thus disagree on the principles that underlie an appropriate choice for the family. Or, some members have difficulty expressing their points of view in a manner others can understand. Finally, some family members are inflexible—that is, they cannot view decisions in a new or unique way.

Deborah Godwin, from the University of Georgia, and John Scanzoni, at the University of Florida, recently identified some factors that are related to consensual decision making between the two members of a couple. They found that when husbands had previous patterns of cooperativeness during conflict situations; when the spouses had more, rather than less, equitable economic resources; when wives had communication styles that were less, rather than more, coercive; and when spouses both had great control, the level of consensus between the two on their decisions increased.[58] Cooperativeness, equitability, low coercion, and increased control are all important to the couple wishing to use consensual decision making.

Consensual decision making may be the best way to make decisions in an ideal world, with all family members fully interacting in each decision. However, we recognize such decision making may only be a goal rather than a reality. While we strive to include all points of view and to make decisions with which all family members can agree, sometimes we do not, or cannot.

■ Flexibility in Decision Making

One of the most important factors distinguishing successful from unsuccessful decision making is flexibility.[59] Family decision-making structures, which handle a great number of problems and a variety of decisions, must retain a great deal of flexibility in their structure.[60] Decision-making structures must be open, decisive, perceptive, and realistic, as well.

Close personal relationships generally are more flexible when they include more flexible and tolerant standards of behavior. Although people sometimes lament the poor treatment they receive at home as compared to the way they are treated by strangers, they might also view such differences in treatment favorably. Close relationships result in cohesive bonds among individuals that make termination of the relationship difficult and that also make spontaneous and emotional behavior possible and permissible.[61] Although family members may sometimes treat their members worse than they treat strangers, they are not likely to dismiss members who behave equally badly. To the extent we are willing to accept discrepant treatment, we are allowed the flexibility of sometimes behaving in a less than ideal manner.

Flexibility also implies creativity, an important aspect of effective decision making. Creativity is a virtue for any group in their endeavors to solve problems and that one measure of creativity is the ability to generate a variety of alternatives.[62] The family that includes individuals who can generate alternatives and can communicate them successfully to others will probably be superior in their decision making. In the next section we will consider the relationship between decision making and a satisfying family life.

■ Successful Decision Making Related to Satisfying Family Life

Our ability to make decisions within the family can lead to greater satisfaction. Overall marital satisfaction can best be indicated by the couple's ability to discuss problems in an effective manner and to express their feelings to each other.[63] Positive problem-solving behaviors and compromises mark the interaction of nondistressed couples.[64] By contrast, distressed couples engage in more conflict but use fewer problem-solving statements and provide less information to their partners.[65]

Nondistressed couples also seem to be better able to modify their spouse's behavior. Marital satisfaction is related to the couple's ability to persuade, rather than coerce, each other. When the number of directions, instructions, suggestions, or requests that alter the behavior of the spouse is compared with the number of similar directives that are unsuccessful, satisfied couples have a higher ratio of successful attempts than dissatisfied couples do.[66] Wives who are in distressed marriages make more unsuccessful attempts to dominate their spouses than wives in nondistressed marriages do.[67]

Two researchers provided additional information about successful decision making among couples. They analyzed decision making and found that couples with satisfying marriages had more extensive repertoires of responses to negative messages. These alternatives inhibited the escalation of conflict and allowed the couple to engage in more issue-oriented, as opposed to personality-oriented, discussions. They responded to each other with supportive comments.[68] Although we cannot impose a cause-effect relationship on the researchers' findings, we can conclude that flexibility in responses, added to an issue orientation and general supportiveness, appear to be related to marital satisfaction. The findings are consistent with other studies reviewed in this text.

Sandra Metts and William Cupach, at Illinois State University, recently provided a fresh approach to our understanding of the decisions made by relational couples. They used a typology provided by another researcher to describe possible decision making responses. This typology includes *voice*, which is an active and constructive response and includes discussion of problems, compromising, and seeking help from third parties. *Loyalty* is passive and constructive and involves waiting for things to get better and maintaining faith both in the relationship and one's partner. *Neglect* is passive and destructive and includes withdrawal by decreasing time with each other, avoiding the discussion of problems, and treating one's partner badly. Finally, *exit* is active and destructive and it involves thinking about leaving the relationship, threatening to leave, and actually destroying the relationship.[69]

For their part, Metts and Cupach hypothesized that the two destructive strategies—exit and neglect—were negatively related to relational satisfaction, and that voice—the constructive, active strategy—was positively related to relational satisfaction. They also conjectured that dysfunctional relationship beliefs (such as: disagreement is destructive, partners cannot change, mind reading is expected, sexual activities between couples should be perfect, and the sexes are different) would be negatively related to the use of voice and positively related to the exit and neglect responses. They found that both of these hypotheses were accurate.[70]

The implications of this research is that couples who are more satisfied tend to use active and constructive responses to decisions, while those who are less satisfied use destructive means of solving problems and making decisions. Too, people who hold self-defeating, negative beliefs about relationships are more likely to use destructive responses and less likely to use constructive, active strategies. While the relationship among these variables is not necessarily cause-effect, couples who want to improve their satisfaction may consider substituting constructive, active responses to problems and decisions for destructive ones.

Successful decision making is additive to marital satisfaction across the life cycle. Two investigators studied couples in retirement. Although, as we observed in Chapter 9, couples in this family stage are generally satisfied, they may have to reorganize, as they are together for many more hours than they previously have been. Dorfman and Hill showed that joint decision making by retired couples consistently resulted in high levels of satisfaction.[71]

Relatively few studies have considered the manner by which couples reach agreement, consensus, or a decision. The literature is clear that to the extent couples are able to reach such an outcome, their marital satisfaction ratings will probably be higher. Future investigations might consider the means by which couples are able to successfully reach consensus.

Do you understand family communication more thoroughly now than when you began reading this book? In the first chapter, a marital quiz was provided. The quiz is reprinted here. In order to test the development of your understanding of family communication, you may wish to retake the marriage quiz.*

1. A husband's marital satisfaction is usually lower if his wife is employed full time than if she is a full-time homemaker.

2. Today most young, single, never-married people will eventually get married.

3. In most marriages having a child improves marital satisfaction for both spouses.

4. The best single predictor of overall marital satisfaction is the quality of a couple's sex life.

5. The divorce rate in America increased from 1960 to 1980.

6. A greater percentage of wives are in the work force today than in 1970.

7. Marital satisfaction for a wife is usually lower if she is employed full time than if she is a full-time homemaker.

8. If my spouse loves me, he/she should instinctively know what I want and need to be happy.

9. In a marriage in which the wife is employed full time, the husband usually assumes an equal share of the housekeeping.

10. For most couples marital satisfaction gradually increases from the first year of marriage through the child-bearing years, the teen years, the empty nest period, and retirement.

11. No matter how I behave, my spouse should love me simply because he/she *is* my spouse.

12. One of the most frequent marital problems is poor communication.

13. Husbands usually make more life style adjustments in marriage than wives.

14. Couples who cohabitated before marriage usually report greater marital satisfaction than couples who did not.

---

*. Items 1, 3, 4, 7, 8, 9, 10, 11, 13, 14, 15, 17, 18, 19, and 20 are false and are marital myths. The other items are true and are included as filler items for the marital myths.

15. I can change my spouse by pointing out his/her inadequacies, errors, etc.

16. Couples who marry when one or both partners are under the age of 18 have more chance of eventually divorcing than those who marry when they are older.

17. Either my spouse loves me or does not love me; nothing I do will affect the way my spouse feels about me.

18. The more a spouse discloses positive and negative information to his/her partner, the greater the marital satisfaction of both partners.

19. I must feel better about my partner before I can change my behavior toward him/her.

20. Maintaining romantic love is *the key* to marital happiness over the life span for most couples.

SUMMARY

In this chapter, we considered stress and decision making in the family. Stress is inevitable within the family. Stress occurs when disruptive or disquieting influences are experienced by family members. Although researchers have attempted to create measures of life events that result in stress, such scales have been criticized on the basis of individual variability. Stress can be harmful to the individual as it is related to a variety of health problems, or it can be welcomed by people who enjoy changes in their lives and are bored when events are not in flux. Stress can occur in response to family developments and to less predictable events.

Families can adjust to the changes and crises occurring in their lives. Some of the factors that affect the manner in which families respond to crises include the nature of the stress, the skills or resources available to perform the task, the individuals' personality characteristics, the individuals' history of stress-arousing experiences, and the available social support. While few studies have examined family coping skills, two conclusions seem warranted. First, the family may be better able to cope with a stressful situation if they define it as less rather than as more severe. Second, discussing the stressful situation may render it more understandable and solvable. Specific coping strategies cannot be offered for all families.

Decision making occurs on a variety of levels in the family. Both one's original family and one's current family influence decision-making patterns. Three kinds of family decision making were considered. De facto decision making occurs when people do nothing but let circumstances and situations govern them. Accommodative decision making occurs when individuals make adaptations or adjustments to others. Consensual decision making occurs when the family reaches a collective decision or general agreement.

Flexibility is key to decision making. Families that are flexible in their decision making probably make better decisions than those who are inflexible. Flexibility in decision making encourages family satisfaction. This final chapter of the text is important to our ability to seek satisfaction within our family relationships because the management of stress and the ability to make appropriate decisions are related to satisfaction.

KEY TERMS

1. *Stress* occurs when disruptive or disquieting influences are experienced by family members.

2. *Stressors* are the life events and related hardships that are of sufficient magnitude to create change in the family

3. The *ABC-X Model* explains stress in regard to: the event and related changes; the resources of the family to meet the crisis; and the definition the family places on the event which results in X, the crisis.

4. Kinds of decision making include *de facto,* which means people do nothing but let the situation and circumstances govern themselves; *accommodation,* which suggests we make adaptations or adjustments to others; and *consensus,* which occurs when members are in general agreement and a collective decision results.

NOTES

CHAPTER 1 NOTES

1. Sven Wahlroos, *Family Communication* (New York: Macmillan, 1983), xi.

2. J. C. Coleman, *Intimate Relationships, Marriage, and Family* (Indianapolis, IN: Bobbs-Merrill, 1984).

3. See, for example, Harold T. Christensen, "Children in the Family: Relationship of Number and Spacing to Marital Success," *Journal of Marriage and the Family* 30 (1968): 283–289; Eleanor B. Luckey and Joyce K. Bain, "Children: A Factor in Marital Satisfaction," *Journal of Marriage and the Family* 32 (1970): 43–44; John E. O'Brien, "Violence in Divorce Prone Families," *Journal of Marriage and the Family* 33 (1971): 692–698; and Norval D. Glenn, "Quantitative Research on Marital Quality in the 1980s: A Critical Review," *Journal of Marriage and the Family* 52 (November 1990): 818–831.

4. Linda K. Acitelli, "When Spouses Talk to Each Other About Their Relationship," *Journal of Social and Personal Relationships* 5 (1988): 185–199; Leslie A. Baxter and William W. Wilmot, "'Secret Tests': Social Strategies for Acquiring Information about the State of the Relationship," *Human Communication Research* 11 (1984): 171–202; Leslie A. Baxter and Connie Bullis, "Turning Points in Developing Romantic Relationships," *Human Communication Research* 12 (1986): 469–493; and R. Burnett, "Thinking and Communicating about Personal Relationships: Some Sex Differences," paper presented at the Second International Conference on Personal Relationship, Madison, WI, July 1984.

5. Linda K. Acitelli, "When Spouses Talk to Each Other About Their Relationship," *Journal of Social and Personal Relationships* 5 (1988): 186.

6. R. Burnett, "Thinking and Communicating about Relationships: Some Sex Differences," paper presented at the Second International Conference on Personal Relationships, Madison, WI, July 1984; and Linda K. Acitelli, "When Spouses Talk to Each Other About Their Relationship," *Journal of Social and Personal Relationships* 5 (1988): 185–199.

7. Robert A. Lewis and Graham B. Spanier, "Theorizing about the Quality and Stability of Marriage," *Contemporary Theories About the Family: Research-Based Theories* 1 (1979): 268–294.

8. See, for example, Kip Jenkins, "Families and Religion," *Family Perspective* 23 (1989): 285–308; Larry L. Bumpass, Teresa Castro Martin, and James A. Sweet, "The Impact of Family Background and Early Marital Factors on Marital Disruption," *Journal of Family Issues* 12 (1991): 22–42; and Suzanne T. Ortega, Hugh P. Whitt, and J. Allen William, Jr., "Religious Homogamy and Marital Happiness," *Journal of Family Issues* 9 (1988): 224–239.

9. See, for example, Martha S. Hill, "Marital Stability and Spouses' Shared Time," *Journal of Family Issues* 9 (1988): 427–451; and Dennis K. Orthner, "Leisure Activity Patterns and Marital Satisfaction Over the Marital Career," *Journal of Marriage and the Family* (1975): 91–102.

10. Jeanette Lauer and Robert Lauer, "Marriages Made to Last," *Psychology Today* 7 (1985 July):22–26.

11. Judy C. Pearson, *Lasting Love: What Keeps Couples Together* (Dubuque, IA: William C. Brown, 1992).

12. Larry L. Bumpass, Teresa Castro Martin, and James A. Sweet, "The Impact of Family Background and Early Marital Factors on Marital Disruption," *Journal of Family Issues* 12 (1991): 22–42.

13. Robert H. Coombs, "Marital Status and Personal Well-Being: A Literature Review," *Family Relations* 40 (1991): 97–102; Walter R. Gove, Carolyn Briggs Style, and Michael Hughes, "The Effects of Marriage on the Well-Being of Adults," *Journal of Family Issues* 11 (1990): 4–35; Norval D. Glenn and Charles N. Weaver "A Note on Family Situation and Global Happiness," *Social Forces* 57 (1979): 960–967; Leonard I. Pearlin, "Sex Roles and Depression," *Life Span Developmental Psychology: Normative Life Crises* (New York: Academic, 1975): 191–197 and Joyce S. Johnson, "Marital Status, Life Strains and Depression," *American Sociological Review* 42 (1977): 704–715; and Norval D. Glenn and Charles N. Weaver, "The Changing Relationship of Marital Status to Reported Happiness," *Journal of Marriage and the Family* 50 (1988): 317–324.

14. See, for example, Jesse S. Bernard, *The Future of Marriage* (New York: Bantam, 1972); Robert H. Coombs, "Marital Status and Personal Well-Being: A Literature Review," *Family Relations* 40 (1991): 97–102; Mary Anne Fitzpatrick, *Between Husbands and Wives: Communication in Marriage* (Newbury Park, CA: Sage, 1988); and Norval D. Glenn and Charles Weaver, "The Changing Relationship of Marital Status to Reported Happiness," *Journal of Marriage and the Family* 50 (1988): 317–324.

15. See, for example, Debra Umberson and Walter R. Gove, "Parenthood and Psychological Well-Being," *Journal of Family Issues* 10 (1989): 440–462; David

Johnson, Lynn White, John Edwards, and Alan Booth, "Dimensions of Marital Quality: Toward Methodological and Conceptual Refinement," *Journal of Family Issues* 7 (1986): 31–50; Boyd C. Rollins and Kenneth L. Cannon, "Marital Satisfaction Over the Family Life Cycle: A Reevaluation," *Journal of Marriage and the Family* 36 (1974): 271–282; and Gary R. Lee, "Marital Satisfaction in Later Life: The Effects of Nonmarital Roles," *Journal of Marriage and the Family* 50 (August 1988): 775–783.

16. M. A. Fitzpatrick and D. M. Badzinski, "All in the Family: Interpersonal Communication in Kin Relationships," *Handbook of Interpersonal Communication* (Newbury Park, CA: Sage, 1985), 692.

17. See, for example, Walter A. Schumm and Margaret A. Bugaighis, "Marital Quality and Marital Stability: Resolving a Controversy," *Journal of Divorce* 9 (1985): 73–77; Richard J. Udry, "The Marital Happiness/Disruption Relationship by Level of Marital Alternatives," *Journal of Marriage and the Family* 45 (1983): 221–222; and Lynn K. White and Alan Booth, "Divorce Over the Life Course: The Role of Marital Happiness," *Journal of Family Issues* 12 (1991): 5–21.

18. William Lederer and Don D. Jackson, *The Mirages of Marriage* (New York: Norton, 1968).

19. See, for example, L. M. Terman and P. Wallin, "The Validity of Marriage Prediction and Marital Adjustment Tests," *American Sociological Review* 14 (1949): 497–504.

20. Edwards, Personal Interview, 1991.

21. Barzicchini, Personal Interview, 1991.

22. Goldstein, Personal Interview, 1991.

23. John Naisbitt, *Megatrends* (New York: Warner Books, 1982), 260.

24. Berger, Personal Interveiw, 1985.

25. Ralph Keyes, *Chancing It: Why We Take Risks* (Boston: Little, Brown, 1985), 74.

26. Arthur P. Bochner, "Conceptual Frontiers in the Study of Communication in Families: An Introduction to the Literature," *Human Communication Research* 2 (1976): 381–397.

27. Frank E. X. Dance and Carl E. Larson, *The Functions of Human Communication* (New York: Holt, Rinehart and Winston, 1976).

28. S. A. Anderson, as cited in Frank E. X. Dance (1970), "The 'Concept' of Communication," *Journal of Communication* 20 (1959): 201–210.

29. Herbert Blumer, *Symbolic Interactionism: Perspective and Method* (Englewood Cliffs, NJ: Prentice-Hall, 1969), 2.

30. Shaw, Personal Interview, 1987.

31. *USA Today,* 13 April 1987, p. 4D.

32. *USA Today,* 13 April 1987, p. 4D.

33. *USA Today,* 13 April 1987, p. 4D.

34. Jane Howard, *Families* (New York: Berkley Books Simon and Schuster, 1978), 13.

35. George P. Murdock, *Social Structure* (New York: Free Press, 1965), 1.

36. The U.S. Census Bureau, 1980.

37. Klee, Schmidt, and Johnson, 1988–1989.

38. Arthur P. Bochner, "Conceptual Frontiers in the Study of Communication in Families: An Introduction to the Literature," *Human Communication Research* 2 (1976): 381–397.

39. Remy, Personal Interview, 1987.

40. S. L. Silverman and M. G. Silverman, *Theory of Relationships* (New York: Philosophical Library, 1963), xi.

41. Richard Q. Bell, "A Reinterpretation of the Direction of Effects in Studies of Socialization," *Psychological Review* 75 (1968): 81–95.

42. M. Lewis and L. A. Rosenblum, eds., *The Effect of the Infant on Its Caregiver* (New York: Wiley, 1974).

43. A. Adams, *Families and Other Survivors* (New York: Penguin, 1974), 69.

44. Bill Cosby, *Fatherhood* (New York: Berkley, 1986), 38–39.

45. See, for example, Mary W. Hicks, Sally L. Hansen, and Leo A. Christie, "Dual-Career/Dual-Work Families: A Systems Approach," *Contemporary Familes and Alternative Lifestyles*, ed. Eleanor D. Macklin and Roger H. Rubin (Newbury Park, CA: Sage, 1983), 164–179; L. Holstrom, *The Two Career Family* (Cambridge, MA: Schenkman, 1978); Rhona Rapoport and Robert Rapoport, eds., *Working Couples* (New York: Harper & Row, 1978); and Denise A. Skinner, "Dual-Career Family Stress and Coping: A Literature Review," *Family Relations* 29 (1980): 473–481.

46. See, for example, Naomi Gerstel and Harriet Gross, *Commuter Marriage: A Study of Work and Family* (New York: Guilford Press, 1984); and H. E. Gross, "Dual-Career Couples Who Live Apart: Two Types," *Journal of Marriage and the Family* 42 (1980): 567–576.

47. B. Kirschner and L. Wallum, "Two-Location Families: Married Singles," *Alternative Lifestyles* 1 (1978): 513–525.

48. George H. Mead, *Mind, Self, and Society* (Chicago: University of Chicago Press, 1934).

49. Hoey, Personal Interview, 1985.

50. Russell Baker, *Growing Up* (New York: Congdon & Weed, 1982), 14.

51. Dean C. Barnlund, "A Transactional Model of Communication," *Foundations of Communication Theory*, ed. Kenneth K. Sereno and C. David Mortensen (New York: Harper & Row, 1970), 83–107.

52. Erica Jong, *Parachutes and Kisses* (New York: New American Library, 1984), 75.

53. Sandra L. Bem, "The Measurement of Psychological Androgyny," *Journal of Consulting and Clinical Psychology* 42 (1974): 155–162; and Janet T. Spence, Robert Helmrich, and J. Stapp, *Masculinity and Femininity: Their Psychological Dimensions, Correlates and Antecedents* (Austin: University of Texas Press, 1975).

54. Paul Hersey and Kenneth H. Blanchard, *Management of Organizational Behavior: Utilizing Human Sources* (Englewood Cliffs, NJ: Prentice-Hall, 1977), 103–104.

55. J. K. Alberts, "A Descriptive Taxonomy of Couples' Complaint Interactions," *The Southern Communication Journal* 54 (1989): 125–143.

56. Sven Wahlroos, 1983, p. xii.

57. See, for example, Janet Bavelas and Lynn Segal, "Family Systems Theory: Background and Implications," *Journal of Communication* 32 (1982): 99–107; Kathleen M. Galvin and Bernard J. Brommel, *Family Communication: Cohesion*

and Change, 2nd ed. (Glenview, IL: Scott, Foresman, 1986); and David Kantor and William Lehr, *Inside the Family* (San Francisco: Jossey-Bass, 1976).

58. Lillian B. Rubin, *Intimate Strangers: Men and Women Together* (New York: Harper & Row, 1984).

59. Tannen, Personal Interview, 1990.

60. Schmidt, Personal Interview, 1985.

61. Berger, Personal Interview, 1985.

62. Berger, Personal Interview, 1985.

63. Sven Wahlroos, 1983, p. xiii.

64. M. Healy and K. S. Peterson, *USA Today,* 17 April 1987, p. 6D.

65. *USA Today,* 13 April 1987, p. 6D.

66. Jeffry H. Larson, "The Marriage Quiz: College Students' Beliefs in Selected Myths," *Family Relations* 37 (January 1988): 59–60.

CHAPTER 2 NOTES

1. Leigh A. Leslie "The Impact of Adolescent Females' Assessments of Parenthood and Employment on Plans for the Future," *Journal of Youth and Adolescence* 15 (1986): 29–49; Lynn M. Blinn and Tricia McClam, "Undergraduates' Views of Their Family Lives in the Future: Exploring the Influence of Selected Variables," *Family Perspective* 23 (1989): 185–200; and Lynn M. Blinn and Gary Pike, "Future Time Perspective: Adolescents' Predictions of Their Interpersonal Lives in the Future," *Adolescence* 24 (1989): 289–301.

2. Jerald G. Bachman, Lloyd D. Johnston, and Patrick O'Malley, *Monitoring the Future* (Ann Arbor: Institute for Social Research, University of Michigan, 1987).

3. Lynn M. Blinn and Gary Pike, "Future Time Perspective: Adolescents' Predictions of Their Interpersonal Lives in the Future," *Adolescence* 24 (1989): 289–301.

4. Gunhild O. Hagestad, "Demographic Change and the Life Course: Some Emerging Trends in the Family Realm," *Family Relations* 37 (1988): 405–410.

5. Jerrold Footlick, "What Happened to the Family?" *Newsweek* Winter/Spring (special edition, 1990): 8–13.

6. John Scanzoni, "Families in the 1980s: Time to Refocus Our Thinking," *Journal of Family Issues* 8 (1988): 394–421.

7. Mary E. Stovall, "Myths of the American Family: A Historical Perspective," *Family Perspective* 23 (1989): 133–145.

8. Mary E. Stovall, "Myths of the American Family: A Historical Perspective," *Family Perspective* 23 (1989): 133–145.

9. Felix M. Bernardo, "Decade Preview: Some Trends and Directions for Family Research and Theory in the 1980s," *Journal of Marriage and the Family* 42 (1980): 723–728; Felix M. Bernardo "The American Family: A Commentary," *Journal of Family Issues* 8 (1987): 426–428.

10. Felix M. Bernardo, "Trends and Directions in Family Research in the 1980s," *Journal of Marriage and the Family* 52 (1990): 809–817.

11. Miriam E. Berger, "Trial Marriage: Harnessing the Trend Constructively," *The Family Coordinator* 20 (1971): 38–43; and H. Rodman, "Illegitimacy in the

Caribbean Social Structure: A Reconsideration," *American Sociological Review* 31 (1966): 673–683.

12. See, for example, Patricia A. Gwartney-Gibbs, "The Institutionalization of Premarital Cohabitation: Estimates from Marriage License Application, 1970 and 1980," *Journal of Marriage and the Family* 48 (1986): 423–434.

13. U.S. Bureau of the Census, *Current Population Reports: Population Profile of the United States: 1991*, Series p-23, No. 173 (Washington, DC: U.S. Government Printing Office, 1991).

14. M. Sheils, D. Weathers, L. Howard, and R. Givens, "A Portrait of America," *Newsweek* (January 17, 1983): 20–32.

15. Jesse Bernard, "The Good-Provider Role: Its Rise and Fall," *American Psychologist* 36 (1981): 1–12.

16. Eleanor D. Macklin, "Relationships: Nonmarital Heterosexual Cohabitation," *Marriage and Family Review* 1(2) (Spring 1978): 1–12.

17. See, for example, Donald W. Bower and Victor A. Christopherson, "University Student Cohabitation: A Regional Comparison of Selected Attitudes and Behavior," *Journal of Marriage and the Family* 39 (1977): 447–453; and Carl Danziger, "Unmarried Heterosexual Cohabitation," diss., Rutgers University, 1976.

18. Eleanor D. Macklin, "Relationships: Nonmarital Heterosexual Cohabitation," *Marriage and Family Review* 1(2) 1978: 1–12.

19. See, for example, B. McCauley, "Self-Esteem in the Cohabiting Relationship," Thesis, University of Delaware, 1977; and D. J. Peterman, Carl A. Ridley, and Susan M. Anderson, "A Comparison of Cohabiting and Non-Cohabiting College Students," *Journal of Marriage and the Family* 36 (1974): 344–354.

20. Barbara J. Risman, Charles T. Hill, Zick Rubin, and Letitia A. Peplau, "Living Together in College: Implications for Courtship," *Journal of Marriage and the Family* 43 (1981): 77–83.

21. See, for example, Laura F. Henze and John W. Hudson, "Personal and Family Characteristics of Cohabitating and Noncohabitation College Students," *Journal of Marriage and the Family* 36 (1974): 722–726; and Eleanor D. Macklin, "Unmarried Heterosexual Cohabitation on the University Campus," *The Social Psychology of Sex*, ed. Jacqueline P. Wiseman (New York: Harper & Row, 1976), 108–142.

22. Ibtihaj Arafat and Betty Yorburg, "On Living Together Without Marriage," *Journal of Sex Research* 9 (1973): 97–106.

23. Michael D. Newcomb, "Cohabitation, Marriage and Divorce Among Adolescents and Young Adults," *Journal of Social and Personal Relationships* 3 (1986): 473–494.

24. Paul Yelsma, "Marriage vs. Cohabitation: Couples' Communication Practices and Satisfaction," *Journal of Communication* 36 (1986): 94–107.

25. Paul R. Newcomb, "Cohabitation in America: An Assessment of Consequences," *Journal of Marriage and the Family* 41 (1978): 597–603.

26. Kersti Yllo and Murray Strauss, "Interpersonal Violence Among Married and Cohabitating Couples," *Family Relations* 30 (1981): 339–347.

27. Philip Blumstein and Pepper Schwartz, *American Couples* (New York: William Morrow, 1983).

28. Roy E. L. Watson and Peter W. DeMeo, "Premarital Cohabitation vs. Traditional Courtship and Subsequent Marital Adjustment: A Replication and Follow-up," *Family Relations* 36 (1987): 193–197.

29. Alfred DeMaris and Gerald R. Leslie, "Cohabitation with Future Spouse: Its Influence Upon Marital Satisfaction and Communication," *Journal of Marriage and the Family* 46 (1984): 77–84.

30. Alan Booth and David Johnson, "Premarital Cohabitation and Marital Success," *Journal of Family Issues* 9 (1988): 255–272.

31. Daniel Yankelovich, *New Rules: Searching for Self-Fulfillment in a World Turned Upside Down* (New York: Random House, 1981).

32. U.S. Bureau of the Census, "Changes in American Family Life," *Current Population Reports*, Series p-23, No. 163 (Washington, DC: Government Printing Office, 1989).

33. U.S. Bureau of the Census, "Fertility of American Women: June 1986," *Current Population Reports*, Series p-20, No. 421 (Washington, DC: Government Printing Office, 1987).

34. U.S. Bureau of the Census, "Fertility of American Women: June 1976," *Current Population Reports* Series p-20, No. 308 (Washington, DC: Government Printing Office, 1977).

35. U.S. Bureau of the Census "Fertility of American Women: June 1983," *Current Population Reports*, Series p-20, No. 395 (Washington, DC: Government Printing Office, 1984).

36. Arland Thornton and Deborah Freedman, "The Changing American Family," *Population Bulletin* 38 (1983); and U.S. Bureau of the Census, "Fertility of American Women: June 1985," *Current Population Reports* Series p-20, No. 406 (Washington, DC: Government Printing Office, 1986).

37. J. E. Veevers, "Voluntary Childlessness: A Neglected Area of Family Study," *Family Coordinator* 22 (1972): 199–205.

38. George Masnick and Mary J. Bane, *The Nation's Families: 1960–1990* (Boston: Auburn House, 1980).

39. Lisa Kay Rogers and Jeffrey H. Larson, "Voluntary Childlessness: A Review of the Literature and a Model of the Childlessness Decision," *Family Perspective* 22 (1988): 43–56.

40. See, for example, E. E. LeMasters, "Parenthood as Crisis," *Marriage and Family Living* 19 (1957): 352–355; Agnus Campbell, *The Sense of Well-Being in America: Recent Patterns and Trends* (New York: McGraw-Hill, 1981).

41. Erik H. Erikson, *Childhood and Society*, 2nd ed. (New York: Norton, 1963); Talcott Parsons and Robert F. Bales, *Family Socialization and Interaction Process* (Glencoe, IL: Free Press, 1955).

42. Debra Umberson, "Parenting and Well-Being," *Journal of Family Issues* 10 (1989): 428.

43. Debra Umberson, "Parenting and Well-Being," *Journal of Family Issues* 10 (1989): 427–439.

44. Masako Ishii-Kuntz and Karen Seccombe, "The Impact of Children upon Social Support Networks throughout the Life Course," *Journal of Marriage and the Family* 51 (1989): 777–790.

45. Ronald M. Sabatelli, Richarl L. Meth, and Stephen M. Gavazzi, "Factors Mediating the Adjustment to Involuntary Childlessness," *Family Relations* 37 (1988): 338–343.

46. U.S. Bureau of the Census, "Population Profile of the United States: 1991," *Current Population Reports,* Series p-23, No. 173 (Washington, DC: Government Printing Office, 1991).

47. Judith Boswell, "The Dual-Career Family: A Model for Egalitarian Family Politics," *Elementary School Guidance and Counseling* 15 (1981): 262–268.

48. Young, Personal Interview, 1987.

49. Nina Darnton, "Women and Stress on Job and at Home," *New York Times,* August 8, 1985, p. 15.

50. Ellen Rock, *Family Relations* 34 (1985): 505–511.

51. Shirley S. Ricks, "Father-Infant Interactions: A Review of Empirical Research," *Family Relations* 34 (1985): 505–511.

52. See, for example, Lee G. Streetman, "Contrasts in the Self-Esteem of Unwed Teenage Mothers," *Adolescence* 22 (1987): 459–464; and Thomas G. Endres, "Rhetorical Visions of Unmarried Mothers," *Communication Quarterly* 37 (1989): 134–150.

53. Elizabeth A. McGee, *Too Little, Too Late: Services for Teenage Parents* (New York: Ford Foundation, 1982).

54. Reed, Personal Interview, 1987.

55. See, for example, Paul C. Glick, "Fifty Years of Family Demography: A Record of Social Change," *Journal of Marriage and the Family* 50 (1988): 861–873; James A. Norton and Paul C. Glick, "One Parent Families: A Social and Economic Profile," *Family Relations* 35 (1986): 9–17; and Charlene E. Depner and James H. Bray, "Modes of Participation for Noncustodial Parents: The Challenge for Research, Policy, Practice, and Education," *Family Relations* 39 (1990): 378–381.

56. Grief, 1985; Barbara J. Risman and Kyung Park, "Just the Two of Us: Parent-Child Relationships in Single-Parent Homes," *Journal of Marriage and the Family* 50 (1988): 1049–1062.

57. Paula W. Dail, "Can Fathers 'Mother'? The Nurturing Characteristics of Noncustodial, Single-Parent Fathers," *Family Perspective* 23 (1989): 219–231.

58. U.S. Bureau of the Census, *Current Population Reports: Marital Status and Living Arrangements,* Series p-20, No. 389 (Washington, DC: U.S. Government Printing Office, 1984).

59. Richard A. Warshak and John W. Santrock, "The Impact of Divorce in Father-Custody and Mother-Custody Homes: The Child's Perspective," *Children and Divorce,* ed. Lawrence A. Kurdek (San Francisco, CA: Jossey-Bass, 1983), 29–46.

60. M. Roman and W. Haddad, *The Disposable Parent: The Case for Joint Custody* (New York: Holt, Rinehart and Winston, 1978).

61. Robert S. Weiss, "Growing Up a Little Faster: The Experience of Growing Up in a Single-Parent Household," *Journal of Social Issues* 35 (1979): 97–111; and Peggy Quinn and Katherine R. Allen, "Facing Challenges and Making Compromises: How Single Mothers Endure," *Family Relations* 38 (1989): 390–395.

62. T. H. Holmes and R. H. Rahe, "The Social Adjustment Rating Scale," *Journal of Psychosomatic Research* 2 (1967): 213–218.

63. Leslie N. Richards, "The Precarious Survival and Hard-Won Satisfactions of White Single-Parent Families," *Family Relations* 38 (1989): 396–403.

64. Maureen Moore, "Female Lone Parenting over the Life Course," *Canadian Journal of Sociology* 14 (1989): 335–352.

65. U.S. Bureau of the Census, *Current Population Reports: Household and Family Characteristics,* Series p-20, No. 398 (Washington, DC: U.S. Government Printing Office, 1985).

66. U.S. Bureau of the Census, *Current Population Reports: Household and Family Characteristics,* Series p-20, Nos. 191–352 (Washington, DC: U.S. Government Printing Office, 1980).

67. George Masnick and Mary J. Bane, *The Nation's Families: 1960–1990* (Boston: Auburn House, 1980).

68. See, for example, Marjorie H. Cantor, "Strain Among Caregivers: A Study of Experiences in the United States," *Gerontologist* 23 (1983): 23–43; Marilyn Coleman, Lawrence H. Ganong, and Patricia Ellis, "Family Structure and Dating Behavior of Adolescents," *Adolescence* 20 (1985): 537–543.

69. Sadi Bayrakal and Teresa M. Kope, "Dysfunctions in the Single-Parent and Only-Child Family," *Adolescence* 25 (1990): 1–7.

70. Thomas S. Parish, "Evaluations of Family by Youth: Do They Vary as a Function of Family Structure, Gender, and Birth Order?" *Adolescence* 25 (1990): 353–356.

71. Amanda McCombs and Rex Forehand, "Adolescent School Performance Following Parental Divorce: Are There Family Factors That Can Enhance Success?" *Adolescence* 24 (1989): 871–879.

72. Judith S. Wallerstein and Joan B. Kelly, "Effects of Divorce on the Visiting Father-Child Relationships," *American Journal of Psychiatry* 137 (1980): 1534–1539.

73. Judith S. Wallerstein and Joan B. Kelly, "The Effects of Parental Divorce: Experiences of the Child in Later Latency," *American Journal of Orthopsychiatry* 46 (1976): 256–269.

74. Cynthia Longfellow, "Divorce in Context: Its Impact on Children," *Divorce and Separation: Context, Causes, and Consequences,* ed. George Levinger and Oliver C. Moles (New York: Basic Books, 1979), 287–306.

75. Lee G. Burchinal, "Characteristics of Adolescents from Unbroken, Broken and Reconstituted Families," *Journal of Marriage and the Family* 26 (1964): 44–51; J. T. Landis, "A Comparison of Children from Divorced and Nondivorced Unhappy Marriages," *The Family Coordinator* 11 (1960): 61–65; and F. Ivan Nye, "Child Adjustment in Broken and Unbroken Homes," *Journal of Marriage and the Family* 19 (1957): 356–361.

76. J. C. Coleman, *Intimate Relationships, Marriage, and Family* (Indianapolis, IN: Bobbs-Merrill, 1984).

77. Remy, Personal Interview, 1987.

78. Sheldon Glueck and Eleanor Glueck, *Unraveling Juvenile Delinquency* (Cambridge, MA: Harvard University Press, 1950).

79. Ruth A. Brandwein, Carol A. Brown, and Elizabeth M. Fox, "Women and Children Last: The Social Situation of Divorced Mothers and Their Families," *Journal of Marriage and the Family* 36 (1974): 498–514.

80. Stanford M. Dornbusch, J. Merrill Carlsmith, Steven J. Bushwall, Philip L. Ritter, Herbert Leiderman, Albert H. Hastorf, and Ruth T. Gross, "Single Parents, Extending Households, and Control of Adolescents," *Child Development* 56 (1985): 326–341.

81. Urie Bronfenbrenner, "Developmental Research, Public Policy, and the Ecology of Childhood," *Child Development* 45 (1974): 1–5; and Daniel Yankelovich, *New Rules: Searching for Self-Fulfillment in a World Turned Upside Down* (New York: Random House, 1981).

82. Penny L. Burge, "Parental Sex-Role Attitudes Related to Self-Concept and Sex-Role Identity of Pre-School Children," diss., Pennsylvania State University, 1979.

83. Ann Goetting, "The Six Stations of Remarriage: Developmental Tasks of Remarriage after Divorce," *Family Relations* 31 (1982): 213–222.

84. See, for example, S. M. Dornbusch, J. M. Carlsmith, S. J. Bushwall, P. L. Ritter, H. Leiderman, A. H. Hastorf, and R. T. Gross, "Single Parents, Extending Households, and Control of Adolescents," *Child Development* 56 (1985): 326–341.

85. Larry Bumpass, James Sweet, and Teresa Castro Martin, "Changing Patterns of Remarriage," *Journal of Marriage and the Family* 52 (1990): 747–756.

86. Marilyn Coleman and Lawrence H. Ganong, "Remarriage and Stepfamily Research in the 1980s: Increased Interest in an Old Family Form," *Journal of Marriage and the Family* 52 (1990): 925–940; Lawrence H. Ganong and Marilyn Coleman, "Preparing for Remarriage: Anticipating the Issues, Seeking Solutions," *Family Relations* 38 (1989): 28–33.

87. Helen Weingarten, "Remarriage and Well-Being: National Survey Evidence of Social and Psychological Effects," *Journal of Family Issues* 1 (1980): 533–560.

88. Paul C. Glick, "Remarried Families, Stepfamilies, and Stepchildren: A Brief Demographic Profile," *Family Relations* 38 (1989): 24–27.

89. Myron Orleans, Bartolomeo J. Palisi, and David Caddell, "Marriage Adjustment and Satisfaction of Stepfathers: Their Feelings and Perceptions of Decision Making and Stepchildren Relations," *Family Relations* 38 (1989): 371–377.

90. A. Herndon, "Do We Know Enough About the Predominant Family Form of the 21st Century?" *Wake Forest* (August 1982): 36–37.

91. Paul C. Glick, "Remarried Families, Stepfamilies, and Stepchildren: A Brief Demographic Profile," *Family Relations* 38 (1989): 24–27.

92. Paul C. Glick, "Prospective Changes in Marriage, Divorce, and Living Arrangement," *Journal of Family Issues* 33 (1983): 7–26.

93. Paul C. Glick, 1983, 7–26

94. Elizabeth Vemer, Marilyn Coleman, Lawrence H. Ganong, and Harris Cooper, "Marital Satisfaction in Remarriage: A Meta-analysis," *Journal of Marriage and the Family* 51 (1989): 713–725.

95. Ester Wald, *The Remarried Family* (New York: Family Service Association of America, 1981).

96. Kathleen M. Galvin and Bernard J. Brommel, *Family Communication: Cohesion and Change,* 2nd ed. (Glenview, IL: Scott, Foresman, 1986), 247–248.

97. Kathleen M. Galvin and Bernard J. Brommel, *Family Communication: Cohesion and Change,* 2nd ed. (Glenview, IL: Scott, Foresman, 1986), 247–248; John S. Visher and Emily B. Visher, "Stepfamilies and Stepparenting," *Normal Family Processes,* ed. Froma Walsh (New York: Guilford Press, 1982), 331–353; E. Einstein, "Stepfamily: Chaotic, Complex, Challenging," *Stepfamily Bulletin* 1 (1982): 1–2; and David Mills, "A Model for Stepfamily Development," *Family Relations* 33 (1984): 365–372.

98. See, for example, Judith A. Seltzer, "Relationships between Fathers and Children Who Live Apart: The Father's Role after Separation," *Journal of Marriage and the Family* 53 (1991): 79–101.

99. Remy, Personal Interview, 1987.

100. See, for example, James H. Bray and Sandra H. Berger, "Noncustodial Father and Paternal Grandparent Relationships in Stepfamilies," *Family Relations* 39 (1990): 414–419.

101. See, for example, Judith A. Seltzer, "Relationships between Fathers and Children Who Live Apart: The Father's Role after Separation," *Journal of Marriage and the Family* 53 (1991): 79–101.

102. John Visher and Emily Visher, "Stepfamilies and Stepparenting," *Normal Family Processes*, ed. F. Walsh (New York: Guilford Press, 1982), 331–353.

103. See, for example, Andrew Cherlin, "Remarriage as an Incomplete Institution," *American Journal of Sociology* 86 (1978); Esther Wald, *The Remarried Family* (New York: Family Service Association of America, 1981); and Lynn White and Alan Booth, "The Quality and Stability of Remarriages: The Role of Stepchildren," *American Sociological Review* (1985): 689–698.

104. Frank F. Furstenberg, Jr., and Graham B. Spanier, "The Risk of Dissolution in Remarriage: An Examination of Cherlin's Hypothesis of Incomplete Institutionalization," *Family Relations* 33 (1984): 433–441.

105. Lawrence H. Ganong and Marilyn Coleman, "Do Mutual Children Cement Bonds in Stepfamilies?" *Journal of Marriage and the Family* 50 (1988): 687–698.

106. Charles W. Hobart, "Perception of Parent-Child Relationships in First Married and Remarried Families," *Family Relations* 37 (1988): 175–182.

107. Lawrence A. Kurdek, "Effects of Child Age on the Marital Quality and Psychological Distress of Newly Married Mothers and Stepfathers," *Journal of Marriage and the Family* 52 (1990): 81–85.

108. Kenneth N. Cissna, Dennis E. Cox, and Arthur H. Bochner, "The Dialectic of Marital and Parental Relationships Within the Stepfamily," *Communication Monographs* 57 (1990): 44–61.

109. See, for example, Myron Orleans, Bartolomeo J. Palisi, and David Caddell, "Marriage Adjustment and Satisfaction of Stepfathers: Their Feelings and Perceptions of Decision Making and Stepchildren Relations," *Family Relations* 38 (1989): 371–377.

110. Lawrence A. Kurdek, "Relationship Quality for Newly Married Husbands and Wives: Marital History, Stepchildren, and Individual-Difference Predictors," *Journal of Marriage and the Family* 51 (1989): 1053–1064.

111. Mark A. Fine, Brenda Donnelly, and Patricia Voydanoff, "The Relationship Between Cognition and Maternal Satisfaction in Stepfather Families," *Family Perspective* 25 (1991): 19–25; and Lawrence A. Kurdek, "Relationship Quality for Newly Married Husbands and Wives: Marital History, Stepchildren, and Individual-Difference Predictors," *Journal of Marriage and the Family* 51 (1989): 1053–1064.

112. Frank F. Furstenberg, "Reflections on Remarriage," *Journal of Family Issues* 1 (1980): 4.

113. Daniel Yankelovich, *New Rules: Searching for Self-Fulfillment in a World Turned Upside Down* (New York: Random House, 1981).

114. See, for example, Sandra S. Tangri and Sharon R. Jenkins, "Stability and Change in Role Innovation and Life Plans," *Sex Roles* 14 (1986): 647–662.

115. U.S. Department of Labor, *Time of Change: 1983 Handbook on Women Workers* (Washington, DC: U.S. Government Printing Office, 1983).

116. U.S. Department of Labor, *Time of Change: 1983 Handbook on Women Workers* (Washington, DC: U.S. Government Printing Office, 1983).

117. U.S. Department of Labor, *Time of Change: 1983 Handbook on Women Workers* (Washington, DC: U.S. Government Printing Office, 1983).

118. Maureen Perry-Jenkins, "Future Directions for Research on Dual-Earner Families: A Young Professional's Perspective," *Family Relations* 37 (1988): 226–228.

119. Smith, Personal Interview, 1987.

120. See, for example, Stephen A. Small and Dave Riley, "Toward a Multidimensional Assessment of Work Spillover into Family Life," *Journal of Marriage and the Family* 52 (1990): 51–61.

121. See, for example, H. Mederer and R. Hill, "Cultural Transitions Over the Family Life Span: Theory and Research," *Social Stress and the Family*, ed. Charles R. Figley and Hamilton McCubbin et al. (New York: Hayworth Press, 1983), 39–60.

122. "More Women Working, Pay Trails, Study Finds," *The Wall Street Journal*, 20 June 1985, p. 24.

123. A. C. Bebbington, "The Function of Stress in the Establishment of the Dual-Career Family," *Journal of Marriage and the Family* 35 (1973): 530–537.

124. Robin A. Deutsch, "Sex-Linked Role Behavior: Philosophical Orientation, and Coping Styles in Three Marital Groups," diss., University of California, Berkeley, 1978.

125. Joseph P. Stokes and Judith S. Peyton, "Attitudinal Differences Between Full-Time Homemakers and Women Who Work Outside the Home," *Sex Roles* 15 (1986): 299–310.

126. Robin A. Deutsch, "Sex-Linked Role Behavior: Philosophical Orientation, and Coping Styles in Three Marital Groups," diss., University of California, Berkeley, 1978.

127. Constantina Safilios-Rothschild, "The Study of Family Power Structure: A Review of 1960–1969," *Journal of Marriage and the Family* 32 (1970): 539–552.

128. Sara Yogev and Jeanne M. Brett, "Professional Couples and Money," *Family Perspective* 23 (1989): 31–38.

129. James H. Russell, "Need for Achievement Across Three Career Patterns of College Educated Mothers Compared with Participation in Marital Decision-Making and Their Husband's Performance of Domestic Activities," diss., Ohio State University, 1975.

130. Marjorie Shaevitz and Morton Shaevitz, *Making it Together as a Two-Career Couple* (Boston: Houghton Mifflin, 1980).

131. David G. Rice, *Dual-Career Marriage: Conflict and Treatment* (New York: Macmillan, 1979).

132. William W. Philliber and Dana Vannoy-Hiller, "The Effect of Husband's Occupational Attainment on Wife's Achievement," *Journal of Marriage and the Family* 52 (1990): 323–329.

133. Caroline Bird, *The Two-Paycheck Marriage* (New York: Rawson Wade, 1979).

134. Theodore N. Greenstein, "Marital Disruption and the Employment of Married Women," *Journal of Marriage and the Family* 52 (1990): 657–676.

135. Frederick R. Ford, "Rules: The Visible Family," *Family Process* 22 (1983): 135–145.

136. Reed, Personal Interview, 1987.

137. Patrick K. Knaub, "Growing Up in a Dual-Career Family: The Children's Perceptions," *Family Relations* 35 (1986): 431–437.

138. Mary Holland Benin and Debra A. Edwards, "Adolescents' Chores: The Difference Between Dual- and Single-Earner Families," *Journal of Marriage and the Family* 52 (1990): 361–373.

139. Ronald C. Kessler and James A. McRae, Jr., "The Effect of Wives' Employment on the Mental Health of Married Men and Women," *American Sociological Review* 47 (1982): 216–227.

140. Ronald J. Burke and Tamara Weir, "Some Personality Differences Between Members of One-Career and Two-Career Families," *Journal of Marriage and the Family* 38 (1976): 453–459.

141. Jeanne Maracek and Deborah J. Ballou, "Family Roles and Women's Mental Health," *Professional Psychology* 12 (1981): 39–46.

142. See, for example, D. St. John-Parsons, "Continuous Dual Career Families: A Case Study," *Psychology of Women Quarterly* 3 (1978): 30–42; Colleen L. Johnson and Frank A. Johnson, "Attitudes Toward Parenting in Dual Career Families," *American Journal of Psychiatry* 134 (1977): 391–395; Mary J. Rotheram and Neil Weiner, "Androgyny, Stress, and Satisfaction: Dual Career and Traditional Relationships," *Sex Roles* 9 (1983): 151–158; and Priscilla White, Alison Mascalo, Sandra Thomas, and Sandra Shoun, "Husbands' and Wives' Perceptions of Marital Intimacy and Wives' Stresses in Dual-Career Marriages," *Family Perspective* 20 (1986): 27–35.

143. See, for example, Maureen G. Guelzow, Gloria W. Bird, and Elizabeth H. Koball, "An Exploratory Path Analysis of the Stress Process for Dual-Career Men and Women," *Journal of Marriage and the Family* 53 (1991): 151–164.

144. Vicki C. Rachlin, "Fair vs. Equal Role Relations in Dual-Career and Dual-Earner Families: Implications for Family Interventions," *Family Relations* 36 (1987): 187–192; Marjorie Shaevitz and Morton Shaevitz, *Making it Together as a Two-Career Couple* (Boston: Houghton Mifflin, 1980); and Sara Yogev, "Happiness in Dual-Career Couples: Changing Research, Changing Values," *Sex Roles* 8 (1982): 593–605.

145. Joseph Pleck and Michael Rustad, *Husbands' and Wives' Time in Family Work and Paid Work in the 1975–1976 Study of Time Use* (Wellesley, MA: Wellesley College Research Center on Women, 1980).

146. Constantina Safilios-Rothschild, "The Study of Family Power Structure: A Review of 1960–1969," *Journal of Marriage and the Family* 32 (1970): 539–552; Margaret Poloma and T. Neal Garland, "The Married Professional Woman: A Study in the Tolerance of Domestication," *Journal of Marriage and the Family* 33 (1971): 531–540; and Rebecca Bryson, Jeff B. Bryson, and Marilyn F. Johnson, "Family Size, Satisfaction, and Productivity in Dual-Career Couples," *Psychology of Women Quarterly* 3 (1978): 67–77.

147. J. Spiegel, *Transaction: The Interplay Between Individual, Family, and Society* (New York: Science House, 1971).

148. Lucia A. Gilbert, Carole K. Holahan, and Linda Manning, "Coping With Conflict Between Professional and Maternal Roles," *Family Relations* 30 (1981): 419–426.

149. Ellen Greenberger and Robin O'Neil, "Parents' Concerns about Their Child's Development: Implications for Fathers' and Mothers' Well-being and Attitudes toward Work," *Journal of Marriage and the Family* 52 (1990): 621–635.

150. B. M. Campbell, "Backlash in the Bedroom," *Savvy* 6 (1985): 56–60.

151. Daniel Yankelovich, *New Rules: Searching for Self-Fulfillment in a World Turned Upside Down* (New York: Random House, 1981).

152. A. Regula Herzog, Jerold G. Bachman, and Lloyd D. Johnston, "Paid Work, Child-Care, and Housework: A National Survey of High School Seniors' Preferences for Sharing Responsibilities Between Husband and Wife," *Sex Roles* 9 (1983): 109–135.

153. Georgia Dullea, "Enough Is Enough for Ex-Superwoman," *New York Times,* 15 November 1985, p. I20.

154. Bruce Lansky, *Mother Murphy's Second Law: Love, Sex, Marriage, and Other Disasters* (New York: Simon & Schuster, 1986), 4.

155. Working Family Project, "Parenting," *Working Couples,* ed. Rhona Rapoport and Robert Rapoport (New York: Harper & Row, 1978), 74–88.

156. Samuel Osherson and Diana Dill, "Varying Work and Family Choices: Their Impact on Men's Work Satisfaction," *Journal of Marriage and the Family* 45 (1983): 339–346.

157. See, for example, Maureen G. Guelzow, Gloria W. Bird, and Elizabeth H. Koball, "An Exploratory Path Analysis of the Stress Process for Dual-Career Men and Women," *Journal of Marriage and the Family* 53 (1991): 151–164.

158. A. Regula Herzog, Jerold G. Bachman, and Lloyd D. Johnston, "Paid Work, Child-Care, and Housework: A National Survey of High School Seniors' Preferences for Sharing Responsibilities Between Husband and Wife," *Sex Roles* 9 (1983): 109–135.

159. Ronald C. Kessler and James A. McRae, Jr., "The Effect of Wives' Employment on the Mental Health of Married Men and Women," *American Sociological Review* 47 (1982): 216–227.

160. B. Dale and J. Dale, *The Working Woman Book: Or, How to Be Everything to Everyone* (New York: Andrews, McMeel & Parker, 1985), 52.

161. Bruce Lansky, *Mother Murphy's Second Law: Love, Sex, Marriage, and Other Disasters* (New York: Simon & Schuster, 1986), 6.

162. Ronald J. Burke and Tamara Weir, "Some Personality Differences Between Members of One-Career and Two-Career Families," *Journal of Marriage and the Family* 38 (1976): 453–458.

163. Catalyst, *Corporations and Two-Career Families: Directions for the Future* (New York: Catalyst, 1982).

164. Mary J. Rotheram and Neil Weiner, "Androgyny, Stress, and Satisfaction: Dual Career and Traditional Relationships," *Sex Roles* 9 (1983): 151–158.165. Rhona N. Rapoport and Robert Rapoport, *Dual-Career Families* (Hardmondsworth, UK: Penguin, 1971).

165. Rhona N. Rapoport and Robert Rapoport, Dual-Career Families

(Hatmondsworth, U.K: Penguin, 1971).

166. F. Hall and D. Hall, *Two-Career Couples* (Reading, MA: Addison-Wesley, 1979).

167. Andree Brooks, "At Work: Problems of Couples," *New York Times,* 17 June 1985, p. C13.

168. Carl A. Ridley, "Exploring the Impact of Work Satisfaction and Involvement on Marital Interaction When Both Partners Are Employed," *Journal of Marriage and the Family* 35 (1973): 229–237.

169. Sara Yogev, "Marital Satisfaction and Sex Role Perceptions Among Dual-Earner Couples," *Journal of Social and Personal Relationships* 4 (1987): 35–45.

170. Sarah A. Hardesty and Nancy E. Betz, "The Relationships of Career Salience, Attitudes Toward Women, and the Demographic and Family Characteristics to Marital Adjustment in Dual-Career Couples," *Journal of Vocational Behavior* 17 (1980): 242–250; and Sara Yogev, "Happiness in Dual-Career Couples: Changing Research, Changing Values," *Sex Roles* 8 (1982): 593–605.

171. Sara Yogev, "Marital Satisfaction and Sex Role Perceptions Among Dual-Earner Couples," *Journal of Social and Personal Relationships* 4 (1987): 35-45.

172. Jane Hopkins and Priscilla White, "The Dual-Career Couple: Constraints and Supports," *Family Coordinator* 27 (1978): 253–259.

173. Sara Yogev, "Happiness in Dual-Career Couples: Changing Research, Changing Values," *Sex Roles* 8 (1982): 593–605.

174. David G. Rice, *Dual-Career Marriage: Conflict and Treatment* (New York: Macmillan, 1979).

175. Helen S. Farmer, "Career and Homemaking Plans for High School Youth," *Journal of Counseling Psychology* 30 (1983): 40–45.

176. Leigh A. Leslie, "Stress in the Dual-Income Couple: Do Social Relationships Help or Hinder?" *Journal of Social and Personal Relationships* 6 (1989): 451–461.

177. Maureen H. Schnittger and Gloria W. Bird, "Coping Among Dual-Career Men and Women Across the Family Life Cycle," *Family Relations* 39 (1990): 199–205.

178. Leigh A. Leslie, "Stress in the Dual-Income Couple: Do Social Relationships Help or Hinder?" *Journal of Social and Personal Relationships* 6 (1989): 451–461.

179. Letty Cottin Pogrebin, "Can Women Really Have It All?" *Ms.* 6 (1978): 47–50.

180. C. L. Johnson and F. A. Johnson, "Attitudes Toward Parenting in Dual Career Families," *American Journal of Psychiatry* 134 (1977): 391–395.

181. Mary F. Maples, "Dual-Career Marriages: Elements for Potential Success," *Personnel and Guidance Journal* 60 (1981): 19–23.

182. Andree Brooks, "At Work: Problems of Couples," *New York Times,* 17 June 1985, p. C13.

183. Rhona N. Rapoport and Robert Rapoport, *Dual-Career Families* (Hardmondsworth, UK: Penguin, 1971).

184. See, for example, Diane Heacock and Christopher H. Spicer, "Communication and the Dual-Career: A Literature Assessment," *The Southern Speech Communication Journal* 51 (1986): 260–266; Dorothy L. Krueger, "Communication Patterns and Egalitarian Decision-Making in Dual-Career Couples," *The Western Journal of Speech Communication* 49 (1985): 126–145; Lawrence B. Rosenfeld and Sharon M. Welsh, "Differences in Self-Disclosure in Dual-Career and Single-Career Marriages," *Communication Monographs* 52

(1985): 253–263; Christopher H. Spicer, "Careers and Relationships: The Interpersonal Intricacies of Maintaining a Dual-Career Relationship," *The Southern Speech Communication Journal* 51 (1986): 256–259; and Julia T. Wood, "Maintaining Dual-Career Bonds: Communicative Dimensions of Internally Structured Relationships," *The Southern Speech Communication Journal* 51 (1986): 267–273.

185. Arthur P. Bochner, "Conceptual Frontiers in the Study of Communication in Families: An Introduction to the Literature," *Human Communication Research* 2 (1976): 381–397; and D. Heacock and Christopher H. Spicer, "Communication and the Dual-Career: A Literature Assessment," *The Southern Speech Communication Journal* 51 (1986): 260–266.

186. Julia T. Wood, "Maintaining Dual-Career Bonds: Communicative Dimensions of Internally Structured Relationships," *The Southern Speech Communication Journal* 51 (1986): 267.

187. T. H. Brubaker, *Later Life Families* (Beverly Hills, CA: Sage, 1985); and Thomas E. Denham and Craig W. Smith, "The Influence of Grandparents on Grandchildren: A Review of the Literature and Resources," *Family Relations* 38 (1989): 345–350.

188. Eileen M. Crimmins and Dominique G. Ingegreri, "Interaction and Living Arrangements of Older Parents and Their Children: Past Trends, Present Determinants, Future Implications," *Research on Aging* 12 (1990): 3–35.

189. U.S. Bureau of the Census, *Current Population Reports: Marital Status and Living Arrangements*, Series p-20, No. 389 (Washington, DC: U.S. Government Printing Office, 1984).

190. Jennifer B. Hull, "Women Find Parents Need Them Just When Careers are Resuming," *Wall Street Journal*, 9 September 1985, p. 23.

191. Shaw, Personal Interview, 1987.

192. Wayne C. Seelbach, "Gender Differences in Expectations for Filial Responsibility," *The Gerontologist* 17 (1978): 421–424; and Rosemary Blieszner and Jay A. Mancini, "Enduring Ties: Older Adults' Parental Role and Responsibilities," *Family Relations* 36 (1987): 176–180.

193. Bert Adams, *Kinship in an Urban Setting* (Chicago: Markham, 1968); and Nancy J. Finley, Diane M. Roberts, and Benjamin F. Banahan III, "Motivators and Inhibitors of Attitudes of Filial Obligation Toward Aging Parents," *The Gerontologist* 28 (1988): 73–78.

194. Victor W. Marshall, Carolyn J. Rosenthal, and Jane Synge, "Concerns About Parental Health," *Older Women*, ed. Elizabeth W. Markson (Lexington, MA: D.C. Heath, 1983), 253–273.

195. Alexis J. Walker, Hwa-Yong Shin, and David N. Bird, "Perceptions of Relationship Change and Caregiver Satisfaction," *Family Relations* 39 (1990): 147–152.

196. Alexis J. Walker and Linda Thompson, "Intimacy and Intergenerational Aid and Contact Among Mothers and Daughters," *Journal of Marriage and the Family* 43 (1983): 841–849.

197. Alexis J. Walker, Clara C. Pratt, Hwa-Yong Shin, and Laura L. Jones, "Motives for Parental Caregiving and Relationship Quality," *Family Relations* 39 (1990): 51–56.

198. Alexis J. Walker, Hwa-Yong Shin, and David N. Bird, "Perceptions of Relationship Change and Caregiver Satisfaction," *Family Relations* 39 (1990): 147–152.

199. Nancy W. Sheehan and Paul Nuttall, "Conflict, Emotion, and Personal Strain Among Family Caregivers," *Family Relations* 37 (1988): 92–98.

200. See, for example, William S. Aquilino, "The Likelihood of Parent-Adult Child Coresidence: Effects of Family Structure and Parental Characteristics," *Journal of Marriage and the Family* 52 (1990): 405–419.

201. Andree Brooks, "Staying On At Home of Parents," *New York Times,* 4 November 1985, p. B11.

202. J. Jill Suitor and Karl Pillemer, "Explaining Intergenerational Conflict When Adult Children and Elderly Parents Live Together," *Journal of Marriage and the Family* 50 (1988): 1037–1047.

203. Robert Strom and Shirley Strom, "Grandparents and Learning," *International Journal of Aging and Human Development* 29 (1989): 163–169.

204. David Nee, "The Intergenerational Movement: A Social Imperative," *Journal of Children in Contemporary Society* 20 (1989): 3–4.

205. John Naisbitt, *Megatrends* (New York: Warner, 1984), 283.

CHAPTER 3 NOTES

1. See, for example, Erving Goffman, *The Presentation of Self in Everyday Life* (New York: Doubleday, Anchor, 1959); Anselm Leonard Strauss, *Mirrors and Masks: The Search For Identity* (Glencoe, IL: Free Press, 1959).

2. Mead, Personal Interview, 1987.

3. See, for example, Alfred B. Heilbrun, "Measurement of Masculine and Feminine Sex Role Identities as Independent Dimensions," *Journal of Consulting and Clinical Psychology* 44 (1976): 183–190.

4. Sandra L. Bem, "The Measurement of Psychological Androgyny," *Journal of Consulting and Clinical Psychology* 42 (1974): 155–162.

5. Nathan B. Epstein, Duane S. Bishop, and Sol Levin, "The McMaster Model of Family Functioning," *Journal of Marriage and Family Counseling* 4 (1978): 19–31.

6. Nathan B. Epstein, Duane S. Bishop, and Lawrence M. Baldwin, "The McMaster Model of Family Functioning," *Journal of Marriage and Family Counseling* 4 (1982): 19–31; Nathan B. Epstein, Duane S. Bishop, and Lawrence M. Baldwin, "The McMaster Model of Family Functioning," *Normal Family Processes,* ed. Froma Walsh (New York: Guilford Press, 1982), 124.

7. Craig L. Israelson, "Family Resource Management," *Family Perspective,* 23 (1989): 311–331.

8. Kathryn M. Krogh, "Women's Motives to Achieve and to Nurture in Different Life Stages," *Sex Roles* 12 (1985): 75–90; and Drake S. Smith, "Wife Employment and Marital Adjustment: A Cumulation of Results," *Family Relations* 34 (1985): 483–490.

9. Young, Personal Interview, 1987.

10. Louise V. Burroughs, Barbara F. Turner, and Castellano B. Turner, "Careers, Contingencies, and Locus of Control Among White College Women," *Sex Roles* 11 (1984): 289–302.

11. Smith, 1985, 483–490.

12. Mary K. Biaggio, Philip J. Mohan, and Cynthia Baldwin, "Relationships Among Attitudes Toward Children, Women's Liberation, and Personality Characteristics," *Sex Roles* 12 (1985): 47–62; and Larry C. Jensen, Robert Christensen, and Diana J. Wilson, "Predicting Young Women's Role Preference for Parenting Work," *Sex Roles* 13 (1985): 507–514.

13. Krogh, 1985, 75–90.

14. Jones, Personal Interview, 1985.

15. Smith, Personal Interview, 1987.

16. Claire Etaugh and Barbara Petroski, "Perceptions of Women: Effects of Employment Status and Marital Status," *Sex Roles* 12 (1985): 329–339.

17. Arthur P. Bochner, Dorothy L. Krueger, and Terrence L. Chmielewski, "Interpersonal Perceptions and Marital Adjustment," *Journal of Communication* 32 (1982): 135–147.

18. George Levinger, "Marital Cohesiveness and Dissolution: An Integrative Review," *Journal of Marriage and the Family* 27 (1965): 19–28; John E. O'Brien, "Violence in Divorce Prone Families," *Journal of Marriage and the Family* 33 (1971): 692–698.

19. Carla R. Dersch and Judy C. Pearson, "Interpersonal Communication Competence and Marital Adjustment Among Dual Career and Dual Worker Women," paper presented to the Annual Meeting of the Central States Speech Association Convention, Cincinnati, Ohio, April 1986; and W. W. Philliber and D. V. Hiller, "A Research Note: Occupational Attainments and Perceptions of Status Among Working Wives," *Journal of Marriage and the Family* 41 (1979): 59–62.

20. Mary Holland Benin and Barbara Cable Nienstedt, "Happiness in Single- and Dual-Earner Families: The Effects of Marital Happiness, Job Satisfaction, and Life Cycle," *Journal of Marriage and the Family* 47 (1985): 975–984; and David L. Gaesser and Susan Krauss Whitbourne, "Work Identity and Marital Adjustment in Blue-Collar Men," *Journal of Marriage and the Family* 47 (1985): 747–751.

21. Judith E. Blakemore, "Interaction with a Baby by Young Adults: A Comparison of Traditional and Feminist Men and Women," *Sex Roles* 13 (1985): 405–411; Elizabeth Maret and Barbara Finlay, "The Distribution of Household Labor Among Women in Dual-Earner Families," *Journal of Marriage and the Family* 46 (1984): 357–364; and Stephen Mugford and Dorothy B. Darroch, "Marital Status and Female Achievement in Australia: A Research Note," *Journal of Marriage and the Family* 42 (1980): 563–656.

22. Margaret Mietus Sanik, "Division of Household Work: A Decade of Comparison—1967–1977," *Home Economics Research Journal* 10 (1981): 175–180.

23. Mohamed Abdel-Ghany and Sharon Y. Nickols, "Husband/Wife Differentials in Household Work Time: The Case of Dual-Earner Families," *Home Economics Research Journal* 12 (1983): 159–167; Craig L. Israelsen, "Family Resource Management," *Family Perspective* 23 (1989): 311–326.

24. J. R. Blaylock and D. M. Smallwood, "Intrahousehold Time Allocation: The Case of Grocery Shopping," *Journal of Consumer Affairs* 21 (1987): 183–201.

25. Sharon Y. Nickols and Mohamed Abdel-Ghany, "Leisure Time of Husbands and Wives," *Home Economic Research Journal* 7 (1983): 85–97.

26. Israelsen, 1989, 311–326.

27. Remy, Personal Interview, 1987.

28. French, 1987, 76.

29. Israelsen, 1989, 311–326.

30. Kretch, Personal Interview, 1987.

31. Poussaint in Cosby, 1986, 9.

32. Reed, Personal Interview, 1987.

33. Gloria W. Bird, Gerald A. Bird, and Marguerite Scruggs, "Determinants of Family Task Sharing: A Study of Husbands and Wives," *Journal of Marriage and Family* 46 (1984): 345–355; Susan Bram, "Voluntarily Childless Women: Traditional or Nontraditional," *Sex Roles* 10 (1984): 195–206; F. Ivan Nye, *Role Structure and Analysis of the Family* (Newbury Park, CA: Sage, 1976); John H. Scanzoni, *Sex Roles, Women's Work, and Marital Conflict: A Study of Family Change* (Lexington, MA: Lexington Books, 1978); and John H. Scanzoni and Greer L. Fox, "Sex Roles, Family and Society: The Seventies and Beyond," *Journal of Marriage and the Family* 42 (1980): 20–33.

34. Bram, 1984, 195–206.

35. Glenna D. Spitze and Linda J. Waite, "Wives' Employment: The Role of Husbands' Perceived Attitudes," *Journal of Marriage and the Family* 43 (1981): 117–124.

36. See, for example, Carolyn C. Perrucci, Harry R. Potter, and Deborah L. Rhoads, "Determinants of Male Family-Role Performance," *Dual Career Couples*, ed. Jeff B. Bryson and Rebecca Bryson (New York: Human Services Press, 1978); John H. Scanzoni, *Sex Roles*, 1978; and Rebecca Stafford, Elaine Backman, and Pamela Dibona, "The Division of Labor Among Cohabiting and Married Couples," *Journal of Marriage and the Family* 39 (1977): 43–57.

37. Bassof, 1974.

38. John D. Adler and Russell L. Boxley, "The Psychological Reactions to Infertility: Sex Roles and Coping Styles," *Sex Roles* 12 (1985): 271–279.

39. Richard A. Berk and Sarah Fenstermaker Berk, *Labor and Leisure at Home: Content and Organization of the Household Day* (Newbury Park, CA: Sage, 1979); Judith E. Blakemore, 1985, 405–411.

40. Donna Hodgkins Berardo, Constance L. Shehan, and Gerald R. Leslie, "A Residue of Tradition: Jobs, Careers and Spouses Time in Housework," *Journal of Marriage and the Family* 49 (1987): 381–390.

41. See, for example, Robert O. Blood and Donald M. Wolfe, *Husbands and Wives: The Dynamics of Married Living* (New York: Free Press, 1960); Elizabeth Marat and Barbara Finlay, "The Distribution of Household Labor Among Women in Dual-Earner Families," *Journal of Marriage and the Family* 46 (1984): 357–364; and K. E. Walker, *Time-Use Patterns For Household Work Related to Homemaker's Employment*, Paper presented at the Agricultural Outlook Conference, Washington, DC, 1970.

42. Maret and Finlay, 1984, 357–364.

43. Zecchio, Personal Interview, 1985.

44. See, for example, L. Bailyn, "Career and Family Orientations of Husbands and Wives in Relation to Marital Happiness," *Human Relations* 23 (1970): 97–113; and Rosabeth Moss Kanter, *Men and Women of the Corporation* (New York: Basic Books, 1977).

45. See, for example, John P. Robinson, *How Americans Use Time: A Social-Psychological Analysis* (New York: Praeger, 1977); Richard A. Berk and Sarah Fenstermaker Berk, *Labor and Leisure At Home: Content and Organization of the Household Day* (Newbury Park, CA: Sage, 1979); and Joseph H. Pleck, "Men's Family Work: Three Perspectives and Some New Data," *Family Coordinator* 28 (1979): 481–488.

46. See, for example, Carolyn C. Perrucci, Harry R. Potter, and Deborah L. Rhoades, "Determinants of Male Family-Role Performance," *Dual Career Couples,* ed. Jeff B. Bryson and Rebecca Bryson (New York: Human Services Press, 1978); and John H. Scanzoni, "Contemporary Marriage Types: A Research Note," *Journal of Family Issues* 1 (1980): 125–140.

47. See, for example, Blood and Wolfe, *Husbands and Wives,* 1960; and Sharon Y. Nickols and Edward J. Metzen, "Household Time For Husband and Wife," *Home Economics Research Journal* 1 (1978): 85–97.

48. S. Model, "Housework By Husbands," *Journal of Family Issues* 2 (1981): 225–237.

49. Strickmaker, Personal Interview, 1987.

50. Bird, Bird, and Scruggs, 1984, 345–355.

51. Lalit K. Masih, "Career Saliency and Its Relation to Certain Needs, Interests, and Job Values," *Journal of Personnel and Guidance* 45 (1967): 653–658.

52. Bailyn, 1970, 97–113.

53. Kanter, *Men and Women,* 1977.

54. Rhona Rapoport and Robert Rapoport, *Dual-Career Families* (Hardmondsworth, UK: Penguin, 1971); Rhona Rapoport and Robert Rapoport, *Dual-Career Families Reexamined: New Integrations of Work and Family* (New York: Harper & Row, 1976).

55. Bird, Bird, and Scruggs, 1984, 345–355.

56. Bird, Bird, and Scruggs, 1984, 345–355; Cynthia Rexroat and Constance Shehan, "The Family Life Cycle and Spouses' Time In Housework," *Journal of Marriage and the Family* 49 (1987): 737–750.

57. See, for example, Michael P. Johnson and Robert M. Milardo, "Network Interference in Pair Relationships: A Social Psychological Recasting of Slater's Theory of Social Regression," *Journal of Marriage and the Family* 46 (1984): 893–899.

58. Jay Belsky and Michael Rovine, "Patterns of Marital Change Across the Transition to Parenthood: Pregnancy to Three Years Postpartum," *Journal of Marriage and the Family* 52 (1984): 5–19; and Thomas G. Power and Ross D. Parke, "Social Network Factors and the Transition to Parenthood," *Sex Roles* 10 (1984): 949–972.

59. Johnson and Milardo, 1984, 893–899; and Leigh A. Leslie and Katherine Grady, "Changes in Mothers' Social Networks and Social Support Following Divorce," *Journal of Marriage and the Family* 47 (1985): 663–673.

60. John M. Gottman, "Emotional Responsiveness in Marital Conversations," *Journal of Communication* 32 (1982): 108–120.

61. Mary Anne Fitzpatrick and Julie Indvik, "Implicit Theories in Enduring Relationships: Psychological Gender Differences in One's Mate," *The Western Journal of Speech Communication* 46 (1982): 311–325; Mary Anne Fitzpatrick and Julie Indvik, "The Instrumental and Expressive Domains of Marital Communication," *Human Communication Research* 8 (1982): 195–213.

62. See, for example, Howard A. Moss, "Sex, Age, and State as Determinants of Mother-Infant Interaction," *Readings in Child Development and Personality*, ed. Paul Henry Mussen, John Janeway Conger, and Jerome Kagan (New York: Harper & Row, 1970), 177–187; and Nancy J. Bell and William Carver, "A Reevaluation of Gender Label Effects: Expectant Mothers' Responses to Infants," *Child Development* 51 (1980): 925–927.

63. Beverly I. Fagot, "A Cautionary Note: Parents' Socialization of Boys and Girls," *Sex Roles* 12 (1985): 471–476.

64. Epstein et al., 1982a; 1982b, 124.

65. Deborah Frank and Anne Maass, "Relationship Factors as Predictors of Causal Attributions about Sexual Experiences," *Sex Roles* 12 (1985): 697–711; and William R. Cupach and Jamie Comstock, "Satisfaction with Sexual Communication in Marriage: Links to Sexual Satisfaction and Dyadic Adjustment," *Journal of Social and Personal Relationships* 7 (1990): 179–186.

66. Juliet Bussey Swieczkowski and Eugene C. Walker, "Sexual Behavior Correlates of Female Orgasm and Marital Happiness," *Journal of Nervous and Mental Disease* 166 (1978): 335–342.

67. Carole S. Kirkpatrick, "Sex Roles and Sexual Satisfaction in Women," *Psychology of Women Quarterly* 4 (1980): 444–459.

68. Sanford A. Weinstein and Gloria Goebel, "The Relationship Between Contraceptive Sex Role Stereotyping and Attitudes Toward Male Contraception Among Males," *The Journal of Sex Research* 15 (1979): 235–242.

69. Clinton J. Jesser, "Male Responses to Direct Verbal Sexual Initiatives of Females," *The Journal of Sex Research* 14 (1978): 118–128.

70. Ellen Frank, Carol Anderson, and Debra Rubinstein, "Marital Role Strain and Sexual Satisfaction," *Journal of Consulting and Clinical Psychology* 47 (1979): 1096–1103.

71. Gail Sheehy, *Passages* (New York: Bantam, 1976); Gail Sheehy, *Pathfinders* (New York: William Morrow, 1981).

72. Angela B. McBride and Kathryn N. Black, "Differences that Suggest Female Investment in, and Male Distance from Children," *Sex Roles* 10 (1984): 231–246.

73. Zolinda Stoneman, Gene H. Brody, and Carol E. MacKinnon, "Same-Sex and Cross-Sex Siblings: Activity Choices, Roles, Behavior, and Gender Stereotypes," *Sex Roles* 15 (1986): 495–512.

74. Linda O. Lavine and John P. Lombardo, "Self-Disclosure: Intimate and Nonintimate Disclosures to Parents and Best Friends as a Function of Bem Sex-Role Category," *Sex Roles* 11 (1984): 735–744.

75. Linda M. Jones and Joanne L. McBride, "Sex-Role Stereotyping in Children as a Function of Maternal Employment," *Journal of Social Psychology* 11 (1980): 219–222.

76. See, for example, Charles M. Schaninger and W. Christian Buss, "The Relationship of Sex-Role Norms to Couple and Parental Demographics," *Sex Roles* 15 (1986): 77–94; and Cooke White Stephan and Judy Corder, "The Effects of Dual-Career Families on Adolescents' Sex-Role Attitudes, Work and Family Plans, and Choices of Important Others," *Journal of Marriage and the Family* 47 (1985): 921–929.

77. See, for example, Marianne N. Bloch, "The Development of Sex Differences in Young Children's Activities at Home: The Effect of the Social Context," *Sex Roles* 16 (1987): 279–302; and Margaret Mietus Sanik and Kathryn Stafford, "Adolescents' Contribution to Household Production: Male and Female Differences," *Adolescence* 20 (1985): 207–215.

78. Harriet K. Light, Doris Hertsgaard, and Ruth E. Martin, "Farm Children's Work in the Family," *Adolescence* 20 (1985): 425–432.

79. Gene H. Brody and Lola Carr Steelman, "Sibling Structure and Parental Sex-Typing of Children's Household Tasks," *Journal of Marriage and the Family* 47 (1985): 265–273.

80. Hoffman, Personal Interview, 1987.

81. Clarke, Personal Interview, 1987.

82. Cooke White Stephan and Judy Corder, "The Effects of Dual-Career Families on Adolescents' Sex-Role Attitudes, Work and Family Plans, and Choices of Important Others," *Journal of Marriage and the Family* 47 (1985): 921–929.

83. Marilyn Coleman and Lawrence H. Ganong, "Effect of Family Structure on Family Attitudes and Expectations," *Family Relations* 33 (1984): 425–432.

84. Lynn H. Turner, "Family Communication: Toward the Development of Androgyny," paper presented at the Central States Speech Association Convention, Milwaukee, Wisconsin, 21 May 1982.

85. Carol J. Ireson, "Adolescent Pregnancy and Sex Roles," *Sex Roles* 11 (1984): 189–201.

86. Jerry Finn, "The Relationship Between Sex Role Attitudes and Attitudes Supporting Marital Violence," *Sex Roles* 14 (1986): 235–244.

87. Poussaint in Cosby, 1986, 10.

88. Margaret J. Intons-Peterson, "Fathers' Expectations and Aspirations for Their Children," *Sex Roles* 12 (1985): 877–895.

89. See, for example, Suzanne M. Allen and Richard A. Kalish, "Professional Women and Marriage," *Journal of Marriage and the Family* 46 (1984): 375–382.

90. Epstein, Bishop, and Baldwin, *Normal Family*, 1982, 124.

91. See, for example, Philip Blumstein and Pepper Schwartz, *American Couples* (New York: William Morrow, 1983); and Dorothy Lenk Krueger, "Marital Decision-Making: A Language-Action Analysis," *Quarterly Journal of Speech* 68 (1982): 273–287.

92. Topping, Personal Interview, 1987.

93. Carolyn J. Rosenthal, "Kinkeeping in the Familial Division of Labor," *Journal of Marriage and the Family* 47 (1985): 965–974.

94. Rosenthal, 1985, 965–974.

95. See, for example, Bert N. Adams, *Kinship in an Urban Setting* (Chicago: Markham, 1968); and Joan Aldous, "Intergenerational Visiting Patterns: Variation in Boundary Maintenance as an Explanation," *Family Process* 6 (1967): 235–251.

96. Eisenberg, 1988.

97. Glenna Spitze and John Logan, "Sons, Daughters, and Intergenerational Social Support," *Journal of Marriage and the Family* 52 (1990): 420–430.

98. Howard M. Bahr, "The Kinship Role," ed. F. Ivan Nye, *Role Structure and Analysis of the Family* 33 (1976): 360–367.

99. Rosenthal, 1985, 965–974.

100. See, for example, Leslie A. Morgan, "Changes in Family Interaction Following Widowhood," *Journal of Marriage and the Family* 46 (1984): 323–332.

101. See, for example, Claude S. Fischer, *To Dwell Among Friends: Personal Networks in Town and City* (Chicago: University of Chicago Press, 1982); James M. Gaudin and Kathryn B. Davis, "Social Networks of Black and White Rural Families: A Research Report," *Journal of Marriage and the Family* 47 (1985): 1015–1021; Gary R. Lee and Margaret L. Cassidy, "Kinship Systems and Extended Family Ties," *The Family in Rural Society*, ed. Raymond T. Coward and William M. Smith, Jr. (Boulder, CO: Westview Press, 1981).

102. Kathleen M. Galvin and Bernard J. Brommel, *Family Communication: Cohesion and Change*, 2nd ed. (Glenview, IL: Scott, Foresman, 1986), 20.

103. Flora L. Williams and Ruth E. Berry, "Intensity of Family Disagreement Over Finances and Associated Factors," *Journal of Consumer Studies and Home Economics* 8 (1984): 33–53.

104. T. K. Hira, "Satisfaction with Money Management: Practices Among Dual-Earner Households," *Journal of Home Economics* 79 (1987): 19–22.

105. Charles M. Schaninger and W. Christian Buss, "A Longitudinal Comparison of Consumption and Finance Handling Between Happily Married and Divorced Couples," *Journal of Marriage and the Family* 48 (1986): 129–136.

106. See, for example, Israelsen, 1989, 311–326.

107. French, 1987, 305.

108. Rapoport and Rapoport, *Dual-Career Families*, 1971.

109. Monique Lortier-Lussier, Christine Schwab, and Joseph de-Konick, "Working Mothers Versus Housemakers: Do Dreams Reflect the Changing Roles of Women?" *Sex Roles* 12 (1985): 1009–1021.

110. Rapoport and Rapoport, *Dual-Career Families*, 1971.

111. Rapoport and Rapoport, *Dual-Career Families*, 1971.

112. Nancy Pistrang, "Women's Work Involvement and Experience of New Motherhood," *Journal of Marriage and the Family* 46 (1984): 433.

113. Ellen Hock, M. Therese Gnezda, and Susan L. McBride, "Mothers of Infants: Attitudes Toward Employment and Motherhood Following Birth of the First Child," *Journal of Marriage and the Family* 46 (1984): 425–431.

114. Good, Personal Interview, 1987.

115. Sheehy, 1976, 25.

116. See, for example, S. Shirley Feldman and Sharon C. Nash, "The Transition from Expectancy to Parenthood: Impact of the Firstborn Child on Men and Woman," *Sex Roles* 11 (1984): 61–78.

117. Shaw, Personal Interview, 1987.

118. Fitzpatrick and Indvik, "Enduring Relationships," 1982, 311–325, and "Marital Communication, 1982, 195–213.

119. James L. Hawkins, Carol Weisberg, and Diurie W. Ray, "Spouse Differences in Communication Style: Preference, Perception, and Behavioral," *Journal of Marriage and the Family* 42 (1980): 585–593.

120. Kathleen F. Slevin and Jack Balswick, "Childrens' Perceptions of Parental Expressiveness," *Sex Roles* 6 (1980): 293–299.

121. See, for example, Lowell J. Krokoff, John M. Gottman, and Anup K. Roy, "Blue-Collar and White-Collar Marital Interaction and Communication Orientation," *Journal of Social and Personal Relationships* 5 (1988): 201–221; and Lynn White and Bruce Keith, "The Effect of Shift Work on the Quality and Stability of Marital Relations," *Journal of Marriage and the Family* 52 (1990): 453–462.

122. Rapoport and Rapoport, *Dual-Career Families*, 1971.

123. F. Ivan Nye and Steven McLaughlin, "Role Competence and Marital Satisfaction," in F. Ivan Nye, ed., *Family Relationships: Rewards and Costs* (Newbury Park, CA: Sage, 1982), 67–79.

124. Epstein, Bishop, and Baldwin, 1982, 125.

125. See, for example, Pistrang, 1984, 433–447.

126. Judy Corder and Cookie White Stephan, "Females' Combination of Work and Family Roles: Adolescents' Aspiration," *Journal of Marriage and the Family* 46 (1984): 391–402.

127. See, for example, Sharon B. Merriam and Patricia Hyer, "Changing Attitudes of Women Towards Family-Related Tasks in Young Adulthood," *Sex Roles* 10 (1984): 231–246.

128. Kathleen F. Slevin and C. Ray Wingrove, "Similarities and Differences Among Three Generations of Women in Attitudes Toward the Female Role in Contemporary Society," *Sex Roles* 9 (1983): 609–624.

129. Connie Lizette Spreadbury and Richard P. Hurzeler, "Attitudes of College Students Toward New Trends in Marriage and the Family," *Family Perspective* 18 (1984): 135–139.

CHAPTER 4 NOTES

1. Julia Wood, "Communication and Relational Culture: Bases for the Study of Human Relationship," *Communication Quarterly* 30 (1982): 75–84.

2. Salvador Minuchin, *Families and Family Therapy* (Boston, MA: Harvard University Press, 1974), 51.

3. See, for example, Michael Argyle and Monica Henderson, "The Rules of Friendship," *Journal of Social and Personal Relationships* 1 (1984): 211–237

4. Kathleen Galvin and Bernard Brommel, *Family Communication: Cohesion and Change*, 2nd ed. (Glenview, IL: Scott, Foresman 1986), 51.

5. Don D. Jackson, "Family Rules: Marital Quid Pro Quo," *Archives of General Psychiatry* 12 (1965): 11.

6. F. R. Ford, "Rules: The Visible Family," *Family Process* 22 (1983): 135.

7. Susan B. Shimanoff, *Communication Rules: Theory and Research* (Newbury Park, CA: Sage, 1980).

8. Ford, 1983, 135.

9. Reed, Personal Interview, 1987.

10. William Meredith, Douglas A. Abbott, Mary Ann Lamanna, and Gregory Sanders, "Rituals and Family Strengths: A Three-Generation Study," *Family Perspective* 23 (1989): 75–83.

11. Petrucelli, Personal Interview, 1986.

12. Stoppelbein, Personal Interview, 1986.

13. Bruggemeyer, Personal Interview, 1986.

14. Forman, Personal Interview, 1986.

15. Vecchio, Personal Interview, 1986.

16. Young, Personal Interview, 1987.

17. Lang, Personal Interview, 1985.

18. Jones, Personal Interview, 1985.

19. Krause, Personal Interview, 1985.

20. Zecchino, Personal Interview, 1985.

21. Anderson, Personal Interview, 1985.

22. Young, Personal Interview, 1987.

23. Young, Personal Interview, 1987.

24. Remy, Personal Interview, 1987.

25. Shaw, Personal Interview, 1987.

26. Marilyn French, *Her Mother's Daughter* (New York: Summit Books, 1987), 241.

27. William H. Meredith, Douglas A. Abbott, Mary Ann Lamanna, and Gregory Sanders, "Rituals and Family Strengths: A Three-Generation Study," *Family Perspective* 23 (1989): 75–83.

28. See, for example, Nancy L. Buerkel-Rothfuss, Bradley S. Greenburg, B. S. Atkin, and Kimberly Neuendorf, "Learning about the Family from Television," *Journal of Communication* 32 (1982): 191–201; Anne Locksley, "Social Class and Marital Attitudes and Behavior," *Journal of Marriage and the Family* 44 (1982): 427–440; Michael E. Roloff and Bradley S. Greenberg, "TV, Peer, and Parent Models for Pro- and Antisocial Conflict Behaviors," *Human Communication Research* 6 (1980): 340–351; Ellen Wartella and Byron Reeves, "Historical Trends in Research on Children and the Media: 1900–1960," *Journal of Communication* 35 (1985): 118–133; and James G. Webster, Judy C. Pearson, and Debra B. Webster, "Children's Television Viewing as Affected by Contextual Variables in the Home," *Communication Research Reports* 3 (1986): 1–8.

29. Russell Baker, *Growing Up* (New York: Congdon & Weed, 1982), 16.

30. See, for example, Carol K. Sigelman, Lee Sigelman, and Margaret Goodlette, "Sex Differences in the Moral Values of College Students and Their Parents," *Sex Roles* 10 (1984): 877–883.

31. Bill Cosby, *Fatherhood* (New York: Berkley, 1986), 19–20.

32. Cosby, 1986, 48.

33. Beth Haslett, "Children's Strategies for Maintaining Cohesion in their Written and Oral Stories," *Communication Education* 32 (1984): 91–105.

34. See, for example, Noam Chomsky, "Three Models for the Description of Language," *Transactions on Information Theory* IT-2 (1956): 113–124; Noam Chomsky, *The Logical Structure of Linguistic Theory* (New York: Plenum, 1975); Noam Chomsky, *Rules and Representations* (New York: Columbia University Press, 1980); Jerry A. Fodor, Thomas G. Bever, and Merrill F. Garrett, *The Psychology of Language: An Introduction to Psycholinguistics and Generative Grammar* (New York: McGraw-Hill, 1974); Gilbert Harmon, *On Noam Chomsky: Critical Essays* (Garden City, NY: Anchor, 1974); and Burrhus F. Skinner, *Verbal Behavior* (New York: Appleton-Century-Crofts, 1957).

35. Beth Haslett, "Acquiring Conversational Competence," *The Western Journal of Speech Communication* 48 (1984): 107–124.

36. James J. Bradac, Charles H. Tardy, and Lawrence A. Hosman, "Disclosure Styles and a Hint at Their Genesis," *Human Communication Research* 6 (1980): 228–238.

37. Tracy Kidder, *House* (Boston: Houghton Mifflin, 1985), 6–7.

38. Debra Kalmuss, "The Intergenerational Transmission of Marital Aggression," *Journal of Marriage and the Family* 46 (1984): 11–19.

39. Linda Thompson, Kevin Clark, and William Gunn, Jr., "Development Stage and Perceptions of Intergenerational Continuity," *Journal of Marriage and the Family* 47 (1985): 913–920.

40. Salvador Minuchin, *Families and Family Therapy* (Boston, MA: Harvard University Press, 1974), 27.

41. Frederick R. Ford, "Rules: The Visible Family," *Family Process* (1983): 139.

42. Marilyn French, *Her Mother's Daughter* (New York: Summit Books, 1987), 126–127.

43. Erik E. Filsinger and Leanne K. Lamke, "The Lineage Transmission of Interpersonal Competence," *Journal of Marriage and the Family* 45 (1983): 75–80.

44. Salvador Minuchin, 1974, 19.

45. Robert Hopper, Mark L. Knapp, and Lorel Scott, "Couples' Personal Idioms: Exploring Intimate Talk," *Journal of Communication* 31 (1981): 23–33.

46. David C. Bellinger and Jean B. Gleason, "Sex Differences in Parental Directions to Young Children," *Sex Roles* 8 (1982): 1123–1139.

47. Kretch, Personal Interview, 1987.

48. Wagner, Personal Interview, 1987.

49. Strickmaker, Personal Interview, 1987.

50. See, for example, Gayle C. Broberg, "Fatherhood: Rediscovered in Empirical Research," *Family Perspective* 22 (1988): 75–83; and Mark D. Baranowski, "The Grandfather-Grandchild Relationship: Meaning and Exchange," *Family Perspective* 24 (1990): 201–212.

51. Ventrelli, Personal Interview, 1987.

52. LeMieux, Personal Interview, 1987.

53. Cox, Personal Interview, 1987.

54. Anderson, Personal Interview, 1987.

55. Hoffman, Personal Interview, 1987.

56. Tocci, Personal Interview, 1987.

57. Strickmaker, Personal Interview, 1987.

58. Remy, Personal Interview, 1987.

59. Mead, Personal Interview, 1987.

60. Ford, Personal Interview, 1987.

61. Knop, Personal Interview, 1987.

62. Thompsen, Personal Interview, 1987.

63. Young, Personal Interview, 1987.

64. Russell Baker, *Growing Up* (New York: New American Library, 1982), 168–169.

65. Shaw, Personal Interview, 1987.

66. S. Zamanou, "A Study of Teenagers' Perceptions of Topic," paper presented at the annual Speech Communication Association Convention, Denver, CO, November 1985.

67. Kay E. Mueller and William G. Powers, "Parent-Child Sexual Discussion: Perceived Communicator Style and Subsequent Behavior," *Adolescence* 25 (1990): 469–482.

68. See, for example, Sandra K. Tucker, "Adolescent Patterns of Communication about Sexually Related Topics," *Adolescence* 94 (1989): 269–278; Terri D. Fisher, "An Extension of the Findings of Moore, Peterson, and Furstenberg (1986) Regarding Family Sexual Communication and Adolescent Sexual Behavior," *Journal of Marriage and the Family* 51 (1989): 637–639; and Kay E. Mueller and William G. Powers, "Parent-Child Sexual Discussion: Perceived Communicator Style and Subsequent Behavior," *Adolescence* 25 (1990): 469–482.

69. Alan L. Sillars, Judith Weisberg, Cynthia S. Burggraf, and Elizabeth A. Wilson, "Content Themes in Marital Conversations," *Human Communication Research* 13 (1987): 495–528.

70. Sillars, Weisberg, Burggraf, and Wilson, 1987, i.

71. Frank E. Millar, E. M. Nunnally, and Daniel Wackman, "Relational Communication and Family Functioning: A Proposed Model," paper presented at the annual conference at the Eastern Communication Association, Philadelphia, PA, February 1979.

72. Wagner, Personal Interview, 1987.

73. Clarke, Personal Interview, 1987.

74. Wesley R. Burr, "Beyond I-Statements in Family Communication," *Family Relations* 39 (1990): 266–273.

75. Susan B. Shimanoff, "Expressing Emotions in Words: Verbal Patterns of Interaction," *Journal of Communication* 35 (1985): 16–31.

76. Susan B. Shimanoff, "Types of Emotional Disclosures and Request Compliance Between Spouses," *Communication Monographs* 54 (1987): 85–100.

77. Wentworth, Personal Interview, 1987.

78. Wagner, Personal Interview, 1987.

79. Thompsen, Personal Interview, 1987.

80. Thomas B. Holman, and Mary Jacquart, "Leisure-Activity Patterns and Marital Satisfaction: A Further Test," *Journal of Marriage and the Family* 50 (1988): 69–77.

81. Alassaf, Personal Interview, 1987.

82. See, for example, Philip J. Glenn and Mark L. Knapp, "The Interactive Framing of Play in Adult Conversations," *Communication Quarterly* 35 (1987): 48–66; William F. Owen, "Mutual Interaction of Discourse Structures and Relational Pragmatics in Conversational Influence Attempts," *The Southern Speech Communication Journal* 52 (1987): 103–127; and Robin N. Williamson and Mary Ann Fitzpatrick, "Two Approaches to Marital Interaction: Relational Control Patterns in Marital Types," *Communication Monographs* 52 (1985): 236–252.

83. Abbott, Personal Interview, 1987.

84. Knop, Personal Interview, 1987.

85. Hoffman, Personal Interview, 1987.

86. Young, Personal Interview, 1987.

87. See, for example, Larry B. Feldman, "Marital Conflict and Marital Intimacy: An Integrative Psychodynamic-Behavioral Systemic Model," *Family Process* 18 (1979): 69–78.

CHAPTER 5 NOTES

1. Timothy G. Hegstrom, "Message Impact: What Percentage is Nonverbal?" *The Western Journal of Speech Communication* 43 (1979): 134–142.

2. Gene H. Brody, Zolinda Stoneman, and Alice K. Sanders, "Effects of Television Viewing on Family Interactions: An Observational Study," *Family Relations* 29 (1980): 216–220.

3. Mark L. Knapp, *Essentials of Nonverbal Communication* (New York: Holt, Rinehart and Winston, 1980); Judee K. Burgoon and Thomas Saine, *The Unspoken Dialogue: An Introduction to Nonverbal Communication* (Boston: Houghton Mifflin, 1978); and Loretta A. Malandro and Larry L. Barker, *NonverbalCommunication* (Reading, MA: Addison-Wesley, 1983).

4. Lilly Sprecher Dimitrovsky, "The Ability to Identify the Emotional Meaning of Vocal Expressions at Successive Age Levels," *The Communication of Emotional Meaning*, ed. Joel Robert Davitz (New York: McGraw-Hill, 1964), 69–86; Robert Rosenthal, J. A. Hall, M. R. DiMatteo, P. O. Rogers, and D. Archer, *Sensitivity to Nonverbal Communications: The PONS Test* (Baltimore: Johns Hopkins University Press, 1979); Daniel Solomon and Judy Yeager, "Determinants of Boy's Perceptions of Verbal Reinforcers," *Developmental Psychology* 1 (1969): 637–645; and Robert L. Woolfolk, Anita E. Woolfolk, and Karen S. Garlinsky, "Nonverbal Behavior of Teachers: Some Empirical Findings," *Environmental Psychology and Nonverbal Behavior* 2 (1977): 45–61.

5. Michael Argyle, *Bodily Communication* (London: Methuen, 1975); Peter D. Blanck, Robert Rosenthal, Sara E. Snodgrass, Bella M. DePaulo and Miron Zuckerman, "Longitudinal and Cross-Sectional Age Effects in Nonverbal Decoding Skills and Style," *Developmental Psychology* 18 (1982): 491–498; Bella M. DePaulo, and Robert Rosenthal, "Age Changes in Nonverbal Decoding as a Function of Increasing Amounts of Information," *Journal of Experimental Child Psychology* 26 (1978): 280–287; Bella M. DePaulo and Robert Rosenthal, "Ambivalence, Discrepancy and Deception in Nonverbal Communication," *Skill in Nonverbal Communication: Individual Differences*, ed. Robert Rosenthal

(Cambridge, MA: Oelgeschlager, Gunn and Hain, 1979), 204–248; Albert Mehrabian, *Nonverbal Communication* (Chicago: Aldine-Atherton, 1972); Albert Mehrabian, and Morton Wiener, "Decoding of Inconsistent Communications," *Journal of Personality and Social Psychology* 6 (1967): 109–114; Daniel Solomon and Faizunisa A. Ali, "Age Trends in the Perception of Verbal Reinforcers," *Developmental Psychology* 7 (1972): 238–243; and Miron Zuckerman, Peter D. Blanck, Bella M. DePaulo, and Robert Rosenthal, "Developmental Changes in Decoding Discrepant and Nondiscrepant Nonverbal Cues," *Developmental Psychology* 16 (1980): 220–228.

6. Robin S. Cohen and Andrew Christensen, "Further Examination of Demand Characteristics in Marital Interaction," *Journal of Consulting and Clinical Psychology* 48 (1980): 121–123.

7. Gregory Bateson, Don D. Jackson, Jay Haley, and John Weakland, "Toward a Theory of Schizophrenia," *Behavioral Science* 1 (1956): 251–264.

8. Patricia Noller, "Misunderstandings in Marital Communication: A Study of Couples' Nonverbal Communication," *Journal of Personality and Social Psychology* 39 (1980): 1135.

9. John Gottman, *Marital Interaction: Experimental Investigations* (New York: Academic Press, 1979).

10. Michael E. Lamb, Ann M. Frodj, Carl Philip Hwang, and Majt Frodj, "Varying Degrees of Paternal Involvement in Infant Care," *Nontraditional Families: Parenting and Child Development*, ed. Michael E. Lamb (Hillsdale, NJ: Lawrence Erlbaum, 1982), 117–137.

11. Michael E. Lamb, Ann M. Frodj, Carl Philip Hwang, and Majt Frodj, "Varying Degrees of Paternal Involvement in Infant Care," *Nontraditional Families: Parenting and Child Development*, ed. Michael E. Lamb (Hillsdale, NJ: Lawrence Erlbaum, 1982), 117–137.

12. Daphne E. Bugental, Leonore R. Love, and Robert M. Gianetto, "Perfidious Feminine Faces," *Journal of Personality and Social Psychology* 17 (1971): 314–318.

13. Gene H. Brody and Zolinda Stoneman, "Parental Nonverbal Behavior Within the Family Context," *Family Relations* 30 (1981): 187–190.

14. Remy, Personal Interview, 1987.

15. Neal Krause, "Conflicting Sex-Role Expectations, Housework, Dissatisfaction, and Depressive Symptoms Among Full-Time Housewives," *Sex Roles* 9 (1983): 1114–1125.

16. Neal Krause, "Conflicting Sex-Role Expectations, Housework, Dissatisfaction, and Depressive Symptoms Among Full-Time Housewives," *Sex Roles* 9 (1983): 1114–1125.

17. Adams, Personal Interview, 1985.

18. Hoey, Personal Interview, 1985.

19. Bell, Personal Interview, 1985.

20. Reed, Personal Interview, 1987.

21. Reed, Personal Interview, 1987.

22. Young, Personal Interview, 1987.

23. Ford, Personal Interview, 1987.

24. Ford, Personal Interview, 1987.

25. Remy, Personal Interview, 1987.

26. Billy A. Barrios, L. Claire Corbitt, J. Philip Estes, and Jeff S. Topping, "Effect of a Social Stigma on Interpersonal Distance," *The Psychological Record* 26 (1976): 346–348; Gloria Leventhal and Michelle Matturro, "Differential Effects of Spatial Crowding and Sex on Behavior," *Perceptual Motor Skills* 51 (1980): 111–119; and C. R. Synder and Janet R. Endelman, "Effects of Degree of Interpersonal Similarity on Physical Distance and Self-Reinforcement Theory Predictions," *Journal of Personality* 47 (1979): 23–26, 71–84.

27. Michael Argyle and Janet Dean, "Eye Contact, Distance and Affiliation," *Sociometry* 28 (1965): 289–304.

28. Judee K. Burgoon, "A Communication Model of Personal Space Violations: Explication and an Initial Test," *Human Communication Research* 4 (1978): 129–142; and James R. Graves and John D. Robinson II, "Proxemic Behavior as a Function of Inconsistent Verbal and Nonverbal Messages," *Journal of Counseling Psychology* 23 (1976): 333–338.

29. Gene H. Brody and Zolinda Stoneman, "Parental Nonverbal Behavior Within the Family Context," *Family Relations* 30 (1981): 187–190.

30. Bill Cosby, *Fatherhood* (New York: Berkley, 1986).

31. Ron Adler, and Neil Towne, *Looking Out/Looking In* (New York: Holt, Rinehart and Winston, 1978); John Bowlby, *Maternal Care and Mental Health* (Geneva: World Health Organization, 1961), 15–29; and Ashley Montague, *Touching: The Human Significance of the Skin* (New York: Harper & Row, 1971).

32. See, for example, Peter A. Anderson and Karen K. Sull, "Out of Touch, Out of Reach: Tactile Predispositions as Predictors of Interpersonal Distance," *The Western Journal of Speech Communication* 49 (1985): 57–72.

33. Shaw, Personal Interview, 1987.

34. Vidal S. Clay, "The Effect of Culture on Mother-Child Tactile Communication," *Family Coordinator* 17 (1968): 204–210; Susan Goldberg and Michael Lewis, "Play Behavior in the Year-Old Infant: Early Sex Differences," *Child Development* 40 (1969): 21–31.

35. Sidney M. Jourard and Jane E. Rubin, "Self-Disclosure and Touching: A Study of Two Modes of Interpersonal Encounter and Their Interrelation," *Journal of Humanistic Psychology* 8 (1968): 39–48.

36. M. Lewis, "Parents and Children: Sex Role Development," *Social Review* 80 (1972): 229–240.

37. Kevin MacDonald and Ross D. Parke, "Parent-Child Physical Play: The Effects of Sex and Age of Children and Parents," *Sex Roles* 15 (1986): 1538–1542.

38. Jay Belsky, "Mother-Father-Infant Interactions: A Naturalistic Observational Study," *Developmental Psychology* 15 (1979): 601–607; and Michael E. Lamb, "The Development of Mother-Infant and Father-Infant Attachments in the Second Year of Life," *Developmental Psychology* 13 (1977): 637–646.

39. Michael E. Lamb, "The Development of Mother-Infant and Father-Infant Attachments in the Second Year of Life," *Developmental Psychology* 13 (1977): 637–646.

40. Michael E. Lamb, Ann M. Frodi, Carl Philip Hwang, and Majt Frodj, "Varying Degrees of paternal Involvement in Infant Care," *Nontraditional Families: Parenting and Child Development,* ed. Michael E. Lamb (Hillsdale, NJ: Lawrence Erlbaum, 1982), 117–137.

41. Gene H. Brody and Zolinda Stoneman, "Parental Nonverbal Behavior Within the Family Context," *Family Relations* 30 (1981): 187–190.

42. Gene H. Brody and Zolinda Stoneman, "Parental Nonverbal Behavior Within the Family Context," *Family Relations* 30 (1981): 187–190.

43. Stephen A. Anderson, "Parental and Marital Role Stress During the School Entry Transition," *Journal of Social and Personal Relationships* 2 (1985): 59–80.

44. Stephen A. Anderson, "Parental and Marital Role Stress During the School Entry Transition," *Journal of Social and Personal Relationships* 2 (1985): 59–80.

45. Ticer, Personal Interview, 1985.

46. Neal Krause, "Conflicting Sex-Role Expectations, Housework Dissatisfaction, and Depressive Symptoms Among Full-Time Housewives," *Sex Roles* 9 (1983): 1114–1125.

47. Rainey, Personal Interview, 1985.

48. Seymour Fisher, "Body Decoration and Camouflage," *Dimensions of Dress and Adornment: A Book of Readings,* 3rd ed., ed. Lois M. Gurel and Marianne S. Beeson (Dubuque, IA: Kendall/Hunt, 1975), 138–149.

49. Lynn Proctor, *Fashion and Anti-Fashion* (London: Cox and Wyman, 1978).

50. Marilyn J. Horn, "Carrying It Off In Style: The Role of Clothing," *Dimensions of Dress and Adornment: A Book of Readings,* ed. Lois M. Gurel and Marianne S. Beeson (Dubuque, IA: Kendall/Hunt, 1975), 120–122.

51. Maureen M. Sweeney and Paul Zionts, "The 'Second Skin': Perceptions of Disturbed and Nondisturbed Early Adolescents on Clothing, Self-Concept, and Body Image," *Adolescence* 24 (1989): 410–419.

52. Marcia O'Reilly, Howard G. Schutz, and Margaret H. Rucker, "Clothing Interest, Self-Actualization, and Demographic Variables," *Home Economics Research Journal* 11 (1983): 280–288.

53. Russell Baker, *Growing Up* (New York: New American Library, 1982), 122.

54. Cook, Personal Interview, 1985.

55. Judee K. Burgoon and Thomas Saine, *The Unspoken Dialogue: An Introduction to Nonverbal Communication* (Boston: Houghton Mifflin, 1978).

56. Richard Stuart Mach, *Postural Carriage and Congruency as Nonverbal Indicators of Status Differentials and Interpersonal Attraction,* diss., U. of Colorado, 1972.

57. Paul Ekman and Wallace V. Friesen, "The Repertoire of Nonverbal Behavior: Categories, Origins, Usage, and Coding," *Semiotica* 1 (1969): 49–98; and Paul Ekman and Wallace V. Friesen, *Unmasking the Face: A Guide to Recognizing Emotions from Facial Cues* (Englewood Cliffs, NJ: Prentice-Hall, 1975).

58. Ross Buck, Robert E. Miller, and William F. Caul, "Sex, Personality, and Physiological Variables in the Communication of Affect Via Facial Expression," *Journal of Personality and Social Psychology* 30 (1974): 587–596; Albert Mehrabian, *Nonverbal Communication* (Chicago: Aldine-Atherton, 1972).

59. Daphne E. Bugental, Leonore R. Love, and Robert M. Gianetto, "Perfidious Feminine Faces," *Journal of Personality and Social Psychology* 17 (1971): 314–318.

60. Charlotte Wolff, *A Psychology of Gesture* (New York: Arno Press, 1972).

61. Paul Ekman and Wallace V. Friesen, "The Repertoire of Nonverbal Behavior: Categories, Origins, Usage, and Coding," *Semiotica* 1 (1969): 49–98; Paul Ekman and Wallace V. Friesen, *Unmasking the Face: A Guide to Recognizing Emotions from Facial Cues* (Englewood Cliffs, NJ: Prentice-Hall, 1975).

62. Starkey Duncan, "Some Signals and Rules for Taking Speaking Turns in Conversations," *Journal of Personality and Social Psychology* 23 (1972): 283–292.

63. Mead, Personal Interview, 1987.

64. Mark L. Knapp, Roderick P. Hart, Gustav W. Friedrich, and Gary M. Shulman, "The Rhetoric of Goodbye: Verbal and Nonverbal Correlates of Human Leave-Taking Behavior," *Speech Monographs* 40 (1973): 182–198.

65. Tracy Kidder, *House* (Boston: Houghton Mifflin, 1985), 316.

66. Mead, Personal Interview, 1987.

CHAPTER 6 NOTES

1. See, for example, Charles P. Loomis, "The Growth of the Farm Family in Relation to Its Activities" (Raleigh, NC: North Carolina State College Agricultural Experiment Station, 1934); Mary Jo Bane and David T. Ellwood, "Slipping Into and Out of Poverty: The Dynamics of Spells," *Journal of Human Resources* 21 (1986): 1–23; and Greg J. Duncan, *Years of Poverty, Years of Plenty: The Changing Economic Fortunes of American Workers and Families* (Ann Arbor, MI: Institute for Social Research, University of Michigan, 1984).

2. See, for example, Lonnie R. Sherrod and Orville G. Brim, Jr., "Epilogue: Retrospective and Prospective Views of Life Course Research on Human Development," *Human Development and the Life Course: Multidisciplinary Perspectives,* ed. Aage E. Sorensen, Franz E. Weinert, and Lonnie R. Sherrod (Hillsdale, NJ: Erlbaum, 1986); and Joan Aldous, "Family Development and the Life Course: Two Perspectives on Family Change," *Journal of Marriage and the Family* 52 (1990): 571–583.

3. See, for example, William W. Wilmot, "Metacommunication: A Re-examination and Extension," *Communication Yearbook 4,* ed. Dan Nimmo (New Brunswick, NJ: Transaction Books, 1980), 61–69.

4. Irwin Altman and Dalmas A. Taylor, *Social Penetration: The Development of Interpersonal Relationships* (New York: Holt, Rinehart and Winston, 1973).

5. Altman and Taylor, *Social Penetration,* 1973.

6. See, for example, Leslie A. Baxter, "Self-Report Disengagement Strategies in Friendship Relationships," paper presented at the Annual Convention of the Western Speech Communication Association, Los Angeles, CA, February 1979; Leslie A. Baxter, "Towards a Dialectical Understanding of Interpersonal Relationships: Research and Theory in the 1980s," keynote address presented to the California State University Fresno annual communication conference, May 1982; Leslie A. Baxter, "An Investigation of Compliance-Gaining as Politeness," *Human Communication Research* 10 (1984): 427–456; Sally A. Lloyd and Rodney M. Cate, "Attributions Associated with Significant Turning Points in Premarital Relationship Development and Dissolution," *Journal of Social and*

Personal Relationships 2 (1985): 419–436; and Mark L. Knapp, *Interpersonal Communication and Human Relationships* (Boston: Allyn and Bacon, 1984).

7. Rebecca J. Cline, "The Acquaintance Process as Relational Communication," *Communication Yearbook* 7, ed. Robert N. Bostrom (Newbury Park, CA: Sage, 1983), 396–413.

8. G. M. Maxwell, "Behaviour of Lovers: Measuring the Closeness of Relationships," *Journal of Social and Personal Relationships* 2 (1985): 215–238.

9. Elaine Walster and G. William Walster, *A New Look at Love* (Reading, MA: Addison-Wesley, 1978).

10. Eric N. Berkowitz, "Role Theory, Attitudinal Constructs, and Actual Performance: A Measurement Issue," *Journal of Applied Psychology* 65 (1980): 240–245.

11. Rebecca J. Cline and Karen E. Musolf, "Disclosure as Social Exchange: Anticipated Length of Relationship, Sex Roles, and Disclosure Intimacy," *Western Journal of Speech Communication* 49 (1985): 44.

12. See, for example, Gerald R. Adams and Judy A. Shea, "Talking and Loving: A Cross-Lagged Panel Investigation," *Basic and Applied Social Psychology* 2 (1981): 81–88; Joseph W. Critelli and Kathleen M. Dupre, "Self-Disclosure and Romantic Attraction," *Journal of Social Psychology* 106 (1978): 127–128; Sidney M. Jourard, "Self-Disclosure and Other-Cathexis," *Journal of Abnormal and Social Psychology* 59 (1959): 428–431; Sidney M. Jourard and Paul Laskow, "Some Factors in Self-Disclosure," *Journal of Abnormal and Social Psychology* 56 (1958): 91–98; and Judy A. Shea and Gerald R. Adams, "Correlates of Romantic Attachment: A Path Analysis Study," *Journal of Youth and Adolescence* 13 (1984): 27–44.

13. Cline and Musolf, 1985, 43–56; Valerian J. Derlega, Barbara A. Winstead, Paul T. Wong, and S. Hunter, "Gender Effects in an Initial Encounter: A Case Where Men Exceed Women in Discourse," *Journal of Social and Personal Relationships* 2 (1985): 25–44.

14. Susan Sprecher, "The Effects of Self-Disclosure Given and Received on Affection for an Intimate Partner and Stability of the Relationship," *Journal of Social and Personal Relationships* 4 (1987): 115–127.

15. James W. Michaels, Alan C. Acock, and John N. Edwards, "Social Exchange and Equity Determinants of Relationship Commitment," *Journal of Social and Personal Relationships* 3 (1986): 161–175.

16. Leslie A. Baxter and William W. Wilmot, "Taboo Topics in Close Relationships," *Journal of Social and Personal Relationships* 2 (1985): 253–269.

17. Evelyn Ruth Millis Duvall, *Family Development*, 2nd ed. (New York: Lippincott, 1962); Boyd C. Rollins and Harold Feldman, "Marital Satisfaction Over the Family Life Cycle," *Journal of Marriage and the Family* 32 (1970): 20–27; Monica McGoldrick and Elizabeth A. Carter, "The Family Life Cycle," *Normal Family Processes*, ed. Froma Walsh (New York: Guilford Press, 1982), 167–195; and Stephen A. Anderson, Candyce J. Russell, and Walter R. Schumm, "Perceived Marital Quality and Family Life-Cycle: A Further Analysis," *Journal of Marriage and the Family* 45 (1983): 127–139.

18. Charles R. Berger and Richard J. Calabrese, "Some Explorations in Initial Interaction and Beyond: Toward a Developmental Theory of Interpersonal Communication," *Human Communication Research* 1 (1975): 99–112.

19. Charles R. Berger and James J. Bradac, *Language and Social Knowledge: Uncertainty in Interpersonal Relations* (Baltimore: Edward Arnold, 1982).

20. William Douglas, "Uncertainty, Information-Seeking, and Liking During Initial Interaction," *Western Journal of Speech Communication* 54 (1990): 66–81.

21. William Douglas, "Affinity-Testing in Initial Interactions," *Journal of Social and Personal Relationships* 4 (1987): 3–15.

22. Sally Planalp and James M. Honeycutt, "Events That Increase Uncertainty in Personal Relationships," *Human Communication Research* 11 (1985): 593–604.

23. Malcolm R. Parks and Mara B. Adelman, "Communication Networks and the Development of Romantic Relationships: An Expansion of Uncertainty Reduction Theory," *Human Communication Research* 10 (1983): 55–79.

24. James McCroskey and Lawrence Wheeless, *Introduction to Human Communication* (Boston, MA: Allyn and Bacon, 1976).

25. Robert A. Bell and John A. Daly, "Affinity-Seeking: Its Nature and Correlates," paper presented at the annual meeting of the International Communication Association, San Francisco, CA, 1984, 1.

26. Douglas, 1987, 3–15.

27. Douglas, 1987, 7.

28. Douglas, 1987, 7.

29. Douglas, 1987, 7.

30. Douglas, 1987, 7.

31. Douglas, 1987, 3–15.

32. Douglas, 1987, 7–8.

33. Douglas, 1987, 8.

34. Douglas, 1987, 8.

35. Leslie A. Baxter and William W. Wilmot, "'Secret Test': Social Strategies for Acquiring Information about the State of Relationship," *Human Communication Research* 11 (1984): 171–201.

36. Robert A. Bell and Nancy L. Burkel-Rothfuss, "S(he) Loves Me, S(he) Loves Me Not: Predictors of Relational Information-Seeking in Courtship and Beyond," *Communication Quarterly* 38 (1990): 64–82.

37. Virginia P. Richmond, Joan S. Gorham, and Brian J. Furio, "Affinity-Seeking Communication in Collegiate Female-Male Relationships," *Communication Quarterly* 35 (1987): 334–348.

38. Peter Young, "Looking for Mr. or Mrs. Right: Self-Presentation in Videodating," *Journal of Marriage and the Family* 51 (1989): 483–488.

39. Ellen Berscheid and Elaine Hatfield Walster, *Interpersonal Attraction*, 2nd ed. (Reading, MA: Addison-Wesley, 1978).

40. See, for example, Thomas Cash, "If You Think Beautiful People Hold All the Cards, You're Right Says a Researcher," *People Weekly* 14 (1980): 74–79.

41. Jack Sparacino and Stephen Hansell, Physical Attractiveness and Academic Performance: Beauty Is Not Always Talent," *Journal of Personality* 47 (1979): 449–469.

42. See, for example, Dennis Krebs and Allen A. Adinolfi, "Physical Attractiveness, Social Relations, and Personality Style," *Journal of Personality and Social Psychology* 31 (1975): 245–253.

43. Harry T. Reis, John Nezlek, and Ladd Wheeler, "Physical Attractiveness in Social Interaction," *Journal of Personality and Social Psychology* 38 (1980): 604–617.

44. Richard W. Brislin and Steven A. Lewis, "Dating and Physical Attractiveness: Replication," *Psychological Reports* 22 (1968): 976; Wolfgang Stroebe, Chester A. Insko, Vaida D. Thompson, and Bruce D. Layton, "Effects of Physical Attractiveness, Attitude Similarity, and Sex on Various Aspects of Interpersonal Attraction," *Journal of Personality and Social Psychology* 18 (1971): 79–91; and Elaine Walster, Vera Aronson, Darcy Abrahams, and Leon Rottman, "Importance of Physical Attractiveness in Dating Behavior," *Journal of Personality and Social Psychology* 4 (1966): 508–516.

45. James Shanteau and Geraldine F. Nagy, "Probability of Acceptance in Dating Choice," *Journal of Personality and Social Psychology* 37 (1979): 522–533.

46. Wolfgang Stroebe, Chester A. Insko, Vaida D. Thompson, and B. D. Layton, "Effects of Physical Attractiveness, Attitude Similarity, and Sex on Various Aspects of Interpersonal Attraction," *Journal of Personality and Social Psychology* 18 (1971): 79–91.

47. Thomas Cash, "Beautiful People," 1980, 74–79; Richard Centers, "The Completion Hypothesis and the Compensatory Dynamic in Intersexual Attraction and Love," *Journal of Psychology* 82 (1972): 111–126; and Bernard I. Murstein and Patricia Christy, "Physical Attractiveness and Marriage Adjustment in Middle-Aged Couples," *Journal of Personality and Social Psychology* 34 (1976): 537–542.

48. Richard Centers, "The Completion Hypothesis and the Compensatory Dynamic in Intersexual Attraction and Love," *Journal of Psychology* 82 (1972): 111–126.

49. Elaine Walster and G. William Walster, *A New Look at Love* (Reading, MA: Addison-Wesley, 1978).

50. Shaw, Personal Interview, 1987.

51. Murstein and Christy, 1976, 537–542.

52. Mary L. Meiners and John P. Sheposh, "Beauty or Brains: Which Image for Your Mate?" *Personality and Social Psychology Bulletin* 3 (1977): 262–265.

53. Daniel Bar-Tal and Leonard Saxe, "Perceptions of Similarly and Dissimilarly Attractive Couples and Individuals," *Journal of Personality and Social Psychology* 33 (1976): 772–781.

54. Rosemary Bolig, Peter J. Stein, and Patrick C. McKenry, "The Self-Advertisment Approach to Dating: Male-Female Differences," *Family Relations* 33 (1984): 591.

55. Remy, Personal Interview, 1987.

56. See, for example, Joseph E. Grush and Janet G. Yehl, "Marital Roles, Sex Differences, and Interpersonal Attraction," *Journal of Personality and Social Psychology* 37 (1979): 116–123.

57. See, for example, Jared Diamond, "'I Want a Girl Just Like The Girl. . .'," *Discover* 7 (1986): 65–68; Verlin B. Hinsz, "Facial Resemblance in Engaged and Married Couples," *Journal of Social and Personal Relationships* 6 (1989): 223–229.

58. Hinsz, 223–229.

59. James Covington Coleman, *Intimate Relationships, Marriage, and Family* (Indianapolis, IN: Bobbs-Merrill, 1984).

60. Elaine Walster, G. William Walster, and Ellen Berscheid, *Equity: Theory and Research* (Boston: Allyn and Bacon, 1978).

61. Remy, Personal Interview, 1987.

62. Shaw, Personal Interview, 1987.

63. Robin Norwood, *Women Who Love Too Much: When You Keep Wishing and Hoping He'll Change* (Los Angeles, CA: Jeremy P. Tarcher, 1985).

64. Mark H. Thelen, M. Daniel Fishbein, and Heather A. Tatten, "Interspousal Similarity: A New Approach to an Old Question," *Journal of Social and Personal Relationships* 2 (1985): 437–446.

65. John M. Drescher, "When Opposites Attract," *Marriage and Family Living* 61 (1979): 9–11.

66. Ellen Berscheid and Elaine Hatfield Walster, *Interpersonal Attraction*, 2nd ed. (Reading, MA: Addison-Wesley, 1978).

67. Elliot Aronson, *The Social Animal*, 3rd ed. (New York: W. H. Freeman, 1980).

68. Shaw, Personal Interview, 1987.

69. Reed, Personal Interview, 1987.

70. See, for example, Faye Grigg, Garth O. Fletcher, and Julie Fitness, "Spontaneous Attributions in Happy and Unhappy Dating Relationships," *Journal of Social and Personal Relationships* 6 (1989): 61–68; and Valerie Manusov, "An Application of Attribution Principles to Nonverbal Behavior in Romantic Dyads," *Communication Monographs* 57 (1990): 104–118.

71. See, for example, Berscheid and Walster, *Interpersonal Attraction*, 1978.

72. Remy, Personal Interview, 1987.

73. Reed, Personal Interview, 1987.

74. Leon Festinger, Stanley Schachter, and Kurt Back, *Social Pressures in Informal Groups: A Study of Human Factors in Housing* (New York: Harper & Row, 1950).

75. Irwin Altman and Dalmas Taylor, *Social Penetration: The Development of Interpersonal Relationships* (New York: Holt, Rinehart and Winston, 1973); and Mark L. Knapp, *Interpersonal Communication and Human Relationships* (Boston, MA: Allyn and Bacon, 1984).

76. See, for example, Michael P. Nofz, "Fantasy-Testing Assessment: A Proposed Model for the Investigation of Mate Selection," *Family Relations* 33 (1984): 273–281.

77. Geoffery K. Leigh, Thomas B. Holman, and Wesley R. Burr, "An Empirical Test of Sequence in Murstein's SVR Theory of Mate Selection," *Family Relations* 33 (1984): 225–231.

78. Catherine A. Surra, *Turning Point Coding Manual*, unpublished manuscript, University of Illinois, 1981.

79. Catherine A. Surra and B. G. Halperin, "Sex Differences in the Decision to Wed," paper presented at the National Council on Family Relations annual meeting, St. Paul, MN, 1983.

80. Catherine A. Surra, "Courtship Types: Variations in Interdependence Between Partners and Social Networks," *Journal of Personality and Social Psychology* 49 (1985): 357–375.

81. Catherine A. Surra, "Reasons for Changes in Commitment: Variations by Courtship Type," *Journal of Social and Personal Relationships* 4 (1987): 17–33.

82. Catherine A. Surra, Peggy Arizzi, and Linda A. Asmussen, "The Association Between Reasons for Commitment and the Development and Outcome of Marital Relationships," *Journal of Social and Personal Relationships* 5 (1988): 47–63.

83. Catherine A. Surra, "Research and Theory on Mate Selection and Premarital Relationships in the 1980s," *Journal of Marriage and the Family* 52 (1990): 844–865.

84. Bruce Lansky, *Mother Murphy's Second Law: Love, Sex, Marriage, and Other Disasters* (New York: Simon & Schuster, 1986), 19.

85. See, for example, Richard Driscoll, Keith E. Davis, and Milton E. Lipetz, "Parental Interference and Romantic Love: The Romeo and Juliet Effect," *Journal of Personality and Social Psychology* 24 (1972): 1–10.

86. See, for example, Ellen Berscheid and Elaine Hatfield Walster, "A Little Bit About Love," *Foundations of Interpersonal Attraction,* ed. Ted L. Huston (New York: Academic Press, 1974), 356–381.

87. Rex A. Wright and Richard J. Contrada, "Dating Selectivity and Interpersonal Attraction: Toward a Better Understanding of the 'Elusive Phenomenon'," *Journal of Social and Personal Relationships* 3 (1986): 131–148.

88. James E. Deal and Karen Smith Wampler, "Dating Violence: The Primacy of Previous Experience," *Journal of Social and Personal Relationships* 3 (1986): 457–471.

89. James M. Makepeace, "Gender Differences in Courtship Violence Victimization," *Family Relations* 35 (1986): 383–388.

90. James M. Makepeace, "Social Factor and Victim-Offender Differences in Courtship Violence," *Family Relations* 36 (1987): 87–91.

91. Young, Personal Interview, 1987.

92. Ford, Personal Interview, 1987.

93. Laura Stafford and James R. Reske, "Idealization and Communication in Long-Distance Premarital Relationships," *Family Relations* 39 (1990): 274–279.

94. D. Austrom, M. De Sousa, and K. Hanel, "The Interpersonal Marketplace: Companion Ads," paper presented at the Annual Meeting of the Canadian Psychological Association, Calgary, Alberta, 1980.

95. Bolig, Stein, and McKenry, 1984, 587–592.

96. See, for example, Judith Frankel D'Augelli and Anthony R. D'Augelli, "Moral Reasoning and Premarital Sexual Behavior: Toward Reasoning About Relationships," *Journal of Social Issues* 33 (1977): 46–66; and F. Scott Christopher and Rodney M. Cate, "Premarital Sexual Pathways and Relationship Development," *Journal of Social and Personal Relationships* 2 (1985): 271–288.

97. F. Scott Christopher and Michela M. Frandsen, "Strategies of Influence in Sex and Dating," *Journal of Social and Personal Relationships* 7 (1990): 89–105.

98. Christopher and Cate, 1985, 271–288.

99. Alp, Personal Interview, 1991.

100. Don Martin and Maggie Martin, "Selected Attitudes Toward Marriage and Family Life Among College Students," *Family Relations* 33 (1984): 293–300.

101. Harriet B. Braiker and Harold H. Kelley, "Conflict in the Development of Close Relationships," *Social Exchange in Developing Relationships,* ed. Robert L. Burgess and Ted L. Huston (New York: Academic Press, 1979), 135–168.

102. Carol Kelly, Ted L. Huston, and Rodney M. Cate, "Premarital Relationship Correlates of the Erosion of Satisfaction in Marriage," *Journal of Social and Personal Relationships* 2 (1985): 167–178.

103. Young, Personal Interview, 1987.

104. Braiker and Kelley, 1979, 149.

105. Karen A. Foss and Belle A. Edson, "What's In a Name? Accounts of Married Women's Name Choices," *Western Journal of Speech Communication* 53 (1989): 356–373.

106. Troy A. Zimmer, "Premarital Anxieties," *Journal of Social and Personal Relationships* 3 (1986): 149–159.

107. J. D. Ball and L. H. Henning, "Rational Suggestions for Premarital Counseling," *Journal of Marriage and Family Therapy* 9 (1981): 69–73.

108. Polk and Dennis, Personal Interview, 1991.

109. Martin and Martin, 1984, 293–300.

110. Martin and Martin, 1984, 293–300.

111. Lynn P. Buckner and Connie J. Salts, "A Premarital Assessment Program," *Family Relations* 34 (1985): 513–520.

112. Mead, Personal Interview, 1987.

113. Moore, Personal Interview, 1991.

114. Herschel, Personal Interview, 1991.

115. Alan and Karen Simms, Personal Interview, 1991.

116. Alan Simms, Personal Interview, 1991.

117. Coleman, *Intimate Relationships,* 1984.

118. Coleman, *Intimate Relationships,* 1984.

119. John Alan Lee, *The Colours of Love: An Exploration of the Ways of Loving* (Toronto, Canada: New Press, 1973).

120. Clyde Hendrick and Susan S. Hendrick, "Lovers Wear Rose Colored Glasses," *Journal of Social and Personal Relationships* 5 (1988): 161–183.

121. Lawrence A. Kurdek, "Marital Stability and Changes in Marital Quality in Newly Wed Couples: A Test of the Contextual Model," *Journal of Social and Personal Relationships* (1991): 27–48.

122. Evelyn Ruth Millis Duvall and Reuben Hill, *Being Married* (New York: Associated Press, 1960), 340.

123. Patricia A. Parmelee, "Sex Role Identity, Role Performance and Marital Satisfaction of Newly-Wed Couples," *Journal of Social and Personal Relationships* 4 (1987): 429–444.

CHAPTER 7 NOTES

1. Judith C. Daniluk and Al Herman, "Parenthood Decision-Making," *Family Relations* 33 (1984): 607–612.

2. Anne V. Gormly, John B. Gormly, and Helen Weiss, "Motivations for Parenthood Among Young Adult College Students," *Sex Roles* 16 (1987): 31–40.

3. Bill Cosby, *Fatherhood* (New York: Berkley, 1986), 18, 23.

4. Lansky, *Mother Murphy*, 1986, 61–62.

5. Luther B. Otto, "America's Youth: A Changing Profile," *Family Relations* 37 (1988): 385–391.

6. Harold L. Hodgkinson, *All One System: Demographics of Education—Kindergarten Through Graduate School* (Washington, DC: Institute for Educational Leadership, 1985).

7. Valena White Plisko and Joyce D. Stern, eds., *The Condition of Education: 1985 Edition* (Washington, DC: U.S. Government Printing Office, 1985).

8. Luther B. Otto, "America's Youth: A Changing Profile," *Family Relations* 37 (1988): 385–391.

9. Hodgkinson, *All One System*, 1985.

10. Hodgkinson, *All One System*, 1985.

11. B. Liebenberg, "Expectant Fathers," *Child and Family* 8 (1969): 265–272.

12. "New Baby Tough on Pop," *Columbus Citizen Journal*, 28 December 1985.

13. Rob Palkovitz, "Predictors of Change in Parental Role Prescriptions and Self-Esteem Across the Transition to Parenthood," *Family Perspective* 22 (1988): 15–26.

14. Lawrence H. Liese, Lonnie R. Snowden, and Lucy K. Ford, "Partner Status, Social Support, and Psychological Adjustment During Pregnancy," *Family Relations* 38 (1989): 311–316.

15. Pamela M. Wallace and Ian H. Gotlib, "Marital Adjustment during the Transition to Parenthood: Stability and Predictors of Change," *Journal of Marriage and the Family* 52 (1990): 21–29.

16. Wallace and Gotlib, 1990, 21–29.

17. Jay Belsky and Michael Rovine, "Patterns of Marital Change Across the Transition to Parenthood: Pregnancy to Three Years Postpartum," *Journal of Marriage and the Family* 52 (1990): 5–19.

18. Ford, Personal Interview, 1987.

19. Hilary M. Lips and Anne Morrison, "Changes in the Sense of Family Among Couples Having Their First Child," *Journal of Social and Personal Relationships* 3 (1986): 393–400.

20. Lips and Morrison, 1986, 393.

21. Eric E. Peterson, "The Stories of Pregnancy: On Interpretation of Small-Group Cultures," *Communication Quarterly* 35 (1987): 39–47.

22. Lucia A. Gilbert and Gary R. Hanson, "Perceptions of Parental Role Responsibilities Among Working People: Development of a Comprehensive Measure," *Journal of Marriage and the Family* 45 (1983): 203–212.

23. Coleman, *Intimate Relationships*, 1984.

24. Robert R. Sears, Eleanor E. Maccoby, and Harry Levin, *Patterns of Child Rearing* (New York: Harper & Row, 1957).

25. Coleman, *Intimate Relationships*, 1984.

26. Patricia M. Crittenden, "Social Networks, Quality of Child Rearing and Child Development," *Child Development* 56 (1985): 1299–1313.

27. Lucia A. Gilbert and Gary R. Hanson, "Perceptions of Parental Role Responsibilities Among Working People: Development of a Comprehensive Measure," *Journal of Marriage and the Family* 45 (1983): 203–212.

28. J. J. Evoy, *The Rejected: Psychological Consequences of Parental Rejection* (University Park, PA: Pennsylvania State University Press, 1982).

29. Victor Goertzel and Mildred George Goertzel, *Cradles of Eminence* (Boston, MA: Little, Brown, 1962).

30. Ellen Galinsky, *Between Generations: The Six Stages of Parenthood* (New York: Times Books, 1981), 5.

31. Galinsky, *Between Generations,* 1981, 122–130.

32. Galinsky, *Between Generations,* 1981, 178.

33. Galinsky, *Between Generations,* 1981, 283.

34. Ford, Personal Interview, 1987.

35. Hilliard, Personal Interview, 1991.

36. Hilliard, Personal Interview, 1991.

37. Hilliard, Personal Interview, 1991.

38. See, for example, Corrine Hutt, "Sex Differences in Human Development," *Human Development* 15 (1972): 153–170.

39. Jaipaul L. Roopnarine, "Mothers' and Fathers' Behavior Toward the Toy Play of Their Infant Sons and Daughters," *Sex Roles* 14 (1986): 59.

40. R. Parke and S. O'Leary, "Father-Mother-Infant Interaction in the Newborn Period: Some Findings, Some Observations, and Some Unresolved Issues," *The Developing Infant in a Changing World,* vol. 2, *Social and Environmental Issues,* ed. K. Reigel and J. Meacham (The Hague: Mouton, 1976).

41. Jay Belsky, "Mother-Father-Infant Interaction: A Naturalistic Observational Study," *Developmental Psychology* 15 (1979): 601–607.

42. Frank A. Pedersen, B. J. Anderson, and R. L. Caine, "Parent-Infant and Husband-Wife Interactions Observed at Age Five Months," *The Father-Infant Relationship: Observational Studies in a Family Setting,* ed. Frank A. Pederson (New York: Praeger, 1980), 71–86.

43. Belsky, "Mother-Father-Infant," 1979, 601–607.

44. Ford, Personal Interview, 1987.

45. Joe F. Pittman, Cherly A. Wright, and Sally A. Lloyd, "Predicting Parenting Difficulty," *Journal of Family Issues* 10 (1989): 267–286.

46. Joan Pinkos Bowker, *The First Baby: Coping or Crisis in the First Three Months,* diss., University of Michigan, Ann Arbor, 1977; Everett Dyer, "Parenthood as Crisis: A Restudy," *Journal of Marriage and the Family* 25 (1963): 196–201; and Daniel Hobbs, Jr., "Parenthood as Crisis: A Third Study," *Journal of Marriage and the Family* 27 (1965): 367–372.

47. S. Shirley Feldman and Sharon C. Nash, "Interest in Babies During Young Adulthood," *Child Development* 49 (1984): 616–622.

48. Barbara Abrahams, S. Shirley Feldman, and Sharon C. Nash, "Sex Role Self-Concept and Sex Role Attitudes: Enduring Personality Characteristics or

Adaptations to Changing Life Situations?" *Developmental Psychology* 14 (1978): 393–400; S. Shirley Feldman, Zeynep C. Biringen, and Sharon C. Nash, "Fluctuations in Sex-Related Self-Attributions as a Function of Stage of Family Life Cycle," *Developmental Psychology* 17 (1981): 24–35; and Lois Wiadis Hoffman and Jean Denby Manis, "Influences of Children on Marital Interaction and Parental Satisfactions and Dissatisfactions," *Child Influences on Marital and Family Interaction: A Life-Span Perspective,* ed. Richard M. Learner and Graham B. Spanier (New York: Academic Press, 1978), 165–214.

49. David Gutmann, "Parenthood: A Key to the Comparative Study of the Life-Cycle," *Life-Span Developmental Psychology: Normative Life Crises,* ed. Nancy Datan and Leon Ginsberg (New York: Academic Press, 1975), 167–184; David L. Gutmann, "The Cross-Cultural Perspective: Notes Toward a Comparative Psychology of Aging," *Handbook on the Psychology of Aging,* ed. James E. Birren and K. Warner Schaie (New York: Van Nostrand Reinhold, 1977), 302–326.

50. S. Shirley Feldman and Sharon C. Nash, "Interest in Babies During Young Adulthood," *Child Development* 49 (1978): 616–622; S. Shirley Feldman and Sharon C. Nash, "Sex Differences in Responsiveness to Babies Among Mature Adults," *Development Psychology* 15 (1979): 430–436; Sharon C. Nash and S. Shirley Feldman, "Responsiveness to Babies: Life-Situation Specific Sex Differences in Adulthood," *Sex Roles* 6 (1980): 751–758; Sharon C. Nash and S. Shirley Feldman, "Sex Role and Sex-Related Attributions: Constancy and Change Across the Life Cycle," *Advances in Developmental Psychology,* ed. Michael E. Lamb and Ann L. Brown (Hillsdale, NJ: Lawrence Erlbaum, 1981), 1–35.

51. Judith E. Blakemore, "Age and Sex Differences in Interaction with a Human Infant," *Child Development* 52 (1981): 386–388.

52. Judith E. Blakemore, "Interaction with a Baby by Young Adults: A Comparison of Traditional and Feminist Men and Women," *Sex Roles* 13 (1985): 405–411.

53. Renee H. Steffensmeier, "A Role Model of the Transition to Parenthood," *Journal of Marriage and the Family* 44 (1982): 319–344; and Holly Waldron and Donald K. Routh, "The Effect of the First Child on the Marital Relationship," *Journal of Marriage and the Family* 43 (1981): 785–788.

54. Boyd C. Rollins and Kenneth L. Cannon, "Marital Satisfaction Over the Family Life Cycle: A Reevaluation," *Journal of Marriage and the Family* 36 (1974): 271–282; B. C. Rollins and R. Galligan, "The Developing Child and Marital Satisfaction of Parents," *Child Influences on Marital and Family Interaction: A Life-Span Perspective,* ed. Richard M. Lerner and Graham B. Spanier (New York: Academic Press, 1978), 71–106.

55. Lucia A. Gilbert, Carole Kovalic Holahan, and Linda Manning, "Coping with Conflict Between Professional and Maternal Roles," *Family Relations* 30 (1981): 419–426.

56. Feldman and Nash, *Expectancy to Parenthood,* 1984, 61–78; Lynda Cooper Harriman, "Marital Adjustment as Related to Personal and Marital Changes Accompanying Parenthood," *Family Relations* 34 (1986): 233–239; and Judith Long Laws, "A Feminist Review of Marital Adjustment Literature: The Rape of the Locke," *Journal of Marriage and the Family* 33 (1971): 483–516.

57. Jay Belsky and Russell A. Isabella, "Marital and Parent-Child Relationships in Family Origin and Marital Charge Following the Birth of a Baby: A Retrospective Analysis," *Child Development* 56 (1985): 342–349.

58. See, for example, Lucia A. Gilbert and Carole K. Holahan, "Conflicts Between Student/Professional, Parental, and Self-Development Roles: A Comparison of High and Low Effective Copers," *Human Relations* 35 (1982): 635–648; and Leonard I. Pearlin and Carmi Schooler, "The Structure of Coping," *Journal of Health and Social Behavior* 19 (1978): 2–21.

59. See, for example, Pearlin and Schooler, "The Structure of Coping," 1978, 2–21.

60. Lucia A. Gilbert, Carole K. Holahan, and Linda Manning, "Coping with Conflict Between Professional and Maternal Roles," *Family Relations* 30 (1981): 419–426.

61. Margaret R. Elman and Lucia A. Gilbert, "Coping Strategies for Role Conflict in Married Professional Women with Children," *Family Relations* 33 (1984): 317–327.

62. Judith A. Myers-Walls, "Balancing Multiple Role Responsibilities During the Transition to Parenthood," *Family Relations* 33 (1984): 267–271.

63. Alan Guttmacher Institute, *The Problem Hasn't Gone Away* (New York: Planned Parenthood Federation of America, 1981).

64. Mark W. Roosa and Linda Vaughan, "A Comparison of Teenage and Older Mothers with Preschool Age Children," *Family Relations* 33 (1984): 259–265.

65. See, for example, Lillian Belmont, Patricia Cohen, Joy Dryfoos, Zena Stein, and Susan Zayac, "Maternal Age and Children's Intelligence," *Teenage Parents and Their Offspring*, ed. Keith G. Scott, Tiffany Field, and Evan G. Robertson (New York: Grune and Stratton, 1981), 177–194; S. H. Broman, "Longterm Development of Children Born to Teenagers," *Teenage Parents and Their Offspring*, ed. Keith G. Scott, Tiffany Field, and Evan G. Robertson (New York: Grune and Stratton, 1981), 195–224; and Roosa and Vaughan, 1984, 259–265.

66. Nancy C. Gunter and Richard C. LaBarba, "Maternal and Perinatal Effects of Adolescent Childbearing," *International Journal of Behavioral Development* 4 (1981): 333–357; and Pearila Brickner Rothenberg and Phylis E. Varga, "The Relationship Between Age of Mother and Child Health and Development," *American Journal of Public Health* 71 (1981): 810–817.

67. Mark W. Roosa, Hiram E. Fitzgerald, and Nancy A. Carlson, "A Comparison of Teenage and Older Mothers: A Systems Analysis," *Journal of Marriage and the Family* 44 (1982): 367–377; and G. L. Schilmoeller and M. D. Baranowski, "Childrearing of Firstborns by Adolescent and Older Mothers," *Adolescence* 20 (1985): 805–822.

68 Ramona T. Mercer, "Teenage Motherhood: The First Year," *Journal of Obstetric, Gynecological and Neonatal Nursing* 9 (1980): 16–27; Roosa and Vaughan, 1984, 259–265.

69. Roosa and Vaughan, 1984, 259–265.

70. Stephen W. Littlejohn, *Theories of Human Communication* (Belmont, CA: Wadsworth, 1983), 47.

71. Charles Horten Cooley, *Human Nature and the Social Order* (New York: Charles Scriber's Sons, 1912).

72. Anne McCreary Juhasz, "Significant Others and Self-Esteem: Methods for Determining Who and Why," *Adolescence* 95 (1989): 580–593.

73. French, *Her Mother's Daughter*, 1987, 404.

74. Littlejohn, 1983, 49.

75. Annie Dillard, *An American Childhood* (New York: Harper & Row, 1987), 15.

76. See, for example, Ellen Wartella and Byron Reeves, "Communication and Children," *Handbook of Communication Science*, ed. Charles R. Berger and Steven H. Chaffee (Newbury Park, CA: Sage, 1987), 619–650.

77. Beth Haslett, "Acquiring Conversational Competence," *The Western Journal of Speech Communication* 48 (1984): 107–124.

78. Haslett, "Conversational Competence," 1984, 107–124.

79. C. Trevarthen, "The Primary Motives for Cooperative Understanding," *Social Cognition*, ed. George Butterworth and Paul Light (Chicago: University of Chicago Press, 1982), 100.

80. David J. Messer, "Adult-Child Relationships and Language Acquisition," *Journal of Social and Personal Relationships* 3 (1986): 101–119.

81. Haslett, "Conversational Competence," 1984, 107–124.

82. Elizabeth Bates, *Language and Context: The Acquisition of Pragmatics* (New York: Academic Press, 1976).

83. Catherine Garvey, "Requests and Responses in Children's Speech," *Journal of Child Language* 2 (1975): 41–63.

84. Laura Stafford, "A Comparison of Illocutionary Force of Maternal Speech to Twin and Singleton Children: Implications for Language Acquisition," paper presented to the Speech Communication Association, Chicago, IL, November 1986, 3.

85. J. B. Gleason, *The Development of Language* (Columbus, OH: Charles E. Merrill, 1985); Lila R. Gleitman, Elissa L. Newport, and Henry Gleitman, "The Current Status of the Motherese Hypothesis," *Journal of Child Language* 11 (1984): 43–79.

86. See, for example, Jerome S. Bruner, "The Ontogenisis of Speech Acts," *Journal of Child Language* 2 (1975): 1–19; Jerome S. Bruner and V. Sherwood, "Early Rule Structure: The Case of Peekaboo," *Play: Its Role in Evolution and Development*, ed. Jerome S. Bruner, Alison Jolly, and Kathy Sylva (Harmondsworth, UK: Penguin, 1976); Anat Ninio and Jerome Bruner, "The Achievement and Antecedents of Labeling," *Journal of Child Language* 5 (1978): 1–15; and Nancy Ratner and Jerome Bruner, "Games, Social Exchange, and the Acquisition of Language," *Journal of Child Language* 5 (1978): 391–401.

87. See, for example, Catherine Snow, "Mothers' Speech Research: From Input to Interaction," *Talking to Children*, ed. Catherine E. Snow and Charles A. Ferguson (Cambridge, MA: Cambridge University Press, 1977), 31–49; and C. Trevathan, "Descriptive Analyses of Infant Communicative Behavior," *Studies in Mother-Infant Interaction*, ed. H. Rudolph Schaffer (London: Academic Press, 1977), 227–270.

88. A. Hayes, "Interaction, Engagement, and the Origins and Growth of Communication: Some Constructive Concerns," *The Origins and Growth of Communication*, ed. Lynne Feagans, Catherine Garvey, and Roberta Golinkoff (Norwood, NJ: Ablex, 1984), 136–161.

89. Mary D. Salter Ainsworth and Silvia M. Bell, "Mother-Infant Interaction and the Development of Competence," *The Growth of Competence*, ed. Kevin Connolly and Jerome Bruner (New York: Academic Press, 1974), 97–119; and Michael Lewis and Susan Goldberg, "Perceptual-Cognitive Development in Infancy: A Generalized Expectancy Model as a Function of the Mother-Infant Interaction," *Merrill-Palmer Quarterly of Behavior and Development* 15 (1969): 81–100.

90. Laura Stafford, "A Conversational Analysis of Turn Allocation Techniques in Mother-Infant Routines," paper presented at the annual Speech Communication Association Convention, Denver, CO, 1985.

91. See, for example, James P. Connell and Ross Thompson, "Emotion and Social Interaction in the Strange Situation: Consistencies and Asymmetric Influences in the Second Year," *Child Development* 57 (1986): 733–745; and Jeanne M. Meadowcroft, "Family Communication Patterns and Political Development: The Child's Role," *Communication Research* 13 (1986): 603–624.

92. Julie Yingling, "Relational Competence in Infant-Caregiver Pairs: Strategies for Constituting Interaction Between Unequal Partners," paper presented to the Speech Communication Association, Chicago, IL, November 1986, 1.

93. See, for example, S. S. Ricks, "Father-Infant Interactions: A Review of Empirical Research," *Family Relations* 34 (1985): 505–511.

94. Michael E. Lamb, Ann M. Frodi, Carl Philip Hwang, and Majt Frodi, "Varying Degrees of Paternal Involvement in Infant Care," *Nontraditional Families: Parenting and Child Development*, ed. Michael E. Lamb (Hillsdale, NJ: Lawrence Erlbaum, 1982), 117–137.

95. Jay Belsky, "A Family Analysis of Parental Influence on Infant Exploratory Competence," *The Father-Infant Relationship: Observational Studies in a Family Setting*, ed. Frank A. Pedersen (New York: Praeger, 1980), 87–110; and F. A. Pedersen, L. J. Yarrow, B. J. Anderson, and R. L. Caine, "Conceptualization of Father Influences in the Infancy Period," *The Child and Its Family*, ed. Michael Lewis and Leonard A. Rosenblum (New York: Plenum, 1979), 45–66.

96. Michael E. Lamb, "Parent-Infant Interaction in Eight-Month-Olds," *Child Psychiatry and Human Development* 7 (1976): 56–63.

97. Milton Kotelchuck, Philip R. Zelazo, Jerome Kagan, and Elizabeth Spelke, "Infant to Parental Separations When Left with Familiar and Unfamiliar Adults," *The Journal of Genetic Psychology* 126 (1975): 255–262.

98. Ross D. Parke and Douglas B. Sawin, "The Family in Early Infancy: Social Interactional and Attitudinal Analysis," *The Father-Infant Relationship: Observational Studies in a Family Setting*, ed. Frank A. Pedersen (New York: Praeger, 1980), 44–70.

99. Frank A. Pedersen, Barbara J. Anderson, and Richard L. Cain, "Parent Infant and Husband Wife Interactions Observed at Age Five Months," *The Father-Infant Relationship: Observational Studies in a Family Setting*, ed. Frank A. Pedersen (New York: Praeger, 1980), 71–86.

100. K. Allison Clarke-Stewart, "And Daddy Makes Three: The Father's Impact on Mother and Child," *Child Development* 49 (1978): 466–478.

101. J. Belsky, "A Family Analysis of Parental Influence on Infant Exploratory Competence," *The Father-Infant Relationship: Observational Studies in a Family Setting*, ed. Frank A. Pedersen (New York: Praeger, 1980), 87–110.

102. Michael E. Lamb, "The Development of Mother-Infant and Father-Infant Attachments in the Second Year of Life," *Developmental Psychology* 13 (1977): 637–646; Ross D. Parke and Douglas B. Sawin, "The Family in Early Infancy: Social Interactional and Attitudinal Analysis," *The Father-Infant Relationship: Observational Studies in a Family Setting*, ed. Frank A. Pedersen (New York: Praeger, 1980), 44–70.

103. Paul Henry Mussen, John J. Conger, Jerome Kagan, and J. Geiwitz, *Psychological Development: A Life-Span Approach* (New York: Harper & Row, 1979).

104. Beth Haslett, "Conversational Competence," 1984, 107–124.

105. Ann R. Eisenberg and Catherine Garvey, "Children's Use of Verbal Strategies in Resolving Conflicts," *Discourse Processes* 4 (1981): 149–170; and Beth Haslett, "Preschooler's Communicative Strategies in Gaining Compliance from Peers: A Developmental Study," *Quarterly Journal of Speech* 69 (1983): 84–99.

106. Catherine Garvey, "Requests and Responses in Children's Speech," 30 (1974): 297–306; Beth Haslett, "Children's Strategies for Maintaining Cohesion in Their Written and Oral Stories," *Communication Education* 32 (1983): 91–105.

107. Marilyn Shatz and Rachel Gelman, "The Development of Communication Skills: Modifications in the Speech of Young Children as a Function of Listener," *Monographs of the Society for Research in Child Development* 38 (1973): Serial No. 152.

108. Richard L. Street, Jr., "Noncontent in Speech Convergence and Divergence in Adult-Child Interactions," *Communication Yearbook* 7, ed. Robert N. Bostrom (Newbury Park, CA: Sage, 1983), 369–395.

109. J. Donald Ragsdale and Rosemary Dauterive, "Relationships Between Age, Sex, and Hesitation Phenomena in Young Children," *The Southern Speech Communication Journal* 52 (1986): 22–34.

110. Mary Louise Willbrand and Richard D. Rieke, "Reason Giving in Children's Supplicatory Compliance Gaining," *Communication Monographs* 53 (1986): 47–60.

111. Haslett, "Conversation Competence," 1984, 221.

112. Lisa D. Kahan and D. Dean Richards, "Effects of Two Types of Familiarity on Children's Referential Communication Abilities," *Communication Monographs* 52 (1985): 280–287.

113. Barbara O'Keefe and Jesse Delia, "Impression Formation and Message Production," *Social Cognition and Communication,* ed. Michael E. Roloff and Charles R. Berger (Newbury Park, CA: Sage, 1982), 33–72.

114. Doran C. French, "Children's Social Interaction with Older, Younger, and Same-Age Peers," *Journal of Social and Personal Relationships* 4 (1987): 63–86.

115. Judy Dunn and Penny Munn, "Becoming a Family Member: Family Conflict and the Development of Social Understanding in the Second Year," *Child Development* 56 (1985): 486–492.

116. Reed Markham, "Teaching Your Child Through Effective Communication," available through EDRS, 1990.

117. Derek Edwards and David Middleton, "Conversation Remembering and Family Relationships: How Children Learn to Remember," *Journal of Social and Personal Relationships* 5 (1988): 3–25.

118. See, for example, John P. Murray and Susan Kippax, "Children's Social Behavior in Three Towns with Differing Television Experience," *Journal of Communication* 28 (1978): 19–29; and James G. Webster, Judy C. Pearson, and Debra B. Webster, "Children's Television Viewing as Affected by Contextual Variables in the Home," *Communication Research Reports* 3 (1986): 1–8.

119. Alan M. Rubin, "Age and Family Control Influences on Children's Television Viewing," *The Southern Speech Communication Journal* 52 (1986): 35–51; and Webster, Pearson, and Webster, 1986, 1–8.

120. Webster, Pearson, and Webster, 1986, 1–8.

121. Roger Jon Desmond, Jerome L. Singer, Dorothy G. Singer, Rachel Calam, and Karen Colimore, "Family Mediation Patterns and Television Viewing: Young

Children's Use and Grasp of the Medium," *Human Communication Research* 11 (1985): 461–480.

122. Mary Strom Larson, "The Portrayal of Families on Prime Time Television," paper presented at the Annual Meeting of the Speech Communication Association, Boston, MA, 5–6 November 1987.

123. Michael Morgan, Alison Alexander, James Shanahan, and Cheryl Harris, "Adolescents, VCRs, and the Family Environment," *Communication Research* 17 (1990): 83–106.

124. Virginia Satir, *Conjoint Family Therapy* (3rd ed.) (Palo Alto, CA: Science and Behavior Books, 1983).

125. Richard B. Felson and Mary A. Zielinski, "Children's Self-Esteem and Parental Support," *Journal of Marriage and the Family* 51 (1989): 727–735.

126. Satir, 1983, 67–68.

127. See, for example, Bonni R. Seegmiller, "Sex-Typed Behavior in Preschoolers: Sex, Age, and Social Class Effects," *Journal of Psychology* 104 (1980): 31–33.

128. Susan S. Haugh, Charles D. Hoffman, and Gloria Cowan, "The Eye of the Very Young Beholder: Sex Typing of Infants by Young Children," *Child Development* 51 (1980): 598–600.

129. See, for example, Sylvia Lee Tibbits, "Sex Role Stereotyping in the Lower Grades: Part of a Solution," *Journal of Vocational Behavior* 6 (1975): 255–261.

130. Nancy Eisenberg, Sharlene A. Wolchik, Robert Hernandez, and Jeanette F. Pasternack, "Parental Socialization of Young Children's Play: A Short-Term Longitudinal Study," *Child Development* 56 (1985): 1506–1513.

131. Barry Schwartz, "The Social Psychology of Privacy," *American Journal of Sociology* 73 (1985): 741–752.

132. A. D. Pellegrini and Jane C. Perlmutter, "Classroom Contextual Effects on Childrens' Play," *Developmental Psychology* 25 (1989): 289–296.

133. Judith E. O. Blakemore, Asenath A. LaRue, and Anthony B. Olenjnik, "Sex Appropriate Preferences and the Ability to Conceptualize Toys as Sex Role Related," *Developmental Psychology* 15 (1979): 339–340; and Marion O'Brien and Aletha C. Huston, "Activity Level and Sex Stereotyped Toy Choice in Toddler Boys and Girls," *The Journal of Genetic Psychology* 146 (1986): 527–528.

134. L. A. Serbin and J. M. Conner, "Sex Typing of Children's Play Preferences and Patterns of Cognitive Performance," *Journal of Genetic Psychology* 134 (1979): 315–316.

135. O'Brien and Huston, 1986, 527–528.

136. Arnie Cann and Susan Palmer, "Children's Assumptions About the Generalizability of Sex-Typed Abilities," *Sex Roles* 15 (1986): 551–558; and Mary L. Trepanier-Street and Jerri Jaudon Kropp, "Children's Recall and Recognition of Sex Role Stereotyped and Discrepant Information," *Sex Roles* 16 (1986): 237–249.

137. Michelle B. Bass, "The Cooperative Family," *Pointer* 33 (1989): 39–42.

138. Satir, *Conjoint Family Therapy*, 1983.

139. Bruce Hilands Peppin, "Parental Understanding, Parental Acceptance and the Self-Concept of Children as a Function of Academic Over- and Under-Achievement," *Dissertation Abstracts* 23 (1963): 4422–4423.

140. Harry Levin, "Permissive Child Rearing and Adult Role Behavior," *Contributions to Modern Psychology*, ed. Don Edwin Dunlany, Russell L. DeValois, David C. Beardsley, and Marion R. Winterbottom (New York: Oxford University Press, 1958), 307–312.

141. K. Purcell, "Assessment of Psychological Determinants in Childhood Asthma," *Readings in a Child Development and Personality*, ed. Paul Henry Mussen, John Janeway Conger, and Jerome Kagan (New York: Harper & Row, 1970), 345–355.

142. E. James Anthony and Therese Benedek, *Parenthood: Its Pscyopathology* (Boston, MA: Little, Brown, 1970).

143. Shear, Personal Interview, 1991.

144. Jacob Chwast, "Sociopathic Behavior in Children," *Manual of Child Psychopathology*, ed. Benjamin B. Wolman (New York: McGraw-Hill, 1972), 436–445.

145. James A. Armentrout and Gary K. Burger, "Children's Reports of Parental Childrearing Behavior at Five Grade Levels," *Developmental Psychology* 7 (1972): 44–48; and E. S. Schaefer, "A Configurational Analysis of Children's Reports of Parent Behavior," *Journal of Consulting Psychology* 29 (1965): 552–557.

146. Mary Anne Fitzpatrick and Diane M. Badzinski, "All in the Family: Interpersonal Communication in Kin Relationships," *Handbook of Interpersonal Communication*, ed. Mark L. Knapp and Gerald R. Miller (Newbury Park, CA: Sage, 1985), 707.

147. Dillard, 1987, 130.

148. Gwendolyn Mettetal, "Fantasy, Gossip, and Self-Disclosure: Children's Conversations with Friends," *Communication Yearbook* 7, ed. Robert B. Bostrom (Newbury Park, CA: Sage, 1983), 717–736.

149. French, "Children's Social Interaction," 1987, 63–86.

150. Brant R. Burleson, James L. Applegate, Julie A. Burke, Ruth Anne Clark, Jesse G. Delia, and Susan L. Kline, "Communicative Correlates of Peer Acceptance," *Communication Education* 35 (1986): 358.

151. Ruth Anne Clark, Shirley C. Willihnganz, and Lisa L. O'Dell, "Training Fourth Graders in Compromising and Persuasive Strategies," *Communication Education* 34 (1985): 340.

152. Ross Homel, Ailsa Burns, and Jacqueline Goodnow, "Parental Social Networks and Child Development," *Journal of Social and Personal Relationships* 4 (1987): 159–177.

153. James C. Coleman, *Intimate Relationships, Marriage, and Family* (Indianapolis, IN: Bobbs-Merrill, 1984).

CHAPTER 8 NOTES

1. A. K. Cohen, 1964.

2. D. Rogers, *Issues in Adolescent Psychology*, 3rd ed. (Englewood Cliffs, NJ: Prentice-Hall, 1977), 3.

3. M. S. Faust, "Somatic Development of Adolescent Girls," *Monographs of the Society for Research in Child Development* 42 (1977): 1, Serial No. 169; J. M. Tanner, "Growth and Physique in Different Populations of Mankind," *The Biology of Human Adaptability*, ed. P. T. Baker and J. S. Weiner (Oxford: Clarendon, 1966); J. M. Tanner, "Physical Growth," *Carmichael's Manual of Child Psychology*, ed. P. H. Mussen, vol. 1 (New York: John Wiley, 1970).

4. See, for example, V. G. Lewis, J. Money, and N. A. Bobrow, "Idiopathic Pubertal Delay Beyond the Age of Fifteen: Psychologic Study of Twelve Boys," *Adolescence* 12 (1977): 1–11; J. Money, "Psychosexual Differentiation," *Sex Research, New Developments*, ed. J. Money (New York: Holt, Rinehart and Winston, 1965); and Arlene McGrory, "Menarche: Responses of Early Adolescent Females," *Adolescence* 25 (1990): 265–270.

5. Lee Shain and Barry A. Farber, "Female Identity Development and Self-Reflection in Late Adolescence," *Adolescence* 24 (1989): 381–392.

6. N. J. Bell, A. W. Avery, D. Jenkins, J. Feld, and C. J. Schoenrock, "Family Relationships and Social Competence During Late Adolescence," *Journal of Youth and Adolescence* 14 (1985): 109–119; L. G. Bell and D. C. Bell, "Family Climate and the Role of the Female Adolescent: Determinants of Adolescent Functioning," *Family Relations* (1982): 519–527; L. G. Bell and D. C. Bell, "Parental Validation and Support in the Development of Adolescent Daughters," *New Directions for Child Development: Adolescent Development in the Family*, ed. H. D. Grotevant and C. R. Cooper (San Francisco, CA: Jossey-Bass, 1983); Dennis R. Papini, Rickard A. Sebby, and Steven Clark, "Affective Quality of Family Relations and Adolescent Identity Exploration," *Adolescence* 24 (1989): 457–466.

7. L. O. Murphy and S. M. Ross, "Gender Differences in the Social Problem-Solving Performance of Adolescents," *Sex Roles* 16 (1987): 251–264.

8. Christine Nelson and Joanne Keith, "Comparisons of Female and Male Early Adolescent Sex Role Attitude and Behavior Development," *Adolescence* (1990): 183–204.

9. Katica Lackovic-Grgin and Maja Dekovic, "The Contribution of Significant Others to Adolescents' Self-Esteem," *Adolescence* 25 (1990): 839–846.

10. Lackovic-Grgin and Dekovic, 1990, 839–846.

11. Thomas Ewin Smith, "Parental Separation and the Academic Self-Concepts of Adolescents: An Effort to Solve the Puzzle of Separation Effects," *Journal of Marriage and the Family* 52 (1990): 107–118.

12. George A. Youngs, Jr., Richard Rathage, Ron Mullis, and Ann Mullis, "Adolescent Stress and Self-Esteem," *Adolescence* 25 (1990): 333–341.

13. Anne B. Hendershott, "Residential Mobility, Social Support and Adolescent Self-Concept," *Adolescence* 24 (1989): 217–232.

14. Scott Hines and David L. Groves, "Sports Competition and Its Influence on Self-Esteem Development," *Adolescence* 24 (1989): 861–869.

15. Lian-Hwang Chiu, "The Relationship of Career Goal and Self-Esteem Among Adolescents," *Adolescence* 25 (1990): 593–597.

16. G. M. Ingersoll, *Adolescence*, 2nd ed. (Englewood Cliffs, NJ: Prentice-Hall, 1989).

17. M. Friedman, *Family Nursing: Theory and Assessment*, 2nd ed. (Norwalk, CT: Appleton-Century-Crofts, 1986).

18. J. A. Williamson and L. P. Campbell, "Parents and Their Children Comment on Adolescence," *Adolescence* 20 (1985): 745–748.

19. A. P. Jurich, W. R. Schumm, and S. R. Bollman, "The Degree of Family Orientation Perceived by Mothers, Fathers, and Adolescents," *Adolescence* 22 (1987): 119–128.

20. Raymond L. Calabrese and Jane Adams, "Alienation: A Cause of Juvenile Delinquency," *Adolescence* 25 (1990): 435–440; Jill A. Daniels, "Adolescent Separation-Individuation and Family Transitions," *Adolescence* 25 (1990): 105–116; A. Therese Miller, Colleen Eggertson-Tacon, and Brian Quigg, "Patterns of Runaway Behavior Within a Larger Systems Context: The Road to Empowerment," *Adolescence* 25 (1990): 271–289; Jean A. Pardeck and John T. Pardeck, "Family Factors Related to Adolescent Autonomy," *Adolescence* 25 (1990): 311–319.

21. R. Montemayer, "The Relationship Between Parent-Adolescent Conflict and the Amount of Time Adolescents Spend Alone and with Parents and Peers," *Child Development* 53 (1982): 1512–1519; Joan Pulakos, "Young Adult Relationships: Siblings and Friends," *Journal of Psychology* 123 (1989): 237–244.

22. Remy, Personal Interview, 1987.

23. Reed, Personal Interview, 1987.

24. See, for example, Linda Bell, Connie S. Cornwell, and David C. Bell, "Peer Relationships of Adolescent Daughters: A Reflection of Family Relationship Patterns," *Family Relations* 37 (1988): 171–174; Ann C. Crouter, Judith H. Carson, Judith A. Vicary, and Janice Butler, "Parent-Child Closeness as an Influence on the Projected Life Course of Rural Adolescent Girls," *Journal of the History of the Behavioral Sciences* 8 (1988): 345–355.

25. Patricia E. Ortman, "Adolescents' Perceptions of and Feelings about Control and Responsibility in Their Lives," *Adolescence* 23 (1988): 913–924; M. E. P. Seligman and M. Miller, "The Psychology of Power: Concluding Comments," *Choice and Perceived Control,* ed. L. C. Perlmutter and R. Monty (Hillsdale, NJ: Lawrence Erlbaum Associates, 1979).

26. Christina E. Mitchell, "Development or Restoration of Trust in Interpersonal Relationships During Adolescence and Beyond," *Adolescence* 25 (1990): 847–854; J. Rotter, "Interpersonal Trust, Trustworthiness and Gullibility," *American Psychologist* 35 (1980): 1–7; J. Tanner, *Loneliness: The Fear of Love* (New York: Perennial Library, 1973); Lawrence Wheeless, "A Follow-Up Study of the Relationship Among Trust, Disclosure, and Interpersonal Solidarity," *Human Communication Research* 4 (1978): 143–157; Lawrence Wheeless and Janice Grotz, "The Measurement of Trust and Its Relationship to Self-Disclosure," *Human Communication Research* 3 (1977): 250–257.

27. Lisa A. Tedesco and Eugene L. Gaier, "Friendship Bond in Adolescence," *Adolescence* 23 (1988): 127–136.

28. William K. Rawlins and Melissa R. Holl, "Adolescents' Interaction with Parents and Friends: Dialetics of Temporal Perspective and Evaluation," *Journal of Social and Personal Relationships* 5 (1988): 27–46.

29. Montemayer, 1982, 1512–1519.

30. S. Zamanou, "A Study of Teenagers' Perceptions of Topic Appropriateness for Discussion with Parents," paper presented at the annual Speech Communication Association Convention, Denver, CO, November 1985.

31. See, for example, Terri D. Fisher, "An Extension of the Findings of Moore, Peterson, and Furstenberg (1986) Regarding Family Sexual Communication and Adolescent Sexual Behavior," *Journal of Marriage and the Family* 51 (1989): 637–639.

32. S. Elizabeth Baldwin and Madelon Visintainer Baranoski, "Family Interactions and Sex Education in the Home," *Adolescence* 25 (1990): 573–592.

33. Gregory F. Sanders and Ronald L. Mullis, "Family Influences on Sexual Attitudes and Knowledge as Reported by College Students," *Adolescence* 23 (1988): 837–846.

34. B. A. Goswick and W. H. Jones, "Components of Loneliness During Adolescence," *Journal of Youth and Adolescence* 11 (1982): 378–389.

35. Stuart H. Traub and Richard A. Dodder, "Intergenerational Conflict of Values and Norms: A Theoretical Model," *Adolescence* 23 (1988): 975–989.

36. H. L. Barnes and D. H. Olson, "Parent-Adolescent Communication and the Circumplex Model," *Child Development* 56 (1985): 438–447.

37. Venus Shirley Masselam, "Parent Adolescent Communication, Family Functioning, and School Performance," diss., University of Maryland, 1989, 23; Venus S. Masselam, Robert F. Marcus, and Clayton L. Strunkard, "Parent-Adolescent Communication, Family Functioning, and School Performance," *Adolescence* 25 (1990): 723–737.

38. Masselam, 1989, 23.

39. French, 1987, 340.

40. H. H. Remmers and D. H. Radler, *The American Teenager* (Indianapolis, IN: Bobbs-Merrill, 1957).

41. Williamson and Campbell, 1985, 745–748.

42. Young, Personal Interview, 1987.

43. Smith, Personal Interview, 1987.

44. Jeffry H. Larson and Wendell Lowe, "Family Cohesion and Personal Space in Families with Adolescents," *Journal of Family Issues* 11 (1990): 101–108.

45. Dennis R. Papini, Frank F. Farmer, Steven M. Clark, Jill C. Micka, and Jawanda K. Barnett, "Early Adolescent Age and Gender Differences in Patterns of Emotional Self-Disclosure to Parents and Friends," *Adolescence* 25 (1990): 959–976.

46. L. L. Eggert and M. R. Parks, "Communication Network Involvement in Adolescents' Friendship and Romantic Relationships," *Communication Yearbook* 10 (Newbury Park, CA: Sage, 1987), 283–322.

47. See, for example, D. W. Proefrock, "The Uncertainty Principle in Adolescent Research," *Adolescence* 18 (1983): 339–343.

48. R. E. Muus, *Theories of Adolescence* (New York: Random House, 1962).

49. N. Kiell, *The Universal Experience of Adolescence* (New York: International Universities Press, 1964).

50. Remy, Personal Interview, 1987.

51. Remy, Personal Interview, 1987.

52. C. Peterson, J. Peterson, and S. Skevington, "Heated Argument and Adolescent Development," *Journal of Social and Personal Relationships* 3 (1986): 229–240.

53. L. S. Wright, "Suicidal Thoughts and Their Relationship to Family Stress and Personal Problems Among High School Seniors and College Graduates," *Adolescence* 20 (1985): 575–580.

54. C. Gurucharri and R. L. Selma, "The Development of Interpersonal Understanding During Childhood, Preadolescence, and Adolescence, a Longitudinal Follow-Up Study," *Child Development* 53 (1982): 924–927; Marcel Danesi, "Adolescent Language as Affectively Coded Behavior: Findings of an Observational Research Project," *Adolescence* 24 (1989): 311–320.

55. Geoffrey Tesson, John H. Lenko, and Brian J. Bigelow, "Adolescent Social Rule Usage in Family, Peer and Adult Relationships," *Sociological Studies of Child Development* 3 (1990): 175–199.

56. Tedesco and Gaier, 1988, 127–136.

57. Elizabeth Paul and Kathleen M. White, "The Development of Intimate Relationships in Late Adolescence," *Adolescence* 25 (1990): 375–400.

58. J. G. Delia, S. L. Kline, and B. R. Burleson, "The Development of Persuasive Communication Strategies in Kindergartners Through Twelfth-Graders," *Communication Monographs* 46 (1979): 241–256.

59. Kim D. White, Judy C. Pearson, and Lyle Flint, "Adolescents' Compliance-Resistance: Effects of Parents' Compliance Strategy and Gender and Adolescents' Gender," paper presented at the International Communication Association Convention, Montreal, May 1987.

60. J. F. Peters, "Adolescents as Socialization Agents to Parents," *Adolescence* 20 (1985): 921–933.

61. Ellen A. Forman, Patriya S. Tansuhaz, and Karin M. Ekstrom, "Family Members' Perceptions of Adolescents' Influence in Family Decision Making," *Journal of Consumer Research* 15 (1989): 482–491.

62. Stephen Rubin, "College Freshmen: Turmoil or Maturity?" *Adolescence* 23 (1988): 585–591.

63. See, for example, F. Herz, "The Impact of Death and Serious Illness on the Family Life Cycle," *The Family Life Cycle: A Framework for Family Therapy*, ed. E. Carter and M. McGoldrick (New York: Gardner Press, 1980).

64. D. Offer and M. Sabshin, *Normality and the Life Cycle* (New York: Basic Books, 1984).

65. B. A. Goswick and W. H. Jones, "Components of Loneliness During Adolescence," *Journal of Youth and Adolescence* 11 (1982): 378–389.

66. M. Davis and S. Franzoi, "Adolescent Self-Disclosure and Loneliness: Private Self-Consciousness and Parental Influence," *Journal of Personality and Social Psychology* 48 (1985): 768–780.

67. Tesson, Lenko, and Bigelow, 1990, 175–199.

68. See, for example, Barbara Newman, "The Changing Nature of the Parent-Adolescent Relationship from Early to Late Adolescence," *Adolescence* 24 (1989): 915–924.

69. Anita L. Vangelisti, "Validity Testing: A Systematic Examination of Social Consensus and Intersubjectivity in Qualitative Observation," paper presented at

the joint meeting of the Central States Speech Association and the Southern Speech Communication Association, St. Louis, MO, April 1987.

CHAPTER 9 NOTES

1. Barbara Mitchell, Andrew V. Wister, and Thomas K. Burch, "The Family Environment and Leaving the Parental Home," *Journal of Marriage and the Family* 51 (1989): 605–613.

2. Stephen A. Anderson, "Changes in Parental Adjustment and Communication During the Leaving-Home Transition," *Journal of Social and Personal Relationships* 7 (1990): 47–68.

3. Anderson, 1990, 47–68.

4. William S. Aqrilino and Khalil R. Supple, "Parent-Child Relations and Parent's Satisfaction with Living Arrangements When Adult Children Live at Home," *Journal of Marriage and the Family* 53 (1991): 13–27.

5. Shaw, Personal Interview, 1987.

6. J. F. Peters, "Youth, Family and Employment," *Adolescence* 22 (1987): 465–474.

7. A. F. Poussaint, Introduction, *Time Flies,* by Bill Cosby (New York: Doubleday, 1987), 3.

8. B. Lansky, *Mother Murphy's Second Law: Love, Sex, Marriage, and Other Disasters* (New York: Simon & Schuster, 1986), 46.

9. D. C. Borland, "A Cohort Analysis Approach to the Empty Nest Syndrome Among Three Ethnic Groups of Women: A Theoretical Position," *Journal of Marriage and the Family* 44 (1982): 117–129.

10. E. Palmore, "Total Chance of Institutionalization Among the Aged," *Gerontologist* 16 (1981): 504–507; H. L. Bee and S. K. Mitchell, *The Developing Person: A Life-Span Approach* (New York: Harper & Row, 1984).

11. S. S. Feldman, Z. C. Biringen, and S. C. Nash, "Fluctuations in Sex-Related Self-Attributions as a Function of Stage of Family Life Cycle," *Developmental Psychology* 17 (1981): 24–35; J. Z. Giele, "Women in Adulthood: Unanswered Questions," *Women in the Middle Years: Current Knowledge and Directions for Research and Policy,* ed. J. Z. Giele (New York: John Wiley and Sons, 1982); G. E. Vaillant, *Adaptation to Life: How the Brightest Come of Age* (Boston, MA: Little, Brown, 1978).

12. L. Neugarten and D. L. Gutmann, "Age-Sex Roles and Personality in Middle Age: A Thematic Apperception Study," *Psychological Monographs* 72 (1958): 1–33.

13. O. G. Brim, Jr., "Dating and Physical Attractiveness: Replication," *Psychological Reports* (1976): 6.

14. S. Model, "Housework by Husbands," *Journal of Family Issues* 2 (1981): 225–237.

15. F. Walsh, "The Family in Later Life," *The Family Life Cycle: A Framework for Family Therapy,* ed. E. A. Carter and M. McGoldrick (New York: Gardner Press, 1980), 197–220.

16. See, for example, V. Wood and J. Robertson, "The Significance of Grandparenthood," *Time, Roles, and Self in Old Age,* ed. J. F. Gubrium (New York: Human Sciences, 1976), 278–304.

17. J. Aldous, "International Visiting Patterns: Variation in Boundary Maintenance as an Explanation," *Family Process* 6 (1967): 235–251; V. L. Bengtson et al., "The

Impact of Social Structure on the Aging Individual," *Handbook of the Psychology of Aging*, ed. J. E. Birren and K. W. Schaie (New York: Van Nostrand Reinhold, 1976); V. R. Kivett, "Aging in Rural Society: Non-Kin Community Relations and Participation," *The Elderly in Rural Society*, ed. R. T. Coward and G. R. Lee (New York: Springer, 1985), 171–191; G. F. Sanders, J. Walters, and J. E. Montgomery, "Married Elderly and Their Families," *Family Perspectives* 18 (1984): 45–52.

18. See, for example, M. Zube, "Continuities and Change in the Life Course and Family Life of Middle-Aged and Older Men," *Family Perspective* 19 (1985): 79–89.

19. National Center for Health Statistics. Reported in M. E. Barrett, "Still married after all these years." *USA Today Weekend*, September 8–10, 1989, p. 18.

20. Lynn White and John N. Edwards, "Emptying the Nest and Parental Well-Being: An Analysis of National Panel Date," *American Sociological Review* 55 (1990): 235–242; N. D. Glenn and S. McLanahan, "Children and Marital Happiness: A Further Specification of the Relationship," *Journal of Marriage and the Family* 44 (1982): 63–72; W. R. Gove and C. Peterson, "An Update of the Literature on Personal and Marital Adjustment: The Effect of Children and the Employment of Wives," *Marriage and Family Review* 3 (1980): 63–96.

21. White and Edwards, 1990, 235–242.

22. M. J. Cain, Personal Interview, 1991.

23. A. F. Poussaint, Introduction, *Time Flies*, by Bill Cosby (New York: Doubleday, 1987), 12–13.

24. Glenn and McLanahan, 1982, 63–72; Gove and Peterson, 1980, 63–96; L. W. Hoffman and J. D. Manis, "Influences of Children on Marital Interaction and Parental Satisfactions and Dissatisfaction," *Child Influences on Marital and Family Interaction: A Life-Span Perspective*, ed. R. M. Dearner and G. B. Spanier (New York: Academic Press, 1978), 165–214; B. C. Rollins and H. Feldman, "Marital Satisfaction Over the Family Life Cycle," *Journal of Marriage and the Family* 32 (1970): 20–27.

25. Christian Kloos, Personal Interview, 1991.

26. Linda Robertson, Personal Interview, 1991.

27. P. M. Keither and T. H. Brubaker, "Male Household Roles in Later Life: A Look at Masculinity and Marital Relationships," *Family Coordinator* 28 (1979): 497–502.

28. Lorraine T. Dorfman and D. Alex Heckert, "Egalitarianism in Retired Rural Couples: Household Tasks, Decision Making, and Leisure Activities," *Family Relations* 37 (1988): 73–78.

29. J. Aldous, *Family Careers: Developmental Changes in Families* (New York: Wiley, 1978); E. A. Hill and L. T. Dorfman, "Reaction of Housewives to the Retirement of Their Husbands," *Family Relations* 31 (1982): 195–200.

30. J. H. Scanzoni and M. Szinovacz, *Family Decisionmaking: A Developmental Sex Role Model* (Newbury Park, CA: Sage, 1980); T. H. Brubaker and C. B. Hennon, "Responsibility for Household Tasks: Comparing Dual-Retired Marriages," *Women's Retirement: Policy Implications of Recent Research*, ed. M. Szinovacz (Beverly Hills, CA: Sage, 1982), 205–219.

31. Pat M. Keith and Andre Nauta, "Old and Single in the City and in the Country: Activities of the Unmarried," *Family Relations* 37 (1988): 79–83.

32. Elizabeth Mutran, "Family, Social Ties and Self-Meaning in Old Age: The Development of an Affective Identity," *Journal of Social and Personal Relationships* 4 (1987): 463.

33. Joyce Baumgard, Personal Interview, 1991

34. A. F. Poussaint Introduction, *Time Flies,* by Bill Cosby (New York: Doubleday, 1987), 2.

35. Bill Cosby, *Time Flies* (New York: Doubleday, 1987), 78–83.

36. Christian Kloos, Personal Interview, 1991

37. Joseph Baumgard, Personal Interview, 1991.

38. Cosby, 1987, 23.

39. Michelle Beaumont, Personal Interview, 1991.

40. Victor Beaumont, Personal Interview, 1991.

41. V. R. Kivett, "The Kinship Network and the Elderly," *Handbook of Aging,* ed. J. E. Montgomery (Washington, DC: American Home Economics Association, 1980).

42. L. Webb, "Common Topics of Conversation Between Young Adults and Their Grandparents," *Communication Research Reports* 2 (1985): 156–163.

43. M. C. Rosebud-Harris, "A Description of the Interactional and Subjective Characteristics of the Relationships Between Black Grandmothers and Their Grandchildren Enrolled in the University of Louisville," *Dissertation Abstracts International* 43 (1982): 2714A.

44. E. Hoffman, "Young Adults' Relations with Their Grandparents: An Exploratory Study," *International Journal of Aging and Human Development* 10 (1979): 299–309.

45. J. F. Robertson, "Interaction in Three Generation Families, Parents as Mediators: Toward a Theoretical Perspective," *International Journal of Aging and Human Development* 6 (1975): 103–110.

46. Webb, 1985, 156–153.

47 E. J. Caltvedt and G. K. Leigh, "Parent-Adult-Child Interaction and Psychological Well-Being of the Elderly," *Family Perspectives* 18 (1984): 93–100.

48. Joyce McDonough Mercier, Lori Paulson, and Earl W. Morris, "Rural and Urban Elderly: Differences in the Quality of the Parent-Child Relationship," *Family Relations* 37 (1988): 68–72.

49. R. Blieszner and J. A. Mancini, "Enduring Ties: Older Adults' Parental Role and Responsibilities," *Family Relations* 36 (1987): 176–180.

50. D. J. Cheal, "Intergenerational Family Transfers," *Journal of Marriage and the Family* 45 (1983): 805–813; G. F. Sanders, J. Walters, and J. E. Montgomery, "Married Elderly and Their Families," *Family Perspectives* 18 (1984): 45–52.

CHAPTER 10 NOTES

1. Leslie A. Baxter and Kathryn Dindia, "Marital Partners' Perceptions of Marital Maintenance Strategies," *Journal of Social and Personal Relationships* 7 (1990): 1.

2. Baxter and Dindia, 1990, 2.

3. Baxter and Dindia, 1990, 2–3.

4. Erich Fromm, *The Art of Loving* (New York: Harper & Row, 1956).

5. Kahlil Gibran, *The Prophet* (New York: Knopf, 1923).

6. Henry Turk, Personal Interview, 1991.

7. Sandra Turk, Personal Interview, 1991.

8. Christian Kloos, Personal Interview, 1991.

9. Tina Kloos, Personal Interview, 1991.

10. Sherry Ehrlich, Personal Interview, 1991.

11. Arnold Lazarus, "Five Most Dangerous Myths About Marriage," *New Woman* May (1986): 73–75.

12. Phil DeLong, Personal Interview, 1991.

13. Phil DeLong, Personal Interview, 1991.

14. Christian Kloos, Personal Interview, 1991.

15. Janeen Nickerson, Personal Interview, 1991.

16. E. Oring, "Dyadic Traditions," *Journal of Folklore Research* 21 (1984): 19–28.

17. Robert Hopper, Mark L. Knapp, and Lorel Scott, "Couples' Personal Idioms: Exploring Intimate Talk," *Journal of Communication* 31 (1981): 23–33.

18. Hopper, Knapp, and Scott, 1981, 23–33.

19. Robert A. Bell, Nancy L. Buerkel-Rothfuss, and Kevin E. Gore, "Did You Bring the Yarmulke for the Cabbatge Patch Kid? The Idomatic Communication of Young Lovers," *Human Communication Research* 14 (1987): 47–67.

20. Lori Strauss and Joel Woods, Personal Interview, 1991.

21. Kathleen M. Galvin and Bernard J. Brommel, *Family Communication: Cohesion and Change*, 2nd ed. (Glenviw, IL: Scott, Foresman, 1986), 65.

22. Bess Pittman, Personal Interview, 1991.

23. Curt Emde, Personal Interview, 1991.

24. Donna Emde, Personal Interview, 1991.

25. Karen Simons, Personal Interview, 1991.

26. Harold D. Grotevant and Catherine R. Cooper, "Patterns of Interaction in Family Relationships and the Development of Identity Exploration in Adolescence," *Child Development* 56 (1985): 415–428.

27. Michelle Healy and Karen S. Peterson, "Talking Is Key to a Healthy Clan," *USA Today*, 17 April 1987, 4D.

28. David H. L. Olson, "Bridging Research, Theory and Application: The Triple Threat in Science," *Treating Relationships*, ed. David H. L. Olson (Lake Mills, IA: Graphic, 1976), 565–579.

29. David H. L. Olson and Hamilton I. McCubbin, *Families: What Makes Them Work* (Newbury Park, CA: 1983), 48.

30. Olson and McCubbin, 1983, 48.

31. See, for example, David H. Olson and A. E. Craddock, "Circumplex Model of Marital and Family Symptoms: Application to Australian Families," *Australian Journal of Sex, Marriage and Family* 1 (1980): 53–69; David H. Olson and Hamilton I. McCubbin, "Circumplex Model of Marital and Family Systems V: Application to Family Stress and Crises Intervention," *Family Stress, Coping and Social Support*, ed. Hamilton I. McCubbin, A. Elizabeth Cauble, and Joan M.

Patterson (Springfield, IL: Charles C. Thomas, 1982), 48–72; David H. Olson, Douglas H. Sprenkle, and Candyce S. Russell, "Circumplex Model of Marital and Family Systems: In Cohesion and Adaptability Dimensions, Family Types and Clinical Application," *Family Process* 18 (1979): 3–28.

32. Virginia Satir, *Conjoint Family Therapy,* 3rd ed. (Palto Alto, CA: Science and Behavior Books, 1983), 9.

33. Ellen Galinsky, *Between Generations: The Six Stages of Parenthood* (New York: Times Book, 1981), 78–79.

34. Paul Lutkenhaus, Klaus E. Grossmann, and Karin Grossmann, "Infant-Mother Attachment at Twelve Months and Style of Interaction with a Stranger at Three Years," *Child Development* 56 (1985): 1538–1542.

35. Satir, *Conjoint Family Therapy,* 1983.

36. Harry Stack Sullivan, *The Interpersonal Theory of Psychiatry,* ed. Helen Swick Perry and Mary Ladd Gewel (New York: Norton, 1953).

37. E. Galinsky, 1981, 189.

38. Joseph Luft, *Group Processes: An Introduction to Group Dynamics* (Palto Alto, CA: Mayfield, 1984).

39. Dysfunctional social behavior and an avoidance of intimacy can occur because of a violation of attachment relationships with particular developmental stages, as well. See, for example, Kim Bartholomew, "Avoidance of Intimacy: An Attachment Perspective," *Journal of Social and Personal Relationships* 7 (1990): 147–178.

40. Erik Erikson, *Identity, Youth, and Crisis* (New York: Norton, 1968).

41. Harold and Stella Hensley, Personal Interview, 1991.

42. Mary Anne Fitzpatrick, "Dyadic Adjustment in Traditional, Independent and Separate Relationships: A Validation Study," paper presented at Speech Communication Association, 1977; Mary Anne Fitzpatrick, "A Typological Approach to Communication in Relationships," *Communication Yearbook 1,* ed. B. Rubin (New Brunswick, NJ: Transaction Books, 1977).

43. Paul C. Rosenblatt and Martha G. Russell, "The Social Psychology of Potential Problems in Family Vacation Travel," *Family Coordinator* 24 (1975): 209–215.

44. Barry Schwartz, "The Social Psychology of Privacy," *American Journal of Sociology* 73 (1968): 741–752.

45. Paul Cozby, "Self-Disclosure: A Literature Review," *Psychological Bulletin* 79 (1973): 73–91; Sidney M. Jourard and Paul Lasakow, "Some Factors in Self-Disclosure," *Journal of Abnormal and Social Psychology* 56 (1958): 91–98; W. Barnett Pearce and Stewart M. Sharp, "Self-Disclosing Communication," *Journal of Marriage and the Family* 23 (1973): 409–425.

46. Irwin Altman, "Reciprocity of Interpersonal Exchange," *Journal for the Theory of Social Behavior* 3 (1973): 249–261; Kenneth N. Anchor, Howard M. Sandler, and Jacqueline H. Cherones, "Maladaptive Antisocial Aggressive Behavior and Outlets for Intimacy," *Journal of Clinical Psychology* 33 (1977): 947–949; Barbara M. Montgomery and Robert W. Norton, "Sex Differences and Similiarities in Communicator Style," *Communication Monographs* 48 (1981): 121–132; Robert W. Norton, "Foundation of a Communicator Style Construct," *Human Communication Research* 4 (1978): 99–112.

47. See, for example, Irwin Altman and Dalmas Taylor, *Social Penetration: The Development of Interpersonal Relationships* (New York: Holt, Rinehart and

Winston, 1973); Cozby, 1973, 73–91; Shirley J. Gilbert, "Self-Disclosure, Intimacy and Communication in Families," *The Family Coordinator* 25 (1976): 221–230; Shirley J. Gilbert and Gale G. Whiteneck, "Toward a Multidimensional Approach to the Study of Self-Disclosure," *Human Communication Research* 2 (1976): 347–355; Lawrence R. Wheeless and Janice Grotz, "Conceptualization and Measurement of Reported Self-Disclosure," *Human Communication Research* 2 (1976): 338–346.

48. John W. Thibaut and Harold H. Kelley, *The Social Psychology of Groups* (New York: Wiley, 1959), 20–21.

49. Elaine Walster, G. William Walster, and Ellen Berscheid, *Equity: Theory and Research* (Boston, MA: Allyn and Bacon, 1978), 6.

50. Anna Kashfi Brando and E. P. Stein, *Brando for Breakfast* (New York: Berkley, 1980).

51. Stephen A. Anderson, "Parental and Marital Role Stress During the School Entry Transition," *Journal of Social and Personal Relationships* 2 (1985): 59–80.

52. Jones, Personal Interview, 1985.

53. James J. Bradac, Charles H. Tardy, and Lawrence A. Hosman, "Disclosure Styles and a Hint at Their Genesis," *Human Communication Research* 6 (1980): 228–238.

54. See, for example, Cozby, 1973, 73–91; Connie DeForest and Gerald L. Stone, "Effects of Sex and Intimacy Level on Self-Disclosure," *Journal of Counseling Psychology* 27 (1980): 93–96; Lynda Greenblatt, James E. Gasenauer, and Vicki S. Freimuth, "Psychological Sex Type and Androgyny in the Study of Communication Variables: Self-Disclosure and Communication Apprehension," *Human Communication Research* 6 (1980): 117–129; Elaine LeVine and Juan N. Franco, "A Reassessment of Self-Disclosure Patterns Among Anglo-Americans and Hispanics," *Journal of Counseling Psychology* 28 (1981): 522–524.

55. Wheeless and Grotz, 1976, 338–346.

56. Wheeless and Grotz, 1976, 338–346.

57. A. George Gitter and Harvey Black, "Is Self-Disclosure Revealing?" *Journal of Counseling Psychology* 23 (1976): 327–332; Darhl M. Pederson and Vincent J. Breglio, "The Correlation of Two Self Disclosure Inventories with Actual Self-Disclosure: A Validity Study," *Journal of Psychology* 68 (1968): 291–298.

58. Lawrence B. Rosenfeld, "Self-Disclosure Avoidance: Why I Am Afraid to Tell You Who I Am," *Communication Monographs* 46 (1979): 63–74.

59. Wheeless and Grotz, 1976, 338–346.

60. Ronald J. Burke, Tamara Weir, and Denise Harrison, "Disclosure of Problems and Tensions Experienced by Marital Partners," *Psychological Reports* 38 (1976): 531–542.

61. Alice Adams, *Families and Other Survivors* (New York: Penguin, 1974), 193.

62. Hazel J. Rozema, "Defensive Communication Climate as a Barrier to Sex Education in the Home," *Family Relations* 35 (1986): 531–537.

63. Charles H. Tardy, Lawrence A. Hosman, and James J. Bradac, "Disclosing Self to Friends and Family: A Reexamination of Initial Questions," *Communication Quarterly* 29 (1981): 263–268.

64. Tardy, Hosman, and Bradac, 1981, 263–268.

65. Jack O. Balswick and James W. Balkwell, "Self-Disclosure to Same- and Opposite-

Sex Parents: An Empirical Test of Insights from Role Theory," *Sociometry* 40 (1977): 282–286; Sidney M. Jourard and Paul Lasakow, "Some Factors in Self-Disclosure," *Journal of Abnormal and Social Psychology* 56 (1958): 91–98; Robert P. Littlefield, "Self-Disclosure Among Some Negro, White, and Mexican-American Adolescents," *Journal of Counseling Psychology* 21 (1974): 133–136; Brian S. Morgan, "Intimacy of Disclosure Topics and Sex Differences in Self-Disclosure," *Sex Roles* 2 (1976): 161–166; Darhl M. Pederson and Kenneth L. Higbee, "Self-Disclosure and Relationship to the Target Person," *Merrill Palmer Quarterly of Behavior and Development* 15 (1969): 213–220; Richard M. Ryckman, Martin F. Sherman, and Gary D. Burgess, "Locus of Control and Self-Disclosure of Public and Private Information by College Men and Women: A Brief Note," *Journal of Psychology* 84 (1973): 317–318.

66. Tardy, Hosman, and Bradac, 1981, 263–268.

67. Howard P. Woodyard and David A. Hines, "Accurate Compared to Inaccurate Self-Disclosure," *Journal of Humanistic Psychology* 13 (1973): 61–67.

68. Tardy, Hosman, and Bradac, 1981, 263–268.

69. Rainey, Personal Interview, 1985.

70. Ticer, Personal Interview, 1985.

71. Gerber, Personal Interview, 1985.

72. Hoey, Personal Interview, 1985.

73. Rader, Personal Interview, 1985.

74. Krause, Personal Interview, 1985.

75. Judy C. Pearson, *Interpersonal Communication: Clarity, Confidence, Concern* (Glenview, IL: Scott, Foresman, 1983), 249.

76. Hoey, Personal Interview, 1985.

77. Harry Stack Sullivan, *The Interpersonal Theory of Psychiatry*, ed. Helen Swick Perry and Mary Ladd Gewel (New York: Norton, 1953), 264.

78. Sven Wahlroos, *Family Communication* (New York: Macmillan, 1983), 303.

79. Wahlroos, 1983, 305.

80. *USA Today*, 13 April 1987, 4D.

81. See, for example, T. B. Holman and G. W. Brock, "Implications for Therapy in the Study of Communication and Marital Quality," *Family Perspective* 20 (1986): 85–94.

82. Gary R. Birchler and Linda J. Webb, "Discriminating Interaction Behaviors in Happy and Unhappy Marriages," *Journal of Consulting and Clinical Psychology* 45 (1977): 494–495; Lenne A. Boyd and Arthur J. Roach, "Interpersonal Communication Skills Differentiating More Satisfying From Less Satisfying Marital Relationships," *Journal of Counseling Psychology* 24 (1977): 540–542; Shirley J. Gilbert, 1976, 221–230; Leslie Navran, "Communication Adjustment in Marriage," *Family Process* 6 (1967): 173–184.

83. Lillian M. Snyder, "The Deserting, Nonsupporting Father: Scapegoat of Family Nonpolicy," *Family Coordinator* 28 (1979): 594–598.

84. Carla R. Dersch and Judy C. Pearson, "Interpersonal Communication Competence and Marital Adjustment Among Dual-Career and Dual-Worker Women," paper presented to the annual meeting of the Central States Speech Association Convention, Cincinnati, OH, April 1986.

85. Sharon Brennan, Personal Interview, 1991.

86. J. B. McGinnis, *Bread and Injustice* (New York: Paulist Press, 1977).

87. Sidney M. Jourard, "A Study of Self-Disclosure," *Scientific American* 198 (1958): 77–82.

88. See, for example, A. P. Bochner and C. W. Kelly, "Interpersonal Competence: Rationale, Philosophy, and Implementation of a Conceptual Framework," *Speech Teacher* 23 (1974): 279–301; Richard L. Johannesen, "The Emerging Concept of Communication as Dialogue," *Quarterly Journal of Speech* 57 (1971): 373–382; Robert A. Lewis, "Emotional Intimacy Among Men," *Journal of Social Issues* 34 (1978): 108–121.

89. Claude M. Steiner, *When a Man Loves a Woman: Sexual and Emotional Literacy for the Modern Man* (New York: Grove Press, 1986), 152.

90. See, for example, Shirley J. Gilbert, 1976, 221–230; George Levinger and David J. Senn, "Disclosure of Feelings in Marriage," *Merrill-Palmer Quarterly of Behavior and Development* 13 (1967): 237–249.

91. Stephen R. Jorgensen and Janis C. Gaudy, "Self-Disclosure and Satisfaction in Marriage: The Relation Examined," *Family Relations* 29 (1980): 286.

92. Patricia Noller, "Negative Communication in Marriage," *Journal of Social and Personal Relationships* 2 (1985): 289–301.

93. Gabrielle M. Maxwell, "Behaviour of Lovers: Measuring the Closeness of Relationships," *Journal of Social and Personal Relationships* 2 (1985): 215–238.

94. Jeffrey E. Hansen and W. John Schuldt, "Marital Self-Disclosure and Marital Satisfaction," *Journal of Marriage and the Family* 46 (1984): 923–926.

95. Burke, Weir, and Harrison, 1976, 531–542; Anthony Fiore and Clifford H. Swenson, "Analysis of Love Relationships in Functional and Dysfunctional Marriages," *Psychological Reports* 40 (1977): 707–714; Shirley J. Gilbert, 1976, 221–230; Levinger and Senn, 1967, 237–249; J. Waterman, "Family Patterns of Self-Disclosure," *Self-Disclosure,* ed. Gordon J. Chelune and Associates (San Francisco: Jossey-Bass, 1979), 225–242.

96. Rainey, Personal Interview, 1985.

97. Shirley J. Gilbert and David Horenstein, "The Communication of Self-Disclosure: Level Versus Valence," *Human Communication Research* 1 (1975): 316–322.

98. See, for example, Richard L. Archer and John H. Berg, "Disclosure Reciprocity and Its Limits: A Reactance Analysis," *Journal of Experimental Social Psychology* 14 (1978): 527–540; Joseph A. Flaherty, "Self-Disclosure in Therapy: Marriage of the Therapist," *American Journal of Psychotherapy* 33 (1979): 442–452.

99. Walter R. Schumm, Howard L. Barnes, Stephen R. Bollman, Anthony P. Jurich, and M. A. Bugaighis, "Self-Disclosure and Marital Satisfaction Revisited," *Family Relations* 34 (1986): 241–247.

100. Alan L. Sillars, Judith Weisberg, Cynthia S. Burggraf, and Elizabeth A. Wilson, "Content Themes in Marital Conversations," *Human Communication Research* 13 (1987): 495–528.

101. Barry Schwartz, "The Social Psychology of Privacy," *American Journal of Sociology* 73 (1968): 741–752.

102. See, for example, Douglas L. Kelley, "Privacy in Marital Relationships," *The Southern Speech Communication Journal* 53 (1988): 441–456.

103. Malcolm R. Parks, "Ideology in Interpersonal Communication: Off the Couch and into the World," *Communication Yearbook 5*, ed. M. Burgoon (New Brunswick, NJ: Transaction Books, 1981), 79–107.

104. Ronny E. Turner, Charles Edgley, and Glen Olmstead, "Information Control in Conversations: Honesty Is Not Always the Best Policy," *Kansas Journal of Sociology* 11 (1975): 69–89.

105. Arthur P. Bochner, "On the Efficacy of Openness in Close Relationships," *Communication Yearbook 5*, ed. Michael Burgoon (New Brunswick, NJ: Transaction Books, 1981), 119.

106. Valerian J. Derlega and Alan L. Chaikin, "Privacy and Self-Disclosure in Social Relationships," *Journal of Social Issues* 33 (1977): 102–115.

107. Shirley P. Glass and Thomas L. Wright, "Sex Differences in Type of Extramarital Involvement and Marital Dissatisfaction," *Sex Roles* 12 (1985): 1101–1120.

108. Stephen R. Jorgensen and Janis C. Gaudy, "Self-Disclosure and Satisfaction in Marriage: The Relation Examined," *Family Relations* 29 (1980): 281–287.

109. Shirley J. Gilbert, "Self-Disclosure, Intimacy and Communication in Families," *The Family Coordinator* 25 (1976): 221–230.

110. Gary R. Pike and Alan L. Sillars, "Reciprocity of Marital Communication," *Journal of Social and Personal Relationships* 2 (1985): 303.

111. Burke, Weir, and Harrison, 1976, 531–542.

112. Davidson, Balswick, and Halverson, 1983.

113. Gerald M. Phillips and H. Lloyd Goodall, *Loving and Living: Improve Your Friendships and Marriage* (Englewood Cliffs, NJ: Prentice-Hall, 1983).

114. Levinger and Senn, 1967, 246

115. See, for example, George Levinger, "Marital Cohesiveness and Dissolution: An Integrative Review," *Journal of Marriage and the Family* 27 (1965): 19–28; Patricia Noller, "Negative Communications in Marriage," *Journal of Social and Personal Relationships* 2 (1985): 289–301; Gary R. Pike and Alan L. Sillars, "Reciprocity of Marital Communication," *Journal of Social and Personal Relationships* 2 (1985): 303–324.

116. Millard J. Bienvenu, "Measurement of Marital Communication," *The Family Coordinator* 19 (1970): 26–31.

117. Susan Sprecher, "The Effects of Self-Disclosure Given and Received on Affection for an Intimate Partner and Stability of the Relationship," *Journal of Social and Personal Relationships* 4 (1987): 125.

118. Stella Ting-Toomey, "An Analysis of Verbal Communication Patterns in High and Low Marital Adjustment Groups," *Human Communication Research* 9 (1983): 306–319.

119. Warren Farrell, *Why Men Are the Way They Are* (New York: McGraw-Hill, 1986), 339.

120. Susan B. Shimanoff, "Types of Emotional Disclosures and Request Compliance Between Spouses," *Communication Monographs* 54 (1987): 85–100.

121. Sandra S. Petronio, "The Effect of Interpersonal Communication on Women's Family Role Satisfaction," *The Western Journal of Speech Communication* 46 (1982): 208–222.

122. Levinger and Senn, 1967, 237–249; Frances Helen Voss, *The Relationships of Disclosure to Marital Satisfaction: An Exploratory Study,* thesis, University of Wisconsin–Milwaukee, 1969.

123. Leslie A. Baxter and William W. Wilmot, "Taboo Topics in Close Relationships," *Journal of Social and Personal Relationships* 2 (1985): 253–269.

124. John M. Gottman, *Marital Interaction: Experimental Investigations* (New York: Academic Press, 1979).

125. Arnold Shapiro and Clifford Swenson, "Patterns of Self-Disclosure Among Married Couples," *Journal of Counseling Psychology* 16 (1969): 179–180.

126. Bernard Davidson, Jack Balswick, and Charles J. Halverson, "Affective Self-Disclosure and Marital Adjustment: A Test of Equity Theory," *Journal of Marriage and the Family* 45 (1983): 93–102.

127. Steven H. Beach and Ileana Arias, "Assessment of Perceptual Discrepancy: Utility of the Primary Communication Inventory," *Family Process* 22 (1983): 309–316.

128. Stephen R. Jorgensen and Janis C. Gaudy, "Self-Disclosure and Satisfaction in Marriage: The Relation Examined," *Family Relations* 29 (1980): 281–287; Susan Sprecher, "The Effects of Self-Disclosure Given and Received on Affection for an Intimate Partner and Stability of the Relationship," *Journal of Social and Personal Relationships* 4 (1987): 115–127.

CHAPTER 11 NOTES

1. P. Watzlawick, J. Beavin, and D. Jackson, *Pragmatics of Human Communication: A Study of Interactional Patterns, Pathologies, and Paradoxes* (New York: Norton, 1967).

2. See, for example, E. J. Posavee and S. J. Pasko, "Interpersonal Attraction and Confidence of Attraction Ratings as a Function of Number of Attitudes and Attitude Similarity," *Psychonomic Science* 23 (1971): 433–436; Arnold Shapiro and Clifford Swensen, "Patterns of Self-Disclosure Among Married Couples," *Journal of Counseling Psychology* 16 (1969): 179–180; Alan L. Sillars and Michael D. Scott, "Interpersonal Perception Between Intimates: An Integrative Review," *Human Communication Research* 10 (1983): 153–176.

3. Joan Aldous, Elisabeth Klaus, and David M. Klein, "The Understanding Heart: Aging Parents and Their Favorite Children," *Child Development* 35 (1985): 613–617; Robert A. Lewis and Graham B. Spanier, "Theorizing About the Quality and Stability of Marriage," *Contemporary Theories About the Family,* vol. 1, ed. Wesley R. Burr, R. Hill, F. E. Nye, and I. C. Reiss (London: Free Press, 1979).

4. J. M. White, "Perceived Similarity and Understanding in Married Couples," *Journal of Social and Personal Relationships* 2 (1985): 45–57.

5. Arthur P. Bochner, Dorothy L. Krueger, and Terrence L. Chmielewski, "Interpersonal Perceptions and Marital Adjustment," *Journal of Communication* 32 (1982): 135–147.

6. B. H. Gottlieb, "Social Support and the Study of Personal Relationships," *Journal of Social and Personal Relationships* 2 (1985): 354.

7. Marilyn French, *Her Mother's Daughter* (New York: Summit Books, 1987), 91.

8. French, 1987, 91–92.

9. Robert N. Bostrom and Carol L. Bryant, "Factors in the Retention of Information   Presented Orally: The Role of Short Term Listening," *Western Journal of Speech Communication* 44 (1980): 137–145.

10. Kenneth B. Clark, "Empathy: A Neglected Topic in Psychological Research," *American Psychologist* 35 (1980): 188.

11. Sandra L. Bem, "Sex-Role Adaptability: One Consequence of Psychological Androgyny," *Journal of Personality and Social Psychology* 31 (1975): 634–643; Malcolm R. MacDonald, "How Do Men and Women Students Rate Empathy?" *American Journal of Nursing* 77 (1977): 998; Neill P. Watson, "A Theoretical and Empirical Study of Empathy and Sex Role Differentiation," diss., Harvard University, 1976.

12. J. A. Hall, "Gender Effects in Decoding Nonverbal Cues," *Psychological Bulletin* 85 (1978): 845–857.

13. Nancy M. Henley, *Body Politics: Power, Sex, and Nonverbal Communication* (Englewood Cliffs, NJ: Prentice-Hall, 1977); Linda Von Feldern Kestenbaum, "Decoding Inconsistent Communications: Importance of Body Versus Voice Cues and An Analysis of Individual Differences," diss., City University of New York (1977); Miron Zuckerman, R. S. DeFrank, J. A. Hall, and Robert Rosenthal, "Encoding and Decoding of Spontaneous and Posed Facial Expressions," *Journal of Personality and Social Psychology* 34 (1979): 966–977.

14. Robert Rosenthal and Bella M. DePaulo, "Sex Differences in Eavesdropping on Nonverbal Cues," *Journal of Personality and Social Psychology* 37 (1979): 273–285.

15. Jeffrey C. Siegal, "Effects of Objective Evidence of Expertness, Nonverbal Behavior and Subject Sex on Client-Perceived Expertness," *Journal of Counseling Psychology* 27 (1980): 117–121.

16. Kretch, Personal Interview, 1987.

17. Sven Wahlroos, *Family Communication* (New York: Macmillan, 1983), 120–121.

18. Julie Indvik and Mary Anne Fitzpatrick, "If You Could Read My Mind, Love. . . ' Understanding and Misunderstanding in the Marital Dyad," *Family Relations* 31 (1982): 43–51.

19. Mark E. Comadena, "Accuracy in Detecting Deception: Intimate and Friendship Relationships," *Communication Yearbook* 6, ed. Michael Burgoon (Newbury Park, CA: Sage, 1982), 446–472.

20. John M. Gottman and Albert L. Porterfield, "Communicative Competence in Nonverbal Behavior of Married Couples," *Journal of Marriage and the Family* 43 (1981): 817–824.

21. Wahlroos, 1983, 164.

22. Wahlroos, 1983, 169.

23. Harold D. Grotevant and Catherine R. Cooper, "Patterns of Interaction in Family Relationships and the Development of Identity Exploration in Adolescence," *Child Development* 56 (1985): 426.

24. See, for example, Catherine R. Cooper, Harold D. Grotevant, and Sherri M. Condon, "Methodological Challenges of Selectivity in Family Interaction:

Assessing Temporal Patterns of Individuation," *Journal of Marriage and the Family* 44 (1982): 749–754; Grotevant and Cooper, 1985, 415–428.

25. D. Bird, "Have You Tried Listening?" *Journal of the American Dietetic Association* 30 (1954): 225–230; Paul Tory Rankin, "The Measurement of the Ability to Understand Spoken Language," *Dissertation Abstracts* 12 (1926): 847.

26. William Smiley Howell, *The Empathic Communicator* (Belmont, CA: Wadsworth, 1982), 3.

27. Howell, 1982, 3.

28. W. R. Burr, R. Hill, F. I. Nye, and I. L. Reiss, *Contemporary Theories About the Family: Research-Based Theories,* vol.1 (New York: Free Press, 1979); Diana R. Garland, "Training Married Couples in Listening Skills: Effects on Behavior, Perceptual Accuracy, and Marital Adjustment," *Family Relations* 30 (1981): 297–306; Ronald B. Tiggle, Mark D. Peters, Harold H. Kelley, and John Vincent, "Correlational and Discrepancy Indices of Understanding and Their Relation to Marital Satisfaction," *Journal of Marriage and the Family* 44 (1982): 209–215.

29. Walter R. Schumm, "Theory and Measurement in Marital Communication Training Programs," *Family Relations* 32 (1983): 3–11.

30. Paul Watzlawick, Janet Beavin, and Don D. Jackson, *Pragmatics of Human Communication: A Study of Interactional Patterns, Pathologies, and Paradoxes* (New York: Norton, 1967).

31. Dehn, Personal Interview, 1985.

32. Evans, Personal Interview, 1985.

33. Fix, Personal Interview, 1985.

34. Elaine Walster, G. William Walster, and Ellen Berscheid, *Equity: Theory and Research* (Boston, MA: Allyn and Bacon, 1978).

35. Jones, Personal Interview, 1985.

36. Topping, Personal Interview, 1985.

37. Wagner, Personal Interview, 1985.

38. Wahlroos, 1983, 261.

39. Bruno Bettelheim, *A Good Enough Parent: A Book on Childrearing* (New York: Alred A. Knopf, 1987), 14.

40. Clarke, Personal Interview, 1987.

41. *USA Today,* 13 April 1987, 4D.

42. Barbara L. Fisher, Paul R. Giblin, and Margaret H. Hoopes, "Healthy Family Functioning: What Therapists Say and What Families Want," *Journal of Marital and Family Therapy* 8 (1982): 273–284.

43. See, for example, James M. Honeycutt, Charmaine Wilson, and Christine Parker, "Effects of Sex and Degrees of Happiness on Perceived Styles of Communication In and Out of the Marital Relationship," *Journal of Marriage and the Family* 44 (1982): 395–406.

44. Lenore Anglin Boyd and Arthur J. Roach, "Interpersonal Communication Skills Differentiating More Satisfying From Less Satisfying Marital Relationships," *Journal of Counseling Psychology* 24 (1977): 540–542.

45. See, for example, Patricia Noller, "Nonverbal Communication in Marriage,"

Intimate Relationships: Development, Dynamics and Deterioration, ed. Daniel Perlman and Steve Duck (Newbury Park, CA: Sage, 1987), 149–175.

46. Stella Ting-Toomey, "An Analysis of Verbal Communication Patterns in High and Low Marital Adjustment Groups," *Human Communication Research* 9 (1983): 306–319.

47. See, for example, Robert A. Lewis and Graham B. Spanier, "Theorizing About the Quality and Stability of Marriage," *Contemporary Theories About the Family,* vol. 1, ed. W. R. Burr, R. Hill, F. I. Nye, and I. C. Reiss (London: Free Press, 1979); Erich Kirchler, "Marital Happiness and Interaction in Everyday Surroundings: A Time-Sample Diary Approach for Couples," *Journal of Social and Personal Relationships* 5 (1988): 375–382.

48. See, for example, Patricia Noller and Calliope Venandos, "Communication Awareness in Married Couples," *Journal of Social and Personal Relationships* 3 (1986): 31–42; Dudley D. Cahn, "Perceived Understanding and Interpersonal Relationships," *Journal of Social and Personal Relationships* 7 (1990): 231–244.

49. Walster, Walster, and Berscheid, 1978.

50. David Reiss, Ronald Costell, Helen Berkman, and Carole Jones, "How One Family Perceives Another: The Relationship Between Social Constructions and Problem-Solving Competence," *Family Process* 19 (1980): 239–256.

51. John Mordechai Gottman, *Marital Interaction: Experimental Investigations* (New York: Academic Press, 1979).

52. Gottman and Porterfield, 1981, 817–824.

53. J. M. Gottman, C. Notarius, H. Markham, S. Banks, B. Yoppi, and M. E. Rubin, "Behavior Exchange Theory and Marital Decision-Making," *Journal of Personality and Social Psychology* 34 (1976): 14–23.

54. Gottman, *Marital Interaction,* 1979; Patricia Noller, "Channel Consistency and Inconsistency in the Communications of Married Couples," *Journal of Personality and Social Psychology* 43 (1982): 732–741.

55. Gottman, *Marital Interaction,* 1979; Patricia Noller, "Couple Communication and Marital Satisfaction," *Australian Journal of Sex, Marriage and Family* 3 (1982): 69–75; Mary Ellen Rubin, "Differences Between Distressed and Nondistressed Couples in Verbal and Nonverbal Communication Codes," diss., Indiana University, 1977.

56. Lillian B. Rubin, *Worlds of Pain: Life in the Working Class Family* (New York: Basic Books, 1976), 116–117.

57. Gottman, *Marital Interaction,* 1979

58. Ronald B. Tiggle, Mark D. Peters, Harold H. Kelley, and John Vincent, "Correlational and Discrepancy Indices of Understanding and Their Relation to Marital Satisfaction," *Journal of Marriage and the Family* 44 (1982): 209–215.

59. Gordon G. Chelune, Lawrence B. Rosenfeld, and E. M. Waring, "Spousal Disclosure Patterns in Distressed and Nondistressed Couples," *American Journal of Family Therapy* 13 (1985): 24–32.

60. Chelune, Roesenfield, and Waring, 1985, 24–32.

61. O'Shea, Personal Interview, 1987.

62. Strickmaker, Personal Interview, 1987.

63. See, for example, Kirchler, 1988, 375–382; Prudence A. Widlack and Carolyn C. Perrucci, "Family Configuration, Family Interaction, and Intellectual Attainment," *Journal of Marriage and the Family* 50 (1988): 33–44.

64. Vincent Jeffries, "Adolescent Love, Perception of Parental Love, and Relationship Quality," *Family Perspective* 24 (1990): 175–196.

65. See, for example, Douglas A. Abbott, Margaret Berry, and William H. Meredith, "Religious Belief and Practice: A Potential Asset in Helping Families," *Family Relations* 39 (1990): 443–448; Betty D. Cooke, Marilyn Martin Rossmann, Hamilton I. McCubbin, and Joan M. Patterson, "Examining the Definition and Assessment of Social Support: A Resource for Individuals and Families," *Family Relations* 37 (1988): 211–216.

66. Gottman, *Marital Interaction*, 1979; Noller, 1982, 69–75; Patricia Noller, "Negative Communication in Marriage," *Journal of Social and Personal Relationships* 2 (1985): 289–301; G. R. Pike and Alan L. Sillars, "Reciprocity of Marital Communication," *Journal of Social and Personal Relationships* 2 (1985): 303–324.

67. John P. Vincent, Lois C. Friedman, Jane Nugent, and Linzy Messerly, "Demand Characteristics in the Observations of Marital Interaction," *Journal of Consulting and Clinical Psychology* 47 (1979): 557–566.

68. Barbara M. Montgomery, "The Form and Function of Quality Communication in Marriage," *Family Relations* 30 (1981): 21–30; V. C. Weatherford, "Confirming and Disconfirming Communication: The Impact on Marital Satisfaction," paper presented at the Speech Communication Association, Chicago, November 1986.

69. Stella Ting-Toomey, 1983, 306–319.

70. See, for example, Jules Riskin and Elaine E. Faunce, "An Evaluative Review of Family Interaction Research," *Family Process* 11 (1972): 365–455; Jon Wuerffel, John DeFrain, and Nick Stinnett, "How Strong Families Use Humor," *Family Perspective* 24 (1990): 129–141.

71. Gottman, *Marital Interaction*, 1979; Riskin and Faunce, 1972, 365–455.

72. Gary Rudolph Birchler, "Differential Patterns of Instrumental and Affilative Behavior as a Function of Degree of Marital Distress and Level of Intimacy," diss., University of Oregon, 1972; Vincent, Friedman, Nugent, and Messerly, 1979, 557–566.

73. Riskin and Faunce, 1972, 402

74. Riskin and Faunce, 1972, 365–455.

75. Edwin J. Thomas, *Marital Communication and Decision Making* (New York: Free Press, 1977).

76. John P. Vincent, Robert L. Weiss, and Gary R. Birchler, "A Behavioral Analysis of Problem Solving in Distressed and Nondistressed Married and Stranger Dyads," *Behavior Therapy* 6 (1975): 475–487.

77. Andrew Billings, "Conflict Resolution in Distressed and Nondistressed Marital Couples," *Journal of Consulting and Clinical Psychology* 47 (1979): 368–376.

78. Neil S. Jacobson, "Behavioral Marital Therapy," *Handbook of Family Therapy*, ed. Alan S. Gurman and David P. Kniskern (New York: Brunner/Mazel, 1981), 556–591.

79. Noller, 1985, 289–301.

80. Vincent, Friedman, Nugent, and Messerly, 1979, 557–566.

81. Douglas Hartman Sprenkle, "A Behavioral Assessment of Creativity, Support and Power in Clinic and Non-Clinic Married Couples," diss., University of Minnesota, 1975; Claus Wegener, Dirk Revenstorf, Kurt Hahlweg, and Ludwig Schindler, "Empirical Analysis of Communication in Distressed and Nondistressed Couples," *Behavior Analysis and Modification* 3 (1979): 178–188.

82. Patricia Noller, "Misunderstandings in Marital Communication: A Study of Couples' Nonverbal Communication," *Journal of Personality and Social Psychology* 39 (1980): 1135–1148.

83. James F. Alexander, "Defensive and Supportive Communications in Family Systems," *Journal of Marriage and the Family* 35 (1973): 613–617.

84. R. B. Stuart, "Operant-Interpersonal Treatment for Marital Discord," *Journal of Consulting and Clinical Psychology* 33 (1969): 675–682.

85. John M. Gottman, Howard Markman, and Cliff Notarius, "The Topography of Marital Conflict: A Sequential Analysis of Verbal and Nonverbal Behavior," *Journal of Marriage and the Family* 39 (1977): 461–477.

86. Gottman, *Marital Interaction*, 1979; Noller, 1985, 289–301; Rubin, diss., 1977.

87. Ernst G. Beier and Daniel P. Stenberg, "Subtle Cues Between Newlyweds," *Journal of Communication* 27 (1977): 92–97.

88. Steven R. H. Beach and Ileana Arias, "Assessment of Perceptual Discrepancy: Utility of the Primary Communication Inventory," *Family Process* 22 (1983): 309–316.

89. George, Personal Interview, 1985.

90. Wahlroos, 1983, 180.

91. Rhea Zakich, "Simple Secrets of Family Communication," *Reader's Digest,* August 1986: 158–159.

92. Hart, Personal Interview, 1985.

93. Judy C. Pearson and Paul E. Nelson, *Understanding and Sharing: An Introduction to Speech Communication* (Dubuque, IA: William C. Brown Company, 1991).

94. Ice, Personal Interview, 1985.

95. Jurma, Personal Interview, 1985.

96. See, for example, Leo Buscaglia, *Loving, Living and Learning* (New York: Ballantine, 1982).

97. Kirk, Personal Interview, 1985.

98. See, for example, Erik E. Filsinger and Stephen J. Thoma, "Behavioral Antecedents of Relationship Stability and Adjustment: A Five-Year Longitudinal Study," *Journal of Marriage and the Family* 50 (1988): 785–795.

99. See, for example, Linda J. Roberts and Lowell Krokoff, "A Time-Series Analysis of Withdrawal, Hostility, and Displeasure in Satisfied and Dissatisfied Marriages," *Journal of Marriage and the Family* 52 (1990): 95–105; Wuerffel, DeFranin, and Stinnett, 1990, 129–141.

100. Wahlroos, 1983, 173

CHAPTER 12 NOTES

1. Bruce Lansky, *Mother Murphy's Second Law: Love, Sex, Marriage, and Other Disasters* (New York: Simon & Schuster, 1986), 81.

2. See, for example, John H. Harvey, A. L. Weber, Kerry L. Yarkin, and B. E. Stewart, "An Attributional Approach to Relationship Breakdown and Resolution," *Personal Relationships 4: Dissolving Personal Relationships,* ed. Steve W. Duck (New York: Academic Press, 1982); Cay Kelly, Ted L. Huston, and Rodney M. Cate, "Premarital Relationship Correlates of the Erosion of Satisfaction in Marriage," *Journal of Social and Personal Relationships* 2 (1985): 167–178.

3. Kelly, Huston, and Cate, 1985, 167–178.

4. Harriet B. Braiker and Harold H. Kelly, "Conflict in the Development of Close Relationships," *Social Exchange in Developing Relationships,* ed. Robert Burgess and Ted Huston (New York: Academic Press, 1979).

5. S. A. Lloyd and R. M. Cate, "The Development Course of Conflict in Dissolution of Premarital Relationships," *Journal of Social and Personal Relationships* 2 (1985): 179–194.

6. Joyce Hocker and William W. Wilmot, *Interpersonal Conflict,* 2nd ed. (Dubuque, IA: William C. Brown Company, 1985), 9.

7. Linda Robertson, Personal Interview, 1991.

8. Kathleen Galvin and Bernard Brommel, *Family Communication: Cohesion and Change,* 2nd ed. (Glenview, IL: Scott, Foresman, 1986), 169.

9. Filley, 1975.

10. Catalyst, *Corporations and Two-Career Families: Directions for the Future* (New York: Catalyst, 1982); Marjorie Shaevitz and Morton Shaevitz, *Making It Together as a Two-Career Couple* (Boston, MA: Houghton Mifflin, 1980); Sara Yogev, "Happiness in Dual-Career Couples: Changing Research, Changing Values," *Sex Roles* 8 (1982): 593–605.

11. See Antonio J. Ferreira and William D. Winter, "Information Exchange and Silence in Normal and Abnormal Families," *Family Process* 7 (1968): 251–276.

12. Ron Hamm, Personal Interview, 1991.

13. Jeannie Hamm, Personal Interview, 1991.

14. Ron Hamm, Personal Interview, 1991.

15. Norma Rogalski, Personal Interview, 1991.

16. Alassaf, Personal Interview, 1987.

17. Sven Wahlroos, *Family Communication* (New York: Macmillan, 1983), 80.

18. Wentworth, Personal Interview, 1987.

19. Bernard Davidson, Jack Balswick, and Charles Halverson, "Affective Self-Disclosure and Marital Adjustment: A Test of Equity Theory," *Journal of Marriage and the Family* 45 (1983): 93–102.

20. Alan L. Sillars and Michael D. Scott, "Interpersonal Perception Between Intimates: An Integrative Review," *Human Communication Research* 10 (1983): 153–176.

21. Jimmy Carter and Rosalynn Carter, *Everything to Gain: Making the Most of the Rest of Your Life* (New York: Random House, 1987), 89–90.

22. Noreen M. Carrocci, "Perceiving and Responding to Interpersonal Conflict," *Central States Speech Journal* 36 (1985): 215–228.

23. William W. Wilmot, *Dyadic Communication: A Transactional Perspective* (Reading, MA: Addison-Wesley, 1979), 95.

24. Wentworth, Personal Interview, 1987.

25. J. Byng-Hall and D. Campbell, "Resolving Conflicts in Family Distance Regulation: An Integrative Approach," *Journal of Marital and Family Therapy* 7 (1981): 321–330.

26. Larry B. Feldman, "Marital Conflict and Marital Intimacy: An Integrative Psychodynamic-Behavioral Systemic Model," *Family Process* 18 (1979): 69–78.

27. See, for example, Rex Forehand, Gene Brody, Nicholas Long, Jerry Slotkin, and Robert Fauber, "Divorce/Divorce Potential and Interparental Conflict: The Relationship to Early Adolescent Social and Cognitive Functioning," *Journal of Adolescent Research* 1 (1986): 389–397.

28. Wahlroos, 1983, 73–74.

29. S. K. Steinmetz, "Monkeys, See, Monkeys, Do: The Learning of Aggressive Behavior," paper presented at the meeting of the National Council on Family Relations, 1973; S. K. Steinmetz, "Intrafamilial Patterns of Conflict Resolution: United States and Canadian Comparisons," paper presented at the meeting of the Society for the Study of Social Problems," 1974; S. K. Steinmetz, "The Use of Force for Resolving Family Conflict: The Training Ground for Abuse," *Family Coordinator* 26 (1977): 19–26; S. K. Steinmetz and M. A. Straus, *Violence in the Family* (New York: Harper & Row, 1974).

30. Helen M. Newman, "Interpretation and Explanation: Influences on Communicative Exchanges Within Intimate Relationships," *Communication Quarterly* 29 (1981): 123–131.

31. Alan L. Sillars, "Interpersonal Perception in Relationships," *Compatible and Incompatible Relationships*, ed. W. J. Ickes (New York: Springer, 1985), 227–305.

32. Guillermo Bernal and Jeffrey Baker, "Toward a Metacommunicational Framework of Couples Interactions," *Family Process* 18 (1979): 293–302.

33. Haim Ginott, *Group Psychotherapy with Children* (New York: McGraw-Hill, 1961); Haim Ginott, *Between Parent and Child* (New York: Macmillan, 1969); Haim Ginott, *Teacher and Child: A Book for Parents and Teachers* (New York: Macmillan, 1972).

34. Ginott, 1969, 231.

35. Tracy Kidder, *House* (Boston, MA: Houghton Mifflin, 1985), 10.

36. Margaret J. Haefner, Sandra Metts, and Ellen Wartella, "Siblings' Strategies for Resolving Conflict Over Television Program Choice," *Communication Quarterly* 37 (1989): 223–230.

37. Paul Yelsma, "Functional Conflict Management in Effective Marital Adjustment," *Communication Quarterly* 32 (1984): 56–61.

38 Carole M. Pistole, "Attachment in Adult Romantic Relationships: Style of Conflict Resolution and Relationship Satisfaction," *Journal of Social and Personal Relationships* 6 (1989): 505–510.

39. Wahlroos, 1983, 82.

40. Hoffman, Personal Interview, 1987.

41. Sally A. Lloyd, "A Behavioral Self-Report Technique for Assessing Conflict in Close Relationships," *Journal of Social and Personal Relationships* 7 (1990): 265–272.

42. Lowell J. Krokoff, John M. Gottman, and Anup K. Roy, "Blue-Collar and White-Collar Marital Interaction and Communication Orientation," *Journal of Social and Personal Relationships* 5 (1988): 201–221.

43. Good, Personal Interview, 1987.

44. Leah Fraley, Personal Interview, 1991.

45. Wahlroos, 1983, 83.

46. Jenson, Personal Interview, 1987.

47. Sole, Personal Interview, 1987.

48. Anderson, Personal Interview, 1987.

49. Janice Rohrbach, Personal Interview, 1991.

50. Steven Rohrbach, Personal Interview, 1991.

51. Strickmaker, Personal Interview, 1987.

52. Tony Gregori, Personal Interview, 1991.

53. Tony Gregori, Personal Interview, 1991.

54. Wagner, Personal Interview, 1987.

55. Carter and Carter, 1987, 90.

56. Paul Yelsma, "Functional Conflict Management in Effective Marital Adjustment," *Communication Quarterly* 32 (1984): 56–61.

57. A. Locksley, "Social Class and Marital Attitudes and Behavior," *Journal of Marriage and the Family* 44 (1982): 427–440.

58. Cynthia Berryman-Fink and Claire C. Brunner, "The Effects of Sex on Source and Target of Interpersonal Conflict Management Styles," *The Southern Speech Communication Journal* 53 (1987): 38–48.

59. Mary Anne Fitzpatrick, "A Typological Approach to Communication in Relationships," *Communication Yearbook 1*, ed. B. Rubin (New Brunswick, NJ: Transaction Books, 1977), 263–275.

60. See, for example, M. A. Fitzpatrick, S. Fallis, and L. Vance, "Multifunctional Coding of Conflict Resolution Strategies in Marital Dyads," *Family Relations* 31 (1982): 61–70.

61. Alan L. Sillars, Gary R. Pike, Tricia S. Jones, and Kathleen Redmon, "Communication and Conflict in Marriage," *Communication Yearbook 7*, ed. Robert Bostrom (Newbury Park, CA: Sage, 1983), 414–429.

62. Thesing, Personal Interview, 1987.

63. Wahlroos, 1983, 71.

64. Thompsen, Personal Interview, 1987.

65. Wahlroos, 1983, 81.

66. Dan Canary and Brian Spitzberg, "Appropriateness and Effectiveness Perceptions of Conflict Strategies," *Human Communication Research* 14 (1987): 93–118.

67. Whitehouse, 1985.

68. Mary Anne Fitzpatrick and Patricia G. Best, "Dyadic Adjustment in Relational Types: Consensus, Cohesion, Affectional Expression, and Satisfaction in Enduring Relationships," *Communication Monographs* 46 (1979): 167–178.

69. John Mordechai Gottman, *Marital Interaction: Experimental Investigations* (New York: Academic Press, 1979), 9–10.

70. Leonard M. Uhr, "Personality Changes During Marriage," diss., University of Michigan, Ann Arbor, 1957.

71. Lempka, Personal Interview, 1987.

72. Paul R. Amato, "Marital Conflict, the Parent-Child Relationship and Child Self-Esteem," *Family Relations* 35 (1986): 403–410.

73. Lloyd S. Wright, "Suicidal Thoughts and Their Relationship to Family Stress and Personal Problems Among High School Seniors and College Graduates," *Adolescence* 20 (1985): 575–580.

74. Murray A. Straus, "Measuring Intrafamily Conflict and Violence: The Conflicts Tactics (CT) Scales," *Journal of Marriage and the Family* 41 (1979): 75–88.

75. Alan L. Sillars, "Attributions and Communication in Roommate Conflicts," *Communication Monographs* 47 (1980): 180–200.

76. Catherine M. Fichten, "Videotape and Verbal Feedback: Effects on Behavior and Attribution in Distressed Couples," diss., McGill University, Canada, 1978.

77. J. H. Harvey, G. L. Wells, and M. D. Alvarez, "Attribution in the Context of Conflict and Separation in Close Relationships," ed. John H. Harvey, William J. Ickes, and Robert F. Kidd, *New Directions in Attribution Research,* vol. 2 (Hillsdale, NJ: Lawrence Erlbaum, 1978).

78. Helen M. Newman, "Interpretation and Explanation: Influences on Communicative Exchanges Within Intimate Relationships," *Communication Quarterly* 29 (1981): 123–131.

79. Alan L. Sillars, "Interpersonal Perception in Relationships," *Compatible and Incompatible Relationships,* ed. W. J. Ickes (New York: Springer, 1985), 227–305.

80. Guillermo Bernal and Jeffry Baker, "Toward a Metacommunicational Framework of Couples Interactions," *Family Process* 18 (1979): 293–302.

81. Suzanne Meeks, Diane Arnkoff, Carol R. Glass, and Clifford Notarius, "Wives' Employment Status, Hassles, Communication, and Relational Efficacy: Intra-Versus Extra-Relationship Factors and Marital Adjustment," *Family Relations* 34 (1985): 249–255.

82. Nora Cate Schaeffer, "The Frequency and Intensity for Parental Conflict: Choosing Response Dimensions," *Journal of Marriage and the Family* 51 (1989): 759–766.

83. William A. Barry, "Conflict in Marriage," diss., University of Michigan, Ann Arbor, 1968; Harold L. Raush, William A. Barry, Richard K. Hertel, and Mary A. Swain, *Communication, Conflict and Marriage* (San Francisco, CA: Jossey-Bass, 1974).

84. Douglas H. Sprenkle, "A Behavioral Assessment of Creativity, Support and Power in Clinic and Non-Clinic Married Couples," diss., University of Minnesota, 1975; Claus Wegener, Dirk Revenstorf, Kurt Hahlweg, and Ludwig Schindler, "Empirical Analysis of Communication in Distressed and Nondistressed Couples," *Behavior Analysis and Modification* 3 (1979): 178–188.

85. Lloyd, 1990, 265.

86. Harold L. Raush, William A. Barry, Richard K. Hertel, and Mary A. Swain, *Communication, Conflict and Marriage* (San Francisco, CA: Jossey-Bass, 1974).

87. Gary R. Pike and Alan L. Sillars, "Reciprocity of Marital Communication," *Journal of Social and Personal Relationships* 2 (1985): 303–324.

88. Fitzpatrick and Best, 1979, 167–178.

89. Mary Anne Fitzpatrick, "Dyadic Adjustment in Traditional, Independent, and Separate Relationships: A Validation Study," paper presented at the annual meeting of the Speech Communication Association, 1977.

90. Pike and Sillars, 1985, 320–321.

91. Paul H. Zietlow and Alan L. Sillars, "Life-Stage Differences in Communication During Marital Conflicts," *Journal of Social and Personal Relationships* 5 (1988): 223–245.

92. Fitzpatrick, Fallis, and Vance, 1982, 62.

93. Dominic Infante, "Trait Argumentativeness as a Predictor of Communicative Behavior in Situations Requiring Argument," *Central States Speech Journal* 32 (1981): 265–272; Dominic Infante, "The Argumentative Student in the Speech Communication Classroom: An Investigation and Implications," *Communication Education* 31 (1982): 141–147; Dominic Infante, "Response to High Argumentatives: Message and Sex Differences," paper presented at the Speech Communication Association, Denver, CO, 1985; Dominic Infante and Andrew Rancer, "A Conceptualization and Measure of Argumentativeness," *Journal of Personality Assessment* 46 (1982): 72–80.

94. Infante, 1981, 273.

95. Infante and Rancer, 1982, 74.

96. David Johnson and Roger Johnson, "Conflict in the Classroom: Controversy and Learning," *Review of Educational Research* 49 (1979): 51–70.

97. Dominic Infante, Teresa A. Chandler, and Jill E. Rudd, "Test of an Argumentative Skill Deficiency Model of Interspousal Violence," *Communication Monographs* 56 (1989): 1989.

98. Gottman, *Marital Interaction,* 1979.

99. J. K. Alberts, "Perceived Effectiveness of Couples' Conversational Complaints," *Communication Studies* 40 (1989): 280–291.

100. See, for example, Neil S. Jacobson and Barclay Martin, "Behavioral Marriage Therapy: Current Status," *Psychological Bulletin* 83 (1976): 540–556; Robert L. Weiss, Gary R. Birchler, and John P. Vincent, "Contractual Models for Negotiation Training in Marital Dyads," *Journal of Marriage and the Family* 36 (1974): 321–330.

101. Andrew Billings, "Conflict Resolution in Distressed and Nondistressed Marital Couples," *Journal of Consulting and Clinical Psychology* 47 (1979): 368–376.

102. Stella Ting-Toomey, "An Analysis of Verbal Communication Patterns in High and Low Marital Adjustment Groups," *Human Communication Research* 9 (1983): 306–319.

103. Robert W. Levenson and John M. Gottman, "Marital Interaction: Physiological Linkage and Affective Exchange," *Journal of Personality and Social Psychology* 45 (1983): 587–597.

104. Pike and Sillars, 1985, 318.

105. Patricia Noller, "Channel Consistency and Inconsistency in the Communications of Married Couples," *Journal of Personality and Social Psychology* 43 (1982): 732–741.

106. John P. Vincent, Lois C. Friedman, Jane Nugent, and Linzy Messerly, "Demand Characteristics in the Observations of Marital Interaction," *Journal of Consulting and Clinical Psychology* 47 (1979): 557–566.

107. John Gottman, Cliff Notarius, Howard Markhan, Steve Banks, Bruce Yoppi, and Mary E. Rubin, "Behavior Exchange Theory and Marital Decision-Making," *Journal of Personality and Social Pschology* 34 (1976): 14–23.

CHAPTER 13 NOTES

1. L. Edna Rogers-Millar and Frank E. Millar, "Domineeringness and Dominance: A Transactional View," *Human Communication Research* 5 (1979): 239.

2. John R. P. French and Bertram H. Raven, "The Bases of Social Power," *Group Dynamics,* ed. Dorwin Cartwright and Alvin Zander (Evanston, IL: Row Peterson, 1962), 607–623.

3. Anderson, Personal Interview, 1985.

4. Ventrelli, Personal Interview, 1987.

5. Wagner, Personal Interview, 1987.

6. Anderson, Personal Interview, 1985.

7. Thesing, Personal Interview, 1987.

8. Wentworth, Personal Interview, 1987.

9. Anderson, Personal Interview, 1985.

10. Thesing, Personal Interview, 1987.

11. Wentworth, Personal Interview, 1987.

12. Elias, Personal Interview, 1985.

13. Anderson, Personal Interview, 1985.

14. Thesing, Personal Interview, 1987.

15. Topping, Personal Interview, 1987.

16. O'Shea, Personal Interview, 1987.

17. Topping, Personal Interview, 1987.

18. Brendan Rule, Gay Bisanz, and Melinda Kahn, "Anatomy of Persuasion Schema: Targets, Goals, and Strategies," *Journal of Personality and Social Psychology* 43 (1985): 304–318.

19. Toni Falbo and Letitia A. Peplau, "Power Strategies in Intimate Relationships," *Journal of Personality and Social Psychology* 38 (1980): 627.

20. Toni Falbo, "PAQ Types and Power Strategies Used in Intimate Relationships," *Psychology of Women Quarterly* 6 (1982): 399–405.

21. Gerald Marwell and David R. Schmitt, "Dimensions of Compliance-Gaining Behavior: An Empirical Analysis," *Sociometry* 30 (1967): 350–364.

22. See, for example, Gerald R. Miller, Frank J. Boster, Michael E. Roloff, and David R. Seibold, "Compliance-Gaining Message Strategies: A Typology and Some Findings Concerning Effects of Situational Differences," *Communication Monographs* 44 (1977): 37–51.

23. Mary Anne Fitzpatrick and Jeff Winke, "You Always Hurt the One You Love: Strategies and Tactics in Interpersonal Conflict," *Communication Quarterly* 27 (1979): 7.

24. See, for example, Michael J. Cody and Margaret L. McLaughlin, "Perceptions of Compliance-Gaining Situations: A Dimensional Analysis," *Communication Monographs* 47 (1980): 132–148; Michael J. Cody, Margaret L. McLaughlin, and Michael J. Schneider, "The Impact of Relational Consequences and Intimacy on the Selection of Interpersonal Persuasion Tactics: A Reanalysis," *Communication Quarterly* 29 (1981): 91–106; Michael J. Cody, Mary L. Woelfel, and William J. Jordan, "Dimensions of Compliance Gaining Situations," *Human Communication Research* 9 (1983): 99–113; Mark A. de Turck, "A Transactional Analysis of Compliance-Gaining Behavior: Effects of Non-Compliance, Relational Context, and Actors' Gender," *Human Communication Research* 12 (1985): 54–78; Mark A. de Turck, "When Communication Fails: Physical Aggression as a Compliance Gaining Strategy," *Communication Monographs* 54 (1987): 106–112; Robert L. Hertzog and James J. Bradac, "Perceptions of Compliance-Gaining Situations: An Extended Analysis," *Communication Research* 11 (1984): 363–391; Michael J. Cody, John Greene, Peter J. Marson, H. Dan O'Hair, Kevin T. Baaske, and Michael J. Schneider, "Situation Perception and Message Strategy Selection," *Communication Yearbook 9,* ed. Margaret L. McLaughlin (Newbury Park, CA: Sage, 1986), 390–420.

25. Myron W. Lustig and Stephen W. King, "The Effect of Communication Apprehension and Situation on Communication Strategy Choices," *Human Communication Research* 7 (1980): 74–82.

26. Ruth Anne Clark, "The Impact of Self Interest and Desire for Liking on the Selection of Communicative Strategies," *Communication Monographs* 46 (1979): 257–273.

27. Clark, 1979, 257–273.

28. Michael E. Roloff and Edwin F. Barnicott, "The Situational Use of Pro- and Anti-Social Compliance-Gaining Strategies by High and Low Machiavellians," *Communication Yearbook 4,* ed. D. Ruben (New Brunswick, NJ: Transaction Books, 1978), 193–205.

29. Michael E. Roloff and E. F. Barnicott, "The Influence of Dogmatism on the Situational Use of Pro- and Anti-Social Compliance-Gaining Strategies," *The Southern Speech Communication Journal* 45 (1979): 37–45.

30. Cody, McLaughlin, and Schneider, "Relational Consequences," 1981, 91–106.

31. Vincent J. Hazelton and William R. Cupach, "An Exploration of Ontological Knowledge: Communication Competence as a Function of the Ability to Describe, Predict, and Explain," *The Western Journal of Speech Communication* 50 (1986): 119–132.

32. See, for example, Schenck-Hamlin, Wiseman, and Georgacarakos, 1982.

33. Cody, McLaughlin, and Schneider, 1981, 91.

34. Mark A. de Turck, "When Communication Fails: Physical Aggression as a

Compliance Gaining Strategy," *Communication Monographs* 54 (1985); James P. Dillard and Mary Anne Fitzpatrick, "The Short and Long Term Outcomes of Compliance-Gaining in Marital Interaction," paper presented at the meeting of the International Communication Association, San Francisco, 1984; Bertram Raven, Richard Centers, and Aroldo Rodrigues, "The Bases of Conjugal Power," *Power in Families,* ed. Ronald E. Cromwell and David H. Olson (New York: Halsted Press, 1975), 217–234.

35. Margaret L. McLaughlin, Michael J. Cody, and Carl S. Robey, "Situational Influences on the Selection of Strategies to Resist Compliance-Gaining Attempts," *Human Communication Research* 1 (1980): 14–36.

36. Leslie A. Baxter, "An Investigation of Compliance-Gaining Politeness," *Human Communication Research* 10 (1984): 427–456.

37. Fitzpatrick and Winke, 1979, 3–11.

38. Hal Witteman and Mary Anne Fitzpatrick, "Compliance-Gaining in Marital Interaction: Power Bases, Processes, and Outcomes," *Communication Monographs* 53 (1986): 131.

39. Witteman and Fitzpatrick, 1986, 140.

40. Witteman and Fitzpatrick, 1986, 140.

41. Dillard and Fitzpatrick, 1984; Witteman and Fitzpatrick, 1986, 130–143.

42. Susan B. Shimanoff, "Types of Emotional Disclosures and Request Compliance Between Spouses," *Communication Monographs* 54 (1987): 85–100.

43. Margaret J. Haefner and Jamie Comstock, "Compliance Gaining on Prime Time Family Programs," *The Southern Communication Journal* 55 (1990): 402–420.

44. Lynn Oldershaw, Gary G. Walters, and Darlene K. Hall, "Control Strategies and Non-Compliance in Abusive Mother-Child Dyads: An Observational Study," *Child Development* 57 (1986): 722–732.

45. Dorothy J. Jessop, "Family Relationships as Viewed by Parents and Adolescents: A Specification," *Journal of Marriage and the Family* 43 (1982): 95–107.

46. See, for example, Dennis N. Thompson, "Parent-Peer Compliance in a Group of Preadolescent Youths," *Adolescence* 20 (1985): 501–508.

47. Wyndol Furman and Duane Buhrmester, "Children's Perceptions of the Qualities of Sibling Relationships," *Child Development* 56 (1985): 448–461.

48. Ruth Anne Clark and Jesse G. Delia, "Cognitive Complexity, Social Perspective-Taking, and Functional Persuasive Skills in Second-to-Ninth Grade Children," *Human Communication Research* 3 (1977): 128–134.

49. Fern Johnson, "Role-Taking and Referential Communication Abilities in First- and Third-Grade Children," *Human Communication Research* 3 (1977): 135–145.

50. Catherine Garvey, "Requests and Responses in Children's Speech," *Journal of Child Language* 2 (1975): 41–63.

51. Beth Haslett, "Communicative Functions and Strategies in Children's Conversations," *Human Communication Research* 9 (1983): 114–129.

52. Mary L. Willbrand and Richard D. Rieke, "Reason Giving in Children's Supplicatory Compliance Gaining," *Communication Monographs* 53 (1986): 47–60.

53. G. E. Finley and C. A. Humphreys, "Naive Psychology and the Development of Persuasive Appeals in Girls," *Canadian Journal of Behavioral Science* 6 (1974): 75–80.

54. McLaughlin, Cody, and Robey, 1980, 14–36.

55. McLaughlin, Cody, and Robey, 1980, 14.

56. See, for example, Michael J. Cody, H. Dan O'Hair, and Michael J. Schneider, "The Impact of Intimacy Rights to Resist Machiavellianism, and Psychological Gender on Compliance-Resisting Strategies: How Persuasive Are Response Effects in Communication Surveys?" paper presented at the International Communication Association, Boston, 1982; de Turck, 1985, 54–78; Jeffrey S. McQuillen, "The Development of Listener-Adapted Compliance-Resisting Strategies," *Human Communication Research* 12 (1986): 359–375; Jeffrey S. McQuillen, Dorothy C. Higgenbotham, and M. Claire Cummings, "Compliance-Resisting Behaviors: The Effects of Age, Agent, and Types of Request," *Communication Yearbook 8*, ed. R. N. Bostrom (Newbury Park, CA: Sage, 1984), 747–762.

57. McQuillen, Higgenbotham, and Cummings, 1984, 747–762.

58. McLaughlin, Cody, and Robey, 1980, 14–46.

59. Fitzpatrick and Winke, 1979, 3–11; Clark, 1979, 257–273; Michael J. Cody, Margaret L. McLaughlin, William J. Jordan, and Michael J. Schneider, *A Proposed Working Typology of Compliance-Gaining Message Strategies*, ms., Department of Speech Communication, Texas Tech University, 1979.

60. McQuillen, Higginbotham, and Cummings, 1984, 749.

61. McLaughlin, Cody, and Robey, 1980, 14–36.

62. Thompson, *Adolescence*, 1985.

63. Oldershaw, Walters, and Hall, 1986, 722–732.

64. McQuillen, Higginbotham, and Cummings, 1984, 749.

65. Jeffrey S. McQuillen and Dorothy C. Higginbotham, "Children's Reasoning About Compliance-Resisting Behaviors," *Communication Yearbook 9*, ed. M. L. McLaughlin (Newbury Park, CA: Sage, 1986), 673–690.

66. McQuillen and Higginbotham, 1986, 673–690.

67. Kim D. White, Judy C. Pearson, and Lyle Flint, "Adolescents' Compliance-Resistance: Effects of Parents' Compliance Strategy and Gender and Adolescents' Gender," *Adolescence* 95 (1989): 595–621.

68. Roxane S. Luloffs, "The Content of Interpersonal Persuasion Episodes and the Relationship of Strategy Use to Perceived Competence and Persuasive Outcomes," paper presented at the Speech Communication Association Convention, Denver, CO, 1985.

69. Donald M. Wolfe, "Power and Authority in the Family," *Studies in Social Power*, ed. D. Cartwright (Ann Arbor, MI: University of Michigan, Institute for Social Research, 1959).

70. See, for example, Rae Lesser Blumberg and Marion Coleman, "A Theoretical Look at the Gender Balance of Power in the American Couple," *Journal of Family Issues* 10 (1989): 225–250; Philip Blumstein and Pepper Schwartz, *American Couples* (New York: William Morrow, 1983).

71. Blumberg and Coleman, 1989, 225–250.

72. Blumstein and Schwartz, *American Couples,* 1983.

73. Mayta A. Caldwell and Letitia A. Peplau, "The Balance of Power in Lesbian Relationships," *Sex Roles* 10 (1984): 587–599.

74. Charles D. Hoffman, Sandra E. Tsuneyoshi, Marilyn Ebina, and Heather Fite, "A Comparison of Adult Males' and Females' Interactions with Girls and Boys," *Sex Roles* 11 (1984): 799–811.

75. Craig M. Allen and Murray A. Straus, "Resources, Power, and Husband-Wife Violence," *The Social Causes of Husband-Wife Violence,* ed. Murray A. Straus and Gerald T. Hotaling (Minneapolis, MN: University of Minnesota Press, 1980); Diane H. Coleman and Murray A. Straus, "Marital Power, Conflict, and Violence in a Nationally Representative Sample of American Couples," *Violence and Victims* 1 (1986): 141–157.

76. D. Kalmuns, "Wife Abuse Continues to Rise," *Marriage and Divorce Today* 7 (1981).

77. Bertram Raven, Richard Centers, and Aroldo Rodrigues, "The Bases of Conjugal Power," *Power in Families,* ed. Ronald E. Cromwell and David H. Olson (New York: Halsted Press, 1975), 217–234.

78. Frank E. Millar, L. Edna Rogers-Millar, and John A. Courtright, "Relational Control and Dyadic Understanding: An Exploratory Regression Model," *Communication Yearbook 3* (New Brunswick, NJ: Transaction Books, 1979), 213–224.

79. See, for example, Mary Anne Fitzpatrick, "Predicting Couples' Communication from Couples' Self-Reports," *Communication Yearbook 7,* ed. Robert Bostrom (Newbury Park, CA: Sage, 1983), 49–82; John M. Gottman, *Marital Interaction: Experimental Investigations* (New York: Academic Press, 1979).

80. See, for example, Stephen J. Bahr and Boyd C. Rollins, "Crisis and Conjugal Power," *Journal of Marriage and the Family* 33 (1971): 360–367; Irvine L. Janis and Leon Mann, *Decision-Making: A Psychological Analysis of Conflict, Choice and Commitment* (New York: Free Press, 1977).

81. Raven, Centers, and Rodrigues, 1975, 217–234; C. Tavris and Toby Jayaratne, "How Happy Is Your Marriage? What 75,000 Wives Say About Their Most Intimate Relationships," *Redbook,* June 1976: 90–92.

82. Gary L. Bowen and Dennis K. Orthner, "Sex-Role Congruency and Marital Quality," *Journal of Marriage and the Family* 45 (1983): 257–266.

83. Neal Krause, "Conflicting Sex-Role Expectations, Housework Dissatisfaction, and Depressive Symptoms Among Full-Time Housewives," *Sex Roles* 9 (1983): 1114–1125.

84. Dana V. Hiller and William W. Philliber, "Predicting Marital and Career Success Among Dual-Worker Couples," *Journal of Marriage and the Family* 44 (1982): 53–62.

85. L. Edna Rogers-Millar and Frank E. Millar, "Domineeringness and Dominance: A Transactional View," *Human Communication Research* 5 (1979): 238–246.

86. Phillip Blumstein and Pepper Schwartz, *American Couples* (New York: William Morrow, 1983).

87. Blumstein and Schwartz, 1983.

88. Caroline Bird, *Born Female: The High Cost of Keeping Women Down* (New York: David McKay, 1968); Blumstein and Schwartz, 1983.

89. See, for example, Dorothy L. Krueger, "Communication Patterns and Egalitarian Decision-Making in Dual-Career Couples," *The Western Journal of Speech Communication* 49 (1985): 126–145.

90. Sandra Pursell, Paul G. Banikiotes, and Richard J. Sebastian, "Androgyny and the Perception of Marital Roles," *Sex Roles* 7 (1981): 201–215.

91. Robert B. Schafer and Patricia M. Keith, "Equity in Marital Roles Across the Family Life Cycle," *Journal of Marriage and the Family* 43 (1981): 359–367.

92. Dorothy L. Krueger, "Marital Decision-Making: A Language-Action Analysis," *Quarterly Journal of Speech* 68 (1982): 273–287.

93. Carol Gilligan, *In a Different Voice: Psychological Theory and Women's Development* (Cambridge, MA: Harvard University Press, 1982); Judy C. Pearson, *Gender and Communication* (Dubuque, IA: Wm. C. Brown, 1985).

94. Krueger, 1985, 126–145.

95. William Schutz, *Firo: A Three-Dimensional Theory of Interpersonal Behavior* (New York: Holt, Rinehart and Winston, 1958).

96. Julie Indvik and Mary Anne Fitzpatrick, "Perceptions of Inclusion, Affiliation, and Control in Five Interpersonal Relationships," *Communication Quarterly* 34 (1986): 1–13.

97. Frank E. Millar and L. Edna Rogers, "A Relational Approach to Interpersonal Communication," *Explorations in Interpersonal Communication*, ed. G. R. Miller (Newbury Park, CA: Sage, 1976), 87–103.

98. See, for example, Millar, Rogers-Millar, and Courtright, 1979, 213–224; Rogers-Millar and Millar, 1979, 238–246.

99. Millar and Rogers, 1976, 87–103.

100. Paul Watzlawick, Janet H. Beavin, and Don S. Jackson, *Pragmatics of Human Communication: A Study of Interactional Patterns, Pathologies, and Paradoxes* (New York: Norton, 1967), 68–69.

101. Robin N. Williamson and Mary Anne Fitzpatrick, "Two Approaches to Marital Interaction: Relational Control Patterns in Marital Types," *Communication Monographs* 52 (1985): 236–252.

102. Edward E. Jones and Harold B. Gerard, *Foundations of Social Psychology* (New York: Wiley, 1967).

CHAPTER 14 NOTES

1. Froma Walsh, "Conceptualization of Normal Family Functioning," *Normal Family Processes*, ed. Froma Walsh (New York: Guilford Press, 1982), 30–31.

2. I-Chiao Huang, "Family Stress and Coping," *Family Perspective* 23 (1989): 225–282.

3. T. H. Holmes and R. H. Rahe, "The Social Adjustment Rating Scale," *Journal of Psychosomatic Research* 2 (1967): 213–218.

4. See, for example, G. Everly, *The Measurement of Occupational Anxiety,* ms., Department of Health Education, University of Maryland, College Park, 1976.

5. John W. Santrock, *Psychology: The Science of Mind and Behavior* (Dubuque, IA: Wm. C. Brown, 1986).

6. See, for example, R. Keyes, *Chancing It: Why We Take Risks* (Boston, MA: Little, Brown, 1985).

7. David Chiriboga, Linda Catron, and Philip Weiler, "Childhood Stress and Adult Functioning During Marital Separation," *Family Relations* 36 (1987): 163–167.

8. Norma Rogalski, Personal Interview, 1991.

9. Richard S. Lazarus and Anita DeLongis, "Psychological Stress and Coping in Aging," *American Psychologist* 38 (1983): 24.

10. Sandra Turk, Personal Interview, 1991.

11. See, for example, O. Siegel, "Personality Development in Adolescence," *Handbook of Development Psychology,* ed. B. B. Wolman (Englewood Cliffs, NJ: Prentice-Hall, 1982), 537–548.

12. John C. Coleman, *Intimate Relationships, Marriage, and Family* (Indianapolis, IN: Bobbs-Merrill, 1984).

13. Jacqueline N. Ventura, "The Stresses of Parenthood Reexamined," *Family Relations* 36 (1987): 26–29.

14. See, for example, H. L. Bee and S. K. Mitchell, *The Developing Person: A Life-Span Approach* (New York: Harper & Row, 1984).

15. See, for example, S. Chese and A. Thomas, "Keeping an Eye on Child Behavior," *Los Angeles Times,* 8 May 1980; J. Larsen, "Family Counseling: A Resource for Adolescent Problems," *Marriage and Family Living* 63 (1981): 21–24; P. York and D. York, *Family Therapy Networker,* September–October 1982: 35–37.

16. Christian Kloos, Personal Interview, 1991.

17. Michael P. Farrell and Stanley D. Rosenberg, *Men at Midlife* (Boston, MA: Auburn House, 1981).

18. Seymour S. Kety, "Foreword: Bringing Knowledge to Bear on the Mental Dysfunctions Associated with Aging," *Handbook of Mental Health and Aging,* ed. James E. Birren and Bruce R. Sloane (Englewood Cliffs, NJ: Prentice-Hall, 1980), xi.

19. Suzanne K. Steinmetz and D. J. Amsden, "Dependent Elders, Family Stress, and Abuse," *Family Relationships in Later Life,* ed. T. H. Brubaker (Newbury Park, CA: Sage, 1983), 173–192.

20. Mary Beth Block, Personal Interview, 1991.

21. Froma Walsh, "Conceptualizations of Normal Family Functioning," *Normal Family Processes,* ed. F. Walsh (New York: Guilford Press, 1982), 169.

22. See, for example, J. C. Coleman, *Intimate Relationships, Marriage, and Family* (Indianapolis, IN: Bobbs-Merrill, 1984); Joe F. Pittman and Sally A. Lloyd, "Quality of Family Life, Social Support, and Stress," *Journal of Marriage and the Family* 50 (1988): 53–67; Patricia Voydanoff, Brenda W. Donnelly, and Mark A. Fine, "Economic Distress, Social Integration, and Family Satisfaction," *Journal of Family Issues* 9 (1988): 545–564.

23. Lowell Krokoff, "Job Distress Is No Laughing Matter in Marriage, Or Is It?" *Journal of Social and Personal Relationships* 8 (1991): 5–25.

24. Cynthia J. Meyer, "Stress: There's No Place Like a First Home," *Family Relations* 36 (1987): 198–203.

25. Ramona Marotz-Baden and Peggy C. Colvin, "Coping Strategies: A Rural-Urban Comparison," *Family Relations* 35 (1986): 281–288.

26. Nicholas Hobbs and James Perrin, eds., *Issues in the Care of Children with Chronic Illness* (San Francisco, CA: Jossey-Bass Publishers, 1985).

27. See, for example, Marilyn A. McCubbin, "Family Stress, Resources, and Family Types: Chronic Illness in Children," *Family Relations* 37 (1988): 203–210.

28. See, for example, Chiriboga, Catron, and Weiler, 1987

29. Stan L. Albrecht, "Reactions and Adustments to Divorce: Differences in the Experiences of Males and Females," *Family Relations* 29 (1980): 59–68.

30. Leone P. Plummer and Alberta Koch-Hattem, "Family Stress and Adjustment to Divorce," *Family Relations* 35 (1986): 253–529.

31. Valerie E. Whiffen and Ian H. Gotlib, "Stress and Coping in Maritally Distressed and Nondistressed Couples," *Journal of Social and Personal Relationships* 6 (1989): 327–344.

32. R. Hill, *Families Under Stress* (New York: Harper & Row, 1949).

33. Wesley R. Burr, *Theory Construction and the Sociology of the Family* (New York: Wiley, 1973).

34. Hamilton I. McCubbin and Joan M. Patterson, "Family Adaptation to Crisis," *Family Stress, Coping and Social Support*, ed. Hamilton McCubbin, A. Elizabeth Cauble, and Joan M. Patterson (Springfield, IL: Charles C. Thomas, 1982).

35. David H. Olson and Hamilton I. McCubbin, *Families: What Makes Them Work* (Newbury Park, CA: Sage, 1983).

36. Irwin Sarason, "Life Stress, Self-Preoccupation, and Social Supports," *Stress and Anxiety*, vol. 7, ed. I. G. Sarason and C. D. Speilberger (Washington, DC: Hemisphere, 1980).

37. Sarason, 1980.

38. Hill, 1949; H. I. McCubbin and Patterson, 1982; Olson and McCubbin, 1983.

39. Hill, 1949.

40. Lois Pratt, *Family Structure and Effective Health Behavior: The Energized Family* (Boston, MA: Houghton Mifflin, 1976).

41. David H. Olson, Douglas H. Sprenkle, and Candyce S. Russell, "Circumplex Model of Marital and Family Systems: In Cohesion and Adaptability Dimensions, Family Types and Clinical Applications," *Family Process* 18 (1979): 3–28.

42. See, for example, Richard L. Kahn and Toni C. Antonucci, "Convoys Over the Life Course: Attachment, Roles, and Social Support," *Life-Span Development and Behavior*, vol. 3, ed. Paul B. Baltes and Orville G. Brim, Jr. (New York: Academic Press, 1980).

43. Olson and McCubbin, 1983.

44. James Robertson, Personal Interview, 1991.

45. Linda Robertson, Personal Interview, 1991.

46. Patty Woodyard, Personal Interview, 1991.

47. Craig Jackson, Personal Interview, 1991.

48. Hamilton McCubbin, C. Joy, A. Cauble, J. Comeau, Joan Patterson, and R. Needle, "Family Stress and Coping: A Decade Review," *Journal of Marriage and the Family* 42 (1980): 125–141.

49. Walsh, 1982, 3–42.

50. See, for example, David Reiss and Mary E. Oliveri, "Family Paradigm and Family Coping: A Proposal for Linking the Family's Intrinsic Adaptive Capacities to Its Responses to Stress," *Family Relations* 29 (1980): 431–444.

51. Aaron Antonovsky and Talma Sourai, "Family Sense of Coherence and Family Adaptation," *Journal of Marriage and the Family* 50 (1988): 79–92.

52. See, for example, Deborah D. Godwin and John Scanzoni, "Couple Decision Making: Commonalities and Differences Across Issues and Spouses," *Journal of Family Issues* 10 (1989): 291–310.

53. William J. Doherty, "Attributional Style and Negative Problem-Solving in Marriage," *Family Relations* 31 (1982): 201–205.

54. John Scanzoni and Karen Polonko, "A Conceptual Approach to Explicit Marital Negotiation," *Journal of Marriage and the Family* 42 (1980): 31–44.

55. Stephen W. Royce and Robert L. Weiss, "Behavioral Cues in the Judgment of Marital Satisfaction: A Linear Regression Analysis," *Journal of Consulting and Clinical Psychology* 43 (1975): 816–824.

56. J. Z. Rubin and B. R. Brown, *The Social Psychology of Bargaining and Negotiation* (New York: Academic Press, 1975); Jetse Sprey, "Conflict Theory and the Study of Marriage and the Family," *Contemporary Theories About the Family*, vol. 2, ed. Wesley R. Burr, Juan F. Nye, and Ira L. Reiss (New York: Free Press, 1979), 130–159.

57. Elaine A. Blechman and Michael J. McEnroe, "Effective Family Problem Solving," *Child Development* 56 (1985): 429–437.

58. Deborah D. Godwin and John Scanzoni, "Couple Consensus During Marital Joint Decision-Making: A Context, Process, Outcome Model," *Journal of Marriage and the Family* 51 (1989): 943–956.

59. Rubin and Brown, 1975; Sprey, 1979, 130–159.

60. Kay P. Edwards, "Agency and Certitude and Rational Family Decision-Making," *Family Perspective* 17 (1983): 183–193.

61. See, for example, Alan L. Sillars, "Attributions and Communication in Roommate Conflicts," *Communication Monographs* 47 (1980): 180–200.

62. Mary T. Warmbrod, "Alternative Generation in Marital Problem-Solving," *Family Relations* 31 (1982): 503–511.

63. Lillian Snyder, "The Deserting, Nonsupporting Father: Scapegoat of Family Nonpolicy," *Family Coordinator* 28 (1979): 594–598.

64. Gary R. Birchler, "Differential Patterns of Instrumental and Affilative Behavior as a Function of Degree of Marital Distress and Level of Intimacy," diss., University of Oregon, 1972; John P. Vincent, Lois C. Friedman, Jane Nugent, and Lingy Messerly, "Demand Characteristics in the Observations of Marital Interaction," *Journal of Consulting and Clinical Psychology* 47 (1979): 557–566.

65. William A. Barry, "Conflict in Marriage," diss., University of Michigan, Ann Arbor, 1968; Harold L. Raush, William A. Barry, Richard K. Hertel, and Mary A.

Swain, *Communication, Conflict and Marriage* (San Francisco, CA: Jossey-Bass, 1974).

66. Douglas H. Sprenkle, "A Behavioral Assessment of Creativity, Support and Power in Clinic and Non-Clinic Married Couples," diss., University of Minnesota, Minneapolis, 1975.

67. Frank E. Millar and L. Edna Rogers, "A Relational Approach to Interpersonal Communication," *Explorations in Interpersonal Communication*, ed. Gerald R. Miller (Newbury Park, CA: Sage, 1976); Sprenkle, diss., 1975.

68. Dorothy L. Krueger and Patricia Smith, "Decision-Making Patterns of Couples: A Sequential Analysis," *Journal of Communication* 32 (1982): 121–134.

69. Caryl E. Rusbult, "Responses to Dissatisfaction in Close Relationships: The Exit-Voice-Loyalty-Neglect Model" *Intimate Relationships*, ed. Daniel Perlman and Steve Duck (Newbury Park, CA: Sage, 1987).

70. Sandra Metts and William R. Cupach, "The Influence of Relationship Beliefs and Problem-Solving Responses on Satisfaction in Romantic Relationships," *Human Communication Research* 17 (1990): 170–185.

71. Lorraine T. Dorfman and Elizabeth A. Hill, "Rural Housewives and Retirement: Joint Decision-Making Matters," *Family Relations* 35 (1986): 507–514.

72. Jeffry H. Larson, "The Marriage Quiz: College Students' Beliefs in Selected Myths." *Family Relations* 37 (January 1988): 59–60.

CREDITS

INDEX